Sally Sondheim and Suzannah Sloan

THE
ACCIDENTAL GOURMET
Weeknights

A YEAR OF FAST AND DELICIOUS MEALS

A FIRESIDE BOOK
PUBLISHED BY SIMON AND SCHUSTER
NEW YORK • LONDON • TORONTO • SYDNEY • SINGAPORE

FIRESIDE
Rockefeller Center
1230 Avenue of the Americas
New York, NY 10020

FIRESIDE and colophon are registered trademarks
of Simon & Schuster, Inc.

For information about special discounts for bulk purchases,
please contact Simon & Schuster Special Sales:
1-800-456-6798 or business@simonandschuster.com

Designed by Elina Nudelman

Manufactured in the United States of America

1   3   5   7   9   10   8   6   4   2

Library of Congress Cataloging-in-Publication Data
Sondheim, Sally.
The accidental gourmet : weeknights / Sally Sondheim and Suzannah Sloan.
p.   cm.
Includes index.
1. Dinners and dining.   2. Quick and easy cookery.   3. Menus.
I. Sloan, Suzannah.   II. Title.
TX737 .S653   2002
641.5'4—dc21   2002067740

ISBN 0-684-86770-2

To Howard,
In Loving Memory

We hope it wasn't the food . . .

ACKNOWLEDGMENTS

We would like to express our profound appreciation to our brave testers and tasters and to our staunch supporters and contributors, without whom this tome would have fallen flat and the task would have been far too overwhelming to undertake:

Kim Aiello

Myrna Black

Cindy, Claudio, and Adrianna Bucceri

Jessa Fassel

Betta Ferrendelli

Tom and Janice Geisness

Roger Haydon

Jo Howe

Sue Klein

Blossom Landau

Cathy, Wilson, Ceanna, Trevor, and Jarett Leake

Tom and Louise McCloskey

Susan Roth

Sara Scribner

Robert Sondheim

Hal Sparks

Linda Wise

We would also like to thank the staff at the Bainbridge Island Town & Country Thriftway. In particular:

Mike Anderson

Bryan Briggs

Katy Cunningham

Todd Kowalski

Rick Nakata

Felix Narte

Linda Papineau

Gary Reese

Su Reith

Steve Vadset

And our sincere gratitude to the helpful folks at the Bainbridge Island Safeway Food & Drug.

THE
ACCIDENTAL GOURMET

Weeknights

A YEAR OF FAST AND DELICIOUS MEALS

INTRODUCTION

Remember "What's for dinner?" And the panicked feeling that gripped you as you heard those dreaded words every evening because, let's face it, your mind had been on other things most of the day and you hadn't even thought about what you were going to put on the table?

Well, thanks to a big little cookbook published a few years ago, called *A Dinner A Day,* the most worrisome question of all time became a thing of the past. And thanks to the tremendous success of *A Dinner A Day,* Sally and Suzannah are at it again—now bringing you *The Accidental Gourmet,* with yet another delicious dinner for every Monday through Friday for an entire year. From now on, you won't have to think about what's for dinner until the moment you walk into your kitchen.

If you already use *A Dinner A Day* and are familiar with the stress-free, fuss-free pleasure of preparing the evening meal, please turn to page 17 and begin your exciting new year of delicious weeknight menus. If not, please take a few moments to read on and see for yourself how effortlessly *The Accidental Gourmet* is going to redefine your relationship with your kitchen. You'll find that our surefire technique makes the evening meal one less thing you have to worry about in your busy day because we have taken the anxiety out of both the planning and the preparation.

Like its predecessor, *The Accidental Gourmet* is designed to complement the way we do things in today's hectic society. Because we believe that an overcommitted lifestyle does not have to shortchange the family, we show you how, even with limited time and resources, you can produce a terrific dinner every single weeknight in less than an hour. One that will have your family licking the plates. The secret is simple. We have redesigned old-fashioned home cooking to fit perfectly into today's more fragmented existence. In other words, the taste that used to take our grandmothers all day to prepare can now be produced by you in a matter of minutes. It's a totally new concept of "fast food."

Statistics show that 70 percent of the families in this country prefer to home-cook on a regular basis. But if you're one of those who depend on packaged entrees for a quick fix, you're not home-cooking. Instead, you're paying for a package filled with sodium, preservatives, and empty calories. For a little more time and a lot less money, you can have a complete, health-conscious meal for every Monday through Friday for an entire year.

Whether you're a single parent, the cooking half of a two-income family, or a multifaceted, stay-at-home mom, *The Accidental Gourmet* will work for you. It's a fool-proof method for putting meals on the table that can make each evening memorable and have even the cook looking forward to dinner.

Big in size, compact in presentation, *The Accidental Gourmet* gives you dinner, in its entirety, on two facing pages. Every meal is composed of main, side, and dessert dishes that have been carefully chosen to complement one another and allow you to maximize your time and enjoyment. Each dinner comes with a step-by-step countdown to ensure that your meal is on the table, start to finish, in less than an hour. And each week we provide a complete shopping list, day-coded for easy reference.

You can use this cookbook every single weeknight. You can use it two or three times a week. You can use it once or twice a month. However you choose to use it, *The Accidental Gourmet* will work for you. Its easy-to-follow format will allow cooks of every level to achieve spectacular results every time.

The Accidental Gourmet presents 260 complete dinner menus without a single repetition. That means more than 950 individual recipes, dovetailed to make each night unique. Every menu has been designed to feed an average family of four. However, most of our recipes can be adapted for more or fewer people, according to the size and appetite of your family. But please keep in mind that altering the portions may also alter some of the cooking times.

In looking over the menus, you will notice that not only does each dish fit perfectly into its meal, but each meal is carefully positioned within its week, each week is properly balanced within its season, and four distinct seasons of fresh fruits and vegetables and fish and meat make up an entire year of cooking variety and pleasure. And when we say that a meal can be prepared, start to finish, in less than an hour, we mean everything having to do with that meal, including assembling all the required ingredients, gathering the necessary cooking equipment, and doing all the peeling, grating, shredding, and chopping. The only thing missing is the time it will take you to get through your supermarket, and you will see that we've even taken the pain out of that.

In our efforts to simplify the entire dinner process, we have made the ritual of purchasing food every bit as important as the ritual of preparing it. Hence, there is a convenient and comprehensive weekly shopping list that provides you with all the ingredients you will need to create a whole week's worth of meals, organized into general categories that correspond with the placement of products in the majority of markets across the country.

In addition to the products to be purchased for each individual meal, we have identified a number of nonperishable ingredients used throughout the book as staple items. We recommend that you keep these items on hand at all times and that each week, before you shop, you take stock of the staples that will be used during that week and add them to your shopping list if necessary. Nothing is more frustrating than starting to prepare a meal, only to discover that you either lack, or lack enough of, a necessary ingredient.

While we have made every effort to be consistent, product availability does vary across the country, and you may find it necessary to make occasional substitutions. For example, products in cans and jars may vary by an ounce or two, depending on the manufacturer, but they can be substituted in recipes with no harm whatsoever. Different kinds of fish can be exchanged for whatever similar variety is available in your area.

You will notice that we use a great deal of fish in this cookbook. If you plan to shop once a week, look for fresh fish that has not been previously frozen so that you can freeze and then thaw the day before you are going to use it. Or purchase already frozen fish and thaw it the day before you use it. Your fishmonger may agree to provide you with frozen fish that would ordinarily be thawed before being sold. Please keep in mind, however, that shellfish, such as clams and mussels, must be purchased fresh and used within a day. If this is not possible because of your location or your time availability, use canned clams instead.

You will note that we offer two different times for cooking pasta because many varieties are now offered in both fresh and dried packages. It does not matter which you choose.

Among the best things about creating a cookbook for an entire year is that we get to make full use of the fresh seasonal products, such as fruits and vegetables, that are showing up in more and more markets across the country. Even so, there may be some products that your market simply does not carry. Feel free to substitute. A small melon will stand in for a papaya; spinach may be used instead of Swiss chard. You are also free to choose a frozen vegetable if fresh is not available. The same is true for berries. We love fresh berries, as you will see by the frequency with which we use them. If you find any of them not available or not cost-effective, you may always use frozen, and simply adjust the instructions.

Breads are another item that can easily be interchanged. French and Italian loaves can always be substituted for each other, as can country loaves and sourdough loaves. And peasant bread, rye bread, and pumpernickel are sufficiently similar to swap out.

It is always a joy to cook with fresh herbs because they greatly enhance the flavor and aroma of foods. We use them frequently—it's one of our rare excesses. However, they can be costly, so you may omit them if you prefer and use the dried variety at a ratio of three parts fresh to one part dried. We use one fresh herb, parsley, with abandon because it does wonderful things for food, is relatively inexpensive, is available all year long, and can be found in every market in the country. There is a dried version, but it's no substitute.

Garlic is another flavoring we use liberally. Not only does it make everything taste wonderful, but it's good for you. You are, of course, free to omit it, but be warned that the dish will not be nearly as flavorful.

Because herbs and spices are such a delicious and healthy way to flavor foods, we almost never call for just plain salt and pepper seasoning. However, we invite you to season to taste in whatever way you choose. Play with the dishes. Adapt them to your particular taste. Experiment. Have fun. You can rarely go very wrong.

While we have created *The Accidental Gourmet* to be a delicious, nutritious way to feed your family, we make no pretensions about its being a diet cookbook. It is, instead, a cookbook for the way most Americans prefer to eat. You are always free to use low-fat alternatives to such ingredients as milk, cream, cheese, and oil, and you may certainly substitute margarine for butter. Desserts are always optional. However, there are now many low-fat pound cakes and cookies on the market, as well as low-fat and fat-free ice creams and frozen yogurts, that will allow you to enjoy many of our desserts without feeling guilty.

Because no two kitchens are exactly alike, and cooks vary so greatly in style, it would be nearly impossible for us to suggest a single list of equipment that would suit every home. Instead, we will briefly discuss the equipment that we used in creating the recipes for this cookbook and leave the details to you.

For openers, there are a few small appliances without which we couldn't function. Tops on the list is an electric mixer, indispensable for mixing, beating, and blending chores that make preparing cakes and puddings seem easy. We love the wok for fast and healthful food preparation. There are stovetop versions as well as electric ones. Both work equally well. A blender is also indispensable. For creating fabulous soups and super sauces and perfect desserts, it's a miracle worker. We love stews almost as much as we love soups. This means a prominent place in our kitchen is reserved for the Dutch oven. And we frequently use a double boiler for rice. You bring water to boil in the bottom saucepot, put your ingredients in the top saucepot, cover it up, and leave it alone. You end up with perfect results every time. An electric rice cooker also delivers fuss-free results, if you happen to have one. If you have an electric steaming appliance for vegetables,

by all means use it. If not, you might want to consider the inexpensive stainless steel, fan-style insert for a saucepan or the bamboo type that is used in a wok or skillet.

Every kitchen has its supply of basic pots and pans. We use them all—and probably more. We call for skillets in small, medium, and large sizes. On occasion, we even call for more than one of the same size at the same time. It's a good idea to have tight-fitting lids for all your skillets.

As with skillets, we use small, medium, and large saucepans. All the time. And a good-sized stockpot for cooking pasta. And a colander to drain it. Like skillets, all your saucepans should have good-fitting lids.

You'll notice that we bake quite a bit in this cookbook—everything from biscuits to puddings, fish to fowl, and casseroles to cakes. So we use baking pans, baking dishes, baking sheets, muffin tins, and casseroles to delightful excess.

We also mix a lot, beat a lot, blend a lot. You can never have too many mixing bowls. We use everything from half-quart bowls to five-quart bowls, as often as possible.

Kitchen knives are definitely our tools of choice. Buy good quality, keep them clean and sharp, and they'll be worth their weight in steel for years to come. You can resort to expensive food processors, but we prefer slicing, dicing, and chopping the old-fashioned way. It may take a little more time, but you control the results, and the cleanup is a lot easier.

Then there are all the miscellaneous utensils that make preparing a meal possible. We wouldn't survive without a whisk in our kitchen. For making everything from sauces to salad dressings, it's a must. A vegetable brush, a vegetable peeler, and vegetable, citrus, and cheese graters all come under the "necessary" category. Something as simple as a pastry brush makes all sorts of jobs easy. Tongs to turn things, a mallet for crushing things, a melon baller, and an ice cream scoop are just a few of the items that keep the food coming but rarely get much praise. From spoons to spreaders to spatulas, every tool has its purpose. And a kitchen can't be called a real kitchen without a complete set of both liquid and dry measures. Unless you're uncommonly good at guessing, you'll use them every single evening.

As with *A Dinner A Day,* we have made a deliberate choice not to include microwave oven recipes in *The Accidental Gourmet.* We're never sure how many cooks truly feel comfortable using the appliance for anything other than defrosting and reheating. If you're one who does, however, you can save time and produce spectacular results by baking fish and steaming vegetables in your microwave oven. You'll find that adapting our recipes is easy.

It's not enough for a cookbook author to tell you that you can produce a whole dinner in less than an hour. The truth is, unless you're a super-well-organized cook, the vegetables are likely to get cold while you're waiting for the meat. Or you're trying to bake the casserole at the same time as the dessert—at different temperatures. Trying to prepare a meal that consists of several different dishes, each with its own set of cooking instructions, isn't always easy. So we don't just tell you that you can get that meal on the table in less than an hour—we show you exactly how.

We call it the "Countdown," and it's a chronology of cooking steps, covering every dish in the dinner, that will guide you through the preparation with the confidence of knowing that it will all be ready when you are. Just as we've taken the stress out of planning the meal and the hassle out of buying the ingredients, we've now taken all the confusion out of the cooking because, at the end of a long day, that should be the last thing for you to have to worry about. With the entire meal in full view, following the Countdown is easy. And everything's included in the hour, from the moment you walk into your kitchen to the moment you sit down at the table. In fact, we've done everything for you but the dishes.

Which means that we've done our job. So you can do yours.

WINTER

WEEK ONE

Monday
The Shell Game
Roll the Rice
Sleight of Salad
Jackpot Cake

Tuesday
Quiche Me Once
Two-Timers
Three's Company

Wednesday
Rhode Island Red
Providential Potatoes
Bristol Broccoli
Snug Harbors

Thursday
Unsurpasta
Beyond Beleaf
French Folly
Pearagon of Virtue

Friday
Upon My Sole
Norman Vincent Pilaf
Bishop Sheen's Beans
Billy Grahams

STAPLES

☐ Butter
☐ Flour
☐ Cornstarch
☐ Granulated sugar
☐ Dark brown sugar
☐ Olive oil
☐ Vegetable oil
☐ Red wine vinegar
☐ Rice vinegar
☐ White wine vinegar
☐ Lemon juice
☐ Lime juice
☐ Chili sauce
☐ Honey
☐ Ketchup
☐ Prepared horseradish
☐ Worcestershire sauce
☐ Grated Parmesan cheese
☐ Celery seeds
☐ Dried basil
☐ Dried marjoram
☐ Dried oregano
☐ Dried thyme
☐ Ground allspice
☐ Ground cardamom
☐ Cayenne pepper
☐ Ground cinnamon
☐ Ground cloves
☐ Curry powder
☐ Dry mustard
☐ Ground nutmeg
☐ Paprika
☐ Black pepper
☐ Red pepper flakes
☐ White pepper
☐ Salt
☐ Turmeric
☐ Vanilla extract

SHOPPING LIST

MEAT & POULTRY

4 boneless, skinless chicken breast halves (about 1 1/2 pounds) (W)

FISH

1 pound medium shrimp, shelled and deveined (M)
1 pound sea scallops (M)
4 sole fillets (about 1 1/2 pounds) (F)

FRESH PRODUCE

VEGETABLES

1 1/2 pounds small new red potatoes (W)
1 medium bunch broccoli (W)
3/4 pound sugar-snap peas (Th)
4 medium carrots (T)
2 stalks celery (W)
2 stalks celery (F)
1/4 pound mushrooms (T)
1 small head lettuce (M)
1 small head lettuce (Th)
1 large ripe avocado (M)
1 medium cucumber (F)
1 small red bell pepper (Th)
1 small yellow bell pepper (Th)
1 large onion (T)
1 small onion (Th)
1 small red onion (M)
1 small red onion (W)
1 medium shallot (M)
3 scallions (green onions) (F)
4 cloves garlic (M)
1 clove garlic (T)
3 cloves garlic (Th)

HERBS

3 tablespoons chives (when chopped) (F)
1/4 cup parsley (when chopped) (M)
1/4 cup parsley (when chopped) (Th)
2 tablespoons parsley (when chopped) (F)

FRUIT

1 small grapefruit (M)
1 large lemon (F)
1 small ripe cantaloupe melon (T)
1 small ripe honeydew melon (T)
1 large red apple (W)
1/4 pound seedless red grapes (T)

CANS, JARS & BOTTLES

SOUPS

1 can (14 ounces) chicken broth (W)
1 can (14 ounces) vegetable broth (F)

INTERNATIONAL FOODS

1 can (8 ounces) sliced water chestnuts (T)

SAUCES

1 can (15 ounces) tomato sauce (Th)

CONDIMENTS

1 jar (6 1/2 ounces) marinated artichoke hearts (Th)
1 jar (4 ounces) sliced pimientos (Th)
1 can (3 1/2 ounces) sliced black olives (Th)

FRUIT

1 can (15 ounces) pear halves (Th)

SPREADS

1 jar (10 ounces) mango chutney (W)

PACKAGED GOODS

PASTA, RICE & GRAINS

1 pound linguini (Th)
1 cup long-grain white rice (M)
1 cup long-grain white rice (F)

BAKED GOODS

1 loaf French bread (Th, F)
1 box (9 ounces) gingersnaps (Th)
1/2 cup graham cracker crumbs (F)

DRIED FRUIT & NUTS

1/2 cup golden raisins (W)

DESSERT & BAKING NEEDS

1 package (3 ounces) lemon gelatin (W)
1 package (3.4 ounces) instant chocolate pudding mix (F)
1/2 cup chocolate chips (W)
1 cup mini-marshmallows (W)
1/2 cup flaked coconut (M)

WINE & SPIRITS

1/2 cup dry white wine (Th)
2 tablespoons dry sherry (M)

REFRIGERATED PRODUCTS

DAIRY

1/2 cup milk (T)
2 cups chocolate milk (F)
1 cup half-and-half (T)
1/2 cup plain yogurt (T)
1/4 cup plain yogurt (F)
Whipped cream for garnish (Th)
Whipped cream for garnish (F)
4 eggs (T)

CHEESE

2 cups shredded Colby/Monterey Jack cheese (T)
1 cup shredded mozzarella cheese (Th)

JUICES

1 cup orange juice (W)

DELI

4 slices bacon (Th)

FROZEN GOODS

VEGETABLES

1 package (10 ounces) chopped spinach (T)
1 package (10 ounces) cut green beans (F)

BAKED GOODS

1 cinnamon swirl pound cake (M)

PASTRY

1 unbaked pie shell (T)

MONDAY

The Shell Game

1 medium shallot
4 cloves garlic
1/4 cup fresh parsley (when chopped)
1 pound medium shrimp, shelled and
    deveined
1 pound sea scallops
2 tablespoons ketchup
1 tablespoon chili sauce
2 tablespoons dry sherry
1/2 teaspoon dry mustard
1 teaspoon prepared horseradish
1/4 cup vegetable oil
1/4 teaspoon red pepper flakes
Seasoning to taste

Roll the Rice

1 cup long-grain white rice
2 1/4 cups water
2 teaspoons turmeric
1/2 teaspoon ground nutmeg

Sleight of Salad

1 small head lettuce
1 small red onion
1 small grapefruit
1 large ripe avocado
3 tablespoons olive oil
2 tablespoons red wine vinegar
1 teaspoon granulated sugar
Seasoning to taste

Jackpot Cake

1 frozen cinnamon swirl pound cake
3 tablespoons butter
3 tablespoons honey
1/2 cup flaked coconut

EQUIPMENT

Double boiler	Whisk
Large skillet	Kitchen knives
Baking sheet	Measuring cups and
Medium mixing bowl	spoons
2 small mixing bowls	Cooking utensils

COUNTDOWN

1. Assemble the ingredients and the
   equipment.
2. Do Steps 1–2 of *Roll the Rice*.
3. Do Step 1 of *Jackpot Cake*.
4. Do Steps 1–3 of *Sleight of Salad*.
5. Do Steps 1–3 of *The Shell Game*.
6. Do Steps 2–4 of *Jackpot Cake*.
7. Do Steps 4–5 of *The Shell Game*.
8. Do Step 3 of *Roll the Rice*.
9. Do Step 6 of *The Shell Game*.
10. Do Step 4 of *Sleight of Salad*.
11. Do Step 5 of *Jackpot Cake*.

MONDAY

The Shell Game

1 Peel and chop the shallot. Peel and mince the garlic. Rinse, stem, and chop the parsley.

2 Rinse and pat dry the shrimp and the scallops.

3 In a small bowl, combine the shallot, the ketchup, the chili sauce, the sherry, the mustard, and the horseradish. Set aside.

4 Heat the oil in a large skillet. Add the garlic and the red pepper flakes and sauté for 3 minutes. Add the shrimp and the scallops and cook until the shrimp turn pink, 3 to 4 minutes.

5 Add the parsley and the sauce mixture, season to taste, and cook for 1 to 2 minutes to heat through.

6 Serve over the rice.

Roll the Rice

1 Bring water to a boil in the bottom of a double boiler.

2 Combine the rice, the 2¼ cups of water, the turmeric, and the nutmeg in the top of the double boiler. Cover, reduce the heat, and simmer until all the water is absorbed and the rice is tender, 30 to 40 minutes.

3 Fluff the rice with a fork.

Sleight of Salad

1 Wash and dry the lettuce and arrange the leaves on individual salad plates.

2 Peel and chop the onion. Peel and section the grapefruit. Halve, pit, peel, and slice the avocado. Combine the ingredients in a medium bowl.

3 In a small bowl, whisk together the oil, the vinegar, and the sugar. Season to taste and toss with the vegetables.

4 Spoon the mixture over the lettuce leaves.

Jackpot Cake

1 Set the pound cake out to thaw. Set the butter out to soften. Grease a baking sheet.

2 Slice the pound cake into 8 equal portions. Spread lightly with the softened butter and the honey. Sprinkle with the coconut. Arrange the cake slices on the baking sheet.

3 Preheat the oven to 375°F.

4 Bake the cake slices until lightly browned, 5 to 10 minutes.

5 Turn off the oven and let the cake remain in the oven until you are ready to serve.

TUESDAY

Quiche Me Once

1 package (10 ounces) frozen chopped
  spinach
1 large onion
1/4 pound mushrooms
3 tablespoons butter
4 eggs
1/2 cup milk
1/2 cup plain yogurt
1 cup half-and-half
2 tablespoons flour
1/2 teaspoon ground allspice
1/4 teaspoon cayenne pepper
1/2 teaspoon white pepper
Seasoning to taste
2 cups shredded Colby/Monterey Jack
  cheese
1/4 cup grated Parmesan cheese
1 unbaked pie shell

Two-Timers

4 medium carrots
1 clove garlic
1 can (8 ounces) sliced water chestnuts
3 tablespoons lemon juice
1/4 teaspoon paprika
1/4 teaspoon ground cinnamon
1/8 teaspoon Worcestershire sauce

Three's Company

1 small ripe cantaloupe melon
1 small ripe honeydew melon
1/4 pound seedless red grapes
3 tablespoons lime juice
2 teaspoons honey
1 teaspoon water
1 teaspoon cornstarch

EQUIPMENT

Small saucepan	Whisk
Medium covered skillet	Vegetable peeler
Medium skillet	Kitchen knives
Large mixing bowl	Measuring cups and spoons
Small mixing bowl	Cooking utensils

COUNTDOWN

1. Assemble the ingredients and the equipment.
2. Do Steps 1–6 of *Quiche Me Once*.
3. Do Steps 1–3 of *Three's Company*.
4. Do Steps 1–3 of *Two-Timers*.
5. Do Step 7 of *Quiche Me Once*.
6. Do Step 4 of *Two-Timers*.
7. Do Step 4 of *Three's Company*.

TUESDAY

Quiche Me Once

1 Place the package of spinach in a small bowl of very warm water to thaw.

2 Peel and chop the onion. Rinse, pat dry, trim, and slice the mushrooms.

3 Melt the butter in a medium skillet. Add the onion and the mushrooms and sauté until the onion is soft, about 5 minutes.

4 Squeeze the spinach dry.

5 In a large bowl, whip the eggs lightly. Add the milk, the yogurt, the half-and-half, the flour, the allspice, the cayenne pepper, and the white pepper, and season to taste. Add the onions, the mushrooms, and the spinach. Fold in the cheeses.

6 Pour the mixture into the pie shell and bake until a knife inserted in the center comes out clean, 35 to 40 minutes.

7 Let the quiche cool for 5 minutes before cutting.

Two-Timers

1 Peel, trim, and julienne the carrots. Peel and mince the garlic. Drain the water chestnuts.

2 Bring a small amount of water to a boil in a medium skillet.

3 Place the carrots and the garlic in the skillet. Cover, reduce the heat, and simmer for 5 minutes.

4 Drain the carrots and return them to the skillet. Add the water chestnuts. Add the lemon juice, the paprika, the cinnamon, and the Worcestershire sauce and toss to combine and heat through.

Three's Company

1 Halve, seed, and slice the melons into thin wedges. Remove the rinds. Rinse, dry, and stem the grapes.

2 Place the melon wedges, alternating colors, on individual plates. Dot with the grapes.

3 Combine the lime juice and the honey in a small saucepan and heat. Mix the water and the cornstarch together and whisk into the lime mixture until well blended and clear, about 2 minutes. Remove from the heat and cover to keep warm.

4 Drizzle the sauce over the fruit.

WEDNESDAY

Rhode Island Red

4 boneless, skinless chicken breast halves
 (about 1 1/2 pounds)
Seasoning to taste
1 cup orange juice
1/2 cup golden raisins
1 jar (10 ounces) mango chutney
1 teaspoon dried thyme
1 teaspoon ground cardamom
1 teaspoon curry powder

Providential Potatoes

1 1/2 pounds small new red potatoes
2 stalks celery
1 can (14 ounces) chicken broth
2 tablespoons butter
1/2 teaspoon ground cloves
Seasoning to taste

Bristol Broccoli

1 medium bunch broccoli
1 small red onion
1 tablespoon butter
Seasoning to taste

Snug Harbors

1 1/4 cups water
1 large red apple
1 package (3 ounces) lemon gelatin
Ice cubes
1/2 cup chocolate chips
1 cup mini-marshmallows

EQUIPMENT

Blender
Medium covered
 saucepan
Medium saucepan
Medium skillet
9 x 13-inch glass
 baking dish
Steamer insert

Small mixing bowl
Whisk
Vegetable brush
Kitchen knives
Measuring cups and
 spoons
Cooking utensils

COUNTDOWN

1. Assemble the ingredients and the equipment.
2. Do Steps 1–5 of *Snug Harbors*.
3. Do Steps 1–3 of *Rhode Island Red*.
4. Do Steps 1–2 of *Providential Potatoes*.
5. Do Steps 1–2 of *Bristol Broccoli*.
6. Do Step 3 of *Providential Potatoes*.
7. Do Steps 3–4 of *Bristol Broccoli*.
8. Do Step 4 of *Providential Potatoes*.
9. Do Step 5 of *Bristol Broccoli*.

WEDNESDAY

Rhode Island Red

1 Preheat the oven to 350°F. Lightly grease a 9 x 13-inch baking dish.

2 Rinse and pat dry the chicken breasts and arrange them in a single layer in the baking dish. Season to taste.

3 In a small bowl, whisk together the orange juice, the raisins, the chutney, the thyme, the cardamom, and the curry powder. Pour the mixture over the chicken and bake until the chicken is tender, 25 to 30 minutes.

Providential Potatoes

1 Scrub the potatoes. Rinse, trim, and slice the celery.

2 Bring the broth to a boil in a medium saucepan. Add the potatoes and cook for 10 minutes.

3 Add the celery and cook until the potatoes are tender, about 5 minutes more.

4 Drain the vegetables. Melt the butter with the cloves in the saucepan. Return the vegetables and toss to coat. Season to taste.

Bristol Broccoli

1 Bring a small amount of water to a boil in a medium saucepan.

2 Rinse and trim the broccoli, discard the tough ends, and cut into bite-sized florets. Arrange the florets in a steamer insert.

Place the insert in the saucepan, cover, and steam until the broccoli is crisp-tender, 6 to 8 minutes.

3 Peel and mince the onion.

4 Melt the butter in a medium skillet and sauté the onion until it is soft, about 5 minutes.

5 Drain the broccoli, add it to the skillet, season to taste, and toss to coat.

Snug Harbors

1 Bring ¾ cup of the water to a boil.

2 Rinse, quarter, and core the apple and cut it into small pieces.

3 Pour the boiling water into a blender. Add the gelatin and blend until the gelatin is completely dissolved, about 30 seconds.

4 Combine the remaining ½ cup water with enough ice cubes to make 1¼ cups. Add to the blender and process until smooth, about 30 seconds.

5 Distribute the apple, the chocolate chips, and the marshmallows among individual dessert glasses. Pour the gelatin mixture over the apples, the chips, and the marsh-mallows. Refrigerate until you are ready to serve.

THURSDAY

Unsurpasta

1 small onion
2 cloves garlic
1 jar (6½ ounces) marinated artichoke
  hearts
1 can (3½ ounces) sliced black olives
1 jar (4 ounces) sliced pimientos
1 pound linguini
1 can (15 ounces) tomato sauce
½ cup dry white wine
2 teaspoons dried basil
2 teaspoons dried oregano
1 teaspoon dried marjoram
Seasoning to taste
1 cup shredded mozzarella cheese

Beyond Beleaf

1 small head lettuce
¾ pound sugar-snap peas
1 small yellow bell pepper
1 small red bell pepper
¼ cup fresh parsley (when chopped)
2 tablespoons honey
2 tablespoons white wine vinegar
Seasoning to taste

French Folly

4 slices bacon
1 clove garlic
2 tablespoons olive oil
1 loaf French bread (reserve both ends for
  use on Friday)

Pearagon of Virtue

1 can (15 ounces) pear halves
1 box (9 ounces) gingersnaps
2 tablespoons butter
2 tablespoons dark brown sugar
Whipped cream for garnish

EQUIPMENT

Stockpot	Small mixing bowl
Small saucepan	Whisk
Large skillet	Plastic bag
Medium skillet	Kitchen knives
Small skillet	Measuring cups and
9-inch cake pan	spoons
Baking sheet	Cooking utensils
Colander	

COUNTDOWN

1. Assemble the ingredients and the equipment.
2. Do Steps 1–5 of *Pearagon of Virtue*.
3. Do Steps 1–2 of *Beyond Beleaf*.
4. Do Step 1 of *French Folly*.
5. Do Steps 1–3 of *Unsurpasta*.
6. Do Steps 2–3 of *French Folly*.
7. Do Steps 3–5 of *Beyond Belief*.
8. Do Step 4 of *French Folly*.
9. Do Steps 4–6 of *Unsurpasta*.
10. Do Step 5 of *French Folly*.
11. Do Step 6 of *Pearagon of Virtue*.

THURSDAY

Unsurpasta

1 Peel and chop the onion. Peel and mince the garlic.

2 Drain the artichoke hearts, reserving the marinade. Coarsely chop the hearts. Drain the olives. Drain the pimientos.

3 Bring water to a boil in a stockpot.

4 Cook the linguini until almost tender, 2 to 3 minutes if you are using fresh pasta, 6 to 7 minutes if you are using dry pasta.

5 In a large skillet, heat the reserved artichoke marinade. Add the onion and the garlic. Sauté, stirring, for 5 minutes. Add the artichokes, the olives, the pimientos, the tomato sauce, the wine, the basil, the oregano, and the marjoram. Season to taste.

6 Drain the pasta, return it to the stockpot, and toss it with the cheese. Top it with the sauce.

Beyond Beleaf

1 Wash and dry the lettuce and arrange the leaves on individual salad plates.

2 Rinse and string the snap peas. Rinse, trim, and seed the bell peppers and cut them into thin strips. Rinse, stem, and chop the parsley.

3 Bring a small amount of water to a boil in a medium skillet. Add the snap peas and cook for 2 minutes.

4 In a small bowl, whisk together the honey and the vinegar. Season to taste.

5 Drain the snap peas and rinse under cold water. Arrange the peas and the pepper strips over the lettuce. Drizzle the dressing over the salads and garnish with the parsley.

French Folly

1 Dice the bacon. Peel and mince the garlic.

2 Sauté the bacon in a small skillet until it is almost crisp, about 5 minutes. Drain on paper towels and discard the bacon grease. Heat the oil in the same skillet and sauté the garlic for 2 minutes.

3 Cut 2 inches off each end of the bread and reserve for use on Friday. Slice the remainder of the bread in half lengthwise. Spread the cut sides with the garlic mixture and sprinkle with the bacon.

4 Preheat the broiler.

5 Place the bread on a baking sheet and broil until lightly toasted, about 2 minutes.

Pearagon of Virtue

1 Preheat the oven to 300°F.

2 Drain the pears and place them cut side up in a 9-inch cake pan.

3 In a plastic bag, finely crush the gingersnaps.

4 In a small saucepan, melt the butter with the brown sugar. Add the gingersnap crumbs, mixing well. Spread the mixture over the pears.

5 Bake for 20 minutes.

6 Garnish with dollops of whipped cream.

FRIDAY

MENU

Upon My Sole

4 sole fillets (about 1 1/2 pounds)
3 scallions (green onions)
1 medium cucumber
2 tablespoons fresh parsley (when chopped)
2 end slices French bread (reserved from Thursday)
2 tablespoons butter
1/4 cup plain yogurt
1 tablespoon rice vinegar
1/2 teaspoon paprika
Seasoning to taste

Norman Vincent Pilaf

1 large lemon
3 tablespoons fresh chives (when chopped)
2 tablespoons vegetable oil
1 cup long-grain white rice
1 can (14 ounces) vegetable broth
1/4 cup water

Bishop Sheen's Beans

1 package (10 ounces) frozen cut green beans
2 stalks celery
1 tablespoon butter
1 teaspoon celery seeds
1/4 teaspoon granulated sugar
Seasoning to taste

Billy Grahams

1 package (3.4 ounces) instant chocolate pudding mix
2 cups chocolate milk
1 teaspoon vanilla extract
Whipped cream for garnish
1/2 cup graham cracker crumbs

EQUIPMENT

Electric mixer
Large covered saucepan
Medium covered saucepan
Large skillet
9 x 9-inch glass baking dish
Baking sheet
Steamer insert
Medium mixing bowl
Small mixing bowl
Vegetable peeler
Citrus grater
Citrus juicer
Toothpicks
Aluminum foil
Kitchen knives
Measuring cups and spoons
Cooking utensils

COUNTDOWN

1. Assemble the ingredients and the equipment.
2. Do Step 1 of *Bishop Sheen's Beans.*
3. Do Steps 1–2 of *Billy Grahams.*
4. Do Step 1 of *Norman Vincent Pilaf.*
5. Do Step 2 of *Bishop Sheen's Beans.*
6. Do Steps 1–5 of *Upon My Sole.*
7. Do Step 2 of *Norman Vincent Pilaf.*
8. Do Step 3 of *Bishop Sheen's Beans.*
9. Do Step 3 of *Norman Vincent Pilaf.*
10. Do Step 4 of *Bishop Sheen's Beans.*
11. Do Step 3 of *Billy Grahams.*

FRIDAY

Upon My Sole

1 Preheat the oven to 350°F. Grease a 9 x 9-inch baking dish.

2 Rinse and pat dry the fish fillets. Rinse, trim, and chop the scallions. Peel, halve, seed, and chop the cucumber. Rinse, stem, and chop the parsley.

3 Lay the French bread ends on a baking sheet and toast in the oven on both sides, about 2 minutes per side. Cut the slices into ¼-inch cubes.

4 Melt the butter in a large skillet. Sauté the scallions until tender, about 2 minutes. Add the cucumber, the parsley, the bread cubes, the yogurt, the vinegar, and the paprika. Season to taste.

5 Spread the scallion stuffing over each fish fillet. Starting at the narrow end, roll each fillet up and skewer with a toothpick. Place the rolls in the pan. Cover with aluminum foil and bake until the fish flakes easily with a fork, about 25 minutes.

Norman Vincent Pilaf

1 Grate the lemon peel. Squeeze 2 tablespoons of lemon juice. Rinse, trim, and chop the chives.

2 Heat the oil in a large saucepan and sauté the rice for 1 minute. Add the chives, the broth, the water, the lemon juice, and the lemon peel. Bring the liquid to a boil. Cover and simmer until all the liquid is absorbed, about 20 minutes.

3 Fluff the rice with a fork.

Bishop Sheen's Beans

1 Set the green beans in a small bowl of warm water to thaw.

2 Rinse, trim, and slice the celery.

3 Bring a small amount of water to a boil in a medium saucepan. Arrange the celery and the beans in a steamer insert. Place the insert in the saucepan, cover, and steam for 5 minutes.

4 Drain the beans and the celery. Melt the butter in the saucepan. Add the vegetables, the celery seeds, and the sugar, and stir to mix. Season to taste.

Billy Grahams

1 In a medium bowl, combine the pudding mix and the chocolate milk and beat until well blended, about 2 minutes. Fold in the vanilla.

2 Pour the mixture into individual dessert bowls and refrigerate until you are ready to serve.

3 Garnish with dollops of whipped cream and the graham cracker crumbs.

WEEK TWO

Monday
Casual Consommé
Funky Fettuccine
Gotcha Focaccia
Chill-Out Pudding

Tuesday
Snap To It!
Practical Potatoes
Eenie Meenie Zucchini
Peach Perfect

Wednesday
The Wabash Mash
La Salad
Hoosits
French Lick

Thursday
Bye-Bye Birdie
Rice Side Story
Show Bean
The Dessert Song

Friday
Green and Bear It
Tomato Things
Maybe Muffins
Sly Pudding

- ❑ Butter
- ❑ Flour
- ❑ Baking powder
- ❑ Baking soda
- ❑ Granulated sugar
- ❑ Dark brown sugar
- ❑ Powdered sugar
- ❑ Olive oil
- ❑ Vegetable oil
- ❑ Red wine vinegar
- ❑ White wine vinegar
- ❑ Lemon juice
- ❑ Mayonnaise
- ❑ Prepared horseradish
- ❑ White Worcestershire sauce
- ❑ Grated Romano cheese
- ❑ Poppy seeds
- ❑ Sesame seeds
- ❑ Dried basil
- ❑ Bay leaf
- ❑ Dried dill
- ❑ Dried oregano
- ❑ Dried savory
- ❑ Dried tarragon
- ❑ Dried thyme
- ❑ Ground allspice
- ❑ Ground cardamom
- ❑ Ground cinnamon
- ❑ Ground cumin
- ❑ Italian seasoning
- ❑ Ground nutmeg
- ❑ Black pepper
- ❑ Salt
- ❑ Rum extract

MEAT & POULTRY

1 1/2 pounds lean cooked ham steak (W)

3 pounds chicken pieces (Th)

FISH

4 red snapper fillets (about 1 1/2 pounds) (T)

FRESH PRODUCE

VEGETABLES

1 1/2 pounds new red potatoes (T)

2 medium zucchini (T)

1 small carrot (T)

1 stalk celery (T)

1 small head red cabbage (T)

1 medium head lettuce (W)

2 large tomatoes (F)

2 medium tomatoes (W)

1 small ripe avocado (W)

1 medium cucumber (W)

1 large green bell pepper (W)

1 large red bell pepper (W)

1 jalapeño pepper (optional) (W)

1 small onion (T)

1 large leek (W)

2 scallions (green onions) (Th)

2 cloves garlic (M)

2 cloves garlic (W)

1 clove garlic (F)

HERBS

2 tablespoons chives (when chopped) (M)

1/4 cup chives (when chopped) (F)

3 tablespoons cilantro (when chopped) (W)

2 tablespoons parsley (when chopped) (T)

2 tablespoons parsley (when chopped) (Th)

FRUIT

1 small lime (Th)

1 large tart green apple (F)

CANS, JARS & BOTTLES

SOUPS

1 can (14 ounces) vegetable broth (M)

2 cans (14 ounces each) chicken broth (W)

1 can (14 ounces) beef broth (W)

1 can (14 ounces) onion beef broth (Th)

VEGETABLES

1 can (15 ounces) cream-style corn (W)

1 can (11 ounces) whole-kernel corn (W)

1 can (14 ounces) hearts of palm (F)

FRUIT

1 can (15 ounces) crushed pineapple (M)

1 can (29 ounces) peach halves (T)

1 can (15 ounces) apricot halves (Th)

SPREADS

1/2 cup raspberry preserves (W)

1 cup apricot preserves (Th)

JUICES

2 cups tomato juice (M)

1 can (6 ounces) V-8 juice (M)

DESSERT & BAKING NEEDS

1/4 cup marshmallow crème for garnish (W)

PACKAGED GOODS

PASTA, RICE & GRAINS

1 pound fettuccine (M)

1 pound spinach tortellini (F)

1/2 cup instant rice (T)

1/2 cup long-grain white rice (Th)

1/2 cup wild rice (Th)

BAKED GOODS

1 loaf focaccia bread (M)

1 angel food loaf cake (Th)

25 vanilla wafers (M)

DRIED FRUIT & NUTS

1/2 cup pecan bits (T)

1/2 cup walnut bits (F)

DESSERT & BAKING NEEDS

1 package (3.4 ounces) instant pistachio pudding mix (M)

1 package (3.4 ounces) instant vanilla pudding mix (F)

1/2 cup mini-marshmallows (M)

1 milk chocolate bar (2.6 ounces) (F)

WINE & SPIRITS

1/4 cup dry white wine (M)

1/2 cup dry white wine (T)

2 tablespoons dry white wine (F)

1/4 cup dry sherry (M)

2 tablespoons dry sherry (W)

REFRIGERATED PRODUCTS

DAIRY

3 1/4 cups milk (F)

1/2 cup sour cream (M)

1 1/2 cups sour cream (W)

1 cup plain yogurt (Th)

1/2 cup whipping cream (W)

1 egg (F)

CHEESE

1/2 cup shredded mozzarella cheese (F)

DELI

1/2 pound prosciutto ham (M)

4 slices bacon (T)

FROZEN GOODS

VEGETABLES

1 package (10 ounces) chopped asparagus (M)

1 package (10 ounces) cut green beans (Th)

1 package (10 ounces) green peas (F)

DESSERTS

1 pint French vanilla ice cream (W)

1 container (8 ounces) whipped topping (M)

1 container (8 ounces) whipped topping (Th)

MONDAY

Casual Consommé

2 tablespoons fresh chives (when chopped)
1 can (14 ounces) vegetable broth
2 cups tomato juice
1 can (6 ounces) V-8 juice
1 teaspoon granulated sugar
Seasoning to taste
1/4 cup dry sherry

Funky Fettuccine

1 package (10 ounces) frozen chopped
    asparagus
1/2 pound prosciutto ham
2 tablespoons butter
1/2 cup sour cream
3/4 cup grated Romano cheese
1/4 cup dry white wine
1 teaspoon dried basil
1/2 teaspoon dried oregano
Seasoning to taste
1 pound fettuccine

Gotcha Focaccia

1 loaf focaccia bread
2 cloves garlic
3 tablespoons olive oil
1 teaspoon poppy seeds
2 teaspoons Italian seasoning

Chill-Out Pudding

1 can (15 ounces) crushed pineapple
1 package (3.4 ounces) instant pistachio
    pudding mix
1/2 cup mini-marshmallows
4 tablespoons butter
25 vanilla wafers
2 tablespoons granulated sugar
1 container (8 ounces) frozen whipped
    topping

EQUIPMENT

Electric mixer	2 small mixing bowls
Stockpot	Whisk
Large covered saucepan	Pastry brush
	Plastic bag
2 medium saucepans	Aluminum foil
9 x 9-inch glass baking dish	Kitchen knives
Colander	Measuring cups and spoons
Medium mixing bowl	Cooking utensils

COUNTDOWN

1. Assemble the ingredients and the equipment.
2. Do Step 1 of *Funky Fettuccine*.
3. Do Steps 1–5 of *Chill-Out Pudding*.
4. Do Step 2 of *Funky Fettuccine*.
5. Do Steps 1–2 of *Casual Consommé*.
6. Do Steps 1–4 of *Gotcha Focaccia*.
7. Do Steps 3–8 of *Funky Fettuccine*.
8. Do Step 3 of *Casual Consommé*.

MONDAY

Casual Consommé

1 Rinse, trim, and chop the chives.

2 In a large saucepan, combine the broth, the tomato juice, the V-8 juice, and the sugar. Season to taste. Bring to a boil. Add the sherry and mix well. Cover, reduce the heat, and simmer until you are ready to serve.

3 Spoon the soup into bowls and sprinkle the chives over each serving.

Funky Fettuccine

1 Set the asparagus in a small bowl of warm water to thaw.

2 Bring water to a boil in a stockpot.

3 Bring a small amount of water to a boil in a medium saucepan.

4 Add the asparagus to the saucepan and cook for 2 minutes. Drain and rinse in cold water.

5 Cut the prosciutto into 1-inch-wide strips.

6 Melt the butter in the saucepan. Blend in the sour cream, the cheese, the wine, the basil, and the oregano. Season to taste. Fold in the asparagus and the prosciutto and simmer until heated through, about 5 minutes.

7 Cook the fettuccine until it is almost tender, 2 to 3 minutes if you are using fresh pasta, 6 to 7 minutes if you are using dry pasta.

8 Drain the pasta and return it to the stockpot. Toss it with the sauce.

Gotcha Focaccia

1 Preheat the oven to 375°F.

2 Cut the bread crosswise into 1-inch-thick slices without slicing all the way through.

3 Peel and mash the garlic.

4 In a small bowl, combine the garlic, the oil, the poppy seeds, and the Italian seasoning. Brush the mixture between the slices. Wrap the bread in aluminum foil and bake until heated through, about 10 minutes.

Chill-Out Pudding

1 In a medium bowl, combine the undrained pineapple with the pudding mix and beat well. Fold in the mini-marshmallows, and let the mixture stand for 20 minutes.

2 Place the vanilla wafers in a plastic bag and crumble them.

3 Melt the butter in a medium saucepan.

4 Combine the cookie crumbs and the sugar with the butter. Reserve 1 cup of the mixture and press the rest evenly into the bottom of a 9 x 9-inch baking dish.

5 Fold the whipped topping into the pineapple mixture and spoon it over the cookie mixture. Sprinkle with the reserved crumbs and chill until firm, about 25 minutes.

TUESDAY

Snap To It!

4 red snapper fillets (about 1 1/2 pounds)
1 small onion
1 small carrot
1 teaspoon dried thyme
1 teaspoon dried dill
1 bay leaf
1/2 cup dry white wine
1/2 cup water
Seasoning to taste
2 tablespoons butter
2 tablespoons flour

Practical Potatoes

1 1/2 pounds new red potatoes
2 tablespoons fresh parsley (when chopped)
4 slices bacon
Seasoning to taste

Eenie Meenie Zucchini

2 medium zucchini
1 small red cabbage
1 stalk celery
2 tablespoons granulated sugar
3 tablespoons olive oil
2 tablespoons white wine vinegar
Seasoning to taste

Peach Perfect

1 can (29 ounces) peach halves
1/2 cup instant rice
1/4 cup water
2 tablespoons dark brown sugar
1 teaspoon ground allspice
1 tablespoon butter
1/2 cup pecan bits

EQUIPMENT

Small covered saucepan
Small saucepan
Large skillet
9 x 13-inch glass baking dish
9 x 9-inch glass baking dish
Large mixing bowl
Small mixing bowl

Whisk
Vegetable brush
Vegetable peeler
Vegetable grater
Aluminum foil
Kitchen knives
Measuring cups and spoons
Cooking utensils

COUNTDOWN

1. Assemble the ingredients and the equipment.
2. Do Steps 1–2 of *Eenie Meenie Zucchini.*
3. Do Steps 1–2 of *Peach Perfect.*
4. Do Steps 1–4 of *Snap To It!*
5. Do Steps 1–2 of *Practical Potatoes.*
6. Do Step 5 of *Snap To It!*
7. Do Steps 3–4 of *Practical Potatoes.*
8. Do Steps 6–7 of *Snap To It!*
9. Do Steps 3–5 of *Peach Perfect.*

TUESDAY

Snap To It!

1 Grease a 9 x 13-inch baking dish.

2 Wash and pat dry the fish fillets. Peel and chop the onion. Peel, trim, and chop the carrot.

3 Place the onion, the carrot, the thyme, the dill, and the bay leaf in the baking dish. Lay the fish over the vegetables. Add the wine and the water and season to taste. Cover the dish with aluminum foil, sealing tightly.

4 Preheat the oven to 375°F.

5 Bake until the fish flakes easily with a fork, 12 to 15 minutes.

6 Melt the butter in a small saucepan. Blend in the flour.

7 With a slotted spoon, remove the fish fillets from the baking dish and arrange them on individual dinner plates. Discard the bay leaf and add the vegetables and the cooking liquid to the butter mixture. Bring to a boil, whisking to blend, and spoon over the fish.

Practical Potatoes

1 Scrub and thinly slice the potatoes. Rinse, stem, and chop the parsley.

2 Sauté the bacon in a large skillet until crisp, about 7 minutes. Remove and drain on paper towels.

3 Sauté the potatoes in the bacon drippings until they are brown and crisp, 12 to 15 minutes.

4 Season the potatoes to taste. Crumble the bacon and sprinkle it and the parsley over the potatoes.

Eenie Meenie Zucchini

1 Scrub, trim, and coarsely grate the zucchini. Rinse, trim, quarter, and grate the cabbage. Rinse, trim, and chop the celery. Place the ingredients in a large bowl.

2 In a small bowl, whisk together the sugar, the oil, and the vinegar. Season to taste and toss with the salad.

Peach Perfect

1 Drain the peaches, reserving ¼ cup of the liquid, and arrange them, cut side up, in a 9 x 9-inch baking dish.

2 Combine the rice, the reserved liquid, and the water in a small saucepan. Bring to a boil, cover, and cook for 1 minute. Remove the saucepan from the heat and let stand for at least 5 minutes.

3 Preheat the broiler.

4 Blend the brown sugar, the allspice, and the butter into the rice.

5 Fill the peach halves with the rice mixture. Top with the pecans. Broil for 3 minutes.

WEDNESDAY

The Wabash Mash

1 large leek
2 cloves garlic
1 large green bell pepper
1 large red bell pepper
2 medium tomatoes
1 1/2 pounds lean cooked ham steak
3 tablespoons fresh cilantro (when
   chopped)
1 jalapeño pepper (optional)
1 tablespoon butter
1 tablespoon olive oil
1 teaspoon ground cumin
1 can (15 ounces) cream-style corn
1 can (11 ounces) whole-kernel corn
2 cans (14 ounces each) chicken broth
1 can (14 ounces) beef broth
2 tablespoons dry sherry
Seasoning to taste

La Salad

1 medium head lettuce
1 medium cucumber
1 small ripe avocado
3 tablespoons olive oil
2 tablespoons red wine vinegar
1/2 teaspoon dried tarragon
Seasoning to taste

Hoosits

2 cups flour
1 1/2 tablespoons granulated sugar
4 teaspoons baking powder
1/2 teaspoon baking soda
1 1/2 cups sour cream

French Lick

1/2 cup raspberry preserves
1/2 cup whipping cream
1 teaspoon butter
1 pint French vanilla ice cream
1/4 cup marshmallow crème for garnish

EQUIPMENT

Stockpot
Small saucepan
Baking sheet
Breadboard
2 large mixing bowls
Small mixing bowl
Whisk

Vegetable peeler
Biscuit cutter
Ice cream scoop
Kitchen knives
Measuring cups and
   spoons
Cooking utensils

COUNTDOWN

1. Assemble the ingredients and the equipment.
2. Do Steps 1–3 of *Hoosits*.
3. Do Steps 1–3 of *The Wabash Mash*.
4. Do Steps 4–5 of *Hoosits*.
5. Do Steps 1–2 of *French Lick*.
6. Do Steps 1–3 of *La Salad*.
7. Do Step 4 of *The Wabash Mash*.
8. Do Step 3 of *French Lick*.

WEDNESDAY

The Wabash Mash

1 Thoroughly wash and chop the leek, discarding the root end and the tough outer leaves. Peel and mince the garlic. Rinse, trim, seed, and chop the bell peppers. Rinse, stem, and chop the tomatoes. Dice the ham. Rinse, stem, and chop the cilantro. Finely chop the jalapeño pepper. Drain the whole-kernel corn.

2 Melt the butter with the oil in a stockpot. Sauté the leek and the garlic with the cumin until the leek is soft, 3 to 4 minutes. Stir in the bell peppers and the jalapeño pepper and cook 5 minutes more.

3 Add the tomatoes, the ham, the corn, the broth, and the sherry. Season to taste, cover, and simmer until hot, about 15 minutes.

4 Garnish with the cilantro.

La Salad

1 Wash and dry the lettuce and tear it into bite-sized pieces. Peel, trim, and slice the cucumber. Halve, pit, peel, and slice the avocado. Combine the ingredients in a large bowl.

2 In a small bowl, whisk together the oil, the vinegar, and the tarragon. Season to taste.

3 Toss the salad with the dressing.

Hoosits

1 Grease a baking sheet.

2 In a large bowl, combine the flour, the sugar, the baking powder, and the baking soda. Mix well. Fold in the sour cream and blend to form a soft ball.

3 Dust a breadboard with flour. Knead the dough 3 or 4 times to blend and then pat it out to a ¾-inch thickness. Cut with a biscuit cutter or a glass that has been dipped in flour and arrange the biscuits on the baking sheet.

4 Preheat the oven to 425°F.

5 Bake until the biscuits are lightly browned, 10 to 12 minutes.

French Lick

1 In a small saucepan, combine the preserves, the cream, and the butter. Bring the mixture just to a boil, stirring constantly. Reduce the heat and simmer, stirring occasionally, until the mixture thickens, about 5 minutes.

2 Remove from the heat and set aside.

3 Place scoops of ice cream in individual dessert bowls. Top with the sauce and dollops of marshmallow crème.

THURSDAY

Bye-Bye Birdie

3 pounds chicken pieces
2 scallions (green onions)
2 tablespoons lemon juice
1 cup plain yogurt
1/2 cup mayonnaise
2 teaspoons white Worcestershire sauce
1 tablespoon prepared horseradish
1/2 teaspoon dried savory
Seasoning to taste

Rice Side Story

2 tablespoons fresh parsley (when chopped)
1/2 cup wild rice
1 can (14 ounces) onion beef broth
1/2 cup water
1/2 cup long-grain white rice
Seasoning to taste

Show Bean

1 package (10 ounces) frozen cut green beans
1 small lime
1 tablespoon butter
1/2 teaspoon dried thyme
Seasoning to taste

The Dessert Song

1 can (15 ounces) apricot halves
1 cup apricot preserves
1/2 teaspoon ground cinnamon
1/4 teaspoon ground nutmeg
1 container (8 ounces) frozen whipped topping
1 angel food loaf cake
2 tablespoons powdered sugar

EQUIPMENT

Medium covered saucepan
Small saucepan
Medium skillet
9 x 13-inch glass baking dish
Large mixing bowl

2 small mixing bowls
Citrus grater
Citrus juicer
Kitchen knives
Measuring cups and spoons
Cooking utensils

COUNTDOWN

1. Assemble the ingredients and the equipment.
2. Do Step 1 of *Show Bean.*
3. Do Steps 1–4 of *Bye-Bye Birdie.*
4. Do Steps 1–2 of *Rice Side Story.*
5. Do Steps 1–4 of *The Dessert Song.*
6. Do Step 3 of *Rice Side Story.*
7. Do Steps 2–4 of *Show Bean.*
8. Do Step 4 of *Rice Side Story.*
9. Do Step 5 of *Bye-Bye Birdie.*

THURSDAY

Bye-Bye Birdie

1 Preheat the oven to 375°F.

2 Rinse and pat dry the chicken pieces. Rinse, trim, and chop the scallions.

3 Arrange the chicken pieces in a 9 x 13-inch baking dish in a single layer, skin side up. Drizzle with the lemon juice.

4 In a small bowl, combine the yogurt, the mayonnaise, the Worcestershire sauce, the horseradish, the savory, and the scallions. Spread the mixture over the chicken. Season to taste and bake until the chicken is tender and the juices run clear, 40 to 45 minutes.

5 Serve over the rice.

Rice Side Story

1 Rinse, stem, and chop the parsley. Rinse the wild rice.

2 In a medium saucepan, combine the wild rice, the broth, and the water. Bring to a boil, cover, and simmer for 25 minutes.

3 Stir in the white rice, season to taste, and return to boiling. Cover, reduce the heat, and simmer until the liquid is absorbed and the rice is tender, about 20 minutes more.

4 Fluff with a fork and sprinkle with the parsley.

Show Bean

1 Set the beans in a small bowl of warm water to thaw.

2 Grate the lime peel and juice the lime.

3 Bring a small amount of water to a boil in a medium skillet. Add the beans and cook through, 3 to 4 minutes.

4 Drain the beans. Melt the butter in the skillet. Add the lime juice and the thyme and combine. Add the beans, season to taste, mix well, and heat through. Sprinkle with the lime peel.

The Dessert Song

1 Drain the apricots, reserving ¼ cup of the liquid.

2 In a small saucepan, heat the reserved apricot liquid, the apricot preserves, the cinnamon, and the nutmeg, stirring to blend. Remove from the heat and let cool.

3 In a large bowl, blend the whipped topping with the cooled apricot mixture.

4 Spread the mixture over the cake, top with the apricot halves, and dust with the powdered sugar.

FRIDAY

Green and Bear It

1 package (10 ounces) frozen green peas
1/4 cup fresh chives (when chopped)
1 can (14 ounces) hearts of palm
3 tablespoons vegetable oil
2 tablespoons dry white wine
1/2 cup walnut bits
Seasoning to taste
1 pound spinach tortellini

Tomato Things

2 large tomatoes
1 clove garlic
1 tablespoon olive oil
1 teaspoon dried basil
Seasoning to taste
1/2 cup shredded mozzarella cheese

Maybe Muffins

4 tablespoons butter
1/4 cup granulated sugar
1/4 cup sesame seeds
1 egg
1 1/4 cups milk
2 cups flour
1 tablespoon baking powder

Sly Pudding

1 large tart green apple
1 milk chocolate bar (2.6 ounces)
1 package (3.4 ounces) instant vanilla
   pudding mix
2 cups milk
1/2 teaspoon rum extract
1/2 teaspoon ground cardamom

EQUIPMENT

Electric mixer	2 large mixing bowls
Stockpot	Medium mixing bowl
Medium saucepan	Small mixing bowl
Small skillet	Kitchen knives
8 x 8-inch glass baking dish	Measuring cups and spoons
Muffin tin	Cooking utensils
Colander	

COUNTDOWN

1. Assemble the ingredients and the equipment.
2. Do Step 1 of *Green and Bear It*.
3. Do Step 1 of *Maybe Muffins*.
4. Do Steps 1–3 of *Sly Pudding*.
5. Do Steps 1–3 of *Tomato Things*.
6. Do Steps 2–6 of *Maybe Muffins*.
7. Do Steps 2–5 of *Green and Bear It*.
8. Do Steps 4–5 of *Tomato Things*.
9. Do Step 6 of *Green and Bear It*.

FRIDAY

Green and Bear It

1 Set the package of peas in a small bowl of warm water to thaw.

2 Bring water to a boil in a stockpot.

3 Rinse, trim, and chop the chives. Drain and slice the hearts of palm.

4 Cook the tortellini until it is almost tender, about 5 minutes if you are using fresh pasta, about 10 minutes if you are using dry pasta.

5 In a medium saucepan, heat the oil with the wine. Add the peas, the chives, the hearts of palm, and the nuts. Season to taste and heat through.

6 Drain the pasta and return it to the stockpot. Toss with the pea mixture.

Tomato Things

1 Rinse, stem, and halve the tomatoes. Place them cut side up in an 8 x 8-inch baking dish.

2 Peel and mince the garlic. Heat the oil in a small skillet and sauté the garlic for 2 minutes.

3 Sprinkle the garlic and the basil on the tomatoes. Season to taste and top with the cheese.

4 Preheat the broiler.

5 Broil until the cheese is melted and bubbly, 2 to 3 minutes.

Maybe Muffins

1 Set the butter out to soften.

2 Preheat the oven to 400°F. Grease a muffin tin.

3 In a medium bowl, cream the softened butter with the sugar until light and fluffy. Add the sesame seeds and the egg and blend well. Blend in the milk.

4 In a large bowl, combine the flour and the baking powder. Make a well in the center, pour in the milk mixture, and stir to combine.

5 Pour the batter into the muffin cups.

6 Bake until the muffins are golden and firm to the touch, 15 to 20 minutes.

Sly Pudding

1 Peel, quarter, core, and chop the apple. Chop the chocolate bar.

2 In a large bowl, combine the pudding mix and the milk. Beat for 2 minutes. Fold in the rum extract, the cardamom, the apple, and the chocolate.

3 Spoon the mixture into individual dessert dishes and refrigerate until you are ready to serve.

Monday

Rooster Cogburn
She Wore a Yellow Ribbon
The Green Berets
True Grit

Tuesday

Pisa Pasta
Romaine Holiday
Pompeii Bread
Siena Sherbet

Wednesday

Name That Tuna
Rice Is Nice
Tomato Melody
Yes, We Have No Bananas

Thursday

Bismarck's Beef
Fargo the Chips
Sioux Slaw
Meadowlark Tarts

Friday

Moroccoroni
Casbah Salad
Bazaar Bread
Pepe Le Mocha

- ❑ Butter
- ❑ Flour
- ❑ Cornstarch
- ❑ Dark brown sugar
- ❑ Powdered sugar
- ❑ Multicolored sprinkles
- ❑ Olive oil
- ❑ Vegetable oil
- ❑ Apple cider vinegar
- ❑ Balsamic vinegar
- ❑ White wine vinegar
- ❑ Lemon juice
- ❑ Dijon mustard
- ❑ Honey
- ❑ Ketchup
- ❑ Mayonnaise
- ❑ Worcestershire sauce
- ❑ White Worcestershire sauce
- ❑ Plain breadcrumbs
- ❑ Instant coffee
- ❑ Poppy seeds
- ❑ Dried dill
- ❑ Dried marjoram
- ❑ Dried rosemary
- ❑ Dried tarragon
- ❑ Cayenne pepper
- ❑ Ground cumin
- ❑ Curry powder
- ❑ Ground ginger
- ❑ Italian seasoning
- ❑ Dry mustard
- ❑ Black pepper
- ❑ Poultry seasoning
- ❑ Salt
- ❑ Vanilla extract

MEAT & POULTRY

1½ pounds lean ground beef (Th)

1 pound sweet Italian sausage (T)

4 boneless, skinless chicken breast halves (about 1½ pounds) (M)

FRESH PRODUCE

VEGETABLES

1½ pounds baking potatoes (Th)

1 medium head cauliflower (F)

1 medium bunch broccoli (F)

1 pound Brussels sprouts (M)

1 medium zucchini (T)

2 medium carrots (Th)

4 stalks celery (M)

2 stalks celery (W)

1 stalk celery (F)

1 package (10 ounces) spinach (T)

1 medium head green cabbage (Th)

1 medium head romaine lettuce (T)

1 small head lettuce (F)

2 medium tomatoes (T)

4 medium tomatoes (W)

1 small cucumber (W)

1 small green bell pepper (W)

1 small orange bell pepper (W)

1 small red bell pepper (Th)

1 large yellow bell pepper (M)

1 medium red onion (T)

1 small red onion (F)

1 small onion (W)

2 small onions (Th)

2 small shallots (M)

2 scallions (green onions) (T)

3 scallions (green onions) (Th)

1 clove garlic (M)

2 cloves garlic (T)

2 cloves garlic (W)

2 cloves garlic (F)

HERBS

2 tablespoons chives (when chopped) (Th)

1 tablespoon chives (when chopped) (F)

2 teaspoons parsley (when chopped) (T)

1 tablespoon parsley (when chopped) (W)

FRUIT

1 medium orange (M)

2 small ripe honeydew melons (T)

4 medium bananas (W)

3 ripe kiwifruit (W)

1 pound seedless red grapes (M)

CANS, JARS & BOTTLES

SOUPS

1 can (10½ ounces) chicken broth (M)

1 can (10¾ ounces) cream of onion soup (W)

VEGETABLES

1 jar (3 ounces) sun-dried tomatoes (F)

1 can (11 ounces) whole-kernel corn (M)

1 can (15 ounces) cream-style corn (M)

FISH

2 cans (6 ounces each) solid white tuna (W)

SAUCES

1 can (15 ounces) tomato sauce (T)

FRUIT

1 can (15 ounces) chunky mixed fruit (M)

1 can (8 ounces) sliced pineapple (F)

1 can (16 ounces) pitted dark cherries (F)

CONDIMENTS

1 can (3½ ounces) sliced black olives (T)

PACKAGED GOODS

PASTA, RICE & GRAINS

12 ounces rotelle (T)

1 pound elbow macaroni (F)

1 cup brown rice (W)

BAKED GOODS

1 small loaf Italian bread (T)

1 loaf French bread (F)

4 hamburger buns (Th)

4 graham cracker tart shells (Th)

DRIED FRUIT & NUTS

¼ cup sliced almonds (Th)

DESSERT & BAKING NEEDS

1 package (3.4 ounces) instant butterscotch pudding mix (M)

1 package (3.4 ounces) instant chocolate pudding mix (F)

1 jar (12 ounces) caramel topping (Th)

½ cup flaked coconut (M)

WINE & SPIRITS

¼ cup dry white wine (M)

3 tablespoons Grand Marnier (W)

REFRIGERATED PRODUCTS

DAIRY

1¼ cups milk (M)

2¾ cups milk (F)

¼ cup half-and-half (M)

1 cup sour cream (W)

½ cup plain yogurt (M)

½ cup plain yogurt (W)

8 ounces coffee yogurt (F)

¾ cup whipping cream (M)

¼ cup whipped cream (F)

Whipped cream for garnish (Th)

CHEESE

½ cup shredded mozzarella cheese (T)

½ cup shredded Cheddar cheese (F)

½ cup crumbled feta cheese (F)

JUICES

¾ cup orange juice (W)

DELI

1 large dill pickle (Th)

FROZEN GOODS

VEGETABLES

1 package (10 ounces) green peas (W)

DESSERTS

1 pint strawberry sherbet (T)

1 pint butter pecan ice cream (Th)

MONDAY

Rooster Cogburn

4 boneless, skinless chicken breast halves
 (about 1 1/2 pounds)
2 small shallots
1 pound seedless red grapes
1 medium orange
2 tablespoons butter
1/4 teaspoon poultry seasoning
1 teaspoon dried rosemary
1/4 cup dry white wine
1 can (10 1/2 ounces) chicken broth
1/4 cup half-and-half
Seasoning to taste

She Wore a Yellow Ribbon

1 large yellow bell pepper
1 can (11 ounces) whole-kernel corn
2 tablespoons butter
1 can (15 ounces) cream-style corn
1/8 teaspoon cayenne pepper
Seasoning to taste

The Green Berets

1 pound Brussels sprouts
4 stalks celery
1 clove garlic
2 tablespoons olive oil
2 tablespoons lemon juice
1/2 teaspoon dried marjoram
Seasoning to taste

True Grit

3/4 cup whipping cream
2 tablespoons powdered sugar
1 package (3.4 ounces) instant butterscotch
 pudding mix
1 1/4 cups milk
1/2 cup plain yogurt
1 can (15 ounces) chunky mixed fruit
1/2 cup flaked coconut

EQUIPMENT

Electric mixer	Small mixing bowl
2 large skillets	Citrus grater
Medium covered skillet	Kitchen knives
2 medium mixing bowls	Measuring cups and spoons
	Cooking utensils

COUNTDOWN

1. Assemble the ingredients and the equipment.
2. Do Step 1 of *True Grit*.
3. Do Steps 1–2 of *Rooster Cogburn*.
4. Do Step 1 of *She Wore a Yellow Ribbon*.
5. Do Step 1 of *The Green Berets*.
6. Do Steps 2–5 of *True Grit*.
7. Do Steps 3–4 of *Rooster Cogburn*.
8. Do Steps 2–3 of *The Green Berets*.
9. Do Steps 2–3 of *She Wore a Yellow Ribbon*.
10. Do Step 5 of *Rooster Cogburn*.

MONDAY

Rooster Cogburn

1 Rinse and pat dry the chicken breasts.

2 Peel and mince the shallots. Rinse and dry the grapes. Separate 4 small clusters of grapes for garnish and stem the remainder. Cut 4 thin slices from the orange and grate 2 teaspoons of the remaining peel.

3 Melt the butter with the poultry seasoning and the rosemary in a large skillet. Sauté the chicken until it is golden, about 5 minutes per side. Remove and reserve the chicken.

4 Add the shallots to the skillet and cook until they are soft, about 2 minutes, stirring to keep from browning. Slowly add the wine and the broth and bring to a boil, scraping up any brown bits from the pan. Add the half-and-half and the orange peel and season to taste. Return the chicken to the pan, add the stemmed grapes, and simmer until the chicken is tender and the sauce thickens, about 15 minutes.

5 Spoon the sauce over the chicken and garnish with the orange slices and the grape clusters.

She Wore a Yellow Ribbon

1 Rinse, trim, seed, and julienne the bell pepper. Drain the whole-kernel corn.

2 Melt the butter in a large skillet and sauté the pepper for 3 minutes.

3 Add the whole-kernel corn, the cream-style corn, and the cayenne pepper. Season to taste, mix well, and heat through.

The Green Berets

1 Rinse, trim, and halve the Brussels sprouts. Rinse, trim, and slice the celery. Peel and mince the garlic.

2 Heat the oil in a medium skillet. Add the garlic and sauté for 1 minute. Add the sprouts and the celery and cook, stirring to coat, for 2 minutes.

3 Add the lemon juice and the marjoram and season to taste. Cover and cook until the sprouts can easily be pricked with a fork, 6 to 7 minutes.

True Grit

1 Chill a medium bowl and the beaters of an electric mixer for 10 minutes.

2 Pour the whipping cream into the chilled bowl and beat until stiff peaks form, about 3 minutes. Fold in the powdered sugar and set aside.

3 Combine the pudding mix, the milk, and the yogurt in another medium bowl and beat until well blended. Fold in the whipped cream.

4 Drain the mixed fruit. In a small bowl, combine the mixed fruit with the coconut.

5 Layer the pudding and the fruit mixture in individual dessert glasses. Refrigerate until you are ready to serve.

TUESDAY

Pisa Pasta

2 cloves garlic
1 medium red onion
1 package (10 ounces) fresh spinach
1 pound sweet Italian sausage
1 tablespoon vegetable oil
1 can (15 ounces) tomato sauce
1 tablespoon Italian seasoning
12 ounces rotelle
Seasoning to taste
1/2 cup shredded mozzarella cheese

Romaine Holiday

1 medium head romaine lettuce
2 scallions (green onions)
1 medium zucchini
2 medium tomatoes
1 can (3 1/2 ounces) sliced black olives
3 tablespoons vegetable oil
2 tablespoons white wine vinegar
1/4 teaspoon dry mustard
1/4 teaspoon white Worcestershire sauce
Seasoning to taste

Pompeii Bread

2 teaspoons fresh parsley (when chopped)
1 small loaf Italian bread
2 tablespoons olive oil
1/2 teaspoon dried tarragon
Seasoning to taste

Siena Sherbet

2 small ripe honeydew melons
1 pint frozen strawberry sherbet
Multicolored sprinkles for garnish

EQUIPMENT

Stockpot	Pastry brush
Large skillet	Ice cream scoop
Colander	Aluminum foil
Large mixing bowl	Kitchen knives
Small mixing bowl	Measuring cups and
Whisk	spoons
Vegetable brush	Cooking utensils

COUNTDOWN

1. Assemble the ingredients and the equipment.
2. Do Steps 1–3 of *Pisa Pasta*.
3. Do Steps 1–4 of *Pompeii Bread*.
4. Do Step 1 of *Romaine Holiday*.
5. Do Steps 4–6 of *Pisa Pasta*.
6. Do Step 2 of *Romaine Holiday*.
7. Do Steps 1–2 of *Siena Sherbet*.

TUESDAY

Pisa Pasta

1 Place the sausage in the freezer for 10 minutes. Bring water to a boil in a stockpot.

2 Peel and mince the garlic. Peel and slice the onion. Rinse, pat dry, and stem the spinach.

3 Slice the sausage into ¼-inch-thick rounds.

4 Heat the oil in a large skillet and sauté the sausage until lightly browned. Remove and reserve. Sauté the garlic and the onion in the skillet until the onion is soft, about 5 minutes. Add the tomato sauce and the Italian seasoning and simmer until hot.

5 Cook the rotelle until it is almost tender, 8 to 10 minutes.

6 Drain the pasta and return it to the stockpot. Add the sausage and the sauce and season to taste. Add the spinach leaves and warm through. Toss with the cheese.

Romaine Holiday

1 Wash and dry the lettuce and tear it into bite-sized pieces. Rinse, trim, and chop the scallions. Scrub, trim, and thinly slice the zucchini. Rinse, stem, and chop the tomatoes. Drain the olives. Combine the ingredients in a large bowl.

2 In a small bowl, whisk together the oil, the vinegar, the mustard, and the Worcester-shire sauce. Season to taste and toss the salad with the dressing.

Pompeii Bread

1 Preheat the oven to 325°F.

2 Rinse, stem, and chop the parsley.

3 Slice the bread in half lengthwise. Brush the cut sides with the oil and sprinkle with the tarragon. Sprinkle with the parsley. Season to taste.

4 Reassemble the loaf and wrap it in aluminum foil. Heat the bread in the oven until you are ready to serve.

Siena Sherbet

1 Halve and seed the melons and place the halves on individual dessert plates.

2 Top each half with a scoop of sherbet and a dash of sprinkles.

WEDNESDAY

Name That Tuna

1 package (10 ounces) frozen green peas
1 small onion
1 small green bell pepper
1 small orange bell pepper
2 stalks celery
2 tablespoons butter
1 cup sour cream
1 can (10¾ ounces) cream of onion soup
2 cans (6 ounces each) solid white tuna
1 teaspoon curry powder
Seasoning to taste

Rice Is Nice

1 clove garlic
1 tablespoon fresh parsley (when chopped)
1 tablespoon olive oil
1 cup brown rice
2¼ cups water
Seasoning to taste

Tomato Melody

4 medium tomatoes
1 small cucumber
1 clove garlic
3 tablespoons olive oil
2 tablespoons balsamic vinegar
½ teaspoon dried dill
Seasoning to taste

Yes, We Have No Bananas

¾ cup orange juice
1 tablespoon cornstarch
3 tablespoons Grand Marnier
½ cup plain yogurt
1 tablespoon honey
½ teaspoon ground ginger
4 medium bananas
3 ripe kiwifruit

EQUIPMENT

Medium covered saucepan	2 small mixing bowls
Small covered saucepan	Whisk
Large covered skillet	Vegetable peeler
Small strainer	Kitchen knives
Medium mixing bowl	Measuring cups and spoons
	Cooking utensils

COUNTDOWN

1. Assemble the ingredients and the equipment.
2. Do Step 1 of *Name That Tuna*.
3. Do Steps 1–2 of *Rice Is Nice*.
4. Do Steps 1–2 of *Yes, We Have No Bananas*.
5. Do Steps 2–5 of *Name That Tuna*.
6. Do Steps 1–3 of *Tomato Melody*.
7. Do Step 3 of *Rice Is Nice*.
8. Do Steps 3–4 of *Yes, We Have No Bananas*.

WEDNESDAY

Name That Tuna

1 Set the package of peas in a small bowl of warm water to thaw.

2 Peel and mince the onion. Rinse, trim, seed, and chop the bell peppers. Rinse, trim, and chop the celery.

3 Melt the butter in a large skillet. Sauté the onion, the bell peppers, and the celery until they are soft, about 5 minutes. Stir in the sour cream and the soup.

4 Drain and flake the tuna and add it to the sour cream mixture. Mix in the peas.

5 Add the curry powder and season to taste. Cover, reduce the heat, and simmer until hot, about 10 minutes.

Rice Is Nice

1 Peel and mince the garlic. Rinse, stem, and chop the parsley.

2 Heat the oil in a medium saucepan and sauté the garlic for 2 minutes. Add the rice and the water and bring to a boil. Season to taste, cover, reduce the heat, and simmer until all the water is absorbed and the rice is tender, 40 to 45 minutes.

3 Fluff the rice and fold in the parsley before serving.

Tomato Melody

1 Rinse, dry, and stem the tomatoes. Cut a thin slice off the top of each tomato and scoop out half of the pulp. Drain and reserve the pulp. Cut a thin slice off the bottom of each tomato.

2 Peel, trim, and chop the cucumber. Peel and mince the garlic.

3 In a small bowl, combine the reserved tomato pulp, the cucumber, the garlic, the oil, the vinegar, and the dill. Season to taste and spoon the mixture into the tomatoes.

Yes, We Have No Bananas

1 Combine the orange juice and the cornstarch in a small saucepan and whisk until smooth. Bring the mixture to a boil, stirring constantly, until it thickens, 3 to 4 minutes. Remove the saucepan from the heat and stir in the Grand Marnier. Cover and let stand until you are ready to serve.

2 Combine the yogurt, the honey, and the ginger in a medium bowl and refrigerate until you are ready to serve.

3 Peel and slice the bananas. Peel and slice the kiwifruit. Reserve 4 kiwi slices for garnish and add the bananas and the remaining kiwi to the yogurt mixture.

4 Spoon the fruit mixture into individual dessert glasses. Top with the orange syrup and garnish with the reserved kiwi slices.

THURSDAY

Bismarck's Beef

2 small onions
1 small red bell pepper
2 tablespoons fresh chives (when chopped)
4 hamburger buns
1 1/2 pounds lean ground beef
1 cup ketchup
1 tablespoon dark brown sugar
1 tablespoon Worcestershire sauce
Seasoning to taste

Fargo the Chips

1 1/2 pounds baking potatoes
Seasoning to taste
4 tablespoons butter
2 teaspoons dried rosemary

Sioux Slaw

1 medium head green cabbage
2 medium carrots
3 scallions (green onions)
1 large dill pickle
3 tablespoons mayonnaise
2 tablespoons apple cider vinegar
1/2 teaspoon Dijon mustard
Seasoning to taste

Meadowlark Tarts

4 graham cracker tart shells
1 pint butter pecan ice cream
1 jar (12 ounces) caramel topping
Whipped cream for garnish
1/4 cup sliced almonds for garnish

EQUIPMENT

Large skillet	Vegetable peeler
Baking sheet	Ice cream scoop
2 large mixing bowls	Kitchen knives
Small mixing bowl	Measuring cups and
Whisk	spoons
Vegetable brush	Cooking utensils
Vegetable grater	

COUNTDOWN

1. Assemble the ingredients and the equipment.
2. Do Steps 1–2 of *Fargo the Chips*.
3. Do Steps 1–2 of *Bismarck's Beef*.
4. Do Steps 3–4 of *Fargo the Chips*.
5. Do Steps 1–2 of *Sioux Slaw*.
6. Do Step 5 of *Fargo the Chips*.
7. Do Steps 3–4 of *Bismarck's Beef*.
8. Do Steps 1–2 of *Meadowlark Tarts*.

THURSDAY

Bismarck's Beef

1 Peel and chop the onions. Rinse, trim, seed, and chop the bell pepper. Rinse, trim, and chop the chives.

2 Split and lightly toast the buns.

3 In a large skillet, sauté the beef with the onions and the bell pepper until lightly browned, about 10 minutes. Add the ketchup, the sugar, and the Worcestershire sauce and season to taste. Reduce the heat and simmer for 5 minutes.

4 Spoon the beef mixture over the toasted buns and top with the chives.

Fargo the Chips

1 Preheat the oven to 375° F. Grease a baking sheet.

2 Scrub the potatoes and cut them into ⅛-inch–thick slices. Put the slices in a large bowl of cold water for 10 minutes.

3 Drain and dry the potatoes. Place them in a single layer on the baking sheet. Season to taste.

4 Melt the butter and drizzle it over the potatoes. Sprinkle with the rosemary. Bake for 15 minutes.

5 Turn the potatoes and bake for 15 minutes more.

Sioux Slaw

1 Rinse, trim, quarter, and grate the cabbage. Peel, trim, and grate the carrots. Rinse, trim, and chop the scallions. Mince the pickle. Combine the ingredients in a large bowl.

2 In a small bowl, whisk together the mayonnaise, the vinegar, and the mustard. Season to taste, toss the salad with the dressing, and refrigerate until you are ready to serve.

Meadowlark Tarts

1 Place the tart shells on individual dessert plates.

2 Fill each tart shell with scoops of ice cream. Spoon the caramel topping over the ice cream. Top with a dollop of whipped cream and a sprinkle of nuts.

FRIDAY

Moroccoroni

1 medium head cauliflower
1 medium bunch broccoli
1 small red onion
1 tablespoon butter
1 tablespoon olive oil
1 pound elbow macaroni
1 1/2 cups milk
3 tablespoons flour
1 teaspoon Dijon mustard
1 teaspoon ground cumin
Seasoning to taste
1/2 cup shredded Cheddar cheese
1 1/2 cups plain breadcrumbs
1/2 cup crumbled feta cheese

Casbah Salad

1 small head lettuce
1 stalk celery
1 can (8 ounces) sliced pineapple
1 can (16 ounces) pitted dark cherries
3 tablespoons vegetable oil
2 tablespoons apple cider vinegar
1 tablespoon lemon juice
1/2 teaspoon poppy seeds

Bazaar Bread

2 cloves garlic
1 tablespoon fresh chives (when chopped)
1 jar (3 ounces) sun-dried tomatoes
Seasoning to taste
1 loaf French bread

Pepe Le Mocha

1 package (3.4 ounces) instant chocolate
    pudding mix
1 1/4 cups milk
1 container (8 ounces) coffee yogurt
1/4 cup whipped cream
1 teaspoon vanilla extract
2 tablespoons powdered sugar
2 tablespoons instant coffee

EQUIPMENT

Electric mixer	Large mixing bowl
Stockpot	Medium mixing bowl
Large skillet	2 small mixing bowls
Small covered skillet	Whisk
9 x 13-inch glass baking dish	Kitchen knives
Baking sheet	Measuring cups and spoons
Colander	Cooking utensils

COUNTDOWN

1. Assemble the ingredients and the equipment.
2. Do Steps 1–2 of Bazaar Bread.
3. Do Steps 1–3 of Pepe Le Mocha.
4. Do Steps 1–8 of Moroccoroni.
5. Do Steps 1–4 of Casbah Salad.
6. Do Steps 3–4 of Bazaar Bread.
7. Do Step 5 of Casbah Salad.

FRIDAY

Moroccoroni

1 Bring water to a boil in a stockpot. Grease a 9 x 13-inch baking dish.

2 Rinse and trim the cauliflower and the broccoli, discard the tough ends, and cut into bite-sized florets. Peel and chop the onion.

3 Melt the butter with the oil in a large skillet and sauté the onion for 3 minutes. Add the cauliflower and the broccoli and sauté for 5 minutes. Transfer to a large bowl.

4 Cook the macaroni in the stockpot until it is almost tender, 8 to 10 minutes.

5 Preheat the oven to 375°F.

6 Add the milk to the skillet, blend in the flour, and whisk until the mixture begins to thicken, 3 to 4 minutes. Blend in the mustard and the cumin and season to taste. Fold in the Cheddar cheese and remove the skillet from the heat.

7 Drain the pasta and return it to the stockpot. Add the contents of the large bowl and the contents of the skillet and blend well. Pour the mixture into the baking dish. Top with the breadcrumbs and sprinkle with the feta cheese.

8 Bake until hot and bubbly, about 20 minutes.

Casbah Salad

1 Wash and dry the lettuce and arrange the leaves on individual salad plates.

2 Rinse, trim, and chop the celery.

3 Drain the pineapple and arrange the slices over the lettuce. Drain the cherries and arrange them in the center of the pineapple. Add the celery to the cherries.

4 In a small bowl, combine the oil, the vinegar, the lemon juice, and the poppy seeds.

5 Drizzle the dressing over the salad.

Bazaar Bread

1 Peel and mince the garlic. Rinse, trim, and chop the chives. Drain and chop the tomatoes, reserving the oil.

2 Heat the reserved oil in a small skillet. Add the garlic and the tomatoes. Season to taste and cook until the tomatoes are heated through, about 3 minutes. Remove from the heat and cover to keep warm.

3 Preheat the broiler.

4 Cut the bread in half lengthwise and place the halves on a baking sheet, cut side up. Spoon the tomato mixture over the bread, sprinkle with the chives, and broil until hot, about 2 minutes.

Pepe Le Mocha

1 In a medium bowl, beat the pudding mix with the milk until blended. Fold in the yogurt and refrigerate.

2 Put the whipped cream in a small bowl and fold in the vanilla, the powdered sugar, and the instant coffee.

3 Spoon the pudding into individual dessert glasses and garnish with the whipped cream. Refrigerate until you are ready to serve.

WEEK FOUR

Monday

Potter's Pasta
Slither In Salad
Muggles Bread
Dumble Delight

Tuesday

Birmingham
Farragut's Asparaguts
Cotton Balls

Wednesday

Ratatouille Fouille
Grab the Greens
Banana Pajamas

Thursday

Extraordinary Eggs
Superior Sausage
Marvelous Muffins
Preposterous Poof

Friday

O-Sole-O-Me-O
Pianissimo Pilaf
Bossa Nova Broccoli
Mango Tango

STAPLES

- [ ] Butter
- [ ] Granulated sugar
- [ ] Powdered sugar
- [ ] Chocolate syrup
- [ ] Chocolate sprinkles
- [ ] Multicolored sprinkles
- [ ] Olive oil
- [ ] Vegetable oil
- [ ] Raspberry vinegar
- [ ] Tarragon vinegar
- [ ] Beef bouillon cube
- [ ] Celery seeds
- [ ] Dried basil
- [ ] Dried oregano
- [ ] Dried rosemary
- [ ] Dried savory
- [ ] Dried thyme
- [ ] Cayenne pepper
- [ ] Lemon-pepper seasoning
- [ ] Paprika
- [ ] Black pepper
- [ ] White pepper
- [ ] Salt
- [ ] Lemon extract
- [ ] Rum extract

MEAT & POULTRY

2 lean cooked ham steaks (about ¾ pound each) (T)

1½ pounds breakfast sausage links (Th)

FISH

48 hard-shell clams (M)

4 sole fillets (about 1½ pounds) (F)

FRESH PRODUCE

VEGETABLES

1 pound new red potatoes (Th)

1 medium bunch broccoli (F)

1 small eggplant (W)

1 medium zucchini (W)

2 stalks celery (W)

½ pound mushrooms (M)

½ pound mushrooms (F)

1 package (10 ounces) spinach (M)

1 medium head red leaf lettuce (M)

1 medium head green leaf lettuce (W)

¼ pound alfalfa sprouts (W)

2 medium tomatoes (W)

2 medium tomatoes (Th)

1 medium cucumber (M)

1 medium cucumber (W)

1 small green bell pepper (T)

1 medium red bell pepper (W)

1 small yellow bell pepper (W)

1 small bunch radishes (M)

1 medium onion (T)

1 medium onion (W)

1 medium onion (F)

1 small red onion (M)

2 scallions (green onions) (W)

3 scallions (green onions) (Th)

2 scallions (green onions) (F)

3 cloves garlic (M)

1 clove garlic (T)

1 clove garlic (F)

HERBS

2 tablespoons basil (when chopped) (Th)

3 tablespoons parsley (when chopped) (M)

¼ cup parsley (when chopped) (W)

2 tablespoons parsley (when chopped) (Th)

FRUIT

1 large orange (T)

1 medium orange (W)

1 small lemon (F)

4 medium bananas (W)

CANS, JARS & BOTTLES

SOUPS

1 can (14 ounces) vegetable broth (F)

VEGETABLES

1 can (14½ ounces) diced tomatoes (T)

1 can (14½ ounces) diced tomatoes (W)

1 can (15 ounces) white beans (W)

FRUIT

1 jar (6 ounces) maraschino cherries (M)

JUICES

1 can (12 ounces) mango nectar (F)

SPREADS

3 tablespoons orange marmalade (Th)

CONDIMENTS

1 tablespoon capers (W)

1 small jar (2 ounces) diced pimientos (F)

PACKAGED GOODS

PASTA, RICE & GRAINS

1 pound spaghetti (M)

½ cup vermicelli (when broken) (F)

1 cup brown rice (T)

1 cup long-grain white rice (F)

BAKED GOODS

1 loaf Italian bread (M)

4 English muffins (Th)

1 angel food loaf cake (T)

INTERNATIONAL FOODS

8 large soft corn tortillas (W)

DRIED FRUIT & NUTS

½ cup pecan bits (M)

½ cup walnut bits (F)

DESSERT & BAKING NEEDS

1 package (3 ounces) strawberry gelatin (Th)

1 package (3 ounces) cook-and-serve vanilla pudding mix (F)

WINE & SPIRITS

1 cup dry white wine (M)

¼ cup dry red wine (W)

2 tablespoons dry sherry (F)

2 tablespoons Grand Marnier (T)

REFRIGERATED PRODUCTS

DAIRY

½ cup milk (F)

1 cup half-and-half (M)

2 tablespoons half-and-half (Th)

1 cup whipping cream (T)

Whipped cream for garnish (M)

Whipped cream for garnish (Th)

Whipped cream for garnish (F)

9 eggs (Th)

CHEESE

1 package (3 ounces) cream cheese (Th)

1 cup Gruyère cheese (when grated) (F)

FROZEN GOODS

VEGETABLES

2 packages (10 ounces each) chopped asparagus (T)

FRUIT

1 package (16 ounces) unsweetened sliced strawberries (Th)

DESSERTS

1 pint caramel yogurt (M)

1 pint vanilla yogurt (W)

MONDAY

Potter's Pasta

1 package (10 ounces) fresh spinach
1 clove garlic
1/2 pound fresh mushrooms
2 tablespoons butter
48 hard-shell clams
1 cup dry white wine
1 cup half-and-half
Seasoning to taste
1 pound spaghetti

Slither In Salad

1 medium head red leaf lettuce
1 small red onion
1 medium cucumber
1 small bunch radishes
3 tablespoons fresh parsley (when
    chopped)
3 tablespoons vegetable oil
2 tablespoons tarragon vinegar
1 teaspoon dried savory
Seasoning to taste

Muggles Bread

2 cloves garlic
4 tablespoons butter
1/2 teaspoon dried oregano
1/8 teaspoon cayenne pepper
1 loaf Italian bread

Dumble Delight

1 pint caramel frozen yogurt
1 jar (6 ounces) maraschino cherries
1/2 cup pecan bits
1 teaspoon rum extract
Whipped cream for garnish

EQUIPMENT

Stockpot	Small mixing bowl
Large covered saucepan	Whisk
	Vegetable brush
Small saucepan	Vegetable peeler
Large skillet	Pastry brush
Baking sheet	Kitchen knives
Colander	Measuring cups and spoons
2 medium mixing bowls	Cooking utensils

COUNTDOWN

1. Assemble the ingredients and the equipment.
2. Do Steps 1–4 of *Dumble Delight*.
3. Do Step 1 of *Potter's Pasta*.
4. Do Steps 1–3 of *Slither In Salad*.
5. Do Steps 2–4 of *Potter's Pasta*.
6. Do Steps 1–4 of *Muggles Bread*.
7. Do Steps 5–6 of *Potter's Pasta*.
8. Do Step 4 of *Slither In Salad*.
9. Do Step 5 of *Muggles Bread*.
10. Do Step 7 of *Potter's Pasta*.

MONDAY

Potter's Pasta

1 Bring water to a boil in a stockpot.

2 Rinse, pat dry, and stem the spinach. Peel and mince the garlic. Rinse, pat dry, trim, and thinly slice the mushrooms.

3 Melt the butter in a large skillet. Sauté the garlic and the mushrooms for 2 minutes. Remove the skillet from the heat and set aside.

4 Scrub the clams, discarding any that do not close when lightly tapped. Place the clams in a large saucepan. Add the wine. Cover and cook until the clams open, about 10 minutes.

5 Reserving the cooking liquid, discard any clams that do not open. Add the reserved liquid to the skillet. Reheat the mixture, slowly adding the half-and-half, and bring it to a boil. Stir in the spinach, tossing to coat. Season to taste and heat through.

6 Cook the spaghetti until it is almost tender, 6 to 7 minutes.

7 Drain the spaghetti and return it to the stockpot. Combine the pasta with the spinach mixture and top with the clams.

Slither In Salad

1 Wash and dry the lettuce and distribute the leaves among individual salad plates.

2 Peel and chop the onion. Peel, trim, and chop the cucumber. Rinse, trim, and slice the radishes. Rinse, stem, and chop the parsley. Combine the ingredients in a medium bowl.

3 In a small bowl, whisk together the oil, the vinegar, and the savory. Season to taste.

4 Toss the vegetables with the dressing and spoon onto the lettuce leaves.

Muggles Bread

1 Peel and mince the garlic. Melt the butter in a small saucepan. Blend in the garlic, the oregano, and the cayenne pepper.

2 Cut the bread into 2-inch-thick slices.

3 Preheat the broiler.

4 Brush the slices with the butter mixture and lay them on a baking sheet.

5 Broil until the bread is lightly toasted, about 1 minute.

Dumble Delight

1 Set the frozen yogurt out to soften slightly.

2 Drain the cherries and cut them in half, reserving 4 whole ones for garnish.

3 Place the yogurt in a medium bowl and fold in the cherries and the pecans. Mix in the rum extract.

4 Spoon the mixture into individual dessert glasses. Top with a dollop of whipped cream and a whole maraschino cherry. Place in the freezer until you are ready to serve.

TUESDAY

Birmingham

1 medium onion
1 clove garlic
1 small green bell pepper
2 lean cooked ham steaks (about 3/4 pound
  each)
3 tablespoons vegetable oil
1 cup brown rice
1 can (14 1/2 ounces) diced tomatoes
1 1/4 cups water
1 beef bouillon cube
Seasoning to taste

Farragut's Asparaguts

2 packages (10 ounces each) chopped
  asparagus
2 tablespoons butter
1/2 teaspoon dried rosemary
1/2 teaspoon celery seeds

Cotton Balls

1 angel food loaf cake
1 large orange
2 tablespoons Grand Marnier
1 cup whipping cream
2 tablespoons powdered sugar
1 teaspoon lemon extract
Chocolate syrup for garnish

EQUIPMENT

Electric mixer
Large covered
  skillet
Medium skillet
Large mixing bowl
2 medium mixing
  bowls

Citrus grater
Citrus juicer
Kitchen knives
Measuring cups and
  spoons
Cooking utensils

COUNTDOWN

1. Assemble the ingredients and the
   equipment.
2. Do Step 1 of Cotton Balls.
3. Do Step 1 of Farragut's Asparaguts.
4. Do Steps 1–6 of Birmingham.
5. Do Steps 2–5 of Cotton Balls.
6. Do Step 2 of Farragut's Asparaguts.
7. Do Step 6 of Cotton Balls.

TUESDAY

Birmingham

1 Peel and chop the onion. Peel and mince the garlic. Rinse, trim, seed, and chop the bell pepper. Cut the ham steaks in half.

2 Heat 2 tablespoons of the oil in a large skillet and brown the ham steaks lightly on both sides, about 5 minutes.

3 Remove the ham and reserve.

4 Heat the remaining 1 tablespoon of oil in the skillet and sauté the onion and the garlic for 2 minutes. Add the bell pepper and sauté for 3 minutes.

5 Add the rice to the skillet and stir to coat for 1 minute. Add the tomatoes, the water, and the bouillon cube, mashing to dissolve. Season to taste and heat through.

6 Place the ham steaks over the rice and vegetables. Cover, reduce the heat, and simmer until all the liquid is absorbed and the rice is tender, about 20 minutes.

Farragut's Asparaguts

1 Set the asparagus in a large bowl of warm water to thaw.

2 Melt the butter in a medium skillet. Blend in the rosemary. Sauté the asparagus until heated through, about 2 minutes. Sprinkle with the celery seeds.

Cotton Balls

1 Place the angel food cake in the freezer for 10 minutes. Chill a medium bowl and the beaters of an electric mixer for 10 minutes.

2 Grate 1 tablespoon of orange peel and juice the orange. Combine the peel, the juice, and the Grand Marnier in a medium bowl.

3 Pour the whipping cream into the chilled bowl and beat until soft peaks form, about 2 minutes. Fold in the powdered sugar and beat until stiff, about 2 minutes more. Fold in the lemon extract.

4 Cube the cake. Add the cubes to the orange mixture and toss to combine.

5 Spoon half of the whipped cream into individual dessert glasses. Add the cake cubes. Top with the remaining whipped cream.

6 Garnish with the chocolate syrup.

WEDNESDAY

Ratatouille Fouille

1 medium onion
1 small eggplant
2 medium tomatoes
1 medium zucchini
1 medium red bell pepper
1 small yellow bell pepper
1 can (15 ounces) white beans
8 large soft corn tortillas
2 tablespoons olive oil
1 can (14½ ounces) diced tomatoes
¼ cup dry red wine
½ tablespoon dried basil
½ teaspoon dried thyme
¼ teaspoon dried oregano
Seasoning to taste
1 tablespoon capers

Grab the Greens

1 medium head green leaf lettuce
2 scallions (green onions)
1 medium cucumber
2 stalks celery
¼ pound alfalfa sprouts
¼ cup fresh parsley (when chopped)
3 tablespoons vegetable oil
2 tablespoons raspberry vinegar
Seasoning to taste

Banana Pajamas

1 medium orange
4 medium bananas
2 tablespoons butter
¼ cup granulated sugar
1 pint vanilla frozen yogurt
Chocolate sprinkles for garnish

EQUIPMENT

Medium covered saucepan
Large covered skillet
Baking sheet
Large mixing bowl
Small mixing bowl
Whisk
Vegetable brush

Vegetable peeler
Citrus grater
Citrus juicer
Ice cream scoop
Kitchen knives
Measuring cups and spoons
Cooking utensils

COUNTDOWN

1. Assemble the ingredients and the equipment.
2. Do Steps 1–2 of *Banana Pajamas*.
3. Do Steps 1–3 of *Grab the Greens*.
4. Do Steps 1–6 of *Ratatouille Fouille*.
5. Do Step 4 of *Grab the Greens*.
6. Do Step 3 of *Banana Pajamas*.

WEDNESDAY

Ratatouille Fouille

1 Preheat the oven to 275°F.

2 Peel and thinly slice the onion. Peel, trim, and cube the eggplant. Rinse, stem, and chop the fresh tomatoes. Scrub, trim, and slice the zucchini. Rinse, trim, seed, and slice the bell peppers. Drain the beans.

3 Place the tortillas on a baking sheet and warm them in the oven for 10 minutes.

4 Heat the oil in a large skillet. Sauté the onion for 5 minutes. Add the eggplant. Cover and cook for 5 minutes, stirring occasionally. Add the fresh tomatoes, the zucchini, the peppers, the beans, the canned tomatoes, the wine, the basil, the thyme, and the oregano. Season to taste. Cook until the vegetables are just tender, 5 to 7 minutes more.

5 Toss the ratatouille with the capers.

6 Lay the warmed tortillas on individual plates. Spoon some of the ratatouille onto one side of each tortilla and fold the other side over the ratatouille.

Grab the Greens

1 Wash and dry the lettuce and tear it into bite-sized pieces. Rinse, trim, and chop the scallions. Peel, trim, and slice the cucumber. Rinse, trim, and slice the celery. Rinse and dry the alfalfa sprouts. Combine the ingredients in a large bowl.

2 Rinse, stem, and chop the parsley.

3 In a small bowl, whisk together the oil and the vinegar. Season to taste.

4 Toss the salad with the dressing and sprinkle with the parsley.

Banana Pajamas

1 Grate the peel from the orange. Juice the orange. Peel and diagonally slice the bananas.

2 Melt the butter with the orange juice in a medium saucepan. Add the sugar and the orange peel. Simmer until the mixture thickens slightly, about 2 minutes. Add the bananas, turning to coat the slices evenly with the syrup. Remove from the heat and cover to keep warm.

3 Place scoops of frozen yogurt in individual dessert dishes and top with the bananas and syrup. Garnish with chocolate sprinkles.

THURSDAY

Extraordinary Eggs

3 scallions (green onions)
2 tablespoons fresh basil (when chopped)
2 tablespoons fresh parsley (when chopped)
2 medium tomatoes
1 package (3 ounces) cream cheese
9 eggs
2 tablespoons half-and-half
1/4 teaspoon white pepper
Seasoning to taste
2 tablespoons butter

Superior Sausage

1 pound new red potatoes
1 1/2 pounds breakfast sausage links
2 tablespoons vegetable oil
2 tablespoons water
Seasoning to taste

Marvelous Muffins

4 English muffins
2 tablespoons butter
3 tablespoons orange marmalade

Preposterous Poof

1 package (16 ounces) unsweetened frozen sliced strawberries
1/2 cup water
1 package (3 ounces) strawberry gelatin
1 cup ice cubes
Whipped cream for garnish
Multicolored sprinkles for garnish

EQUIPMENT

Blender	Vegetable grater
Large covered skillet	Kitchen knives
Large skillet	Measuring cups and spoons
Medium mixing bowl	Cooking utensils
Vegetable brush	

COUNTDOWN

1. Assemble the ingredients and the equipment.
2. Do Steps 1–3 of *Preposterous Poof*.
3. Do Steps 1–3 of *Superior Sausage*.
4. Do Steps 1–2 of *Extraordinary Eggs*.
5. Do Step 1 of *Marvelous Muffins*.
6. Do Step 4 of *Superior Sausage*.
7. Do Step 3 of *Extraordinary Eggs*.
8. Do Step 2 of *Marvelous Muffins*.
9. Do Step 4 of *Extraordinary Eggs*.
10. Do Step 4 of *Preposterous Poof*.

THURSDAY

Extraordinary Eggs

1 Rinse, trim, and chop the scallions. Rinse, stem, and chop the basil. Rinse, stem, and chop the parsley. Rinse, stem, and chop the tomatoes. Cube the cream cheese.

2 Beat the eggs in a medium bowl. Add the half-and-half, the white pepper, the cream cheese, the scallions, the basil, and the parsley. Season to taste.

3 Melt the butter in a large skillet. Add the egg mixture and stir to scramble and fluff.

4 Blend in the tomatoes and heat through.

Superior Sausage

1 Scrub and coarsely grate the potatoes. Separate the sausage links.

2 Heat the oil in a large skillet.

3 Sauté the potatoes and the sausage until the sausage is browned on all sides and the potatoes are crisp, about 10 minutes.

4 Add the water, season to taste, cover, and steam for 2 minutes more.

Marvelous Muffins

1 Split the muffins and toast them.

2 Spread lightly with the butter and the marmalade.

Preposterous Poof

1 Set the strawberries out to soften.

2 Bring the water to a boil.

3 Place the gelatin in a blender. Add the boiling water and blend until the gelatin is dissolved, 2 to 3 minutes. Add the ice cubes and process until the mixture is thick and frothy. Pour into individual dessert glasses and freeze until you are ready to serve.

4 Top the poof with the sliced strawberries, dollops of whipped cream, and the sprinkles.

FRIDAY

O-Sole-O-Me-O

1 medium onion
1/2 pound fresh mushrooms
1 cup Gruyère cheese (when grated)
4 sole fillets (about 1 1/2 pounds)
2 tablespoons butter
1/4 teaspoon lemon-pepper seasoning
1/2 teaspoon paprika

Pianissimo Pilaf

1 clove garlic
2 tablespoons butter
1/2 cup vermicelli (when broken)
1 cup long-grain white rice
1 can (14 ounces) vegetable broth
1/2 cup water
2 tablespoons dry sherry
Seasoning to taste

Bossa Nova Broccoli

1 medium bunch broccoli
2 scallions (green onions)
1 small lemon
1 tablespoon butter
1 small jar (2 ounces) diced pimientos
1 teaspoon dried savory
Seasoning to taste

Mango Tango

1 package (3 ounces) cook-and-serve
   vanilla pudding mix
1 can (12 ounces) mango nectar
1/2 cup milk
Whipped cream for garnish
1/2 cup walnut bits for garnish

EQUIPMENT

Medium covered
   saucepan
Medium saucepan
Large covered skillet
Medium skillet
Small skillet
9 x 13-inch glass
   baking dish

Steamer insert
Cheese grater
Citrus grater
Citrus juicer
Kitchen knives
Measuring cups and
   spoons
Cooking utensils

COUNTDOWN

1. Assemble the ingredients and the
   equipment.
2. Do Steps 1–2 of *Mango Tango*.
3. Do Steps 1–3 of *Pianissimo Pilaf*.
4. Do Steps 1–4 of *O-Sole-O-Me-O*.
5. Do Steps 1–2 of *Bossa Nova Broccoli*.
6. Do Step 4 of *Pianissimo Pilaf*.
7. Do Steps 3–5 of *Bossa Nova Broccoli*.
8. Do Step 5 of *O-Sole-O-Me-O*.
9. Do Step 3 of *Mango Tango*.

FRIDAY

O-Sole-O-Me-O

1 Preheat the oven to 400°F. Grease a 9 x 13-inch baking dish.

2 Peel and thinly slice the onion. Rinse, pat dry, trim, and slice the mushrooms. Grate the cheese. Rinse and pat dry the fish fillets.

3 Melt the butter in a medium skillet. Sauté the onion and the mushrooms until soft, about 5 minutes.

4 Cover the bottom of the baking dish with half of the onion and mushrooms. Sprinkle with half of the cheese. Lay the fish fillets over the cheese. Sprinkle with the lemon-pepper seasoning and the paprika. Cover the fish with the remaining onion and mushrooms. Sprinkle on the rest of the cheese. Bake until the fish flakes easily with a fork, about 10 minutes.

5 Preheat the broiler. Broil the fish until the cheese bubbles, about 1 minute.

Pianissimo Pilaf

1 Peel and mince the garlic.

2 Melt the butter in a large skillet and sauté the garlic for 1 minute. Break the vermicelli into small pieces and add it to the skillet, stirring until browned, 2 to 3 minutes.

3 Add the rice, the broth, the water, and the sherry and season to taste. Cover the skillet, reduce the heat, and simmer for 15 minutes.

4 Remove the skillet from the heat and let stand for 15 minutes.

Bossa Nova Broccoli

1 Bring water to a boil in a medium saucepan.

2 Rinse and trim the broccoli, discard the tough ends, and cut into bite-sized florets. Arrange the florets in a steamer insert, place the insert in the saucepan, cover, and steam until the broccoli is crisp-tender, 6 to 8 minutes.

3 Rinse, trim, and chop the scallions. Grate the peel from the lemon and squeeze 2 tablespoons of lemon juice.

4 Melt the butter in a small skillet. Sauté the scallions for 2 minutes. Add the undrained pimientos, the savory, the lemon juice, and the lemon peel and season to taste.

5 Drain the broccoli and serve with the sauce.

Mango Tango

1 In a medium saucepan, combine the pudding mix, the nectar, and the milk, stirring constantly until the mixture comes to a boil, 5 to 7 minutes.

2 Pour the mixture into individual dessert glasses and refrigerate until you are ready to serve.

3 Garnish the pudding with dollops of whipped cream and sprinkle with the nuts.

WEEK FIVE

STAPLES

Monday

Fowling Up
Noodling Around
Appearently Pie

Tuesday

Snap Out of It
Recovering Rice
Wake-Up Salad
Just-a-Minute Tapioca

Wednesday

Paducah Pasta
Bowling Greens
Thoroughbread
Appalachians

Thursday

Cider House Ham
Yam Dankees
Caraway Cabbage
Pineapple Dapple

Friday

The Spice Gills
Sporty Rice
Posh Salad
Scary Cream

- ☐ Butter
- ☐ Flour
- ☐ Cornstarch
- ☐ Cream of tartar
- ☐ Granulated sugar
- ☐ Dark brown sugar
- ☐ Corn syrup
- ☐ Chocolate sprinkles
- ☐ Olive oil
- ☐ Sesame oil
- ☐ Vegetable oil
- ☐ Apple cider vinegar
- ☐ Red wine vinegar
- ☐ Tarragon vinegar
- ☐ White wine vinegar
- ☐ Lemon juice
- ☐ Lime juice
- ☐ Dijon mustard
- ☐ Honey
- ☐ Soy sauce
- ☐ Tabasco sauce
- ☐ Worcestershire sauce
- ☐ Grated Parmesan cheese
- ☐ Caraway seeds
- ☐ Dried basil
- ☐ Dried tarragon
- ☐ Ground allspice
- ☐ Cayenne pepper
- ☐ Ground cinnamon
- ☐ Ground cloves
- ☐ Ground ginger
- ☐ Ground nutmeg
- ☐ Black pepper
- ☐ Red pepper flakes
- ☐ Saffron threads
- ☐ Salt
- ☐ Brandy extract
- ☐ Rum extract
- ☐ Vanilla extract

SHOPPING LIST

MEAT & POULTRY

2 lean cooked ham steaks (about ³/₄ pound each) (Th)
1 ¹/₂ pounds boneless, skinless chicken breast (M)

FISH

4 red snapper fillets (about 1 ¹/₂ pounds) (T)
4 white fish fillets (about 1 ¹/₂ pounds) (F)

FRESH PRODUCE

VEGETABLES

4 small yams (Th)
1 medium head cauliflower (W)
2 small Japanese eggplants (M)
2 medium zucchini (W)
1 medium carrot (M)
3 medium carrots (W)
2 stalks celery (W)
1 stalk celery (F)
1 large head cabbage (Th)
1 medium head red leaf lettuce (T)
1 medium head green leaf lettuce (W)
1 head Boston lettuce (F)
1 large ripe avocado (T)
1 medium green bell pepper (M)
1 medium red bell pepper (W)
1 small green bell pepper (F)
1 medium onion (M)
1 medium onion (W)
2 medium onions (F)
1 small red onion (T)
1 small shallot (T)
2 scallions (green onions) (T)
3 scallions (green onions) (W)
1 clove garlic (F)

HERBS

¹/₄ cup chives (when chopped) (T)
2 tablespoons chives (when chopped) (W)
¹/₄ cup parsley (when chopped) (W)

FRUIT

2 large oranges (F)
1 small lemon (M)
2 medium bananas (F)
1 large tart green apple (T)
2 large sweet apples (W)
2 small tart green apples (F)
5 medium ripe pears (M)
2 medium ripe pears (W)

CANS, JARS & BOTTLES

SOUPS

1 can (14 ounces) chicken broth with roasted garlic (M)
1 can (14 ounces) vegetable broth (F)

VEGETABLES

1 can (14¹/₂ ounces) diced tomatoes (F)
1 can (11 ounces) whole-kernel corn (F)

FISH

1 tube (2 ounces) anchovy paste (W)

INTERNATIONAL FOODS

1 can (8 ounces) sliced water chestnuts (M)

FRUIT

1 can (20 ounces) pineapple rings (Th)

JUICES

1 cup apple juice (W)
1 cup apple cider (Th)

CONDIMENTS

1 jar (6¹/₂ ounces) marinated artichoke hearts (W)

PACKAGED GOODS

PASTA, RICE & GRAINS

12 ounces elbow macaroni (W)
1 cup brown rice (T)
1 cup long-grain white rice (F)

BAKED GOODS

1 loaf Italian bread (W)

INTERNATIONAL FOODS

8 ounces Japanese soba noodles (M)

DRIED FRUIT & NUTS

¹/₂ cup sliced almonds (F)

DESSERT & BAKING NEEDS

3 tablespoons instant tapioca (T)
1 cup mini-marshmallows (Th)

WINE AND SPIRITS

¹/₄ cup dry white wine (F)
3 tablespoons dry sherry (M)

REFRIGERATED PRODUCTS

DAIRY

2 cups milk (T)
2 tablespoons milk (Th)
¹/₄ cup milk (F)
2 eggs (T)

CHEESE

1 cup small-curd cottage cheese (W)

FROZEN GOODS

PASTRY

1 unbaked pie shell (M)

DESSERTS

1 pint pineapple sorbet (Th)
1 pint vanilla ice cream (F)

MONDAY

Fowling Up

1 1/2 pounds boneless, skinless chicken breast
1 medium carrot
1 medium onion
1 medium green bell pepper
2 small Japanese eggplants
1 can (8 ounces) sliced water chestnuts
1 tablespoon cornstarch
2 tablespoons soy sauce
3 tablespoons dry sherry
1 tablespoon honey
1/4 teaspoon red pepper flakes
1/2 teaspoon ground ginger
2 tablespoons vegetable oil
Seasoning to taste

Noodling Around

1 can (14 ounces) chicken broth with
   roasted garlic
1 cup water
8 ounces dry Japanese soba noodles
1 teaspoon sesame oil

Appearently Pie

1 unbaked frozen pie shell
1 small lemon
5 medium ripe pears
3/4 cup granulated sugar
1/2 teaspoon ground cinnamon
1 teaspoon rum extract
3 tablespoons butter
1/4 cup dark brown sugar
1/4 cup flour
1/8 teaspoon ground nutmeg

EQUIPMENT

Wok	Vegetable brush
Medium covered saucepan	Vegetable peeler
	Citrus grater
Small saucepan	Citrus juicer
Colander	Kitchen knives
Large mixing bowl	Measuring cups and spoons
Small mixing bowl	
Whisk	Cooking utensils

COUNTDOWN

1. Assemble the ingredients and the equipment.
2. Do Steps 1–4 of *Appearently Pie.*
3. Do Steps 1–3 of *Fowling Up.*
4. Do Steps 1–2 of *Noodling Around.*
5. Do Step 4 of *Fowling Up.*
6. Do Step 3 of *Noodling Around.*

MONDAY

Fowling Up

1 Rinse and pat dry the chicken and cut it into 1-inch-wide strips.

2 Peel, trim, and thinly slice the carrot. Peel and thinly slice the onion. Rinse, trim, seed, and chunk the bell pepper. Scrub, trim, and slice the eggplants. Drain the water chestnuts.

3 In a small bowl, combine the cornstarch, the soy sauce, the sherry, the honey, the red pepper flakes, and the ginger. Blend well.

4 Heat the oil in a wok. Add the chicken and stir-fry until it is opaque, about 2 minutes. Add the carrot and stir-fry for 1 minute. Add the onion, the bell pepper, the eggplants, and the water chestnuts. Stir-fry for 2 minutes. Add the soy sauce mixture, season to taste, and stir-fry until the vegetables are heated through and the sauce is thickened, 1 to 2 minutes.

Noodling Around

1 Bring the broth and the water to a boil in a medium saucepan.

2 Cook the noodles until almost tender, about 3 minutes.

3 Drain the noodles, toss with the oil, and cover to keep warm.

Appearently Pie

1 Set out the pie shell. Preheat the oven to 400°F.

2 Grate the lemon peel and juice the lemon. Peel, halve, and core the pears. Thinly slice them and place them in a large bowl. Blend in the lemon juice, the lemon peel, the granulated sugar, the cinnamon, and the rum extract.

3 Prick the pie shell all over the bottom with the tines of a fork. Pour the pear mixture into the pie shell.

4 Melt the butter in a small saucepan. Add the brown sugar, the flour, and the nutmeg. Sprinkle the mixture over the pears and bake until hot and bubbly, 25 to 30 minutes.

TUESDAY

Snap Out of It

1 small shallot
4 red snapper fillets (about 1 1/2 pounds)
3 tablespoons butter
2 tablespoons Dijon mustard
1 tablespoon lemon juice
1/8 teaspoon cayenne pepper
Seasoning to taste

Recovering Rice

1 small red onion
2 scallions (green onions)
1/4 cup fresh chives (when chopped)
1 tablespoon butter
1 cup brown rice
2 cups water
1/4 teaspoon ground cloves
Seasoning to taste

Wake-Up Salad

1 medium head red leaf lettuce
1 large ripe avocado
1 large tart green apple
3 tablespoons olive oil
2 tablespoons tarragon vinegar
1/2 teaspoon granulated sugar
Seasoning to taste

Just-a-Minute Tapioca

2 eggs
2 cups milk
1/3 cup plus 1 tablespoon dark brown sugar
2 tablespoons butter
3 tablespoons instant tapioca
1/8 teaspoon salt
1/4 teaspoon cream of tartar
2 teaspoons vanilla extract

EQUIPMENT

Electric mixer	2 small mixing bowls
Double boiler	Whisk
Medium saucepan	Kitchen knives
Small saucepan	Measuring cups and
9 x 13-inch glass	spoons
baking dish	Cooking utensils
Large mixing bowl	

COUNTDOWN

1. Assemble the ingredients and the equipment.
2. Do Steps 1–3 of *Recovering Rice*.
3. Do Steps 1–2 of *Wake-Up Salad*.
4. Do Steps 1–5 of *Just-a-Minute Tapioca*.
5. Do Steps 1–4 of *Snap Out of It*.
6. Do Step 4 of *Recovering Rice*.
7. Do Step 3 of *Wake-Up Salad*.

TUESDAY

Snap Out of It

1 Preheat the broiler.

2 Peel and mince the shallot.

3 Rinse and pat dry the fish fillets and arrange them in a 9 x 13-inch baking dish.

4 Melt the butter in a small saucepan. Blend in the mustard, the lemon juice, and the cayenne pepper. Season to taste and whisk until creamy. Spoon the sauce over the fish and broil until the fish flakes easily with a fork and is nicely browned, about 6 minutes.

Recovering Rice

1 Peel and mince the onion. Rinse, trim, and chop the scallions. Rinse, trim, and chop the chives.

2 Bring water to a boil in the bottom of a double boiler.

3 Melt the butter in the top of the double boiler. Add the onion, the rice, the 2 cups water, and the cloves. Season to taste, cover, reduce the heat, and simmer until all the liquid is absorbed and the rice is tender, 40 to 45 minutes.

4 Fold in the scallions and the chives and fluff with a fork.

Wake-Up Salad

1 Wash and dry the lettuce, tear it into bite-sized pieces, and arrange it on individual salad plates. Halve, pit, peel, and chunk the avocado. Rinse, core, and chop the apple. Combine the avocado and the apple in a small bowl.

2 In another small bowl, whisk together the oil, the vinegar, and the sugar. Season to taste and toss with the fruit.

3 Spoon the fruit over the lettuce.

Just-a-Minute Tapioca

1 Separate the eggs, placing the whites in a large bowl and the yolks in a medium saucepan.

2 Whisk the milk into the yolks. Add $\frac{1}{3}$ cup of the brown sugar, the butter, the tapioca, and the salt. Mix well.

3 Beat the egg whites with the cream of tartar until stiff. Gradually add the remaining 1 tablespoon of brown sugar and beat until the whites are very stiff and glossy.

4 Bring the tapioca mixture to a boil, stirring constantly. Remove from the heat and blend in the vanilla.

5 Fold the tapioca mixture slowly into the whipped egg whites and let stand until you are ready to serve.

WEDNESDAY

Paducah Pasta

1 medium head cauliflower
3 medium carrots
2 medium zucchini
2 stalks celery
1 medium onion
1/4 cup fresh parsley (when chopped)
12 ounces elbow macaroni
1 tablespoon olive oil
1 cup small-curd cottage cheese
Seasoning to taste
1/2 cup grated Parmesan cheese

Bowling Greens

1 medium head green leaf lettuce
3 scallions (green onions)
1 medium red bell pepper
1 jar (6 1/2 ounces) marinated artichoke
   hearts
2 tablespoons white wine vinegar
1/2 teaspoon Dijon mustard
1/4 teaspoon dried tarragon
Seasoning to taste

Thoroughbread

2 tablespoons fresh chives (when chopped)
3 tablespoons butter
1 tube (2 ounces) anchovy paste
1 tablespoon lemon juice
1 loaf Italian bread

Appalachians

2 large sweet apples
2 medium ripe pears
2 tablespoons lime juice
1 cup apple juice
2 teaspoons ground allspice
1 tablespoon honey

EQUIPMENT

Stockpot	Vegetable brush
Small saucepan	Vegetable peeler
Baking sheet	Kitchen knives
Colander	Measuring cups and
Large mixing bowl	spoons
2 small mixing bowls	Cooking utensils
Whisk	

COUNTDOWN

1. Assemble the ingredients and the equipment.
2. Do Steps 1–2 of *Paducah Pasta*.
3. Do Steps 1–2 of *Bowling Greens*.
4. Do Steps 1–2 of *Appalachians*.
5. Do Steps 1–4 of *Thoroughbread*.
6. Do Steps 3–4 of *Paducah Pasta*.
7. Do Step 3 of *Bowling Greens*.
8. Do Step 3 of *Appalachians*.

WEDNESDAY

Paducah Pasta

1 Bring water to a boil in a stockpot.

2 Rinse and trim the cauliflower and cut it into bite-sized florets. Peel, trim, and thinly slice the carrots. Scrub, trim, and slice the zucchini. Rinse, trim, and slice the celery. Peel and chop the onion. Rinse, stem, and chop the parsley.

3 Cook the macaroni, the cauliflower, the carrots, the zucchini, the celery, and the onion until the pasta is almost tender and the vegetables are crisp-tender, about 8 minutes.

4 Drain the pasta and vegetables well and return them to the stockpot. Add the oil, the parsley, and the cottage cheese and season to taste. Toss with the Parmesan cheese.

Bowling Greens

1 Wash and dry the lettuce and arrange 4 of the leaves on individual salad plates. Tear the remaining leaves into bite-sized pieces. Rinse, trim, and chop the scallions. Rinse, trim, and seed the bell pepper and cut it into thin strips. Drain the artichoke hearts, reserving the marinade, and cut the hearts in half. Combine the vegetables in a large bowl.

2 In a small bowl, whisk together the reserved artichoke marinade, the vinegar, the mustard, and the tarragon. Season to taste.

3 Toss with the vegetables and spoon over the lettuce leaves.

Thoroughbread

1 Preheat the oven to 350°F.

2 Rinse, trim, and chop the chives.

3 Combine the butter, the anchovy paste, and the lemon juice in a small bowl and blend well.

4 Cut the bread in half lengthwise. Spread the cut sides with the anchovy mixture. Lay the bread halves on a baking sheet. Sprinkle with the chives and bake until lightly golden, about 10 minutes.

Appalachians

1 Rinse, core, and thinly slice the apples and the pears and arrange the slices on individual dessert plates. Sprinkle with half of the lime juice to keep them from browning.

2 Combine the apple juice, the allspice, the honey, and the remaining lime juice in a small saucepan. Whisk to blend and bring the mixture just to a boil. Remove from the heat and set aside.

3 Drizzle the sauce over the fruit.

THURSDAY

Cider House Ham

2 lean cooked ham steaks (about ¾ pound each)
1 cup apple cider
2 teaspoons Dijon mustard
2 tablespoons dark brown sugar
1 tablespoon apple cider vinegar
Seasoning to taste

Yam Dankees

4 small yams
2 tablespoons butter
2 tablespoons milk
Seasoning to taste
1 cup mini-marshmallows

Caraway Cabbage

1 large head cabbage
4 tablespoons butter
1 tablespoon caraway seeds
2 tablespoons water
Seasoning to taste

Pineapple Dapple

1 can (20 ounces) pineapple rings
1 pint frozen pineapple sorbet
1 tablespoon granulated sugar
½ teaspoon ground cinnamon

EQUIPMENT

Electric mixer
Medium saucepan
Large covered skillet
9 x 13-inch baking pan
Baking sheet
Small mixing bowl
Whisk
Vegetable brush
Vegetable grater
Ice cream scoop
Kitchen knives
Measuring cups and spoons
Cooking utensils

COUNTDOWN

1. Assemble the ingredients and the equipment.
2. Do Steps 1–4 of *Cider House Ham*.
3. Do Step 1 of *Yam Dankees*.
4. Do Steps 1–2 of *Caraway Cabbage*.
5. Do Steps 2–4 of *Yam Dankees*.
6. Do Steps 1–3 of *Pineapple Dapple*.

THURSDAY

Cider House Ham

1 Preheat the oven to 350°F.

2 Trim any fat from the ham steaks and place them in a 9 x 13-inch baking pan.

3 In a small bowl, combine the cider, the mustard, the brown sugar, and the vinegar. Spread the mixture over the ham steaks and season to taste.

4 Bake until the flavors are blended and the topping is crisp, about 10 minutes.

Yam Dankees

1 Scrub, trim, and quarter the yams. Place them in a medium saucepan and cover them with water. Bring the water to a boil and cook until the yams are tender, 10 to 15 minutes.

2 Preheat the broiler. Grease a baking sheet.

3 Drain the yams and rinse them under cold water. Peel them, return them to the saucepan, and whip them with the butter and the milk. Season to taste.

4 With an ice cream scoop, divide the potatoes into 4 portions and place them on the baking sheet. Top each portion with marshmallows and broil until the potatoes are hot and the marshmallows are golden, 1 to 2 minutes.

Caraway Cabbage

1 Rinse, trim, quarter, and coarsely grate the cabbage.

2 Melt the butter in a large skillet and sauté the cabbage for 1 minute. Add the caraway seeds and the water. Season to taste and bring the mixture to a boil. Cover the skillet, remove it from the heat, and let the cabbage steam until it is crisp-tender, 7 to 8 minutes.

Pineapple Dapple

1 Drain the pineapple and distribute the rings among individual dessert dishes.

2 Top with scoops of sorbet.

3 Combine the sugar and the cinnamon and sprinkle over the sorbet.

FRIDAY

The Spice Gills

1 medium onion
1 clove garlic
1 small green bell pepper
4 white fish fillets (about 1 1/2 pounds)
1 tablespoon olive oil
1 can (14 1/2 ounces) diced tomatoes
1 tablespoon Worcestershire sauce
2 teaspoons red wine vinegar
1/2 teaspoon dried basil
1/4 teaspoon red pepper flakes
1/8 teaspoon Tabasco sauce
Seasoning to taste

Sporty Rice

1 medium onion
1 can (11 ounces) whole-kernel corn
2 tablespoons butter
1 cup long-grain white rice
1 can (14 ounces) vegetable broth
1/4 cup dry white wine
1 1/2 teaspoons saffron threads
Seasoning to taste

Posh Salad

1 head Boston lettuce
2 small tart green apples
2 medium bananas
2 large oranges
1 stalk celery
2 tablespoons granulated sugar
2 tablespoons lemon juice
2 tablespoons vegetable oil
1/2 cup sliced almonds

Scary Cream

1 1/2 tablespoons butter
1/2 cup dark brown sugar
1 tablespoon corn syrup
1/4 cup milk
1/2 teaspoon brandy extract
1 pint vanilla ice cream
Chocolate sprinkles for garnish

EQUIPMENT

Small covered
  saucepan
Small saucepan
2 large covered
  skillets
Large mixing bowl

Ice cream scoop
Kitchen knives
Measuring cups and
  spoons
Cooking utensils

COUNTDOWN

1. Assemble the ingredients and the equipment.
2. Do Steps 1–3 of *Sporty Rice*.
3. Do Steps 1–3 of *Posh Salad*.
4. Do Step 1 of *Scary Cream*.
5. Do Steps 1–5 of *The Spice Gills*.
6. Do Step 4 of *Posh Salad*.
7. Do Step 4 of *Sporty Rice*.
8. Do Step 2 of *Scary Cream*.

FRIDAY

The Spice Gills

1 Peel and mince the onion. Peel and mince the garlic. Rinse, trim, seed, and chop the bell pepper. Rinse and pat dry the fish fillets.

2 Heat the oil in a large skillet. Sauté the onion, the garlic, and the bell pepper until tender, about 5 minutes.

3 Add the tomatoes, the Worcestershire sauce, the vinegar, the basil, the red pepper flakes, and the Tabasco sauce. Season to taste.

4 Bring the mixture to a boil, stirring to blend the flavors. Add the fish, cover, reduce the heat, and simmer for 3 minutes.

5 Spoon the sauce over the fish and continue to simmer until the fish flakes easily with a fork, 3 to 4 minutes.

Sporty Rice

1 Peel and chop the onion. Drain the corn.

2 Melt the butter in a large skillet. Sauté the onion until it is lightly browned, about 7 minutes. Add the rice and brown lightly, 1 to 2 minutes.

3 Add the broth, the wine, the corn, and the saffron. Season to taste. Cover and simmer until the liquid is absorbed and the rice is tender, about 20 minutes.

4 Fluff the rice with a fork.

Posh Salad

1 Wash and dry the lettuce and arrange the leaves on individual salad plates.

2 Rinse, core, and chop the apples. Peel and slice the bananas. Peel and section the oranges. Rinse, trim, and dice the celery. Combine the ingredients in a large bowl.

3 In a small saucepan, heat the sugar with the lemon juice until the sugar is dissolved. Blend in the oil and toss with the fruit.

4 Mound the fruit on the lettuce leaves and sprinkle with the nuts.

Scary Cream

1 In a small saucepan, combine the butter, the brown sugar, the corn syrup, and the milk. Cook until just bubbly, about 2 minutes. Remove the saucepan from the heat and blend in the brandy extract. Cover and keep warm.

2 Place scoops of ice cream in individual dessert dishes, add the sauce, and top with a splash of sprinkles.

WEEK SIX

WEEK AT A GLANCE

Monday
Topsy-Turvy Pie
Hurry-Scurry Beans
Higgledy-Piggledy Pudding

Tuesday
Scooter Soup
Tipper Salad
Jake Chips
Frosty Fruit

Wednesday
Prosperous Pasta
Spiffy Salad
Big-Hearted Bread
Deep Pockets

Thursday
Scarlett O'Salmon
Tara Gone
Rhett Broccoli
Twelve Oats

Friday
Holyolk
Harvard Beets
Back Bay Biscuits
Plymouth Rocks

STAPLES

- ❑ Butter
- ❑ Flour
- ❑ Bisquick
- ❑ Baking powder
- ❑ Granulated sugar
- ❑ Dark brown sugar
- ❑ Olive oil
- ❑ Vegetable oil
- ❑ Rice vinegar
- ❑ Tarragon vinegar
- ❑ Lemon juice
- ❑ Chili sauce
- ❑ Mayonnaise
- ❑ Prepared horseradish
- ❑ Steak sauce
- ❑ Worcestershire sauce
- ❑ Grated Parmesan cheese
- ❑ Caraway seeds
- ❑ Celery seeds
- ❑ Sesame seeds
- ❑ Dried dill
- ❑ Dried oregano
- ❑ Dried rosemary
- ❑ Dried savory
- ❑ Curry powder
- ❑ Ground ginger
- ❑ Dry mustard
- ❑ Black pepper
- ❑ Saffron threads
- ❑ Salt
- ❑ Almond extract
- ❑ Orange extract

MEAT & POULTRY

1 1/2 pounds lean ground beef (M)

1 1/2 pounds boneless, skinless chicken breast (T)

FISH

4 salmon steaks (about 1 1/2 pounds) (Th)

FRESH PRODUCE

VEGETABLES

1 1/2 pounds small new potatoes (Th)

1 medium bunch broccoli (Th)

1 pound green beans (M)

3/4 pound Chinese snow peas (T)

2 medium zucchini (F)

1 large carrot (T)

2 stalks celery (T)

1 stalk celery (W)

1/4 pound mushrooms (T)

1/2 pound mushrooms (F)

1 medium head lettuce (W)

1 small head lettuce (T)

1 small head Boston lettuce (F)

2 large tomatoes (F)

12 cherry tomatoes (W)

1 large red bell pepper (T)

1 small green bell pepper (W)

1 small orange bell pepper (W)

1 small bunch radishes (W)

1 medium onion (M)

1 medium onion (T)

1 small onion (F)

1 small red onion (W)

1 small shallot (Th)

4 scallions (green onions) (W)

4 scallions (green onions) (F)

2 cloves garlic (T)

2 cloves garlic (W)

HERBS

3 tablespoons chives (when chopped) (W)

1/4 cup dill (when chopped) (F)

2 tablespoons parsley (when chopped) (Th)

2 tablespoons tarragon (when chopped) (Th)

FRUIT

2 large oranges (F)

4 medium oranges (T)

1 large lemon (W)

1 medium apple (T)

1 small tart apple (F)

2 large ripe pears (Th)

4 ripe kiwifruit (T)

CANS, JARS & BOTTLES

SOUPS

2 cans (14 ounces each) chicken broth (T)

1 can (10 3/4 ounces) tomato soup (M)

VEGETABLES

1 can (11 ounces) whole-kernel corn (W)

1 can (15 ounces) diced Harvard beets (F)

INTERNATIONAL FOODS

1 can (4 ounces) diced green chilies (M)

SPREADS

1/4 cup red currant jelly (T)

DESSERT & BAKING NEEDS

1 jar (7 ounces) marshmallow crème (M)

PACKAGED GOODS

PASTA, RICE & GRAINS

1 pound linguini (W)

1 cup long-grain white rice (T)

BAKED GOODS

4 medium pita bread rounds (T)

1 loaf Italian bread (W)

4 graham cracker tart shells (W)

12 small oatmeal cookies (Th)

DRIED FRUIT & NUTS

1/4 cup walnut bits (M)

DESSERT & BAKING NEEDS

1 package (3.4 ounces) instant butterscotch pudding mix (M)

4 squares (1 ounce each) semisweet chocolate (Th)

WINE & SPIRITS

1/3 cup dry white wine (W)

2 tablespoons Grand Marnier (F)

REFRIGERATED PRODUCTS

DAIRY

2 2/3 cups milk (M)

1/2 cup milk (T)

2/3 cup milk (W)

1 cup milk (F)

1 cup half-and-half (T)

1/3 cup whipping cream (Th)

Whipped cream for garnish (T)

Whipped cream for garnish (W)

Whipped cream for garnish (F)

3 eggs (W)

9 eggs (F)

CHEESE

1/2 cup shredded Cheddar cheese (M)

2 cups shredded Colby/Monterey Jack cheese (W)

1 cup Swiss cheese (when grated) (F)

JUICES

1 tablespoon orange juice (Th)

FROZEN GOODS

FRUIT

1 package (16 ounces) cranberries (F)

DESSERTS

1 pint orange sherbet (F)

MONDAY

Topsy-Turvy Pie

2 cups Bisquick
2/3 cup milk
1 medium onion
1 can (4 ounces) diced green chilies
1 tablespoon vegetable oil
1 1/2 pounds lean ground beef
1/2 teaspoon dried oregano
Seasoning to taste
1 can (10 3/4 ounces) tomato soup
1/2 cup shredded Cheddar cheese

Hurry-Scurry Beans

1 pound fresh green beans
1 tablespoon butter
2 tablespoons rice vinegar
1/4 teaspoon Worcestershire sauce
1/2 teaspoon dried savory
Seasoning to taste

Higgledy-Piggledy Pudding

1 package (3.4 ounces) instant butterscotch
  pudding mix
2 cups milk
1 jar (7 ounces) marshmallow crème
1/4 cup walnut bits

EQUIPMENT

Electric mixer
Medium covered
  saucepan
Large ovenproof
  skillet
2 medium mixing
  bowls

Waxed paper
Kitchen knives
Measuring cups and
  spoons
Cooking utensils

COUNTDOWN

1. Assemble the ingredients and the equipment.
2. Do Step 1 of *Higgledy-Piggledy Pudding.*
3. Do Steps 1–6 of *Topsy-Turvy Pie.*
4. Do Steps 1–3 of *Hurry-Scurry Beans.*
5. Do Step 7 of *Topsy-Turvy Pie.*
6. Do Step 2 of *Higgledy-Piggledy Pudding.*

MONDAY

Topsy-Turvy Pie

1 Preheat the oven to 425°F.

2 Dust a sheet of waxed paper with flour.

3 In a medium bowl, combine the Bisquick and the milk. Blend to form a soft dough. Turn the dough out on the waxed paper, knead lightly, and pat it out to form a 10-inch round.

4 Peel and chop the onion. Drain the chilies.

5 Heat the oil in a large ovenproof skillet. Sauté the onion and the beef until the onion is soft and the beef is browned, about 5 minutes. Blend in the chilies and the oregano and season to taste. Blend in the tomato soup. Remove the skillet from the heat, invert the dough onto the beef mixture, and peel away the waxed paper.

6 Bake until the dough is lightly browned and the beef mixture is heated through, about 20 minutes.

7 Turn the mixture upside down and sprinkle with the cheese.

Hurry-Scurry Beans

1 Bring water to a boil in a medium saucepan.

2 Rinse and trim the green beans. Cook until they are crisp-tender, about 7 minutes.

3 Drain the beans and return them to the saucepan. Blend in the butter, the vinegar, the Worcestershire sauce, and the savory. Season to taste, cover, and keep warm until you are ready to serve.

Higgledy-Piggledy Pudding

1 In a medium bowl, beat the pudding mix with the milk until well blended, about 2 minutes. Pour the mixture into individual dessert dishes and refrigerate for at least 20 minutes.

2 Spoon the marshmallow crème over the pudding and sprinkle with the nuts.

TUESDAY

Scooter Soup

1½ pounds boneless, skinless chicken breast
1 medium onion
1 clove garlic
2 stalks celery
1 large carrot
1 medium apple
3 tablespoons butter
1 cup long-grain white rice
2 teaspoons curry powder
1½ teaspoons saffron threads
2 cans (14 ounces each) chicken broth
¼ cup flour
½ cup milk
Seasoning to taste
1 cup half-and-half

Tipper Salad

1 small head lettuce
¾ pound Chinese snow peas
¼ pound fresh mushrooms
1 large red bell pepper
1 clove garlic
3 tablespoons vegetable oil
2 tablespoons rice vinegar
1 teaspoon granulated sugar
1 tablespoon sesame seeds
Seasoning to taste

Jake Chips

4 tablespoons butter
4 medium pita bread rounds
1 tablespoon dried dill
2 tablespoons grated Parmesan cheese
Seasoning to taste

Frosty Fruit

4 medium oranges
4 ripe kiwifruit
¼ cup red currant jelly
1 teaspoon ground ginger
Whipped cream for garnish

EQUIPMENT

Stockpot
Small saucepan
Medium skillet
Baking sheet
Medium mixing bowl
2 small mixing bowls
Whisk
Vegetable peeler

Citrus grater
Citrus juicer
Pastry brush
Kitchen knives
Measuring cups and
    spoons
Cooking utensils

COUNTDOWN

1. Assemble the ingredients and the equipment.
2. Do Steps 1–3 of *Frosty Fruit*.
3. Do Steps 1–3 of *Scooter Soup*.
4. Do Steps 1–5 of *Tipper Salad*.
5. Do Steps 4–5 of *Scooter Soup*.
6. Do Steps 1–4 of *Jake Chips*.
7. Do Step 6 of *Scooter Soup*.
8. Do Step 6 of *Tipper Salad*.
9. Do Step 7 of *Scooter Soup*.
10. Do Step 4 of *Frosty Fruit*.

TUESDAY

Scooter Soup

1 Rinse and pat dry the chicken.

2 Peel and chop the onion. Peel and mince the garlic. Rinse, trim, and chop the celery. Peel, trim, and chop the carrot. Rinse, core, and chop the apple.

3 Place the chicken in a stockpot, cover with water, and cook until the chicken is tender and cooked through, about 10 minutes.

4 Remove the chicken, let cool, and chop it. Reserve 1 cup of the cooking liquid.

5 Melt the butter in the stockpot. Add the rice and sauté for 3 minutes. Add the onion, the garlic, the celery, and the carrot and sauté until the vegetables soften slightly, about 3 minutes. Add the apple, the curry powder, the saffron, the broth, and the reserved cooking liquid. Bring the mixture to a boil, cover, reduce the heat, and simmer for 15 minutes.

6 In a small bowl, whisk together the flour and the milk until smooth. Blend the mixture into the soup. Add the chicken to the soup and season to taste. Return the soup to a boil and cook for 5 minutes.

7 Slowly add the half-and-half. Heat through but do not boil.

Tipper Salad

1 Wash and dry the lettuce and arrange the leaves on individual salad plates.

2 Rinse and string the snow peas. Rinse, pat dry, trim, and slice the mushrooms. Rinse, trim, and seed the bell pepper and cut it into thin strips. Peel and mince the garlic.

3 Bring a small amount of water to a boil in a medium skillet. Add the snow peas and blanch until they turn bright green, about 1 minute. Drain the snow peas, rinse under cold water, and pat dry.

4 In a small bowl, whisk together the garlic, the oil, the vinegar, and the sugar. Add the sesame seeds and season to taste.

5 Combine the snow peas, the mushrooms, and the bell pepper in a medium bowl. Toss with the dressing.

6 Mound the vegetables over the lettuce.

Jake Chips

1 Preheat the oven to 350°F.

2 Melt the butter.

3 Cut the pita rounds into quarters. Separate each piece. Brush the inside of each piece with the butter. Place the bread, buttered side up, on a baking sheet. Sprinkle with the dill and the cheese and season to taste.

4 Bake until the bread is crisp and golden, about 10 minutes.

Frosty Fruit

1 Grate 2 tablespoons of orange peel. Cut 1 orange in half and juice it. Peel and slice the remaining half and the remaining oranges and cut the slices in half. Peel and slice the kiwifruit.

2 Arrange the orange slices on individual dessert plates. Arrange the kiwi slices over the orange slices. Refrigerate until you are ready to serve.

3 In a small saucepan, combine the orange juice, the orange peel, the currant jelly, and the ginger. Bring the mixture to a boil, remove from the heat, and let cool.

4 Spoon the syrup over the fruit. Top with dollops of whipped cream.

WEDNESDAY

Prosperous Pasta

1 small red onion
1 small green bell pepper
1 small orange bell pepper
4 scallions (green onions)
2 cloves garlic
1 can (11 ounces) whole-kernel corn
3 tablespoons butter
1 tablespoon flour
2/3 cup milk
1/3 cup dry white wine
2 cups shredded Colby/Monterey Jack
   cheese
1 pound linguini
Seasoning to taste

Spiffy Salad

1 medium head lettuce
12 cherry tomatoes
1 small bunch radishes
1 stalk celery
3 tablespoons olive oil
2 tablespoons tarragon vinegar
1/2 teaspoon granulated sugar
1 teaspoon Worcestershire sauce
1/2 teaspoon celery seeds
1/4 teaspoon dry mustard
Seasoning to taste

Big-Hearted Bread

1 loaf Italian bread
3 tablespoons fresh chives (when chopped)
1 tablespoon dried rosemary
1/4 cup olive oil

Deep Pockets

1 large lemon
3 eggs
1 cup granulated sugar
4 tablespoons butter
1 teaspoon orange extract
4 graham cracker tart shells
Whipped cream for garnish

EQUIPMENT

Electric mixer	Small bowl
Stockpot	Whisk
Medium saucepan	Citrus grater
Large skillet	Citrus juicer
2-quart casserole	Pastry brush
Baking sheet	Plastic wrap
Colander	Kitchen knives
Large mixing bowl	Measuring cups and
Medium mixing	spoons
bowl	Cooking utensils

COUNTDOWN

1. Assemble the ingredients and the equipment.
2. Do Steps 1–3 of *Deep Pockets*.
3. Do Steps 1–7 of *Prosperous Pasta*.
4. Do Step 4 of *Deep Pockets*.
5. Do Steps 1–2 of *Spiffy Salad*.
6. Do Steps 1–5 of *Big-Hearted Bread*.
7. Do Step 3 of *Spiffy Salad*.
8. Do Step 5 of *Deep Pockets*.

WEDNESDAY

Prosperous Pasta

1 Preheat the oven to 350°F.

2 Bring water to a boil in a stockpot.

3 Peel and chop the onion. Rinse, trim, seed, and chop the bell peppers. Rinse, trim, and slice the scallions. Peel and mince the garlic. Drain the corn.

4 Melt 2 tablespoons of the butter in a large skillet. Sauté the onion, the peppers, the scallions, and the garlic for 3 minutes. Add the corn and sauté for 1 minute more. Remove the vegetables from the skillet and set aside.

5 Melt the remaining 1 tablespoon butter in the skillet and blend in the flour. Gradually add the milk, stirring until smooth and thick, about 4 minutes. Blend in the wine. Add 1 cup of the cheese and cook just until the cheese is melted, about 3 minutes.

6 Cook the linguini 2 to 3 minutes if you are using fresh pasta, 6 to 7 minutes if you are using dry pasta.

7 Drain the pasta, return it to the stockpot, and combine it with the cheese mixture and the vegetables. Season to taste and pour into a 2-quart casserole. Top with the remaining 1 cup cheese and bake until the cheese is hot and bubbly, about 20 minutes.

Spiffy Salad

1 Wash and dry the lettuce and tear it into bite-sized pieces. Rinse and halve the tomatoes. Rinse, trim, and slice the radishes. Rinse, trim, and chop the celery. Combine the ingredients in a large bowl.

2 In a small bowl, whisk together the oil, the vinegar, the sugar, the Worcestershire sauce, the celery seeds, and the mustard. Season to taste.

3 Toss the salad with the dressing.

Big-Hearted Bread

1 Preheat the broiler.

2 Cut the bread in half and then into quarters.

3 Rinse, trim, and chop the chives and combine them with the rosemary.

4 Brush the cut sides of the bread with the oil and sprinkle with the herb mixture.

5 Place the bread quarters on a baking sheet and broil until lightly toasted, about 2 minutes.

Deep Pockets

1 Grate 3 tablespoons of lemon peel and squeeze $1/4$ cup lemon juice.

2 Beat the eggs in a medium bowl until they are thick and lemony, about 3 minutes.

3 In a medium saucepan, combine the eggs, the sugar, the butter, the lemon peel, the lemon juice, and the orange extract. Bring to a simmer and stir gently until the mixture is thick, 12 to 15 minutes.

4 Remove the saucepan from the heat, cover it with plastic wrap, and let it cool.

5 Spoon the lemon mixture into the tart shells and top with dollops of whipped cream.

Scarlett O'Salmon

4 salmon steaks (about 1 1/2 pounds)
1 teaspoon prepared horseradish
3 tablespoons olive oil
3 tablespoons vegetable oil
2 tablespoons chili sauce
1 tablespoon steak sauce
3 tablespoons lemon juice
Seasoning to taste

Tara Gone

1 1/2 pounds small new potatoes
2 tablespoons fresh tarragon (when chopped)
2 tablespoons fresh parsley (when chopped)
2 tablespoons vegetable oil
Seasoning to taste

Rhett Broccoli

1 medium bunch broccoli
1 small shallot
2 tablespoons butter
Seasoning to taste

Twelve Oats

12 small oatmeal cookies
2 large ripe pears
1 tablespoon orange juice
4 squares (1 ounce each) semisweet chocolate
1/3 cup whipping cream
1 teaspoon almond extract

EQUIPMENT

Small saucepan	Vegetable brush
Large skillet	Plastic bag
9 x 13-inch glass baking dish	Plastic wrap
9 x 9-inch baking pan	Kitchen knives
Small mixing bowl	Measuring cups and spoons
Whisk	Cooking utensils

COUNTDOWN

1. Assemble the ingredients and the equipment.
2. Do Steps 1–4 of *Tara Gone*.
3. Do Steps 1–2 of *Scarlett O'Salmon*.
4. Do Steps 1–2 of *Twelve Oats*.
5. Do Step 3 of *Scarlett O'Salmon*.
6. Do Steps 1–2 of *Rhett Broccoli*.
7. Do Step 5 of *Tara Gone*.
8. Do Steps 3–4 of *Twelve Oats*.

THURSDAY

Scarlett O'Salmon

1 Rinse and pat dry the salmon steaks and place them in a 9 x 13-inch baking dish.

2 In a small bowl, combine the horseradish, the oils, the chili sauce, the steak sauce, and the lemon juice and season to taste. Pour the mixture over the salmon. Cover the dish with plastic wrap and marinate for 15 minutes, turning the steaks once or twice.

3 Place the salmon in a 400°F oven and bake until the fish flakes easily with a fork, about 12 minutes.

Tara Gone

1 Preheat the oven to 400° F.

2 Scrub and halve the potatoes. Rinse, stem, and chop the tarragon. Rinse, stem, and chop the parsley.

3 Place the potatoes in a 9 x 9-inch baking pan. Toss with the oil to coat. Sprinkle with the tarragon and season to taste.

4 Bake, stirring occasionally, until the potatoes are golden and tender, 35 to 40 minutes.

5 Sprinkle with the parsley.

Rhett Broccoli

1 Rinse and trim the broccoli, discard the tough ends, and cut into bite-sized florets. Peel and chop the shallot.

2 Melt the butter in a large skillet. Add the broccoli and the shallot, season to taste, and sauté until the broccoli is just tender, about 5 minutes.

Twelve Oats

1 Place the cookies in a plastic bag and crumble them. Arrange the crumbs on individual dessert plates and set aside.

2 Rinse and core the pears and cut them in half lengthwise. Sprinkle them with the orange juice, cover with plastic wrap, and set aside.

3 Slice the pear halves almost through, leaving them attached at the stem end, and push the slices out into a fan. Place over the cookie crumbs.

4 In a small saucepan, melt the chocolate with the cream. Blend in the almond extract. Drizzle the sauce over the pears.

FRIDAY

Holyolk

1/2 pound fresh mushrooms
2 medium zucchini
4 scallions (green onions)
2 large tomatoes
1/4 cup fresh dill (when chopped)
1 cup Swiss cheese (when grated)
4 tablespoons butter
9 eggs
1/4 cup milk
Seasoning to taste

Harvard Beets

1 small head Boston lettuce
1 small onion
1 small tart apple
1 can (15 ounces) diced Harvard beets
3 tablespoons vegetable oil
2 tablespoons lemon juice
Seasoning to taste

Back Bay Biscuits

2 cups flour
4 teaspoons baking powder
1/2 teaspoon salt
1 1/2 tablespoons caraway seeds
1/4 cup mayonnaise
3/4 cup milk

Plymouth Rocks

1 package (16 ounces) frozen cranberries
2 large oranges
3/4 cup dark brown sugar
2 tablespoons Grand Marnier
1 pint orange sherbet
Whipped cream for garnish

EQUIPMENT

Electric mixer	Whisk
Medium saucepan	Cheese grater
Large covered skillet	Vegetable brush
9 x 13-inch glass baking dish	Citrus grater
	Citrus peeler
Baking sheet	Biscuit cutter
Breadboard	Ice cream scoop
Large mixing bowl	Kitchen knives
3 medium mixing bowls	Measuring cups and spoons
2 small mixing bowls	Cooking utensils

COUNTDOWN

1. Assemble the ingredients and the equipment.
2. Do Steps 1–4 of *Plymouth Rocks*.
3. Do Steps 1–5 of *Holyolk*.
4. Do Steps 1–3 of *Back Bay Biscuits*.
5. Do Step 6 of *Holyolk*.
6. Do Step 4 of *Back Bay Biscuits*.
7. Do Steps 1–5 of *Harvard Beets*.
8. Do Step 5 of *Plymouth Rocks*.

FRIDAY

Holyolk

1 Preheat the oven to 350°F. Butter a 9 x 13-inch baking dish.

2 Rinse, pat dry, trim, and chop the mushrooms. Scrub, trim, and chop the zucchini. Rinse, trim, and chop the scallions. Rinse, stem, and chop the tomatoes. Rinse, stem, and chop the dill. Grate the cheese.

3 Melt 2 tablespoons of the butter in a large skillet. Sauté the mushrooms, the zucchini, the scallions, and the tomatoes until just tender, 2 to 3 minutes. Cover the skillet and remove it from the heat.

4 Separate the eggs. In a large bowl, beat the whites until they are stiff, about 4 minutes. In a medium bowl, combine the yolks, the milk, and the dill. Season to taste and beat until thick, about 3 minutes. Fold the yolks into the whites.

5 Melt the remaining 2 tablespoons butter in the baking dish. Add the vegetables. Pour the egg mixture over the vegetables and sprinkle the cheese on top.

6 Bake until the eggs are fluffy and set and the cheese has melted, 20 to 25 minutes.

Harvard Beets

1 Wash and dry the lettuce and distribute the leaves among individual salad plates.

2 Peel and chop the onion. Rinse, core, and chop the apple. Combine the onion and the apple in a medium bowl.

3 Drain the beets well.

4 In a small bowl, whisk together the oil and the lemon juice, season to taste, and toss with the onion-apple mixture.

5 Spoon the mixture over the lettuce. Top with the beets.

Back Bay Biscuits

1 In a medium bowl, combine the flour, the baking powder, the salt, and the caraway seeds. Make a well in the center of the flour mixture.

2 In a small bowl, combine the mayonnaise and the milk. Pour the mixture into the flour well. Stir gently until a soft dough forms.

3 Flour a breadboard. Lay the dough on the board, knead it 8 to 10 times, and pat it out to a ¼-inch thickness. Cut the dough into rounds and place them on a baking sheet.

4 Bake the biscuits at 350°F until they are lightly browned, about 25 minutes.

Plymouth Rocks

1 Grate 2 tablespoons of orange peel and squeeze ½ cup juice from the oranges.

2 Rinse the cranberries in warm water to thaw, discarding any that are soft or discolored.

3 In a medium saucepan, combine the cranberries, the brown sugar, the orange juice, half of the orange peel, and the Grand Marnier. Bring the mixture to a boil and cook until the cranberries begin to pop, about 5 minutes.

4 Remove the saucepan from the heat and set aside.

5 Place scoops of sherbet in the bottom of individual dessert dishes. Top with the cranberry mixture. Garnish with dollops of whipped cream and the remaining orange peel.

WEEK SEVEN

Monday

Sometimes You Feel Like a Nut
All Choked Up
Sometimes You Doughn't
Juicy Fruit

Tuesday

Halibut Holiday
Potatoes On Parade
Mardi Slaw
Carnival Cream

Wednesday

Chicken Out
Rice 'n' Ready
Dill We Meet Again
Chocolate Tizzy

Thursday

Beefuddled
Numb Noodles
Muddled Melon
Puzzled Pound Cake

Friday

Macon Bacon
Savannah Salad
Southern Belles
Georgia Peach

STAPLES

- ☐ Butter
- ☐ Flour
- ☐ Bisquick
- ☐ Yellow cornmeal
- ☐ Granulated sugar
- ☐ Dark brown sugar
- ☐ Powdered sugar
- ☐ Maple syrup
- ☐ Chocolate sprinkles
- ☐ Multicolored sprinkles
- ☐ Olive oil
- ☐ Vegetable oil
- ☐ Apple cider vinegar
- ☐ Red wine vinegar
- ☐ Rice vinegar
- ☐ White wine vinegar
- ☐ Lemon juice
- ☐ Lime juice
- ☐ Dijon mustard
- ☐ Mayonnaise
- ☐ Prepared horseradish
- ☐ Grated Romano cheese
- ☐ Poppy seeds
- ☐ Dried marjoram
- ☐ Dried rosemary
- ☐ Dried thyme
- ☐ Ground allspice
- ☐ Cayenne pepper
- ☐ Dry mustard
- ☐ Black pepper
- ☐ Salt
- ☐ Almond extract
- ☐ Brandy extract
- ☐ Vanilla extract

MEAT & POULTRY

1 1/2 pounds lean beefsteak (Th)
4 boneless, skinless chicken breast halves (about 1 1/2 pounds) (W)

FISH

4 halibut or other firm white fish fillets (about 1 1/2 pounds) (T)

FRESH PRODUCE

VEGETABLES

1 1/2 pounds yellow potatoes (T)
1 1/2 pounds sweet potatoes (F)
1 medium carrot (T)
1 medium carrot (W)
2 stalks celery (M)
2 stalks celery (T)
1 package (10 ounces) spinach (F)
1/4 pound mushrooms (W)
1 small head red cabbage (T)
1 small head green cabbage (Th)
1 small head red leaf lettuce (M)
1 medium head red leaf lettuce (W)
1 small head Boston lettuce (Th)
3 medium tomatoes (M)
1 medium cucumber (F)
1 small cucumber (T)
2 medium red bell peppers (F)
1 medium yellow bell pepper (Th)
1 small bunch radishes (W)
1 large onion (F)
1 small onion (M)
1 small red onion (F)
1 medium shallot (W)
1 small shallot (Th)
3 scallions (green onions) (T)
4 scallions (green onions) (Th)
2 cloves garlic (M)
1 clove garlic (T)
2 cloves garlic (W)

HERBS

3 tablespoons chives (when chopped) (M)
2 tablespoons chives (when chopped) (T)

1/4 cup cilantro (when chopped) (F)
2 tablespoons dill (when chopped) (W)
4 tablespoons dill (when chopped) (Th)
3 tablespoons parsley (when chopped) (M)
3 tablespoons parsley (when chopped) (W)

FRUIT

1 medium lemon (M)
1 medium lime (T)
1 large ripe honeydew melon (Th)
1/2 pound seedless green grapes (Th)

CANS, JARS & BOTTLES

SOUPS

1 can (14 ounces) chicken broth (W)
3 cans (14 ounces each) vegetable broth (F)

VEGETABLES

1 can (28 ounces) diced tomatoes (F)
1 can (6 ounces) French fried onions (T)

FRUIT

1 can (29 ounces) apricot halves (M)
1 can (29 ounces) sliced peaches (F)

SPREADS

1/4 cup red currant jelly (T)

CONDIMENTS

1 jar (6 1/2 ounces) marinated artichoke hearts (M)
1 jar (7 ounces) pitted green olives (M)
2 tablespoons capers (Th)

DESSERT & BAKING NEEDS

1/4 cup marshmallow crème for garnish (F)

PACKAGED GOODS

PASTA, RICE & GRAINS

1 pound rotini (M)
8 ounces medium egg noodles (Th)
1 cup long-grain white rice (W)

BAKED GOODS

8 brown-and-serve butterflake rolls (M)
1 package (10 ounces) shortbread cookies (F)

DRIED FRUIT & NUTS

1 cup pistachio nuts (M)
2 tablespoons pecan bits (T)
1/2 cup sliced almonds (Th)

DESSERT & BAKING NEEDS

1 package (3.4 ounces) instant vanilla pudding mix (W)

WINE & SPIRITS

2 tablespoons dry sherry (F)

REFRIGERATED PRODUCTS

DAIRY

1/2 cup milk (T)
1 1/4 cups milk (W)
2/3 cup milk (F)
1/2 cup sour cream (M)
1/4 cup sour cream (T)
1/2 cup sour cream (F)
1 container (6 ounces) chocolate yogurt (W)
1/2 cup whipped cream (W)
1 egg (F)

JUICES

2 teaspoons orange juice (M)

DELI

1 pound bacon (F)

FROZEN GOODS

VEGETABLES

1 package (10 ounces) Brussels sprouts (M)
1 package (10 ounces) chopped spinach (W)

FRUIT

1 package (16 ounces) whole raspberries (T)

BAKED GOODS

1 pound cake (Th)

DESSERTS

1 pint raspberry swirl ice cream (T)
1 pint vanilla yogurt (F)

MONDAY

Sometimes You Feel Like a Nut

1 package (10 ounces) frozen Brussels sprouts
2 cloves garlic
1 small onion
1 cup pistachio nuts
3 tablespoons fresh parsley (when chopped)
1 medium lemon
1 jar (7 ounces) pitted green olives
1 pound rotini
2 tablespoons olive oil
Seasoning to taste
1/2 cup grated Romano cheese

All Choked Up

1 small head red leaf lettuce
2 stalks celery
3 medium tomatoes
1 jar (6 1/2 ounces) marinated artichoke hearts
1/4 cup mayonnaise
1 tablespoon rice vinegar
1/2 teaspoon dried marjoram
Seasoning to taste

Sometimes You Doughn't

3 tablespoons fresh chives (when chopped)
3 tablespoons butter
2 teaspoons orange juice
8 brown-and-serve butterflake rolls

Juicy Fruit

1 can (29 ounces) apricot halves
1/2 cup sour cream
2 tablespoons maple syrup
1 teaspoon brandy extract

EQUIPMENT

Stockpot	Citrus grater
Small saucepan	Citrus juicer
Medium skillet	Pastry brush
Muffin tin	Kitchen knives
Colander	Measuring cups and spoons
Medium mixing bowl	
3 small mixing bowls	Cooking utensils
Whisk	

COUNTDOWN

1. Assemble the ingredients and the equipment.
2. Do Steps 1–2 of *Sometimes You Feel Like a Nut*.
3. Do Steps 1–3 of *All Choked Up*.
4. Do Steps 1–5 of *Sometimes You Doughn't*.
5. Do Steps 3–5 of *Sometimes You Feel Like a Nut*.
6. Do Step 4 of *All Choked Up*.
7. Do Steps 1–2 of *Juicy Fruit*.

MONDAY

Sometimes You Feel Like a Nut

1 Set the Brussels sprouts in a small bowl of warm water to thaw. Bring water to a boil in a stockpot.

2 Peel and chop the garlic. Peel and mince the onion. Shell and chop the nuts. Rinse, stem, and chop the parsley. Grate 1 teaspoon of lemon peel and squeeze 2 teaspoons of lemon juice. Drain and slice the olives.

3 Cook the rotini until it is almost tender, 8 to 10 minutes.

4 Heat the oil in a medium skillet and sauté the garlic and the onion until the onion is soft, about 5 minutes. Add the Brussels sprouts, the nuts, the olives, the parsley, the lemon peel, and the lemon juice. Season to taste and cook until the Brussels sprouts are heated through.

5 Drain the pasta and return it to the stockpot. Toss it with the Brussels sprouts mixture and sprinkle with the cheese.

All Choked Up

1 Wash and dry the lettuce and arrange the leaves on individual salad plates.

2 Rinse, trim, and chop the celery. Rinse, stem, and chop the tomatoes. Drain and chop the artichoke hearts. Combine the ingredients in a medium bowl.

3 In a small bowl, combine the mayonnaise, the vinegar, and the marjoram. Season to taste and toss with the artichoke mixture.

4 Spoon the artichoke mixture over the lettuce leaves.

Sometimes You Doughn't

1 Preheat the oven to 400°F.

2 Rinse and chop the chives.

3 Melt the butter in a small saucepan and blend in the orange juice.

4 Partially separate the sections of the rolls and brush with the butter mixture. Sprinkle with the chives.

5 Place the rolls in the muffin tin and bake until lightly browned, 10 to 12 minutes.

Juicy Fruit

1 Drain the apricots, reserving 2 tablespoons of the liquid, and arrange them, cut side up, on individual dessert plates.

2 In a small bowl, combine the sour cream, the maple syrup, the reserved apricot liquid, and the brandy extract. Mix well and spoon over the apricots.

TUESDAY

Halibut Holiday

4 halibut or other firm white fish fillets
   (about 1 1/2 pounds)
1 clove garlic
3 tablespoons vegetable oil
1 tablespoon lime juice
1/8 teaspoon dry mustard
1/4 teaspoon dried thyme
Seasoning to taste
1 can (6 ounces) French fried onions

Potatoes On Parade

2 tablespoons fresh chives (when chopped)
1 1/2 pounds yellow potatoes
2 tablespoons butter
2 tablespoons dark brown sugar
1/2 cup milk
2 tablespoons pecan bits

Mardi Slaw

1 small head red cabbage
1 medium carrot
2 stalks celery
1 small cucumber
3 scallions (green onions)
1/4 cup sour cream
2 tablespoons mayonnaise
1 teaspoon granulated sugar
1 tablespoon apple cider vinegar
Seasoning to taste

Carnival Cream

1 package (16 ounces) frozen whole
   raspberries
1 pint raspberry swirl ice cream
1 medium lime
1/4 cup red currant jelly
Multicolored sprinkles for garnish

EQUIPMENT

Electric mixer	Whisk
Blender	Vegetable peeler
Medium covered saucepan	Vegetable grater
Small saucepan	Citrus grater
9 x 13-inch glass baking dish	Citrus juicer
Large shallow bowl	Ice cream scoop
Large mixing bowl	Kitchen knives
3 small mixing bowls	Measuring cups and spoons
	Cooking utensils

COUNTDOWN

1. Assemble the ingredients and the equipment.
2. Do Steps 1–4 of *Carnival Cream*.
3. Do Steps 1–3 of *Halibut Holiday*.
4. Do Steps 1–3 of *Mardi Slaw*.
5. Do Steps 1–3 of *Potatoes On Parade*.
6. Do Steps 4–6 of *Halibut Holiday*.
7. Do Step 4 of *Potatoes On Parade*.
8. Do Steps 5–6 of *Carnival Cream*.

TUESDAY

Halibut Holiday

1 Butter a 9 x 13-inch baking dish.

2 Rinse and pat dry the fish fillets and place them in a large shallow bowl. Peel and mince the garlic.

3 In a small bowl, whisk together the garlic, the oil, the lime juice, the mustard, and the thyme. Season to taste and pour the mixture over the fish. Marinate for 20 minutes, turning once or twice.

4 Preheat the oven to 450°F.

5 Place the fillets in the baking dish. Crumble the French fried onions over the fish.

6 Bake until the fish flakes easily with a fork, about 10 minutes.

Potatoes On Parade

1 Bring water to a boil in a medium saucepan.

2 Rinse, trim, and chop the chives. Peel and cube the potatoes.

3 Cook the potatoes until they are tender, about 10 minutes.

4 Drain the potatoes well, add the butter and the brown sugar, and blend well. Add the milk and beat until smooth. Top with the chives and the pecan bits. Cover to keep warm.

Mardi Slaw

1 Rinse, trim, quarter, and grate the cabbage. Peel, trim, and grate the carrot. Rinse, trim, and chop the celery. Peel, trim, and chop the cucumber. Rinse, trim, and chop the scallions. Combine the vegetables in a large bowl.

2 In a small bowl, whisk together the sour cream, the mayonnaise, the sugar, and the vinegar. Season to taste.

3 Toss the vegetables with the dressing, and refrigerate until you are ready to serve.

Carnival Cream

1 Set the raspberries in a small bowl of warm water to thaw. Set the ice cream out to soften.

2 Grate 1 tablespoon of lime peel and juice the lime.

3 Place the softened ice cream in a blender. Add the lime peel and the lime juice and process until well blended.

4 Refreeze the ice cream until you are ready to serve.

5 In a small saucepan, combine the raspberries and their liquid with the currant jelly and cook until the jelly has melted, 2 to 3 minutes. Remove from the heat and let cool slightly.

6 Place scoops of ice cream into individual dessert glasses and spoon the raspberry sauce on top. Garnish with the sprinkles.

WEDNESDAY

Chicken Out

4 boneless, skinless chicken breast halves
   (about 1 1/2 pounds)
2 cloves garlic
1/4 pound fresh mushrooms
3 tablespoons fresh parsley (when
   chopped)
2 tablespoons olive oil
2 tablespoons flour
1 teaspoon dried rosemary
Seasoning to taste
1/4 cup lemon juice
1/4 cup chicken broth

Rice 'n' Ready

1 package (10 ounces) frozen chopped
   spinach
1 medium shallot
1 cup long-grain white rice
1 1/2 cups chicken broth
1/2 cup water
2 tablespoons butter

Dill We Meet Again

1 medium head red leaf lettuce
1 small bunch radishes
1 medium carrot
2 tablespoons fresh dill (when chopped)
3 tablespoons olive oil
2 tablespoons red wine vinegar
1 teaspoon Dijon mustard
Seasoning to taste

Chocolate Tizzy

1 package (3.4 ounces) instant vanilla
   pudding mix
1 1/4 cups milk
1 container (6 ounces) chocolate yogurt
1/2 cup whipped cream
Chocolate sprinkles for garnish

EQUIPMENT

Electric mixer
Double boiler
Large covered skillet
Small skillet
Large mixing bowl
Medium mixing bowl
3 small mixing bowls

Whisk
Vegetable peeler
Waxed paper
Kitchen knives
Measuring cups and
   spoons
Cooking utensils

COUNTDOWN

1. Assemble the ingredients and the
   equipment.
2. Do Steps 1–3 of *Chocolate Tizzy*.
3. Do Steps 1–4 of *Rice 'n' Ready*.
4. Do Steps 1–5 of *Chicken Out*.
5. Do Steps 1–3 of *Dill We Meet Again*.
6. Do Steps 5–6 of *Rice 'n' Ready*.
7. Do Step 6 of *Chicken Out*.
8. Do Step 4 of *Chocolate Tizzy*.

WEDNESDAY

Chicken Out

1 Rinse and pat dry the chicken breasts.

2 Peel and chop the garlic. Rinse, pat dry, trim, and slice the mushrooms. Rinse, stem, and chop the parsley.

3 Heat the oil in a large skillet. Sauté the garlic and the mushrooms for 3 minutes. Remove them from the skillet and reserve.

4 Combine the flour and the rosemary on a sheet of waxed paper and season to taste. Coat the chicken breasts with the mixture and brown them in the skillet, about 4 minutes per side.

5 Add the lemon juice and the broth to the skillet, bring to a boil, and scrape any brown bits from the bottom of the pan. Return the garlic and the mushrooms to the skillet. Cover, reduce the heat, and simmer until the flavors are blended and the chicken is cooked through, about 15 minutes.

6 Sprinkle with the parsley.

Rice 'n' Ready

1 Set the spinach in a small bowl of very warm water to thaw.

2 Bring water to a boil in the bottom of a double boiler.

3 Peel and chop the shallot.

4 In the top of the double boiler, combine the rice, the broth, and the ½ cup water. Cover, reduce the heat, and simmer until all the liquid is absorbed and the rice is tender, 30 to 40 minutes.

5 Squeeze the spinach dry. Melt the butter in a small skillet and sauté the shallot for 1 minute. Add the spinach and cook until soft, about 2 minutes.

6 Fold the spinach mixture into the rice.

Dill We Meet Again

1 Wash and dry the lettuce and tear it into bite-sized pieces. Rinse, trim, and slice the radishes. Peel, trim, and julienne the carrot. Combine the ingredients in a large bowl. Rinse, stem, and chop the dill.

2 In a small bowl, whisk together the oil, the vinegar, the mustard, and the dill. Season to taste.

3 Toss the salad with the dressing.

Chocolate Tizzy

1 In a medium bowl, beat the pudding mix and the milk until well blended, about 2 minutes.

2 Place the yogurt in a small bowl and fold in the whipped cream.

3 Add the yogurt mixture to the pudding, stirring lightly so that ribbons of chocolate form. Spoon the mixture into individual dessert glasses and refrigerate until you are ready to serve.

4 To serve, dust with the sprinkles.

THURSDAY

Beefuddled

1 1/2 pounds lean beefsteak
1 small head green cabbage
1 small shallot
1 medium yellow bell pepper
4 scallions (green onions)
4 tablespoons fresh dill (when chopped)
2 tablespoons capers
2 tablespoons white wine vinegar
2 teaspoons prepared horseradish
1/4 teaspoon cayenne pepper
2 tablespoons vegetable oil
Seasoning to taste

Numb Noodles

8 ounces medium egg noodles
2 tablespoons butter
1 teaspoon poppy seeds
Seasoning to taste

Muddled Melon

1 small head Boston lettuce
1 large ripe honeydew melon
1/2 pound seedless green grapes
1/2 cup mayonnaise
2 teaspoons lime juice
1 teaspoon powdered sugar

Puzzled Pound Cake

1 frozen pound cake
3 tablespoons butter
3 tablespoons dark brown sugar
1/2 teaspoon almond extract
1/2 teaspoon vanilla extract
1/2 cup sliced almonds

EQUIPMENT

Wok	Vegetable grater
Large saucepan	Kitchen knives
Small saucepan	Measuring cups and
Colander	spoons
2 small mixing bowls	Cooking utensils
Whisk	

COUNTDOWN

1. Assemble the ingredients and the equipment.
2. Do Steps 1–3 of *Puzzled Pound Cake*.
3. Do Step 1 of *Numb Noodles*.
4. Do Steps 1–3 of *Beefuddled*.
5. Do Steps 1–3 of *Muddled Melon*.
6. Do Step 4 of *Beefuddled*.
7. Do Step 2 of *Numb Noodles*.
8. Do Step 5 of *Beefuddled*.
9. Do Step 3 of *Numb Noodles*.
10. Do Step 6 of *Beefuddled*.
11. Do Step 4 of *Muddled Melon*.
12. Do Step 4 of *Puzzled Pound Cake*.

THURSDAY

Beefuddled

1 Rinse and pat dry the steak and cut it across the grain into thin strips.

2 Rinse, trim, quarter, and grate the cabbage. Peel and mince the shallot. Rinse, trim, seed, and chop the bell pepper. Rinse, trim, and chop the scallions. Rinse, stem, and chop the dill. Drain the capers.

3 In a small bowl, combine the vinegar, the horseradish, the cayenne pepper, the capers, and the scallions.

4 Heat 1 tablespoon of the oil in a wok. Stir-fry the beef until the meat is no longer red, 2 to 3 minutes. Remove the beef and reserve it.

5 Heat the remaining 1 tablespoon oil in the wok. Add the cabbage, the shallot, and the bell pepper and stir-fry until the vegetables are crisp-tender, 2 to 3 minutes. Return the beef to the wok and season to taste.

6 Toss the caper mixture with the beef and vegetables and sprinkle with the dill.

Numb Noodles

1 Bring water to a boil in a large saucepan.

2 Cook the noodles until they are almost tender, 6 to 7 minutes.

3 Drain the noodles and return them to the saucepan. Stir in the butter and the poppy seeds. Season to taste.

Muddled Melon

1 Wash and dry the lettuce and arrange the leaves on individual salad plates.

2 Quarter, seed, and cut the melons into thin slices. Remove the rinds. Wash, dry, and stem the grapes. Arrange the melon slices and the grapes over the lettuce.

3 In a small bowl, combine the mayonnaise, the lime juice, and the powdered sugar.

4 Spoon the mixture over the fruit.

Puzzled Pound Cake

1 Set the pound cake out to thaw.

2 Melt the butter in a small saucepan. Add the brown sugar, the almond extract, the vanilla extract, and the almonds and simmer until the sugar is dissolved and the mixture thickens, about 5 minutes.

3 Remove the saucepan from the heat and set aside.

4 Slice the cake and place the slices on individual dessert plates. Spoon the sauce over the cake.

FRIDAY

Macon Bacon

1 pound bacon
1 large onion
2 medium red bell peppers
1 1/2 pounds sweet potatoes
1 can (28 ounces) diced tomatoes
3 cans (14 ounces each) vegetable broth
2 tablespoons dry sherry
1 teaspoon dried thyme
1/2 teaspoon ground allspice
Seasoning to taste
1/2 cup sour cream

Savannah Salad

1 package (10 ounces) fresh spinach
1/4 cup fresh cilantro (when chopped)
1 medium cucumber
1 small red onion
3 tablespoons olive oil
2 tablespoons lemon juice
Seasoning to taste

Southern Belles

2/3 cup milk
2 tablespoons vegetable oil
1 egg
1 1/2 cups Bisquick
3/4 cup yellow cornmeal
2 tablespoons granulated sugar

Georgia Peach

1 package (10 ounces) shortbread cookies
1 can (29 ounces) sliced peaches
1 pint vanilla frozen yogurt
1/4 cup marshmallow crème for garnish

EQUIPMENT

Blender	Ice cream scoop
Dutch oven	Plastic bag
Muffin tin	Kitchen knives
2 large mixing bowls	Measuring cups and
2 small mixing bowls	spoons
Whisk	Cooking utensils
Vegetable peeler	

COUNTDOWN

1. Assemble the ingredients and the equipment.
2. Do Steps 1–2 of *Georgia Peach*.
3. Do Steps 1–2 of *Southern Belles*.
4. Do Steps 1–4 of *Macon Bacon*.
5. Do Step 3 of *Southern Belles*.
6. Do Steps 1–2 of *Savannah Salad*.
7. Do Step 5 of *Macon Bacon*.
8. Do Step 3 of *Savannah Salad*.
9. Do Step 3 of *Georgia Peach*.

FRIDAY

Macon Bacon

1 Dice the bacon. Peel and chop the onion. Rinse, trim, seed, and chop the bell peppers. Peel and dice the potatoes.

2 Sauté the bacon in a Dutch oven until crisp, about 10 minutes.

3 Remove the bacon and blot on paper towels. Discard all but 2 tablespoons of the drippings. Sauté the onion and the bell peppers in the drippings until soft, about 5 minutes.

4 Add the potatoes, the tomatoes, the broth, the sherry, the thyme, and the allspice. Season to taste and bring to a boil. Cover, reduce the heat, and simmer until the potatoes are soft, 15 to 20 minutes.

5 Transfer 2 cups of the vegetables to a blender and process until smooth, about 1 minute. Return the puree to the Dutch oven. Blend in the sour cream and the bacon and simmer for 2 minutes more.

Savannah Salad

1 Rinse, pat dry, and stem the spinach leaves. Rinse, stem, and chop the cilantro. Peel, trim, and thinly slice the cucumber. Peel and thinly slice the onion. Combine the ingredients in a large bowl.

2 In a small bowl, whisk together the oil and the lemon juice and season to taste.

3 Toss the spinach mixture with the dressing.

Southern Belles

1 Preheat the oven to 400°F. Grease a muffin tin.

2 In a large bowl, combine the milk, the oil, and the egg. Add the Bisquick, the cornmeal, and the sugar and stir to combine. Spoon the batter into the muffin cups.

3 Bake until golden, about 15 minutes.

Georgia Peach

1 Place the cookies in a plastic bag and crumble.

2 Drain the peaches.

3 Place half the crumbled cookies in the bottom of individual dessert glasses. Add scoops of yogurt and a layer of peaches. Repeat. Top with the marshmallow crème.

WEEK EIGHT

WEEK AT A GLANCE

Monday

Mexicali Chicken
Señorita Rice
Baja Broccoli
Tijuana Tapioca

Tuesday

Shelly Winters
Ava Gardener
Bread MacMurray
Peter Loaford

Wednesday

Boris Burgers
Bunwinkles
Natasha Slaw
Rocky's Dessert

Thursday

Hamlet
As You Rice It
Romeo and Julienne
Shakespears

Friday

Spotsylvania Soup
The Virgin Green
Coal Slaw
Applemattox

STAPLES

- ❏ Butter
- ❏ Granulated sugar
- ❏ Dark brown sugar
- ❏ Powdered sugar
- ❏ Multicolored sprinkles
- ❏ Olive oil
- ❏ Vegetable oil
- ❏ Apple cider vinegar
- ❏ Balsamic vinegar
- ❏ Red wine vinegar
- ❏ Rice vinegar
- ❏ White wine vinegar
- ❏ Lemon juice
- ❏ Chili sauce
- ❏ Honey
- ❏ Ketchup
- ❏ Mayonnaise
- ❏ Prepared horseradish
- ❏ Steak sauce
- ❏ Grated Parmesan cheese
- ❏ Poppy seeds
- ❏ Sesame seeds
- ❏ Dried dill
- ❏ Ground allspice
- ❏ Ground cardamom
- ❏ Ground cinnamon
- ❏ Italian seasoning
- ❏ Lemon-pepper seasoning
- ❏ Ground nutmeg
- ❏ Black pepper
- ❏ White pepper
- ❏ Saffron threads
- ❏ Salt
- ❏ Banana extract
- ❏ Vanilla extract

MEAT & POULTRY

1 1/2 pounds lean ground beef (W)
4 loin pork chops (about 1 1/2 pounds) (Th)
1 1/2 pounds boneless, skinless chicken breast (M)

FISH

1 pound small shrimp, shelled and deveined (T)

FRESH PRODUCE

VEGETABLES

1 large bunch broccoli (M)
1 large eggplant (T)
1 small bunch beets (F)
2 medium zucchini (Th)
2 medium yellow zucchini (Th)
1 medium carrot (W)
2 stalks celery (T)
1 stalk celery (Th)
1 small head cabbage (W)
1 small head red cabbage (F)
1 large head lettuce (T, W)
1 large tomato (W)
1 large tomato (F)
2 medium tomatoes (T)
1 medium cucumber (T)
1 small red bell pepper (Th)
1 small yellow bell pepper (W)
1 large onion (M)
1 medium onion (Th)
1 small onion (F)
2 scallions (green onions) (T)
2 scallions (green onions) (Th)
3 scallions (green onions) (F)
2 cloves garlic (T)
1 clove garlic (Th)
1 clove garlic (F)

HERBS

3/4 cup basil leaves (when chopped) (F)
2 tablespoons chives (when chopped) (T)
1/4 cup chives (when chopped) (W)
1 tablespoon parsley (when chopped) (M)

FRUIT

1 medium lime (M)
3 medium tart apples (F)
4 medium ripe pears (Th)

CANS, JARS & BOTTLES

SOUPS

1 can (14 ounces) chicken broth (M)
2 cans (14 ounces each) vegetable broth (F)
1 can (10 1/2 ounces) chicken broth (Th)
1 can (10 1/2 ounces) beef broth (Th)

VEGETABLES

1 can (28 ounces) diced tomatoes (T)
1 can (28 ounces) crushed tomatoes in puree (F)

INTERNATIONAL FOODS

2 cans (4 ounces each) diced green chilies (M)

FRUIT

1 can (11 ounces) mandarin oranges (M)
1 can (8 ounces) crushed pineapple (Th)
6 maraschino cherries (T)

PACKAGED GOODS

PASTA, RICE & GRAINS

1 pound medium pasta shells (T)
1 cup long-grain white rice (M)
1 cup long-grain white rice (Th)

BAKED GOODS

1 loaf Italian bread (T)
4 hamburger buns (W)
1 angel food loaf cake (T)
1 package (9 ounces) chocolate wafers (W)

DRIED FRUIT & NUTS

1/4 cup pecan bits (T)

DESSERT & BAKING NEEDS

1 package (3.4 ounces) instant vanilla pudding mix (W)
1/4 cup instant tapioca (M)
6 ounces chocolate chips (W)
1 cup mini-marshmallows (W)

WINE & SPIRITS

1 tablespoon dry sherry (Th)
2 tablespoons dry sherry (F)
2 tablespoons Marsala wine (T)

REFRIGERATED PRODUCTS

DAIRY

1/3 cup milk (M)
1/4 cup milk (T)
2 cups milk (W)
1 pint sour cream (M)
1/4 cup sour cream (W)
2 cups apple-cinnamon yogurt (F)
Whipped cream for garnish (M)
6 eggs (F)

CHEESE

1 cup shredded Cheddar cheese (M)
1 container (15 ounces) ricotta cheese (F)
2 cups shredded Colby/Monterey Jack cheese (F)

JUICES

2 1/2 cups orange juice (M)
1/4 cup orange juice (Th)

DELI

1/4 pound prosciutto ham (Th)

FROZEN GOODS

VEGETABLES

1 package (10 ounces) green peas (T)
2 packages (14 ounces each) spinach soufflé (F)

PASTRY

1 sheet puff pastry (F)

MONDAY

Mexicali Chicken

1 large onion
1 1/2 pounds boneless, skinless chicken breast
2 tablespoons butter
2 tablespoons vegetable oil
2 cans (4 ounces each) diced green chilies
1/3 cup milk
1 pint sour cream
Seasoning to taste
1 cup shredded Cheddar cheese

Señorita Rice

1 tablespoon fresh parsley (when chopped)
2 tablespoons butter
1 cup long-grain white rice
1 can (14 ounces) chicken broth
1/4 cup water
1 1/2 teaspoons saffron threads
Seasoning to taste

Baja Broccoli

1 medium lime
1 large bunch broccoli
2 tablespoons vegetable oil
1/2 teaspoon ground cinnamon
Seasoning to taste

Tijuana Tapioca

1 can (11 ounces) mandarin oranges
2 1/2 cups orange juice
1/4 cup instant tapioca
1/4 cup granulated sugar
1 teaspoon banana extract
Whipped cream for garnish

EQUIPMENT

Blender
2 medium saucepans
Small saucepan
Large covered skillet
Large skillet
2-quart casserole

Citrus grater
Citrus juicer
Kitchen knives
Measuring cups and
  spoons
Cooking utensils

COUNTDOWN

1. Assemble the ingredients and the equipment.
2. Do Steps 1–3 of *Tijuana Tapioca*.
3. Do Steps 1–6 of *Mexicali Chicken*.
4. Do Steps 1–2 of *Señorita Rice*.
5. Do Steps 1–5 of *Baja Broccoli*.
6. Do Step 3 of *Señorita Rice*.
7. Do Step 4 of *Tijuana Tapioca*.

MONDAY

Mexicali Chicken

1 Preheat the oven to 350°F. Butter a 2-quart casserole.

2 Peel and thinly slice the onion.

3 Rinse and pat dry the chicken and cut it into thin strips.

4 Melt the butter with the oil in a large skillet and lightly brown the chicken strips, about 4 minutes. Remove and reserve. Add the onion and sauté until it is soft, about 5 minutes. Remove the skillet from the heat.

5 Drain the chilies. In a blender, combine the chilies with the milk and the sour cream. Season to taste and puree until smooth.

6 Layer half the chicken and half the onion in the casserole. Cover with half the sour cream mixture. Repeat. Sprinkle with the cheese and bake until heated through and bubbly, about 20 minutes.

Señorita Rice

1 Rinse, stem, and chop the parsley.

2 Melt the butter in a large skillet and sauté the rice until it is lightly browned, about 2 minutes. Add the broth, the water, and the saffron. Season to taste, cover the skillet, and reduce the heat. Simmer until all the liquid is absorbed and the rice is tender, about 20 minutes.

3 Fluff with a fork and sprinkle with the parsley.

Baja Broccoli

1 Bring water to a boil in a medium saucepan.

2 Grate 1 teaspoon of lime peel and squeeze 1 tablespoon of lime juice.

3 Rinse and trim the broccoli, discarding the tough ends, and cut it into bite-sized florets. Cook until it is crisp-tender, 6 to 8 minutes.

4 In a small saucepan, combine the oil, the lime juice, and the cinnamon. Cook the mixture until it is hot, about 1 minute. Remove the saucepan from the heat and cover to keep warm.

5 Drain the broccoli, return it to the saucepan, and toss it with the heated dressing. Season to taste and sprinkle with the lime peel.

Tijuana Tapioca

1 Drain the mandarin oranges.

2 In a medium saucepan, combine the orange juice, the tapioca, and the sugar. Bring the mixture to a boil and cook until it begins to thicken, about 5 minutes. Blend in the banana extract.

3 Reserve 4 mandarin orange sections and fold the rest into the tapioca. Spoon the mixture into individual dessert dishes and set aside.

4 Top each serving with a dollop of whipped cream and a section of orange.

TUESDAY

Shelly Winters

2 cloves garlic
1 large eggplant
2 medium tomatoes
1 pound small shrimp, shelled and deveined
1 pound medium pasta shells
2 tablespoons olive oil
1 can (28 ounces) diced tomatoes
2 tablespoons chili sauce
1 tablespoon dark brown sugar
2 tablespoons Marsala wine
Seasoning to taste
1/2 cup grated Parmesan cheese

Ava Gardener

1 package (10 ounces) frozen green peas
1 large head lettuce (reserve 4 leaves for
   use on Wednesday)
2 scallions (green onions)
1 medium cucumber
2 stalks celery
3 tablespoons vegetable oil
2 tablespoons white wine vinegar
1/2 teaspoon dried dill
1 teaspoon granulated sugar
Seasoning to taste

Bread MacMurray

2 tablespoons fresh chives (when chopped)
3 tablespoons olive oil
1 teaspoon Italian seasoning
1 loaf Italian bread

Peter Loaford

4 tablespoons butter
6 maraschino cherries
2 cups powdered sugar
1/4 cup milk
1/4 cup pecan bits
1 angel food loaf cake

EQUIPMENT

Stockpot
Large covered skillet
Colander
Large mixing bowl
Medium mixing bowl
3 small mixing bowls
Whisk

Vegetable peeler
Pastry brush
Aluminum foil
Kitchen knives
Measuring cups and
   spoons
Cooking utensils

COUNTDOWN

1. Assemble the ingredients and the
   equipment.
2. Do Step 1 of *Peter Loaford*.
3. Do Steps 1–2 of *Ava Gardener*.
4. Do Steps 2–4 of *Peter Loaford*.
5. Do Steps 1–2 of *Shelly Winters*.
6. Do Step 3 of *Ava Gardener*.
7. Do Steps 1–4 of *Bread MacMurray*.
8. Do Steps 3–5 of *Shelly Winters*.
9. Do Step 4 of *Ava Gardener*.

TUESDAY

Shelly Winters

1 Bring water to a boil in a stockpot.

2 Peel and mince the garlic. Rinse, trim, peel, and chunk the eggplant. Rinse, stem, and chop the fresh tomatoes. Rinse and pat dry the shrimp.

3 Cook the pasta shells until just tender, 8 to 10 minutes.

4 Heat the oil in a large skillet. Add the garlic and the eggplant, cover, and cook for 3 minutes. Add the shrimp, the fresh tomatoes, the canned tomatoes, the chili sauce, the brown sugar, and the Marsala. Season to taste and simmer until heated through and the shrimp turn bright pink, about 3 minutes.

5 Drain the pasta. Top it with the sauce and sprinkle with the cheese.

Ava Gardener

1 Set the peas in a small bowl of warm water to thaw.

2 Wash and dry the lettuce and tear it into bite-sized pieces. Rinse, trim, and chop the scallions. Peel, trim, and chop the cucumber. Rinse, trim, and chop the celery. Combine the ingredients in a large bowl. Add the peas.

3 In a small bowl, combine the oil, the vinegar, the dill, and the sugar. Season to taste.

4 Toss the salad with the dressing.

Bread MacMurray

1 Preheat the oven to 350°F.

2 Rinse, trim, and chop the chives.

3 In a small bowl, combine the chives with the oil and the Italian seasoning.

4 Cut the bread in half lenghtwise. Brush the cut sides with the chive mixture. Reassemble the loaf, wrap it in a sheet of aluminum foil, and bake until hot, 10 to 15 minutes.

Peter Loaford

1 Set the butter out to soften.

2 Chop the maraschino cherries.

3 In a medium bowl, combine the softened butter and the powdered sugar. Slowly add the milk and blend well. Fold in the cherries and the nuts.

4 Frost the top and the sides of the angel food loaf with the mixture.

WEDNESDAY

Boris Burgers

1/4 cup fresh chives (when chopped)
1 1/2 pounds lean ground beef
1 teaspoon prepared horseradish
1/4 cup sour cream
1/2 teaspoon white pepper

Bunwinkles

4 hamburger buns
1 large tomato
2 tablespoons mayonnaise
1 tablespoon ketchup
4 lettuce leaves (reserved from Tuesday)

Natasha Slaw

1 small head cabbage
1 medium carrot
1 small yellow bell pepper
3 tablespoons vegetable oil
2 tablespoons apple cider vinegar
2 teaspoons granulated sugar
1 teaspoon dried dill
Seasoning to taste

Rocky's Dessert

1 package (9 ounces) chocolate wafers
1 package (3.4 ounces) instant vanilla
   pudding mix
2 cups milk
1 teaspoon vanilla extract
6 ounces chocolate chips
1 cup mini-marshmallows

EQUIPMENT

Electric mixer
Baking sheet
2 large mixing bowls
Medium mixing bowl
2 small mixing bowls
Whisk
Vegetable peeler

Vegetable grater
Plastic bag
Kitchen knives
Measuring cups and
   spoons
Cooking utensils

COUNTDOWN

1. Assemble the ingredients and the
   equipment.
2. Do Steps 1–2 of *Rocky's Dessert.*
3. Do Steps 1–2 of *Natasha Slaw.*
4. Do Steps 1–4 of *Boris Burgers.*
5. Do Steps 1–4 of *Bunwinkles.*
6. Do Step 3 of *Rocky's Dessert.*

WEDNESDAY

Boris Burgers

1 Preheat the broiler.

2 Rinse, trim, and chop the chives.

3 In a large bowl, combine the chives, the beef, the horseradish, the sour cream, and the white pepper.

4 Form the mixture into 4 hamburger patties. Place the patties on a baking sheet and broil to taste.

Bunwinkles

1 Split the buns and toast them.

2 Rinse, stem, and slice the tomato.

3 In a small bowl, combine the mayonnaise and the ketchup. Spread the mixture on the toasted buns.

4 Lay a lettuce leaf and a tomato slice on each bun. Top with a hamburger.

Natasha Slaw

1 Rinse, trim, quarter, and grate the cabbage. Peel and grate the carrot. Rinse, trim, seed, and chunk the bell pepper. Combine the vegetables in a large bowl.

2 In a small bowl, whisk together the oil, the vinegar, the sugar, and the dill. Season to taste and toss with the salad.

Rocky's Dessert

1 Crush the chocolate wafers in a plastic bag.

2 In a medium bowl, combine the pudding mix and the milk and beat with an electric mixer for 2 minutes. Fold in the vanilla and the chocolate chips and refrigerate until you are ready to serve.

3 Put half of the cookie crumbs into individual dessert glasses. Spoon the pudding mixture over the crumbs. Top with the remaining crumbs and garnish with the marshmallows.

THURSDAY

Hamlet

4 loin pork chops (about 1 1/2 pounds)
Seasoning to taste
1 clove garlic
1 tablespoon vegetable oil
1 can (8 ounces) crushed pineapple
2 tablespoons steak sauce
1/2 teaspoon ground allspice
1/4 pound prosciutto ham
1 medium onion
1 small red bell pepper

As You Rice It

2 scallions (green onions)
1 stalk celery
1 tablespoon vegetable oil
1 cup long-grain white rice
1 can (10 1/2 ounces) chicken broth
1 can (10 1/2 ounces) beef broth

Romeo and Julienne

2 medium zucchini
2 medium yellow zucchini
1 tablespoon rice vinegar
1 tablespoon dry sherry
1 1/2 teaspoons granulated sugar
2 tablespoons butter
1 teaspoon sesame seeds

Shakespears

4 medium ripe pears
1 tablespoon lemon juice
1/4 cup honey
1/4 cup orange juice
1/2 teaspoon ground cardamom

EQUIPMENT

Medium covered saucepan
Small saucepan
2 large skillets
9 x 13-inch glass baking dish
2 small mixing bowls
Whisk

Vegetable brush
Plastic wrap
Aluminum foil
Kitchen knives
Measuring cups and spoons
Cooking utensils

COUNTDOWN

1. Assemble the ingredients and the equipment.
2. Do Steps 1–4 of *Hamlet*.
3. Do Steps 1–3 of *As You Rice It*.
4. Do Steps 1–2 of *Romeo and Julienne*.
5. Do Step 1 of *Shakespears*.
6. Do Steps 5–6 of *Hamlet*.
7. Do Steps 3–4 of *Romeo and Julienne*.
8. Do Step 4 of *As You Rice It*.
9. Do Step 2 of *Shakespears*.

THURSDAY

Hamlet

1 Preheat the oven to 350°F.

2 Rinse and pat dry the pork chops and season them to taste. Peel and mince the garlic.

3 Heat the oil in a large skillet and brown the chops lightly, about 5 minutes per side. Remove the chops from the skillet and arrange them in a 9 x 13-inch baking dish.

4 In a small bowl, combine the garlic, the undrained pineapple, the steak sauce, and the allspice. Pour the mixture over the chops, cover with aluminum foil, and bake for 25 minutes.

5 Dice the prosciutto. Peel and thinly slice the onion. Rinse, trim, seed, and thinly slice the bell pepper.

6 Arrange the prosciutto, the onion, and the bell pepper over the chops. Cover and bake 10 minutes more.

As You Rice It

1 Rinse, trim, and chop the scallions. Rinse, trim, and chop the celery.

2 Heat the oil in a medium saucepan and sauté the scallions and the celery for 2 minutes.

3 Add the rice and sauté for 1 minute. Add the broths and bring to a boil. Cover, reduce the heat, and simmer until all the liquid is absorbed and the rice is tender, about 20 minutes.

4 Fluff the rice with a fork.

Romeo and Julienne

1 Scrub, trim, and julienne the zucchini.

2 In a small bowl, whisk together the vinegar, the sherry, and the sugar.

3 Melt the butter in a large skillet and sauté the zucchini until crisp-tender, about 3 minutes.

4 Toss the zucchini with the sherry mixture until heated through. Sprinkle with the sesame seeds.

Shakespears

1 Rinse, core, and slice the pears. Arrange the slices on individual dessert plates. Sprinkle with the lemon juice, cover with plastic wrap, and set aside.

2 In a small saucepan, combine the honey, the orange juice, and the cardamom. Bring to a boil and drizzle over the pears.

FRIDAY

Spotsylvania Soup

1 small onion
1 clove garlic
1 large tomato
3/4 cup fresh basil leaves (when chopped)
2 tablespoons olive oil
2 cans (14 ounces each) vegetable broth
1 can (28 ounces) crushed tomatoes in
  puree
2 teaspoons granulated sugar
1 tablespoon balsamic vinegar
2 tablespoons dry sherry
Seasoning to taste

The Virgin Green

1 sheet frozen puff pastry
2 packages (14 ounces each) frozen
  spinach soufflé
6 eggs
1 container (15 ounces) ricotta cheese
1 teaspoon ground nutmeg
1 teaspoon lemon-pepper seasoning
2 cups shredded Colby/Monterey Jack
  cheese

Coal Slaw

1 small head red cabbage
1 small bunch beets
3 scallions (green onions)
3 tablespoons vegetable oil
2 tablespoons red wine vinegar
1 teaspoon poppy seeds
Seasoning to taste

Applemattox

3 medium tart apples
2 cups apple-cinnamon yogurt
3 tablespoons powdered sugar
1 teaspoon vanilla extract
Multicolored sprinkles for garnish

EQUIPMENT

Blender	Whisk
Large covered saucepan	Vegetable peeler
Small skillet	Vegetable grater
9 x 13-inch glass baking dish	Rolling pin
Breadboard	Kitchen knives
3 large mixing bowls	Measuring cups and spoons
Small mixing bowl	Cooking utensils

COUNTDOWN

1. Assemble the ingredients and the equipment.
2. Do Steps 1–3 of *Applemattox*.
3. Do Steps 1–5 of *The Virgin Green*.
4. Do Steps 1–4 of *Spotsylvania Soup*.
5. Do Steps 1–2 of *Coal Slaw*.
6. Do Step 6 of *The Virgin Green*.
7. Do Step 4 of *Applemattox*.

FRIDAY

Spotsylvania Soup

1 Peel and mince the onion. Peel and mince the garlic. Rinse, stem, and chop the tomato. Rinse, pat dry, and stem the basil leaves.

2 Heat 1 tablespoon of the oil in a small skillet and sauté the onion and the garlic until the onion is soft, about 5 minutes.

3 Scrape the onion and the garlic into a blender. Add the remaining 1 tablespoon oil, the chopped fresh tomato, 1 can of the broth, and the basil leaves. Puree until smooth.

4 Turn the mixture into a large saucepan. Add the canned crushed tomatoes and the remaining can of broth. Stir in the sugar, the vinegar, and the sherry. Season to taste and bring to a boil. Cover, reduce the heat, and simmer for 15 minutes.

The Virgin Green

1 Set the puff pastry out to thaw. Set the spinach in a large bowl of very warm water to thaw.

2 Preheat the oven to 450°F. Flour a breadboard.

3 In a large bowl, combine the eggs, the ricotta cheese, the nutmeg, and the lemon-pepper seasoning. Blend in the spinach.

4 On the breadboard, roll the pastry out just enough to fit in the bottom of a 9 x 13-inch baking dish. Spread the spinach mixture evenly over the pastry. Sprinkle with the Colby/Monterey Jack cheese.

5 Bake until a toothpick inserted in the center comes out clean, 20 to 25 minutes.

6 Let the dish cool for 5 minutes before cutting.

Coal Slaw

1 Rinse, trim, quarter, and grate the cabbage. Peel, trim, and grate the beets. Rinse, trim, and chop the scallions. Combine the ingredients in a large bowl.

2 In a small bowl, whisk together the oil, the vinegar, and the poppy seeds. Season to taste and toss with the salad.

Applemattox

1 Peel, core, and slice the apples.

2 In a blender, combine the apples, the yogurt, the powdered sugar, and the vanilla. Puree until smooth.

3 Pour the mixture into individual dessert glasses and freeze for at least 30 minutes.

4 Garnish with the sprinkles.

WEEK NINE

Monday
Must-Go Soup
So-Be-It Salad
Balkin' Bread
Cry-Me-a Pudding

Tuesday
Chattanooga Chicken
Mashville
Cucumberland Gap
Monkey Business

Wednesday
The Scalloping Gourmet
Epicurean Rice
Bon Appetites
The Catered Kiwi

Thursday
Beefitting Pie
Appropriate Asparagus
Pertinent Tomatoes
Suitable Sundaes

Friday
Paul Onion
Bacos Bill
Annie Oatleys
Cake Carson

- ❑ Butter
- ❑ Flour
- ❑ Bisquick
- ❑ Baking powder
- ❑ Granulated sugar
- ❑ Dark brown sugar
- ❑ Cocoa powder
- ❑ Chocolate syrup
- ❑ Olive oil
- ❑ Vegetable oil
- ❑ Balsamic vinegar
- ❑ Rice vinegar
- ❑ Red wine vinegar
- ❑ White wine vinegar
- ❑ Dijon mustard
- ❑ Honey
- ❑ Mayonnaise
- ❑ Tabasco sauce
- ❑ Caraway seeds
- ❑ Dried basil
- ❑ Dried dill
- ❑ Dried oregano
- ❑ Dried rosemary
- ❑ Dried tarragon
- ❑ Ground allspice
- ❑ Chili powder
- ❑ Ground cinnamon
- ❑ Ground cloves
- ❑ Curry powder
- ❑ Ground nutmeg
- ❑ Paprika
- ❑ Black pepper
- ❑ White pepper
- ❑ Salt
- ❑ Almond extract
- ❑ Banana extract
- ❑ Brandy extract
- ❑ Vanilla extract

MEAT & POULTRY

1 1/2 pounds lean ground beef (Th)

1 pound sweet Italian sausage (M)

4 boneless, skinless chicken breast halves (about 1 1/2 pounds) (T)

FISH

1 1/2 pounds sea scallops (W)

FRESH PRODUCE

VEGETABLES

1 1/2 pounds small new potatoes (T)

1 pound asparagus (Th)

1/4 pound mushrooms (W)

1 medium head lettuce (F)

1 package (10 ounces) mixed salad greens (M)

4 large tomatoes (Th)

2 medium cucumbers (T)

1 medium cucumber (F)

1 small green bell pepper (T)

1 small jicama (F)

1 large red onion (F)

1 large yellow onion (F)

2 medium onions (M)

1 small onion (W)

1 small onion (Th)

3 scallions (green onions) (M)

2 small shallots (W)

1 clove garlic (M)

1 clove garlic (W)

2 cloves garlic (Th)

HERBS

2 tablespoons parsley (when chopped) (W)

1/4 cup parsley (when chopped) (Th)

3 tablespoons parsley (when chopped) (F)

FRUIT

1 large orange (M)

1 large lemon (W)

4 medium bananas (T)

2 ripe kiwifruit (W)

CANS, JARS & BOTTLES

SOUPS

2 cans (14 ounces each) beef broth (M)

1 can (14 ounces) chicken broth (M)

1 can (14 ounces) chicken broth (W)

VEGETABLES

1 jar (22 ounces) sauerkraut (M)

1 can (15 ounces) sliced beets (F)

1 can (2.8 ounces) French fried onions (Th)

INTERNATIONAL FOODS

1 can (8 ounces) sliced water chestnuts (W)

FRUIT

1 can (15 ounces) almond-flavored apricots (W)

SPREADS

1/2 cup chunky peanut butter (Th)

JUICES

1/4 cup apple juice (Th)

1 can (6 ounces) pineapple juice (F)

CONDIMENTS

1 jar (2 ounces) diced pimientos (T)

PACKAGED GOODS

PASTA, RICE & GRAINS

1 cup long-grain white rice (W)

3/4 cup rolled oats (F)

BAKED GOODS

1 loaf black bread (M)

DRIED FRUIT & NUTS

1/2 cup pecan bits (T)

1/2 cup whole shelled peanuts (Th)

WINE & SPIRITS

1/4 cup dry sherry (W)

REFRIGERATED PRODUCTS

DAIRY

1/3 cup milk (M)

1/4 cup milk (T)

1 cup milk (F)

1 egg (T)

1 egg (Th)

10 eggs (F)

CHEESE

1 package (3 ounces) cream cheese (T)

1 container (15 ounces) ricotta cheese (Th)

1/2 cup shredded Cheddar cheese (Th)

1/2 cup Swiss cheese (when grated) (F)

DELI

4 slices bacon (M)

2 slices bacon (F)

FROZEN GOODS

VEGETABLES

1 package (10 ounces) petite green peas (W)

BAKED GOODS

1 pound cake (F)

PASTRY

1 unbaked pie shell (Th)

DESSERTS

1 pint banana-fudge-walnut (Chunky Monkey) frozen yogurt (T)

1 pint vanilla ice cream (Th)

MONDAY

Must-Go Soup

1 pound sweet Italian sausage
4 slices bacon
2 medium onions
1 clove garlic
1 jar (22 ounces) sauerkraut
1 teaspoon caraway seeds
1 teaspoon paprika
2 cans (14 ounces each) beef broth
1 can (14 ounces) chicken broth
Seasoning to taste
1/4 cup flour
1/2 cup water

So-Be-It Salad

1 package (10 ounces) mixed salad greens
3 scallions (green onions)
1 large orange
3 tablespoons olive oil
3 tablespoons balsamic vinegar
1/2 teaspoon granulated sugar
Seasoning to taste

Balkin' Bread

4 tablespoons butter
1 loaf black bread
1/2 teaspoon white pepper

Cry-Me-a Pudding

2 tablespoons butter
3/4 cup flour
2/3 cup granulated sugar
5 tablespoons cocoa powder
1 1/2 teaspoons baking powder
1/3 cup milk
1 teaspoon vanilla extract
3/4 cup dark brown sugar
1 teaspoon ground cinnamon
1 1/3 cups hot water

EQUIPMENT

Electric mixer
Dutch oven
2-quart casserole
Large mixing bowl
3 small mixing bowls
Whisk

Citrus grater
Kitchen knives
Measuring cups and
  spoons
Cooking utensils

COUNTDOWN

1. Assemble the ingredients and the equipment.
2. Do Step 1 of *Balkin' Bread.*
3. Do Steps 1–5 of *Cry-Me-a Pudding.*
4. Do Steps 1–5 of *Must-Go Soup.*
5. Do Steps 1–3 of *So-Be-It Salad.*
6. Do Step 6 of *Must-Go Soup.*
7. Do Steps 2–3 of *Balkin' Bread.*
8. Do Step 6 of *Cry-Me-a Pudding.*

MONDAY

Must-Go Soup

1 Chill the sausage in the freezer for 10 minutes.

2 Dice the bacon. Cut the sausage into ¼-inch-thick slices.

3 Peel and slice the onions. Peel and mince the garlic. Drain and rinse the sauerkraut.

4 Cook the bacon in a Dutch oven for 3 minutes. Add the onions and the garlic and sauté for 3 minutes. Add the sausage and cook until browned, about 10 minutes.

5 Add the sauerkraut, the caraway seeds, the paprika, and the broths. Season to taste and bring the mixture to a boil. Cover, reduce the heat, and simmer for 30 minutes.

6 Blend the flour with the water and stir it into the soup. Continue cooking for 5 minutes more.

So-Be-It Salad

1 Rinse and dry the salad greens and distribute them among individual salad plates.

2 Rinse, trim, and chop the scallions. Grate 1 tablespoon of orange peel. Peel and slice the orange into very thin rounds. Arrange the orange slices on the salad plates and sprinkle the scallions over them.

3 In a small bowl, whisk together the oil, the vinegar, and the sugar. Season to taste and spoon the dressing over the salad.

Balkin' Bread

1 Set the butter out to soften.

2 Cut the bread into thick slices.

3 In a small bowl, blend the softened butter with the pepper. Spread the mixture on the bread slices.

Cry-Me-a Pudding

1 Set the butter out to soften.

2 Preheat the oven to 350°F. Butter a 2-quart casserole.

3 In a large bowl, combine the flour, the granulated sugar, 2 tablespoons of the cocoa powder, and the baking powder. Add the milk, the butter, and the vanilla and beat well. Pour the mixture into the casserole.

4 In a small bowl, combine the brown sugar, the remaining 3 tablespoons cocoa, and the cinnamon. Sprinkle the mixture over the casserole. Slowly pour the hot water over the top. Do not stir.

5 Bake for 40 minutes.

6 Spoon the pudding into individual dessert dishes and top with the sauce remaining in the casserole.

TUESDAY

Chattanooga Chicken

4 boneless, skinless chicken breast halves
(about 1 1/2 pounds)
1/2 cup pecan bits
1/2 teaspoon dried tarragon
Seasoning to taste
1 egg
1 tablespoon butter
1 tablespoon olive oil

Cucumberland Gap

1 small green bell pepper
2 medium cucumbers
2 tablespoons butter
1 teaspoon rice vinegar
1 teaspoon granulated sugar
1/2 teaspoon dried dill
1/4 teaspoon Dijon mustard
Seasoning to taste

Mashville

1 package (3 ounces) cream cheese
1 1/2 pounds small new potatoes
1 jar (2 ounces) diced pimientos
2 tablespoons butter
1/4 cup milk
1/4 teaspoon ground allspice
Seasoning to taste

Monkey Business

4 medium bananas
1/4 cup honey
2 teaspoons brandy extract
1 pint banana-fudge-walnut (Chunky
Monkey) frozen yogurt

E Q U I P M E N T

Electric mixer	Mallet
Large covered saucepan	Ice cream scoop
	Plastic bag
Large covered skillet	Waxed paper
Medium covered skillet	Assorted kitchen knives
Medium skillet	Measuring cups and spoons
Colander	
Large shallow bowl	Assorted cooking utensils
Vegetable peeler	

C O U N T D O W N

1. Assemble the ingredients and the equipment.
2. Do Step 1 of *Mashville*.
3. Do Steps 1–3 of *Monkey Business*.
4. Do Step 2 of *Mashville*.
5. Do Step 1 of *Cucumberland Gap*.
6. Do Steps 1–2 of *Chattanooga Chicken*.
7. Do Step 3 of *Mashville*.
8. Do Steps 3–5 of *Chattanooga Chicken*.
9. Do Step 4 of *Mashville*.
10. Do Steps 2–3 of *Cucumberland Gap*.
11. Do Step 4 of *Monkey Business*.

TUESDAY

Chattanooga Chicken

1 Rinse and pat dry the chicken breasts.

2 Place the pecans in a plastic bag and pound with a mallet until they are crushed. On a sheet of waxed paper, combine the crushed nuts with the tarragon and season to taste.

3 In a shallow bowl, beat the egg lightly. Dip the chicken breasts into the egg, then roll them in the pecan mixture.

4 Melt the butter with the oil in a large skillet. Add the chicken breasts and cook until nicely browned and cooked through, 8 to 10 minutes per side.

5 Remove the skillet from the heat and cover to keep warm.

Mashville

1 Set the cream cheese out to soften.

2 Peel and cube the potatoes. Drain the pimientos.

3 In a large saucepan, cover the potatoes with water, bring to a boil, cover, and cook until tender, about 10 minutes.

4 Drain the potatoes and return them to the saucepan. Blend in the butter and the milk. Beat in the cream cheese and the allspice. Fold in the pimientos and season to taste.

Cucumberland Gap

1 Rinse, trim, seed, and chop the bell pepper. Peel, trim, and slice the cucumbers.

2 Melt the butter in a medium skillet and sauté the bell pepper for 2 minutes. Add the cucumbers and sauté for 2 minutes.

3 Blend in the vinegar, the sugar, the dill, and the mustard. Season to taste and toss until heated through.

Monkey Business

1 Peel and slice the bananas.

2 Melt the honey in a medium skillet. Add the bananas and cook until heated through, about 2 minutes.

3 Blend in the brandy extract, cover, and remove from the heat

4 Place scoops of yogurt in individual dessert bowls and top with the banana mixture.

WEDNESDAY

The Scalloping Gourmet

1 1/2 pounds sea scallops
1 clove garlic
2 small shallots
2 tablespoons fresh parsley (when chopped)
2 tablespoons butter
2 tablespoons olive oil
1 teaspoon dried basil
1 teaspoon dried oregano
1/4 teaspoon Tabasco sauce
1/4 cup dry sherry
1/2 teaspoon granulated sugar
Seasoning to taste
1 tablespoon flour

Epicurean Rice

1 small onion
1 large lemon
2 tablespoons butter
1 cup long-grain white rice
1 can (14 ounces) chicken broth
Seasoning to taste

Bon Appetites

1 package (10 ounces) frozen petite green peas
1/4 pound fresh mushrooms
1 can (8 ounces) sliced water chestnuts
2 tablespoons vegetable oil
2 tablespoons red wine vinegar
Seasoning to taste

The Catered Kiwi

2 ripe kiwifruit
1 can (15 ounces) almond-flavored apricots
3 tablespoons dark brown sugar
2 teaspoons almond extract
1 tablespoon ground nutmeg

EQUIPMENT

Medium covered saucepan	Citrus grater
Large skillet	Citrus juicer
Medium covered skillet	Plastic wrap
Medium mixing bowl	Kitchen knives
Small mixing bowl	Measuring cups and spoons
Whisk	Cooking utensils

COUNTDOWN

1. Assemble the ingredients and the equipment.
2. Do Step 1 of *Bon Appetites*.
3. Do Step 1 of *The Catered Kiwi*.
4. Do Steps 1–2 of *Epicurean Rice*.
5. Do Steps 1–2 of *The Scalloping Gourmet*.
6. Do Steps 2–3 of *Bon Appetites*.
7. Do Steps 3–4 of *The Scalloping Gourmet*.
8. Do Step 3 of *Epicurean Rice*.
9. Do Step 2 of *The Catered Kiwi*.

WEDNESDAY

The Scalloping Gourmet

1 Rinse and pat dry the scallops.

2 Peel and mince the garlic. Peel and chop the shallots. Rinse, stem, and chop the parsley.

3 Melt the butter with the oil in a large skillet. Sauté the garlic and the shallots for 3 minutes. Add the scallops, the basil, and the oregano and sauté for 4 minutes. Add the Tabasco sauce, the sherry, and the sugar. Season to taste. Remove the scallops from the skillet and keep them warm.

4 Add the flour to the skillet and whisk to thicken the sauce, about 2 minutes. Return the scallops to the skillet and toss to combine. Sprinkle with the parsley.

Epicurean Rice

1 Peel and mince the onion. Grate the lemon peel and juice the lemon.

2 Melt the butter in a medium saucepan. Sauté the onion until it is soft, about 5 minutes. Add the rice and stir to coat. Add the broth and the lemon juice and season to taste. Bring the mixture to a boil, cover, reduce the heat, and simmer until all the liquid is absorbed and the rice is tender, about 20 minutes.

3 Fluff the rice with a fork and fold in the lemon peel.

Bon Appetites

1 Set the peas in a small bowl of warm water to thaw.

2 Rinse, pat dry, trim, and chop the mushrooms. Drain the water chestnuts.

3 Heat the oil in a medium skillet. Add the mushrooms and sauté for 2 minutes. Add the peas, the water chestnuts, and the vinegar and season to taste. Cover and cook until the peas are heated through, about 3 minutes. Remove from the heat and cover to keep warm.

The Catered Kiwi

1 Peel and chunk the kiwifruit. Drain the apricots, reserving 2 tablespoons of the liquid. Combine the kiwis and the apricots in a medium bowl. Add the reserved liquid, the brown sugar, and the almond extract and toss to coat. Cover the bowl with plastic wrap and refrigerate until you are ready to serve.

2 Spoon the fruit into individual dessert glasses and sprinkle with the nutmeg.

THURSDAY

Beefitting Pie

1 small onion
1 clove garlic
1/4 cup fresh parsley (when chopped)
1 tablespoon vegetable oil
1 1/2 pounds lean ground beef
Seasoning to taste
1 frozen unbaked pie shell
1 egg
1 container (15 ounces) ricotta cheese
1/2 cup shredded Cheddar cheese

Appropriate Asparagus

1 pound fresh asparagus
2 tablespoons butter
1/2 teaspoon ground cloves
1/4 cup apple juice

Pertinent Tomatoes

4 large tomatoes
1 clove garlic
1 tablespoon olive oil
1 tablespoon mayonnaise
1/2 teaspoon curry powder
1/4 teaspoon chili powder
1 can (2.8 ounces) French fried onions
Seasoning to taste

Suitable Sundaes

1/2 cup whole shelled peanuts
1/2 cup chocolate syrup
1/2 cup chunky peanut butter
1 pint vanilla ice cream

EQUIPMENT

Large skillet	Ice cream scoop
Medium covered skillet	Plastic bag
Small skillet	Kitchen knives
Baking sheet	Measuring cups and spoons
2 small mixing bowls	Cooking utensils
Mallet	

COUNTDOWN

1. Assemble the ingredients and the equipment.
2. Do Steps 1–2 of *Suitable Sundaes.*
3. Do Steps 1–5 *Beefitting Pie.*
4. Do Step 1 of *Appropriate Asparagus.*
5. Do Steps 1–2 of *Pertinent Tomatoes.*
6. Do Step 6 of *Beefitting Pie.*
7. Do Step 3 of *Pertinent Tomatoes.*
8. Do Step 2 of *Appropriate Asparagus.*
9. Do Step 7 of *Beefitting Pie.*
10. Do Step 3 of *Appropriate Asparagus.*
11. Do Steps 4–5 of *Pertinent Tomatoes.*
12. Do Step 3 of *Suitable Sundaes.*

THURSDAY

Befitting Pie

1 Preheat the oven to 375°F. Set the pie shell out to thaw.

2 Peel and mince the onion. Peel and mince the garlic. Rinse, stem, and chop the parsley.

3 Heat the oil in a large skillet and sauté the onion and the garlic for 1 minute. Add the beef and sauté until browned, 7 to 8 minutes. Season to taste.

4 Turn the mixture into the pie shell.

5 In a small bowl, combine the egg, the ricotta cheese, and the parsley. Spread over the beef mixture and bake for 15 minutes.

6 Sprinkle with the Cheddar cheese and bake until hot and bubbly, about 10 minutes more.

7 Let the pie cool for several minutes before cutting into wedges.

Appropriate Asparagus

1 Rinse the asparagus, remove the tough ends, and cut the spears into 2-inch pieces.

2 Melt the butter with the cloves in a medium skillet and sauté the asparagus for 2 minutes. Add the apple juice, cover, and steam until the asparagus is crisp-tender, 3 to 5 minutes, depending on thickness.

3 Remove from the heat and cover to keep warm.

Pertinent Tomatoes

1 Rinse the tomatoes. Cut small slices off the tops and bottoms to remove the stems and allow the tomatoes to sit upright. Arrange the tomatoes on a baking sheet.

2 Peel and mince the garlic. Heat the oil in a small skillet and sauté the garlic for 1 minute. Blend in the mayonnaise, the curry, and the chili powder. Crumble the French-fried onions and stir them into the mayonnaise mixture. Season to taste.

3 Spoon the mixture over the tomatoes, pressing down lightly to allow for even browning.

4 Preheat the broiler.

5 Broil the tomatoes until golden, 3 to 4 minutes.

Suitable Sundaes

1 Place the peanuts in a plastic bag and crush with a mallet.

2 In a small bowl, combine the chocolate syrup with the peanut butter.

3 Place scoops of ice cream in individual dessert glasses. Top with the chocolate-peanut butter sauce and sprinkle with the crushed peanuts.

FRIDAY

Paul Onion

1 large red onion
1 large yellow onion
3 tablespoons vegetable oil
3 tablespoons fresh parsley (when chopped)
1/2 cup Swiss cheese (when grated)
9 eggs
1/3 cup milk
1/2 teaspoon dried rosemary
Seasoning to taste
3 tablespoons butter

Bacos Bill

2 slices bacon
1 medium head lettuce
1 medium cucumber
1 small jicama
1 can (15 ounces) sliced beets
3 tablespoons vegetable oil
2 tablespoons white wine vinegar
1/2 teaspoon granulated sugar
Seasoning to taste

Annie Oatleys

1 1/2 cups Bisquick
3/4 cup rolled oats
1/4 cup granulated sugar
1 teaspoon ground cinnamon
2/3 cup milk
2 tablespoons vegetable oil
1 egg

Cake Carson

1 frozen pound cake
1 can (6 ounces) pineapple juice
2 tablespoons granulated sugar
4 tablespoons butter
1/2 teaspoon banana extract

EQUIPMENT

Small saucepan	Vegetable peeler
Large ovenproof skillet	Cheese grater
Muffin tin	Kitchen knives
2 large mixing bowls	Measuring cups and spoons
2 small mixing bowls	Cooking utensils
Whisk	

COUNTDOWN

1. Assemble the ingredients and the equipment.
2. Do Step 1 of *Cake Carson*.
3. Do Steps 1–2 of *Paul Onion*.
4. Do Steps 1–2 of *Bacos Bill*.
5. Do Steps 1–3 of *Annie Oatleys*.
6. Do Steps 3–7 of *Paul Onion*.
7. Do Steps 2–3 of *Cake Carson*.
8. Do Steps 3–6 of *Bacos Bill*.
9. Do Step 4 of *Cake Carson*.

FRIDAY

Paul Onion

1 Peel and cut the onions into 8 wedges each. Place the wedges in a large ovenproof skillet, add the oil, toss to coat, and let stand for 5 minutes, turning occasionally.

2 Rinse, stem, and chop the parsley. Grate the cheese.

3 Cook the onions until they are golden and tender underneath, about 5 minutes. Turn the onions over and cook until they are very tender, 5 to 7 minutes more.

4 Remove the onions and reserve.

5 In a large bowl, whip the eggs with the milk until blended. Mix in the cheese and the rosemary and season to taste.

6 Melt the butter in the skillet. Add the egg mixture, arrange the onions on top, and sprinkle with the parsley.

7 Bake at 350°F until the eggs are cooked through and the top is golden, about 15 minutes.

Bacos Bill

1 Dice the bacon.

2 Sauté the bacon until crisp, about 10 minutes. Drain on paper towels.

3 Wash and dry the lettuce and arrange the leaves on individual salad plates.

4 Peel, trim, and slice the cucumber. Peel, trim, and slice the jicama. Drain and rinse the beets. Arrange the vegetables over the lettuce.

5 In a small bowl, combine the oil, the vinegar, and the sugar. Season to taste.

6 Drizzle the dressing over the salad.

Annie Oatleys

1 Preheat the oven to 350°F. Grease a muffin tin.

2 In a large bowl, combine the Bisquick, the oats, the sugar, and the cinnamon.

3 In a small bowl, combine the milk, the oil, and the egg. Fold the egg mixture into the Bisquick mixture until just moistened. Spoon the batter into the muffin cups and bake until golden, about 20 minutes.

Cake Carson

1 Set the pound cake out to thaw.

2 In a small saucepan, combine the pineapple juice, the sugar, and the butter. Bring the mixture to a boil, reduce the heat, and cook until it thickens slightly, about 5 minutes.

3 Remove the saucepan from the heat, blend in the banana extract, and let stand.

4 Slice the pound cake, arrange the slices on individual dessert plates, and drizzle the sauce over the cake.

WEEK TEN

Monday
Bronco Beef
Steamboat Rice
Boulder Beans
The Denver Mint

Tuesday
Three-Penne Opera
Pagliacci and Peppers
Toastca
Aïda Pudding

Wednesday
Curry in a Hurry
No-Excuse Couscous
Pearishables
Quick Cake

Thursday
Soup of Fools
Salad 17
Battle of the Bulge

Friday
Elbows On the Table
Slouch Salad
Bungled Biscuits
Persnickety Pudding

STAPLES

- ☐ Butter
- ☐ Vegetable shortening
- ☐ Flour
- ☐ Baking powder
- ☐ Baking soda
- ☐ Cornstarch
- ☐ Granulated sugar
- ☐ Dark brown sugar
- ☐ Corn syrup
- ☐ Olive oil
- ☐ Vegetable oil
- ☐ Apple cider vinegar
- ☐ Balsamic vinegar
- ☐ Rice vinegar
- ☐ Lemon juice
- ☐ Honey
- ☐ Soy sauce
- ☐ Worcestershire sauce
- ☐ Grated Parmesan cheese
- ☐ Plain breadcrumbs
- ☐ Chicken bouillon cube
- ☐ Caraway seeds
- ☐ Dried basil
- ☐ Bay leaf
- ☐ Dried oregano
- ☐ Dried tarragon
- ☐ Ground cardamom
- ☐ Cayenne pepper
- ☐ Ground cinnamon
- ☐ Curry powder
- ☐ Dry mustard
- ☐ Ground nutmeg
- ☐ Paprika
- ☐ Black pepper
- ☐ Saffron threads
- ☐ Salt
- ☐ Orange extract
- ☐ Rum extract

MEAT & POULTRY

1 1/2 pounds lean ground beef (M)

1 pound spicy Italian sausage (Th)

4 boneless, skinless chicken breast halves (about 1 1/2 pounds) (W)

FRESH PRODUCE

VEGETABLES

1 large bunch broccoli (T)

2 medium carrots (Th)

1 large head lettuce (T, W)

1 medium head lettuce (F)

1 small head lettuce (Th)

1 large tomato (T)

4 medium cucumbers (Th)

1 large green bell pepper (Th)

1 medium green bell pepper (M)

2 small red bell peppers (T)

1 large onion (Th)

2 small onions (M)

2 small onions (W)

1 small red onion (M)

4 scallions (green onions) (T)

2 scallions (green onions) (Th)

1 clove garlic (M)

2 cloves garlic (T)

1 clove garlic (W)

2 cloves garlic (Th)

1 clove garlic (F)

HERBS

3 tablespoons chives (when chopped) (T)

1 tablespoon chives (when chopped) (F)

1/4 cup parsley (when chopped) (M)

2 tablespoons parsley (when chopped) (T)

1/2 cup parsley (when chopped) (F)

FRUIT

2 large oranges (F)

1 large pink grapefruit (F)

2 medium bananas (T)

4 medium ripe pears (W)

CANS, JARS & BOTTLES

SOUPS

1 can (14 ounces) beef broth (M)

2 cans (14 ounces each) beef broth (Th)

VEGETABLES

1 can (14 1/2 ounces) diced tomatoes (Th)

1 can (11 ounces) whole-kernel corn (Th)

1 can (4 ounces) sliced mushrooms (W)

FRUIT

1 can (8 ounces) pineapple chunks (M)

4 maraschino cherries (M)

SPREADS

1/2 cup red current jelly (Th)

CONDIMENTS

1 jar (6 1/2 ounces) marinated artichoke hearts (T)

1 can (3 1/2 ounces) sliced black olives (T)

DESSERT & BAKING NEEDS

1 jar (7 ounces) marshmallow crème (M)

1/4 cup marshmallow crème for garnish (Th)

PACKAGED GOODS

PASTA, RICE & GRAINS

1 pound penne (T)

1 pound elbow macaroni (F)

1 cup long-grain white rice (M)

1 cup couscous (W)

BAKED GOODS

4 hard rolls (T)

1 loaf French bread (Th)

DRIED FRUIT & NUTS

1/2 cup cashew pieces (T)

DESSERT & BAKING NEEDS

1 package (3.4 ounces) instant banana cream pudding mix (T)

1 package (3.4 ounces) instant butterscotch pudding mix (F)

2 peppermint patties (1.5 ounces each) (M)

1 Snickers candy bar (2.7 ounces) (F)

2 squares (1 ounce each) semisweet chocolate (T)

1/3 cup flaked coconut (W)

WINE & SPIRITS

1/2 cup dry white wine (W)

3 tablespoons dry sherry (Th)

REFRIGERATED PRODUCTS

DAIRY

2 cups plus 2 tablespoons milk (T)

2 cups milk (F)

3/4 cup buttermilk (F)

1/2 cup sour cream (Th)

1 container (6 ounces) plain yogurt (W)

Whipped cream for garnish (T)

Whipped cream for garnish (F)

2 eggs (M)

CHEESE

1 cup shredded mozzarella cheese (F)

JUICES

2 tablespoons orange juice (F)

FROZEN GOODS

VEGETABLES

1 package (10 ounces) green beans (M)

1 package (10 ounces) wax beans (M)

2 packages (10 ounces each) chopped spinach (F)

FRUIT

1 package (16 ounces) whole raspberries (Th)

BAKED GOODS

1 pound cake (W)

DESSERTS

1 pint chocolate mint chip ice cream (M)

1 pint vanilla ice cream (Th)

MONDAY

Bronco Beef

2 small onions
1 medium green bell pepper
1/4 cup fresh parsley (when chopped)
1 can (8 ounces) pineapple chunks
1 1/2 pounds lean ground beef
2 eggs
1/2 cup plain breadcrumbs
1 cup water
1 teaspoon dry mustard
Seasoning to taste
2 tablespoons vegetable oil
1/4 cup apple cider vinegar
1 tablespoon soy sauce
1/4 cup dark brown sugar
2 tablespoons cornstarch

Steamboat Rice

1 cup long-grain white rice
1 can (14 ounces) beef broth
1/4 cup water

Boulder Beans

1 package (10 ounces) frozen green beans
1 package (10 ounces) frozen wax beans
1 clove garlic
1 small red onion
1 tablespoon vegetable oil
1 tablespoon lemon juice
1 teaspoon honey

The Denver Mint

2 peppermint patties (1.5 ounces each)
1 jar (7 ounces) marshmallow crème
1 pint chocolate mint chip ice cream
4 maraschino cherries for garnish

EQUIPMENT

Double boiler	Small mixing bowl
Medium covered saucepan	Mallet
	Ice cream scoop
Large covered skillet	Plastic bag
Large skillet	Kitchen knives
Steamer insert	Measuring cups and spoons
Large mixing bowl	
Medium mixing bowl	Cooking utensils

COUNTDOWN

1. Assemble the ingredients and the equipment.
2. Do Step 1 of *Boulder Beans*.
3. Do Steps 1–2 of *Steamboat Rice*.
4. Do Steps 1–2 of *The Denver Mint*.
5. Do Steps 1–5 of *Bronco Beef*.
6. Do Steps 2–4 of *Boulder Beans*.
7. Do Step 6 of *Bronco Beef*.
8. Do Steps 5–6 of *Boulder Beans*.
9. Do Step 3 of *Steamboat Rice*.
10. Do Step 3 of *The Denver Mint*.

MONDAY

Bronco Beef

1 Peel and mince 1 onion. Peel and slice 1 onion. Rinse, trim, seed, and chop the bell pepper. Rinse, stem, and chop the parsley. Drain the pineapple, reserving the liquid.

2 In a large bowl, combine the minced onion and the parsley with the meat, the eggs, the breadcrumbs, the water, and the mustard. Season to taste. Form the mixture into 2-inch balls.

3 Heat 1 tablespoon of the oil in a large skillet and sauté the meatballs until well browned and cooked through, 12 to 15 minutes. Remove and drain on paper towels. Wipe out the skillet.

4 Heat the remaining 1 tablespoon oil in the skillet and sauté the sliced onion and the bell pepper until the onion is soft, about 5 minutes. Add the reserved pineapple liquid, the vinegar, the soy sauce, the brown sugar, and the cornstarch. Bring the mixture to a boil and cook until the sauce is clear and slightly thickened, about 4 minutes.

5 Return the meatballs to the skillet, add the pineapple, and reduce the heat. Cover and simmer for 5 minutes more.

6 Remove the skillet from the heat and keep covered.

Steamboat Rice

1 Bring water to a boil in the bottom of a double boiler.

2 In the top of the double boiler, combine the rice, the broth, and the ¼ cup water. Cover, reduce the heat, and simmer until all the liquid is absorbed and the rice is tender, 30 to 40 minutes.

3 Fluff the rice with a fork.

Boulder Beans

1 Set the beans in a medium bowl of warm water to thaw.

2 Bring a small amount of water to a boil in a medium saucepan.

3 Peel and mince the garlic. Peel and mince the onion.

4 Place the beans in a steamer insert in the saucepan. Cover and steam until crisp-tender, about 5 minutes.

5 Heat the oil in a large skillet and sauté the garlic and onion for 5 minutes.

6 Drain the beans and add them to the skillet. Add the lemon juice and the honey, toss to coat, and cover to keep warm.

The Denver Mint

1 Place the mint patties in a plastic bag and crush with a mallet.

2 In a small bowl, combine the crushed candy with the marshmallow crème.

3 Place scoops of ice cream in individual dessert bowls and top with the mint mixture. Garnish each serving with a maraschino cherry.

TUESDAY

Three-Penne Opera

2 cloves garlic
1 large tomato
1 large bunch broccoli
1 can (3½ ounces) sliced black olives
4 tablespoons butter
1 teaspoon dried oregano
1 teaspoon dried basil
Seasoning to taste
1 pound pénne
½ cup grated Parmesan cheese
½ cup cashew pieces

Pagliacci and Peppers

1 large head lettuce (reserve 4 leaves for
  use on Wednesday)
1 jar (6½ ounces) marinated artichoke
  hearts
2 small red bell peppers
4 scallions (green onions)
2 tablespoons lemon juice
½ teaspoon Worcestershire sauce
Seasoning to taste

Toastca

4 hard rolls
3 tablespoons fresh chives (when chopped)
2 tablespoons fresh parsley (when
  chopped)
2 tablespoons olive oil
Seasoning to taste

Aïda Pudding

1 package (3.4 ounces) instant banana
  cream pudding mix
2 cups plus 2 tablespoons milk
2 squares (1 ounce each) semisweet
  chocolate
2 medium bananas
Whipped cream for garnish

EQUIPMENT

Electric mixer
Stockpot
Small saucepan
Large covered skillet
Baking sheet
Colander
Medium mixing bowl

2 small mixing
  bowls
Whisk
Kitchen knives
Measuring cups and
  spoons
Cooking utensils

COUNTDOWN

1. Assemble the ingredients and the
   equipment.
2. Do Step 1 of *Aïda Pudding.*
3. Do Steps 1–2 of *Three-Penne Opera.*
4. Do Steps 1–4 of *Pagliacci and Peppers.*
5. Do Steps 3–5 of *Three-Penne Opera.*
6. Do Steps 1–4 of *Toastca.*
7. Do Step 6 of *Three-Penne Opera.*
8. Do Step 5 of *Pagliacci and Peppers.*
9. Do Steps 2–3 of *Aïda Pudding.*

TUESDAY

Three-Penne Opera

1 Bring water to a boil in a stockpot.

2 Peel and mince the garlic. Rinse, stem, and chop the tomato. Rinse and trim the broccoli, discarding the tough ends, and cut into bite-sized florets. Drain the olives.

3 Melt 2 tablespoons of the butter in a large skillet and sauté the garlic for 3 minutes. Add the broccoli, cover, reduce the heat, and cook until crisp-tender, 6 to 8 minutes.

4 Cook the penne until it is almost tender, 8 to 10 minutes.

5 Add the olives, the oregano, and the basil to the skillet. Fold in the tomato and season to taste.

6 Drain the pasta and return it to the stockpot. Toss it with the remaining 2 tablespoons butter and the broccoli mixture. Sprinkle with the cheese and the nuts.

Pagliacci and Peppers

1 Wash and dry the lettuce, tear it into bite-sized pieces, and distribute it among individual salad plates.

2 Drain the artichoke hearts, reserving the marinade, and cut them in half. Rinse, trim, seed, and julienne the bell peppers. Rinse, trim, and chop the scallions.

3 Arrange the artichokes and bell pepper strips over the lettuce and sprinkle with the scallions.

4 In a small bowl, whisk together the reserved marinade, the lemon juice, and the Worcestershire sauce. Season to taste.

5 Drizzle the dressing over the salad.

Toastca

1 Preheat the broiler.

2 Cut the rolls in half lengthwise.

3 Rinse, trim, and chop the chives. Rinse, stem, and chop the parsley. In a small bowl, combine the chives, the parsley, and the oil. Season to taste and spread the mixture on the bread.

4 Place the rolls on a baking sheet and toast until golden, 2 to 3 minutes.

Aïda Pudding

1 Combine the pudding mix and 2 cups of the milk in a medium bowl and beat with an electric mixer for 2 minutes. Refrigerate the mixture for at least 20 minutes.

2 Melt the chocolate with the remaining 2 tablespoons milk in a small saucepan, whisking until smooth, about 2 minutes. Remove the saucepan from the heat.

3 Peel and slice the bananas. Layer the bananas and the pudding in individual dessert glasses. Drizzle with the melted chocolate and garnish with a dollop of whipped cream.

WEDNESDAY

Curry in a Hurry

4 boneless, skinless chicken breast halves
    (about 1 1/2 pounds)
1 small onion
1 can (4 ounces) sliced mushrooms
1/2 teaspoon paprika
Seasoning to taste
1 chicken bouillon cube
1/2 cup dry white wine
2 teaspoons curry powder

No-Excuse Couscous

2 cups water
1 small onion
1 clove garlic
2 tablespoons butter
1 cup couscous
1 1/2 teaspoons saffron threads

Pearishables

4 lettuces leaves (reserved from Tuesday)
4 medium ripe pears
2 tablespoons lemon juice
1 container (6 ounces) plain yogurt
2 tablespoons honey
1 teaspoon ground cardamom

Quick Cake

1 frozen pound cake
2 tablespoons butter
1/4 cup dark brown sugar
2 tablespoons corn syrup
1 teaspoon orange extract
1/3 cup flaked coconut for garnish

EQUIPMENT

Medium covered
    saucepan
2 small saucepans
9 x 13-inch glass
    baking dish
Small mixing bowl

Whisk
Aluminum foil
Kitchen knives
Measuring cups and
    spoons
Cooking utensils

COUNTDOWN

1. Assemble the ingredients and the
   equipment.
2. Do Step 1 of *Quick Cake.*
3. Do Steps 1–4 of *Curry in a Hurry.*
4. Do Steps 1–2 of *Pearishables.*
5. Do Steps 1–4 of *No-Excuse Couscous.*
6. Do Step 5 of *Curry in a Hurry.*
7. Do Step 5 of *No-Excuse Couscous.*
8. Do Steps 2–3 of *Quick Cake.*

WEDNESDAY

Curry in a Hurry

1 Preheat the oven to 350°F.

2 Rinse and pat dry the chicken breasts. Peel and mince the onion. Drain the mushrooms, reserving the liquid.

3 Sprinkle the chicken with the paprika, season to taste, and place in a 9 x 13-inch baking dish.

4 In a small saucepan, heat the reserved mushroom liquid with the bouillon cube until the cube is dissolved. Add the onion, the mushrooms, the wine, and the curry powder. Pour the mixture over the chicken. Cover the dish with aluminum foil and bake for 15 minutes.

5 Uncover the chicken and bake until the juice runs clear when the chicken is pricked with a fork, about 10 minutes.

No-Excuse Couscous

1 Bring the water to a boil.

2 Peel and mince the onion. Peel and mince the garlic.

3 Melt the butter in a medium saucepan and sauté the onion and the garlic for 5 minutes.

4 Add the couscous and sauté for 3 minutes. Add the saffron and the boiling water, mix well, cover, remove from the heat, and let stand for 10 minutes.

5 Fluff before serving.

Pearishables

1 Arrange the lettuce leaves on individual salad plates. Peel, core, and slice the pears and arrange them on the lettuce. Drizzle with the lemon juice.

2 In a small bowl, combine the yogurt, the honey, and the cardamom. Drizzle the mixture over the pears.

Quick Cake

1 Set the pound cake out to thaw.

2 In a small saucepan, melt the butter with the brown sugar and the corn syrup. Add the orange extract and cook until the mixture is bubbly, 2 to 3 minutes.

3 Drizzle the mixture over the cake and sprinkle with the coconut.

THURSDAY

Soup of Fools

1 pound spicy Italian sausage
1 large onion
2 cloves garlic
2 medium carrots
1 large green bell pepper
1 can (11 ounces) whole-kernel corn
2 tablespoons vegetable oil
1 can (14½ ounces) diced tomatoes
2 cans (14 ounces each) beef broth
1 cup water
1 bay leaf
3 tablespoons dry sherry
1 teaspoon granulated sugar
1 teaspoon dried tarragon
½ teaspoon cayenne pepper
Seasoning to taste
1 loaf French bread

Salad 17

1 small head lettuce
4 medium cucumbers
2 scallions (green onions)
½ cup sour cream
1½ tablespoons rice vinegar
¼ teaspoon granulated sugar
Seasoning to taste
½ teaspoon paprika for garnish

Battle of the Bulge

1 package (16 ounces) frozen whole
  raspberries
1½ teaspoons cornstarch
½ cup red currant jelly
1 teaspoon ground cinnamon
1 pint vanilla ice cream
¼ cup marshmallow crème for garnish

EQUIPMENT

Dutch oven	Vegetable peeler
Small saucepan	Ice cream scoop
Large covered skillet	Kitchen knives
Medium mixing bowl	Measuring cups and
2 small mixing bowls	spoons
Whisk	Cooking utensils

COUNTDOWN

1. Assemble the ingredients and the equipment.
2. Do Step 1 of *Battle of the Bulge.*
3. Do Steps 1–5 of *Soup of Fools.*
4. Do Steps 1–3 of *Salad 17.*
5. Do Steps 2–3 of *Battle of the Bulge.*
6. Do Step 4 of *Salad 17.*
7. Do Step 6 of *Soup of Fools.*
8. Do Step 4 of *Battle of the Bulge.*

THURSDAY

Soup of Fools

1 Place the sausage in the freezer for 10 minutes.

2 Peel and chop the onion. Peel and mince the garlic. Peel, trim, and chop the carrots. Rinse, trim, seed, and chop the bell pepper. Drain the corn. Slice the sausage.

3 Heat the oil in a large skillet. Add the onion, the garlic, and the sausage and sauté until the sausage is lightly browned, about 10 minutes. Add the carrots and the bell pepper. Cover and cook until the vegetables are crisp-tender, about 5 minutes. Remove the skillet from the heat.

4 In a Dutch oven, combine the corn, the tomatoes, the broth, the water, and the bay leaf. Bring the mixture to a boil.

5 Add the sausage mixture, the sherry, the sugar, the tarragon, and the cayenne pepper. Season to taste, reduce the heat, and simmer until heated through, about 25 minutes.

6 Remove the bay leaf before serving. Serve with chunks of French bread.

Salad 17

1 Wash and dry the lettuce and distribute the leaves among individual salad plates.

2 Peel, trim, and slice the cucumbers. Rinse, trim, and chop the scallions. Combine the cucumbers and the scallions in a medium bowl.

3 In a small bowl, combine the sour cream, the vinegar, and the sugar. Season to taste. Pour the dressing over the cucumber mixture and toss to coat.

4 Mound the cucumber mixture on the lettuce leaves and sprinkle with the paprika.

Battle of the Bulge

1 Set the raspberries in a small bowl of warm water to thaw.

2 Blend the cornstarch with 2 tablespoons of the raspberry liquid.

3 Combine the raspberries with the currant jelly in a small saucepan. Add the cornstarch mixture and the cinnamon. Bring the mixture to a boil and cook, stirring, until it is thick and clear, about 3 minutes. Cover, remove from the heat, and keep warm.

4 Place scoops of ice cream in individual dessert glasses. Add some of the raspberry sauce. Add more ice cream and top with the remaining sauce. Garnish with the marshmallow crème.

FRIDAY

Elbows On the Table

2 packages (10 ounces each) frozen
   chopped spinach
1 clove garlic
1/2 cup fresh parsley (when chopped)
1 pound elbow macaroni
1/4 cup vegetable oil
2 cups plain breadcrumbs
1/2 cup grated Parmesan cheese
1 teaspoon ground nutmeg
Seasoning to taste
1 cup shredded mozzarella cheese

Slouch Salad

1 medium head lettuce
2 large oranges
1 large pink grapefruit
1 tablespoon fresh chives (when chopped)
3 tablespoons vegetable oil
2 tablespoons orange juice
1 tablespoon balsamic vinegar
Seasoning to taste

Bungled Biscuits

2 cups flour
1 tablespoon baking powder
1/2 teaspoon baking soda
1/2 teaspoon salt
1 tablespoon caraway seeds
1/2 cup vegetable shortening
3/4 cup buttermilk

Persnickety Pudding

1 Snickers candy bar (2.7 ounces)
1 package (3.4 ounces) instant butterscotch
   pudding mix
2 cups milk
1 teaspoon rum extract
Whipped cream for garnish

EQUIPMENT

Electric mixer	Small mixing bowl
Stockpot	Whisk
Large skillet	Citrus grater
9 x 13-inch glass baking dish	Mallet
Baking sheet	Pastry blender
Breadboard	Biscuit cutter
Colander	Plastic bag
Large mixing bowl	Kitchen knives
2 medium mixing bowls	Measuring cups and spoons
	Cooking utensils

COUNTDOWN

1. Assemble the ingredients and the equipment.
2. Do Step 1 of *Elbows On the Table*.
3. Do Steps 1–2 of *Persnickety Pudding*.
4. Do Steps 2–8 of *Elbows On the Table*.
5. Do Steps 1–3 of *Slouch Salad*.
6. Do Steps 1–4 of *Bungled Biscuits*.
7. Do Step 4 of *Slouch Salad*.
8. Do Step 3 of *Persnickety Pudding*.

FRIDAY

Elbows On the Table

1 Set the spinach in a medium bowl of very warm water to thaw.

2 Preheat the oven to 350°F. Lightly grease a 9 x 13-inch baking dish.

3 Bring water to a boil in a stockpot.

4 Peel and mince the garlic. Rinse, stem, and chop the parsley. Squeeze the thawed spinach to remove any excess liquid.

5 Cook the macaroni until it is almost tender, 8 to 10 minutes.

6 Heat the oil in a large skillet and sauté the garlic for 3 minutes. Add the spinach, the parsley, the breadcrumbs, the Parmesan cheese, and the nutmeg. Season to taste and blend well.

7 Drain the pasta. Put half of the pasta in the bottom of the baking dish and layer with half of the spinach mixture, the remaining pasta, and the remaining spinach mixture. Sprinkle with the mozzarella cheese.

8 Bake until hot and bubbly, about 30 minutes.

Slouch Salad

1 Wash and dry the lettuce and arrange the leaves on individual salad plates.

2 Grate 1 teaspoon of orange peel. Peel and slice the oranges and arrange the slices on the lettuce leaves. Peel and section the grapefruit and arrange the sections on the lettuce leaves. Rinse, trim, and chop the chives.

3 In a small bowl, combine the oil, the orange juice, and the vinegar. Season to taste.

4 Spoon the dressing over the fruit. Sprinkle with the chives and the orange peel.

Bungled Biscuits

1 In a large bowl, combine the flour, the baking powder, the baking soda, the salt, and the caraway seeds. Cut in the shortening with a pastry blender until the mixture resembles coarse crumbs. Fold in the buttermilk.

2 Flour a breadboard. Turn the dough out onto the breadboard and knead about 10 times. Pat out the dough to a ½-inch thickness. Cut it with a biscuit cutter.

3 Place the biscuits 1 inch apart on a baking sheet.

4 Increase the oven temperature to 450°F. Bake the biscuits until golden, about 10 minutes.

Persnickety Pudding

1 Place the candy bar in a plastic bag and crush with a mallet.

2 In a medium bowl, beat the pudding mix with the milk until smooth, about 2 minutes. Fold in the candy and the rum extract. Spoon into individual dessert bowls and refrigerate until you are ready to serve.

3 Top with dollops of whipped cream.

WEEK ELEVEN

Monday
Tortilla Flats
Mexican Standoff
Zapáta Coládas

Tuesday
Going Dutch
Saving Your Bacon
An Apple a Day

Wednesday
On the Other Ham
Yam Session
Snap Happy
Chill We Meet Again

Thursday
Milwokee
Watomato Salad
Badger Sticks
Eau Claires

Friday
Small Investor
Ticker Tape
Stalk Market
Frozen Assets

STAPLES

- ☐ Butter
- ☐ Flour
- ☐ Granulated sugar
- ☐ Dark brown sugar
- ☐ Powdered sugar
- ☐ Corn syrup
- ☐ Chocolate syrup
- ☐ Olive oil
- ☐ Vegetable oil
- ☐ Balsamic vinegar
- ☐ Red wine vinegar
- ☐ White wine vinegar
- ☐ Lemon juice
- ☐ Dijon mustard
- ☐ Honey
- ☐ Prepared horseradish
- ☐ Worcestershire sauce
- ☐ White Worcestershire sauce
- ☐ Instant coffee
- ☐ Dried marjoram
- ☐ Dried oregano
- ☐ Dried rosemary
- ☐ Dried thyme
- ☐ Ground allspice
- ☐ Chili powder
- ☐ Ground cinnamon
- ☐ Lemon-pepper seasoning
- ☐ Dry mustard
- ☐ Ground nutmeg
- ☐ Paprika
- ☐ Black pepper
- ☐ Salt
- ☐ Orange extract
- ☐ Rum extract

SHOPPING LIST

MEAT & POULTRY

2 lean cooked ham steaks (about 3/4 pound each) (W)

1 1/2 pounds boneless, skinless chicken breast (M)

FISH

1 1/2 pounds medium shrimp, shelled and deveined (F)

FRESH PRODUCE

VEGETABLES

4 small yams (W)

1 pound sugar-snap peas (W)

1 stalk celery (W)

8 large stalks celery (F)

1/4 pound mushrooms (T)

1 package (12 ounces) spinach (T)

1 medium head romaine lettuce (M)

1 medium head lettuce (Th)

3 medium tomatoes (M)

1 container cherry tomatoes (Th)

1 medium ripe avocado (M)

1 medium cucumber (M)

1 large green bell pepper (M)

1 small red bell pepper (F)

1 small jicama (M)

2 large onions (M)

1 small onion (Th)

1 small red onion (T)

1 medium shallot (Th)

1 medium shallot (F)

3 scallions (green onions) (F)

1 clove garlic (M)

2 cloves garlic (Th)

2 cloves garlic (F)

HERBS

2 tablespoons chives (when chopped) (Th)

3 tablespoons parsley (when chopped) (F)

FRUIT

2 medium oranges (M)

1 medium banana (M)

4 tart green apples (T)

CANS, JARS & BOTTLES

VEGETABLES

1 can (15 ounces) diced beets (Th)

1 can (11 ounces) whole-kernel corn (Th)

INTERNATIONAL FOODS

1 jar (12 ounces) salsa (M)

FRUIT

1 can (8 ounces) crushed pineapple (M)

SPREADS

1/4 cup grape jelly (W)

CONDIMENTS

1 can (3 1/2 ounces) sliced black olives (M)

DESSERT & BAKING NEEDS

1 jar (7 ounces) marshmallow crème (T)

1 jar (12 ounces) chocolate fudge topping (Th)

PACKAGED GOODS

PASTA, RICE & GRAINS

1 pound fettuccine (Th)

8 ounces vermicelli (F)

BAKED GOODS

4 small croissants (Th)

1 prepared chocolate pie shell (W)

INTERNATIONAL FOODS

8 large soft flour tortillas (M)

DRIED FRUIT & NUTS

3 tablespoons golden raisins (T)

1/2 cup sliced almonds (T)

1/4 cup pecan bits (Th)

DESSERT & BAKING NEEDS

3 tablespoons flaked coconut (M)

6 ounces cinnamon chips (F)

REFRIGERATED PRODUCTS

DAIRY

1 1/2 cups milk (T)

2 tablespoons milk (F)

1 1/3 cups half-and-half (Th)

1 cup sour cream (M)

1 cup whipped cream (Th)

Whipped cream for garnish (W)

9 eggs (T)

CHEESE

1 cup pepper Jack cheese (when grated) (M)

1/2 cup shredded Cheddar cheese (Th)

DELI

4 slices bacon (T)

1 package (10 ounces) breadsticks (Th)

FROZEN GOODS

VEGETABLES

1 package (10 ounces) green peas (Th)

1 package (10 ounces) cut green beans (Th)

BAKED GOODS

1 pound cake (F)

DESSERTS

1 pint vanilla sherbet (M)

1 pint coffee ice cream (W)

1 container (8 ounces) whipped topping (F)

MONDAY

Tortilla Flats

1 1/2 pounds boneless, skinless chicken breast
2 large onions
1 clove garlic
1 large green bell pepper
3 medium tomatoes
1 medium ripe avocado
1 tablespoon lemon juice
1 cup pepper Jack cheese (when grated)
8 large soft flour tortillas
2 tablespoons vegetable oil
1 tablespoon Worcestershire sauce
Seasoning to taste
1 cup sour cream
1 jar (12 ounces) salsa

Mexican Standoff

1 medium head romaine lettuce
2 medium oranges
1 medium cucumber
1 small jicama
1 can (3 1/2 ounces) sliced black olives
3 tablespoons vegetable oil
2 tablespoons red wine vinegar
1 teaspoon granulated sugar
1/4 teaspoon chili powder
1/4 teaspoon dried oregano
Seasoning to taste

Zapáta Coládas

1 medium banana
1 can (8 ounces) crushed pineapple
1 pint vanilla sherbet
1 1/2 teaspoons rum extract
3 tablespoons flaked coconut

EQUIPMENT

Large skillet	Cheese grater
Baking sheet	Ice cream scoop
Large mixing bowl	Kitchen knives
Small mixing bowl	Measuring cups and
Whisk	spoons
Vegetable peeler	Cooking utensils

COUNTDOWN

1. Assemble the ingredients and the equipment.
2. Do Steps 1–2 of *Mexican Standoff*.
3. Do Steps 1–7 of *Tortilla Flats*.
4. Do Step 3 of *Mexican Standoff*.
5. Do Steps 1–2 of *Zapáta Coládas*.

MONDAY

Tortilla Flats

1 Warm the oven to 200°F.

2 Rinse and pat dry the chicken breast and cut it into ½-inch-wide strips.

3 Peel and slice the onions. Peel and mince the garlic. Rinse, trim, seed, and chop the bell pepper. Rinse, stem, and chop the tomatoes. Halve, pit, peel, and slice the avocado and sprinkle the slices with the lemon juice to prevent browning. Grate the cheese.

4 Place the tortillas on a baking sheet in the oven to warm for 5 minutes.

5 Heat the oil in a large skillet and sauté the chicken strips until they are lightly browned, about 5 minutes. Remove the chicken and set aside.

6 Add the onions, the garlic, the bell pepper, and the Worcestershire sauce to the skillet. Sauté until the vegetables are soft, about 5 minutes. Return the chicken to the skillet, season to taste, and mix to combine and heat through.

7 Spread the chicken mixture over the tortillas and serve with the tomatoes, the avocado, the cheese, the sour cream, and the salsa.

Mexican Standoff

1 Wash and dry the lettuce and tear it into bite-sized pieces. Peel and section the oranges and cut the sections in half. Peel, trim, and slice the cucumber. Peel, trim, and slice the jicama. Drain the olives. Combine the ingredients in a large bowl.

2 In a small bowl, whisk together the oil, the vinegar, the sugar, the chili powder, and the oregano. Season to taste.

3 Toss the salad with the dressing.

Zapáta Coládas

1 Peel and chop the banana. Drain the pineapple.

2 Place scoops of the sherbet in individual dessert glasses. Add the banana and the pineapple. Drizzle with the rum extract and sprinkle with the coconut.

TUESDAY

Going Dutch

6 tablespoons butter
9 eggs
1 1/2 cups milk
1 1/2 cups flour
1/4 cup powdered sugar
1 teaspoon ground cinnamon

Saving Your Bacon

1 package (12 ounces) fresh spinach
4 slices bacon
1/4 pound fresh mushrooms
1 small red onion
1/2 cup sliced almonds
3 tablespoons olive oil
2 tablespoons lemon juice
1 teaspoon Dijon mustard
1 teaspoon honey

An Apple a Day

4 tart green apples
2 tablespoons butter
1 teaspoon ground nutmeg
3 tablespoons golden raisins
2 tablespoons dark brown sugar
1 jar (7 ounces) marshmallow crème

EQUIPMENT

Blender	Small mixing bowl
Large ovenproof skillet	Whisk
Medium covered skillet	Kitchen knives
Small skillet	Measuring cups and spoons
Large mixing bowl	Cooking utensils

COUNTDOWN

1. Assemble the ingredients and the equipment.
2. Do Steps 1–2 of *An Apple a Day*.
3. Do Steps 1–4 of *Going Dutch*.
4. Do Steps 1–5 of *Saving Your Bacon*.
5. Do Step 5 of *Going Dutch*.
6. Do Step 3 of *An Apple a Day*.

TUESDAY

Going Dutch

1 Preheat the oven to 425°F.

2 Melt the butter in a large ovenproof skillet in the oven until bubbly but not brown.

3 Place the eggs in a blender and process for 1 minute. Slowly add the milk and blend for 1 minute. Slowly add the flour and blend for 2 minutes more.

4 Pour the mixture into the hot skillet and bake until puffy and golden, 20 to 25 minutes.

5 Combine the powdered sugar with the cinnnamon and sprinkle over the eggs.

Saving Your Bacon

1 Rinse, pat dry, and stem the spinach and tear it into bite-sized pieces. Place it in a large bowl.

2 Dice the bacon and sauté it in a small skillet until crisp, about 5 minutes.

3 Drain the bacon on paper towels and add it to the spinach.

4 Rinse, pat dry, trim, and slice the mushrooms. Peel and thinly slice the onion. Add the mushrooms, the onion, and the almonds to the spinach.

5 In a small bowl, whisk together the oil, the lemon juice, the mustard, and the honey. Toss the salad with the dressing.

An Apple a Day

1 Peel, core, and thinly slice the apples.

2 Melt the butter with the nutmeg in a medium skillet and sauté the apples with the raisins and the brown sugar until the apples are tender, about 10 minutes. Cover and keep warm.

3 Spoon into individual dessert bowls and top with dollops of marshmallow crème.

WEDNESDAY

On the Other Ham

$1/4$ cup grape jelly
$1/2$ teaspoon dry mustard
2 teaspoons prepared horseradish
2 lean cooked ham steaks (about $3/4$ pound each)

Yam Session

4 small yams
2 tablespoons butter
2 tablespoons lemon juice
1 tablespoon dark brown sugar
$1/2$ teaspoon ground allspice
Seasoning to taste

Snap Happy

1 pound sugar-snap peas
1 stalk celery
2 tablespoons butter
1 teaspoon dried rosemary
Seasoning to taste

Chill We Meet Again

1 pint coffee ice cream
1 prepared chocolate pie shell
$1/2$ cup chocolate syrup
Whipped cream for garnish
1 tablespoon instant coffee for garnish

EQUIPMENT

Medium covered saucepan	Vegetable brush
Large skillet	Pastry brush
Medium skillet	Kitchen knives
9 x 13-inch baking pan	Measuring cups and spoons
Small mixing bowl	Cooking utensils

COUNTDOWN

1. Assemble the ingredients and the equipment.
2. Do Step 1 of *Chill We Meet Again*.
3. Do Step 1 of *Snap Happy*.
4. Do Step 2 of *Chill We Meet Again*.
5. Do Steps 1–3 of *Yam Session*.
6. Do Steps 1–4 of *On the Other Ham*.
7. Do Steps 4–5 of *Yam Session*.
8. Do Step 2 of *Snap Happy*.
9. Do Step 3 of *Chill We Meet Again*.

WEDNESDAY

On the Other Ham

1 Preheat the oven to 350°F.

2 In a small bowl, combine the jelly, the mustard, and the horseradish.

3 Place the ham steaks in a 9 x 13-inch baking pan and brush with the jelly mixture.

4 Bake until the ham is heated through and well glazed, 10 to 15 minutes.

Yam Session

1 Bring water to a boil in a medium saucepan.

2 Scrub, trim, and halve the yams.

3 Cook the yams, covered, until they are tender, 10 to 15 minutes.

4 Melt the butter in a large skillet. Stir in the lemon juice, the brown sugar, and the allspice. Season to taste, bring the mixture to a boil, reduce the heat, and simmer for 2 minutes.

5 Drain the yams, rinse them in cold water, peel, and slice them. Add them to the skillet and toss to coat and reheat.

Snap Happy

1 Rinse, trim, and string the snap peas. Rinse, trim, and chop the celery.

2 Melt the butter with the rosemary in a medium skillet and sauté the celery for 2 minutes. Add the snap peas and sauté until crisp-tender, about 4 minutes. Season to taste.

Chill We Meet Again

1 Set the ice cream out to soften.

2 Spoon the softened ice cream into the pie shell and place in the freezer until you are ready to serve.

3 Drizzle the chocolate syrup over the pie. Top with dollops of whipped cream and a sprinkle of instant coffee.

THURSDAY

Milwokee

1 package (10 ounces) frozen green peas
1 package (10 ounces) frozen cut green
   beans
1 can (15 ounces) diced beets
1 can (11 ounces) whole-kernel corn
1 small onion
3 tablespoons butter
1 pound fettuccine
1 1/3 cups half-and-half
1/2 cup shredded Cheddar cheese
1/2 teaspoon ground nutmeg
1/2 teaspoon paprika
Seasoning to taste

Watomato Salad

1 medium head lettuce
1 container cherry tomatoes
1 medium shallot
3 tablespoons vegetable oil
2 tablespoons balsamic vinegar
1/2 teaspoon dried marjoram
1/2 teaspoon granulated sugar
Seasoning to taste

Badger Sticks

1 package (10 ounces) refrigerated
   breadsticks
2 cloves garlic
2 tablespoons fresh chives (when chopped)
2 tablespoons olive oil

Eau Claires

1 jar (12 ounces) chocolate fudge topping
1 teaspoon orange extract
4 small croissants
1 cup whipped cream
1/4 cup pecan bits

EQUIPMENT

Wok	2 small mixing bowls
Stockpot	Whisk
Small saucepan	Pastry brush
Baking sheet	Kitchen knives
Colander	Measuring cups and
Large mixing bowl	spoons
Medium mixing bowl	Cooking utensils

COUNTDOWN

1. Assemble the ingredients and the equipment.
2. Do Step 1 of *Milwokee*.
3. Do Steps 1–2 of *Watomato Salad*.
4. Do Steps 1–5 of *Badger Sticks*.
5. Do Steps 2–7 of *Milwokee*.
6. Do Step 3 of *Watomato Salad*.
7. Do Step 1–2 of *Eau Claires*.

THURSDAY

Milwokee

1 Set the packages of peas and beans in a medium bowl of warm water to thaw.

2 Drain the beets well. Drain the corn. Peel and chop the onion.

3 Bring water to a boil in a stockpot.

4 Melt the butter in a wok and stir-fry the onion for 3 minutes. Add the peas, the beans, the beets, and the corn and stir-fry for 3 minutes.

5 Cook the fettuccine until it is almost tender, 2 to 3 minutes if you are using fresh pasta, 6 to 7 minutes if you are using dry pasta.

6 Blend the half-and-half, the cheese, the nutmeg, and the paprika into the wok. Season to taste and heat through.

7 Drain the pasta and top with the vegetable mixture.

Watomato Salad

1 Wash and dry the lettuce and tear it into bite-sized pieces. Rinse, stem, and halve the tomatoes. Peel and mince the shallot. Combine the ingredients in a large bowl.

2 In a small bowl, whisk together the oil, the vinegar, the marjoram, and the sugar. Season to taste.

3 Toss the salad with the dressing.

Badger Sticks

1 Preheat the oven to 375°F.

2 Separate the breadsticks.

3 Peel and mash the garlic. Rinse, trim, and chop the chives. Combine the garlic, the chives, and the oil in a small bowl.

4 Brush the breadsticks with the mixture.

5 Lay the breadsticks on a baking sheet and bake until golden, about 15 minutes.

Eau Claires

1 In a small saucepan, combine the fudge topping and the orange extract. Heat until well blended.

2 Cut the croissants in half lengthwise. Fill with the whipped cream. Spoon the warm sauce over the top. Sprinkle with the nuts.

FRIDAY

Small Investor

2 cloves garlic
3 scallions (green onions)
3 tablespoons fresh parsley (when chopped)
1 1/2 pounds medium shrimp, shelled and deveined
2 tablespoons butter
1 tablespoon lemon juice
1/4 teaspoon lemon-pepper seasoning
Seasoning to taste

Ticker Tape

1 small red bell pepper
1 medium shallot
8 ounces vermicelli
2 tablespoons vegetable oil
1/2 teaspoon dried thyme
1 tablespoon white wine vinegar
Seasoning to taste

Stalk Market

8 large stalks celery
3 tablespoons vegetable oil
1 tablespoon white Worcestershire sauce
1/2 teaspoon granulated sugar
Seasoning to taste

Frozen Assets

1 frozen pound cake
6 ounces cinnamon chips
2 tablespoons butter
1 1/2 tablespoons corn syrup
2 tablespoons milk
1 container (8 ounces) frozen whipped topping

EQUIPMENT

Large covered saucepan
Small saucepan
Large skillet
Medium skillet
Colander

Large mixing bowl
Kitchen knives
Measuring cups and spoons
Cooking utensils

COUNTDOWN

1. Assemble the ingredients and the equipment.
2. Do Step 1 of *Frozen Assets*.
3. Do Step 1 of *Small Investor*.
4. Do Steps 1–2 of *Ticker Tape*.
5. Do Step 1 of *Stalk Market*.
6. Do Steps 2–4 of *Frozen Assets*.
7. Do Steps 3–5 of *Ticker Tape*.
8. Do Step 2 of *Stalk Market*.
9. Do Step 2 of *Small Investor*.

FRIDAY

Small Investor

1 Peel and mince the garlic. Rinse, trim, and chop the scallions. Rinse, stem, and chop the parsley. Rinse and pat dry the shrimp.

2 Melt the butter in a large skillet and sauté the garlic with the shrimp until the shrimp turn bright pink, 3 to 4 minutes. Add the scallions, the lemon juice, and the lemon-pepper seasoning. Season to taste and toss to combine. Sprinkle with the parsley.

Ticker Tape

1 Bring water to a boil in a large saucepan.

2 Rinse, trim, seed, and mince the bell pepper. Peel and mince the shallot.

3 Cook the vermicelli until almost tender, 2 to 3 minutes.

4 Drain the vermicelli.

5 Heat the oil in the saucepan and sauté the pepper and the shallot until the shallot is soft, 3 to 4 minutes. Return the vermicelli to the saucepan. Add the thyme and the vinegar. Season to taste and toss to coat and heat through. Cover to keep warm.

Stalk Market

1 Rinse and trim the celery and cut the stalks diagonally into 1-inch-thick slices.

2 Heat the oil in a medium skillet. Add the celery and sauté until crisp-tender, about 5 minutes. Add the Worcestershire sauce and the sugar and toss to combine. Season to taste and cover to keep warm.

Frozen Assets

1 Set the pound cake out to thaw slightly.

2 In a small saucepan, combine the cinnamon chips, the butter, the corn syrup, and the milk. Simmer until melted and smooth, about 2 minutes. Place the saucepan in the refrigerator for 5 minutes.

3 In a large bowl, combine the cooled cinnamon mixture with the whipped topping.

4 Spread the mixture evenly over the top and sides of the cake and refrigerate until you are ready to serve.

WEEK TWELVE

Monday
Foiled Again!
Stooged Tomatoes
Butt of the Biscuits
Second Banana

Tuesday
State of the Onion
Conservative Salad
Democratic Dessert

Wednesday
Raleigh 'Round the Chicken
Carolina Couscous
Blue Ridge Beets
Bragging Rights

Thursday
Mission Impastable
Slaw and Order
Bananacek

Friday
Oxford Omelet
Eatin' Muffins
Cambridge Cordials

- ☐ Butter
- ☐ Flour
- ☐ Baking powder
- ☐ Cornstarch
- ☐ Granulated sugar
- ☐ Dark brown sugar
- ☐ Cocoa powder
- ☐ Olive oil
- ☐ Vegetable oil
- ☐ Lemon juice
- ☐ Dijon mustard
- ☐ Honey
- ☐ Worcestershire sauce
- ☐ Grated Parmesan cheese
- ☐ Dried savory
- ☐ Dried tarragon
- ☐ Ground allspice
- ☐ Ground cinnamon
- ☐ Ground ginger
- ☐ Lemon-pepper seasoning
- ☐ Paprika
- ☐ Black pepper
- ☐ Red pepper flakes
- ☐ Salt
- ☐ Banana extract
- ☐ Vanilla extract

MEAT & POULTRY

1 pound mild Italian sausage (Th)

4 boneless, skinless chicken breast halves (about 1 1/2 pounds) (W)

FISH

4 sole fillets (about 1 1/2 pounds) (M)

FRESH PRODUCE

VEGETABLES

1 medium zucchini (W)

1 small turnip (Th)

4 medium carrots (W)

1 medium carrot (Th)

1 stalk celery (Th)

1/2 pound mushrooms (W)

1 package (16 ounces) spinach (F)

1 medium head lettuce (Th)

1 small head lettuce (T)

2 large tomatoes (F)

4 medium tomatoes (M)

1 large ripe avocado (T)

1 medium cucumber (T)

1 medium green bell pepper (Th)

1 medium red bell pepper (T)

1 large fennel bulb (Th)

5 large onions (T)

1 medium onion (Th)

1 small red onion (W)

1 small red onion (Th)

2 medium shallots (F)

4 scallions (green onions) (M)

1 clove garlic (M)

1 clove garlic (W)

2 cloves garlic (Th)

HERBS

3 tablespoons chives (when chopped) (M)

3 tablespoons chives (when chopped) (F)

1/4 cup parsley (when chopped) (Th)

FRUIT

3 large bananas (Th)

2 medium bananas (M)

2 medium red apples (M)

2 ripe kiwifruit (M)

CANS, JARS & BOTTLES

SOUPS

2 cans (14 ounces each) beef broth (T)

1 can (14 ounces) chicken broth (T)

1 can (14 ounces) chicken broth (W)

1 can (10 3/4 ounces) cream of celery soup (W)

VEGETABLES

1 can (14 1/2 ounces) Italian stewed tomatoes (Th)

1 can (15 ounces) julienne beets (W)

SAUCES

1 jar (16 ounces) Parmesan Alfredo sauce (Th)

JUICES

1 cup apple juice (W)

PACKAGED GOODS

PASTA, RICE & GRAINS

1 pound rigatoni (Th)

1 cup couscous (W)

1 cup corn flakes (Th)

BAKED GOODS

1 small loaf dark rye bread, unsliced (T)

4 English muffins (F)

1 angel food loaf cake (W)

DRIED FRUIT & NUTS

1/2 cup hazelnuts (T)

WINE & SPIRITS

2 tablespoons dry white wine (M)

1/4 cup dry white wine (W)

1/3 cup dry red wine (T)

REFRIGERATED PRODUCTS

DAIRY

3/4 cup milk (M)

1 cup milk (W)

3 tablespoons milk (F)

3 tablespoons half-and-half (Th)

1/4 cup half-and-half (F)

1 cup sour cream (F)

1 container (6 ounces) strawberry yogurt (M)

3/4 cup whipping cream (T)

Whipped cream for garnish (Th)

1 egg (W)

9 eggs (F)

CHEESE

1 cup shredded Cheddar cheese (M)

4 slices Swiss cheese (about 1/2 pound) (T)

JUICE

1/4 cup orange juice (M)

FROZEN GOODS

VEGETABLES

1 package (10 ounces) chopped spinach (F)

FRUIT

1 package (16 ounces) whole pitted cherries (F)

DESSERTS

1 pint butter brickle ice cream (T)

MONDAY

Foiled Again!

4 scallions (green onions)
4 sole fillets (about 1 ½ pounds)
1 teaspoon dried tarragon
1 teaspoon lemon-pepper seasoning
2 tablespoons dry white wine
2 tablespoons lemon juice
Seasoning to taste

Stooged Tomatoes

4 medium tomatoes
1 clove garlic
3 tablespoons fresh chives (when chopped)
Seasoning to taste
2 tablespoons olive oil

Butt of the Biscuits

2 cups flour
4 teaspoons baking powder
2 tablespoons granulated sugar
¼ teaspoon salt
⅓ cup vegetable oil
¾ cup milk
1 cup shredded Cheddar cheese

Second Banana

2 medium bananas
2 medium red apples
2 ripe kiwifruit
¼ cup orange juice
1 container (6 ounces) strawberry yogurt
¼ teaspoon ground ginger

EQUIPMENT

8 x 8-inch glass
    baking dish
Baking sheet
Breadboard
2 medium mixing
    bowls
Biscuit cutter

Plastic wrap
Aluminum foil
Kitchen knives
Measuring cups and
    spoons
Cooking utensils

COUNTDOWN

1. Assemble the ingredients and the equipment.
2. Do Step 1 of *Second Banana*.
3. Do Steps 1–7 of *Stooged Tomatoes*.
4. Do Steps 1–4 of *Foiled Again!*
5. Do Steps 1–4 of *Butt of the Biscuits*.
6. Do Step 2 of *Second Banana*.

MONDAY

Foiled Again!

1 Rinse, trim, and chop the scallions.

2 Rinse and pat dry the fish fillets and lay each one on a sheet of aluminum foil.

3 Sprinkle the scallions, the tarragon, and the lemon-pepper seasoning over the fish. Drizzle on the wine and the lemon juice. Season to taste and wrap the fillets in the foil, sealing the edges.

4 Place the foil packets in the oven and bake at 425°F until the fish flakes easily with a fork, about 10 minutes.

Stooged Tomatoes

1 Preheat the oven to 425°F. Grease an 8 x 8-inch baking dish.

2 Rinse and stem the tomatoes and cut a ½-inch-thick slice off the top. Using a sharp knife, make several cuts across the tomato flesh.

3 Place the tomatoes in the baking dish.

4 Peel and mince the garlic. Rinse, trim, and chop the chives. Sprinkle both over the tomatoes. Season to taste.

5 Drizzle 1 tablespoon of the oil over the tomatoes.

6 Replace the tomato lids and drizzle with the remaining 1 tablespoon oil.

7 Bake until the tomatoes are soft but not mushy, 20 to 25 minutes.

Butt of the Biscuits

1 Flour a breadboard.

2 In a medium bowl, combine the flour, the baking powder, the sugar, and the salt. Blend in the oil and the milk. Fold in the cheese and turn the mixture out onto the breadboard.

3 Knead gently 8 to 10 times to make a soft dough. Pat out the dough to a ¾-inch thickness and cut it into rounds with a biscuit cutter or glass.

4 Place the biscuits on a baking sheet, 1 inch apart, and bake at 425°F until golden, about 10 minutes.

Second Banana

1 Peel and slice the bananas. Rinse, core, and chunk the apples. Peel and slice the kiwifruit. Combine the fruit in a medium bowl. Pour the orange juice over the fruit, cover with plastic wrap, and refrigerate until you are ready to serve.

2 Combine the yogurt with the ginger. Pour over the fruit and blend well.

TUESDAY

State of the Onion

5 large onions
3 tablespoons butter
1 tablespoon vegetable oil
1 teaspoon granulated sugar
2 tablespoons flour
2 cans (14 ounces each) beef broth
1 can (14 ounces) chicken broth
1/3 cup dry red wine
Seasoning to taste
1 small loaf dark rye bread, unsliced
4 slices Swiss cheese (about 1/2 pound)

Conservative Salad

1 small head lettuce
1 medium red bell pepper
1 medium cucumber
1 large ripe avocado
1/2 cup hazelnuts
3 tablespoons vegetable oil
2 tablespoons lemon juice
1/2 teaspoon Dijon mustard
1/4 teaspoon Worcestershire sauce
1/2 teaspoon honey
Seasoning to taste

Democratic Dessert

3 tablespoons butter
3/4 cup whipping cream
1 cup dark brown sugar
1 teaspoon vanilla extract
1 pint butter brickle ice cream

EQUIPMENT

Dutch oven
Medium covered
  saucepan
4 ovenproof bowls,
  16 ounces each
Large mixing bowl
Small mixing bowl

Whisk
Vegetable peeler
Ice cream scoop
Kitchen knives
Measuring cups and
  spoons
Cooking utensils

COUNTDOWN

1. Assemble the ingredients and the equipment.
2. Do Steps 1–3 of *State of the Onion.*
3. Do Steps 1–2 of *Conservative Salad.*
4. Do Step 4 of *State of the Onion.*
5. Do Steps 1–2 of *Democratic Dessert.*
6. Do Steps 5–7 of *State of the Onion.*
7. Do Step 3 of *Conservative Salad.*
8. Do Step 3 of *Democratic Dessert.*

TUESDAY

State of the Onion

1 Peel and thinly slice the onions.

2 Melt the butter with the oil in a Dutch oven and sauté the onions until they turn golden, about 15 minutes.

3 Add the sugar, cover, and simmer for 15 minutes.

4 Add the flour and blend well. Add the broths and the wine, season to taste, and simmer for 20 minutes.

5 Preheat the broiler.

6 Cut the bread into 4 thick slices and toast them lightly.

7 Pour the onion soup into individual ovenproof bowls. Top each bowl with a slice of bread. Top each slice of bread with a slice of cheese and broil until the cheese melts, about 5 minutes.

Conservative Salad

1 Wash and dry the lettuce and tear it into bite-sized pieces. Rinse, trim, seed, and slice the bell pepper. Peel, trim, and slice the cucumber. Halve, pit, peel, and slice the avocado. Chop the nuts. Combine the ingredients in a large bowl.

2 In a small bowl, combine the oil, the lemon juice, the mustard, the Worcestershire sauce, and the honey. Season to taste.

3 Toss the salad with the dressing.

Democratic Dessert

1 Melt the butter in a medium saucepan. Stir in the cream and the brown sugar and bring to a boil. Reduce the heat and simmer, stirring occasionally, until the mixture thickens, 3 to 4 minutes.

2 Remove the saucepan from the heat, fold in the vanilla, and cover to keep warm.

3 Place scoops of ice cream in individual dessert bowls and top with the sauce.

WEDNESDAY

Raleigh 'Round the Chicken

4 boneless, skinless chicken breast halves
  (about 1 1/2 pounds)
1 clove garlic
1/2 pound fresh mushrooms
4 medium carrots
1/2 cup flour
1/2 teaspoon paprika
1 teaspoon ground allspice
Seasoning to taste
3 tablespoons olive oil
1 can (10 3/4 ounces) cream of celery soup
1 cup apple juice
1/4 cup dry white wine
1 tablespoon dark brown sugar

Carolina Couscous

1 medium zucchini
1 can (14 ounces) chicken broth
1/4 cup water
1 tablespoon olive oil
1 tablespoon lemon juice
1 cup couscous
Seasoning to taste

Blue Ridge Beets

1 small red onion
1 can (15 ounces) julienne beets
2 tablespoons butter
1/2 teaspoon dried savory

Bragging Rights

1 egg
1 tablespoon cornstarch
2 teaspoons granulated sugar
1 cup milk
1/2 teaspoon ground cinnamon
1 angel food loaf cake

EQUIPMENT

Medium covered saucepan	Vegetable brush
Small covered saucepan	Vegetable peeler
Large covered skillet	Vegetable grater
Medium skillet	Kitchen knives
Large shallow bowl	Measuring cups and spoons
2 small mixing bowls	Cooking utensils

COUNTDOWN

1. Assemble the ingredients and the equipment.
2. Do Steps 1–5 of *Raleigh 'Round the Chicken*.
3. Do Steps 1–2 of *Carolina Couscous*.
4. Do Steps 1–4 of *Bragging Rights*.
5. Do Step 6 of *Raleigh 'Round the Chicken*.
6. Do Steps 1–3 of *Blue Ridge Beets*.
7. Do Step 5 of *Bragging Rights*.

WEDNESDAY

Raleigh 'Round the Chicken

1 Rinse and pat dry the chicken breasts.

2 Peel and mince the garlic. Rinse, pat dry, trim, and slice the mushrooms. Peel, trim, and slice the carrots.

3 In a large shallow bowl, combine the flour, the paprika, and the allspice and season to taste. Dredge the chicken in the flour mixture.

4 Heat the oil in a large skillet. Add the garlic and the chicken and cook until the chicken is lightly browned, about 5 minutes per side.

5 In a small bowl, combine the soup, the apple juice, and the wine. Add the brown sugar. Pour the mixture over the chicken, cover the skillet, reduce the heat, and simmer for 10 minutes.

6 Turn the chicken, add the carrots and the mushrooms, and continue cooking until the chicken is tender, about 10 minutes more.

Carolina Couscous

1 Scrub, trim, and grate the zucchini.

2 In a medium saucepan, combine the zucchini, the broth, the water, the oil, and the lemon juice. Bring the mixture to a boil. Add the couscous, season to taste, and stir to blend. Cover the saucepan, remove it from the heat, and let stand for at least 10 minutes.

Blue Ridge Beets

1 Peel and mince the onion. Drain the beets.

2 Melt the butter with the savory in a medium skillet and sauté the onion until it is soft, about 5 minutes.

3 Add the beets and sauté until heated through, about 2 minutes.

Bragging Rights

1 Beat the egg in a small bowl.

2 In a small saucepan, combine the cornstarch and the sugar. Gradually stir in the milk and bring the mixture to a boil, stirring constantly, until it thickens, about 5 minutes.

3 Stir half of the milk mixture into the egg and pour the egg mixture back into the saucepan. Simmer, stirring constantly, until thick, about 3 minutes.

4 Remove the saucepan from the heat, stir in the cinnamon, and cover to keep warm.

5 Slice the cake, arrange the slices on individual dessert plates, and drizzle with the sauce.

THURSDAY

Mission Impastable

1 pound mild Italian sausage
2 cloves garlic
1 medium onion
1 medium green bell pepper
1/4 cup fresh parsley (when chopped)
1 tablespoon olive oil
1 can (14 1/2 ounces) Italian stewed
   tomatoes
1 jar (16 ounces) Parmesan Alfredo sauce
Seasoning to taste
1 pound rigatoni

Slaw and Order

1 medium head lettuce
1 medium carrot
1 small turnip
1 large fennel bulb
1 small red onion
1 stalk celery
1/4 cup olive oil
3 tablespoons lemon juice
2 teaspoons Dijon mustard
1 teaspoon dried tarragon
Seasoning to taste

Bananacek

3 large bananas
2 tablespoons lemon juice
3 tablespoons butter
1/2 cup dark brown sugar
1 teaspoon banana extract
3 tablespoons half-and-half
1 cup corn flakes
Whipped cream for garnish

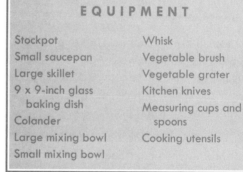

EQUIPMENT

Stockpot	Whisk
Small saucepan	Vegetable brush
Large skillet	Vegetable grater
9 x 9-inch glass	Kitchen knives
baking dish	Measuring cups and
Colander	spoons
Large mixing bowl	Cooking utensils
Small mixing bowl	

COUNTDOWN

1. Assemble the ingredients and the
   equipment.
2. Do Steps 1–2 of *Bananacek.*
3. Do Steps 1–7 of *Mission Impastable.*
4. Do Steps 1–3 of *Slaw and Order.*
5. Do Step 8 of *Mission Impastable.*
6. Do Steps 3–5 of *Bananacek.*

THURSDAY

Mission Impastable

1 Place the sausage in the freezer to chill for 10 minutes.

2 Bring water to a boil in a stockpot.

3 Peel and mince the garlic. Peel and chop the onion. Rinse, trim, seed, and chop the bell pepper. Rinse, stem, and chop the parsley. Cut the sausage into ½-inch-thick rounds.

4 Heat the oil in a large skillet and brown the sausage on both sides, about 10 minutes.

5 Remove the sausage and drain it on paper towels. Drain off all but 1 tablespoon of the fat. Add the garlic, the onion, and the bell pepper to the skillet and sauté until the onion is soft, about 5 minutes.

6 Add the tomatoes and the Alfredo sauce. Bring the mixture to a boil and reduce the heat. Return the sausage to the skillet, season to taste, and simmer for 10 minutes.

7 Cook the rigatoni until it is almost tender, 8 to 10 minutes.

8 Drain the pasta, return it to the stockpot, and toss it with the sauce. Sprinkle with the parsley.

Slaw and Order

1 Wash and dry the lettuce and distribute the leaves among individual salad plates.

2 Peel, trim, and grate the carrot. Peel, trim, and grate the turnip. Scrub, trim, and coarsely grate the fennel bulb. Peel and grate the onion. Rinse, trim, and mince the celery. Combine the ingredients in a large bowl.

3 In a small bowl, whisk together the oil, the lemon juice, the mustard, and the tarragon. Season to taste and toss with the vegetables. Spoon the mixture over the lettuce.

Bananacek

1 Peel the bananas, cut them in half lengthwise, and halve them crosswise. Place them in a 9 x 9-inch baking dish and sprinkle them with the lemon juice.

2 Melt the butter in a small saucepan. Stir in the brown sugar, the banana extract, and the half-and-half. Bring just to a boil and remove from the heat. Blend in the corn flakes and spoon over the bananas.

3 Preheat the broiler.

4 Broil until bubbly, 3 to 4 minutes.

5 Top with dollops of whipped cream.

FRIDAY

Oxford Omelet

2 medium shallots
1 package (16 ounces) fresh spinach
2 tablespoons butter
1/4 teaspoon red pepper flakes
1 cup sour cream
9 eggs
3 tablespoons milk
Seasoning to taste

Eatin' Muffins

4 English muffins
1 tablespoon olive oil
2 large tomatoes
3 tablespoons fresh chives (when chopped)
Seasoning to taste
4 tablespoons grated Parmesan cheese

Cambridge Cordials

1 package (16 ounces) frozen whole pitted
  cherries
1/4 cup granulated sugar
1/4 cup water
2 tablespoons cocoa powder
1/4 cup half-and-half
1 teaspoon vanilla extract

EQUIPMENT

Medium saucepan
Large skillet
9 x 13-inch glass
  baking dish
Baking sheet
Pie plate
2 medium mixing
  bowls

Small mixing bowl
Whisk
Pastry brush
Kitchen knives
Measuring cups and
  spoons
Cooking utensils

COUNTDOWN

1. Assemble the ingredients and the
   equipment.
2. Do Steps 1–4 of *Cambridge Cordials.*
3. Do Steps 1–5 of *Oxford Omelet.*
4. Do Steps 1–5 of *Eatin' Muffins.*
5. Do Steps 5–6 of *Cambridge Cordials.*

FRIDAY

Oxford Omelet

1 Peel and chop the shallots. Rinse, pat dry, and stem the spinach.

2 Preheat the oven to 350°F. Butter a 9 x 13-inch baking dish.

3 Melt the butter in a large skillet and sauté the shallots for 1 minute. Add the spinach and sauté for 1 minute. Add the pepper flakes and the sour cream and blend well. Spoon the mixture into the baking dish.

4 Whip the eggs with the milk in a medium bowl until they are light and frothy. Pour the mixture over the shallots and the spinach. Season to taste.

5 Bake until the eggs are set, about 20 minutes.

Eatin' Muffins

1 Cut the muffins in half and brush the cut sides lightly with the oil.

2 Rinse, stem, and slice the tomatoes. Rinse, trim, and chop the chives.

3 Place a tomato slice on each muffin half. Season to taste and sprinkle with the chives and the cheese.

4 Preheat the broiler.

5 Place the muffins on a baking sheet and broil until the cheese is bubbly, about 3 minutes.

Cambridge Cordials

1 Set the cherries in a medium bowl of warm water to thaw.

2 Combine the sugar and the water in a medium saucepan and bring the mixture to a boil. Add the cherries, stirring to combine, and cook for 2 minutes. Remove the saucepan from the heat.

3 With a slotted spoon, remove the cherries to a pie plate, reserving the cooking liquid.

4 In a small bowl, combine the cocoa powder and the half-and-half. Slowly add the cocoa mixture to the saucepan, blending it into the reserved cooking liquid, and bring the mixture to a boil. Reduce the heat and simmer for 5 minutes. Remove from the heat and cover to keep warm.

5 Preheat the broiler.

6 Stir the vanilla into the saucepan. Pour the mixture over the cherries and place the pie plate under the broiler until the cherries are bubbly, about 2 minutes.

WEEK THIRTEEN

Monday
Corn Biscayne
Mihami Beach
The Orange Bowl
Cake Canaveral

Tuesday
Dapper Snapper
Gnarly Barley
Bean There Done That
Mum Plums

Wednesday
The Teutonic Tomato
Scandinavian Sandwiches
A Celtic Compote

Thursday
Porkfolio
Using Your Noodle
Double Entry
You're Pudding Me On

Friday
Deep In My Tart
Man of La Muncha
A Slaw Is Born
Birth of the Blueberries

- ☐ Butter
- ☐ Flour
- ☐ Baking powder
- ☐ Cornstarch
- ☐ Granulated sugar
- ☐ Dark brown sugar
- ☐ Powdered sugar
- ☐ Olive oil
- ☐ Vegetable oil
- ☐ Apple cider vinegar
- ☐ Rice vinegar
- ☐ Lemon juice
- ☐ Honey
- ☐ Mayonnaise
- ☐ Worcestershire sauce
- ☐ Seasoned breadcrumbs
- ☐ Poppy seeds
- ☐ Dried basil
- ☐ Bay leaf
- ☐ Dried oregano
- ☐ Dried rosemary
- ☐ Dried thyme
- ☐ Ground allspice
- ☐ Ground cinnamon
- ☐ Dried dill
- ☐ Italian seasoning
- ☐ Dry mustard
- ☐ Ground nutmeg
- ☐ Paprika
- ☐ Black pepper
- ☐ Saffron threads
- ☐ Salt
- ☐ Almond extract
- ☐ Orange extract

MEAT & POULTRY

2 lean cooked ham steaks (about ¾ pound each) (M)
4 loin pork chops (about 1½ pounds) (Th)

FISH

4 red snapper fillets (about 1½ pounds) (T)
½ pound baby cooked shrimp (F)

FRESH PRODUCE

VEGETABLES

½ pound asparagus (Th)
½ pound Chinese snow peas (Th)
¾ pound sugar-snap peas (F)
1 small carrot (T)
1 stalk celery (T)
2 stalks celery (F)
1 small turnip (W)
1 medium head red cabbage (F)
1 medium head lettuce (M)
2 medium tomatoes (W)
1 small ripe avocado (M)
1 small ripe avocado (F)
1 medium cucumber (W)
1 small cucumber (F)
1 medium green bell pepper (W)
1 medium red onion (W)
1 small onion (T)
1 small onion (Th)
1 large shallot (F)
1 small shallot (Th)
4 scallions (green onions) (M)
3 scallions (green onions) (F)
1 clove garlic (M)
1 clove garlic (T)

HERBS

¼ cup dill (when chopped) (W)
¼ cup parsley (when chopped) (T)

FRUIT

1 large orange (F)
2 medium oranges (M)
1 large lemon (Th)
1 large banana (W)
2 medium ripe pears (W)
½ pound seedless green grapes (W)
1 pint strawberries (W)

CANS, JARS & BOTTLES

SOUPS

1 can (14 ounces) vegetable broth (M)
1 can (14 ounces) chicken broth (T)
1 can (14 ounces) onion beef broth (W)

VEGETABLES

1 can (28 ounces) crushed tomatoes (W)
1 can (14½ ounces) stewed tomatoes (T)
1 can (11 ounces) whole-kernel corn (M)
1 can (15 ounces) cream-style corn (M)
1 can (8 ounces) button mushrooms (M)

FISH

2 cans (6 ounces each) minced clams (F)
1 tin (2 ounces) anchovy fillets (W)

FRUIT

1 can (15 ounces) purple plums (T)
4 maraschino cherries for garnish (Th)

CONDIMENTS

1 jar (2 ounces) diced pimientos (M)
2 tablespoons capers (W)

PACKAGED GOODS

PASTA, RICE & GRAINS

8 ounces broad egg noodles (Th)
1 cup quick-cooking barley (T)

BAKED GOODS

1 loaf pumpernickel bread, unsliced (W)
1 package (10 ounces) shortbread cookies (Th)

DRIED FRUIT & NUTS

½ cup golden raisins (M)
2 tablespoons sliced almonds (Th)

DESSERT & BAKING NEEDS

1 package (3.4 ounces) instant butterscotch pudding mix (Th)

WINE & SPIRITS

2 tablespoons dry sherry (M)
2 tablespoons dry sherry (W)

REFRIGERATED PRODUCTS

DAIRY

½ cup milk (M)
1 cup milk (W)
2 cups milk (Th)
1 cup half-and-half (M)
1 cup half-and-half (F)
Whipped cream for garnish (M)
Whipped cream for garnish (Th)
2 eggs (W)
4 eggs (F)

CHEESE

1 container (5 ounces) herbed cream cheese (W)
½ pound thinly sliced Swiss cheese (W)

JUICES

3 tablespoons orange juice (W)

DELI

4 slices bacon (F)

FROZEN GOODS

VEGETABLES

1 package (10 ounces) green peas and pearl onions (M)
1 package (10 ounces) cut green beans (T)

FRUIT

1 package (12 ounces) blueberries (F)

PASTRY

1 unbaked pie shell (F)

DESSERTS

1 pint boysenberry sorbet (T)
1 pint blueberry swirl ice cream (F)

MONDAY

Corn Biscayne

1 can (11 ounces) whole-kernel corn
1 jar (2 ounces) diced pimientos
1 can (15 ounces) cream-style corn
1 can (14 ounces) vegetable broth
1/2 teaspoon granulated sugar
1/2 teaspoon dried oregano
1 cup half-and-half
2 tablespoons dry sherry
Seasoning to taste

Mihami Beach

1 package (10 ounces) frozen green peas
   and pearl onions
1 clove garlic
1 can (8 ounces) button mushrooms
2 tablespoons honey
1 teaspoon dry mustard
2 lean cooked ham steaks (about 3/4 pound
   each)
2 tablespoons butter
Seasoning to taste

The Orange Bowl

1 medium head lettuce
2 medium oranges
1 small ripe avocado
4 scallions (green onions)
3 tablespoons olive oil
2 tablespoons lemon juice
1/2 teaspoon dried dill
Seasoning to taste

Cake Canaveral

1 cup flour
2/3 cup granulated sugar
1 tablespoon baking powder
1/2 cup golden raisins
1/2 cup milk
2 cups water
1 cup dark brown sugar
2 tablespoons butter
1 teaspoon orange extract
Whipped cream for garnish

EQUIPMENT

Medium covered
   saucepan
Medium saucepan
Large covered skillet
9 x 9-inch glass
   baking dish
Baking sheet
Large mixing bowl

3 small mixing bowls
Whisk
Pastry brush
Kitchen knives
Measuring cups and
   spoons
Cooking utensils

COUNTDOWN

1. Assemble the ingredients and the
   equipment.
2. Do Step 1 of *Mihami Beach*.
3. Do Steps 1–5 of *Cake Canaveral*.
4. Do Steps 2–4 of *Mihami Beach*.
5. Do Steps 1–4 of *The Orange Bowl*.
6. Do Steps 1–2 of *Corn Biscayne*.
7. Do Steps 5–7 of *Mihami Beach*.
8. Do Step 5 of *The Orange Bowl*.
9. Do Step 6 of *Cake Canaveral*.

MONDAY

Corn Biscayne

1 Drain the whole-kernel corn. Drain the pimientos.

2 In a medium saucepan, combine the whole-kernel corn, the pimientos, the cream-style corn, the broth, the sugar, the oregano, the half-and-half, and the sherry. Season to taste, cover, and simmer until hot.

Mihami Beach

1 Place the peas and onions in a small bowl of warm water to thaw.

2 Preheat the broiler.

3 Peel and mince the garlic. Drain the mushrooms.

4 In a small bowl, combine the honey and the mustard.

5 Lay the ham steaks on a baking sheet. Brush them lightly with the honey mixture and broil until lightly browned, about 4 minutes.

6 Melt the butter in a large skillet and sauté the garlic for 1 minute. Add the peas and onions and the mushrooms and season to taste. Cover the skillet, reduce the heat, and simmer until heated through, about 4 minutes.

7 Cut the ham steaks in half and top them with the vegetable mixture.

The Orange Bowl

1 Wash and dry the lettuce and arrange the leaves on individual salad plates.

2 Peel and slice the oranges and arrange the slices over the lettuce.

3 Halve, pit, peel, and slice the avocado. Rinse, trim, and chop the scallions. Arrange both over the oranges.

4 In a small bowl, whisk together the oil, the lemon juice, and the dill. Season to taste.

5 Drizzle the dressing over the salad.

Cake Canaveral

1 Preheat the oven to 350°F. Grease a 9 x 9-inch baking dish.

2 In a large bowl, combine the flour, the granulated sugar, and the baking powder. Add the raisins and the milk, stir to combine, and pour the mixture into the baking dish.

3 Bring the water and the brown sugar to a boil in a medium saucepan. Add the butter and stir until melted. Remove the saucepan from the heat and stir in the orange extract.

4 Slowly pour the syrup over the flour mixture in the baking dish. Do not mix.

5 Bake for 40 minutes.

6 Serve warm with a dollop of whipped cream for garnish.

TUESDAY

Dapper Snapper

1/4 cup fresh parsley (when chopped)
4 red snapper fillets (about 1 1/2 pounds)
Seasoning to taste
1 can (14 1/2 ounces) stewed tomatoes
1/2 teaspoon Italian seasoning
2 tablespoons butter
1/4 cup seasoned breadcrumbs

Gnarly Barley

1 small onion
1 clove garlic
1 small carrot
1 tablespoon vegetable oil
1 cup quick-cooking barley
1 can (14 ounces) chicken broth
1/4 cup water
Seasoning to taste

Bean There Done That

1 package (10 ounces) frozen cut green
  beans
1 stalk celery
2 tablespoons butter
1/2 teaspoon dried rosemary
1/4 cup hot water
Seasoning to taste

Mum Plums

1 can (15 ounces) purple plums
2 tablespoons powdered sugar
1 teaspoon ground nutmeg
1 pint boysenberry sorbet

EQUIPMENT

Medium covered saucepan	Whisk
Small saucepan	Vegetable peeler
Medium covered skillet	Vegetable grater
9 x 9-inch glass baking dish	Ice cream scoop
2 small mixing bowls	Kitchen knives
	Measuring cups and spoons
	Cooking utensils

COUNTDOWN

1. Assemble the ingredients and the equipment.
2. Do Steps 1–5 of Dapper Snapper.
3. Do Steps 1–3 of Gnarly Barley.
4. Do Step 6 of Dapper Snapper.
5. Do Steps 1–2 of Mum Plums.
6. Do Steps 1–4 of Bean There Done That.
7. Do Step 3 of Mum Plums.

TUESDAY

Dapper Snapper

1 Preheat the oven to 350°F.

2 Rinse, stem, and chop the parsley.

3 Rinse and pat dry the fish fillets and season them to taste.

4 Spread half the tomatoes in a 9 x 9-inch baking dish. Arrange the fish in a single layer over the tomatoes. Cover with the remaining tomatoes. Sprinkle with the Italian seasoning.

5 Melt the butter in a small saucepan. Blend in the parsley and the breadcrumbs and spread the mixture over the top.

6 Bake until the fish flakes easily with a fork, about 15 minutes.

Gnarly Barley

1 Peel and mince the onion. Peel and mince the garlic. Peel, trim, and grate the carrot.

2 Heat the oil in a medium saucepan and sauté the onion, the garlic, and the carrot for 3 minutes.

3 Add the barley and sauté it for 1 minute. Add the broth and the water and season to taste. Bring the mixture to a boil, cover, reduce the heat, and simmer until all the liquid is absorbed and the barley is tender, 20 to 25 minutes.

Bean There Done That

1 Set the green beans in a small bowl of warm water to thaw.

2 Rinse, trim, and chop the celery.

3 Melt the butter in a medium skillet and sauté the celery with the rosemary for 3 minutes. Add the thawed beans and sauté for 2 minutes.

4 Add the water and season to taste. Cover the skillet, reduce the heat, and let the vegetables simmer for 5 minutes.

Mum Plums

1 Drain, halve, pit, and chop the plums, reserving 2 tablespoons of the liquid.

2 In a small bowl, whisk together the powdered sugar, the nutmeg, and the reserved plum liquid. Fold in the plums.

3 Place scoops of sorbet in individual dessert bowls and top with the plum mixture.

WEDNESDAY

The Teutonic Tomato

1 small turnip
2 tablespoons butter
2 tablespoons flour
1 can (28 ounces) crushed tomatoes
1 can (14 ounces) onion beef broth
2 tablespoons dry sherry
1/2 teaspoon dried basil
1/2 teaspoon dried thyme
1 bay leaf
1 cup milk
Seasoning to taste

Scandinavian Sandwiches

2 eggs
1 container (5 ounces) herbed cream
   cheese
1/4 cup fresh dill (when chopped)
1 medium red onion
2 medium tomatoes
1 medium cucumber
1 medium green bell pepper
2 tablespoons capers
1 tin (2 ounces) anchovy fillets
1 loaf pumpernickel bread, unsliced
1/2 pound Swiss cheese, thinly sliced

A Celtic Compote

1 pint fresh strawberries
2 medium ripe pears
1 large banana
1/2 pound seedless green grapes
3 tablespoons orange juice
2 tablespoons lemon juice
2 tablespoons dark brown sugar

EQUIPMENT

Blender
Large covered
   saucepan
Small saucepan
2 large mixing bowls
Small mixing bowl
Whisk

Vegetable peeler
Vegetable grater
Kitchen knives
Measuring cups and
   spoons
Cooking utensils

COUNTDOWN

1. Assemble the ingredients and the equipment.
2. Do Steps 1–2 of *A Celtic Compote*.
3. Do Step 1 of *Scandinavian Sandwiches*.
4. Do Steps 1–2 of *The Teutonic Tomato*.
5. Do Steps 2–6 of *Scandinavian Sandwiches*.
6. Do Steps 3–4 of *The Teutonic Tomato*.

WEDNESDAY

The Teutonic Tomato

1 Peel, trim, and grate the turnip.

2 Melt the butter in a large saucepan and sauté the turnip for 3 minutes. Whisk in the flour and cook for 1 minute. Add the tomatoes, the broth, the sherry, the basil, the thyme, and the bay leaf. Bring the mixture to a boil, cover, reduce the heat, and simmer for 15 minutes, stirring frequently.

3 Remove and discard the bay leaf.

4 Place half the soup in a blender and process until pureed, about 1 minute. Remove the soup to a large bowl. Repeat with the remaining soup. Return the soup to the saucepan, blend in the milk, and season to taste. Simmer until heated through, 3 to 5 minutes. Do not let boil.

Scandinavian Sandwiches

1 Cover the eggs with water in a small saucepan. Bring the water to a boil and hard-cook the eggs, 10 to 12 minutes.

2 Set the cream cheese out to soften. Rinse, stem, and chop the dill. Peel and slice the onion. Rinse, stem, and slice the tomatoes. Peel, trim, and slice the cucumber. Rinse, trim, seed, and slice the bell pepper. Drain the capers. Drain and chop the anchovies.

3 Drain the eggs, rinse them in cold water, and set them in the freezer for 5 minutes to cool.

4 Slice the pumpernickel into 1½-inch-thick slices.

5 Spread the bread slices with the cream cheese. Sprinkle with the dill. Add the Swiss cheese and the vegetables.

6 Peel and slice the eggs and lay them over the vegetables. Top with the capers and the anchovies and serve open-faced.

A Celtic Compote

1 Rinse, dry, hull, and slice the berries. Peel, core, and slice the pears. Peel and chunk the banana. Rinse and stem the grapes. Combine the fruit in a large bowl.

2 In a small bowl, whisk together the orange and lemon juices and the brown sugar. Pour the mixture over the fruit, tossing to coat, and refrigerate until you are ready to serve.

THURSDAY

Porkfolio

1 small onion
1 large lemon
2 tablespoons vegetable oil
4 loin pork chops (about 1 1/2 pounds)
1 tablespoon dark brown sugar
1 tablespoon honey
1 tablespoon Worcestershire sauce
1 teaspoon cornstarch
2 tablespoons rice vinegar
Seasoning to taste
2 tablespoons sliced almonds

Using Your Noodle

8 ounces broad egg noodles
2 teaspoons saffron threads
2 tablespoons butter
1/2 tablespoon poppy seeds
1/2 teaspoon paprika

Double Entry

1/2 pound Chinese snow peas
1/2 pound fresh asparagus
1 small shallot
1 tablespoon butter
1 tablespoon vegetable oil
1/4 cup water
Seasoning to taste

You're Pudding Me On

1 package (3.4 ounces) instant butterscotch
   pudding mix
2 cups milk
1 package (10 ounces) shortbread cookies
Whipped cream for garnish
4 maraschino cherries for garnish

EQUIPMENT

Electric mixer	Whisk
Large saucepan	Citrus juicer
2 large covered skillets	Plastic bag
Colander	Kitchen knives
Medium mixing bowl	Measuring cups and spoons
Small mixing bowl	Cooking utensils

COUNTDOWN

1. Assemble the ingredients and the equipment.
2. Do Steps 1–2 of *You're Pudding Me On*.
3. Do Step 1 of *Using Your Noodle*.
4. Do Steps 1–3 of *Porkfolio*.
5. Do Step 1 of *Double Entry*.
6. Do Step 2 of *Using Your Noodle*.
7. Do Step 2 of *Double Entry*.
8. Do Step 4 of *Porkfolio*.
9. Do Step 3 of *Using Your Noodle*.
10. Do Step 3 of *You're Pudding Me On*.

THURSDAY

Porkfolio

1 Peel and thinly slice the onion. Cut the lemon in half. Juice one half and thinly slice the other half.

2 Heat the oil in a large skillet and sauté the onion for 1 minute. Add the pork chops and brown lightly, about 5 minutes per side.

3 In a small bowl, combine the lemon juice, the brown sugar, the honey, the Worcestershire sauce, the cornstarch, and the vinegar. Season to taste and pour the mixture over the chops. Cover the skillet, reduce the heat, and simmer until the chops are no longer pink inside, about 25 minutes.

4 During the last minute of cooking, top each chop with a lemon slice and a sprinkle of almonds.

Using Your Noodle

1 Bring water to a boil in a large saucepan.

2 Cook the noodles with the saffron until they are almost tender, 6 to 7 minutes.

3 Drain the noodles and return them to the saucepan. Toss them with the butter and the poppy seeds and sprinkle with the paprika.

Double Entry

1 Rinse and string the snow peas and cut them in half. Rinse and trim the asparagus, discard the tough ends, and cut the spears into 2-inch pieces. Peel and mince the shallot.

2 Melt the butter with the oil in a large skillet. Add the shallot and the asparagus and sauté for 3 minutes. Add the snow peas and the water, season to taste, and toss to combine. Bring to a boil, cover, remove from the heat, and let steam for 2 minutes.

You're Pudding Me On

1 Combine the pudding mix and the milk in a medium bowl and beat with an electric mixer for 2 minutes. Refrigerate until you are ready to serve.

2 Place the shortbread cookies in a plastic bag and crumble them.

3 Layer half the cookie crumbs in the bottom of individual dessert glasses. Add a layer of the pudding and repeat. Top each serving with dollops of whipped cream and a maraschino cherry.

FRIDAY

Deep In My Tart

4 slices bacon
1 large shallot
½ pound baby cooked shrimp
2 cans (6 ounces each) minced clams
1 frozen unbaked pie shell
4 eggs
2 tablespoons lemon juice
1 cup half-and-half
½ teaspoon ground nutmeg
Seasoning to taste

Man of La Muncha

¾ pound sugar-snap peas
2 stalks celery
1 tablespoon butter
½ teaspoon ground allspice

A Slaw Is Born

1 medium head red cabbage
3 scallions (green onions)
1 small cucumber
1 small ripe avocado
1 tablespoon lemon juice
¼ cup mayonnaise
3 tablespoons apple cider vinegar
1 teaspoon granulated sugar
1 teaspoon dried dill
Seasoning to taste

Birth of the Blueberries

1 package (12 ounces) frozen blueberries
1 large orange
1 tablespoon honey
½ teaspoon almond extract
½ teaspoon ground cinnamon
1 pint blueberry swirl ice cream

EQUIPMENT

Small covered
  saucepan
Medium skillet
Small skillet
Large mixing bowl
Medium mixing bowl
2 small mixing bowls
Whisk
Vegetable peeler

Vegetable grater
Citrus grater
Citrus juicer
Ice cream scoop
Kitchen knives
Measuring cups and
  spoons
Cooking utensils

COUNTDOWN

1. Assemble the ingredients and the equipment.
2. Do Step 1 of *Birth of the Blueberries*.
3. Do Steps 1–9 of *Deep In My Tart*.
4. Do Steps 1–4 of *A Slaw Is Born*.
5. Do Steps 1–2 of *Man of La Muncha*.
6. Do Steps 2–4 of *Birth of the Blueberries*.

FRIDAY

Deep In My Tart

1 Preheat the oven to 400°F.

2 Dice the bacon. Peel and mince the shallot. Chop the shrimp. Drain the clams.

3 Bake the pie shell for 7 minutes.

4 Cook the bacon in a small skillet until crisp, about 7 minutes.

5 Drain the bacon on paper towels.

6 Remove the pie shell and reduce the oven temperature to 375°F.

7 Sauté the shallot in the bacon drippings until soft, about 5 minutes.

8 Whip the eggs in a medium bowl. Add the lemon juice, the half-and-half, and the nutmeg. Season to taste, blend until smooth, and stir in the shrimp and the clams.

9 Scrape the shallot and the drippings into the shrimp mixture. Crumble the bacon and add it to the shrimp mixture. Pour the mixture into the pie shell and bake until a toothpick inserted in the center comes out clean, about 30 minutes.

Man of La Muncha

1 Rinse and string the snap peas. Rinse, trim, and slice the celery.

2 Melt the butter with the allspice in a medium skillet and sauté the snap peas and the celery until they are crisp-tender, about 3 minutes.

A Slaw Is Born

1 Rinse, trim, quarter, and grate the cabbage. Rinse, trim, and slice the scallions. Peel, trim, and chop the cucumber. Combine the ingredients in a large bowl.

2 Halve, pit, peel, and slice the avocado and sprinkle with the lemon juice to prevent browning.

3 In a small bowl, combine the mayonnaise, the vinegar, the sugar, and the dill. Season to taste and toss with the cabbage mixture. Refrigerate until you are ready to serve.

4 Garnish the slaw with the slices of avocado.

Birth of the Blueberries

1 Set the package of blueberries in a small bowl of warm water to thaw.

2 Grate 2 tablespoons of orange peel and juice the orange.

3 In a small saucepan, combine the thawed blueberries, the orange juice, the honey, the almond extract, and the cinnamon. Bring the mixture to a boil, remove from the heat, and cover to keep warm.

4 Place scoops of ice cream in individual dessert bowls. Top with the blueberry sauce and garnish with the orange peel.

SPRING

WEEK ONE

Monday

San Juan Salmon
The Space Noodle
Evergreens
Grand Coolee

Tuesday

Quiche and Tell
Smooching Salad
Hot Date

Wednesday

The Game Is Up
The Rice Squad
Handcuffs
Paroles

Thursday

Run Right Pasta
Snub the Salad
Cold Shoulder Pudding

Friday

Sole Custody
Joint Potatoes
Sidekick Slaw
Freeze Spirit

STAPLES

- ☐ Butter
- ☐ Flour
- ☐ Cream of tartar
- ☐ Granulated sugar
- ☐ Dark brown sugar
- ☐ Olive oil
- ☐ Vegetable oil
- ☐ Apple cider vinegar
- ☐ Red wine vinegar
- ☐ Rice vinegar
- ☐ White wine vinegar
- ☐ Lemon juice
- ☐ Dijon mustard
- ☐ Honey
- ☐ Mayonnaise
- ☐ Tabasco sauce
- ☐ White Worcestershire sauce
- ☐ Bay leaf
- ☐ Dried dill
- ☐ Dried tarragon
- ☐ Cayenne pepper
- ☐ Ground cloves
- ☐ Black pepper
- ☐ Poultry seasoning
- ☐ Red pepper flakes
- ☐ Salt

MEAT & POULTRY

1 pound lean cooked ham steak (T)

4 boneless, skinless chicken breast halves (about 1 1/2 pounds) (W)

FISH

4 salmon steaks (about 1 1/2 pounds) (M)

4 sole fillets (about 1 1/2 pounds) (F)

FRESH PRODUCE

VEGETABLES

1/2 pound yams (F)

1/2 pound sweet potatoes (F)

1/2 pound small new red potatoes (F)

1 large bunch broccoli (M)

1 pound green beans (T)

2 medium carrots (W)

2 stalks celery (T)

1 stalk celery (Th)

1 medium turnip (F)

1/2 pound mushrooms (T)

1 medium head cabbage (F)

1 small head lettuce (Th)

3 pounds tomatoes (Th)

2 medium orange bell peppers (W)

1 large red bell pepper (T)

2 medium leeks (F)

1 small onion (T)

1 large sweet onion (M)

1 small red onion (M)

1 medium shallot (W)

2 scallions (green onions) (Th)

1 clove garlic (T)

3 cloves garlic (Th)

HERBS

1 cup basil leaves (when chopped) (Th)

2 tablespoons chives (when chopped) (M)

2 tablespoons dill (when chopped) (F)

3 tablespoons parsley (when chopped) (M)

1/4 cup parsley (when chopped) (W)

FRUIT

2 large oranges (T)

1 large orange (F)

1 small lemon (M)

1 medium red apple (F)

CANS, JARS & BOTTLES

SOUPS

1 can (14 ounces) chicken broth (W)

VEGETABLES

1 can (14 ounces) whole artichoke hearts (T)

1 jar (3 ounces) sun-dried tomatoes (Th)

JUICES

1 can (6 ounces) tomato juice (Th)

1/2 cup grape juice (F)

DESSERT & BAKING NEEDS

1 jar (12 ounces) caramel topping (M)

PACKAGED GOODS

PASTA, RICE & GRAINS

8 ounces fine egg noodles (M)

1 pound fettuccine (Th)

1 cup long-grain white rice (W)

BAKED GOODS

2/3 cup vanilla wafers (when crumbled) (Th)

DRIED FRUIT & NUTS

1 package (5 ounces) apple chips (M)

1/2 cup dates (T)

1/2 cup raisins (W)

1/4 cup pine nuts (M)

1/2 cup sliced almonds (W)

1/2 cup walnut bits (Th)

DESSERT & BAKING NEEDS

1 package (3 ounces) cook-and-serve lemon pudding mix (Th)

1 package (7 ounces) peppermint candies (M)

1 cup mini-marshmallows (T)

1/4 cup flaked coconut (T)

WINE & SPIRITS

2 tablespoons dry white wine (M)

1/2 cup dry white wine (F)

1/4 cup dry red wine (Th)

2 tablespoons Grand Marnier (T)

REFRIGERATED PRODUCTS

DAIRY

1 cup milk (M)

1 1/2 cups milk (Th)

1 cup sour cream (T)

1 container (8 ounces) vanilla yogurt (F)

1 egg (M)

4 eggs (T)

2 eggs (Th)

2 eggs (F)

CHEESE

1 cup small-curd cottage cheese (T)

2 cups shredded Colby/Monterey Jack cheese (Th)

1 cup shredded mozzarella cheese (Th)

1 package (3 ounces) cream cheese (Th)

DELI

1 package (9 ounces) cinnamon rolls (W)

FROZEN GOODS

VEGETABLES

1 package (10 ounces) green peas (Th)

JUICES

1 can (12 ounces) lemonade concentrate (Th)

DESSERTS

1 pint vanilla ice cream (M)

San Juan Salmon

4 salmon steaks (about 1½ pounds)
1 small red onion
1 small lemon
3 tablespoons fresh parsley (when chopped)
1 bay leaf
3 tablespoons butter
1½ tablespoons flour
½ teaspoon dried dill
2 teaspoons Dijon mustard
1 cup milk
1 egg
2 tablespoons lemon juice
Seasoning to taste

The Space Noodle

2 tablespoons fresh chives (when chopped)
8 ounces fine egg noodles
2 tablespoons butter
½ teaspoon ground cloves

Evergreens

1 large bunch broccoli
1 large sweet onion
¼ cup pine nuts
½ cup water
1 tablespoon butter
1 tablespoon olive oil
2 tablespoons dry white wine
Seasoning to taste

Grand Coolee

1 pint vanilla ice cream
1 package (5 ounces) apple chips
1 package (7 ounces) peppermint candies
1 jar (12 ounces) caramel topping

EQUIPMENT

Large covered saucepan
2 large covered skillets
Medium skillet
Colander
Large mixing bowl
Medium mixing bowl

Small mixing bowl
Whisk
Mallet
Plastic bag
Kitchen knives
Measuring cups and spoons
Cooking utensils

COUNTDOWN

1. Assemble the ingredients and the equipment.
2. Do Steps 1–3 of *Grand Coolee*.
3. Do Step 1 of *San Juan Salmon*.
4. Do Steps 1–2 of *The Space Noodle*.
5. Do Steps 1–2 of *Evergreens*.
6. Do Steps 2–3 of *San Juan Salmon*.
7. Do Step 3 of *The Space Noodle*.
8. Do Step 3 of *Evergreens*.
9. Do Step 4 of *San Juan Salmon*.
10. Do Steps 4–5 of *The Space Noodle*.
11. Do Steps 4–5 of *Evergreens*.
12. Do Step 5 of *San Juan Salmon*.
13. Do Step 6 of *The Space Noodle*.
14. Do Step 4 of *Grand Coolee*.

MONDAY

San Juan Salmon

1 Rinse and pat dry the salmon steaks. Peel and thinly slice the onion. Thinly slice the lemon. Rinse, stem, and chop the parsley.

2 Melt the butter in a medium skillet. Stir in the flour, the dill, and the mustard. Gradually add the milk, whisking to keep smooth, and blend well.

3 Beat the egg in a small bowl. Stir in a teaspoon of the hot milk mixture to blend. Whisk the egg into the milk mixture and cook for 1 minute. Remove the skillet from the heat, blend in the lemon juice, and season to taste.

4 Place the salmon in a large skillet. Add the onion slices and half of the lemon slices. Add water to almost cover the fish. Add the bay leaf. Bring the water to a boil. Cover the skillet, reduce the heat, and simmer until the fish flakes easily with a fork, 5 to 7 minutes.

5 Garnish the salmon with the parsley and the remaining lemon slices and serve with the sauce.

The Space Noodle

1 Bring water to a boil in a large saucepan.

2 Rinse, trim, and chop the chives.

3 Cook the noodles until they are almost tender, about 3 minutes.

4 Drain the noodles.

5 Melt the butter with the cloves in the saucepan. Return the noodles and toss to coat and heat through. Cover to keep warm.

6 Sprinkle with the chives.

Evergreens

1 Rinse and trim the broccoli, discarding the tough ends, and cut into bite-sized florets. Peel and chop the onion.

2 Place the pine nuts in a large skillet and lightly toast them, 2 to 3 minutes. Remove and reserve.

3 Place the broccoli in the skillet. Add the water and bring to a boil. Cover the skillet and cook until the broccoli is crisp-tender, 6 to 8 minutes.

4 Drain the broccoli, remove, and reserve.

5 Melt the butter with the oil in the same skillet. Sauté the onion until soft, about 5 minutes. Return the broccoli and the pine nuts to the skillet. Add the wine, season to taste, and toss to combine and heat through. Remove from the heat and cover until you are ready to serve.

Grand Coolee

1 Set the ice cream out to soften. Lightly grease a medium bowl.

2 Place the apple chips and the peppermint candies in a plastic bag and crush them with a mallet.

3 In a large bowl, combine the softened ice cream and the crushed apple chips and peppermint candies and blend well. Spoon the mixture into the medium bowl, smoothing to even, and place the bowl in the freezer until you are ready to serve.

4 Invert the bowl onto a plate, remove the ice cream mold, and drizzle it with the caramel topping.

TUESDAY

Quiche and Tell

½ pound fresh mushrooms
1 small onion
1 pound lean cooked ham steak
1 can (14 ounces) whole artichoke hearts
2 tablespoons butter
4 eggs
1 cup sour cream
1 cup small-curd cottage cheese
¼ cup flour
⅛ teaspoon Tabasco sauce
Seasoning to taste
2 cups shredded Colby/Monterey Jack
  cheese

Smooching Salad

1 pound fresh green beans
1 large red bell pepper
2 stalks celery
1 clove garlic
¼ cup olive oil
3 tablespoons red wine vinegar
½ teaspoon dried dill
Seasoning to taste

Hot Date

2 large oranges
½ cup dates
2 tablespoons Grand Marnier
¼ cup flaked coconut
½ cup water
1 cup mini-marshmallows

EQUIPMENT

Medium covered saucepan	2 large mixing bowls
Medium skillet	Small mixing bowl
9 x 9-inch glass baking dish	Whisk
Pie plate	Kitchen knives
Steamer insert	Measuring cups and spoons
	Cooking utensils

COUNTDOWN

1. Assemble the ingredients and the equipment.
2. Do Steps 1–5 of *Quiche and Tell*.
3. Do Steps 1–3 of *Hot Date*.
4. Do Steps 1–5 of *Smooching Salad*.
5. Do Step 6 of *Quiche and Tell*.
6. Do Step 6 of *Smooching Salad*.
7. Do Step 4 of *Hot Date*.

TUESDAY

Quiche and Tell

1 Preheat the oven to 350°F. Grease a pie plate.

2 Rinse, pat dry, trim, and slice the mushrooms. Peel and mince the onion. Dice the ham. Drain and quarter the artichokes.

3 Melt the butter in a medium skillet. Sauté the mushrooms and the onion until the onion is soft and the mushrooms are lightly browned, about 5 minutes. Drain on paper towels.

4 Whip the eggs in a large bowl. Add the sour cream, the cottage cheese, and the flour. Blend in the Tabasco sauce and season to taste. Fold in the mushrooms, the onion, the ham, the artichokes, and the Colby/Monterey Jack cheese.

5 Pour the mixture into the pie plate and bake until a knife inserted in the center comes out clean, 35 to 40 minutes.

6 Let the quiche stand for 5 minutes before cutting into wedges.

Smooching Salad

1 Bring water to a boil in a medium saucepan.

2 Rinse and trim the green beans and cut them into 2-inch lengths. Arrange the beans in a steamer insert, place the insert in the saucepan, cover, and cook until crisp-tender, 6 to 8 minutes.

3 Rinse, trim, seed, and chop the bell pepper. Rinse, trim, and chop the celery. Combine the ingredients in a large bowl.

4 Peel and mince the garlic. In a small bowl, whisk together the garlic, the oil, the vinegar, and the dill and season to taste.

5 Drain the beans and rinse them under cold water to cool. Add them to the bowl.

6 Toss the salad with the dressing.

Hot Date

1 Cut the oranges in half. Scoop out the orange pulp and place it in a medium bowl. Cut a zigzag pattern around the edges of the shells and reserve.

2 Chop the pulp. Chop the dates. Add the dates to the orange pulp and combine the mixture with the Grand Marnier and the coconut.

3 Spoon the mixture into the orange shells and place the shells in an 9 x 9-inch baking dish. Dribble the water around the shells, place the dish in the oven, and bake at 350°F for 15 minutes.

4 Sprinkle the marshmallows over the orange shells and bake until golden, about 5 minutes more.

WEDNESDAY

The Game Is Up

4 boneless, skinless chicken breast halves
    (about 1 1/2 pounds)
1 medium shallot
1/2 cup flour
1/2 teaspoon poultry seasoning
Seasoning to taste
2 tablespoons butter
1 tablespoon vegetable oil
1 cup white wine vinegar
1 teaspoon dark brown sugar

The Rice Squad

1 cup long-grain white rice
1 can (14 ounces) chicken broth
1/2 cup water
Seasoning to taste
1/4 cup fresh parsley (when chopped)

Handcuffs

2 medium carrots
2 medium orange bell peppers
2 tablespoons vegetable oil
1/4 teaspoon white Worcestershire sauce
Seasoning to taste
1/4 cup water

Paroles

3 tablespoons butter
1/2 cup sliced almonds
1 package (9 ounces) refrigerated
    cinnamon rolls
1/2 cup granulated sugar
1/2 cup raisins

EQUIPMENT

Double boiler	Pastry brush
Large covered skillet	Mallet
Medium covered skillet	Plastic bag
Baking sheet	Kitchen knives
Large shallow bowl	Measuring cups and spoons
Vegetable peeler	Cooking utensils

COUNTDOWN

1. Assemble the ingredients and the equipment.
2. Do Steps 1–3 of *The Rice Squad.*
3. Do Step 1 of *Handcuffs.*
4. Do Steps 1–6 of *The Game Is Up.*
5. Do Steps 1–4 of *Paroles.*
6. Do Steps 2–3 of *Handcuffs.*
7. Do Step 4 of *The Rice Squad.*
8. Do Step 7 of *The Game Is Up.*

WEDNESDAY

The Game Is Up

1 Rinse and pat dry the chicken breasts. Peel and mince the shallot.

2 Combine the flour and the poultry seasoning in a large shallow bowl and season to taste. Lightly dredge the chicken in the seasoned flour.

3 Melt the butter with the oil in a large skillet. Sauté the chicken until lightly browned, about 5 minutes per side.

4 Remove the chicken and reserve.

5 Add the shallot to the skillet and sauté for 5 minutes.

6 Add the vinegar and deglaze the skillet. Blend in the brown sugar. Bring the mixture to a boil and cook for 1 minute. Return the chicken, cover, reduce the heat, and simmer until the chicken is tender and cooked through, 10 to 15 minutes.

7 Top the chicken with the sauce.

The Rice Squad

1 Bring water to a boil in the bottom of a double boiler.

2 In the top of the double boiler, combine the rice, the broth, and the ½ cup water. Season to taste, cover, and reduce the heat. Simmer until the liquid is absorbed and the rice is tender, 30 to 40 minutes.

3 Rinse, stem, and chop the parsley.

4 Fluff the rice with a fork and sprinkle with the parsley.

Handcuffs

1 Peel, trim, and thinly slice the carrots. Rinse, trim, seed, and thinly slice the bell peppers.

2 Heat the oil in a medium skillet and sauté the carrots and the bell peppers for 2 minutes.

3 Blend in the Worcestershire sauce and season to taste. Add the water, cover the skillet, remove it from the heat, and let the vegetables steam for 5 minutes.

Paroles

1 Preheat the oven to 400°F.

2 Melt the butter. Place the almonds in a plastic bag and crush with a mallet.

3 Separate and unroll the cinnamon rolls. Brush the insides with the butter. Sprinkle with the sugar, the almonds, and the raisins. Roll the cinnamon rolls back up and arrange them on a baking sheet.

4 Bake until golden and bubbly, about 10 minutes.

THURSDAY

Run Right Pasta

3 pounds tomatoes
3 cloves garlic
1 cup fresh basil leaves (when chopped)
1 jar (3 ounces) sun-dried tomatoes
3 tablespoons olive oil
1/4 cup dry red wine
1 can (6 ounces) tomato juice
1/2 teaspoon red pepper flakes
Seasoning to taste
1 pound fettuccine
1 cup shredded mozzarella cheese

Snub the Salad

1 package (10 ounces) frozen green peas
1 small head lettuce
2 scallions (green onions)
1 stalk celery
3 tablespoons vegetable oil
2 tablespoons rice vinegar
1/2 teaspoon dark brown sugar
Seasoning to taste
1/2 cup walnut bits

Cold Shoulder Pudding

1 package (3 ounces) cream cheese
1 can (12 ounces) frozen lemonade
  concentrate
2/3 cup vanilla wafers (when crumbled)
2 eggs
1 1/2 cups milk
2 tablespoons butter
1/4 teaspoon cream of tartar
1/4 cup granulated sugar
1 package (3 ounces) cook-and-serve
  lemon pudding mix

EQUIPMENT

Electric mixer
Stockpot
Large saucepan
Small saucepan
Large skillet
Baking sheet
Colander
Medium mixing bowl

2 small mixing bowls
Whisk
Plastic bag
Kitchen knives
Measuring cups and
  spoons
Cooking utensils

COUNTDOWN

1. Assemble the ingredients and the equipment.
2. Do Steps 1–6 of Cold Shoulder Pudding.
3. Do Steps 1–4 of Snub the Salad.
4. Do Steps 1–7 of Run Right Pasta.
5. Do Step 5 of Snub the Salad.
6. Do Step 7 of Cold Shoulder Pudding.

THURSDAY

Run Right Pasta

1 Preheat the oven to 400°F.

2 Bring water to a boil in a stockpot.

3 Rinse and stem the tomatoes and cut them into wedges. Peel and mince the garlic. Rinse, stem, and chop the basil. Drain the sun-dried tomatoes.

4 Brush a baking sheet with 1½ tablespoons of the oil. Spread the tomato wedges on the sheet and roast them until the skins are lightly browned, about 10 minutes.

5 Heat the remaining 1½ tablespoons oil in a large skillet. Add the garlic, the roasted tomatoes, and the sun-dried tomatoes. Add the basil. Stir in the wine and the tomato juice. Add the pepper flakes and season to taste. Cook until the liquid is slightly reduced, about 7 minutes.

6 Cook the fettuccine until it is almost tender, 2 to 3 minutes if you are using fresh pasta, 6 to 7 minutes if you are using dry pasta.

7 Drain the pasta and toss with the sauce. Sprinkle with the cheese.

Snub the Salad

1 Set the peas in a small bowl of warm water to thaw.

2 Wash and dry the lettuce and arrange the leaves on individual salad plates to form cups.

3 Rinse, trim, and chop the scallions. Rinse, trim, and chop the celery. Rinse the peas. Combine the ingredients in a medium bowl.

4 In a small bowl, whisk together the oil, the vinegar, and the brown sugar. Season to taste and toss with the pea mixture.

5 Pile the pea mixture in the center of each lettuce cup and sprinkle with the nuts.

Cold Shoulder Pudding

1 Set the cream cheese out to soften. Set the lemonade concentrate out to thaw.

2 Place the cookies in a plastic bag and crumble them.

3 Separate the eggs, placing the whites in a medium bowl. Combine the yolks with the milk in a large saucepan.

4 Melt the butter in a small saucepan. Blend in the cookie crumbs.

5 Beat the egg whites with the cream of tartar until soft peaks form. Gradually add the sugar and beat until very stiff and glossy, about 5 minutes.

6 Add the pudding mix to the milk mixture and stir to blend. Cook, stirring, until the mixture comes to a boil. Add the softened cream cheese and whisk to combine. Stir in the lemonade. Remove the saucepan from the heat and let it stand for 10 minutes. Fold in the egg whites. Refrigerate until you are ready to serve.

7 Place half of the cookie crumb mixture in individual dessert glasses. Add the pudding and top with the remaining crumbs.

FRIDAY

Sole Custody

4 sole fillets (about 1 1/2 pounds)
2 medium leeks
1 large orange
1/2 cup dry white wine
1 teaspoon dried tarragon
Seasoning to taste
2 egg yolks
2 tablespoons butter

Joint Potatoes

1/2 pound yams
1/2 pound sweet potatoes
1/2 pound small new red potatoes
2 tablespoons fresh dill (when chopped)
2 tablespoons butter
2 tablespoons vegetable oil
1/4 teaspoon cayenne pepper
Seasoning to taste

Sidekick Slaw

1 medium head cabbage
1 medium turnip
1 medium red apple
3 tablespoons mayonnaise
2 tablespoons apple cider vinegar
1/4 teaspoon white Worcestershire sauce
1 teaspoon granulated sugar
Seasoning to taste

Freeze Spirit

2 egg whites
1/4 teaspoon cream of tartar
1 container (8 ounces) vanilla yogurt
1/2 cup grape juice
1/4 cup honey
1 tablespoon lemon juice
1/8 teaspoon salt

EQUIPMENT

Electric mixer
Medium skillet
Large saucepan
Large skillet
9 x 13-inch glass baking dish
2 large mixing bowls
Medium mixing bowl
Small mixing bowl
Whisk

Vegetable brush
Vegetable peeler
Vegetable grater
Citrus grater
Citrus juicer
Aluminum foil
Kitchen knives
Measuring cups and spoons
Cooking utensils

COUNTDOWN

1. Assemble the ingredients and the equipment.
2. Do Steps 1–3 of *Freeze Spirit*.
3. Do Steps 1–2 of *Sidekick Slaw*.
4. Do Steps 1–3 of *Joint Potatoes*.
5. Do Steps 1–7 of *Sole Custody*.
6. Do Steps 4–5 of *Joint Potatoes*.
7. Do Step 8 of *Sole Custody*.

FRIDAY

RECIPES

Sole Custody

1 Preheat the oven to 350°F.

2 Rinse the fish fillets and pat them dry.

3 Thoroughly wash the leeks, discarding the root ends and the tough outer leaves, and thinly slice them.

4 Grate 2 tablespoons of orange peel and juice the orange.

5 Place half the leeks in the bottom of a 9 x 13-inch baking dish. Place the fillets on top. Add the remaining leeks.

6 Drizzle the orange juice and the wine over the fish. Sprinkle with the orange peel and the tarragon and season to taste.

7 Cover the dish with aluminum foil and bake until the fish is opaque and flakes easily with a fork, about 10 minutes.

8 Remove the fish and keep it warm. Pour the liquid from the baking dish into a medium skillet. Beat in the reserved egg yolks. Bring the mixture to a boil and reduce it slightly, 3 to 4 minutes. Add the butter and cook for 2 minutes more. To serve, pour the sauce over the fish.

Joint Potatoes

1 Bring water to a boil in a large saucepan.

2 Scrub and quarter the yams. Scrub and quarter the sweet potatoes. Scrub the new potatoes. Rinse, stem, and chop the dill.

3 Cook the potatoes until they are just tender, about 10 minutes.

4 Drain the potatoes. Peel and slice the yams.

Peel and slice the sweet potatoes. Cut the new potatoes in half.

5 Melt the butter with the oil in a large skillet. Blend in the dill and the cayenne pepper. Sauté the potatoes until they are crisp, about 5 minutes. Season to taste.

Sidekick Slaw

1 Rinse, trim, quarter, and grate the cabbage. Peel, trim, and grate the turnip. Rinse, core, and chop the apple. Combine the ingredients in a large bowl.

2 In a small bowl, combine the mayonnaise, the vinegar, the Worcestershire sauce, and the sugar and season to taste. Toss the cabbage mixture with the dressing and refrigerate until you are ready to serve.

Freeze Spirit

1 Separate the eggs, reserving the yolks for use with the fish. In a medium bowl, beat the egg whites with the cream of tartar until very stiff, about 5 minutes.

2 In a large bowl, combine the yogurt, the grape juice, the honey, the lemon juice, and the salt. Whip until thick. Fold in the egg whites.

3 Spoon the mixture into dessert glasses and freeze until set, about 30 minutes.

WEEK TWO

Monday

Pretty In Pink
Head of the Class
Biscuit Beaus
Can't Elope

Tuesday

Porky and Bess
I Say Potato
I Got Plenty of Nuttin'
Rhapsody In Blue

Wednesday

Shell We Dance?
Tomato Two-Step
Cakewalk

Thursday

Minneapolis
Go For Beans
Mini-Soda Biscuits
Moccasin Pie

Friday

Smart Soup
Egghead
Wise Fries
Bright Berries

STAPLES

- ☐ Butter
- ☐ Vegetable shortening
- ☐ Flour
- ☐ Bisquick
- ☐ Baking soda
- ☐ Cornstarch
- ☐ Cream of tartar
- ☐ Granulated sugar
- ☐ Dark brown sugar
- ☐ Powdered sugar
- ☐ Multicolored sprinkles
- ☐ Olive oil
- ☐ Vegetable oil
- ☐ Lemon juice
- ☐ Dijon mustard
- ☐ White Worcestershire sauce
- ☐ Grated Parmesan cheese
- ☐ Chicken bouillon cube
- ☐ Dried basil
- ☐ Bay leaf
- ☐ Dried marjoram
- ☐ Dried oregano
- ☐ Ground allspice
- ☐ Whole allspice
- ☐ Ground cinnamon
- ☐ Ground cumin
- ☐ Ground nutmeg
- ☐ Black pepper
- ☐ Salt
- ☐ Lemon extract
- ☐ Rum extract
- ☐ Vanilla extract

MEAT & POULTRY

- 4 loin pork chops (about 1½ pounds) (T)
- 4 boneless, skinless chicken breast halves (about 1½ pounds) (Th)

FISH

- 1 pound medium shrimp, shelled and deveined (M)

FRESH PRODUCE

VEGETABLES

- 1½ pounds yellow potatoes (T)
- 1½ pounds baking potatoes (F)
- 1 medium head cauliflower (M)
- 1 small bunch broccoli (W)
- 1 pound green beans (Th)
- 1 medium zucchini (F)
- 1 medium yellow zucchini (F)
- 1 medium carrot (F)
- 2 stalks celery (T)
- 2 stalks celery (F)
- 1 medium parsnip (F)
- 1 package (16 ounces) spinach (T)
- 4 medium tomatoes (W)
- 2 medium tomatoes (F)
- 1 pint cherry tomatoes (M)
- 1 large green bell pepper (T)
- 1 large orange bell pepper (W)
- 1 large red bell pepper (W)
- 1 large yellow bell pepper (W)
- 1 large leek (F)
- 2 medium onions (Th)
- 1 small onion (M)
- 1 small onion (W)
- 1 small red onion (F)
- 1 small shallot (T)
- 2 scallions (green onions) (F)
- 2 cloves garlic (M)
- 3 cloves garlic (W)

HERBS

- ½ cup basil leaves (when chopped) (W)
- 3 tablespoons chives (when chopped) (M)
- 2 tablespoons dill (when chopped) (Th)
- 2 tablespoons parsley (when chopped) (M)
- 1 cup parsley (when chopped) (W)
- 3 tablespoons tarragon (when chopped) (W)
- 3 tablespoons thyme (when chopped) (W)

FRUIT

- 2 medium ripe cantaloupe melons (M)
- 3 small tart apples (Th)
- 1 medium banana (M)
- ½ pound seedless red grapes (M)
- 1 pint strawberries (F)

CANS, JARS & BOTTLES

SOUPS

- 2 cans (14 ounces each) vegetable broth (F)

VEGETABLES

- 1 can (11 ounces) whole-kernel corn (Th)

SAUCES

- 1 can (15 ounces) tomato sauce (T)
- 1 jar (16 ounces) Alfredo mushroom sauce (W)

FRUIT

- 1 can (8 ounces) pineapple chunks (T)

JUICES

- 1 cup clam juice (M)
- 1 cup apple juice (Th)
- 1 cup V-8 juice (F)

CONDIMENTS

- 1 jar (10 ounces) roasted red peppers (M)

PACKAGED GOODS

PASTA, RICE & GRAINS

- 12 ounces fusilli (M)
- 1 pound medium pasta shells (W)

BAKED GOODS

- 1 loaf Italian bread (W)
- 1 angel food loaf cake (W)

DRIED FRUIT & NUTS

- ¼ cup pine nuts (T)

DESSERT & BAKING NEEDS

- 1 package (3.4 ounces) instant lemon pudding mix (W)
- 1 package (3.4 ounces) instant vanilla pudding mix (F)
- 8 ounces chocolate chips (Th)

WINE & SPIRITS

- ¼ cup dry sherry (F)

REFRIGERATED PRODUCTS

DAIRY

- 1 cup milk (W)
- 1 cup milk (Th)
- 2 cups milk (F)
- ⅔ cup buttermilk (M)
- 1 cup half-and-half (W)
- 2 tablespoons half-and-half (F)
- ½ cup sour cream (T)
- Whipped cream for garnish (T)
- Whipped cream for garnish (W)
- 2 eggs (Th)
- 9 eggs (F)

CHEESE

- 1 package (3 ounces) cream cheese (T)
- ¼ cup shredded mozzarella cheese (W)

FROZEN GOODS

FRUIT

- 1 package (12 ounces) blueberries (T)

PASTRY

- 1 unbaked pie shell (Th)

DESSERTS

- 1 pint boysenberry sorbet (T)

MONDAY

Pretty In Pink

2 cloves garlic
1 pint cherry tomatoes
1 small onion
1 pound medium shrimp, shelled and
  deveined
1 jar (10 ounces) roasted red peppers
12 ounces fusilli
2 tablespoons olive oil
1 cup clam juice
1 teaspoon dried oregano
1 teaspoon dried basil
Seasoning to taste
$^1/_2$ cup grated Parmesan cheese

Head of the Class

1 medium head cauliflower
2 tablespoons fresh parsley (when
  chopped)
2 tablespoons butter
Seasoning to taste

Biscuit Beaus

2 tablespoons butter
3 tablespoons fresh chives (when chopped)
2$^1/_4$ cups Bisquick
$^2/_3$ cup buttermilk

Can't Elope

2 medium ripe cantaloupe melons
$^1/_2$ pound seedless red grapes
1 medium banana
1$^1/_2$ tablespoons lemon juice
2 teaspoons granulated sugar
$^1/_2$ teaspoon ground cinnamon
1 tablespoon powdered sugar for garnish

EQUIPMENT

Blender	2 medium mixing
Stockpot	bowls
Medium covered	Small mixing bowl
saucepan	Whisk
Large skillet	Biscuit cutter
Baking sheet	Kitchen knives
Steamer insert	Measuring cups or
Breadboard	spoons
Colander	Cooking utensils

COUNTDOWN

1. Assemble the ingredients and the equipment.
2. Do Steps 1–3 of Can't Elope.
3. Do Step 1 of Pretty In Pink.
4. Do Steps 1–5 of Biscuit Beaus.
5. Do Steps 2–3 of Pretty In Pink.
6. Do Steps 1–3 of Head of the Class.
7. Do Step 6 of Biscuit Beaus.
8. Do Steps 4–5 of Pretty In Pink.
9. Do Step 7 of Biscuit Beaus.
10. Do Step 4 of Head of the Class.
11. Do Step 6 of Pretty In Pink.
12. Do Step 4 of Can't Elope.

MONDAY

Pretty In Pink

1 Bring water to a boil in a stockpot.

2 Peel and mince the garlic. Rinse and halve the tomatoes. Peel and chop the onion. Rinse and pat dry the shrimp.

3 Place the roasted red peppers and their juice in a blender and puree.

4 Cook the fusilli until it is almost tender, 8 to 10 minutes.

5 Heat the oil in a large skillet. Sauté the garlic and the onion until the onion is soft, about 5 minutes. Add the shrimp and sauté until they turn bright pink, about 3 minutes. Add the tomatoes, the pureed peppers, the clam juice, the oregano, and the basil. Season to taste, bring the mixture to a simmer, and cook until heated through, about 3 minutes.

6 Drain the pasta and return it to the stockpot. Add the shrimp mixture and toss to coat. Sprinkle with the Parmesan cheese.

Head of the Class

1 Rinse and trim the cauliflower and cut into bite-sized florets. Rinse, stem, and chop the parsley.

2 Bring water to a boil in a medium saucepan.

3 Arrange the cauliflower in a steamer insert and place the insert in the saucepan. Cover and steam until the cauliflower is crisp-tender, about 7 minutes.

4 Drain the cauliflower. Melt the butter in the saucepan, add the cauliflower and the parsley, season to taste, and toss to coat. Cover to keep warm.

Biscuit Beaus

1 Grease a baking sheet. Flour a breadboard.

2 Melt the butter.

3 Rinse, trim, and chop the chives.

4 In a medium bowl, combine the butter, the chives, the Bisquick, and the buttermilk. Blend well.

5 Turn the mixture out onto the breadboard. Knead gently 8 to 10 times to make a soft dough. Pat the dough out to a ¾-inch thickness and cut with a biscuit cutter. Place the biscuits on the baking sheet.

6 Preheat the oven to 450°F.

7 Bake the biscuits until golden, 8 to 10 minutes.

Can't Elope

1 Cut each cantaloupe in half and remove the seeds. Rinse and stem the grapes. Peel and slice the banana.

2 Combine the grapes and the banana in a medium bowl.

3 In a small bowl, whisk together the lemon juice, the granulated sugar, and the cinnamon. Toss with the grapes and the banana and spoon the mixture into the cantaloupe halves. Chill until ready to serve.

4 Dust the fruit with the powdered sugar.

TUESDAY

Porky and Bess

4 loin pork chops (about 1 1/2 pounds)
1 tablespoon butter
2 tablespoons olive oil
1 can (15 ounces) tomato sauce
1 tablespoon Dijon mustard
1 tablespoon dark brown sugar
1 teaspoon ground cumin
Seasoning to taste

I Say Potato

1 package (3 ounces) cream cheese
1 1/2 pounds yellow potatoes
1/2 cup sour cream
1/4 teaspoon ground nutmeg
Seasoning to taste

I Got Plenty of Nuttin'

1 small shallot
1 large green bell pepper
2 stalks celery
1 package (16 ounces) fresh spinach
2 tablespoons butter
1/2 teaspoon white Worcestershire sauce
Seasoning to taste
1/4 cup pine nuts

Rhapsody In Blue

1 package (12 ounces) frozen blueberries
1 can (8 ounces) pineapple chunks
2 teaspoons cornstarch
1 pint boysenberry sorbet
Whipped cream for garnish
Multicolored sprinkles for garnish

EQUIPMENT

Electric mixer	Vegetable peeler
Large saucepan	Ice cream scoop
Medium saucepan	Plastic wrap
2 large covered skillets	Kitchen knives
Medium mixing bowl	Measuring cups and spoons
2 small mixing bowls	Cooking utensils

COUNTDOWN

1. Assemble the ingredients and the equipment.
2. Do Step 1 of *Rhapsody In Blue.*
3. Do Steps 1–3 of *Porky and Bess.*
4. Do Steps 2–3 of *Rhapsody In Blue.*
5. Do Steps 1–3 of *I Say Potato.*
6. Do Steps 1–2 of *I Got Plenty of Nuttin'.*
7. Do Step 4 of *I Say Potato.*
8. Do Steps 4–5 of *Rhapsody In Blue.*

TUESDAY

Porky and Bess

1 Rinse and pat dry the pork chops and trim off any excess fat.

2 Melt the butter with the oil in a large skillet. Sauté the chops until they are browned, 5 to 6 minutes per side.

3 In a small bowl, blend together the tomato sauce, the mustard, the brown sugar, and the cumin. Add to the skillet. Season to taste, cover, reduce the heat, and simmer until the pork is tender and white throughout, 25 to 30 minutes.

I Say Potato

1 Cut the cream cheese into cubes and set out to soften.

2 Bring water to a boil in a large saucepan.

3 Peel and cube the potatoes, then boil them until they are tender, 10 to 15 minutes.

4 Drain the potatoes and return them to the saucepan. Shake the pan over low heat until the potatoes are dry. Remove from the heat, add the cream cheese, and beat to blend. Add the sour cream and the nutmeg and season to taste. Beat until the potatoes are creamy and smooth.

I Got Plenty of Nuttin'

1 Peel and mince the shallot. Rinse, trim, seed, and julienne the bell pepper. Rinse, trim, and slice the celery. Rinse, pat dry, and stem the spinach.

2 Melt the butter in a large skillet and sauté the shallot for 2 minutes. Add the bell pepper and the celery and sauté for 2 minutes more. Blend in the Worcestershire sauce. Add the spinach, tossing to combine. Season to taste, cover the skillet, remove it from the heat, and let the vegetables steam for 5 minutes.

3 Sprinkle with the pine nuts.

Rhapsody In Blue

1 Set the blueberries in a small bowl of warm water to thaw.

2 Drain the pineapple, reserving the liquid in a medium saucepan. Combine the pineapple and the thawed blueberries in a medium bowl. Cover with plastic wrap and refrigerate until you are ready to use.

3 Add the cornstarch to the reserved pineapple liquid and bring the mixture to a boil. Cook until thick and clear, about 2 minutes. Remove from the heat and set aside.

4 Place scoops of sorbet in individual dessert glasses. Spoon half of the fruit over the sorbet. Add another scoop of sorbet, top with the remaining fruit, and spoon the sauce over the fruit.

5 Garnish with a dollop of whipped cream and sprinkles.

WEDNESDAY

Shell We Dance?

3 cloves garlic
1 small bunch broccoli
1 large orange bell pepper
1 large red bell pepper
1 large yellow bell pepper
1 cup fresh parsley (when chopped)
3 tablespoons fresh tarragon (when chopped)
3 tablespoons fresh thyme (when chopped)
1 pound medium pasta shells
3 tablespoons butter
1 jar (16 ounces) Alfredo mushroom sauce
Seasoning to taste

Tomato Two-Step

1 loaf Italian bread
1 small onion
4 medium tomatoes
1/2 cup fresh basil leaves (when chopped)
1/4 cup olive oil
1/4 cup shredded mozzarella cheese
Seasoning to taste

Cakewalk

1 angel food loaf cake
1 package (3.4 ounces) instant lemon pudding mix
1 cup half-and-half
1 cup milk
1 teaspoon lemon extract
Whipped cream for garnish

EQUIPMENT

Electric mixer
Stockpot
Medium skillet
Baking sheet
Colander
Large mixing bowl

Small mixing bowl
Pastry brush
Kitchen knives
Measuring cups and spoons
Cooking utensils

COUNTDOWN

1. Assemble the ingredients and the equipment.
2. Do Steps 1–2 of *Cakewalk*.
3. Do Step 1 of *Shell We Dance?*
4. Do Steps 1–5 of *Tomato Two-Step*.
5. Do Step 2 of *Shell We Dance?*
6. Do Step 6 of *Tomato Two-Step*.
7. Do Steps 3–5 of *Shell We Dance?*
8. Do Step 3 of *Cakewalk*.

WEDNESDAY

Shell We Dance?

1 Bring water to a boil in a stockpot.

2 Peel and mince the garlic. Rinse and trim the broccoli, discarding the tough ends, and cut into bite-sized florets. Rinse, trim, seed, and chop the bell peppers. Rinse, stem, and chop the parsley. Rinse, stem, and chop the tarragon. Rinse, stem, and chop the thyme.

3 Cook the pasta shells until almost tender, 8 to 10 minutes.

4 Melt the butter in a medium skillet and sauté the garlic for 2 minutes. Add the parsley, the tarragon, and the thyme. Blend in the Alfredo sauce, season to taste, and heat through.

5 Drain the pasta, return it to the stockpot, and toss with the sauce.

Tomato Two-Step

1 Cut the bread in half and then into quarters.

2 Peel and mince the onion. Rinse, core, and chop the tomatoes. Rinse, stem, and chop the basil.

3 Brush the cut sides of the bread with the oil.

4 In a small bowl, combine the onion, the tomatoes, the basil, and the cheese. Season to taste. Spread the mixture on the bread quarters.

5 Preheat the oven to 350°F.

6 Place the bread on a baking sheet and bake until hot and bubbly, about 10 minutes.

Cakewalk

1 Tear the cake into 1-inch cubes.

2 In a large bowl, combine the pudding mix, the half-and-half, the milk, and the lemon extract. Beat until the mixture is well blended and the pudding begins to thicken, about 2 minutes. Fold the cake cubes into the pudding and pour the mixture into individual dessert glasses. Chill until you are ready to serve.

3 Garnish with dollops of whipped cream.

THURSDAY

Minneapolis

2 medium onions
4 boneless, skinless chicken breast halves
(about 1 1/2 pounds)
2 tablespoons butter
1 cup apple juice
1/4 teaspoon ground cinnamon
1/4 teaspoon ground allspice
Seasoning to taste
3 small tart apples

Go For Beans

1 pound fresh green beans
1 can (11 ounces) whole-kernel corn
2 tablespoons fresh dill (when chopped)
Seasoning to taste

Mini-Soda Biscuits

2 cups flour
1/2 teaspoon baking soda
1 teaspoon cream of tartar
1/2 teaspoon salt
1/4 cup vegetable shortening
1 cup milk

Moccasin Pie

1 unbaked pie shell
8 tablespoons butter
2 eggs
3/4 cup granulated sugar
1/2 cup flour
1 teaspoon vanilla extract
8 ounces chocolate chips

EQUIPMENT

Electric mixer	Large mixing bowl
Medium covered saucepan	Medium mixing bowl
Small saucepan	Vegetable peeler
Large covered skillet	Pastry blender
Steamer insert	Small biscuit cutter
1 pie plate	Kitchen knives
Baking sheet	Measuring cups and spoons
Breadboard	Cooking utensils

COUNTDOWN

1. Assemble the ingredients and the equipment.
2. Do Steps 1–5 of *Moccasin Pie*.
3. Do Steps 1–4 of *Minneapolis*.
4. Do Steps 1–4 of *Mini-Soda Biscuits*.
5. Do Steps 1–3 of *Go For Beans*.
6. Do Steps 5–6 of *Minneapolis*.
7. Do Step 4 of *Go For Beans*.

THURSDAY

Minneapolis

1 Peel and thinly slice the onions.

2 Rinse and pat dry the chicken breasts.

3 Melt the butter in a large skillet and sauté the onions for 5 minutes. Add the chicken and lightly brown it, about 5 minutes per side.

4 Add the apple juice, the cinnamon, and the allspice and season to taste. Cover the skillet, reduce the heat, and simmer for 15 minutes.

5 Core and slice the apples. Add them to the skillet and simmer for 5 minutes more.

6 Uncover the skillet, remove the chicken, and keep it warm. Bring the sauce to a boil and cook, stirring, until it thickens, about 2 minutes. Return the chicken to the skillet and turn to coat.

Go For Beans

1 Bring water to a boil in a medium saucepan.

2 Rinse and trim the green beans. Drain the corn. Rinse, stem, and chop the dill.

3 Combine the beans, the corn, and the dill in a steamer insert. Place the insert in the saucepan, cover, and steam until the beans are crisp-tender, 6 to 8 minutes.

4 Season to taste.

Mini-Soda Biscuits

1 Increase the oven temperature to 450°F. Flour a breadboard.

2 In a medium bowl, combine the flour, the baking soda, the cream of tartar, and the salt and blend well.

3 Cut the shortening into the flour mixture until it resembles coarse meal. Add the milk and blend until a soft dough is formed. Turn the dough onto the breadboard and knead 2 to 3 times.

4 Pat the dough out into a ½-inch thickness, and cut with a small biscuit cutter. Place the rounds on a baking sheet and bake until golden, 10 to 12 minutes.

Moccasin Pie

1 Preheat the oven to 350°F.

2 Place the pie shell in a pie plate.

3 Melt the butter in a small saucepan.

4 Beat the eggs in a large bowl until light, about 5 minutes. Add the butter, the sugar, and the flour and mix well to combine. Blend in the vanilla. Fold in the chocolate chips. Spoon the mixture into the pie shell.

5 Bake until the center is firm, 30 to 35 minutes.

FRIDAY

Smart Soup

1 large leek
1 medium parsnip
1 medium carrot
2 stalks celery
2 cans (14 ounces each) vegetable broth
1 cup V-8 juice
1/4 cup dry sherry
1 bay leaf
3 whole allspice
Seasoning to taste

Egghead

2 scallions (green onions)
1 medium zucchini
1 medium yellow zucchini
2 medium tomatoes
1 small red onion
1 chicken bouillon cube
3 tablespoons hot water
1/2 teaspoon dried marjoram
1/2 cup grated Parmesan cheese
9 eggs
2 tablespoons half-and-half
2 tablespoons butter
Seasoning to taste

Wise Fries

1 1/2 pounds baking potatoes
3 tablespoons vegetable oil
Seasoning to taste

Bright Berries

1 pint fresh strawberries
1 small package (3.4 ounces) instant vanilla
   pudding mix
2 cups milk
1 teaspoon rum extract

EQUIPMENT

Electric mixer	Large mixing bowl
Large covered saucepan	2 medium mixing bowls
Medium covered saucepan	Vegetable brush
Large covered skillet	Kitchen knives
10 x 15-inch baking pan	Measuring cups and spoons
Strainer	Cooking utensils

COUNTDOWN

1. Assemble the ingredients and the equipment.
2. Do Steps 1–2 of *Bright Berries*.
3. Do Steps 1–3 of *Smart Soup*.
4. Do Steps 1–4 of *Wise Fries*.
5. Do Steps 1–4 of *Egghead*.
6. Do Step 5 of *Wise Fries*.
7. Do Steps 5–7 of *Egghead*.
8. Do Step 3 of *Bright Berries*.

FRIDAY

Smart Soup

1 Thoroughly wash and trim the leek and remove the root end. Cut the leek into quarters. Peel, trim, and chunk the parsnip. Peel, trim, and chunk the carrot. Rinse, trim, and chunk the celery.

2 In a large saucepan, combine the vegetables with the broth, the juice, the sherry, the bay leaf, and the allspice. Season to taste and bring the mixture to a boil. Cover the saucepan, reduce the heat, and simmer for 30 minutes.

3 Strain the soup, discarding the vegetables, the bay leaf, and the allspice and return it to the saucepan. Cover and simmer until you are ready to serve.

Egghead

1 Rinse, trim, and chop the scallions. Scrub, trim, and cube the zucchini. Rinse, stem, and chop the tomatoes. Peel and chop the onion.

2 In a medium saucepan, dissolve the bouillon cube in three tablespoons of hot water. Add the zucchini and the onion. Cover and simmer for 5 minutes.

3 Add the marjoram, fold in the cheese, and cook until the cheese has melted, 1 to 2 minutes. Set aside.

4 In a medium bowl, beat the eggs with the half-and-half.

5 Melt the butter in a large skillet. Add the eggs, cover, and simmer for 1 minute. Uncover, gently lift the edges of the omelet, and tilt the pan so that the top part runs to the bottom and cooks evenly. Cook for 1 minute more.

6 Spread the zucchini mixture evenly over the eggs. Add the tomatoes. Cover and simmer until the eggs are set and the vegetables are hot, about 5 minutes.

7 Season to taste, fold half of the omelet over the other half, slide out of the pan, and cut into individual portions.

Wise Fries

1 Preheat the oven to 475°F.

2 Scrub the potatoes and cut them into ½-inch-thick strips. Rinse the potato strips in cold water to remove the starch and pat dry with paper towels.

3 Place the potatoes in a large bowl. Add the oil and toss to coat the strips evenly.

4 Place the potatoes in a single layer in a 10 x 15-inch baking pan. Season to taste and bake for 15 minutes.

5 Turn the potatoes over and bake until lightly browned, about 15 minutes more.

Bright Berries

1 Wash the berries, reserving 4 for garnish. Hull and slice the remaining berries and divide them among individual dessert glasses.

2 Combine the pudding mix and the milk in a medium bowl and beat until well blended, 2 to 3 minutes. Add the rum extract and blend. Pour the pudding mixture over the berries and refrigerate until you are ready to serve.

3 Garnish each pudding with a whole berry.

WEEK THREE

Monday
Chickago
O'Hair
Peoria
Decakur

Tuesday
Funny Gill
Fanny Rice
Zucchfeld Follies
Nuts

Wednesday
Pork Out Pasta
Salad Splurge
The Bountiful Baguette
The Prodigal Pear

Thursday
Sam 'n' Eggs
Spear Me the Details
Roll In the Hay
Berry Up to the Bar

Friday
Busy Burritos
Messy Rice
Rind Over Matter

STAPLES

- Butter
- Flour
- Baking powder
- Granulated sugar
- Dark brown sugar
- Powdered sugar
- Olive oil
- Vegetable oil
- Red wine vinegar
- Rice vinegar
- Lemon juice
- Mayonnaise
- Worcestershire sauce
- Poppy seeds
- Dried basil
- Dried savory
- Dried tarragon
- Dried thyme
- Ground allspice
- Ground cardamom
- Cayenne pepper
- Chili powder
- Ground cinnamon
- Dry mustard
- Paprika
- Black pepper
- Poultry seasoning
- Salt
- Brandy extract
- Orange extract
- Vanilla extract

SHOPPING LIST

MEAT & POULTRY

- ½ pound Italian sausage (W)
- ½ pound lean cooked ham steak (W)
- 4 boneless, skinless chicken breast halves (about 1½ pounds) (M)

FISH

- 4 white fish fillets (about 1½ pounds) (T)

FRESH PRODUCE

VEGETABLES

- ¾ pound sugar-snap peas (M)
- 1 pound asparagus (Th)
- 2 medium zucchini (T)
- 2 medium carrots (W)
- 1 small head lettuce (W)
- 1 small head lettuce (F)
- 3 medium tomatoes (F)
- 1 large ripe avocado (F)
- 2 medium cucumbers (W)
- 1 large green bell pepper (M)
- 1 large red bell pepper (Th)
- 1 large yellow bell pepper (W)
- 1 small green bell pepper (F)
- 1 medium onion (W)
- 1 medium onion (F)
- 1 small onion (T)
- 1 small onion (F)
- 1 small red onion (Th)
- 2 small shallots (T)
- 3 scallions (green onions) (F)
- 2 cloves garlic (M)
- 2 cloves garlic (W)
- 2 cloves garlic (F)

HERBS

- ⅓ cup basil leaves (when chopped) (W)
- ¼ cup chives (when chopped) (W)
- ½ cup chives (when chopped) (Th)
- 2 tablespoons dill (when chopped) (T)
- 2 tablespoons parsley (when chopped) (T)

FRUIT

- 1 medium orange (M)
- 1 medium lemon (T)
- 2 small grapefruit (F)

CANS, JARS & BOTTLES

SOUPS

- 1 can (14 ounces) chicken broth (M)
- 1 can (14 ounces) vegetable broth (T)

VEGETABLES

- 1 can (28 ounces) diced tomatoes (W)
- 1 can (4 ounces) sliced mushrooms (T)

INTERNATIONAL FOODS

- 1 can (30 ounces) refried beans (F)

FRUIT

- 1 can (15 ounces) sliced pears (W)

JUICES

- 1 cup tomato juice (F)

CONDIMENTS

- 1 jar (2 ounces) diced pimientos (T)

PACKAGED GOODS

PASTA, RICE & GRAINS

- 8 ounces angel hair pasta (M)
- 1 pound linguini (W)
- 1 cup long-grain white rice (T)
- 1 cup long-grain white rice (F)

BAKED GOODS

- 1 large French baguette (W)
- 4 bagels (Th)

INTERNATIONAL FOODS

- 4 large soft corn tortillas (F)

DRIED FRUIT & NUTS

- ¼ cup raisins (M)
- ½ cup sliced almonds (M)
- ½ cup walnut bits (T)

DESSERT & BAKING NEEDS

- 1 package (3½ ounces) orange gelatin (Th)
- ½ cup chocolate chips (T)

WINE & SPIRITS

- 2 tablespoons dry sherry (T)
- 1 tablespoon Grand Marnier (Th)

REFRIGERATED PRODUCTS

DAIRY

- ½ cup milk (W)
- ¼ cup milk (Th)
- ⅓ cup half-and-half (T)
- ¼ cup sour cream (F)
- 1 cup piña colada yogurt (F)
- 1 cup whipping cream (Th)
- 3 eggs (M)
- 2 eggs (W)
- 9 eggs (Th)

CHEESE

- 1 container (8 ounces) salmon cream cheese spread (Th)
- 1½ cups shredded Cheddar cheese (F)

JUICES

- 2 tablespoons orange juice (T)

DELI

- 4 slices bacon (W)
- ¼ pound smoked salmon (Th)

FROZEN GOODS

FRUIT

- 1 package (10 ounces) raspberries (Th)

DESSERTS

- 1 pint vanilla ice cream (T)

MONDAY

Chickago

4 boneless, skinless chicken breast halves
   (about 1 1/2 pounds)
2 cloves garlic
1 large green bell pepper
1 medium orange
1/2 cup flour
1/2 teaspoon poultry seasoning
Seasoning to taste
1/2 cup sliced almonds
4 tablespoons butter
1 cup chicken broth

O'Hair

8 ounces angel hair pasta
3 tablespoons butter
1/2 teaspoon ground allspice

Peoria

3/4 pound sugar-snap peas
3/4 cup chicken broth
3/4 cup water
1/2 teaspoon dried thyme
Seasoning to taste

Decakur

3 eggs
1 cup dark brown sugar
3 tablespoons flour
1 teaspoon baking powder
1 teaspoon vanilla extract
1/4 cup raisins
1/2 teaspoon ground cardamom
1 tablespoon powdered sugar

EQUIPMENT

Electric mixer
Large covered
   saucepan
Medium covered
   saucepan
Large covered skillet
Mini-muffin tin
Steamer insert
Colander

Large shallow bowl
Large mixing bowl
Citrus grater
Citrus juicer
Kitchen knives
Measuring cups and
   spoons
Cooking utensils

COUNTDOWN

1. Assemble the ingredients and the
   equipment.
2. Do Steps 1–2 of Decakur.
3. Do Step 1 of O'Hair.
4. Do Step 1 of Peoria.
5. Do Steps 1–4 of Chickago.
6. Do Steps 3–4 of Decakur.
7. Do Steps 5–7 of Chickago.
8. Do Steps 2–3 of Peoria.
9. Do Steps 2–3 of O'Hair.
10. Do Step 8 of Chickago.
11. Do Step 5 of Decakur.

MONDAY

Chickago

1 Rinse and pat dry the chicken breasts. Peel and mince the garlic. Rinse, trim, seed, and julienne the bell pepper. Grate the orange peel and cut the orange in half. Squeeze the juice from half the orange over the chicken breasts. Reserve the other orange half.

2 In a large shallow bowl, combine the orange peel, the flour, and the poultry seasoning. Season to taste. Roll the chicken breasts in the flour mixture to coat.

3 Spread the almonds in a large skillet and toss them until lightly toasted, about 1 minute. Remove and reserve.

4 Melt 2 tablespoons of the butter in the skillet and sauté the garlic for 1 minute. Add the chicken, reserving the remaining flour mixture, and cook until golden, about 5 minutes per side. Remove the chicken and keep it warm.

5 Melt the remaining 2 tablespoons butter in the skillet and sauté the bell pepper for 2 minutes. Remove and reserve.

6 Add the broth to the skillet and bring it to a boil, scraping up any brown bits.

7 Squeeze the remaining orange juice into the reserved flour mixture and whisk until smooth. Add the mixture to the skillet and bring to a boil, whisking to blend. Return the chicken to the skillet. Cover and simmer until the chicken is tender and cooked through, about 15 minutes.

8 Return the peppers and the almonds to the skillet and heat through, about 2 minutes.

O'Hair

1 Bring water to a boil in a large saucepan.

2 Cook the pasta until it is almost tender, about 2 minutes.

3 Drain the pasta, return it to the saucepan, and toss it with the butter and the allspice. Cover to keep warm.

Peoria

1 Rinse and string the snap peas.

2 Bring the broth and the water to a boil in a medium saucepan.

3 Place the snap peas in a steamer insert. Sprinkle with the thyme and season to taste. Place the insert in the saucepan, cover, and steam until the snap peas are crisp-tender, about 5 minutes.

Decakur

1 Preheat the oven to 350°F. Grease a mini-muffin tin.

2 Beat the eggs in a large bowl until they are light and fluffy, about 2 minutes. Add the brown sugar, the flour, the baking powder, the vanilla, and the raisins. Blend well and let the mixture stand for 10 minutes.

3 Stir in the cardamom and spoon the mixture into the muffin cups.

4 Bake until the cakes are golden and firm to the touch, about 15 minutes.

5 Dust the cakes with the powdered sugar.

TUESDAY

Funny Gill

4 white fish fillets (about 1 1/2 pounds)
2 small shallots
2 tablespoons fresh parsley (when chopped)
1 medium lemon
2 tablespoons butter
1/2 teaspoon dried tarragon
1/4 cup vegetable broth
2 tablespoons dry sherry
1/4 teaspoon paprika
Seasoning to taste

Fanny Rice

1 cup long-grain white rice
1 1/2 cups vegetable broth
1/2 cup water
1 can (4 ounces) sliced mushrooms
1 jar (2 ounces) diced pimientos
Seasoning to taste

Zucchfeld Follies

2 medium zucchini
1 small onion
2 tablespoons fresh dill (when chopped)
2 tablespoons butter
1 teaspoon granulated sugar
2 tablespoons orange juice
Seasoning to taste

Nuts

1/2 cup walnut bits
1 pint vanilla ice cream
1/2 cup chocolate chips
2 tablespoons butter
1/2 cup powdered sugar
1/3 cup half-and-half
1 teaspoon brandy extract

EQUIPMENT

Double boiler	Citrus juicer
Small covered saucepan	Ice cream scoop
Large covered skillet	Waxed paper
Large skillet	Kitchen knives
Vegetable brush	Measuring cups and spoons
Vegetable grater	Cooking utensils
Citrus grater	

COUNTDOWN

1. Assemble the ingredients and the equipment.
2. Do Steps 1–2 of *Fanny Rice*.
3. Do Steps 1–3 of *Nuts*.
4. Do Steps 1–4 of *Funny Gill*.
5. Do Steps 1–3 of *Zucchfeld Follies*.
6. Do Step 3 of *Fanny Rice*.
7. Do Step 5 of *Funny Gill*.
8. Do Step 4 of *Nuts*.

TUESDAY

Funny Gill

1 Rinse and pat dry the fish fillets. Peel and mince the shallots. Rinse, stem, and chop the parsley. Grate 1 teaspoon of lemon peel and juice the lemon.

2 Melt the butter in a large skillet and sauté the shallots with the tarragon for 2 minutes. Add the fish. Sprinkle the lemon juice over the fillets and cook until the fish flakes easily with a fork, about 3 minutes per side.

3 Remove the fish and cover to keep warm.

4 Add the broth and the sherry to the skillet and cook for 1 minute. Return the fish to the skillet. Add the lemon peel and the paprika. Season to taste and heat through.

5 Sprinkle with the parsley.

Fanny Rice

1 Bring water to a boil in the bottom of a double boiler.

2 Combine the rice, the broth, the ½ cup water, the undrained mushrooms, and the undrained pimientos in the top of the double boiler. Season to taste, cover, and reduce the heat. Simmer until the liquid is absorbed and the rice is tender, 30 to 40 minutes.

3 Fluff the rice with a fork.

Zucchfeld Follies

1 Scrub, trim, and grate the zucchini. Peel and grate the onion. Rinse, stem, and chop the dill.

2 Melt the butter in a large skillet. Add the onion, the zucchini, the dill, the sugar, and the orange juice and sauté until the zucchini is crisp-tender, 2 to 3 minutes.

3 Season to taste and cover to keep warm.

Nuts

1 Place the nuts on a sheet of waxed paper. Using an ice cream scoop, form 4 balls of ice cream, roll them in the nuts, and place them in individual dessert glasses. Freeze until you are ready to serve.

2 Melt the chocolate with the butter in a small saucepan over low heat. Stir in the powdered sugar, the half-and-half, and the brandy extract. Blend well and heat through, about 2 minutes.

3 Remove from the heat and cover to keep warm.

4 Remove the ice cream from the freezer and top with the fudge sauce.

WEDNESDAY

Pork Out Pasta

½ pound Italian sausage
1 medium onion
2 cloves garlic
1 large yellow bell pepper
⅓ cup fresh basil leaves (when chopped)
4 slices bacon
½ pound lean cooked ham steak
1 can (28 ounces) diced tomatoes
½ teaspoon Worcestershire sauce
½ teaspoon granulated sugar
Seasoning to taste
1 pound linguini

Salad Splurge

1 small head lettuce
2 medium cucumbers
2 medium carrots
3 tablespoons vegetable oil
2 tablespoons rice vinegar
½ teaspoon dry mustard

The Bountiful Baguette

1 large French baguette
¼ cup fresh chives (when chopped)
2 tablespoons mayonnaise
¼ teaspoon dried savory

The Prodigal Pear

2 eggs
5 tablespoons butter
¾ cup granulated sugar
1½ cups flour
2 teaspoons baking powder
½ cup milk
1 can (15 ounces) sliced pears
½ cup dark brown sugar
1 teaspoon ground cinnamon

EQUIPMENT

Electric mixer
Stockpot
Large skillet
9 x 9-inch glass baking dish
Colander
2 medium mixing bowls
4 small mixing bowls

Whisk
Vegetable peeler
Vegetable grater
Aluminum foil
Kitchen knives
Measuring cups and spoons
Cooking utensils

COUNTDOWN

1. Assemble the ingredients and the equipment.
2. Do Steps 1–6 of *The Prodigal Pear*.
3. Do Steps 1–2 of *Pork Out Pasta*.
4. Do Steps 1–3 of *Salad Splurge*.
5. Do Steps 1–3 of *The Bountiful Baguette*.
6. Do Steps 3–6 of *Pork Out Pasta*.
7. Do Step 4 of *Salad Splurge*.

WEDNESDAY

Pork Out Pasta

1 Bring water to a boil in a stockpot. Place the sausage in the freezer to chill for 10 minutes.

2 Peel and chop the onion. Peel and mince the garlic. Rinse, trim, seed, and chop the bell pepper. Rinse, stem, and chop the basil. Dice the bacon. Chop the ham. Slice the sausage.

3 Sauté the bacon in a large skillet until almost crisp, about 5 minutes. Drain on paper towels. Add the sausage to the skillet and sauté until browned, about 7 minutes. Drain on paper towels.

4 In the drippings, sauté the onion and the garlic until the onion is soft, about 5 minutes. Add the bell pepper and sauté for 3 minutes. Add the tomatoes, the Worcestershire sauce, the bacon, the sausage, the ham, the basil, and the sugar, and season to taste. Bring the mixture to a boil, reduce the heat, and simmer for 3 minutes more.

5 Cook the linguini until it is almost tender, 2 to 3 minutes if you are using fresh pasta, 6 to 7 minutes if you are using dry pasta.

6 Drain the pasta and toss it with the sauce.

Salad Splurge

1 Wash and dry the lettuce and arrange the leaves on individual salad plates.

2 Peel, trim, and grate the cucumbers. Peel, trim, and grate the carrots. Combine the ingredients in a medium bowl.

3 In a small bowl, whisk together the oil, the vinegar, and the mustard.

4 Toss the dressing with the cucumber mixture and spoon the mixture over the lettuce.

The Bountiful Baguette

1 Cut the bread diagonally in 1-inch-thick slices without cutting all the way through. Rinse, trim, and chop the chives.

2 In a small bowl, combine the chives with the mayonnaise and the savory. Spread the mixture between the bread slices.

3 Lay the bread on a sheet of aluminum foil and bake at 350°F until it is heated through, about 10 minutes.

The Prodigal Pear

1 Preheat the oven to 350°F. Grease a 9 x 9-inch baking dish.

2 Separate the eggs, placing the whites in a small bowl. In a medium bowl, combine the egg yolks, 4 tablespoons of the butter, and the granulated sugar. Beat until fluffy. Gradually add the flour and the baking powder. Slowly add the milk and blend well.

3 Beat the egg whites until stiff. Fold into the batter. Pour into the pan.

4 Drain the pears and arrange the slices over the batter.

5 In a small bowl, combine the brown sugar, the remaining 1 tablespoon butter, and the cinnamon. Sprinkle the mixture over the fruit.

6 Bake until a toothpick inserted in the center of the cake comes out clean, 30 to 35 minutes.

THURSDAY

Sam 'n' Eggs

1 container (8 ounces) salmon cream cheese
  spread
1/4 pound smoked salmon
1/2 cup fresh chives (when chopped)
9 eggs
1/4 cup milk
Seasoning to taste
3 tablespoons butter

Spear Me the Details

1 pound fresh asparagus
1 large red bell pepper
2 tablespoons olive oil
Seasoning to taste
1 teaspoon dried basil

Roll In the Hay

1 small red onion
4 hard rolls
3 tablespoons butter
1 teaspoon poppy seeds

Berry Up to the Bar

1 package (3 1/2 ounces) orange gelatin
1 cup water
1 package (10 ounces) frozen raspberries
1 cup whipping cream
1 tablespoon Grand Marnier
2 tablespoons powdered sugar
1 teaspoon orange extract

EQUIPMENT

Electric mixer	Whisk
Large covered skillet	Aluminum foil
Small skillet	Kitchen knives
9 x 13-inch glass baking dish	Measuring cups and spoons
2 large mixing bowls	Cooking utensils
Medium mixing bowl	

COUNTDOWN

1. Assemble the ingredients and the equipment.
2. Do Step 1 of *Berry Up to the Bar.*
3. Do Steps 1–3 of *Sam 'n' Eggs.*
4. Do Steps 2–3 of *Berry Up to the Bar.*
5. Do Steps 1–4 of *Spear Me the Details.*
6. Do Steps 1–5 of *Roll In the Hay.*
7. Do Steps 4–6 of *Sam 'n' Eggs.*

THURSDAY

Sam 'n' Eggs

1 Set the cream cheese out to soften.

2 Chop the salmon. Rinse, trim, and chop the chives.

3 In a large bowl, combine the eggs and the milk and whip lightly. Season to taste.

4 Melt the butter in a large skillet. Pour in the egg mixture, tilting the pan in all directions to spread the eggs evenly. Simmer for 3 minutes.

5 Cover the skillet and simmer for 2 minutes more.

6 Uncover the skillet. Spread the cream cheese over the eggs, sprinkle with the chives, and add the salmon. Cover the skillet, remove it from the heat, and let stand for 3 minutes.

Spear Me the Details

1 Preheat the oven to 450°F. Grease a 9 x 13-inch baking dish.

2 Rinse the asparagus and discard the tough ends. Rinse, trim, seed, and slice the bell pepper.

3 Arrange the asparagus and the pepper slices in the baking pan. Drizzle with the oil. Season to taste and sprinkle with the basil.

4 Bake until crisp-tender, about 10 minutes.

Roll In the Hay

1 Reduce the oven temperature to 250°F.

2 Peel and chop the onion. Split the rolls in half.

3 Melt the butter in a small skillet and sauté the onion for 3 minutes. Blend in the poppy seeds.

4 Place the rolls on a sheet of aluminum foil in the warm oven until just heated, about 5 minutes.

5 Spread the onion mixture on the rolls.

Berry Up to the Bar

1 Chill a medium bowl and the beaters of an electric mixer for 10 minutes.

2 Bring the gelatin and the water to a boil in a small saucepan, stirring to dissolve the gelatin. Pour the mixture into a large bowl, add the frozen raspberries, and stir to mix. Refrigerate for at least 30 minutes.

3 Pour the whipping cream into the chilled bowl and beat until it is stiff, about 5 minutes. Fold in the Grand Marnier, the powdered sugar, and the orange extract. Combine the whipped cream with the raspberry mixture, spoon into individual dessert glasses, and refrigerate until you are ready to serve.

FRIDAY

Busy Burritos

1 medium onion
2 cloves garlic
3 scallions (green onions)
1 small head lettuce
3 medium tomatoes
1 large ripe avocado
1 1/2 tablespoons lemon juice
1 tablespoon vegetable oil
1 1/2 teaspoons chili powder
1/2 teaspoon cayenne pepper
1/2 cup water
1 can (30 ounces) refried beans
4 large soft corn tortillas
1 1/2 cups shredded Cheddar cheese
1/4 cup sour cream

Messy Rice

1 small onion
1 small green bell pepper
1 tablespoon vegetable oil
1 cup long-grain white rice
1 cup tomato juice
1 cup water
2 tablespoons red wine vinegar

Rind Over Matter

2 small grapefruit
1 cup piña colada yogurt
2 tablespoons dark brown sugar

EQUIPMENT

Double boiler
Large skillet
Small skillet
9 x 9-inch glass
   baking dish
Baking sheet

Grapefruit knife
Kitchen knives
Measuring cups and
   spoons
Cooking utensils

COUNTDOWN

1. Assemble the ingredients and the equipment.
2. Do Steps 1–4 of *Messy Rice*.
3. Do Step 1 of *Rind Over Matter*.
4. Do Steps 1–7 of *Busy Burritos*.
5. Do Step 5 of *Messy Rice*.
6. Do Steps 2–3 of *Rind Over Matter*.

FRIDAY

RECIPES

Busy Burritos

1 Preheat the oven to 250°F.

2 Peel and chop the onion. Peel and mince the garlic. Rinse, trim, and chop the scallions. Wash, dry, and shred the lettuce. Rinse, stem, and chop the tomatoes. Halve, pit, peel, and chop the avocado and sprinkle with the lemon juice.

3 Heat the oil in a large skillet and sauté the onion and the garlic for 3 minutes. Add the chili powder, the cayenne pepper, and the water. Bring to a boil and cook until the water has evaporated, about 5 minutes.

4 Add the refried beans to the skillet, blend well, and cook until hot, about 3 minutes.

5 Place the tortillas on a baking sheet in the oven to warm, about 3 minutes.

6 Add the cheese to the skillet and continue cooking until it has melted.

7 Spoon the bean mixture onto the warm tortillas and top with the lettuce, the tomatoes, the scallions, the avocado, and a dollop of sour cream.

Messy Rice

1 Bring water to a boil in the bottom of a double boiler.

2 Peel and mince the onion. Rinse, trim, seed, and chop the bell pepper.

3 Heat the oil in a small skillet and sauté the onion and the bell pepper for 3 minutes.

4 In the top of the double boiler, combine the onion, the bell pepper, the rice, the tomato juice, the 1 cup water, and the vinegar. Cover, reduce the heat, and simmer until the liquid is absorbed and the rice is tender, 30 to 40 minutes.

5 Fluff with a fork.

Rind Over Matter

1 Cut the grapefruit in half and loosen the sections with a grapefruit knife. Place the halves in a 9 x 9-inch baking dish.

2 Preheat the broiler.

3 Spread the yogurt lightly over the grapefruit halves and sprinkle with the brown sugar. Broil until the topping is hot and bubbly, about 3 minutes.

WEEK FOUR

Monday

Never Beefore
Not Agrain
Carrot Not
Mousseunderstood

Tuesday

Dancin' Chick to Chick
Corny Weather
In the Dill of the Night
I Get a Cake Out of You

Wednesday

Friendship Frittata
Lone-Star Salad
El Paso the Biscuits
Banana Alamo-de

Thursday

Over the Rainbow
Munchkin Tomatoes
Scarecrow Salad
Dorothy's Dessert

Friday

Nuclear Fishion
Pilaf Fer Me
Proton Peas
Icetope Pie

STAPLES

- ☐ Butter
- ☐ Flour
- ☐ Baking powder
- ☐ Cornstarch
- ☐ Cream of tartar
- ☐ Granulated sugar
- ☐ Dark brown sugar
- ☐ Powdered sugar
- ☐ Molasses
- ☐ Multicolored sprinkles
- ☐ Olive oil
- ☐ Vegetable oil
- ☐ Apple cider vinegar
- ☐ Red wine vinegar
- ☐ Rice vinegar
- ☐ Lemon juice
- ☐ Dijon mustard
- ☐ Ketchup
- ☐ Mayonnaise
- ☐ Soy sauce
- ☐ Worcestershire sauce
- ☐ Plain breadcrumbs
- ☐ Seasoned breadcrumbs
- ☐ Celery seeds
- ☐ Dried marjoram
- ☐ Dried tarragon
- ☐ Ground allspice
- ☐ Ground cardamom
- ☐ Ground cinnamon
- ☐ Chinese 5-spice
- ☐ Ground ginger
- ☐ Italian seasoning
- ☐ Dry mustard
- ☐ Ground nutmeg
- ☐ Paprika
- ☐ Black pepper
- ☐ Salt
- ☐ Banana extract
- ☐ Rum extract

MEAT & POULTRY

1 1/2 pounds lean sirloin steak (M)

4 boneless, skinless chicken breast halves (about 1 1/2 pounds) (T)

FISH

4 sea bass fillets (about 1 1/2 pounds) (F)

FRESH PRODUCE

VEGETABLES

1 pound Brussels sprouts (T)
3/4 pound sugar-snap peas (F)
2 medium zucchini (W)
1 pound baby carrots (M)
3 medium carrots (Th)
2 stalks celery (Th)
3 stalks celery (F)
1/2 pound mushrooms (M)
1/2 pound mushrooms (W)
1 medium head lettuce (W)
1 medium head lettuce (Th)
1 large tomato (W)
4 medium tomatoes (Th)
1 medium cucumber (Th)
1 small cucumber (W)
2 medium orange bell peppers (T)
1 large red bell pepper (Th)
2 medium red bell peppers (T)
1 small daikon radish (W)
1 small bunch radishes (Th)
1 medium onion (T)
2 medium red onions (W)
4 scallions (green onions) (M)
2 scallions (green onions) (Th)
2 scallions (green onions) (F)
3 cloves garlic (T)
1 clove garlic (W)
1 clove garlic (Th)

HERBS

2 tablespoons chives (when chopped) (T)
2 tablespoons chives (when chopped) (W)
2 tablespoons chives (when chopped) (F)

3 tablespoons cilantro (when chopped) (W)
2 tablespoons dill (when chopped) (T)
4 mint sprigs for garnish (M)
1/4 cup parsley (when chopped) (M)
1/4 cup parsley (when chopped) (T)
2 tablespoons parsley (when chopped) (F)

FRUIT

1 ripe mango (F)
4 medium bananas (W)

CANS, JARS & BOTTLES

SOUPS

1 can (14 ounces) vegetable broth (F)
1 can (10 1/2 ounces) beef broth (M)

VEGETABLES

1 can (15 ounces) cream-style corn (T)
1 can (11 ounces) whole-kernel corn (T)

FRUIT

1 can (15 ounces) apricots in syrup (M)
1 can (8 ounces) crushed pineapple (F)

JUICES

1 can (12 ounces) mango nectar (F)

PACKAGED GOODS

PASTA, RICE & GRAINS

8 ounces wide curly egg noodles (M)
1 pound rainbow spiral pasta (Th)
1 cup couscous (F)

BAKED GOODS

1 prepared pie shell (F)

DRIED FRUIT & NUTS

1/4 cup sliced almonds (T)
1/2 cup pecan bits (W)

DESSERT & BAKING NEEDS

1 envelope unflavored gelatin (M)
1 envelope unflavored gelatin (F)
1 package (3.4 ounces) instant pistachio pudding mix (Th)

WINE & SPIRITS

1/4 cup dry white wine (Th)
1/4 cup dry sherry (M)
2 tablespoons Grand Marnier (M)

REFRIGERATED PRODUCTS

DAIRY

1 1/2 cups + 2 tablespoons milk (T)
3/4 cup milk (W)
1 1/4 cups milk (Th)
1 cup sour cream (M)
3/4 cup sour cream (Th)
1 cup whipped cream (M)
Whipped cream for garnish (Th)
1 egg (T)
9 eggs (W)
4 eggs (F)

CHEESE

1/2 cup shredded Colby/Monterey Jack cheese (W)
1/2 cup shredded mozzarella cheese (Th)

DELI

1/2 pound bacon (Th)

FROZEN GOODS

VEGETABLES

1 package (10 ounces) green peas (Th)

BAKED GOODS

1 pound cake (T)

DESSERTS

1 pint vanilla ice cream (W)
1 container (8 ounces) whipped topping (T)

MONDAY

Never Beefore

1½ pounds lean sirloin steak
½ pound fresh mushrooms
4 scallions (green onions)
2 tablespoons vegetable oil
2 tablespoons butter
¼ cup dry sherry
1 can (10½ ounces) beef broth
3 tablespoons cornstarch
1 cup sour cream
½ tablespoon Dijon mustard
1 teaspoon Worcestershire sauce
Seasoning to taste

Not Agrain

¼ cup fresh parsley (when chopped)
8 ounces wide curly egg noodles
1 tablespoon butter

Carrot Not

1 pound baby carrots
1 tablespoon butter
½ teaspoon dried marjoram
½ teaspoon ground cardamom

Mousseunderstood

1 can (14 ounces) apricots in syrup
1 envelope unflavored gelatin
2 tablespoons lemon juice
2 tablespoons Grand Marnier
1 cup whipped cream
2 tablespoons powdered sugar
4 mint sprigs for garnish

EQUIPMENT

Blender	Medium mixing bowl
Large covered saucepan	Small mixing bowl
	Colander
Medium covered saucepan	Whisk
	Kitchen knives
Small saucepan	Measuring cups and spoons
Large skillet	
Steamer insert	Cooking utensils

COUNTDOWN

1. Assemble the ingredients and the equipment.
2. Do Steps 1–4 of *Mousseunderstood*.
3. Do Steps 1–2 of *Not Agrain*.
4. Do Steps 1–4 of *Never Beefore*.
5. Do Steps 1–2 of *Carrot Not*.
6. Do Step 3 of *Not Agrain*.
7. Do Step 5 of *Never Beefore*.
8. Do Step 3 of *Carrot Not*.
9. Do Step 4 of *Not Agrain*.
10. Do Steps 6–8 of *Never Beefore*.
11. Do Step 5 of *Mousseunderstood*.

MONDAY

Never Beefore

1 Trim any excess fat from the beef and cut it diagonally across the grain into thin strips.

2 Rinse, pat dry, trim, and slice the mushrooms. Rinse, trim, and chop the scallions.

3 Heat the oil in a large skillet and sauté the beef until it is browned, about 5 minutes.

4 Remove the beef from the skillet and keep it warm.

5 Add the butter to the skillet and sauté the mushrooms and the scallions until the mushrooms are tender, about 5 minutes. Add the sherry, bring the mixture to a boil, and cook for 2 minutes.

6 In a small bowl, combine the broth and the cornstarch. Add it to the skillet, return to a boil, and cook, stirring, until the mixture begins to thicken, about 4 minutes.

7 Stir in the sour cream, the mustard, and the Worcestershire sauce. Season to taste and blend well.

8 Return the beef to the skillet and heat through but do not boil, 1 to 2 minutes.

Not Agrain

1 Bring water to a boil in a large saucepan.

2 Rinse, stem, and chop the parsley.

3 Cook the noodles until they are almost tender, about 6 minutes.

4 Drain the noodles, return them to the saucepan, and toss them with the butter and the parsley. Remove from the heat and cover to keep warm.

Carrot Not

1 Bring a small amount of water to a boil in a medium saucepan.

2 Rinse and trim the carrots. Put them in a steamer insert and place the insert in the saucepan. Cover and steam until the carrots are crisp-tender, about 10 minutes.

3 Drain the carrots. Melt the butter with the marjoram and the cardamom in the saucepan. Return the carrots to the saucepan and toss them to coat. Remove from the heat and cover to keep warm.

Mousseunderstood

1 Drain the apricots, reserving $\frac{1}{4}$ cup of the liquid. Place the reserved liquid in a small saucepan. Sprinkle the gelatin over the liquid and let it stand until softened, about 5 minutes.

2 Heat the liquid mixture until the gelatin is dissolved, about 1 minute.

3 Place all but 4 apricot halves in a blender. Add the lemon juice, the Grand Marnier, and the gelatin mixture and puree for 1 minute.

4 In a medium bowl, combine the whipped cream with the powdered sugar. Fold in the apricot mixture. Pour the mousse into individual dessert glasses and chill for 30 minutes, or until you are ready to serve.

5 Garnish each mousse with an apricot half and a sprig of mint.

TUESDAY

Dancin' Chick to Chick

4 boneless, skinless chicken breast halves
   (about 1 1/2 pounds)
3 cloves garlic
1 medium onion
2 medium red bell peppers
2 medium orange bell peppers
1/4 cup fresh parsley (when chopped)
3 tablespoons butter
2 tablespoons olive oil
Seasoning to taste

Corny Weather

1 1/2 cups milk
2 tablespoons butter
1/4 cup flour
1/4 teaspoon paprika
1 teaspoon dry mustard
1 egg
1/2 teaspoon Worcestershire sauce
1 can (15 ounces) cream-style corn
1 can (11 ounces) whole-kernel corn
Seasoning to taste
3/4 cup seasoned breadcrumbs

In the Dill of the Night

1 pound Brussels sprouts
2 tablespoons fresh dill (when chopped)
2 tablespoons fresh chives (when chopped)
1/4 cup sliced almonds
2 tablespoons butter

I Get a Cake Out of You

1 frozen pound cake
4 tablespoons butter
1/2 cup dark brown sugar
1/2 teaspoon ground ginger
1/2 teaspoon ground allspice
1/2 teaspoon ground nutmeg
2 tablespoons milk
1 teaspoon rum extract
1 container (8 ounces) whipped topping

EQUIPMENT

Large covered skillet
Large skillet
Medium saucepan
Small saucepan
1 1/2-quart casserole
Small mixing bowl

Whisk
Kitchen knives
Measuring cups and
   spoons
Cooking utensils

COUNTDOWN

1. Assemble the ingredients and the equipment.
2. Do Step 1 of *I Get a Cake Out of You*.
3. Do Steps 1–5 of *Corny Weather*.
4. Do Steps 2–3 of *I Get a Cake Out of You*.
5. Do Steps 1–5 of *Dancin' Chick to Chick*.
6. Do Steps 1–4 of *In the Dill of the Night*.
7. Do Step 4 of *I Get a Cake Out of You*.

TUESDAY

Dancin' Chick to Chick

1 Rinse and pat dry the chicken breasts.

2 Peel and mince the garlic. Peel and chop the onion. Rinse, trim, seed, and chop the bell peppers. Rinse, stem, and chop the parsley.

3 Melt 2 tablespoons of the butter with 1 tablespoon of the oil in a large skillet. Cook the chicken until lightly browned, about 5 minutes per side.

4 Remove the chicken and reserve.

5 Add the remaining 1 tablespoon butter and the remaining 1 tablespoon oil to the skillet. Sauté the garlic and the onion until the onion is soft, about 5 minutes. Add the peppers and the parsley. Return the chicken. Season to taste. Cover and simmer until the chicken is cooked through and the peppers are tender, about 15 minutes.

Corny Weather

1 Preheat the oven to 325°F. Butter a 1½-quart casserole.

2 Scald the milk in a medium saucepan. Remove from the heat and add the butter, stirring to melt.

3 Combine the flour, the paprika, and the mustard in a small bowl. Gradually add the mixture to the milk, stirring constantly to blend. Return to the heat and cook, stirring, until the mixture is thickened, 7 to 8 minutes.

4 In the same bowl, lightly whip the egg with the Worcestershire sauce. Combine with the milk mixture. Add the cream-style corn. Drain the whole-kernel corn and add

it to the mixture, stirring to combine. Season to taste. Pour into the casserole and top with the breadcrumbs.

5 Bake until the breadcrumbs are golden and the custard is set, 20 to 25 minutes.

In the Dill of the Night

1 Rinse, trim, and cut the Brussels sprouts in half. Rinse, stem, and chop the dill. Rinse, trim, and chop the chives.

2 Place the almonds in a large skillet and toast lightly for 3 minutes. Remove and reserve.

3 Melt the butter with the dill in the skillet and sauté the Brussels sprouts until they are crisp-tender, about 5 minutes.

4 Toss with the nuts and the chives.

I Get a Cake Out of You

1 Set the pound cake out to thaw slightly.

2 Cut the cake into 3 layers.

3 Melt the butter in a small saucepan. Stir in the brown sugar, the ginger, the allspice, and the nutmeg. Bring the mixture to a boil, stirring constantly, for 2 minutes. Add the milk and return the mixture to a boil. Remove from the heat, blend in the rum extract, and set aside.

4 Spread the bottom layer of the cake with half of the whipped topping. Add the second layer and spread with the remaining whipped topping. Add the top layer and spoon the sauce over the cake.

WEDNESDAY

Friendship Frittata

1 clove garlic
2 medium red onions
2 medium zucchini
1/2 pound fresh mushrooms
2 tablespoons fresh chives (when chopped)
3 tablespoons fresh cilantro (when chopped)
9 eggs
3 tablespoons vegetable oil
Seasoning to taste
1/2 cup shredded Colby/Monterey Jack cheese

Lone-Star Salad

1 medium head lettuce
1 large tomato
1 small cucumber
1 small daikon radish
3 tablespoons olive oil
2 tablespoons apple cider vinegar
1 teaspoon granulated sugar
1 teaspoon celery seeds
Seasoning to taste

El Paso the Biscuits

2 cups flour
4 teaspoons baking powder
1/4 teaspoon salt
1/4 cup mayonnaise
3/4 cup milk

Banana Alamo-de

4 medium bananas
2 tablespoons butter
1 teaspoon banana extract
3 tablespoons molasses
1/2 cup dark brown sugar
1 pint vanilla ice cream
1/2 cup pecan bits for garnish

EQUIPMENT

Large ovenproof skillet
9 x 9-inch glass baking dish
Baking sheet
Breadboard
3 large mixing bowls
2 small mixing bowls
Whisk

Large biscuit cutter
Vegetable brush
Vegetable peeler
Ice cream scoop
Kitchen knives
Measuring cups and spoons
Cooking utensils

COUNTDOWN

1. Assemble the ingredients and the equipment.
2. Do Steps 1–2 of *Friendship Frittata*.
3. Do Steps 1–2 of *Lone-Star Salad*.
4. Do Steps 1–4 of *Banana Alamo-de*.
5. Do Steps 1–5 of *El Paso the Biscuits*.
6. Do Step 5 of *Banana Alamo-de*.
7. Do Step 6 of *El Paso the Biscuits*.
8. Do Steps 3–7 of *Friendship Frittata*.
9. Do Step 3 of *Lone-Star Salad*.
10. Do Step 6 of *Banana Alamo-de*.

WEDNESDAY

Friendship Frittata

1 Peel and mince the garlic. Peel and slice the onions. Scrub, trim, and chop the zucchini. Rinse, pat dry, trim, and slice the mushrooms. Rinse, trim, and chop the chives. Rinse, stem, and chop the cilantro.

2 Lightly beat the eggs in a large bowl.

3 Heat 2 tablespoons of the oil in a large ovenproof skillet. Sauté the garlic and the onions until the onions are soft, about 5 minutes. Stir in the zucchini and the mushrooms. Cook, stirring, until the vegetables are crisp-tender, 3 to 4 minutes. Stir in the chives and the cilantro and season to taste.

4 Add the vegetables to the eggs and mix in the cheese.

5 Add the remaining 1 tablespoon oil to the skillet. Pour in the egg mixture and simmer until the eggs are lightly browned on the bottom and the top is almost set, about 5 minutes.

6 Preheat the broiler.

7 Place the skillet under the broiler and broil until the top of the frittata is lightly browned, about 2 minutes.

Lone-Star Salad

1 Wash and dry the lettuce and tear it into bite-sized pieces. Rinse, stem, and chop the tomato. Peel, trim, and slice the cucumber. Peel, trim, and slice the daikon. Combine the ingredients in a large bowl.

2 In a small bowl, whisk together the oil, the vinegar, the sugar, and the celery seeds. Season to taste.

3 Toss the salad with the dressing.

El Paso the Biscuits

1 Flour a breadboard.

2 Combine the flour, the baking powder, and the salt in a large bowl. Make a well in the center.

3 Combine the mayonnaise and the milk in a small bowl and pour the mixture into the flour well. Mix lightly until a soft dough forms.

4 Place the dough in the center of the bread-board, knead 8 to 10 times, and pat into a 6-inch round. Cut with a large biscuit cutter and place the biscuits on a baking sheet.

5 Increase the oven temperature to 425°F.

6 Bake until the biscuits are lightly browned, 10 to 12 minutes.

Banana Alamo-de

1 Preheat the oven to 350°F.

2 Peel and slice the bananas.

3 Melt the butter with the banana extract in a 9 x 9-inch baking dish. Add the bananas. Drizzle the molasses over the bananas. Sprinkle with the brown sugar and mix to combine.

4 Bake for 10 minutes.

5 Spoon the banana mixture into individual dessert glasses and set aside until you are ready to serve.

6 Top with scoops of ice cream and sprinkle with the nuts.

THURSDAY

Over the Rainbow

1 package (10 ounces) frozen green peas
1/2 pound bacon
3 medium carrots
1 large red bell pepper
1 pound rainbow spiral pasta
1/4 cup vegetable oil
1 teaspoon Italian seasoning
1/4 cup dry white wine
1/2 cup shredded mozzarella cheese
Seasoning to taste

Munchkin Tomatoes

4 medium tomatoes
1 clove garlic
2 tablespoons butter
2 teaspoons Dijon mustard
1 teaspoon Worcestershire sauce
1/2 cup plain breadcrumbs
Seasoning to taste

Scarecrow Salad

1 medium head lettuce
2 scallions (green onions)
2 stalks celery
1 medium cucumber
1 small bunch radishes
3 tablespoons olive oil
2 tablespoons red wine vinegar
1 teaspoon granulated sugar
2 teaspoons ketchup
1/2 teaspoon dried tarragon
Seasoning to taste

Dorothy's Dessert

1 package (3.4 ounces) instant pistachio
    pudding mix
1 1/4 cups milk
3/4 cup sour cream
2 teaspoons ground cinnamon
Whipped cream for garnish
Multicolored sprinkles for garnish

EQUIPMENT

Electric mixer	2 small mixing bowls
Stockpot	Vegetable peeler
Small saucepan	Whisk
Large skillet	Kitchen knives
Baking sheet	Measuring cups and
Colander	spoons
Large mixing bowl	Cooking utensils
Medium mixing bowl	

COUNTDOWN

1. Assemble the ingredients and the equipment.
2. Do Steps 1–2 of *Dorothy's Dessert*.
3. Do Steps 1–2 of *Scarecrow Salad*.
4. Do Steps 1–2 of *Munchkin Tomatoes*.
5. Do Steps 1–5 of *Over the Rainbow*.
6. Do Steps 3–4 of *Munchkin Tomatoes*.
7. Do Steps 6–7 of *Over the Rainbow*.
8. Do Step 3 of *Scarecrow Salad*.
9. Do Step 3 of *Dorothy's Dessert*.

THURSDAY

Over the Rainbow

1 Set the peas in a small bowl of warm water to thaw.

2 Bring water to a boil in a stockpot.

3 Dice the bacon. Peel, trim, and grate the carrots. Rinse, trim, seed, and chop the bell pepper.

4 Cook the pasta spirals until almost tender, 8 to 10 minutes.

5 Sauté the bacon in a large skillet until it is crisp, about 7 minutes. Drain on paper towels.

6 Drain the pasta, return it to the stockpot, and cover to keep warm.

7 Discard all but 2 tablespoons of the bacon drippings. Heat the oil with the remaining drippings and sauté the carrots and the bell pepper for 2 minutes. Fold in the peas, the bacon, the Italian seasoning, the wine, and the cheese. Season to taste and heat through. Toss with the pasta.

Munchkin Tomatoes

1 Rinse, stem, and halve the tomatoes, and place them on a baking sheet, cut side up. Peel and mince the garlic.

2 Melt the butter in a small saucepan. Add the garlic, the mustard, and the Worcestershire sauce. Mix well to blend. Stir in the breadcrumbs and season to taste. Spread the mixture over the tomato halves, pressing lightly on the tops.

3 Preheat the broiler.

4 Broil the tomatoes until lightly browned, 3 to 4 minutes.

Scarecrow Salad

1 Wash and dry the lettuce and tear it into bite-sized pieces. Rinse, trim, and chop the scallions. Rinse, trim, and chop the celery. Peel, trim, and slice the cucumber. Rinse, trim, and slice the radishes. Combine the ingredients in a large bowl.

2 In a small bowl, whisk together the oil, the vinegar, the sugar, the ketchup, and the tarragon. Season to taste.

3 Toss the salad with the dressing.

Dorothy's Dessert

1 In a medium bowl, beat the pudding mix with the milk and the sour cream until well blended, about 2 minutes. Fold in the cinnamon.

2 Spoon the mixture into individual dessert glasses and refrigerate until you are ready to serve.

3 Top each pudding with a dollop of whipped cream and a generous splash of sprinkles.

FRIDAY

Nuclear Fishion

4 sea bass fillets (about 1 1/2 pounds)
Seasoning to taste
2 tablespoons fresh chives (when chopped)
1 1/2 teaspoons cornstarch
1/4 cup water
1 can (8 ounces) crushed pineapple
1/2 teaspoon ground ginger
1 teaspoon granulated sugar
1 tablespoon soy sauce

Pilaf Fer Me

2 scallions (green onions)
2 tablespoons fresh parsley (when chopped)
1 can (14 ounces) vegetable broth
2 tablespoons rice vinegar
1 cup couscous

Proton Peas

3/4 pound sugar-snap peas
3 stalks celery
2 tablespoons butter
1/4 teaspoon Chinese 5-spice

Icetope Pie

1 envelope unflavored gelatin
1 tablespoon lemon juice
4 eggs
1 can (12 ounces) mango nectar
1/2 cup granulated sugar
1/4 teaspoon cream of tartar
1 prepared pie shell
1 ripe mango

EQUIPMENT

Electric mixer	Large mixing bowl
Medium covered saucepan	Small mixing bowl
Medium saucepan	Aluminum foil
Small saucepan	Kitchen knives
Large skillet	Measuring cups and spoons
9 x 13-inch glass baking dish	Cooking utensils

COUNTDOWN

1. Assemble the ingredients and the equipment.
2. Do Steps 1–5 of *Icetope Pie*.
3. Do Steps 1–4 of *Nuclear Fishion*.
4. Do Step 1 of *Proton Peas*.
5. Do Steps 1–3 of *Pilaf Fer Me*.
6. Do Steps 5–6 of *Nuclear Fishion*.
7. Do Steps 2–3 of *Proton Peas*.
8. Do Step 7 of *Nuclear Fishion*.
9. Do Step 4 of *Pilaf Fer Me*.
10. Do Step 6 of *Icetope Pie*.

FRIDAY

Nuclear Fishion

1 Preheat the oven to 400°F. Grease a 9 x 13-inch baking dish.

2 Rinse and pat dry the fish fillets, season to taste, and arrange in a single layer in the baking dish.

3 Rinse, trim, and chop the chives.

4 In a small saucepan, blend the cornstarch and the water.

5 Add the undrained pineapple, the ginger, the sugar, and the soy sauce to the saucepan and cook until the mixture comes to a boil and thickens, 2 to 3 minutes.

6 Spread the sauce over the fish. Cover the dish with a sheet of aluminum foil and bake until the fish flakes easily with a fork, about 10 minutes.

7 Sprinkle with the chives.

Pilaf Fer Me

1 Rinse, trim, and chop the scallions. Rinse, stem, and chop the parsley.

2 In a medium saucepan, bring the broth and the vinegar to a boil.

3 Add the couscous, the scallions, and the parsley to the saucepan. Cover, remove from the heat, and let stand until the liquid is absorbed and the couscous is tender, at least 10 minutes.

4 Fluff the couscous with a fork.

Proton Peas

1 Rinse and string the snap peas. Rinse, trim, and slice the celery.

2 Melt the butter with the Chinese 5-spice in a large skillet.

3 Sauté the snap peas and the celery until they are crisp-tender, about 3 minutes.

Icetope Pie

1 In a small bowl, soften the gelatin in the lemon juice.

2 Separate the eggs, placing the yolks in a medium saucepan and the whites in a large bowl.

3 Add the mango nectar and ¼ cup of the sugar to the egg yolks. Blend well and cook until the mixture thickens, about 5 minutes.

4 Add the gelatin mixture to the saucepan and stir until melted, about 2 minutes. Remove the saucepan from the heat and let it stand for 2 minutes. Refrigerate for 10 minutes.

5 Beat the egg whites with the remaining ¼ cup sugar and the cream of tartar until stiff peaks form, about 5 minutes. Fold the gelatin mixture into the egg white mixture and pour into the pie shell. Refrigerate until you are ready to serve.

6 Peel, halve, pit, and slice the mango. Arrange the slices around the pie.

WEEK FIVE

STAPLES

Monday
Alleggheny
Panhandle Potatoes
Morgan Morgan Melon
Wheeling Dervishes

Tuesday
Flounder de Foil
Rice à l'Orange
Bois du Beans
Tête-à-Tart

Wednesday
Leaning Tower of Pizza
Sigh Salad
Ciao

Thursday
Where's the Beef?
Here's the Salad
What's Your Hurry?

Friday
Clair de Tuna
I'll Take Romaine
Rock on Down the Road

- ❑ Butter
- ❑ Cornstarch
- ❑ Cream of tartar
- ❑ Granulated sugar
- ❑ Powdered sugar
- ❑ Cocoa powder
- ❑ Olive oil
- ❑ Vegetable oil
- ❑ Red wine vinegar
- ❑ Lemon juice
- ❑ Lime juice
- ❑ Dijon mustard
- ❑ Honey
- ❑ Mayonnaise
- ❑ Worcestershire sauce
- ❑ Grated Parmesan cheese
- ❑ Dried basil
- ❑ Dried rosemary
- ❑ Dried tarragon
- ❑ Chili powder
- ❑ Ground cumin
- ❑ Ground nutmeg
- ❑ Black pepper
- ❑ Salt
- ❑ Banana extract
- ❑ Orange extract
- ❑ Vanilla extract

MEAT & POULTRY

1 ½ pounds lean ground beef (Th)

1 ½ pounds breakfast link sausage (M)

FISH

4 flounder fillets (about 1 ½ pounds) (T)

FRESH PRODUCE

VEGETABLES

1 ½ pounds small new red potatoes (M)

1 pound green beans (T)

1 stalk celery (T)

2 stalks celery (Th)

½ pound mushrooms (W)

1 small head Boston lettuce (Th)

1 large head romaine lettuce (F)

1 package (10 ounces) mixed salad greens (W)

1 large tomato (M)

2 medium tomatoes (W)

1 large ripe avocado (W)

1 medium cucumber (W)

2 medium green bell peppers (W)

1 medium onion (T)

2 medium onions (W)

1 small onion (F)

1 small red onion (M)

1 medium shallot (M)

3 scallions (green onions) (M)

3 scallions (green onions) (Th)

2 tablespoons chives (when chopped) (W)

1 clove garlic (T)

3 cloves garlic (F)

HERBS

¼ cup basil leaves (when chopped) (W)

4 sprigs dill (T)

1 tablespoon parsley (when chopped) (T)

2 tablespoons parsley (when chopped) (M)

¼ cup parsley (when chopped) (F)

FRUIT

2 medium oranges (M)

1 small orange (T)

1 large lemon (T)

1 small lemon (Th)

1 medium honeydew melon (M)

1 small banana (Th)

4 medium ripe pears (Th)

1 quart strawberries (T)

CANS, JARS & BOTTLES

SOUPS

1 can (14 ounces) beef broth (Th)

1 can (10 ¾ ounces) golden mushroom soup (Th)

VEGETABLES

1 can (14 ½ ounces) diced tomatoes (F)

FISH

2 cans (6 ounces each) solid white tuna (F)

SAUCES

1 jar (14 ounces) pizza sauce (W)

FRUIT

1 can (20 ounces) cherry pie filling (M)

1 can (15 ounces) sliced peaches in syrup (Th)

CONDIMENTS

1 can (3 ½ ounces) sliced black olives (W)

1 jar (2 ounces) diced pimientos (Th)

PACKAGED GOODS

PASTA, RICE & GRAINS

1 pound penne (F)

1 cup long-grain white rice (T)

1 cup couscous (Th)

BAKED GOODS

4 small Boboli pizza crusts (W)

1 small French baguette (F)

1 cup potato chips (when crushed) (Th)

4 prepared tart shells (T)

4 individual sponge cake dessert shells (Th)

8 large chocolate cookies (F)

DRIED FRUIT & NUTS

½ cup slivered almonds (T)

¼ cup walnut bits (F)

DESSERT & BAKING NEEDS

1 package (3 ½ ounces) strawberry gelatin (T)

3 tablespoons instant tapioca (W)

¼ cup mini-marshmallows (F)

WINE & SPIRITS

2 tablespoons dry white wine (T)

½ cup dry white wine (F)

3 tablespoons dry sherry (Th)

REFRIGERATED PRODUCTS

DAIRY

2 tablespoons milk (M)

2 cups chocolate milk (W)

1 cup whipping cream (M)

9 eggs (M)

2 eggs (W)

1 egg (F)

CHEESE

1 package (3 ounces) cream cheese (M)

½ pound shredded mozzarella cheese (W)

1 cup small-curd cottage cheese (Th)

JUICES

¼ cup orange juice (M)

FROZEN GOODS

VEGETABLES

1 package (10 ounces) green peas (Th)

FRUIT

1 package (12 ounces) blueberries (Th)

BAKED GOODS

8 round waffles (M)

DESSERTS

1 pint chocolate ice cream (F)

MONDAY

Alleggheny

1 1/2 pounds breakfast link sausage
1 medium shallot
3 scallions (green onions)
1 large tomato
9 eggs
2 tablespoons milk
1 teaspoon chili powder
1 tablespoon vegetable oil
Seasoning to taste

Panhandle Potatoes

1 small red onion
1 1/2 pounds small new red potatoes
2 tablespoons fresh parsley (when
    chopped)
2 tablespoons lemon juice
1 tablespoon olive oil
1 teaspoon ground cumin
1/2 teaspoon dried basil
Seasoning to taste

Morgan Morgan Melon

1/4 cup orange juice
1/4 cup lime juice
1 tablespoon honey
1/2 teaspoon orange extract
2 medium oranges
1 medium ripe honeydew melon

Wheeling Dervishes

8 frozen round waffles
1 package (3 ounces) cream cheese
1/4 cup powdered sugar
1 cup whipping cream
1 can (20 ounces) cherry pie filling

EQUIPMENT

Electric mixer	Vegetable brush
Large covered saucepan	Citrus grater
	Plastic wrap
Small saucepan	Kitchen knives
Large covered skillet	Measuring cups and spoons
Large mixing bowl	
Medium mixing bowl	Cooking utensils
Whisk	

COUNTDOWN

1. Assemble the ingredients and the equipment.
2. Do Step 1 of *Morgan Morgan Melon*.
3. Do Steps 1–3 of *Wheeling Dervishes*.
4. Do Steps 1–2 of *Panhandle Potatoes*.
5. Do Steps 2–3 of *Morgan Morgan Melon*.
6. Do Steps 1–5 of *Alleggheny*.
7. Do Step 3 of *Panhandle Potatoes*.
8. Do Step 6 of *Alleggheny*.
9. Do Step 4 of *Morgan Morgan Melon*.
10. Do Steps 4–5 of *Wheeling Dervishes*.

MONDAY

Alleggheny

1 Place the sausage in the freezer for 10 minutes.

2 Peel and mince the shallot. Rinse, trim, and chop the scallions. Rinse, stem, and chop the tomato. Slice the sausage.

3 In a large bowl, whip the eggs with the milk and the chili powder.

4 Heat the oil in a large skillet. Add the sausage and the shallot and sauté until the sausage is well browned, about 10 minutes.

5 Pour the egg mixture over the sausage and shallot. Add the tomato and the scallions. Season to taste and cook until the eggs are set, about 5 minutes.

6 Cover the skillet, remove it from the heat, and let stand until you are ready to serve.

Panhandle Potatoes

1 Peel and chop the onion. Scrub the potatoes and cut them in half. Rinse, stem, and chop the parsley.

2 In a large saucepan, cover the potatoes with water. Bring to a boil, cover the saucepan, reduce the heat, and simmer until the potatoes are tender, 10 to 12 minutes.

3 Drain the potatoes. Add the onion, the lemon juice, the oil, the cumin, and the basil. Season to taste and sprinkle with the parsley.

Morgan Morgan Melon

1 In a small saucepan, combine the orange juice, the lime juice, the honey, and the orange extract. Heat until well blended. Remove from the heat and set aside.

2 Grate 1 tablespoon of orange peel. Peel and section the oranges. Halve, seed, and slice the melon. Remove the rind.

3 Arrange the melon slices and the orange sections on individual plates.

4 Drizzle the sauce over the fruit and sprinkle with the orange peel.

Wheeling Dervishes

1 Set the waffles out to thaw.

2 Cut the cream cheese into small pieces and place in a medium bowl. Blend in the powdered sugar and beat until fluffy, about 2 minutes.

3 Gradually beat in the cream until well blended and thick, about 3 minutes. Cover with plastic wrap and refrigerate until you are ready to use.

4 Toast the waffles.

5 On individual dessert plates, spread 2 tablespoons of the cream on each of 4 waffles. Spread 2 tablespoons of the pie filling over the cream. Cover with the remaining waffles and spoon the remainder of the cream and the remainder of the pie filling over the top, letting it run down the sides.

TUESDAY

Flounder de Foil

2 teaspoons butter
1 medium onion
1 large lemon
4 flounder fillets (about 1½ pounds)
4 sprigs fresh dill
2 tablespoons dry white wine
Seasoning to taste

Rice à l'Orange

1 clove garlic
1 stalk celery
1 tablespoon fresh parsley (when chopped)
1 small orange
½ cup slivered almonds
1 tablespoon butter
1 cup long-grain white rice
2¼ cups water
¼ teaspoon ground nutmeg

Bois du Beans

1 pound fresh green beans
1 tablespoon butter
1 teaspoon red wine vinegar
Seasoning to taste

Tête-à-Tart

1 quart fresh strawberries
1 cup granulated sugar
1 cup water
2 tablespoons cornstarch
1 tablespoon butter
1 tablespoon lemon juice
1 package (3½ ounces) strawberry gelatin
4 prepared tart shells
2 tablespoons powdered sugar for garnish

EQUIPMENT

Medium covered
  saucepan
Medium saucepan
Large covered skillet
Steamer insert
Medium mixing bowl
Baking sheet

Citrus grater
Aluminum foil
Kitchen knives
Measuring cups and
  spoons
Cooking utensils

COUNTDOWN

1. Assemble the ingredients and the equipment.
2. Do Steps 1–2 of Tête-à-Tart.
3. Do Steps 1–5 of Rice à l'Orange.
4. Do Steps 3–4 of Tête-à-Tart.
5. Do Steps 1–5 of Flounder de Foil.
6. Do Steps 1–3 of Bois du Beans.
7. Do Step 6 of Flounder de Foil.
8. Do Steps 4–5 of Bois du Beans.
9. Do Step 6 of Rice à l'Orange.

TUESDAY

Flounder de Foil

1 Melt the butter.

2 Peel and thinly slice the onion. Grate the peel from the lemon and slice the lemon.

3 Rinse and pat dry the fish fillets.

4 Lay each flounder fillet on a sheet of aluminum foil. Drizzle the fish with the melted butter. Top with a slice of onion, a slice of lemon, and a sprig of dill. Drizzle the wine over the top and season to taste.

5 Fold the foil around the fish, seal it, and place the packets on a baking sheet.

6 Bake at 400°F until the fish flakes easily with a fork, about 10 minutes.

Rice à l'Orange

1 Preheat the oven to 400°F.

2 Peel and mince the garlic. Rinse, trim, and chop the celery. Rinse, stem, and chop the parsley. Grate 1 tablespoon of orange peel. Peel and section the orange and cut the sections in half.

3 Lay the almonds on a baking sheet and bake until lightly toasted, about 5 minutes.

4 Melt the butter in a large skillet and sauté the garlic and the celery for 3 minutes. Add the rice and sauté for 1 minute.

5 Add the water and the nutmeg, bring to a boil, cover, and reduce the heat. Simmer until all the liquid is absorbed and the rice is tender, about 20 minutes.

6 Fold the parsley, the orange peel, the orange sections, and the almonds into the rice and fluff with a fork.

Bois du Beans

1 Bring a small amount of water to a boil in a medium saucepan.

2 Rinse and trim the green beans.

3 Put the beans in a steamer insert and place the insert in the saucepan. Cover and steam until the beans are crisp-tender, 6 to 8 minutes.

4 Drain the beans.

5 Melt the butter with the vinegar in the saucepan. Season to taste, add the beans, and toss to coat.

Tête-à-Tart

1 Wash and hull the berries, reserving 4 for garnish. Mash 1 cup of the berries, leaving the rest whole.

2 In a medium saucepan, combine the mashed berries, the granulated sugar, the water, and the cornstarch. Bring the mixture to a boil and cook for 2 minutes. Add the butter and remove from the heat. Add the lemon juice and the gelatin, stirring to dissolve. Pour the mixture into a medium bowl and refrigerate until partially set, at least 10 minutes.

3 Spoon half of the gelatin into individual tart shells, fill with the whole strawberries, and spoon the remaining gelatin over the top.

4 Top the tarts with the reserved strawberries and dust with the powdered sugar. Refrigerate until you are ready to serve.

WEDNESDAY

Leaning Tower of Pizza

2 medium onions
2 medium green bell peppers
1/2 pound fresh mushrooms
2 medium tomatoes
1/4 cup fresh basil leaves (when chopped)
1 can (3 1/2 ounces) sliced black olives
4 small Boboli pizza crusts
1 jar (14 ounces) pizza sauce
1/2 pound shredded mozzarella cheese
1 cup grated Parmesan cheese
Seasoning to taste

Sigh Salad

1 package (10 ounces) mixed salad greens
1 medium cucumber
1 large ripe avocado
2 tablespoons fresh chives (when chopped)
3 tablespoons olive oil
2 tablespoons red wine vinegar
1 teaspoon dried tarragon
2 teaspoons Dijon mustard
1/2 teaspoon granulated sugar
Seasoning to taste

Ciao

2 eggs
2 cups chocolate milk
1/3 cup plus 2 tablespoons granulated sugar
3 tablespoons instant tapioca
3 tablespoons cocoa powder
1/4 teaspoon cream of tartar
1 teaspoon vanilla extract

EQUIPMENT

Electric mixer
Medium saucepan
Baking sheet
2 large mixing bowls
Small mixing bowl
Whisk

Vegetable brush
Kitchen knives
Measuring cups and
  spoons
Cooking utensils

COUNTDOWN

1. Assemble the ingredients and the equipment.
2. Do Steps 1–2 of Ciao.
3. Do Steps 1–4 of Leaning Tower of Pizza.
4. Do Steps 3–4 of Ciao.
5. Do Steps 1–2 of Sigh Salad.

WEDNESDAY

Leaning Tower of Pizza

1 Preheat the oven to 450°F.

2 Peel and thinly slice the onions. Rinse, trim, seed, and thinly slice the bell peppers. Rinse, pat dry, trim, and slice the mushrooms. Rinse, stem, and thinly slice the tomatoes. Rinse, stem, and chop the basil. Drain the olives.

3 Spread the Boboli pizza crusts with the pizza sauce. Spread the mozzarella cheese over the sauce. Sprinkle the Parmesan cheese over the mozzarella. Add the onions, the bell peppers, the mushrooms, the tomatoes, the olives, and the basil. Season to taste.

4 Lay the pizzas on a baking sheet and bake until the cheese has melted and the vegetables are hot, about 20 minutes.

Sigh Salad

1 Wash and dry the mixed greens. Scrub, trim, and slice the cucumber. Halve, pit, peel, and chop the avocado. Rinse, trim, and chop the chives. Combine the ingredients in a large bowl.

2 In a small bowl, whisk together the oil, the vinegar, the tarragon, the mustard, and the sugar. Season to taste and toss the salad with the dressing.

Ciao

1 Separate the eggs, placing the yolks in a medium saucepan and the whites in a large bowl.

2 To the yolks, add the milk, ⅓ cup of the sugar, the tapioca, and the cocoa powder. Whisk to combine and let stand for 5 minutes.

3 Beat the egg whites with the cream of tartar until frothy, about 2 minutes. Gradually add the remaining 2 tablespoons sugar and beat well until stiff peaks form, about 3 minutes.

4 Bring the tapioca mixture to a boil, stirring. Remove the saucepan from the heat, fold in the vanilla, and slowly pour the mixture into the beaten egg whites. Blend well and set the pudding aside until you are ready to serve.

THURSDAY

Where's the Beef?

1 package (10 ounces) frozen green peas
1 can (14 ounces) beef broth
1 cup couscous
2 stalks celery
3 scallions (green onions)
1 jar (2 ounces) diced pimientos
1 cup potato chips (when crushed)
1½ pounds lean ground beef
1 can (10¾ ounces) golden mushroom soup
3 tablespoons dry sherry
Seasoning to taste

Here's the Salad

1 small head Boston lettuce
4 medium ripe pears
1 small lemon
2 teaspoons honey
¼ cup mayonnaise
1 cup small-curd cottage cheese

What's Your Hurry?

1 package (12 ounces) frozen blueberries
1 can (15 ounces) sliced peaches in syrup
1 teaspoon cornstarch
½ teaspoon banana extract
1 small banana
4 individual sponge cake dessert shells

EQUIPMENT

Medium covered saucepan
Small saucepan
1½-quart flameproof casserole
Medium mixing bowl
3 small mixing bowls
Citrus grater
Citrus juicer
Plastic bag
Kitchen knives
Measuring cups and spoons
Cooking utensils

COUNTDOWN

1. Assemble the ingredients and the equipment.
2. Do Steps 1–7 of Where's the Beef?
3. Do Steps 1–3 of What's Your Hurry?
4. Do Steps 1–3 of Here's the Salad.
5. Do Steps 4–5 of What's Your Hurry?

THURSDAY

Where's the Beef?

1 Set the peas in a small bowl of warm water to thaw.

2 Bring the broth to a boil in a medium saucepan. Add the couscous, cover tightly, remove from the heat, and let stand for 5 minutes.

3 Preheat the oven to 375°F.

4 Rinse, trim, and chop the celery. Rinse, trim, and chop the scallions. Drain the pimientos. Place the potato chips in a plastic bag and crush them.

5 In a 1½-quart flameproof casserole, sauté the beef until browned and crumbly, about 5 minutes.

6 Drain off any fat. Spread the beef evenly in the bottom of the casserole. Spread the couscous over the beef. Layer the peas over the couscous. Layer the celery over the peas.

7 In a small bowl, combine the soup, the sherry, the scallions, and the pimientos. Season to taste and spread over the casserole. Sprinkle the potato chips on top and bake until hot and bubbly, about 30 minutes.

Here's the Salad

1 Wash and dry the lettuce and distribute the leaves among individual salad plates. Peel, halve, and core the pears.

2 Grate 1 teaspoon of lemon peel and squeeze 1½ teaspoons lemon juice. Combine the lemon juice, the honey, the mayonnaise, and the cottage cheese in a medium bowl.

3 Place 2 pear halves on each lettuce bed and fill the cavities with scoops of the cottage cheese mixture. Sprinkle the lemon peel on top.

What's Your Hurry?

1 Set the blueberries in a small bowl of warm water to thaw.

2 Drain the peaches, reserving the liquid.

3 In a small saucepan, combine the reserved liquid with the cornstarch and the banana extract. Bring to a boil and cook, stirring, until the mixture is clear and begins to thicken, about 2 minutes. Set aside.

4 Peel and slice the banana. Add the blueberries and the peaches and combine.

5 Arrange the fruit in individual sponge cake dessert shells and drizzle with the glaze.

FRIDAY

Clair de Tuna

1 small onion
1 clove garlic
1/4 cup fresh parsley (when chopped)
2 cans (6 ounces each) solid white tuna
1 pound penne
2 tablespoons olive oil
1 can (14 1/2 ounces) diced tomatoes
1/2 cup dry white wine
1 teaspoon dried basil
1/2 teaspoon dried rosemary
Seasoning to taste

I'll Take Romaine

2 cloves garlic
1 large head romaine lettuce
1 small French baguette
4 tablespoons olive oil
1 tablespoon Worcestershire sauce
3 tablespoons vegetable oil
Seasoning to taste
1 egg
1/4 cup lemon juice
1/2 cup grated Parmesan cheese

Rock on Down the Road

1 pint chocolate ice cream
1/4 cup mini-marshmallows
1/4 cup walnut bits
8 large chocolate cookies

EQUIPMENT

Stockpot	Colander
Large saucepan	Plastic wrap
Small saucepan	Kitchen knives
Medium skillet	Measuring cups and
Large mixing bowl	spoons
Small mixing bowl	Cooking utensils
Whisk	

COUNTDOWN

1. Assemble the ingredients and the equipment.
2. Do Step 1 of *Rock on Down the Road*.
3. Do Steps 1–5 of *I'll Take Romaine*.
4. Do Steps 2–4 of *Rock on Down the Road*.
5. Do Steps 1–7 of *Clair de Tuna*.
6. Do Step 6 of *I'll Take Romaine*.

FRIDAY

Clair de Tuna

1 Bring water to a boil in a stockpot.

2 Peel and chop the onion. Peel and mince the garlic. Rinse, stem, and chop the parsley. Drain and flake the tuna.

3 Cook the penne until it is tender but still firm, 8 to 10 minutes.

4 Heat the oil in a large saucepan. Sauté the onion and the garlic until the onion is soft, about 4 minutes. Stir in the tomatoes, the wine, the basil, and the rosemary. Simmer, uncovered, until the flavors are combined, about 4 minutes.

5 Add the tuna to the tomato mixture, season to taste, and cook until heated through, about 2 minutes.

6 Drain the pasta and return it to the stockpot.

7 Toss the tuna mixture with the pasta and sprinkle with the parsley.

I'll Take Romaine

1 Peel and mince the garlic. Wash, dry, and tear the lettuce into bite-sized pieces. Place it in a large bowl.

2 Cut the bread into small cubes. Combine the cubes with 2 tablespoons of the olive oil in a medium skillet and sauté until crisp and golden, about 5 minutes. Set aside.

3 Bring water to a boil in a small saucepan. Cook the egg for 1 minute. Drain and rinse under cold water.

4 In a small bowl, whisk together the remaining 2 tablespoons olive oil with the garlic, the Worcestershire sauce, and the vegetable oil. Season to taste. Add the egg and the lemon juice and blend well.

5 Add the croutons to the lettuce and toss. Add the cheese and toss again.

6 Add the dressing and toss to coat.

Rock on Down the Road

1 Set the ice cream out to soften slightly.

2 Snip the marshmallows into small pieces.

3 Combine the marshmallows and the nuts with the softened ice cream.

4 Spread the ice cream mixture on each of 4 cookies and top with a second cookie. Wrap each cookie sandwich in plastic wrap and freeze until firm, at least 20 minutes.

WEEK SIX

WEEK AT A GLANCE

Monday
MacBeef
FitzSalad
O'Shake

Tuesday
The Thigh's the Limit
Nutty Pilaf
Broc-and-Roll
Kooky Fruit

Wednesday
Pirate's Pasta
High Seas Salad
Crescent Moons
Raspberry Plunder

Thursday
Sing-a-Pork
Raffles
Panda Parfait

Friday
How's Bayou?
Baton Rouge
Bourbon Street Bananas

STAPLES

- ☐ Butter
- ☐ Cornstarch
- ☐ Granulated sugar
- ☐ Dark brown sugar
- ☐ Powdered sugar
- ☐ Chocolate syrup
- ☐ Cocoa powder
- ☐ Multicolored sprinkles
- ☐ Olive oil
- ☐ Sesame oil
- ☐ Vegetable oil
- ☐ Red wine vinegar
- ☐ Rice vinegar
- ☐ White wine vinegar
- ☐ Lemon juice
- ☐ Lime juice
- ☐ Dijon mustard
- ☐ Honey
- ☐ Ketchup
- ☐ Mayonnaise
- ☐ Prepared horseradish
- ☐ Tabasco sauce
- ☐ Worcestershire sauce
- ☐ Dried dill
- ☐ Dried thyme
- ☐ Ground allspice
- ☐ Cayenne pepper
- ☐ Ground cinnamon
- ☐ Curry powder
- ☐ Italian seasoning
- ☐ Dry mustard
- ☐ Paprika
- ☐ Black pepper
- ☐ Salt
- ☐ Turmeric
- ☐ Banana extract
- ☐ Orange extract
- ☐ Vanilla extract

MEAT & POULTRY

1 1/2 pounds lean ground beef (M)
1 1/2 pounds lean boneless pork loin (Th)
1 1/2 pounds boneless, skinless chicken thighs (T)

FISH

1 pound clams (W)
1 pound mussels (W)
1/2 pound sea scallops (W)

FRESH PRODUCE

VEGETABLES

1 large bunch broccoli (T)
2 small zucchini (Th)
2 stalks celery (F)
1 small head red cabbage (Th)
1 medium head green leaf lettuce (W)
1 medium head red leaf lettuce (F)
1 small head lettuce (M)
2 medium tomatoes (W)
1 large ripe avocado (M)
1 medium ripe avocado (F)
1 medium cucumber (F)
1 small cucumber (W)
1 medium green bell pepper (F)
1 medium red bell pepper (F)
1 small red bell pepper (T)
1 small yellow bell pepper (Th)
1 large leek (W)
1 large onion (W)
1 large onion (F)
1 medium onion (T)
1 medium red onion (Th)
2 scallions (green onions) (T)
4 scallions (green onions) (W)
2 cloves garlic (W)
1 clove garlic (Th)
3 cloves garlic (F)

HERBS

3 tablespoons basil leaves (when chopped) (W)
1/4 cup chives (when chopped) (M)
1/4 cup chives (when chopped) (Th)

2 tablespoons chives (when chopped) (F)
1/2 cup parsley (when chopped) (W)
2 tablespoons parsley (when chopped) (F)

FRUIT

2 large oranges (T)
1 small ripe honeydew melon (M)
1 large banana (T)
4 medium bananas (F)
2 ripe kiwifruit (T)

CANS, JARS & BOTTLES

SOUPS

1 can (14 ounces) chicken broth (T)
2 cans (14 ounces each) vegetable broth (F)
1 can (10 3/4 ounces) Cheddar cheese soup (M)

VEGETABLES

2 cans (14 1/2 ounces each) Cajun-style stewed tomatoes (F)
1 can (2.8 ounces) French fried onions (M)
1 can (11 ounces) whole-kernel corn (F)
1 can (15 ounces) white beans (F)
1 can (8 ounces) julienne beets (F)

FRUIT

1 can (11 ounces) mandarin oranges (Th)

JUICES

1 can (6 ounces) grapefruit juice (T)

CONDIMENTS

1 jar (6 1/2 ounces) marinated artichoke hearts (W)
2 tablespoons capers (F)

PACKAGED GOODS

PASTA, RICE & GRAINS

8 ounces elbow macaroni (M)
1 pound fettuccine (W)
1 cup brown rice (T)

1 1/2 cups long-grain white rice (F)

BAKED GOODS

1 loaf French bread (F)

INTERNATIONAL FOODS

8 ounces Chinese-style soft noodles (Th)

DRIED FRUIT & NUTS

1/2 cup sliced almonds (T)

DESSERT & BAKING NEEDS

1 package (3.4 ounces) instant devil's food pudding mix (Th)
1/2 cup flaked coconut (Th)

WINE & SPIRITS

1 cup dry white wine (W)
2 tablespoons bourbon (F)

REFRIGERATED PRODUCTS

DAIRY

3 cups milk (M)
1 3/4 cups milk (Th)
1/4 cup sour cream (F)
1/2 cup plain yogurt (T)
1 cup whipping cream (W)
Whipped cream for garnish (M)
Whipped cream for garnish (F)

CHEESE

1 package (8 ounces) cream cheese (W)

JUICES

1/4 cup orange juice (T)

DELI

1 package crescent rolls (W)

FROZEN GOODS

VEGETABLES

1 package (10 ounces) cut green beans (M)

FRUIT

1 package (16 ounces) raspberries (W)

DESSERTS

1 pint chocolate mint chip ice cream (M)
1 container (8 ounces) whipped topping (Th)

MONDAY

MacBeef

1 package (10 ounces) frozen cut green
  beans
2 tablespoons vegetable oil
1 1/2 pounds lean ground beef
8 ounces elbow macaroni
1/2 cup water
1 teaspoon dry mustard
1 teaspoon Italian seasoning
1 can (10 3/4 ounces) Cheddar cheese soup
Seasoning to taste
1 can (2.8 ounces) French fried onions
1/2 teaspoon paprika

FitzSalad

1 small head lettuce
1/4 cup fresh chives (when chopped)
1 small ripe honeydew melon
1 large ripe avocado
1/4 cup mayonnaise
1 teaspoon lemon juice
2 teaspoons honey

O'Shake

1 pint chocolate mint chip ice cream
3 cups milk
1/2 cup chocolate syrup
Whipped cream for garnish
Cocoa powder for garnish

EQUIPMENT

Blender	Whisk
Large saucepan	Kitchen knives
Large skillet	Measuring cups and
2-quart casserole	spoons
Colander	Cooking utensils
2 small mixing bowls	

COUNTDOWN

1. Assemble the ingredients and the
   equipment.
2. Do Steps 1–10 of *MacBeef*.
3. Do Steps 1–5 of *FitzSalad*.
4. Do Steps 1–2 of *O'Shake*.

MONDAY

MacBeef

1 Preheat the oven to 350°F.

2 Set the green beans in a small bowl of warm water to thaw.

3 Bring water to a boil in a large saucepan.

4 Heat the oil in a large skillet and sauté the beef until browned, about 8 minutes. Turn the beef into a 2-quart casserole.

5 Cook the macaroni until it is almost tender, about 10 minutes.

6 Bring the ½ cup water to a boil in the skillet. Add the beans, the mustard, and the Italian seasoning and cook until the beans are crisp-tender, about 3 minutes.

7 Drain the beans and add them to the casserole. Mix in the soup.

8 Drain the pasta, add it to the casserole, season to taste, and blend well.

9 Crumble the French fried onions over the top of the casserole and sprinkle with the paprika.

10 Bake until hot and bubbly, 20 to 25 minutes.

FitzSalad

1 Wash and dry the lettuce and distribute the leaves among individual salad plates. Rinse, trim, and chop the chives.

2 Cut the melon in half and remove the seeds. Cut the halves into quarters, remove the rind, and slice. Arrange the slices on the lettuce.

3 Halve, pit, peel, and slice the avocado. Arrange the slices with the melon.

4 In a small bowl, whisk together the mayonnaise, the lemon juice, and the honey. Spoon the mixture over the fruit.

5 Sprinkle the chives over the salad.

O'Shake

1 Place half of the ice cream, half of the milk, and half of the chocolate syrup in a blender and process until smooth, about 1 minute. Pour into individual dessert glasses and repeat.

2 Top each shake with a dollop of whipped cream and a sprinkle of cocoa powder.

TUESDAY

The Thigh's the Limit

1 1/2 pounds boneless, skinless chicken thighs
1 1/2 tablespoons Dijon mustard
1/2 cup plain yogurt
2 teaspoons curry powder
1/2 teaspoon cayenne pepper
1 teaspoon turmeric
2 tablespoons lemon juice
2 tablespoons vegetable oil
Seasoning to taste

Nutty Pilaf

1 medium onion
1/2 cup sliced almonds
2 tablespoons butter
1 cup brown rice
1 can (14 ounces) chicken broth
1 cup water

Broc-and-Roll

1 large bunch broccoli
1 small red bell pepper
2 scallions (green onions)
1 tablespoon butter
1 tablespoon vegetable oil
Seasoning to taste

Kooky Fruit

1 can (6 ounces) grapefruit juice
1/4 cup lime juice
1/4 cup orange juice
3 tablespoons granulated sugar
2 tablespoons cornstarch
1 teaspoon banana extract
2 large oranges
1 large banana
2 ripe kiwifruit
1 teaspoon ground cinnamon

EQUIPMENT

Medium covered
  saucepan
Small covered
  saucepan
2 large skillets
Medium mixing bowl

Whisk
Plastic wrap
Kitchen knives
Measuring cups and
  spoons
Cooking utensils

COUNTDOWN

1. Assemble the ingredients and the equipment.
2. Do Steps 1–2 of *The Thigh's the Limit*.
3. Do Steps 1–3 of *Nutty Pilaf*.
4. Do Steps 1–2 of *Kooky Fruit*.
5. Do Step 3 of *The Thigh's the Limit*.
6. Do Steps 1–2 of *Broc-and-Roll*.
7. Do Step 4 of *Nutty Pilaf*.
8. Do Steps 3–4 of *Kooky Fruit*.

TUESDAY

The Thigh's the Limit

1 Rinse and pat dry the chicken thighs.

2 Combine the mustard, the yogurt, the curry powder, the cayenne pepper, the turmeric, and the lemon juice in a medium bowl. Add the chicken, turning to coat. Cover the bowl with plastic wrap and marinate for 10 minutes, turning several times.

3 Heat the oil in a large skillet. Carefully remove the chicken from the marinade and sauté until it is lightly browned, about 5 minutes per side. Add the marinade to the skillet, season to taste, and reduce the heat. Simmer the chicken, turning once or twice until it is fork-tender, 15 to 20 minutes.

Nutty Pilaf

1 Peel and chop the onion.

2 Place the almonds in a medium saucepan and brown lightly, about 2 minutes.

3 Remove the almonds and reserve. Melt the butter in the same saucepan. Sauté the onion until it is soft, about 5 minutes. Add the rice, the broth, and the water and bring the mixture to a boil. Cover, reduce the heat, and simmer until all the liquid is absorbed and the rice is tender, 40 to 45 minutes.

4 Fluff the rice with a fork and top with the almonds.

Broc-and-Roll

1 Rinse and trim the broccoli and cut it into bite-sized florets, discarding the tough ends. Rinse, trim, seed, and chop the bell pepper. Rinse, trim, and chop the scallions.

2 Melt the butter with the oil in a large skillet and sauté the broccoli for 3 minutes. Add the bell pepper and the scallions and sauté for 3 minutes more. Season to taste.

Kooky Fruit

1 Combine the juices and the sugar in a small saucepan. Blend in the cornstarch and cook until the mixture has thickened, about 3 minutes.

2 Remove the saucepan from the heat and stir in the banana extract. Cover and let stand.

3 Peel and section the oranges. Peel and slice the banana. Peel and slice the kiwifruit.

4 Spoon the sauce onto individual dessert plates. Arrange the fruit slices over the sauce. Sprinkle with the cinnamon.

WEDNESDAY

Pirate's Pasta

1 pound fresh clams
1 pound fresh mussels
1/2 pound sea scallops
1 large leek
1 large onion
2 medium tomatoes
1/2 cup fresh parsley (when chopped)
1 cup dry white wine
1 pound fettuccine
2 tablespoons olive oil
1 teaspoon dried thyme
Seasoning to taste

High Seas Salad

1 medium head green leaf lettuce
4 scallions (green onions)
3 tablespoons fresh basil leaves (when
    chopped)
1 small cucumber
1 jar (6 1/2 ounces) marinated artichoke
    hearts
2 tablespoons white wine vinegar
1 teaspoon granulated sugar
Seasoning to taste

Crescent Moons

2 cloves garlic
1 package refrigerated crescent rolls
2 tablespoons olive oil

Raspberry Plunder

1 package (8 ounces) cream cheese
1 package (16 ounces) frozen raspberries
1/3 cup powdered sugar
1 teaspoon vanilla extract
1 cup whipping cream
Multicolored sprinkles for garnish

EQUIPMENT

Electric mixer	Medium mixing bowl
Blender	Small mixing bowl
Stockpot	Whisk
Large covered saucepan	Vegetable brush
Large covered skillet	Vegetable peeler
Baking sheet	Pastry brush
Colander	Kitchen knives
Large mixing bowl	Measuring cups and spoons
	Cooking utensils

COUNTDOWN

1. Assemble the ingredients and the equipment.
2. Do Step 1 of *Raspberry Plunder*.
3. Do Steps 1–3 of *Pirate's Pasta*.
4. Do Steps 1–2 of *High Seas Salad*.
5. Do Steps 2–3 of *Raspberry Plunder*.
6. Do Steps 1–3 of *Crescent Moons*.
7. Do Steps 4–9 of *Pirate's Pasta*.
8. Do Step 3 of *High Seas Salad*.

WEDNESDAY

Pirate's Pasta

1 Bring water to a boil in a stockpot.

2 Scrub the clams. Scrub the mussels and remove the beards. Discard any of the shellfish that are open and do not close when lightly tapped. Rinse and pat dry the scallops.

3 Trim the leek, discarding the tough ends. Wash thoroughly and slice. Peel and chop the onion. Rinse, stem, and chop the tomatoes. Rinse, stem, and chop the parsley.

4 In a large saucepan, combine the clams, the mussels, and the wine. Bring the wine to a boil and cook, covered, just until the shells open, about 4 minutes.

5 Remove the shellfish, reserving the cooking liquid. Separate the clams and mussels from the shells, discarding any that have not opened.

6 Cook the fettuccine until it is almost tender, 2 to 3 minutes if you are using fresh pasta, 6 to 7 minutes if you are using dry pasta.

7 Heat the oil in a large skillet. Add the onion and sauté until it is soft, about 5 minutes. Add the leek, the tomatoes, the thyme, the reserved clam liquid, and the scallops. Bring to a boil, cover, reduce the heat, and simmer until the leeks are tender, about 5 minutes.

8 Drain the pasta and return it to the stockpot.

9 Add the shellfish to the saucepan and combine. Pour the mixture over the pasta, season to taste, and toss with the parsley.

High Seas Salad

1 Rinse and dry the lettuce and tear it into bite-sized pieces. Rinse, trim, and chop the scallions. Rinse, stem, and chop the basil. Peel, trim, and slice the cucumber. Drain and chop the artichoke hearts, reserving the marinade. Combine the ingredients in a large bowl.

2 In a small bowl, combine 3 tablespoons of the reserved marinade with the vinegar and the sugar. Season to taste.

3 Toss the salad with the dressing.

Crescent Moons

1 Preheat the oven to 375°F.

2 Peel and mince the garlic.

3 Separate the rolls and open them into triangles. Brush the insides lightly with the oil. Sprinkle with the garlic. Roll the rolls back up. Place them on a baking sheet, seam side down, and bake until they are golden, 10 to 12 minutes.

Raspberry Plunder

1 Chill a medium bowl and the beaters of an electric mixer for 10 minutes.

2 Cut up the cream cheese and place it in a blender. Add the raspberries, the sugar, and the vanilla, and process until the mixture is thoroughly blended, 2 to 3 minutes.

3 Pour the whipping cream into the chilled bowl and beat until stiff, about 3 minutes. Fold the raspberry mixture into the whipped cream. Spoon into individual dessert glasses. Top with the sprinkles and chill until you are ready to serve.

THURSDAY

Sing-a-Pork

1 1/2 pounds lean boneless pork loin
1 medium red onion
2 small zucchini
1 small yellow bell pepper
1 small head red cabbage
1 clove garlic
2 tablespoons vegetable oil
2 tablespoons dark brown sugar
1 tablespoon ketchup
1 tablespoon rice vinegar
2 tablespoons water
1/2 teaspoon prepared horseradish
1 teaspoon cornstarch
Seasoning to taste

Raffles

1/4 cup fresh chives (when chopped)
8 ounces Chinese-style soft noodles
1 teaspoon sesame oil

Panda Parfait

1 container (8 ounces) frozen whipped
  topping
1 package (3.4 ounces) instant devil's food
  pudding mix
1 3/4 cups milk
1 teaspoon orange extract
1 can (11 ounces) mandarin oranges
1/2 cup flaked coconut

EQUIPMENT

Electric mixer	Vegetable brush
Wok	Vegetable grater
Large saucepan	Kitchen knives
Large mixing bowl	Measuring cups and
Small mixing bowl	spoons
Colander	Cooking utensils
Whisk	

COUNTDOWN

1. Assemble the ingredients and the
   equipment.
2. Do Step 1 of *Panda Parfait*.
3. Do Steps 1–2 of *Raffles*.
4. Do Steps 1–2 of *Sing-a-Pork*.
5. Do Steps 2–5 of *Panda Parfait*.
6. Do Steps 3–4 of *Sing-a-Pork*.
7. Do Step 3 of *Raffles*.

THURSDAY

Sing-a-Pork

1 Trim the pork and cut it into thin strips.

2 Peel and slice the onion. Scrub, trim, and slice the zucchini. Rinse, trim, seed, and chunk the bell pepper. Rinse, trim, quarter, and grate the cabbage. Peel and chop the garlic.

3 Heat the oil in a wok. Add the pork and stir-fry until it is tender and lightly browned, about 5 minutes. Add the onion, the zucchini, the bell pepper, and the garlic and stir-fry for 2 minutes. Add the cabbage and stir-fry for 1 minute.

4 In a small bowl, combine the brown sugar, the ketchup, the vinegar, the water, the horseradish, and the cornstarch. Whisk to blend and pour the mixture over the pork and vegetables. Toss to combine. Season to taste. Cook until the sauce just thickens, about 3 minutes.

Raffles

1 Bring water to a boil in a large saucepan.

2 Rinse, trim, and chop the chives.

3 Cook the noodles until they rise, about 1 minute. Drain and toss with the oil and the chives.

Panda Parfait

1 Set the topping out to thaw.

2 In a large bowl, combine the pudding mix with the milk. Beat until well blended, about 2 minutes.

3 Fold the orange extract into the whipped topping.

4 Drain the mandarin oranges.

5 Layer the pudding, the oranges, and the whipped topping in individual dessert glasses. Sprinkle with the coconut and refrigerate until you are ready to serve.

FRIDAY

How's Bayou?

1 large onion
1 medium red bell pepper
1 medium green bell pepper
3 cloves garlic
2 stalks celery
1 can (11 ounces) whole-kernel corn
1 can (15 ounces) white beans
2 tablespoons olive oil
1 1/2 cups long-grain white rice
2 cans (14 ounces each) vegetable broth
2 cans (14 ounces each) Cajun-style stewed
   tomatoes
2 tablespoons capers
1 tablespoon Worcestershire sauce
1/4 teaspoon Tabasco sauce
1/8 teaspoon cayenne pepper
Seasoning to taste
1 medium ripe avocado
2 tablespoons fresh parsley (when
   chopped)
1 loaf French bread

Baton Rouge

1 medium head red leaf lettuce
1 medium cucumber
2 tablespoons fresh chives (when chopped)
1 small can (8 ounces) julienne beets
1/4 cup sour cream
2 tablespoons mayonnaise
2 teaspoons red wine vinegar
1 teaspoon dried dill
Seasoning to taste

Bourbon Street Bananas

4 medium bananas
3 tablespoons butter
2 tablespoons bourbon
3 tablespoons granulated sugar
Whipped cream for garnish
1 teaspoon ground allspice for garnish

EQUIPMENT

Dutch oven
Large covered skillet
Large mixing bowl
Small mixing bowl
Whisk

Kitchen knives
Measuring cups and
   spoons
Cooking utensils

COUNTDOWN

1. Assemble the ingredients and the
   equipment.
2. Do Steps 1–3 of *How's Bayou?*
3. Do Steps 1–2 of *Baton Rouge.*
4. Do Steps 1–3 of *Bourbon Street
   Bananas.*
5. Do Step 3 of *Baton Rouge.*
6. Do Step 4 of *How's Bayou?*
7. Do Step 4 of *Bourbon Street Bananas.*

FRIDAY

How's Bayou?

1 Peel and chop the onion. Rinse, trim, seed, and chop the bell peppers. Peel and mince the garlic. Rinse, trim, and chop the celery. Drain the corn. Drain the beans.

2 Heat the oil in a Dutch oven. Sauté the onion, the peppers, the garlic, and the celery until the vegetables are soft, about 5 minutes.

3 Add the rice and cook, stirring, for 3 minutes. Add the broth, the undrained tomatoes, the corn, the beans, the capers, the Worcestershire sauce, the Tabasco sauce, and the cayenne pepper. Season to taste. Bring the mixture to a boil, cover, reduce the heat, and simmer for 25 minutes.

4 Halve, pit, peel, and chop the avocado. Rinse, stem, and chop the parsley. Sprinkle both over the jambalaya. Serve with chunks of French bread.

Baton Rouge

1 Wash and dry the lettuce and tear it into bite-sized pieces. Peel, trim, and chop the cucumber. Rinse, trim, and chop the chives. Combine the ingredients in a large bowl.

2 Drain the beets.

3 In a small bowl, whisk together the sour cream, the mayonnaise, the vinegar, and the dill. Season to taste. Toss the salad with the dressing and top with the beets.

Bourbon Street Bananas

1 Peel the bananas and cut them in half lengthwise and crosswise.

2 Melt the butter with the bourbon in a large skillet. Add the bananas, cut side down, and cook until they are lightly browned, about 5 minutes.

3 Add the sugar, turning the bananas until the sugar has melted and all the pieces are glazed, about 2 minutes. Cover, remove from the heat, and keep warm.

4 Top with dollops of whipped cream and a sprinkle of allspice.

WEEK SEVEN

Monday

Silence of the Hams
Romaines of the Day
Amisbread
Legend of the Pears

Tuesday

Make It Snappy
Rice Plus
The Art of Tart

Wednesday

Orson Beans
Maple Sugar Muffins
St. Johnsberries

Thursday

You're Egging Me On
Yes I Yam
Bluffin' Muffins
Tomfool Tapioca

Friday

Clever Cod
Witty Pasta
Little Guys
Sweet Tooth

STAPLES

- ☐ Butter
- ☐ Vegetable shortening
- ☐ Flour
- ☐ Baking powder
- ☐ Baking soda
- ☐ Dark brown sugar
- ☐ Powdered sugar
- ☐ Corn syrup
- ☐ Maple syrup
- ☐ Olive oil
- ☐ Vegetable oil
- ☐ Apple cider vinegar
- ☐ Red wine vinegar
- ☐ White wine vinegar
- ☐ Lemon juice
- ☐ Dijon mustard
- ☐ Dried basil
- ☐ Bay leaf
- ☐ Dried dill
- ☐ Dried thyme
- ☐ Whole allspice
- ☐ Cayenne pepper
- ☐ Ground cloves
- ☐ Italian seasoning
- ☐ Dry mustard
- ☐ Ground nutmeg
- ☐ Paprika
- ☐ Black pepper
- ☐ Salt
- ☐ Turmeric
- ☐ Orange extract
- ☐ Rum extract
- ☐ Vanilla extract

MEAT & POULTRY

1/2 pound lean cooked ham steak (M)

1/2 pound sweet Italian sausage (M)

1 1/2 pounds boneless, skinless chicken breast (W)

FISH

4 red snapper fillets (about 1 1/2 pounds) (T)

4 cod fillets (about 1 1/2 pounds) (F)

FRESH PRODUCE

VEGETABLES

1 pound baking potatoes (W)

1 1/2 pounds yams (Th)

1/2 pound green beans (W)

2 medium carrots (W)

1 pound baby carrots (F)

2 stalks celery (W)

1 package (10 ounces) spinach (W)

1 medium head romaine lettuce (M)

2 medium tomatoes (Th)

2 medium ripe avocados (Th)

1 medium cucumber (M)

1 medium green bell pepper (M)

1 small green bell pepper (Th)

1 large onion (W)

2 large onions (F)

1 medium onion (M)

1 small sweet onion (Th)

1 medium shallot (T)

3 scallions (green onions) (M)

2 scallions (green onions) (Th)

2 cloves garlic (M)

1 clove garlic (W)

HERBS

1/4 cup chives (when chopped) (F)

3 tablespoons parsley (when chopped) (T)

2 tablespoons parsley (when chopped) (F)

FRUIT

2 small ripe honeydew melons (W)

2 large ripe pears (M)

1 pint strawberries (W)

CANS, JARS & BOTTLES

SOUPS

2 cans (14 ounces each) chicken broth (W)

1 can (10 1/2 ounces) onion soup (T)

1 can (10 1/2 ounces) beef consommé (W)

VEGETABLES

1 can (28 ounces) diced tomatoes (M)

1 can (15 ounces) kidney beans (W)

1 can (11 ounces) whole-kernel corn (W)

SAUCES

1 can (6 ounces) tomato paste (M)

FRUIT

4 tablespoons apricot preserves (Th)

PACKAGED GOODS

PASTA, RICE & GRAINS

1 pound spaghetti (M)

8 ounces spinach noodles (F)

1 cup long-grain white rice (T)

3 cups Rice Krispies cereal (F)

BAKED GOODS

4 small French baguettes (M)

4 English muffins (Th)

DRIED FRUIT & NUTS

3/4 cup raisins (T)

1/4 cup walnut bits (W)

1/2 cup sliced almonds (F)

DESSERT & BAKING NEEDS

1/4 cup instant tapioca (Th)

4 ounces butterscotch chips (M)

8 ounces chocolate chips (F)

1 chocolate candy bar (7 ounces) (F)

WINE & SPIRITS

1/2 cup dry red wine (M)

3 tablespoons dry sherry (W)

2 tablespoons dry sherry (F)

REFRIGERATED PRODUCTS

DAIRY

1/4 cup milk (T)

1 cup milk (W)

2 cups plus 3 tablespoons milk (Th)

2 tablespoons milk (F)

1 cup sour cream (F)

1/3 cup whipping cream (M)

Whipped cream for garnish (Th)

Whipped cream for garnish (F)

1 egg (T)

1 egg (W)

9 eggs (Th)

CHEESE

1/4 cup shredded mozzarella cheese (M)

1/2 pound Jarlsberg cheese (Th)

FROZEN GOODS

VEGETABLES

1 package (10 ounces) mixed vegetables (T)

PASTRY

4 unbaked tart shells (T)

DESSERTS

1 pint orange sherbet (W)

MONDAY

Silence of the Hams

1/2 pound sweet Italian sausage
1/2 pound lean cooked ham steak
1 medium onion
2 cloves garlic
2 tablespoons olive oil
1 can (28 ounces) diced tomatoes
1 can (6 ounces) tomato paste
1 tablespoon Italian seasoning
1/2 cup dry red wine
Seasoning to taste
1 pound spaghetti
1/4 cup shredded mozzarella cheese

Romaines of the Day

1 medium head romaine lettuce
3 scallions (green onions)
1 medium cucumber
1 medium green bell pepper
3 tablespoons olive oil
2 tablespoons white wine vinegar
1/2 teaspoon dry mustard
Seasoning to taste

Amisbread

4 small French baguettes
2 tablespoons olive oil
1 tablespoon dried basil
1 teaspoon paprika
1 teaspoon ground pepper

Legend of the Pears

2 large ripe pears
1 tablespoon lemon juice
4 ounces butterscotch chips
1/3 cup whipping cream
1 teaspoon rum extract
Powdered sugar for garnish

C O U N T D O W N

1. Assemble the ingredients and the equipment.
2. Do Steps 1–2 of *Silence of the Hams*.
3. Do Steps 1–2 of *Romaines of the Day*.
4. Do Step 3 of *Silence of the Hams*.
5. Do Step 1 of *Legend of the Pears*.
6. Do Steps 1–3 of *Amisbread*.
7. Do Step 4 of *Silence of the Hams*.
8. Do Step 3 of *Romaines of the Day*.
9. Do Step 5 of *Silence of the Hams*.
10. Do Step 2 of *Legend of the Pears*.

E Q U I P M E N T

Stockpot	Vegetable peeler
Small saucepan	Pastry brush
Large covered skillet	Aluminum foil
Colander	Kitchen knives
Large mixing bowl	Measuring cups and spoons
Small mixing bowl	Cooking utensils
Whisk	

MONDAY

Silence of the Hams

1 Remove the sausage meat from the casings. Cube the ham steak. Peel and chop the onion. Peel and mince the garlic.

2 Heat the oil in a large skillet and sauté the sausage and the ham cubes until browned, about 10 minutes. Add the onion and the garlic and sauté for 5 minutes. Add the tomatoes, the tomato paste, and the Italian seasoning. Stir in the wine and season to taste. Cover the skillet, reduce the heat, and simmer for 30 minutes.

3 Bring water to a boil in a stockpot.

4 Cook the spaghetti 6 to 7 minutes until it is almost tender.

5 Drain the pasta, top it with the sauce, and sprinkle with the cheese.

Romaines of the Day

1 Wash and dry the lettuce and tear it into bite-sized pieces. Rinse, trim, and chop the scallions. Peel, trim, and chop the cucumber. Rinse, trim, seed, and slice the bell pepper. Combine the ingredients in a large bowl.

2 In a small bowl, whisk together the oil, the vinegar, and the mustard. Season to taste.

3 Toss the salad with the dressing.

Amisbread

1 Preheat the broiler.

2 Cut the baguettes in half lengthwise. Brush the cut sides with the oil and sprinkle with the basil, the paprika, and the pepper.

3 Lay the baguettes on a sheet of aluminum foil and broil until lightly toasted, about 1 minute.

Legend of the Pears

1 Rinse, halve, and core the pears. Cut almost through in $1/8$-inch-thick slices, leaving the pears attached at the stem end. Spread the halves like fans on individual dessert plates and sprinkle the cut sides with the lemon juice.

2 In a small saucepan, melt the butterscotch chips with the cream over low heat, about 3 minutes. Remove the saucepan from the heat, stir in the rum extract, and spoon over the pears. Dust with the powdered sugar.

TUESDAY

Make It Snappy

4 red snapper fillets (about 1 1/2 pounds)
1 medium shallot
3 tablespoons fresh parsley (when chopped)
1/4 cup milk
1/4 cup flour
3 tablespoons butter
3 tablespoons lemon juice
Seasoning to taste

Rice Plus

1 package (10 ounces) frozen mixed vegetables
1 tablespoon butter
1 cup long-grain white rice
1 can (10 1/2 ounces) onion soup
1 1/4 cups water

The Art of Tart

4 frozen unbaked tart shells
1/2 cup dark brown sugar
1/4 cup vegetable shortening
1/2 cup corn syrup
1 egg
1 teaspoon vanilla extract
3/4 cup raisins

EQUIPMENT

Electric mixer
Large covered skillet
Large skillet
Baking sheet
Large shallow bowl
Large mixing bowl
Medium mixing bowl
Waxed paper
Kitchen knives
Measuring cups and spoons
Cooking utensils

COUNTDOWN

1. Assemble the ingredients and the equipment.
2. Do Step 1 of *The Art of Tart*.
3. Do Steps 1–2 of *Make It Snappy*.
4. Do Steps 1–3 of *Rice Plus*.
5. Do Steps 2–6 of *The Art of Tart*.
6. Do Step 4 of *Rice Plus*.
7. Do Steps 3–4 of *Make It Snappy*.
8. Do Step 5 of *Rice Plus*.
9. Do Step 5 of *Make It Snappy*.

TUESDAY

Make It Snappy

1 Rinse and pat dry the fish fillets.

2 Peel and mince the shallot. Rinse, stem, and chop the parsley.

3 Put the milk in a shallow bowl. Put the flour on a sheet of waxed paper. Dip the fish into the milk, then into the flour to coat.

4 Melt the butter in a large skillet. Cook the fish until it is golden, 3 to 4 minutes per side. Remove the fish from the skillet and cover to keep warm. Add the lemon juice and the shallot to the skillet and sauté until the shallot is lightly browned, about 5 minutes. Add the parsley, season to taste, and cook for 1 minute.

5 Pour the sauce over the fish.

Rice Plus

1 Set the vegetables in a medium bowl of warm water to thaw.

2 Melt the butter in a large skillet and sauté the rice for 1 minute. Add the soup and the water, blend well, and bring the mixture to a boil.

3 Cover the skillet, reduce the heat, and simmer for 15 minutes.

4 Stir the thawed vegetables into the rice, cover again, and continue cooking until all the liquid is absorbed and the rice is tender, about 10 minutes more.

5 Fluff the rice and vegetables with a fork before serving.

The Art of Tart

1 Set the tart shells out to thaw.

2 Preheat the oven to 400°F.

3 In a large bowl, beat the brown sugar and the shortening until well blended. Add the corn syrup, the egg, and the vanilla and blend well.

4 Distribute the raisins evenly in the tart shells.

5 Pour the sugar mixture over the raisins.

6 Place the tart shells on a baking sheet and bake until the top is set and the crust is lightly browned, 12 to 15 minutes.

WEDNESDAY

Orson Beans

1 1/2 pounds boneless, skinless chicken breast
1 large onion
1 clove garlic
1 pound baking potatoes
2 stalks celery
1/2 pound fresh green beans
2 medium carrots
1 package (10 ounces) fresh spinach
1 can (15 ounces) kidney beans
1 can (11 ounces) whole-kernel corn
1 tablespoon butter
1 tablespoon vegetable oil
2 cans (14 ounces each) chicken broth
1 can (10 1/2 ounces) beef consommé
1 bay leaf
3 whole allspice
1 teaspoon dried dill
Seasoning to taste
3 tablespoons dry sherry

Maple Sugar Muffins

1/4 cup dark brown sugar
4 tablespoons butter
1/4 cup maple syrup
1 egg
1 cup milk
2 cups flour
2 teaspoons baking powder
1/2 teaspoon baking soda
1/4 cup walnut bits
1/2 teaspoon ground nutmeg

St. Johnsberries

1 pint fresh strawberries
4 tablespoons powdered sugar
2 tablespoon lemon juice
2 small ripe honeydew melons
1 pint frozen orange sherbet

EQUIPMENT

Dutch oven
Medium skillet
Muffin tin
2 large mixing bowls
Medium mixing bowl
Small mixing bowl
Whisk

Vegetable peeler
Ice cream scoop
Kitchen knives
Measuring cups and
 spoons
Cooking utensils

COUNTDOWN

1. Assemble the ingredients and the equipment.
2. Do Step 1 of *St. Johnsberries*.
3. Do Steps 1–4 of *Orson Beans*.
4. Do Steps 1–5 of *Maple Sugar Muffins*.
5. Do Step 5 of *Orson Beans*.
6. Do Step 2 of *St. Johnsberries*.
7. Do Step 6 of *Orson Beans*.
8. Do Step 3 of *St. Johnsberries*.

WEDNESDAY

Orson Beans

1 Rinse, pat dry, and cut the chicken into 1-inch cubes.

2 Peel and chop the onion. Peel and mince the garlic. Peel and cube the potatoes. Rinse, trim, and chop the celery. Rinse, trim, and cut the green beans into 1-inch pieces. Peel, trim, and slice the carrots. Rinse, pat dry, stem, and chop the spinach. Drain and rinse the kidney beans. Drain the corn.

3 Melt the butter with the oil in a medium skillet. Sauté the chicken, the onion, and the garlic for 5 minutes.

4 Bring the broth to a boil in a Dutch oven. Add the potatoes, return to a boil, cover, reduce the heat, and simmer for 10 minutes.

5 Add the chicken, the onion, the garlic, the celery, the green beans, the carrots, the kidney beans, the corn, the consommé, the bay leaf, the allspice, and the dill to the Dutch oven. Season to taste, return to a boil, reduce the heat, and simmer for 10 minutes more.

6 Stir in the sherry and the spinach. Return the soup to a boil and cook for 1 minute. Remove the bay leaf and the allspice.

Maple Sugar Muffins

1 Preheat the oven to 400°F. Grease a muffin tin.

2 In a large bowl, cream the brown sugar and the butter until smooth. Blend in the maple syrup.

3 In a small bowl, whip the egg with the milk and combine it with the maple syrup mixture.

4 In a large bowl, combine the flour, the baking powder, and the baking soda. Fold into the maple syrup mixture and blend well. Add the nuts and the nutmeg.

5 Spoon the batter into the muffin cups and bake until the muffins are lightly browned and firm to the touch, about 15 minutes.

St. Johnsberries

1 Rinse, hull, and mash the strawberries. Combine in a medium bowl with the powdered sugar and the lemon juice. Chill until you are ready to serve

2 Cut the melons in half and remove the seeds.

3 Place scoops of sherbet in the honeydew cavities and top with the strawberry sauce.

THURSDAY

You're Egging Me On

2 scallions (green onions)
2 medium tomatoes
2 medium ripe avocados
1/2 pound Jarlsberg cheese
9 eggs
3 tablespoons milk
Seasoning to taste
3 tablespoons butter
1/2 teaspoon dried basil

Yes I Yam

1 1/2 pounds yams
1 small sweet onion
1 small green bell pepper
2 tablespoons vegetable oil
3 tablespoons red wine vinegar
1/4 teaspoon dried thyme
Seasoning to taste

Bluffin' Muffins

4 English muffins
3 tablespoons butter
1/4 cup apricot preserves
1/4 teaspoon cayenne pepper

Tomfool Tapioca

2 cups milk
1/4 cup instant tapioca
1/2 cup dark brown sugar
2 tablespoons butter
1/8 teaspoon salt
1 teaspoon orange extract
Whipped cream for garnish

EQUIPMENT

Medium covered saucepan	Whisk
Medium saucepan	Cheese grater
Small saucepan	Kitchen knives
Large covered skillet	Measuring cups and spoons
Large mixing bowl	Cooking utensils

COUNTDOWN

1. Assemble the ingredients and the equipment.
2. Do Steps 1–3 of *Yes I Yam*.
3. Do Step 1 of *Tomfool Tapioca*.
4. Do Steps 1–2 of *You're Egging Me On*.
5. Do Steps 4–5 of *Yes I Yam*.
6. Do Steps 2–4 of *Tomfool Tapioca*.
7. Do Step 3 of *You're Egging Me On*.
8. Do Step 1 of *Bluffin' Muffins*.
9. Do Step 4 of *You're Egging Me On*.
10. Do Step 2 of *Bluffin' Muffins*.
11. Do Step 5 of *Tomfool Tapioca*.

THURSDAY

You're Egging Me On

1 Rinse, trim, and mince the scallions. Rinse, stem, and chop the tomatoes. Halve, pit, peel, and chop the avocados. Grate the cheese.

2 In a large bowl, combine the scallions, the eggs, and the milk and whisk until frothy. Season to taste.

3 Melt the butter in a large skillet. Add the eggs, cover, and reduce the heat. Cook until the eggs begin to set, 3 to 4 minutes.

4 Arrange the tomatoes, the avocados, and the cheese over half of the eggs. Sprinkle with the basil. Fold the plain egg side over the filling side, cover, and cook for 1 minute more.

Yes I Yam

1 Bring water to a boil in a medium saucepan.

2 Scrub, trim, and slice the yams. Peel and chop the onion. Rinse, trim, seed, and chop the bell pepper.

3 Cook the yams until tender, about 10 minutes.

4 In a small saucepan, combine the oil, the vinegar, and the thyme. Season to taste and bring just to a boil. Remove the saucepan from the heat.

5 Drain and peel the yams and return them to the saucepan. Add the onion and the bell pepper and combine. Toss with the warm dressing. Cover to keep warm.

Bluffin' Muffins

1 Cut the muffins in half and toast them lightly.

2 Spread the muffins with the butter and the preserves and dust with the cayenne pepper.

Tomfool Tapioca

1 Combine the milk and the tapioca in a medium saucepan and let stand for 5 minutes.

2 Cook the milk mixture over medium heat, stirring constantly, until it comes to a boil, about 6 minutes.

3 Stir in the brown sugar, the butter, and the salt and continue cooking until the butter and sugar have melted and blended, about 2 minutes.

4 Remove the saucepan from the heat and stir in the orange extract. Spoon the mixture into individual dessert dishes and set aside.

5 Top each serving with a dollop of whipped cream.

FRIDAY

Clever Cod

4 cod fillets (about 1 1/2 pounds)
2 large onions
1 tablespoon vegetable oil
2 tablespoons apple cider vinegar
3 tablespoons dark brown sugar
1/2 teaspoon turmeric
1 teaspoon Dijon mustard
Seasoning to taste

Witty Pasta

1/4 cup fresh chives (when chopped)
8 ounces spinach noodles
1 cup sour cream
2 tablespoons milk
Seasoning to taste

Little Guys

1 pound baby carrots
2 tablespoons fresh parsley (when chopped)
3 tablespoons butter
1/4 teaspoon ground cloves
2 tablespoons dry sherry
Seasoning to taste

Sweet Tooth

1 chocolate candy bar (7 ounces)
6 tablespoons butter
3 cups Rice Krispies cereal
8 ounces chocolate chips
Whipped cream for garnish
1/2 cup sliced almonds for garnish

EQUIPMENT

2 large saucepans	Colander
2 small saucepans	Aluminum foil
Large covered skillet	Kitchen knives
Large skillet	Measuring cups and
9 x 13-inch glass baking dish	spoons
	Cooking utensils
9 x 9-inch baking pan	

COUNTDOWN

1. Assemble the ingredients and the equipment.
2. Do Steps 1–5 of *Sweet Tooth*.
3. Do Steps 1–4 of *Clever Cod*.
4. Do Step 1 of *Witty Pasta*.
5. Do Steps 1–3 of *Little Guys*.
6. Do Step 5 of *Clever Cod*.
7. Do Steps 2–3 of *Witty Pasta*.
8. Do Steps 4–5 of *Little Guys*.
9. Do Steps 4–5 of *Witty Pasta*.
10. Do Step 6 of *Sweet Tooth*.

FRIDAY

Clever Cod

1 Preheat the oven to 400°F. Grease a 9 x 13-inch glass baking dish.

2 Rinse and pat dry the fish fillets.

3 Peel and slice the onions.

4 Heat the oil in a large skillet. Add the vinegar, the brown sugar, the turmeric, and the mustard. Stir to combine. Add the onions and sauté until they are deep golden in color, about 10 minutes.

5 Spoon half of the onions into the baking dish. Top with the fish and season to taste. Spoon the remaining onions over the fish, cover with aluminum foil, and bake until the fish flakes easily with a fork, about 15 minutes.

Witty Pasta

1 Bring water to a boil in a large saucepan.

2 Rinse, trim, and chop the chives.

3 Cook the noodles until almost tender, 6 to 7 minutes.

4 In a small saucepan, combine the sour cream, the milk, and the chives. Season to taste and bring just to a boil.

5 Drain the pasta and return it to the saucepan. Fold in the sour cream mixture.

Little Guys

1 Bring water to a boil in a large skillet.

2 Rinse and trim the carrots. Rinse, stem, and chop the parsley.

3 Place the carrots in the skillet, cover, and cook until they are crisp-tender, about 10 minutes.

4 Drain the carrots.

5 Melt the butter with the cloves in the skillet. Add the sherry and bring the mixture to a boil. Return the carrots to the skillet, season to taste, and toss to coat. Sprinkle with the parsley.

Sweet Tooth

1 Grease a 9 x 9-inch baking pan.

2 Chop the candy bar into small pieces.

3 Melt 4 tablespoons of the butter in a large saucepan. Add the candy and cook, stirring, over low heat, until the candy has melted.

4 Fold in the Rice Krispies and stir to coat well. Spread the mixture evenly in the baking pan.

5 Melt the chocolate chips with the remaining 2 tablespoons butter in a small saucepan, stirring until smooth. Spread the mixture evenly over the cereal and refrigerate until you are ready to serve.

6 Top with dollops of whipped cream and the almonds.

WEEK EIGHT

Monday
Wok On By
Step Gingerly
Awe Sum Sherbet

Tuesday
Montana Macaroni
Butteful Beets
Custard's Last Stand

Wednesday
Pork-U-Pine
Pot Shots
The Incredible Lightness of Bean
Strawberry Dippers

Thursday
Alley-Soup
Tunaville Trolley
Macaroon Mullins

Friday
Pasta Point of No Return
Leaf Me Alone
Bag It
Jell-Out

STAPLES

- ☐ Butter
- ☐ Flour
- ☐ Baking powder
- ☐ Cornstarch
- ☐ Granulated sugar
- ☐ Powdered sugar
- ☐ Olive oil
- ☐ Sesame oil
- ☐ Vegetable oil
- ☐ Apple cider vinegar
- ☐ Rice vinegar
- ☐ White wine vinegar
- ☐ Lemon juice
- ☐ Honey
- ☐ Mayonnaise
- ☐ Soy sauce
- ☐ Poppy seeds
- ☐ Dried dill
- ☐ Dried rosemary
- ☐ Dried sage
- ☐ Ground allspice
- ☐ Chinese 5-spice
- ☐ Ground cloves
- ☐ Ground ginger
- ☐ Italian seasoning
- ☐ Lemon-pepper seasoning
- ☐ Black pepper
- ☐ White pepper
- ☐ Salt
- ☐ Vanilla extract

MEAT & POULTRY

4 lean boneless pork chops (about 1 1/2 pounds) (W)

1 1/2 pounds boneless, skinless chicken breast (M)

FISH

1 pound small shrimp, shelled and deveined (F)

FRESH PRODUCE

VEGETABLES

1 1/2 pounds new potatoes (W)

1 medium bunch broccoli (M)

1 pound green beans (W)

1 small bunch beets (T)

1/4 pound Chinese snow peas (M)

2 small zucchini (F)

2 medium carrots (T)

2 small carrots (F)

2 stalks celery (Th)

1 small head Napa cabbage (M)

1 medium head romaine lettuce (T)

1 small head lettuce (F)

2 large tomatoes (T)

2 large tomatoes (Th)

1 large cucumber (T)

1 medium green bell pepper (Th)

1 large red bell pepper (M)

1 large onion (T)

1 large sweet onion (F)

1 medium onion (Th)

2 small shallots (W)

3 scallions (green onions) (M)

3 scallions (green onions) (Th)

1 clove garlic (T)

1 clove garlic (F)

HERBS

1/4 cup chives (when chopped) (T)

2 tablespoons chives (when chopped) (F)

1 tablespoon parsley (when chopped) (M)

2 tablespoons parsley (when chopped) (F)

FRUIT

1 large orange (W)

2 large oranges (F)

1 quart strawberries with stems (W)

1/2 pint raspberries (Th)

CANS, JARS & BOTTLES

SOUPS

2 cans (14 ounces each) chicken broth (Th)

1 can (10 1/2 ounces) chicken broth (M)

1 can (10 3/4 ounces) nacho cheese soup (T)

VEGETABLES

1 can (14 1/2 ounces) diced tomatoes (T)

1 can (11 ounces) whole-kernel corn (Th)

FISH

2 cans (6 ounces each) solid white tuna (Th)

FRUIT

1 can (8 ounces) crushed pineapple (M)

JUICES

8 ounces clam juice (F)

PACKAGED GOODS

PASTA, RICE & GRAINS

12 ounces elbow macaroni (T)

1 pound small pasta shells (F)

1 cup long-grain white rice (M)

BAKED GOODS

4 English muffins (Th)

4 small French baguettes (F)

4 fortune cookies for garnish (M)

1 package (10 ounces) macaroons (Th)

DRIED FRUIT & NUTS

1/4 cup pine nuts (W)

DESSERT & BAKING NEEDS

1 1/2 ounces lemon gelatin (F)

1/4 cup flaked coconut for garnish (M)

6 ounces chocolate chips (W)

WINE & SPIRITS

1/4 cup dry white wine (F)

3 tablespoons dry sherry (Th)

REFRIGERATED PRODUCTS

DAIRY

2 cups milk (T)

1 tablespoon milk (F)

2 tablespoons half-and-half (W)

3 eggs (T)

1 egg (Th)

1 egg (F)

CHEESE

2 cups shredded Colby/Monterey Jack cheese (T)

8 slices American cheese (Th)

JUICES

1 cup orange juice (W)

DELI

1/2 pound bacon (T)

FROZEN GOODS

DESSERTS

1 pint pineapple sherbet (M)

1 pint vanilla ice cream (Th)

MONDAY

MENU

Wok On By

1 1/2 pounds boneless, skinless chicken breast
3 scallions (green onions)
1 large red bell pepper
1 medium bunch broccoli
1/4 pound fresh Chinese snow peas
1 small head Napa cabbage
1 tablespoon vegetable oil
2 teaspoons sesame oil
1 teaspoon Chinese 5-spice
1 can (10 1/2 ounces) chicken broth
2 teaspoons rice vinegar
1 tablespoon soy sauce
1 tablespoon honey
2 teaspoons cornstarch
2 tablespoons water

Step Gingerly

1 tablespoon fresh parsley (when chopped)
1 cup long-grain white rice
2 1/4 cups water
1/2 teaspoon ground ginger

Awe Sum Sherbet

1 can (8 ounces) crushed pineapple
2 tablespoons granulated sugar
2 teaspoons cornstarch
2 teaspoons lemon juice
1 pint pineapple sherbet
1/4 cup flaked coconut for garnish
4 fortune cookies for garnish

EQUIPMENT

Wok	Ice cream scoop
Double boiler	Kitchen knives
Small saucepan	Measuring cups and
Small mixing bowl	spoons
Whisk	Cooking utensils

COUNTDOWN

1. Assemble the ingredients and the equipment.
2. Do Steps 1–2 of *Awe Sum Sherbet*.
3. Do Steps 1–2 of *Step Gingerly*.
4. Do Steps 1–4 of *Wok On By*.
5. Do Step 3 of *Step Gingerly*.
6. Do Step 3 of *Awe Sum Sherbet*.

MONDAY

Wok On By

1 Rinse, pat dry, and cut the chicken breast into strips.

2 Rinse, trim, and chop the scallions. Rinse, trim, seed, and chop the bell pepper. Rinse and trim the broccoli and cut it into bite-sized florets, discarding the tough ends. Rinse and string the snow peas. Rinse, trim, and slice the cabbage.

3 Heat both oils in a wok and stir-fry the chicken for 2 minutes. Add the scallions, the bell pepper, the broccoli, and the Chinese 5-spice to the wok and stir-fry for 3 minutes. Add the snow peas and stir-fry for 1 minute.

4 In a small bowl, combine the broth, the vinegar, the soy sauce, and the honey. Combine the cornstarch with the water and add it to the broth. Add the mixture to the wok, cover, and steam for 1 minute. Fold in the cabbage and stir-fry until the greens are crisp-tender, about 1 minute more.

Step Gingerly

1 Bring water to a boil in the bottom of a double boiler. Rinse, stem, and chop the parsley.

2 Combine the parsley, the rice, the 2¼ cups water, and the ginger in the top of the double boiler. Cover, reduce the heat, and simmer until all the liquid is absorbed and the rice is tender, 30 to 40 minutes.

3 Fluff the rice with a fork before serving.

Awe Sum Sherbet

1 Combine the undrained pineapple, the sugar, the cornstarch, and the lemon juice in a small saucepan. Cook until the sugar is dissolved and the mixture begins to thicken, about 3 minutes.

2 Remove from the heat and set aside.

3 Place a scoop of sherbet in individual dessert dishes. Top with the sauce. Sprinkle with the coconut and serve with a fortune cookie.

TUESDAY

Montana Macaroni

½ pound bacon
1 large onion
2 large tomatoes
¼ cup fresh chives (when chopped)
12 ounces elbow macaroni
1 can (10¾ ounces) nacho cheese soup
1 can (14½ ounces) diced tomatoes
2 cups shredded Colby/Monterey Jack
   cheese

Butteful Beets

1 medium head romaine lettuce
1 large cucumber
1 small bunch beets
2 medium carrots
1 clove garlic
3 tablespoons olive oil
2 tablespoons white wine vinegar
½ teaspoon dried dill
Seasoning to taste

Custard's Last Stand

2 cups milk
½ cup granulated sugar
2 teaspoons ground allspice
3 eggs

EQUIPMENT

Stockpot
2-quart casserole
Medium saucepan
Medium skillet
9 x 13-inch baking
   pan
4 custard cups
Colander
Large mixing bowl

Medium mixing bowl
Small mixing bowl
Whisk
Vegetable peeler
Vegetable grater
Kitchen knives
Measuring cups and
   spoons
Cooking utensils

COUNTDOWN

1. Assemble the ingredients and the
   equipment.
2. Do Steps 1–5 of *Custard's Last Stand*.
3. Do Steps 1–8 of *Montana Macaroni*.
4. Do Steps 1–2 of *Butteful Beets*.
5. Do Step 9 of *Montana Macaroni*.
6. Do Step 6 of *Custard's Last Stand*.

TUESDAY

Montana Macaroni

1 Bring water to a boil in a stockpot.

2 Dice the bacon. Peel and chop the onion. Rinse, stem, and slice the tomatoes. Rinse, trim, and chop the chives.

3 Sauté the bacon in a medium skillet until almost crisp, about 5 minutes. Drain on paper towels.

4 Cook the macaroni in the stockpot until it is almost tender, 8 to 10 minutes.

5 Sauté the onion in the bacon drippings until soft, about 5 minutes.

6 In a 2-quart casserole, combine the soup, the canned tomatoes, the bacon, and the onion.

7 Increase the oven temperature to 425°F.

8 Drain the pasta, add it to the casserole, and combine. Sprinkle 1½ cups of the cheese over the casserole and bake for 20 minutes.

9 Arrange the sliced tomatoes over the cheese. Sprinkle with the remaining ½ cup cheese and the chives and bake for 5 minutes more.

Butteful Beets

1 Wash and dry the lettuce and tear it into bite-sized pieces. Peel, trim, and slice the cucumber. Peel, trim, and grate the beets. Peel, trim, and grate the carrots. Combine the ingredients in a large bowl.

2 Peel and mince the garlic. In a small bowl, whisk together the garlic, the oil, the vinegar, and the dill. Season to taste and toss with the salad.

Custard's Last Stand

1 Preheat the oven to 350°F.

2 Set 4 custard cups in a 9 x 13-inch baking pan. Fill the pan halfway with water.

3 In a medium saucepan, combine the milk, the sugar, and 1 teaspoon of the allspice. Bring to a boil, stirring constantly, about 5 minutes.

4 Whip the eggs in a medium bowl. Gradually add the hot milk mixture and blend well.

5 Pour the mixture into the custard cups and bake until the center of the custard is firm and the top is lightly browned, 25 to 30 minutes.

6 Sprinkle with the remaining 1 teaspoon allspice.

WEDNESDAY

Pork-U-Pine

2 small shallots
1 large orange
3 tablespoons butter
1/4 cup pine nuts
4 lean boneless pork chops (about 1 1/2
    pounds)
1 teaspoon dried sage
1 tablespoon granulated sugar
1 cup orange juice
Seasoning to taste

Pot Shots

1 1/2 pounds new potatoes
3 tablespoons butter
1/2 teaspoon dried rosemary
1 tablespoon water
Seasoning to taste

The Incredible Lightness of Bean

1 pound fresh green beans
Seasoning to taste
1/2 teaspoon ground cloves

Strawberry Dippers

1 quart fresh strawberries with stems
    attached
6 ounces chocolate chips
2 tablespoons half-and-half
1 teaspoon vanilla extract

EQUIPMENT

Medium covered saucepan	Vegetable peeler
Small saucepan	Citrus grater
Large covered skillet	Waxed paper
Medium covered skillet	Kitchen knives
Steamer insert	Measuring cups and spoons
Whisk	Cooking utensils

COUNTDOWN

1. Assemble the ingredients and the equipment.
2. Do Steps 1–3 of *Strawberry Dippers*.
3. Do Step 1 of *Pork-U-Pine*.
4. Do Steps 1–2 of *Pot Shots*.
5. Do Steps 2–3 of *Pork-U-Pine*.
6. Do Step 3 of *Pot Shots*.
7. Do Steps 1–3 of *The Incredible Lightness of Bean*.
8. Do Step 4 of *Pot Shots*.

WEDNESDAY

Pork-U-Pine

1 Peel and mince the shallots. Grate the orange peel. Peel the orange and slice it into thin rounds.

2 Melt the butter in a large skillet and sauté the shallots and the pine nuts for 1 minute. Add the pork chops, the sage, and the sugar and sauté until the chops are browned, 5 to 6 minutes per side.

3 Add the orange juice to the skillet, scraping up any brown bits from the bottom of the pan. Add the orange peel and the orange slices and season to taste. Cover the skillet, reduce the heat, and simmer until the pork is tender and white throughout, about 25 minutes.

Pot Shots

1 Peel and cube the potatoes.

2 Place the potatoes in a medium skillet, cover with water, and cook until almost tender, about 12 minutes.

3 Drain the potatoes. Melt the butter with the rosemary in the skillet, tilting the pan to cover the bottom. Press the potatoes into the skillet to cover the bottom evenly. Sprinkle the 1 tablespoon water over the potatoes and season to taste. Cover, reduce the heat, and simmer until the potato bottom is golden and crusty, about 15 minutes.

4 Loosen the potato all the way around with a spatula and invert onto a serving plate. Cut into wedges.

The Incredible Lightness of Bean

1 Bring a small amount of water to a boil in a medium saucepan.

2 Rinse and trim the green beans.

3 Arrange the beans in a steamer insert and place the insert in the saucepan. Season to taste and sprinkle with the ground cloves. Cover and steam until the beans are crisp-tender, about 7 minutes.

Strawberry Dippers

1 Rinse and pat dry the strawberries.

2 In a small saucepan, combine the chocolate chips, the half-and-half, and the vanilla. Heat the mixture, whisking constantly, until the chips are melted and the sauce is well blended.

3 Dip each strawberry in the chocolate sauce, place on sheets of waxed paper, and refrigerate until you are ready to serve.

THURSDAY

Alley-Soup

3 scallions (green onions)
1 can (11 ounces) whole-kernel corn
2 cans (14 ounces each) chicken broth
3 tablespoons dry sherry
1 egg
Seasoning to taste

Tunaville Trolley

2 stalks celery
1 medium onion
1 medium green bell pepper
2 cans (6 ounces each) solid white tuna
1/2 cup mayonnaise
2 tablespoons apple cider vinegar
1/4 teaspoon lemon-pepper seasoning
Seasoning to taste
2 large tomatoes
8 slices American cheese
4 English muffins

Macaroon Mullins

1 package (10 ounces) macaroons
1/2 pint fresh raspberries
1 pint vanilla ice cream
1 tablespoon powdered sugar for garnish

EQUIPMENT

Medium covered saucepan	Ice cream scoop
Baking sheet	Plastic bag
Large mixing bowl	Kitchen knives
Small mixing bowl	Measuring cups and spoons
Whisk	Cooking utensils

COUNTDOWN

1. Assemble the ingredients and the equipment.
2. Do Steps 1–2 of *Macaroon Mullins*.
3. Do Steps 1–4 of *Tunaville Trolley*.
4. Do Steps 1–3 of *Alley-Soup*.
5. Do Steps 5–7 of *Tunaville Trolley*.
6. Do Step 3 of *Macaroon Mullins*.

THURSDAY

Alley-Soup

1 Rinse, trim, and chop the scallions. Drain the corn.

2 In a medium saucepan, combine the scallions, the corn, the broth, and the sherry. Bring the mixture to a boil and cook for 2 minutes.

3 Whip the egg in a small bowl. Slowly pour the egg into the boiling soup, whisking constantly until well blended. Season to taste, cover, reduce the heat, and simmer until you are ready to serve.

Tunaville Trolley

1 Rinse, trim, and dice the celery. Peel and dice the onion. Rinse, trim, seed, and dice the bell pepper. Combine the ingredients in a large bowl.

2 Drain and flake the tuna and add it to the bowl. Blend in the mayonnaise, the vinegar, and the lemon-pepper seasoning and season to taste.

3 Rinse, stem, and slice the tomatoes. Separate the cheese slices.

4 Preheat the broiler.

5 Split the English muffins. Place them on a baking sheet and toast them under the broiler for 1 minute.

6 Spread the tuna mixture on the toasted muffin halves and top each half with a slice of tomato. Run under the broiler for another minute.

7 Top each melt with a slice of cheese and run under the broiler for 1 minute more.

Macaroon Mullins

1 Place the macaroons in a plastic bag and crumble them.

2 Rinse and pat dry the raspberries.

3 Place a scoop of ice cream in the bottom of individual dessert glasses. Add half of the crumbled macaroons and half of the berries. Repeat. Dust with the powdered sugar.

FRIDAY

Pasta Point of No Return

1 clove garlic
2 small zucchini
2 small carrots
2 tablespoons fresh parsley (when chopped)
1 pound small shrimp, shelled and deveined
8 ounces clam juice
1/4 cup dry white wine
1 pound small pasta shells
2 tablespoons flour
1/4 teaspoon white pepper
4 tablespoons butter
1/2 teaspoon dried rosemary
Seasoning to taste

Leaf Me Alone

1 small head lettuce
2 large oranges
1 large sweet onion
3 tablespoons mayonnaise
2 tablespoons white wine vinegar
1 teaspoon poppy seeds
Seasoning to taste

Bag It

4 tablespoons butter
2 tablespoons fresh chives (when chopped)
1 tablespoon milk
1 teaspoon Italian seasoning
4 small French baguettes

Jell-Out

6 tablespoons butter
3/4 cup granulated sugar
1 egg
1 1/2 ounces lemon gelatin
1 teaspoon baking powder
1/4 teaspoon salt
1 1/4 cups flour

EQUIPMENT

Electric mixer	Vegetable brush
Stockpot	Vegetable peeler
Medium saucepan	Vegetable grater
Large skillet	Citrus grater
2 baking sheets	Kitchen knives
Colander	Measuring cups and spoons
Large mixing bowl	
3 small mixing bowls	Cooking utensils
Whisk	

COUNTDOWN

1. Assemble the ingredients and the equipment.
2. Do Step 1 of *Bag It*.
3. Do Steps 1–5 of *Jell-Out*.
4. Do Steps 1–2 of *Pasta Point of No Return*.
5. Do Steps 1–3 of *Leaf Me Alone*.
6. Do Steps 2–4 of *Bag It*.
7. Do Steps 3–7 of *Pasta Point of No Return*.
8. Do Step 5 of *Bag It*.

FRIDAY

Pasta Point of No Return

1 Bring water to a boil in a stockpot.

2 Peel and mince the garlic. Scrub, trim, and coarsely grate the zucchini. Peel, trim, and coarsely grate the carrots. Rinse, stem, and chop the parsley. Rinse and pat dry the shrimp.

3 Bring the clam juice and the wine to a boil in a medium saucepan and cook the shrimp until they turn bright pink, about 3 minutes.

4 Cook the pasta shells until almost tender, 8 to 10 minutes.

5 Drain and set aside the shrimp, reserving the cooking liquid. Blend the flour into the reserved cooking liquid, add the white pepper, and cook over medium heat until the sauce begins to thicken, about 3 minutes.

6 Melt the butter in a large skillet and sauté the garlic for 1 minute. Add the zucchini and the carrots and sauté for 2 minutes. Blend in the rosemary and season to taste. Add the shrimp and the sauce to the skillet and toss to combine and heat through.

7 Drain the pasta and return it to the stockpot. Toss with the shrimp mixture, and sprinkle with the parsley. Cover to keep warm.

Leaf Me Alone

1 Wash and dry the lettuce and arrange the leaves on individual salad plates.

2 Grate 2 teaspoons of peel from one of the oranges. Peel and thinly slice the oranges. Peel and thinly slice the onion. Alternate the orange and onion slices over the lettuce.

3 In a small bowl, combine the mayonnaise, the vinegar, and the poppy seeds. Season to taste and drizzle the dressing over the salad. Sprinkle with the orange peel.

Bag It

1 Set the butter out to soften.

2 Rinse, trim, and chop the chives.

3 In a small bowl, cream the butter with the milk. Fold in the chives and the Italian seasoning.

4 Preheat the broiler.

5 Split the baguettes in half and spread the cut sides with the seasoned butter. Lay the bread on a baking sheet and broil until bubbly, 1 to 2 minutes.

Jell-Out

1 Preheat the oven to 350°F.

2 In a large bowl, cream the butter with ½ cup of the sugar. Add the egg and beat until well blended. Blend in the gelatin. Beat in the baking powder, the salt, and the flour.

3 Roll the dough into 2-inch balls and arrange them on a baking sheet.

4 Place the remaining ¼ cup sugar in a small bowl. Grease the bottom of a small glass. Dip it in the sugar and flatten each dough ball.

5 Bake until the cookies are golden, 5 to 8 minutes.

WEEK NINE

Monday

Impasta
Phony Baloney
Impeachable Tarts

Tuesday

Messy Bessies
Slippery Salad
Devious Pudding

Wednesday

Eggs In a Basket
Finich Your Spinach
Cookie Surprise

Thursday

Chicken de Cristo
Albuquirky Beans
Carl's Bad Cantaloupe

Friday

Little Whippersnapper
Double or Nothing
Nobody's Biscuits
Ice Creammm

STAPLES

- ☐ Butter
- ☐ Vegetable shortening
- ☐ Flour
- ☐ Baking powder
- ☐ Baking soda
- ☐ Granulated sugar
- ☐ Powdered sugar
- ☐ Silver shots
- ☐ Olive oil
- ☐ Vegetable oil
- ☐ Apple cider vinegar
- ☐ Red wine vinegar
- ☐ Rice vinegar
- ☐ Lemon juice
- ☐ Lime juice
- ☐ Honey
- ☐ Ketchup
- ☐ Soy sauce
- ☐ Worcestershire sauce
- ☐ Plain breadcrumbs
- ☐ Dried basil
- ☐ Bay leaf
- ☐ Ground allspice
- ☐ Cayenne pepper
- ☐ Ground cumin
- ☐ Dry mustard
- ☐ Ground nutmeg
- ☐ Black pepper
- ☐ Saffron threads
- ☐ Salt
- ☐ Peppermint extract

SHOPPING LIST

MEAT & POULTRY

1 1/2 pounds lean ground beef (T)

1/2 pound smoked sausage links (Th)

1 1/2 pounds boneless, skinless chicken breast (Th)

FISH

4 red snapper fillets (about 1 1/2 pounds) (F)

FRESH PRODUCE

VEGETABLES

1 1/2 pounds baking potatoes (W)

1 pound green beans (Th)

3/4 pound asparagus (F)

1 medium eggplant (M)

1 package (16 ounces) spinach (W)

3/4 pound Chinese snow peas (F)

2 medium carrots (T)

1/2 pound mushrooms (M)

1 small head lettuce (T)

2 medium tomatoes (M)

1 small green bell pepper (Th)

1 medium onion (M)

1 small onion (T)

1 small shallot (Th)

1 clove garlic (M)

1 clove garlic (T)

2 cloves garlic (W)

1 clove garlic (F)

HERBS

6 ounces basil leaves (M)

2 tablespoons chives (when chopped) (W)

1/2 cup parsley (when chopped) (M)

FRUIT

2 large oranges (T)

2 small ripe cantaloupe melons (Th)

2 large apples (T)

2 large ripe peaches (M)

1 pint blueberries (M)

1 pint raspberries (Th)

CANS, JARS & BOTTLES

SOUPS

1 can (14 ounces) beef broth (T)

1 can (14 ounces) chicken broth (Th)

VEGETABLES

1 can (14 1/2 ounces) stewed tomatoes (Th)

CONDIMENTS

1 jar (3 ounces) pimiento-stuffed olives (Th)

SPREADS

1/4 cup red currant jelly (M)

1/2 cup creamy peanut butter (W)

1/3 cup fruit jam (W)

DESSERT & BAKING NEEDS

1/4 cup chocolate fudge topping for garnish (F)

PACKAGED GOODS

PASTA, RICE & GRAINS

1 pound spaghetti (M)

1 cup instant rice (Th)

BAKED GOODS

1 loaf Italian bread (T)

4 prepared tart shells (M)

8 large chocolate cookies (W)

DESSERT & BAKING NEEDS

1 package (3.4 ounces) devil's food pudding mix (T)

1/4 cup chocolate chips (T)

1 1/2 cups M&M's plain candies (F)

WINE & SPIRITS

1 tablespoon dry sherry (F)

1 tablespoon crème de menthe (Th)

REFRIGERATED PRODUCTS

DAIRY

1/2 cup milk (M)

2 cups milk (T)

1/2 cup milk (W)

3/4 cup buttermilk (F)

8 tablespoons whipping cream (T)

8 eggs (W)

CHEESE

1/2 pound mozzarella cheese (M)

JUICES

1 tablespoon orange juice (T)

DELI

1/2 pound sliced salami (M)

FROZEN GOODS

DESSERTS

1 pint vanilla ice cream (F)

MONDAY

Impasta

1 medium onion
1/2 pound fresh mushrooms
1/2 cup fresh parsley (when chopped)
2 tablespoons butter
2 tablespoons vegetable oil
1 pound spaghetti
1 tablespoon flour
1 teaspoon ground nutmeg
1/2 cup milk
1 tablespoon lemon juice
Seasoning to taste

Phony Baloney

1 medium eggplant
4 tablespoons olive oil
2 medium tomatoes
6 ounces fresh basil leaves
1/2 pound mozzarella cheese
1 clove garlic
2 tablespoons red wine vinegar
1/2 teaspoon dry mustard
1/2 teaspoon granulated sugar
Seasoning to taste
1/2 pound sliced salami

Impeachable Tarts

1 cup water
1/2 cup granulated sugar
2 large ripe peaches
1 pint fresh blueberries
1/4 cup red currant jelly
4 prepared tart shells

EQUIPMENT

Stockpot	Whisk
Medium saucepan	Pastry brush
Large skillet	Kitchen knives
Baking sheet	Measuring cups and
Colander	spoons
3 small mixing bowls	Cooking utensils

COUNTDOWN

1. Assemble the ingredients and the equipment.
2. Do Steps 1–6 of *Impeachable Tarts*.
3. Do Steps 1–4 of *Phony Baloney*.
4. Do Steps 1–2 of *Impasta*.
5. Do Steps 5–7 of *Phony Baloney*.
6. Do Steps 3–6 of *Impasta*.

MONDAY

Impasta

1 Bring water to a boil in a stockpot.

2 Peel and chop the onion. Rinse, pat dry, trim, and slice the mushrooms. Rinse, stem, and chop the parsley.

3 Melt the butter with the oil in a large skillet and sauté the onion until it is soft, about 3 minutes. Add the mushrooms and sauté for 2 minutes more.

4 Cook the spaghetti until it is almost tender, 6 to 7 minutes.

5 In a small bowl, blend the flour and the nutmeg with the milk and the lemon juice. Whisk the mixture into the skillet, season to taste, and heat through, about 2 minutes.

6 Drain the pasta and return it to the stockpot. Toss with the sauce and sprinkle with the parsley.

Phony Baloney

1 Preheat the broiler.

2 Rinse, trim, and slice the eggplant and arrange the slices on a baking sheet. Brush the slices with ½ tablespoon of the oil and broil until golden, about 3 minutes.

3 Turn the eggplant, brush with ½ tablespoon of the oil, and broil again until tender, about 3 minutes more.

4 Remove the eggplant from the broiler and refrigerate it for 15 minutes.

5 Rinse, stem, and slice the tomatoes. Rinse and stem the basil leaves. Slice the cheese.

6 Peel and mince the garlic. In a small bowl, whisk together the garlic, the remaining 3 tablespoons oil, the vinegar, the mustard, and the sugar. Season to taste.

7 On a platter, alternate the eggplant, tomatoes, salami, basil leaves, and cheese. Drizzle with the dressing.

Impeachable Tarts

1 Bring the water and the sugar to a boil in a medium saucepan.

2 Peel, halve, pit, and thinly slice the peaches. Add them to the saucepan and simmer until tender, about 5 minutes.

3 Rinse the blueberries and place them in a small bowl.

4 Remove the peaches with a slotted spoon and set aside to cool. Pour the hot syrup over the berries and let stand for 4 minutes.

5 Melt the currant jelly in the saucepan.

6 Arrange the cooled peach slices in the bottom of the tart shells. Drain the berries and spoon them over the peaches. Drizzle the currant jelly over the top and set aside until you are ready to serve.

TUESDAY

Messy Bessies

1 small onion
1 clove garlic
1 tablespoon vegetable oil
1 1/2 pounds lean ground beef
2 tablespoons flour
1 can (14 ounces) beef broth
1 teaspoon Worcestershire sauce
3 tablespoons ketchup
1 bay leaf
1/2 teaspoon dried basil
1/2 teaspoon granulated sugar
Seasoning to taste
1 loaf Italian bread

Slippery Salad

2 medium carrots
2 large oranges
2 large apples
1 tablespoon orange juice
1 small head lettuce
3 tablespoons olive oil
2 tablespoons apple cider vinegar
1 tablespoon honey
Seasoning to taste

Devious Pudding

1/4 cup chocolate chips
8 tablespoons whipping cream
2 tablespoons powdered sugar
1 teaspoon peppermint extract
1 package (3.4 ounces) instant devil's food
 pudding mix
2 cups milk
Silver shots for garnish

EQUIPMENT

Electric mixer	Whisk
Large skillet	Vegetable peeler
Small saucepan	Vegetable grater
Large mixing bowl	Kitchen knives
2 medium mixing bowls	Measuring cups and spoons
Small mixing bowl	Cooking utensils

COUNTDOWN

1. Assemble the ingredients and the equipment.
2. Do Step 1 of *Devious Pudding*.
3. Do Step 1 of *Slippery Salad*.
4. Do Steps 2–5 of *Devious Pudding*.
5. Do Steps 1–3 of *Messy Bessies*.
6. Do Steps 2–3 of *Slippery Salad*.
7. Do Steps 4–5 of *Messy Bessies*.
8. Do Step 4 of *Slippery Salad*.
9. Do Step 6 of *Devious Pudding*.

TUESDAY

Messy Bessies

1 Peel and mince the onion. Peel and mince the garlic.

2 Heat the oil in a large skillet and sauté the onion and the garlic for 1 minute. Add the beef and brown well, about 7 minutes.

3 Stir in the flour. Stir in the broth. Blend in the Worcestershire sauce, the ketchup, the bay leaf, the basil, and the sugar. Season to taste, reduce the heat, and simmer for 20 minutes.

4 Remove the ends from the bread and cut the loaf into 1½-inch-thick slices.

5 Remove the bay leaf from the skillet and spoon the beef mixture over the bread.

Slippery Salad

1 Peel, trim, and grate the carrots. Peel and slice the oranges. Rinse and core the apples and cut them into thin slices. Combine the ingredients in a large bowl and sprinkle with the orange juice.

2 Wash and dry the lettuce and arrange the leaves on individual salad plates.

3 In a small bowl, combine the oil, the vinegar, and the honey and season to taste.

4 Toss the carrot and fruit mixture with the dressing and spoon onto the lettuce.

Devious Pudding

1 Chill a medium bowl and the beaters of an electric mixer for 10 minutes.

2 Melt the chocolate chips in a small saucepan with 2 tablespoons of the cream.

3 Whip the remaining 6 tablespoons cream until soft peaks form, about 3 minutes. Add the melted chocolate, the powdered sugar, and the peppermint extract and beat until smooth.

4 Beat the pudding mix and the milk in a medium bowl until well blended.

5 Reserve 4 tablespoons of the chocolate cream for garnish and fold the remainder into the pudding. Spoon into individual dessert glasses and refrigerate until you are ready to serve.

6 Garnish the puddings with the reserved chocolate cream and the silver shots.

WEDNESDAY

Eggs In a Basket

1 1/2 pounds baking potatoes
2 tablespoons fresh chives (when chopped)
1/2 cup milk
4 tablespoons butter
8 eggs
Seasoning to taste
1/2 cup plain breadcrumbs
1/2 teaspoon ground nutmeg

Finich Your Spinach

1 package (16 ounces) fresh spinach
2 cloves garlic
1 tablespoon vegetable oil
Seasoning to taste

Cookie Surprise

1/2 cup creamy peanut butter
8 large chocolate cookies
1/3 cup fruit jam
1 tablespoon powdered sugar

EQUIPMENT

Electric mixer	Vegetable peeler
Large covered saucepan	Kitchen knives
Large covered skillet	Measuring cups and spoons
1 1/2-quart casserole	Cooking utensils

COUNTDOWN

1. Assemble the ingredients and the equipment.
2. Do Steps 1–3 of *Eggs In a Basket*.
3. Do Steps 1–3 of *Cookie Surprise*.
4. Do Steps 4–6 of *Eggs In a Basket*.
5. Do Steps 1–3 of *Finich Your Spinach*.
6. Do Step 7 of *Eggs In a Basket*.

WEDNESDAY

Eggs In a Basket

1 Peel and quarter the potatoes and cover them with water in a large saucepan. Bring the water to a boil, cover, and cook until the potatoes are tender, about 15 minutes.

2 Rinse, trim, and chop the chives.

3 Preheat the oven to 425°F. Grease a 1½-quart casserole.

4 Drain the potatoes and return them to the saucepan. Add the milk and mash until well blended. Add 3 tablespoons of the butter and beat until smooth. Spread the potatoes evenly in the casserole.

5 With the back of a spoon, hollow out 8 nests in the potatoes. Break an egg into each nest. Season to taste.

6 Spread the breadcrumbs over the casserole, dot with the remaining 1 tablespoon butter, and sprinkle with the nutmeg. Bake until the eggs are set, 8 to 10 minutes.

7 Sprinkle with the chives.

Finich Your Spinach

1 Rinse, pat dry, and stem the spinach. Peel and mince the garlic.

2 Heat the oil in a large skillet and sauté the garlic for 2 minutes.

3 Add the spinach to the skillet, season to taste, and toss to combine. Cover, remove from the heat, and let stand for 3 minutes.

Cookie Surprise

1 Lightly spread a layer of peanut butter on 4 of the cookies.

2 Lightly spread a layer of jam over the peanut butter.

3 Top with a second cookie and dust with the powdered sugar.

THURSDAY

Chicken de Cristo

1 small shallot
1 small green bell pepper
1 1/2 pounds boneless, skinless chicken breast
1/2 pound smoked sausage links
1 jar (3 ounces) pimiento-stuffed olives
2 tablespoons olive oil
1/4 teaspoon saffron threads
1 can (14 ounces) chicken broth
1 can (14 1/2 ounces) stewed tomatoes
1 cup instant rice
1/2 teaspoon Worcestershire sauce
1/4 teaspoon ground cumin
1/4 teaspoon cayenne pepper
Seasoning to taste

Albuquirky Beans

1 pound fresh green beans
1 tablespoon butter
1/4 teaspoon ground allspice
1 teaspoon lemon juice
Seasoning to taste

Carl's Bad Cantaloupe

1 tablespoon crème de menthe
2 tablespoons lime juice
1 teaspoon granulated sugar
2 small ripe cantaloupe melons
1 pint fresh raspberries

EQUIPMENT

2 small saucepans
Large covered skillet
Large skillet
Whisk

Kitchen knives
Measuring cups and
  spoons
Cooking utensils

COUNTDOWN

1. Assemble the ingredients and the equipment.
2. Do Steps 1–3 of *Carl's Bad Cantaloupe.*
3. Do Step 1 of *Albuquirky Beans.*
4. Do Steps 1–4 of *Chicken de Cristo.*
5. Do Steps 2–3 of *Albuquirky Beans.*
6. Do Step 4 of *Carl's Bad Cantaloupe.*

THURSDAY

Chicken de Cristo

1 Peel and chop the shallot. Rinse, trim, seed, and chop the bell pepper. Rinse and pat dry the chicken breast and cut into strips. Slice the sausage. Drain and slice the olives.

2 Heat the oil in a large skillet and sauté the shallot and the bell pepper for 3 minutes. Add the chicken and the sausage and sauté until the chicken is cooked through and the sausage is lightly browned, about 10 minutes.

3 In a small saucepan, combine the saffron and the broth. Bring the mixture to a boil, whisking to dissolve the saffron.

4 Add the tomatoes, the rice, the Worcestershire sauce, the cumin, and the cayenne to the skillet. Stir in the saffron broth. Stir in the olives and season to taste. Bring the mixture to a boil, cover, and remove it from the heat. Let stand until the liquid is absorbed, about 5 minutes.

Albuquirky Beans

1 Rinse and trim the green beans and cut them in half.

2 Melt the butter with the allspice in a large skillet. Sauté the beans until they are crisp-tender, 6 to 8 minutes.

3 Add the lemon juice, season to taste, and toss to combine.

Carl's Bad Cantaloupe

1 In a small saucepan, heat the crème de menthe, the lime juice, and the sugar, whisking until the sugar is dissolved, about 1 minute. Remove from the heat and let cool.

2 Cut the melons in half and remove the seeds. Place each half on an individual dessert plate.

3 Rinse and pat dry the berries and spoon them into the melon cavities.

4 Spoon the sauce over the berries.

FRIDAY

MENU

Little Whippersnapper

4 red snapper fillets (about 1 1/2 pounds)
2 tablespoons lemon juice
1 clove garlic
2 tablespoons butter
1/2 cup ketchup
2 tablespoons soy sauce
1 teaspoon dry mustard
1 tablespoon dry sherry
Seasoning to taste

Double or Nothing

3/4 pound fresh asparagus
3/4 pound Chinese snow peas
1 tablespoon vegetable oil
1 tablespoon rice vinegar
1/2 teaspoon granulated sugar
Seasoning to taste

Nobody's Biscuits

2 cups flour
1 teaspoon salt
2 teaspoons baking powder
1/2 teaspoon baking soda
1/4 cup vegetable shortening
3/4 cup buttermilk

Ice Creammm

1 1/2 cups M&M's plain candies
1 pint vanilla ice cream
1/4 cup chocolate fudge topping for garnish

EQUIPMENT

Small saucepan
Large skillet
9 x 13-inch glass
   baking dish
Baking sheet
Breadboard
Large mixing bowl
Pastry blender

Biscuit cutter
Mallet
Ice cream scoop
Plastic bag
Kitchen knives
Measuring cups and
   spoons
Cooking utensils

COUNTDOWN

1. Assemble the ingredients and the equipment.
2. Do Step 1 of *Ice Creammm*.
3. Do Step 1 of *Double or Nothing*.
4. Do Steps 1–5 of *Nobody's Biscuits*.
5. Do Steps 1–5 of *Little Whippersnapper*.
6. Do Step 6 of *Nobody's Biscuits*.
7. Do Steps 2–3 of *Double or Nothing*.
8. Do Step 2 of *Ice Creammm*.

FRIDAY

Little Whippersnapper

1 Rinse and pat dry the fish fillets. Place them in a 9 x 13-inch baking dish and sprinkle them with the lemon juice.

2 Peel and mince the garlic.

3 Melt the butter in a small saucepan and sauté the garlic for 1 minute. Add the ketchup, the soy sauce, the mustard, and the sherry. Season to taste. Bring the mixture to a boil and pour it over the fish.

4 Reduce the oven temperature to 350°F.

5 Bake until the fish flakes easily with a fork, 12 to 15 minutes.

Double or Nothing

1 Rinse the asparagus, remove the tough ends, and cut the spears in half. Rinse and string the snow peas.

2 Heat the oil in a large skillet and sauté the asparagus for 3 minutes. Add the snow peas and sauté for 2 minutes.

3 Add the vinegar and the sugar. Season to taste and toss to coat.

Nobody's Biscuits

1 Preheat the oven to 425°F. Lightly flour a breadboard.

2 In a large bowl, combine the flour, the salt, the baking powder, and the baking soda.

3 Cut in the shortening until the mixture resembles coarse crumbs.

4 Add the buttermilk, stirring lightly to make a soft dough. Turn the mixture out on the breadboard and knead until well blended, 8 to 10 times. Pat the roll to a ½-inch thickness and cut into rounds with a biscuit cutter.

5 Lay the biscuits on a baking sheet and bake until they are golden, 12 to 15 minutes.

6 Cover to keep warm.

Ice Creammm

1 Place the M&M's in a plastic bag and lightly crush them with a mallet.

2 Place a scoop of ice cream in each individual dessert glass. Add the crushed candy and another layer of ice cream. Top with a dollop of fudge topping.

WEEK TEN

Monday
Scuttlebutt Scallops
Confidential Couscous
Scandalous Salad
Rumorings

Tuesday
Poultrygeist
Monster Mash
Spirited Beans
Lemonic Pudding

Wednesday
Great Plains Pizza
Yellowstones
Nellie's Jelly

Thursday
In My Soletude
Asparagus Alone
Marooned
Desserted

Friday
Unravioli
Together Tomatoes
Twisted Biscuits
Never-Mind Nectarines

STAPLES

- [ ] Butter
- [ ] Vegetable shortening
- [ ] Flour
- [ ] Baking powder
- [ ] Cornstarch
- [ ] Granulated sugar
- [ ] Dark brown sugar
- [ ] Olive oil
- [ ] Vegetable oil
- [ ] Balsamic vinegar
- [ ] Raspberry vinegar
- [ ] Red wine vinegar
- [ ] Rice vinegar
- [ ] Lemon juice
- [ ] Ketchup
- [ ] Soy sauce
- [ ] Grated Parmesan cheese
- [ ] Seasoned breadcrumbs
- [ ] Celery seeds
- [ ] Sesame seeds
- [ ] Dried marjoram
- [ ] Dried oregano
- [ ] Dried tarragon
- [ ] Ground cinnamon
- [ ] Ground cloves
- [ ] Ground cumin
- [ ] Ground ginger
- [ ] Ground nutmeg
- [ ] Paprika
- [ ] Black pepper
- [ ] Saffron threads
- [ ] Salt
- [ ] Almond extract
- [ ] Vanilla extract

MEAT & POULTRY

1/2 pound Italian sausage (W)

4 boneless, skinless chicken breast halves (about 1 1/2 pounds) (T)

FISH

1 1/2 pounds sea scallops (M)

4 sole fillets (about 1 1/2 pounds) (Th)

FRESH PRODUCE

VEGETABLES

1 1/2 pounds baking potatoes (T)

1 pound sugar-snap peas (M)

3/4 pound green beans (T)

1 pound asparagus (Th)

1 pound green peas, unshelled (F)

1 package (10 ounces) spinach (F)

1 medium carrot (M)

1 stalk celery (M)

1/4 pound mushrooms (W)

1 medium head red cabbage (Th)

1 small head lettuce (M)

4 large tomatoes (F)

2 medium tomatoes (W)

2 medium red bell peppers (T)

1/4 pound bean sprouts (M)

1 small daikon radish (M)

1 small onion (F)

1 medium red onion (W)

1 small red onion (T)

1 small shallot (Th)

1 clove garlic (M)

2 cloves garlic (W)

1 clove garlic (F)

HERBS

2 tablespoons basil leaves (when chopped) (F)

1/4 cup parsley (when chopped) (M)

3 tablespoons parsley (when chopped) (Th)

FRUIT

1 large orange (W)

1 large lemon (Th)

1 large ripe honeydew melon (M)

4 medium ripe peaches (W)

4 large ripe nectarines (F)

CANS, JARS & BOTTLES

SOUPS

1 can (10 1/2 ounces) chicken broth (T)

INTERNATIONAL FOODS

1 can (4 ounces) diced green chilies (W)

JUICES

1 cup ginger ale (W)

SPREADS

1 cup chunky peanut butter (W)

1/4 cup red currant jelly (Th)

CONDIMENTS

1 can (3 1/2 ounces) sliced black olives (W)

DESSERT & BAKING NEEDS

1/4 cup chocolate fudge topping for garnish (T)

PACKAGED GOODS

PASTA, RICE & GRAINS

1 pound cheese ravioli (F)

1 cup couscous (M)

BAKED GOODS

1 large Boboli pizza crust (W)

DRIED FRUIT & NUTS

1/4 cup raisins (Th)

1/2 cup walnut pieces (F)

DESSERT & BAKING NEEDS

1 package (3.4 ounces) instant lemon pudding mix (T)

1 1/2 ounces lemon-flavored gelatin (T)

1 package (3 ounces) orange-flavored gelatin (W)

1/4 cup marshmallow crème for garnish (M)

WINE & SPIRITS

3 tablespoons dry sherry (M)

REFRIGERATED PRODUCTS

DAIRY

1 1/4 cups milk (T)

2/3 cup milk (F)

1/4 cup half-and-half (T)

1/2 cup half-and-half (F)

1/4 cup sour cream (W)

1 container (6 ounces) vanilla yogurt (T)

2 eggs (Th)

1 egg (F)

CHEESE

1/2 cup shredded Cheddar cheese (W)

1/2 cup shredded Monterey Jack cheese (W)

1/2 cup shredded mozzarella cheese (F)

DELI

2 slices bacon (T)

1/4 pound sliced pepperoni (W)

FROZEN GOODS

DESSERTS

1 pint peach sorbet (M)

MONDAY

MENU

Scuttlebutt Scallops

1 1/2 pounds sea scallops
1 pound sugar-snap peas
1 clove garlic
1 cup plus 2 tablespoons water
1/2 teaspoon ground ginger
2 tablespoons soy sauce
1 tablespoon ketchup
3 tablespoons dry sherry
1 tablespoon cornstarch

Confidential Couscous

1 stalk celery
1/4 cup fresh parsley (when chopped)
1 teaspoon vegetable oil
2 cups water
2 teaspoons saffron threads
1 cup couscous
Seasoning to taste

Scandalous Salad

1 small head lettuce
1/4 pound fresh bean sprouts
1 small daikon radish
1 medium carrot
3 tablespoons vegetable oil
2 tablespoons rice vinegar
1/2 teaspoon granulated sugar
Seasoning to taste

Rumorings

1 large ripe honeydew melon
1 pint peach sorbet
1/4 cup marshmallow crème for garnish

EQUIPMENT

Medium covered saucepan	Vegetable grater
Large skillet	Ice cream scoop
Medium mixing bowl	Kitchen knives
2 small mixing bowls	Measuring cups and spoons
Whisk	Cooking utensils
Vegetable peeler	

COUNTDOWN

1. Assemble the ingredients and the equipment.
2. Do Steps 1–3 of *Scandalous Salad*.
3. Do Step 1 of *Rumorings*.
4. Do Steps 1–4 of *Confidential Couscous*.
5. Do Steps 1–4 of *Scuttlebutt Scallops*.
6. Do Step 5 of *Confidential Couscous*.
7. Do Step 4 of *Scandalous Salad*.
8. Do Step 2 of *Rumorings*.

MONDAY

Scuttlebutt Scallops

1 Rinse and pat dry the scallops. Rinse and string the snap peas. Peel and mince the garlic.

2 Bring 1 cup of the water to a boil in a large skillet. Add the scallops and the snap peas and cook for 3 minutes.

3 In a small bowl, combine the garlic, the ginger, the soy sauce, the ketchup, the sherry, the cornstarch, and the remaining 2 tablespoons water and blend well.

4 Add the mixture to the skillet, return to a boil, and cook until the sauce is thick and clear, about 2 minutes.

Confidential Couscous

1 Rinse, trim, and mince the celery. Rinse, stem, and chop the parsley.

2 Heat the oil in a medium saucepan and sauté the celery for 1 minute.

3 Add the water and the saffron to the saucepan, blend well, and bring to a boil.

4 Add the couscous, season to taste, cover the saucepan, and remove it from the heat. Let stand until all the liquid is absorbed, at least 5 minutes.

5 Sprinkle with the parsley.

Scandalous Salad

1 Wash and dry the lettuce and arrange the leaves on individual salad plates.

2 Rinse and dry the sprouts. Peel, trim, and grate the radish. Peel, trim, and grate the carrot. Combine the ingredients in a medium bowl.

3 In a small bowl, combine the oil, the vinegar, and the sugar. Season to taste and toss with the bean sprout mixture.

4 Spoon the mixture over the lettuce.

Rumorings

1 Remove the ends from the melon and discard. Cut the remainder into 4 equal rings. Remove the seeds. Run the tip of a sharp knife around the edge of the rings to remove the rind. Place the melon rings on individual dessert plates.

2 Place scoops of sorbet in the center of each melon ring and top with the marshmallow crème.

TUESDAY

MENU

Poultrygeist

1 small red onion
4 boneless, skinless chicken breast halves
    (about 1 1/2 pounds)
2 tablespoons butter
2 tablespoons raspberry vinegar
1/4 teaspoon dried tarragon
1/2 teaspoon granulated sugar
Seasoning to taste

Monster Mash

1 1/2 pounds baking potatoes
1 can (10 1/2 ounces) chicken broth
1/4 cup half-and-half
Seasoning to taste

Spirited Beans

2 slices bacon
3/4 pound fresh green beans
2 medium red bell peppers
1/2 teaspoon celery seeds

Lemonic Pudding

1 package (3.4 ounces) instant lemon
    pudding mix
1 1/2 ounces lemon gelatin
1 1/4 cups milk
1 container (6 ounces) vanilla yogurt
1/4 cup chocolate fudge topping for garnish

EQUIPMENT

Electric mixer
Large covered
    saucepan
Large covered skillet
Large skillet
Medium mixing bowl

Vegetable peeler
Kitchen knives
Measuring cups and
    spoons
Cooking utensils

COUNTDOWN

1. Assemble the ingredients and the equipment.
2. Do Steps 1–2 of Lemonic Pudding.
3. Do Steps 1–2 of Monster Mash.
4. Do Step 1 of Spirited Beans.
5. Do Steps 1–3 of Poultrygeist.
6. Do Steps 3–5 of Monster Mash.
7. Do Steps 2–4 of Spirited Beans.
8. Do Step 3 of Lemonic Pudding.

TUESDAY

Poultrygeist

1 Peel and mince the onion.

2 Rinse and pat dry the chicken breasts.

3 Melt the butter in a large skillet and sauté the onion for 1 minute. Add the chicken and cook until golden, about 4 minutes per side. Add the vinegar, the tarragon, and the sugar. Season to taste, cover, and reduce the heat. Simmer until the chicken is tender, about 15 minutes.

Monster Mash

1 Peel and cube the potatoes.

2 In a large saucepan, cover the potatoes with water. Bring to a boil, cover, and cook until tender, 10 to 15 minutes.

3 Drain the potatoes and return them to the saucepan. Reduce the heat and gently shake the saucepan over the burner until the potatoes are dry, about 1 minute.

4 In a small saucepan, bring the broth just to boiling.

5 Beat small amounts of the broth into the potatoes until smooth. Fold in the half-and-half, season to taste, and beat vigorously until the potatoes are light and fluffy. Cover to keep warm.

Spirited Beans

1 Dice the bacon. Rinse and trim the green beans and cut them in half. Rinse, trim, seed, and julienne the bell peppers.

2 Sauté the bacon in a large skillet until almost crisp, about 5 minutes. Drain on paper towels.

3 Sauté the beans in the bacon drippings for 5 minutes. Add the bell peppers and continue to sauté until the beans and the peppers are crisp-tender, about 3 minutes.

4 Sprinkle with the diced bacon and the celery seeds.

Lemonic Pudding

1 Combine the pudding mix, the gelatin, and the milk in a medium bowl and beat until well blended, about 2 minutes. Beat in the yogurt and blend well.

2 Spoon the mixture into individual dessert glasses and refrigerate until you are ready to serve.

3 Garnish each pudding with a dollop of fudge topping.

WEDNESDAY

Great Plains Pizza

$1/2$ pound Italian sausage
1 medium red onion
2 cloves garlic
2 medium tomatoes
$1/4$ pound fresh mushrooms
1 can (4 ounces) diced green chilies
1 can ($3 1/2$ ounces) sliced black olives
1 tablespoon olive oil
1 large Boboli pizza crust
$1/4$ pound sliced pepperoni
$1/2$ teaspoon dried oregano
$1/2$ teaspoon ground cumin
$1/2$ cup shredded Cheddar cheese
$1/2$ cup shredded Monterey Jack cheese
$1/4$ cup grated Parmesan cheese

Yellowstones

4 medium ripe peaches
1 tablespoon lemon juice
$1/4$ cup sour cream
$1/2$ teaspoon ground cinnamon

Nellie's Jelly

$1/2$ cup water
1 large orange
1 package (3 ounces) orange gelatin
3 ice cubes
1 cup ginger ale

EQUIPMENT

Blender	Citrus grater
Medium skillet	Kitchen knives
Baking sheet	Measuring cups and
Small mixing bowl	spoons
Whisk	Cooking utensils

COUNTDOWN

1. Assemble the ingredients and the equipment.
2. Do Steps 1–3 of *Nellie's Jelly.*
3. Do Steps 1–2 of *Yellowstones.*
4. Do Step 1 of *Great Plains Pizza.*
5. Do Step 4 of *Nellie's Jelly.*
6. Do Steps 2–5 of *Great Plains Pizza.*

WEDNESDAY

Great Plains Pizza

1 Remove the sausage meat from the casings. Peel and slice the onion. Peel and mince the garlic. Rinse, stem, and chop the tomatoes. Rinse, pat dry, trim, and slice the mushrooms. Drain the chilies. Drain the olives.

2 Heat the oil in a medium skillet and brown the sausage, about 5 minutes. Add the onion and the garlic and sauté for 3 minutes.

3 Preheat the broiler.

4 Spread the sausage mixture over the Boboli pizza crust. Arrange the pepperoni over the sausage and onion. Add the tomatoes, the mushrooms, the chilies, and the olives. Sprinkle with the oregano and the cumin. Top with the Cheddar, the Monterey Jack, and the Parmesan cheeses.

5 Place the pizza on a baking sheet and broil until the cheese is hot and bubbly, 4 to 5 minutes.

Yellowstones

1 Peel, halve, pit, and slice the peaches. Distribute the slices among individual bowls and sprinkle them with the lemon juice.

2 In a small bowl, whisk together the sour cream and the cinnamon and spoon the mixture over the peaches.

Nellie's Jelly

1 Bring the water to a boil.

2 Grate 1 tablespoon of orange peel. Peel and section the orange.

3 Combine the boiling water with the gelatin in a blender and process until dissolved. Add the ice cubes, the ginger ale, and the orange peel and process again until well blended. Refrigerate the mixture in the blender until it has thickened but not set, about 20 minutes.

4 Remove the blender from the refrigerator and process until light and fluffy. Spoon the mixture into individual dessert glasses and garnish with the orange sections. Refrigerate until you are ready to serve.

THURSDAY

In My Soletude

4 sole fillets (about 1 1/2 pounds)
1 small shallot
3 tablespoons fresh parsley (when chopped)
1/3 cup flour
1 teaspoon paprika
Seasoning to taste
1 egg
1/4 cup seasoned breadcrumbs
1/4 cup sesame seeds
2 tablespoons vegetable oil

Asparagus Alone

1 pound fresh asparagus
1 large lemon
1/4 teaspoon dried marjoram

Marooned

1 medium head red cabbage
2 tablespoons butter
1 tablespoon red wine vinegar
1/4 cup red currant jelly

Desserted

1 cup chunky peanut butter
1/2 cup dark brown sugar
1/4 cup granulated sugar
1 egg
1 teaspoon vanilla extract
1/4 cup raisins

EQUIPMENT

Electric mixer
Medium covered saucepan
Large covered skillet
Large skillet
Steamer insert
Baking sheet
Medium mixing bowl

3 shallow bowls
Citrus grater
Citrus juicer
Kitchen knives
Measuring cups and spoons
Cooking utensils

COUNTDOWN

1. Assemble the ingredients and the equipment.
2. Do Steps 1–4 of *Desserted*.
3. Do Steps 1–4 of *In My Soletude*.
4. Do Steps 1–5 of *Asparagus Alone*.
5. Do Steps 1–3 of *Marooned*.
6. Do Step 6 of *Asparagus Alone*.
7. Do Steps 5–8 of *In My Soletude*.

THURSDAY

In My Soletude

1 Rinse and pat dry the fish fillets. Peel and mince the shallot. Rinse, stem, and chop the parsley.

2 Combine the flour and the paprika in a shallow bowl. Season to taste.

3 In a second shallow bowl, beat the egg.

4 In a third shallow bowl, combine the breadcrumbs and the sesame seeds.

5 Heat the oil in a large skillet and sauté the shallot for 1 minute.

6 Dip the fish in the seasoned flour, then in the egg, and then in the breadcrumb mixture.

7 Sauté the fish in the skillet until it flakes easily with a fork, about 3 minutes per side.

8 Sprinkle with the parsley.

Asparagus Alone

1 Rinse the asparagus and remove the tough ends.

2 Bring a small amount of water to a boil in a medium saucepan.

3 Grate the lemon peel and juice the lemon.

4 Arrange the asparagus spears in a steamer insert and place the insert in the saucepan.

5 Sprinkle the asparagus with the lemon juice and the marjoram, cover, and steam until crisp-tender, 5 to 8 minutes, depending on thickness.

6 Drain the asparagus, return it to the saucepan, sprinkle with the lemon peel, and cover to keep warm.

Marooned

1 Rinse, trim, and thinly slice the cabbage.

2 Melt the butter in a large skillet and sauté the cabbage until it is wilted, about 3 minutes.

3 Add the vinegar and the jelly and cook, stirring, to combine and heat through, about 2 minutes. Cover, remove from the heat, and let stand.

Desserted

1 Preheat the oven to 350°F.

2 In a medium bowl, combine the peanut butter, the brown sugar, the granulated sugar, the egg, and the vanilla. Beat until well blended. Fold in the raisins.

3 Drop the dough by spoonfuls, 2 inches apart, onto a baking sheet and flatten each cookie in a crisscross pattern with the tines of a fork.

4 Bake until golden, 8 to 10 minutes.

FRIDAY

Unravioli

1 small onion
1 pound fresh green peas, unshelled
1 package (10 ounces) fresh spinach
1 pound cheese ravioli
2 tablespoons vegetable oil
1 teaspoon dried tarragon
1/2 cup half-and-half
Seasoning to taste
1/2 cup shredded mozzarella cheese
1/2 cup walnut pieces

Together Tomatoes

1 clove garlic
2 tablespoons fresh basil leaves (when chopped)
4 large tomatoes
2 tablespoons olive oil
1 tablespoon balsamic vinegar
Seasoning to taste

Twisted Biscuits

2 cups flour
1 tablespoon granulated sugar
1/4 teaspoon ground cloves
4 teaspoons baking powder
1/4 teaspoon salt
1/2 cup vegetable shortening
1 egg
2/3 cup milk

Never-Mind Nectarines

1 cup water
3 tablespoons lemon juice
1/4 teaspoon ground nutmeg
1/4 teaspoon ground cinnamon
1/4 teaspoon ground ginger
1/3 cup granulated sugar
1 teaspoon almond extract
4 large ripe nectarines

EQUIPMENT

Stockpot	Whisk
Small saucepan	Pastry blender
Large covered skillet	Biscuit cutter
Baking sheet	Kitchen knives
Colander	Measuring cups and
Breadboard	spoons
Large mixing bowl	Cooking utensils
2 small mixing bowls	

COUNTDOWN

1. Assemble the ingredients and the equipment.
2. Do Steps 1–2 of *Never-Mind Nectarines.*
3. Do Steps 1–2 of *Unravioli.*
4. Do Steps 1–3 of *Together Tomatoes.*
5. Do Steps 1–5 of *Twisted Biscuits.*
6. Do Steps 3–5 of *Unravioli.*
7. Do Step 3 of *Never-Mind Nectarines.*

FRIDAY

Unravioli

1 Bring water to a boil in a stockpot.

2 Peel and chop the onion. Shell the peas. Rinse, pat dry, stem, and chop the spinach.

3 Cook the ravioli until it is almost tender, 6 to 7 minutes if you are using fresh pasta, 8 to 10 minutes if you are using dry pasta.

4 Heat the oil in a large skillet and sauté the onion until soft, about 5 minutes. Add the peas and cook for 3 minutes. Fold in the spinach and the tarragon and cook for 1 minute. Stir in the half-and-half and bring the mixture just to a boil. Season to taste, cover the skillet, and remove it from the heat.

5 Drain the ravioli and return it to the stockpot. Toss it with the sauce. Sprinkle with the cheese and the nuts.

Together Tomatoes

1 Peel and mince the garlic. Rinse, stem, and chop the basil.

2 Rinse, stem, and slice the tomatoes and arrange them on individual salad plates.

3 In a small bowl, combine the garlic, the basil, the oil, and the vinegar. Season to taste and drizzle over the tomatoes.

Twisted Biscuits

1 Preheat the oven to 450°F. Flour a breadboard.

2 In a large bowl, blend together the flour, the sugar, the cloves, the baking powder, and the salt. Add the shortening and cut it in with a pastry blender until it resembles coarse crumbs.

3 In a small bowl, combine the egg and the milk. Add to the flour mixture. Stir with a fork until a dough is formed, about 2 minutes.

4 Turn the dough out onto the breadboard and knead until smooth, 8 to 10 times. Pat the dough out to a ½-inch thickness and cut into rounds with a biscuit cutter.

5 Place the biscuits on a baking sheet and bake until golden, 10 to 12 minutes.

Never-Mind Nectarines

1 In a small saucepan, combine the water, the lemon juice, the nutmeg, the cinnamon, the ginger, the sugar, and the almond extract. Bring the mixture to a boil and cook until thickened, about 3 minutes.

2 Remove the saucepan from the heat and let cool.

3 Peel, halve, pit, and slice the nectarines and distribute them among individual dessert plates. Top with the sauce.

WEEK ELEVEN

WEEK AT A GLANCE

Monday
Oodles of Noodles
The Spinach Grinch
Star-Struck

Tuesday
Winsome White Fish
Yam-Packed
Seeing Double
Flagrant Fruit

Wednesday
Hamdinger
Spicy Rice
Sly Slaw
Pound of Pleasure

Thursday
Pearl River Chicken
Pastagoula
Okra Winfrey
Biloxi Blues

Friday
Bow Tides
Cast-Off Carrots
Bulkhead Biscuits
Sea Foam

STAPLES

- ☐ Butter
- ☐ Vegetable shortening
- ☐ Flour
- ☐ Bisquick
- ☐ Baking powder
- ☐ Cornstarch
- ☐ Granulated sugar
- ☐ Powdered sugar
- ☐ Olive oil
- ☐ Vegetable oil
- ☐ Red wine vinegar
- ☐ Rice vinegar
- ☐ Lemon juice
- ☐ Lime juice
- ☐ Dijon mustard
- ☐ Steak sauce
- ☐ Grated Romano cheese
- ☐ Plain breadcrumbs
- ☐ Dried basil
- ☐ Dried dill
- ☐ Dried savory
- ☐ Dried thyme
- ☐ Ground allspice
- ☐ Ground cloves
- ☐ Ground nutmeg
- ☐ Black pepper
- ☐ Salt
- ☐ Peppermint extract
- ☐ Vanilla extract

MEAT & POULTRY

2 lean cooked ham steaks (about ³/₄ pound each) (W)
3 pounds chicken pieces (Th)

FISH

4 flounder fillets (about 1¹/₂ pounds) (T)

FRESH PRODUCE

VEGETABLES

4 small yams (T)
¹/₂ pound green beans (T)
¹/₂ pound wax beans (or butter beans) (T)
1 pound okra (Th)
1 small bunch broccoli (F)
1 package (16 ounces) spinach (M)
1 medium carrot (W)
1 pound baby carrots (F)
2 stalks celery (M)
2 stalks celery (W)
1 medium head cabbage (W)
1 medium green bell pepper (W)
12 pearl onions (Th)
1 medium red onion (F)
1 small red onion (M)
1 medium shallot (T)
1 clove garlic (Th)

HERBS

2 tablespoon chives (when chopped) (M)
2 tablespoons chives (when chopped) (W)
¹/₄ cup chives (when chopped) (Th)
2 tablespoons parsley (when chopped) (T)
2 tablespoons parsley (when chopped) (Th)
1 tablespoon parsley (when chopped) (F)

FRUIT

1 large orange (W)
2 medium limes (F)
2 small ripe cantaloupe melons (Th)
2 large ripe peaches (T)
1 pint raspberries (T)
1 pint blueberries (Th)

CANS, JARS & BOTTLES

SOUPS

1 can (10¹/₂ ounces) chicken broth (W)
1 can (10¹/₂ ounces) beef broth (W)
1 can (10³/₄ ounces) tomato soup (Th)
1 can (10³/₄ ounces) golden mushroom soup (Th)

INTERNATIONAL FOODS

1 can (8 ounces) sliced water chestnuts (M)

FISH

2 cans (6 ounces each) solid white tuna (F)
1 tin (2 ounces) anchovy fillets (F)

JUICES

1 can (12 ounces) ginger ale (F)

CONDIMENTS

1 jar (2 ounces) diced pimientos (Th)

SPREADS

¹/₂ cup red currant jelly (W)

PACKAGED GOODS

PASTA, RICE & GRAINS

12 ounces fine egg noodles (M)
¹/₂ cup vermicelli (when broken) (W)
8 ounces spinach noodles (Th)
12 ounces bow-tie pasta (F)
1 cup long-grain white rice (W)

DESSERT & BAKING NEEDS

1 package (5.1 ounces) instant vanilla pudding mix (M)
1 package (3 ounces) lime gelatin (F)
1 package (8 ounces) chocolate stars (M)
6 ounces cinnamon chips (W)

WINE & SPIRITS

3 tablespoons dry white wine (T)
¹/₂ cup dry red wine (W)
1 tablespoon dry sherry (Th)
1 tablespoon crème de menthe (T)

REFRIGERATED PRODUCTS

DAIRY

1¹/₄ cups milk (F)
¹/₂ cup half-and-half (M)
Whipped cream for garnish (Th)
2 eggs (M)

CHEESE

¹/₂ cup Swiss cheese (when grated) (M)

DELI

6 slices bacon (M)

FROZEN GOODS

BAKED GOODS

1 pound cake (W)

DESSERTS

1 pint vanilla ice cream (Th)
1 container (8 ounces) whipped topping (F)

MONDAY

Oodles of Noodles

2 stalks celery
1/2 cup Swiss cheese (when grated)
2 tablespoons fresh chives (when chopped)
12 ounces fine egg noodles
4 tablespoons butter
1/2 cup half-and-half
Seasoning to taste

The Spinach Grinch

1 package (16 ounces) fresh spinach
1 small red onion
1 can (8 ounces) sliced water chestnuts
6 slices bacon
3 tablespoons vegetable oil
2 tablespoons red wine vinegar
1 teaspoon Dijon mustard
1/2 teaspoon granulated sugar
Seasoning to taste

Star-Struck

4 tablespoons butter
1 package (5.1 ounces) instant vanilla
   pudding mix
2 eggs
1 teaspoon peppermint extract
1 1/2 cups Bisquick
1 package (8 ounces) chocolate stars

EQUIPMENT

Electric mixer
Large saucepan
Small saucepan
Medium skillet
Small skillet
Baking sheet
Colander
2 large mixing bowls

Small mixing bowl
Cheese grater
Whisk
Kitchen knives
Measuring cups and
   spoons
Cooking utensils

COUNTDOWN

1. Assemble the ingredients and the
   equipment.
2. Do Steps 1–4 of *Star-Struck*.
3. Do Steps 1–4 of *The Spinach Grinch*.
4. Do Steps 1–6 of *Oodles of Noodles*.

MONDAY

Oodles of Noodles

1 Bring water to a boil in a large saucepan.

2 Rinse, trim, and chop the celery. Grate the cheese. Rinse, trim, and chop the chives.

3 Cook half the noodles until tender, about 5 minutes.

4 Melt 2 tablespoons of the butter in a medium skillet and sauté the celery for 2 minutes. Add the remaining, uncooked noodles and sauté until they are golden, about 4 minutes.

5 Drain the boiled noodles and return them to the saucepan. Blend in the remaining 2 tablespoons butter, the cheese, and the half-and-half.

6 Toss both noodles together, season to taste, and sprinkle with the chives.

The Spinach Grinch

1 Rinse, pat dry, and stem the spinach. Peel and thinly slice the onion. Drain the water chestnuts. Combine the ingredients in a large bowl.

2 Dice the bacon and cook it in a small skillet until crisp, about 8 minutes. Drain on paper towels.

3 In a small bowl, whisk together the oil, the vinegar, the mustard, and the sugar and season to taste.

4 Toss the salad with the dressing and top with the bacon.

Star-Struck

1 Preheat the oven to 350°F.

2 Melt the butter in a small saucepan.

3 In a large bowl, combine the pudding mix, the eggs, and the peppermint extract and beat well. Add the Bisquick and blend well.

4 Drop by teaspoons on a baking sheet. Bake until lightly golden and set, about 10 minutes. Remove from the oven and press a chocolate star into the center of each cookie.

TUESDAY

Winsome White Fish

4 flounder fillets (about 1 1/2 pounds)
2 tablespoons fresh parsley (when chopped)
1 tablespoon butter
2 tablespoons steak sauce
3 tablespoons dry white wine
1 teaspoon dried dill
Seasoning to taste

Yam-Packed

2 tablespoons butter
4 small yams
1/2 teaspoon ground cloves

Seeing Double

1/2 pound fresh green beans
1/2 pound fresh wax beans (or butter beans)
1 medium shallot
2 tablespoons olive oil
1/2 teaspoon dried savory
Seasoning to taste

Flagrant Fruit

2 tablespoons lime juice
1 tablespoon granulated sugar
1 tablespoon crème de menthe
2 teaspoons cornstarch
2 tablespoons water
2 large ripe peaches
1 pint fresh raspberries

EQUIPMENT

Small saucepan	Whisk
Large covered skillet	Kitchen knives
Large skillet	Measuring cups and spoons
9 x 9-inch baking pan	
2 small mixing bowls	Cooking utensils

COUNTDOWN

1. Assemble the ingredients and the equipment.
2. Do Steps 1–4 of *Yam-Packed*.
3. Do Step 1 of *Flagrant Fruit*.
4. Do Step 1 of *Winsome White Fish*.
5. Do Steps 1–3 of *Seeing Double*.
6. Do Steps 2–4 of *Winsome White Fish*.
7. Do Step 5 of *Yam-Packed*.
8. Do Step 2 of *Flagrant Fruit*.

TUESDAY

Winsome White Fish

1 Rinse and pat dry the fish fillets. Rinse, stem, and chop the parsley.

2 Melt the butter in a large skillet and sauté the fish until it flakes easily with a fork, about 3 minutes per side.

3 In a small bowl, combine the steak sauce, the wine, and the dill and pour the mixture over the fish fillets. Season to taste, reduce the heat, and simmer until hot, about 2 minutes.

4 Garnish with the parsley.

Yam-Packed

1 Set the butter out to soften.

2 Preheat the oven to 450°F.

3 Scrub and trim the yams. Prick several times with a sharp knife. Place in a 9 x 9-inch baking pan.

4 Bake until soft to the touch, about 45 minutes.

5 In a small bowl, combine the softened butter with the ground cloves.

6 Open the potatoes and top each with a dollop of the mixture.

Seeing Double

1 Rinse and trim the green beans. Peel and chop the shallot.

2 Heat the oil in a large skillet and sauté the shallot until it is soft, about 5 minutes.

3 Add the beans and the savory and sauté until the beans are crisp-tender, 6 to 8 minutes. Season to taste and cover to keep warm.

Flagrant Fruit

1 In a small saucepan, combine the lime juice, the sugar, the crème de menthe, the cornstarch, and the water. Bring the mixture to a boil and cook for 1 minute. Remove from the heat and set aside to cool slightly.

2 Peel, halve, pit, and slice the peaches. Rinse and pat dry the raspberries. Distribute the peach slices and the raspberries among individual dessert dishes and drizzle with the sauce.

WEDNESDAY

Hamdinger

2 lean cooked ham steaks (about ¾ pound each)
½ cup red currant jelly
½ cup dry red wine
1 tablespoon Dijon mustard
Seasoning to taste

Spicy Rice

2 tablespoons fresh chives (when chopped)
½ cup vermicelli (when broken)
1 cup long-grain white rice
1 can (10½ ounces) chicken broth
1 can (10½ ounces) beef broth
¼ teaspoon ground allspice

Sly Slaw

1 medium head cabbage
1 medium green bell pepper
2 stalks celery
1 medium carrot
3 tablespoons vegetable oil
2 tablespoons rice vinegar
1 teaspoon granulated sugar
Seasoning to taste

Pound of Pleasure

1 frozen pound cake
1 large orange
2 tablespoons powdered sugar
2 tablespoons butter
6 ounces cinnamon chips

EQUIPMENT

Double boiler
Small covered saucepan
Small saucepan
Baking sheet
Large mixing bowl
Small mixing bowl
Whisk
Vegetable peeler

Vegetable grater
Citrus grater
Citrus juicer
Pastry brush
Kitchen knives
Measuring cups and spoons
Cooking utensils

COUNTDOWN

1. Assemble the ingredients and the equipment.
2. Do Step 1 of *Pound of Pleasure*.
3. Do Steps 1–3 of *Spicy Rice*.
4. Do Steps 1–2 of *Sly Slaw*.
5. Do Step 2 of *Pound of Pleasure*.
6. Do Steps 1–4 of *Hamdinger*.
7. Do Step 4 of *Spicy Rice*.
8. Do Step 3 of *Pound of Pleasure*.

WEDNESDAY

Hamdinger

1 Preheat the broiler.

2 Rinse and pat dry the ham steaks and place them on a baking sheet.

3 In a small saucepan, combine the jelly, the wine, and the mustard. Season to taste. Bring to a boil to dissolve the jelly, stirring to blend.

4 Brush the ham steaks with some of the jelly mixture and broil until the glaze begins to bubble, about 2 minutes. Turn the steaks, brush with the remaining jelly mixture, and return to the broiler to heat through. To serve, cut the steaks in half.

Spicy Rice

1 Bring water to a boil in the bottom of a double boiler.

2 Rinse, trim, and chop the chives. Break the vermicelli into 1-inch pieces.

3 Combine the chives, the vermicelli, the rice, the broths, and the allspice in the top of the double boiler. Cover, reduce the heat, and simmer until all the liquid is absorbed and the vermicelli and rice are tender, 30 to 40 minutes.

4 Fluff with a fork before serving.

Sly Slaw

1 Rinse, trim, and thinly slice the cabbage. Rinse, trim, seed, and chop the bell pepper. Rinse, trim, and chop the celery. Rinse, peel, trim, and grate the carrot. Combine the ingredients in a large bowl.

2 In a small bowl, combine the oil, the vinegar, and the sugar. Season to taste and toss with the slaw.

Pound of Pleasure

1 Set the pound cake out to thaw.

2 Grate 2 tablespoons of orange peel. Juice the orange. In a small saucepan, combine the orange juice, the powdered sugar, and the butter. Bring the mixture to a boil. Reduce the heat, fold in the cinnamon chips, and simmer, stirring, until the chips have melted and the sauce has thickened slightly, about 2 minutes. Cover and set aside.

3 Slice the cake and spoon the sauce over the slices. Sprinkle with the orange peel.

THURSDAY

Pearl River Chicken

12 fresh pearl onions
3 pounds chicken pieces
2 tablespoons butter
1 tablespoon vegetable oil
1 can (10¾ ounces) tomato soup
1 can (10¾ ounces) golden mushroom soup
1 tablespoon dry sherry
Seasoning to taste

Pastagoula

¼ cup fresh chives (when chopped)
2 tablespoons fresh parsley (when chopped)
8 ounces spinach noodles
2 tablespoons butter
½ teaspoon ground nutmeg
Seasoning to taste

Okra Winfrey

1 pound fresh okra
1 clove garlic
1 jar (2 ounces) diced pimientos
½ teaspoon dried thyme
1 teaspoon granulated sugar
Seasoning to taste

Biloxi Blues

1 pint fresh blueberries
2 small ripe cantaloupe melons
3 tablespoons powdered sugar
1 tablespoon lemon juice
1 tablespoon vanilla extract
1 pint vanilla ice cream
Whipped cream for garnish

EQUIPMENT

Electric mixer	Vegetable peeler
Blender	Ice cream scoop
Dutch oven	Kitchen knives
Large covered saucepan	Measuring cups and spoons
Large covered skillet	Cooking utensils
Small mixing bowl	

COUNTDOWN

1. Assemble the ingredients and the equipment.
2. Do Steps 1–3 of *Biloxi Blues*.
3. Do Steps 1–3 of *Pearl River Chicken*.
4. Do Steps 1–3 of *Pastagoula*.
5. Do Steps 1–2 of *Okra Winfrey*.
6. Do Step 4 of *Pastagoula*.
7. Do Steps 3–4 of *Okra Winfrey*.
8. Do Step 4 of *Biloxi Blues*.

THURSDAY

Pearl River Chicken

1 Peel the onions. Rinse and pat dry the chicken pieces.

2 Melt the butter with the oil in a Dutch oven. Add the onions and the chicken pieces and sauté until the chicken is lightly browned on all sides, about 15 minutes.

3 Combine the soups and the sherry in a small bowl and pour the mixture over the chicken, turning to coat well. Season to taste. Reduce the heat and simmer until the chicken is tender, about 30 minutes.

Pastagoula

1 Bring water to a boil in a large saucepan.

2 Rinse, trim, and chop the chives. Rinse, stem, and chop the parsley.

3 Cook the noodles until they are almost tender, 6 to 7 minutes.

4 Drain the noodles and return them to the saucepan. Toss with the butter, the chives, the parsley, and the nutmeg. Season to taste. Cover to keep warm.

Okra Winfrey

1 Bring a small amount of water to a boil in a large skillet.

2 Rinse and pat dry the okra. Peel and mince the garlic. Drain the pimientos.

3 Add the okra, the garlic, and the thyme to the skillet. Reduce the heat, cover, and simmer until the okra is tender, about 5 minutes.

4 Drain the okra and return it to the skillet. Add the pimientos and the sugar, season to taste, and heat through.

Biloxi Blues

1 Rinse the blueberries, reserving several for garnish.

2 Cut the melons in half and remove the seeds.

3 Place the berries, the powdered sugar, the lemon juice, and the vanilla in a blender and puree. Chill the mixture in the refrigerator until you are ready to serve.

4 Top each melon half with a scoop of ice cream, top the ice cream with the sauce, and garnish with a dollop of whipped cream and the reserved berries.

FRIDAY

MENU

Bow Tides

1 medium red onion
1 small bunch broccoli
2 cans (6 ounces) solid white tuna
1 tin (2 ounces) anchovy fillets
3 tablespoons butter
1 tablespoon vegetable oil
12 ounces bow-tie pasta
1/2 cup milk
Seasoning to taste
1/2 cup plain breadcrumbs
1/4 cup grated Romano cheese

Cast-Off Carrots

1 tablespoon fresh parsley (when chopped)
1 pound baby carrots
1 can (12 ounces) ginger ale
1 tablespoon butter
Seasoning to taste

Bulkhead Biscuits

2 cups flour
2 teaspoons dried basil
1 tablespoon baking powder
1 teaspoon salt
1 teaspoon pepper
1/2 teaspoon granulated sugar
1/2 cup vegetable shortening
3/4 cup milk

Sea Foam

3/4 cup water
2 medium limes
1 package (3 ounces) lime gelatin
3 ice cubes
1 container (8 ounces) frozen whipped
   topping

EQUIPMENT

Blender	Large mixing bowl
Stockpot	Medium mixing bowl
Medium covered	Citrus grater
saucepan	Citrus juicer
Large skillet	Pastry blender
9 x 13-inch glass	Biscuit cutter
baking dish	Kitchen knives
Baking sheet	Measuring cups and
Breadboard	spoons
Colander	Cooking utensils

COUNTDOWN

1. Assemble the ingredients and the equipment.
2. Do Steps 1–3 of *Sea Foam.*
3. Do Steps 1–2 of *Bow Tides.*
4. Do Steps 1–2 of *Cast-Off Carrots.*
5. Do Steps 1–4 of *Bulkhead Biscuits.*
6. Do Step 3 of *Cast-Off Carrots.*
7. Do Steps 3–7 of *Bow Tides.*

FRIDAY

Bow Tides

1 Peel and chop the onion. Rinse the broccoli, discard the tough ends, and cut into bite-sized florets. Drain and flake the tuna. Drain, blot, and chop the anchovies.

2 Bring water to a boil in a stockpot.

3 Melt the butter with the oil in a large skillet. Sauté the onion for 5 minutes. Add the broccoli and cook until the onion is golden, about 5 minutes.

4 Cook the bow-ties until tender but still firm, 8 to 10 minutes.

5 Add the milk, the anchovies, and the tuna to the skillet.

6 Preheat the broiler.

7 Drain the pasta and return it to the stock-pot. Add the tuna mixture to the pasta and mix well. Season to taste. Turn the pasta mixture into a 9 x 13-inch baking dish. Top with the breadcrumbs and the cheese and broil until bubbly, about 5 minutes.

Cast-Off Carrots

1 Rinse, stem, and chop the parsley. Rinse and trim the carrots.

2 Place the carrots in a medium saucepan. Add the ginger ale and bring to a boil. Cover, reduce the heat, and simmer until the carrots are tender, about 10 minutes.

3 Drain the carrots, add the butter, season to taste, and toss to coat. Sprinkle with the parsley and cover to keep warm.

Bulkhead Biscuits

1 Preheat the oven to 450°F. Flour a bread-board.

2 In a large bowl, combine the flour, the basil, the baking powder, the salt, the pepper, and the sugar. With a pastry blender, cut in the shortening until it resembles coarse meal. Stir in the milk until the dry ingredients are well blended.

3 Turn the dough out onto the breadboard and knead until smooth, 8 to 10 times. Pat the dough out to a ½-inch thickness and cut with a biscuit cutter.

4 Place the biscuits on a baking sheet and bake until lightly golden, 10 to 12 minutes.

Sea Foam

1 Bring the water to a boil.

2 Grate 1 tablespoon of lime peel. Juice the lime.

3 Put the gelatin in a blender, add the boiling water, and blend for 30 seconds. Add the lime juice and the ice cubes and blend for 30 seconds more. Pour the mixture into a medium bowl and blend in the whipped topping. Spoon into individual dessert glasses and sprinkle with the lime peel. Refrigerate until you are ready to serve.

WEEK TWELVE

Monday

Tulsa Turkey
Couscous Crude
Sooner Stir-Fry
Pottawatomie Pudding

Tuesday

Wild Scramble
High Spearited
Bite the Crust
Split Shakes

Wednesday

Can-Do Salmon
Up-Beet Salad
You Cannoli Imagine

Thursday

Stew Biz
Stopovers
Sour Grapes

Friday

Peter Penne
Hare Today, Gone Tomato
Bunny Hop Pudding

STAPLES

- ☐ Butter
- ☐ Flour
- ☐ Granulated sugar
- ☐ Dark brown sugar
- ☐ Powdered sugar
- ☐ Cocoa powder
- ☐ Multicolored sprinkles
- ☐ Olive oil
- ☐ Vegetable oil
- ☐ Red wine vinegar
- ☐ Rice vinegar
- ☐ Lemon juice
- ☐ Prepared horseradish
- ☐ Worcestershire sauce
- ☐ White Worcestershire sauce
- ☐ Grated Parmesan cheese
- ☐ Instant coffee
- ☐ Poppy seeds
- ☐ Dried basil
- ☐ Dried oregano
- ☐ Dried savory
- ☐ Lemon-pepper seasoning
- ☐ Dry mustard
- ☐ Black pepper
- ☐ Salt
- ☐ Rum extract

MEAT & POULTRY

1½ pounds lean ground beef (Th)

1½ pounds boneless, skinless turkey breast (M)

FRESH PRODUCE

VEGETABLES

1 small bunch broccoli (M)

1 small head cauliflower (F)

1 pound asparagus (T)

2 medium carrots (M)

2 medium carrots (F)

2 stalks celery (T)

3 stalks celery (W)

¼ pound mushrooms (F)

1 small head red leaf lettuce (W)

4 large tomatoes (F)

1 medium green bell pepper (Th)

1 large red bell pepper (T)

1 medium onion (Th)

1 medium red onion (F)

1 medium sweet onion (F)

3 scallions (green onions) (M)

1 clove garlic (M)

1 clove garlic (Th)

1 clove garlic (F)

HERBS

2 tablespoons parsley (when chopped) (M)

2 tablespoons parsley (when chopped) (F)

FRUIT

1 large orange (W)

1 small orange (F)

2 large bananas (T)

2 medium ripe peaches (Th)

2 medium ripe nectarines (Th)

1 pound seedless green grapes (Th)

CANS, JARS & BOTTLES

SOUPS

1 can (14 ounces) chicken broth (M)

1 can (14 ounces) chicken broth (W)

1 can (10½ ounces) onion soup (T)

1 can (10½ ounces) beef consommé (Th)

VEGETABLES

1 can (14½ ounces) diced tomatoes (Th)

1 can (15 ounces) julienne beets (W)

1 can (11 ounces) whole-kernel corn (T)

2 cans (11 ounces each) whole-kernel corn (Th)

1 can (15 ounces) black beans (Th)

INTERNATIONAL FOODS

1 jar (10 ounces) salsa (M)

FISH

2 cans (6 ounces each) salmon (W)

FRUIT

1 maraschino cherry (F)

CONDIMENTS

1 jar (2 ounces) diced pimientos (F)

DESSERT & BAKING NEEDS

1 can (14 ounces) sweetened condensed milk (T)

PACKAGED GOODS

PASTA, RICE & GRAINS

1 pound penne (F)

½ cup wild rice (T)

1 cup long-grain white rice (W)

1 cup couscous (M)

BAKED GOODS

1 loaf French bread (T)

4 cannoli shells (W)

DRIED FRUIT & NUTS

8 raisins (F)

4 whole almonds (F)

DESSERT & BAKING NEEDS

1 package (3.4 ounces) instant vanilla pudding mix (M)

1 package (3.4 ounces) instant white chocolate pudding mix (F)

WINE & SPIRITS

¼ cup dry white wine (M)

½ cup dry white wine (F)

¼ cup dry red wine (Th)

REFRIGERATED PRODUCTS

DAIRY

2 cups milk (M)

1 cup milk (Th)

1¼ cups milk (F)

½ cup half-and-half (M)

½ cup half-and-half (T)

1 cup half-and-half (W)

¼ cup sour cream (W)

¾ cup sour cream (F)

1 cup whipping cream (W)

Whipped cream for garnish (T)

9 eggs (T)

3 eggs (Th)

CHEESE

½ cup shredded Cheddar cheese (W)

JUICES

½ cup orange juice (Th)

DELI

4 slices bacon (F)

FROZEN GOODS

VEGETABLES

1 package (10 ounces) green peas and pearl onions (W)

DESSERTS

1 pint peach sorbet (Th)

MONDAY

Tulsa Turkey

1 1/2 pounds boneless, skinless turkey breast
2 tablespoons vegetable oil
1 jar (10 ounces) salsa
1/4 cup dry white wine
1 teaspoon white Worcestershire sauce
1/2 teaspoon dry mustard
Seasoning to taste

Couscous Crude

3 scallions (green onions)
2 tablespoons fresh parsley (when chopped)
1 can (14 ounces) chicken broth
1/4 cup water
1 teaspoon granulated sugar
1 cup couscous

Sooner Stir-Fry

1 clove garlic
1 small bunch broccoli
2 medium carrots
3 tablespoons olive oil
3 tablespoons rice vinegar
1 teaspoon granulated sugar
Seasoning to taste

Pottawatomie Pudding

3 tablespoons butter
1/2 cup dark brown sugar
1/2 cup half-and-half
1 teaspoon rum extract
1 package (3.4 ounces) instant vanilla pudding mix
2 cups milk

EQUIPMENT

Electric mixer
Medium covered saucepan
Small saucepan
Medium skillet
9 x 13-inch glass baking dish
Medium mixing bowl

Small mixing bowl
Whisk
Vegetable peeler
Aluminum foil
Kitchen knives
Measuring cups and spoons
Cooking utensils

COUNTDOWN

1. Assemble the ingredients and the equipment.
2. Do Steps 1–2 of *Pottawatomie Pudding*.
3. Do Steps 1–3 of *Tulsa Turkey*.
4. Do Step 1 of *Couscous Crude*.
5. Do Step 1 of *Sooner Stir-Fry*.
6. Do Step 2 of *Couscous Crude*.
7. Do Steps 2–3 of *Sooner Stir-Fry*.
8. Do Step 3 of *Couscous Crude*.
9. Do Step 3 of *Pottawatomie Pudding*.

MONDAY

Tulsa Turkey

1 Preheat the oven to 375°F. Grease a 9 x 13-inch baking dish.

2 Rinse and pat dry the turkey, cut it into 4 portions, and place in the baking dish.

3 In a small bowl, combine the oil, the salsa, the wine, the Worcestershire sauce, and the mustard. Season to taste and pour over the turkey. Cover the dish with aluminum foil and bake until the turkey is tender and cooked through, 30 to 35 minutes.

Couscous Crude

1 Rinse, trim, and chop the scallions. Rinse, stem, and chop the parsley.

2 In a medium saucepan, bring the broth and the water to a boil. Add the sugar and the couscous, stirring to blend. Cover, remove from the heat, and let stand until all the liquid is absorbed, at least 5 minutes.

3 Fold in the scallions. Sprinkle with the parsley.

Sooner Stir-Fry

1 Peel and mince the garlic. Rinse the broccoli, discard the tough ends, and cut into bite-sized florets. Peel, trim, and julienne the carrots.

2 Heat the oil in a medium skillet. Add the garlic and sauté for 1 minute.

3 Add the broccoli and the carrots and sauté until the vegetables are crisp-tender, about 5 minutes. Add the vinegar and the sugar, season to taste, and toss to combine.

Pottawatomie Pudding

1 In a small saucepan, combine the butter, the brown sugar, the half-and-half, and the rum extract. Stir until the butter has melted, reduce the heat, and simmer for 2 minutes. Remove from the heat and set aside to cool.

2 Beat the pudding mix and the milk in a medium bowl until well blended. Pour into individual dessert glasses and chill until you are ready to serve.

3 Garnish each pudding with spoonfuls of the topping.

TUESDAY

Wild Scramble

½ cup wild rice
1 can (10½ ounces) onion soup
¼ cup water
2 stalks celery
1 large red bell pepper
1 can (11 ounces) whole-kernel corn
9 eggs
½ cup half-and-half
Seasoning to taste
2 tablespoons butter

High Spearited

1 pound fresh asparagus
1 tablespoon butter
2 teaspoons lemon juice
½ teaspoon prepared horseradish

Bite the Crust

1 loaf French bread
3 tablespoons olive oil
2 teaspoons lemon-pepper seasoning
1 teaspoon dried savory

Split Shakes

2 large bananas
1 can (14 ounces) sweetened condensed milk
4 cups ice cubes
Whipped cream for garnish
Multicolored sprinkles for garnish

EQUIPMENT

Blender
Medium covered saucepan
Large skillet
Medium covered skillet
Strainer
Large mixing bowl

Whisk
Pastry brush
Aluminum foil
Kitchen knives
Measuring cups and spoons
Cooking utensils

COUNTDOWN

1. Assemble the ingredients and the equipment.
2. Do Steps 1–2 of *Wild Scramble*.
3. Do Steps 1–2 of *Split Shakes*.
4. Do Steps 1–4 of *Bite the Crust*.
5. Do Steps 3–4 of *Wild Scramble*.
6. Do Steps 1–3 of *High Spearited*.
7. Do Steps 5–7 of *Wild Scramble*.
8. Do Steps 4–5 of *High Spearited*.
9. Do Step 3 of *Split Shakes*.

TUESDAY

Wild Scramble

1 Rinse the wild rice.

2 Combine the rice, the soup, and the water in a medium saucepan. Bring to a boil, cover, and reduce the heat. Simmer until the liquid is absorbed and the rice is tender, about 45 minutes.

3 Rinse, trim, and dice the celery. Rinse, trim, seed, and chop the bell pepper. Drain the corn.

4 In a large bowl, whisk the eggs with the half-and-half. Season to taste.

5 Melt the butter in a large skillet and sauté the celery and the bell pepper for 3 minutes.

6 Add the cooked rice and the corn and combine.

7 Pour the egg mixture into the skillet and scramble until the eggs are set, about 4 minutes.

High Spearited

1 Bring a small amount of water to a boil in a medium skillet.

2 Rinse the asparagus and remove the tough ends.

3 Arrange the asparagus in the skillet, cover, and steam until crisp-tender, 3 to 8 minutes, depending on thickness.

4 Drain the asparagus.

5 Melt the butter in the skillet. Blend in the lemon juice and the horseradish. Return the asparagus and toss to combine and heat through.

Bite the Crust

1 Preheat the oven to 325°F.

2 Cut the bread in half lengthwise.

3 Brush the cut sides of the bread with the oil. Sprinkle with the lemon-pepper seasoning and the savory. Reassemble the loaf and wrap it in aluminum foil.

4 Heat for 15 minutes.

Split Shakes

1 Peel and chunk the bananas.

2 In a blender, combine the bananas, the condensed milk, and half the ice cubes. Process for 3 minutes. Add the remaining ice cubes and process until smooth, 2 minutes more. Refrigerate until you are ready to serve.

3 Pour into individual glasses and top with a dollop of whipped cream and a splash of sprinkles.

WEDNESDAY

Can-Do Salmon

1 package (10 ounces) frozen green peas
   and pearl onions
3 stalks celery
2 cans (6 ounces each) salmon
1 cup long-grain white rice
1 can (14 ounces) chicken broth
1/4 cup water
2 tablespoons vegetable oil
1/2 cup shredded Cheddar cheese
1 teaspoon dried basil
2 teaspoons flour
1 cup half-and-half
1/4 cup sour cream
Seasoning to taste

Up-Beet Salad

1 small head red leaf lettuce
1 large orange
1 can (15 ounces) julienne beets
3 tablespoons vegetable oil
2 tablespoons red wine vinegar
1/2 teaspoon poppy seeds
1/2 teaspoon granulated sugar

You Cannoli Imagine

1 cup whipping cream
1 tablespoon instant coffee
1 tablespoon cocoa powder
1/4 cup powdered sugar
4 cannoli shells

EQUIPMENT

Electric mixer	Citrus grater
Double boiler	Kitchen knives
Large skillet	Measuring cups and spoons
Medium mixing bowl	
2 small mixing bowls	Cooking utensils
Whisk	

COUNTDOWN

1. Assemble the ingredients and the equipment.
2. Do Step 1 of *You Cannoli Imagine*.
3. Do Steps 1–4 of *Can-Do Salmon*.
4. Do Step 2 of *You Cannoli Imagine*.
5. Do Steps 1–3 of *Up-Beet Salad*.
6. Do Steps 5–7 of *Can-Do Salmon*.
7. Do Step 4 of *Up-Beet Salad*.
8. Do Step 3 of *You Cannoli Imagine*.

WEDNESDAY

Can-Do Salmon

1 Set the peas and onions in a small bowl of warm water to thaw.

2 Bring water to a boil in the bottom of a double boiler.

3 Rinse, trim, and mince the celery. Drain and flake the salmon.

4 Combine the rice, the broth, and the ¼ cup water in the top of the double boiler. Cover, reduce the heat, and simmer until all the liquid is absorbed and the rice is tender, 30 to 40 minutes.

5 Heat the oil in a large skillet and sauté the celery for 2 minutes.

6 Add the salmon, the cheese, the basil, and the flour and stir to combine. Stir in the peas and onions. Slowly add the half-and-half and the sour cream. Season to taste and heat through.

7 Add the rice to the skillet and combine.

Up-Beet Salad

1 Wash and dry the lettuce and distribute the leaves among individual salad plates.

2 Grate 1 tablespoon of orange peel. Peel and section the orange. Drain the beets. Arrange the orange sections and the beets over the lettuce.

3 In a small bowl, combine the oil, the vinegar, the poppy seeds, and the sugar.

4 Drizzle the dressing over the salad and sprinkle with the orange peel.

You Cannoli Imagine

1 Chill a medium bowl and the beaters of an electric mixer for 10 minutes.

2 Beat the cream until soft peaks form, about 3 minutes. Fold in the instant coffee, the cocoa powder, and the powdered sugar. Beat until stiff, about 1 minute longer, and refrigerate until you are ready to serve.

3 Spoon the mixture into the cannoli shells from both ends and place a dollop on top for garnish.

THURSDAY

Stew Biz

1 clove garlic
1 medium onion
1 medium green bell pepper
2 cans (11 ounces each) whole-kernel corn
1 can (15 ounces) black beans
2 tablespoons vegetable oil
$1\frac{1}{2}$ pounds lean ground beef
1 can ($14\frac{1}{2}$ ounces) diced tomatoes
1 can ($10\frac{1}{2}$ ounces) beef consommé
2 teaspoons Worcestershire sauce
$\frac{1}{4}$ cup dry red wine
$\frac{1}{2}$ teaspoon dried oregano
Seasoning to taste

Stopovers

3 eggs
1 cup milk
1 cup flour
$\frac{1}{4}$ teaspoon salt

Sour Grapes

2 medium ripe peaches
2 medium ripe nectarines
1 pound seedless green grapes
$\frac{1}{2}$ cup orange juice
1 pint peach sorbet

EQUIPMENT

Electric mixer
Dutch oven
Muffin tin
2 large mixing bowls
Ice cream scoop

Plastic wrap
Kitchen knives
Measuring cups and
    spoons
Cooking utensils

COUNTDOWN

1. Assemble the ingredients and the equipment.
2. Do Steps 1–2 of Sour Grapes.
3. Do Steps 1–3 of Stopovers.
4. Do Steps 1–3 of Stew Biz.
5. Do Step 4 of Stopovers.
6. Do Step 3 of Sour Grapes.

THURSDAY

Stew Biz

1 Peel and mince the garlic. Peel and chop the onion. Rinse, trim, seed, and slice the bell pepper. Drain the corn. Rinse and drain the beans.

2 Heat the oil in a Dutch oven and sauté the garlic for 1 minute. Add the onion and the beef and sauté until the beef is browned and the onion is tender, about 7 minutes. Stir in the corn, the beans, the tomatoes, the consommé, the Worcestershire sauce, the wine, and the oregano. Season to taste and blend well. Add the bell pepper slices.

3 Cover, reduce the heat, and simmer until the stew is heated through and the bell pepper slices are tender, about 15 minutes.

Stopovers

1 Preheat the oven to 400°F. Grease a muffin tin.

2 Beat the eggs in a large bowl until frothy, about 2 minutes. Beat in the milk. Add the flour and the salt and beat until smooth, about 2 minutes.

3 Fill the muffin cups half way. Bake until the popovers are puffy and golden, 25 to 30 minutes.

4 With a sharp knife, make a slit in each popover to let the steam escape and keep the popovers from falling.

Sour Grapes

1 Peel, halve, pit, and slice the peaches. Peel, halve, pit, and slice the nectarines. Wash, dry, and stem the grapes. Combine the fruit in a large bowl and toss with the orange juice.

2 Cover the bowl with plastic wrap and refrigerate until you are ready to serve.

3 Distribute the fruit among individual dessert glasses and top each serving with a scoop of sorbet.

FRIDAY

Peter Penne

4 slices bacon
2 medium carrots
1 small head cauliflower
¼ pound fresh mushrooms
1 clove garlic
2 tablespoons fresh parsley (when chopped)
1 pound penne
1 jar (2 ounces) diced pimientos
½ cup dry white wine
½ cup grated Parmesan cheese
Seasoning to taste

Hare Today, Gone Tomato

4 large tomatoes
1 medium red onion
1 medium sweet onion
¾ cup vegetable oil
½ cup lemon juice
1 tablespoon Worcestershire sauce
2 teaspoons dried basil
1 teaspoon granulated sugar
Seasoning to taste

Bunny Hop Pudding

1 small orange
1 package (3.4 ounces) instant white chocolate pudding mix
1¼ cups milk
¾ cup sour cream
8 raisins
4 whole almonds
1 maraschino cherry

EQUIPMENT

Electric mixer	Small mixing bowl
Stockpot	Whisk
Medium covered saucepan	Citrus grater
Large skillet	Vegetable peeler
9 x 13-inch glass baking dish	Plastic wrap
Steamer insert	Kitchen knives
Colander	Measuring cups and spoons
Medium mixing bowl	Cooking utensils

COUNTDOWN

1. Assemble the ingredients and the equipment.
2. Do Steps 1–2 of *Bunny Hop Pudding*.
3. Do Steps 1–3 of *Hare Today, Gone Tomato*.
4. Do Steps 1–6 of *Peter Penne*.
5. Do Step 4 of *Hare Today, Gone Tomato*.
6. Do Step 3 of *Bunny Hop Pudding*.

FRIDAY

Peter Penne

1 Bring water to a boil in a stockpot. Bring water to a boil in a medium saucepan.

2 Dice the bacon. Peel, trim, and slice the carrots. Rinse and trim the cauliflower and cut it into bite-sized florets. Rinse, pat dry, trim, and slice the mushrooms. Peel and mince the garlic. Rinse, stem, and chop the parsley.

3 Cook the penne until it is almost tender, 8 to 10 minutes.

4 Arrange the carrots and the cauliflower in a steamer insert. Place the insert in the saucepan, cover, and reduce the heat. Steam until the vegetables are crisp-tender, about 5 minutes.

5 Sauté the bacon in a large skillet for 5 minutes. Add the garlic and sauté for 2 minutes. Add the mushrooms and sauté for 2 minutes. Add the carrots and the cauliflower and combine. Add the undrained pimientos, the wine, and the cheese. Season to taste and heat through.

6 Drain the pasta, return it to the stockpot, and toss with the sauce. Sprinkle with the parsley.

Hare Today, Gone Tomato

1 Rinse, stem, and slice the tomatoes. Peel and thinly slice the onions. Lay the tomatoes and the onions in a 9 x 13-inch baking dish.

2 In a small bowl, combine the oil, the lemon juice, the Worcestershire sauce, the basil, and the sugar. Season to taste and pour over the tomatoes and the onions.

3 Cover with plastic wrap and refrigerate for 30 minutes.

4 Drain the marinade and alternate tomato and onion slices on individual salad plates.

Bunny Hop Pudding

1 Grate 2 tablespoons of orange peel. Peel and section the orange.

2 In a medium bowl, beat the pudding mix, the milk, and the sour cream until well blended. Pour into individual dessert bowls and refrigerate until you are ready to serve.

3 To make bunny faces, set the orange sections upright for the ears; add raisins for the eyes and almonds for the mouths. Cut the cherry into 4 pieces for the noses and use the orange peel for the whiskers.

WEEK THIRTEEN

WEEK AT A GLANCE

Monday
Getty Spaghetti
Louvre Leaves
Pradough
Victoria and Apple

Tuesday
Never a Dill Moment
Babes In the Woods
It's the Pits
Double Your Pleasure

Wednesday
Slick Chick
Ozark Orzo
Arkanslaw
Little Rock Pudding

Thursday
You Gotta Have Hearts
Too Cuke For Words
Say It Isn't Dough
Pretty Cheesy

Friday
Cool as a Cucumber
Hot Potato
Snap Your Fingers
Short 'n' Sweet

STAPLES

- ☐ Butter
- ☐ Bisquick
- ☐ Granulated sugar
- ☐ Dark brown sugar
- ☐ Powdered sugar
- ☐ Chocolate syrup
- ☐ Olive oil
- ☐ Vegetable oil
- ☐ Raspberry vinegar
- ☐ Red wine vinegar
- ☐ Rice vinegar
- ☐ Tarragon vinegar
- ☐ White wine vinegar
- ☐ Lemon juice
- ☐ Dijon mustard
- ☐ Honey
- ☐ White Worcestershire sauce
- ☐ Grated Parmesan cheese
- ☐ Chicken bouillon cube
- ☐ Poppy seeds
- ☐ Dried marjoram
- ☐ Dried thyme
- ☐ Italian seasoning
- ☐ Ground nutmeg
- ☐ Paprika
- ☐ Black pepper
- ☐ Saffron threads
- ☐ Salt
- ☐ Almond extract
- ☐ Lemon extract
- ☐ Orange extract

MEAT & POULTRY

1 pound hot Italian bulk sausage (M)

4 boneless, skinless chicken breast halves (about 1½ pounds) (W)

FISH

4 white fish fillets (about 1½ pounds) (T)

FRESH PRODUCE

VEGETABLES

1½ pounds small new red potatoes (T)

4 medium baking potatoes (F)

¾ pound sugar-snap peas (F)

3 medium zucchini (M)

1 small zucchini (W)

1 medium carrot (W)

2 stalks celery (M)

1 medium turnip (M)

1 small head cabbage (W)

1 medium head lettuce (M)

1 medium head lettuce (T)

1 package (10 ounces) mixed salad greens (Th)

1 medium tomato (T)

2 medium tomatoes (Th)

2 small ripe avocados (T)

1 medium cucumber (Th)

3 medium cucumbers (F)

1 small bunch radishes (T)

1 medium onion (M)

1 small onion (Th)

4 small onions (F)

1 large shallot (W)

2 scallions (green onions) (T)

3 scallions (green onions) (Th)

6 cloves garlic (M)

1 clove garlic (T)

1 clove garlic (Th)

1 clove garlic (F)

HERBS

¼ cup dill (when chopped) (T)

3 tablespoons dill (when chopped) (F)

2 tablespoons parsley (when chopped) (W)

2 tablespoons parsley (when chopped) (Th)

2 tablespoons parsley (when chopped) (F)

FRUIT

1 medium lime (T)

4 medium McIntosh apples (M)

1 small ripe honeydew melon (T)

1 small ripe pink honeydew melon (T)

1 pint blueberries (T)

1 pint raspberries (T)

1 pint strawberries (F)

CANS, JARS & BOTTLES

VEGETABLES

1 can (14½ ounces) diced tomatoes (M)

1 can (14½ ounces) crushed tomatoes (Th)

1 jar (6½ ounces) marinated artichoke hearts (M)

JUICES

1 can (6 ounces) tomato juice (F)

PACKAGED GOODS

PASTA, RICE & GRAINS

12 ounces spaghetti (M)

8 ounces orzo (W)

1 pound linguini (Th)

BAKED GOODS

1 loaf French bread (M)

1 loaf Italian bread (Th)

DESSERT & BAKING NEEDS

1 package (3.4 ounces) instant coconut cream pudding mix (W)

1 package (4 ounces) M&M's plain candies (W)

1 package (8 ounces) candied orange slices for garnish (Th)

WINE & SPIRITS

¼ cup dry sherry (T)

REFRIGERATED PRODUCTS

DAIRY

1¼ cups milk (W)

½ cup milk (F)

½ cup half-and-half (F)

¾ cup sour cream (W)

1 cup plain yogurt (F)

Whipped cream for garnish (F)

8 eggs (F)

CHEESE

¼ cup crumbled blue cheese (M)

1 cup shredded Cheddar cheese (Th)

1 container (15 ounces) ricotta cheese (Th)

1 package (8 ounces) cream cheese (M)

JUICES

3 tablespoons orange juice (Th)

DELI

4 slices bacon (W)

FROZEN GOODS

VEGETABLES

1 package (10 ounces) artichoke hearts (Th)

BAKED GOODS

1 pound cake (Th)

MONDAY

Getty Spaghetti

6 cloves garlic
1 1/2 teaspoons Italian seasoning
2 tablespoons vegetable oil
1 medium onion
3 medium zucchini
12 ounces spaghetti
1 pound hot Italian bulk sausage
Seasoning to taste
1 can (14 1/2 ounces) diced tomatoes

Louvre Leaves

1 medium head lettuce
2 stalks celery
1 medium turnip
1 jar (6 1/2 ounces) marinated artichoke
   hearts
2 tablespoons red wine vinegar
Seasoning to taste

Pradough

1 loaf French bread
3 tablespoons olive oil
1 teaspoon poppy seeds
1/4 cup crumbled blue cheese

Victoria and Apple

4 medium McIntosh apples
1 package (8 ounces) cream cheese
2 tablespoons powdered sugar
1 tablespoon lemon juice
1 teaspoon lemon extract
1 tablespoon dark brown sugar

EQUIPMENT

Electric mixer	Whisk
Stockpot	Vegetable peeler
Large skillet	Vegetable grater
2-quart casserole	Pastry brush
Baking sheet	Aluminum foil
Colander	Kitchen knives
Large mixing bowl	Measuring cups and
Medium mixing bowl	spoons
2 small mixing bowls	Cooking utensils

COUNTDOWN

1. Assemble the ingredients and the equipment.
2. Do Steps 1–3 of *Victoria and Apple*.
3. Do Steps 1–2 of *Getty Spaghetti*.
4. Do Steps 1–4 of *Louvre Leaves*.
5. Do Steps 3–9 of *Getty Spaghetti*.
6. Do Step 1 of *Pradough*.
7. Do Step 10 of *Getty Spaghetti*.
8. Do Step 2 of *Pradough*.
9. Do Step 5 of *Louvre Leaves*.

MONDAY

Getty Spaghetti

1 Preheat the oven to 450°F. Bring water to a boil in a stockpot.

2 Peel the garlic and place the cloves on a sheet of aluminum foil. Sprinkle with the Italian seasoning and drizzle with the oil. Fold the foil around the garlic and seal tightly. Roast for 20 minutes.

3 Peel and chop the onion. Rinse, trim, and coarsely grate the zucchini.

4 Break the spaghetti into 3-inch pieces and cook until almost tender, 6 to 7 minutes.

5 Sauté the sausage and the onion in a large skillet until the sausage is golden and the onion is soft, 5 to 6 minutes. Add the zucchini and sauté for 2 minutes.

6 Drain the pasta and return it to the stockpot.

7 Combine the sausage mixture with the pasta. Season to taste.

8 Remove the garlic from the oven and mash it.

9 Reduce the oven temperature to 350°F.

10 Spoon the pasta mixture into a 2-quart casserole. Spread the tomatoes over the top and sprinkle with the garlic. Bake for 10 minutes.

Louvre Leaves

1 Wash and dry the lettuce and tear it into bite-sized pieces. Rinse, trim, and chop the celery. Trim, peel, and grate the turnip.

2 Reserving 3 tablespoons of the marinade, drain the artichoke hearts and cut them in half.

3 Combine the lettuce, the celery, and the artichoke hearts in a large bowl.

4 In a small bowl, combine the artichoke marinade and the vinegar. Season to taste.

5 Toss the salad with the dressing and top with the grated turnip.

Pradough

1 Split the bread in half lengthwise. Brush the cut sides with the oil. Sprinkle with the poppy seeds and the blue cheese.

2 Place on a baking sheet and bake at 350°F for 10 minutes.

Victoria and Apple

1 Rinse, core, and chop the apples.

2 In a medium bowl, beat together the cream cheese, the powdered sugar, the lemon juice, and the lemon extract.

3 Place a layer of apples in individual dessert glasses. Top with half of the cream cheese mixture. Add the remaining apples and the remaining cream cheese mixture. Dust with the brown sugar and refrigerate until you are ready to serve.

TUESDAY

Never a Dill Moment

4 white fish fillets (about 1 1/2 pounds)
1/4 cup fresh dill (when chopped)
1 clove garlic
1/4 cup lemon juice
1/4 cup dry sherry
1/2 teaspoon paprika
Seasoning to taste

Babes In the Woods

1 1/2 pounds small new red potatoes
2 tablespoons butter
1 teaspoon dried marjoram
Seasoning to taste

It's the Pits

1 medium head lettuce
1 medium tomato
1 small bunch radishes
2 medium ripe avocados
2 scallions (green onions)
3 tablespoons olive oil
2 tablespoons rice vinegar
1/2 teaspoon Dijon mustard
Seasoning to taste

Double Your Pleasure

1 small ripe honeydew melon
1 small ripe pink honeydew melon
1 medium lime
1 pint fresh blueberries
1 pint fresh raspberries
2 tablespoons honey

EQUIPMENT

Medium covered saucepan	Vegetable brush
9 x 13-inch glass baking dish	Citrus juicer
Large mixing bowl	Plastic wrap
3 small mixing bowls	Kitchen knives
Whisk	Measuring cups and spoons
	Cooking utensils

COUNTDOWN

1. Assemble the ingredients and the equipment.
2. Do Steps 1–4 of *Double Your Pleasure*.
3. Do Steps 1–5 of *Never a Dill Moment*.
4. Do Steps 1–2 of *Babes In the Woods*.
5. Do Steps 1–2 of *It's the Pits*.
6. Do Steps 6–7 of *Never a Dill Moment*.
7. Do Step 3 of *Babes In the Woods*.
8. Do Step 3 of *It's the Pits*.

TUESDAY

Never a Dill Moment

1 Grease a 9 x 13-inch baking dish.

2 Rinse and pat dry the fish fillets.

3 Rinse, stem, and chop the dill. Peel and mince the garlic.

4 In a small bowl, combine the dill, the garlic, the lemon juice, the sherry, and the paprika. Season to taste.

5 Arrange the fish in the baking dish and pour the marinade over it. Cover with plastic wrap and refrigerate for 20 minutes.

6 Preheat the oven to 425°F.

7 Drain the excess marinade from the fish and bake until it flakes easily with a fork, about 10 minutes.

Babes In the Woods

1 Scrub the potatoes.

2 Cover the potatoes with water in a medium saucepan. Bring the water to a boil, cover, and cook until the potatoes are tender, 10 to 12 minutes.

3 Drain the potatoes and return them to the saucepan. Add the butter and the marjoram. Season to taste and toss to coat.

It's the Pits

1 Wash and dry the lettuce and tear it into bite-sized pieces. Rinse, stem, and chop the tomato. Rinse, trim, and slice the radishes. Halve, pit, peel, and chop the avocados. Rinse, trim, and slice the scallions. Combine the ingredients in a large bowl.

2 In a small bowl, whisk together the oil, the vinegar, and the mustard. Season to taste.

3 Toss the salad with the dressing.

Double Your Pleasure

1 Remove the ends and cut each melon into 4 rings. Remove the seeds and the peel.

2 Juice the lime. Rinse and pat dry the blueberries. Rinse and pat dry the raspberries.

3 In a small bowl, combine the lime juice and the honey.

4 Place rings of green honeydew on individual dessert plates. Top each with a ring of the pink honeydew. Fill the center of each set of rings with a combination of the berries. Spoon on the lime juice mixture. Refrigerate until you are ready to serve.

WEDNESDAY

Slick Chick

4 slices bacon
4 boneless, skinless chicken breast halves
    (about 1 1/2 pounds)
1 large shallot
1/2 cup red wine vinegar
Seasoning to taste

Ozark Orzo

2 tablespoons fresh parsley (when
    chopped)
8 ounces orzo
1/4 cup water
1 chicken bouillon cube
2 teaspoons saffron threads
Seasoning to taste

Arkanslaw

1 small head cabbage
1 small zucchini
1 medium carrot
2 tablespoons vegetable oil
1/2 teaspoon ground nutmeg
1/2 teaspoon granulated sugar
Seasoning to taste

Little Rock Pudding

1 package (3.4 ounces) instant coconut
    cream pudding mix
1 1/4 cups milk
3/4 cup sour cream
1 teaspoon almond extract
1 package (4 ounces) M&M's plain candies

EQUIPMENT

Electric mixer
Large covered
    saucepan
Large covered skillet
Large skillet
Strainer
Medium mixing bowl

Vegetable peeler
Vegetable grater
Kitchen knives
Measuring cups and
    spoons
Cooking utensils

COUNTDOWN

1. Assemble the ingredients and the
   equipment.
2. Do Steps 1–2 of *Little Rock Pudding*.
3. Do Step 1 of *Ozark Orzo*.
4. Do Steps 1–5 of *Slick Chick*.
5. Do Steps 2–3 of *Ozark Orzo*.
6. Do Step 1 of *Arkanslaw*.
7. Do Steps 4–5 of *Ozark Orzo*.
8. Do Step 2 of *Arkanslaw*.

WEDNESDAY

Slick Chick

1 Dice the bacon. Rinse and pat dry the chicken breasts.

2 Peel and mince the shallot.

3 Sauté the bacon in a large skillet for 3 minutes. Add the shallot and sauté for 2 minutes.

4 Add the chicken and sauté until golden, about 5 minutes per side.

5 Add the vinegar, season to taste, cover, and reduce the heat. Simmer until the chicken is cooked through, 10 to 15 minutes.

Ozark Orzo

1 Bring water to a boil in a large saucepan.

2 Rinse, stem, and chop the parsley.

3 Cook the orzo until it is just tender, 6 to 8 minutes.

4 Combine the ¼ cup water, the bouillon cube, and the saffron in a small saucepan. Bring the mixture to a boil and cook for 1 minute.

5 Drain the orzo and return it to the saucepan. Add the bouillon liquid and the parsley. Season to taste, toss to combine, and cover to keep warm.

Arkanslaw

1 Rinse, trim, quarter, and grate the cabbage. Rinse, trim, and grate the zucchini. Peel, trim, and grate the carrot.

2 Heat the oil in a large skillet. Blend in the nutmeg and the sugar and sauté the vegetables until they are crisp-tender, about 3 minutes. Season to taste and toss to combine.

Little Rock Pudding

1 In a medium bowl, beat the pudding mix, the milk, the sour cream, and the almond extract until well blended. Fold in the M&M's candies.

2 Spoon the mixture into individual dessert dishes and refrigerate until you are ready to serve.

THURSDAY

You Gotta Have Hearts

1 package (10 ounces) frozen artichoke
  hearts
1 clove garlic
1 small onion
2 medium tomatoes
2 tablespoons fresh parsley (when
  chopped)
2 tablespoons vegetable oil
2 tablespoons lemon juice
1 can (14½ ounces) crushed tomatoes
1 teaspoon Italian seasoning
Seasoning to taste
1 pound linguini
1 cup shredded Cheddar cheese

Too Cuke For Words

1 package (10 ounces) mixed salad greens
1 medium cucumber
3 scallions (green onions)
3 tablespoons olive oil
2 tablespoons tarragon vinegar
Seasoning to taste

Say It Isn't Dough

3 tablespoons butter
1 loaf Italian bread
½ teaspoon dried marjoram
½ teaspoon dried thyme

Pretty Cheesy

1 frozen pound cake
1 container (15 ounces) ricotta cheese
3 tablespoons orange juice
1 teaspoon orange extract
½ cup chocolate syrup
1 package (8 ounces) candied orange slices
  for garnish

COUNTDOWN

1. Assemble the ingredients and the
   equipment.
2. Do Steps 1–5 of *Pretty Cheesy*.
3. Do Step 1 of *You Gotta Have Hearts*.
4. Do Step 1 of *Say It Isn't Dough*.
5. Do Steps 2–3 of *You Gotta Have
   Hearts*.
6. Do Steps 2–4 of *Say It Isn't Dough*.
7. Do Step 4 of *You Gotta Have Hearts*.
8. Do Step 1 of *Too Cuke For Words*.
9. Do Step 5 of *You Gotta Have Hearts*.
10. Do Step 2 of *Too Cuke For Words*.
11. Do Step 6 of *You Gotta Have Hearts*.
12. Do Step 3 of *Too Cuke For Words*.

EQUIPMENT

Electric mixer
Stockpot
Large covered skillet
Colander
Large mixing bowl
Medium mixing bowl
2 small mixing bowls

Whisk
Vegetable peeler
Aluminum foil
Kitchen knives
Measuring cups and
  spoons
Cooking utensils

THURSDAY

You Gotta Have Hearts

1 Set the artichoke hearts in a small bowl of warm water to thaw.

2 Peel and mince the garlic. Peel and chop the onion. Rinse, stem, and chop the fresh tomatoes. Rinse, stem, and chop the parsley. Chop the artichoke hearts.

3 Heat the oil in a large skillet. Add the garlic and the onion and sauté for 1 minute. Add the chopped tomatoes, the parsley, the artichoke hearts, the lemon juice, the crushed tomatoes, and the Italian seasoning. Season to taste. Cover, reduce the heat, and simmer until the vegetables are tender and the flavors are blended, about 20 minutes.

4 Bring water to a boil in a stockpot.

5 Cook the linguini until it is almost tender, 2 to 3 minutes if you are using fresh pasta, 6 to 7 minutes if you are using dry pasta.

6 Drain the pasta and toss it with the cheese. Top with the sauce.

Too Cuke For Words

1 Wash and dry the salad greens. Peel, trim, and slice the cucumber. Rinse, trim, and chop the scallions. Combine the ingredients in a large bowl.

2 In a small bowl, whisk together the oil and the vinegar. Season to taste.

3 Toss the salad with the dressing.

Say It Isn't Dough

1 Set the butter out to soften.

2 Preheat the oven to 325°F.

3 Cut the bread in half lengthwise.

4 Butter the cut sides of the bread and sprinkle with the marjoram and the thyme. Reassemble the loaf, wrap it in aluminum foil, and heat for 15 minutes.

Pretty Cheesy

1 Set the pound cake out to thaw.

2 In a medium bowl, beat together the ricotta cheese and the orange juice until smooth, about 2 minutes. Blend in the orange extract.

3 Slice the cake into 3 equal layers. Spread a quarter of the ricotta mixture over the bottom layer. Repeat with the second layer. Spread the remaining ricotta mixture over the top layer and down the sides.

4 Spread the chocolate syrup over the top, letting it drizzle down the sides.

5 Lay the candied orange slices down the middle of the top layer.

FRIDAY

Cool as a Cucumber

3 medium cucumbers
1 clove garlic
3 tablespoons fresh dill (when chopped)
1 cup plain yogurt
1 can (6 ounces) tomato juice
2 tablespoons white wine vinegar
1/2 cup half-and-half
1/2 teaspoon white Worcestershire sauce
Seasoning to taste

Hot Potato

4 medium baking potatoes
4 small onions
2 tablespoons fresh parsley (when
    chopped)
2 tablespoons vegetable oil
8 eggs
1/2 cup grated Parmesan cheese
1/2 teaspoon paprika
Seasoning to taste

Snap Your Fingers

3/4 pound sugar-snap peas
3 tablespoons butter
1 tablespoon raspberry vinegar
1/2 teaspoon granulated sugar
Seasoning to taste

Short 'n' Sweet

3 tablespoons butter
2 1/2 cups Bisquick
1/2 cup milk
1/4 cup dark brown sugar
1 pint fresh strawberries
Whipped cream for garnish

EQUIPMENT

Blender	Whisk
Large skillet	Vegetable peeler
Medium skillet	Kitchen knives
9 x 13-inch glass baking dish	Measuring cups and spoons
Baking sheet	Cooking utensils
2 large mixing bowls	

COUNTDOWN

1. Assemble the ingredients and the equipment.
2. Do Steps 1–2 of Cool as a Cucumber.
3. Do Steps 1–6 of Short 'n' Sweet.
4. Do Steps 1–3 of Hot Potato.
5. Do Step 7 of Short 'n' Sweet.
6. Do Steps 4–5 of Hot Potato.
7. Do Steps 1–2 of Snap Your Fingers.
8. Do Step 6 of Hot Potato.
9. Do Step 8 of Short 'n' Sweet.

FRIDAY

Cool as a Cucumber

1 Peel and trim the cucumbers. Cut them in half lengthwise, remove the seeds, and chunk. Peel and chop the garlic. Rinse, stem, and chop the dill.

2 Put the cucumbers, the garlic, the dill, the yogurt, the tomato juice, the vinegar, the half-and-half, and the Worcestershire sauce in a blender and puree. Season to taste and refrigerate until you are ready to serve.

Hot Potato

1 Grease a 9 x 13-inch baking dish.

2 Peel and slice the potatoes. Peel and mince the onions. Rinse, stem, and chop the parsley.

3 Heat the oil in a large skillet. Add the potatoes and sauté until they are golden and tender, 10 to 15 minutes. Remove and set aside. Add the onions to the skillet and sauté until they are tender, about 7 minutes.

4 Reduce the oven temperature to 350°F.

5 Whip the eggs in a large bowl. Blend in the cheese and the paprika. Pour the egg mixture into the baking dish. Add the potatoes and the onions. Season to taste. Bake until the eggs are set, 15 to 20 minutes.

6 Sprinkle with the parsley.

Snap Your Fingers

1 Rinse and string the snap peas.

2 Melt the butter in a medium skillet. Mix in the vinegar and the sugar. Season to taste. Sauté the snap peas until they are crisp-tender, 2 to 3 minutes.

Short 'n' Sweet

1 Preheat the oven to 425°F.

2 Melt the butter.

3 In a large bowl, combine the Bisquick, the milk, and the brown sugar. Blend in the melted butter and stir until a soft dough forms.

4 Drop the dough by heaping tablespoons on an ungreased baking sheet. Using the back of the spoon, level each mound of the dough.

5 Rinse, hull, and slice the berries and set aside.

6 Bake the shortcakes until they are lightly golden, 10 to 12 minutes.

7 Remove the shortcakes from the oven and let them cool.

8 Cut the cooled shortcakes in half. Place half of the berries on the cut sides. Replace the tops. Spoon the remaining berries over the tops and garnish each serving with a dollop of whipped cream.

SUMMER

WEEK ONE

Monday

Salmon on the Green
Park and Rice
Tomaître d'
Candlelight Cantaloupe

Tuesday

Chiba Chicken
Sesame Soba
Rickshaw Slaw
Dynasty Dessert

Wednesday

Cuban Missiles
Red Potatoes
Grated Antilles
Havana Banana

Thursday

Bela Linguini
Basil Rathbean
Gilbert Rolland
John Berrymore

Friday

Chesapeake Cakes
Potomac Peas
Baltomato Salad
Black-Eyed Susans

STAPLES

- ❑ Butter
- ❑ Cornstarch
- ❑ Granulated sugar
- ❑ Dark brown sugar
- ❑ Powdered sugar
- ❑ Multicolored sprinkles
- ❑ Olive oil
- ❑ Sesame oil
- ❑ Vegetable oil
- ❑ Red wine vinegar
- ❑ Rice vinegar
- ❑ Tarragon vinegar
- ❑ Ketchup
- ❑ Soy sauce
- ❑ White Worcestershire sauce
- ❑ Grated Parmesan cheese
- ❑ Plain breadcrumbs
- ❑ Sesame seeds
- ❑ Dried basil
- ❑ Dried oregano
- ❑ Dried thyme
- ❑ Ground allspice
- ❑ Cayenne pepper
- ❑ Ground ginger
- ❑ Paprika
- ❑ Black pepper
- ❑ White pepper
- ❑ Salt

MEAT & POULTRY

4 beef cube steaks (about 1 1/2 pounds) (W)

4 boneless, skinless chicken breast halves (about 1 1/2 pounds) (T)

FISH

4 salmon steaks (about 1 1/2 pounds) (M)

3/4 pound cooked crabmeat (F)

FRESH PRODUCE

VEGETABLES

1 1/2 pounds small new red potatoes (W)

1 pound green beans (Th)

1 1/2 pounds green peas, unshelled (F)

2 medium carrots (W)

2 stalks celery (M)

1 pound mushrooms (Th)

1 cup bean sprouts (T)

1 head Napa cabbage (T)

1 head green leaf lettuce (W)

1 medium head lettuce (F)

1 package (10 ounces) mixed salad greens (M)

4 medium tomatoes (M)

4 medium tomatoes (F)

1 medium cucumber (F)

1 small green bell pepper (W)

1 small green bell pepper (F)

1 small red bell pepper (T)

1 small jicama (W)

1 small onion (F)

1 small red onion (W)

2 small shallots (Th)

2 scallions (green onions) (T)

4 scallions (green onions) (F)

1 clove garlic (T)

1 clove garlic (W)

HERBS

2 tablespoons basil leaves (when chopped) (Th)

2 tablespoons parsley (when chopped) (M)

3 tablespoons parsley (when chopped) (Th)

3 tablespoons parsley (when chopped) (F)

FRUIT

1 large lemon (M)

2 medium lemons (Th)

1 large lime (T)

2 small ripe cantaloupe melons (M)

4 medium bananas (W)

4 large ripe peaches (F)

1 pint raspberries (M)

1 pint blueberries (Th)

1 pint strawberries (Th)

CANS, JARS & BOTTLES

SOUPS

1 can (14 ounces) vegetable broth (M)

1 can (14 ounces) beef broth (W)

INTERNATIONAL FOODS

1 can (8 ounces) sliced water chestnuts (T)

FRUIT

1 can (8 ounces) pineapple chunks (M)

1 can (11 ounces) mandarin oranges (T)

SAUCES

1 can (8 ounces) tomato sauce (W)

SPREADS

1/4 cup red currant jelly (Th)

CONDIMENTS

1 jar (3 ounces) pimiento-stuffed green olives (W)

DESSERT & BAKING NEEDS

1/4 cup chocolate fudge topping for garnish (T)

PACKAGED GOODS

PASTA, RICE & GRAINS

1 pound linguini (Th)

1 cup brown rice (M)

BAKED GOODS

4 sourdough rolls (Th)

4 prepared graham cracker tart shells (Th)

INTERNATIONAL FOODS

8 ounces Japanese soba noodles (T)

DRIED FRUIT & NUTS

1 cup golden raisins (W)

1/2 cup pecan bits (M)

3 tablespoons sliced almonds for garnish (T)

DESSERT & BAKING NEEDS

1 package (3.4 ounces) instant vanilla pudding mix (F)

4 Hershey's kisses (F)

WINE & SPIRITS

1/2 cup dry white wine (M)

3 tablespoons dry white wine (Th)

1/2 cup dry red wine (W)

2 tablespoons dry sherry (T)

REFRIGERATED PRODUCTS

DAIRY

2 cups milk (F)

1/2 cup half-and-half (Th)

1/2 cup whipped cream (M)

1/2 cup whipped cream (Th)

3 eggs (F)

FROZEN GOODS

DESSERTS

1 pint chocolate ice cream (T)

MONDAY

Salmon on the Green

1 package (10 ounces) mixed salad greens
1 large lemon
4 salmon steaks (about 1 1/2 pounds)
2 tablespoons vegetable oil
1/2 cup dry white wine
1/2 teaspoon cayenne pepper
Seasoning to taste

Park and Rice

2 tablespoons fresh parsley (when
   chopped)
2 tablespoons butter
1 cup brown rice
1 can (14 ounces) vegetable broth
1/4 cup water
1/2 cup pecan bits

Tomaître d'

4 medium tomatoes
2 stalks celery
2 tablespoons butter
1 teaspoon dark brown sugar
1/2 teaspoon dried oregano
Seasoning to taste

Candlelight Cantaloupe

1 can (8 ounces) pineapple chunks
1 pint fresh raspberries
2 small ripe cantaloupe melons
2 tablespoons powdered sugar
1/2 cup whipped cream
Multicolored sprinkles for garnish

EQUIPMENT

Double boiler	Citrus juicer
2 large covered skillets	Kitchen knives
Medium mixing bowl	Measuring cups and spoons
Whisk	Cooking utensils

COUNTDOWN

1. Assemble the ingredients and the equipment.
2. Do Step 1 of *Salmon on the Green.*
3. Do Step 1 of *Tomaître d'.*
4. Do Steps 1–3 of *Park and Rice.*
5. Do Step 2 of *Tomaître d'.*
6. Do Steps 1–3 of *Candlelight Cantaloupe.*
7. Do Step 2 of *Salmon on the Green.*
8. Do Step 3 of *Tomaître d'.*
9. Do Step 4 of *Park and Rice.*
10. Do Step 3 of *Salmon on the Green.*
11. Do Step 4 of *Candlelight Cantaloupe.*

MONDAY

Salmon on the Green

1 Wash and dry the mixed greens and distribute them among individual plates. Juice the lemon. Rinse and pat dry the salmon steaks.

2 Heat the oil in a large skillet and sauté the salmon steaks until they are opaque, about 4 minutes per side. Add the lemon juice, the wine, and the cayenne pepper. Season to taste, cover, and reduce the heat. Simmer until the salmon flakes easily with a fork, 2 to 3 minutes more.

3 Pour half the pan juices over the greens. Top with the salmon steaks and spoon the remaining pan juices over the salmon.

Park and Rice

1 Bring water to a boil in the bottom of a double boiler.

2 Rinse, stem, and chop the parsley.

3 Combine the parsley, the butter, the rice, the broth, and the ¼ cup water in the top of the double boiler. Cover, reduce the heat, and simmer until all the liquid is absorbed and the rice is tender, 40 to 45 minutes.

4 Fold the pecan bits into the rice and fluff with a fork.

Tomaître d'

1 Rinse and stem the tomatoes and cut them in half. Rinse, trim, and chop the celery.

2 Melt the butter in a large skillet. Add the brown sugar and the tomatoes. Cover, reduce the heat, and simmer for 5 minutes.

3 Add the celery and the oregano and season to taste. Simmer, uncovered, for 3 minutes more.

Candlelight Cantaloupe

1 Drain the pineapple, reserving 2 tablespoons of the liquid. Rinse and pat dry the berries.

2 Cut the melons in half, remove the seeds, and place the halves on individual dessert plates. Refrigerate until you are ready to use.

3 In a medium bowl, whisk together the reserved pineapple liquid and the powdered sugar. Fold in the whipped cream and refrigerate until you are ready to use.

4 Fill the melon centers with the berries and the pineapple. Top with the whipped cream mixture and a splash of sprinkles.

TUESDAY

Chiba Chicken

4 boneless, skinless chicken breast halves
   (about 1 1/2 pounds)
1 large lime
1 teaspoon ground ginger
1/2 teaspoon ground allspice
2 teaspoons dark brown sugar
2 tablespoons soy sauce
2 tablespoons dry sherry
2 tablespoons vegetable oil

Sesame Soba

1 clove garlic
2 teaspoons sesame oil
8 ounces Japanese soba noodles
2 cups water
Seasoning to taste
2 tablespoons sesame seeds

Rickshaw Slaw

1 head Napa cabbage
1 small red bell pepper
2 scallions (green onions)
1 cup fresh bean sprouts
1 can (8 ounces) sliced water chestnuts
3 tablespoons vegetable oil
2 tablespoons rice vinegar
2 teaspoons ketchup
Seasoning to taste

Dynasty Dessert

1 can (11 ounces) mandarin oranges
1 pint chocolate ice cream
1/4 cup chocolate fudge topping for garnish
3 tablespoons sliced almonds for garnish

EQUIPMENT

2 large covered skillets	Citrus juicer
Colander	Ice cream scoop
Large mixing bowl	Plastic wrap
Small mixing bowl	Kitchen knives
Large shallow bowl	Measuring cups and spoons
Whisk	Cooking utensils
Citrus grater	

COUNTDOWN

1. Assemble the ingredients and the equipment.
2. Do Steps 1–2 of *Chiba Chicken*.
3. Do Steps 1–2 of *Rickshaw Slaw*.
4. Do Steps 3–4 of *Chiba Chicken*.
5. Do Step 1 of *Dynasty Dessert*.
6. Do Steps 1–3 of *Sesame Soba*.
7. Do Steps 5–6 of *Chiba Chicken*.
8. Do Step 2 of *Dynasty Dessert*.

TUESDAY

Chiba Chicken

1 Rinse and pat dry the chicken breasts. Grate 1 teaspoon of lime peel and juice the lime.

2 In a large shallow bowl, combine the lime juice, the ginger, the allspice, the brown sugar, the soy sauce, and the sherry. Place the chicken in the bowl, turning to coat. Cover with plastic wrap and refrigerate for 20 minutes.

3 Drain the chicken, reserving the marinade.

4 Heat the oil in a large skillet. Add the chicken and brown lightly, about 5 minutes per side. Reduce the heat, cover, and cook until the chicken is tender, 10 to 15 minutes.

5 Remove the chicken and cover to keep warm.

6 Add the marinade to the skillet and bring to a boil. Return the chicken to the skillet and coat in the sauce. Sprinkle with the lime peel.

Sesame Soba

1 Peel and chop the garlic.

2 Heat the oil in a large skillet and sauté the garlic for 1 minute. Add the noodles and sauté for 1 minute. Add the water, bring to a boil, and reduce the heat. Simmer until the noodles are tender, about 2 minutes.

3 Drain the noodles and return them to the skillet. Season to taste, sprinkle with the sesame seeds, and toss to combine. Cover to keep warm.

Rickshaw Slaw

1 Rinse, trim, quarter, and chop the cabbage. Rinse, trim, seed, and chop the bell pepper. Rinse, trim, and chop the scallions. Rinse and dry the bean sprouts. Drain the water chestnuts. Combine the ingredients in a large bowl.

2 In a small bowl, whisk together the oil, the vinegar, and the ketchup. Season to taste and toss with the slaw.

Dynasty Dessert

1 Drain the mandarin oranges.

2 Place scoops of chocolate ice cream in individual dessert dishes. Top with the orange slices. Drizzle the fudge topping over the oranges and sprinkle with the almonds.

WEDNESDAY

Cuban Missiles

1 cup golden raisins
1 clove garlic
1 small green bell pepper
1 jar (3 ounces) pimiento-stuffed green
    olives
1 tablespoon olive oil
4 beef cube steaks (about 1 1/2 pounds)
1 can (8 ounces) tomato sauce
1/2 cup dry red wine
1/2 teaspoon dried basil
Seasoning to taste

Red Potatoes

1 1/2 pounds small new red potatoes
1 can (14 ounces) beef broth
3 tablespoons butter
1/2 teaspoon paprika
Seasoning to taste

Grated Antilles

1 head green leaf lettuce
1 small red onion
1 small jicama
2 medium carrots
3 tablespoons vegetable oil
2 tablespoons tarragon vinegar
1/2 teaspoon granulated sugar
Seasoning to taste

Havana Banana

4 medium bananas
1/2 cup powdered sugar
3 tablespoons butter

EQUIPMENT

Large saucepan	Vegetable brush
Large skillet	Vegetable peeler
Medium skillet	Vegetable grater
Large mixing bowl	Kitchen knives
2 small mixing bowls	Measuring cups and
Shallow bowl	spoons
Whisk	Cooking utensils

COUNTDOWN

1. Assemble the ingredients and the
   equipment.
2. Do Steps 1–2 of *Grated Antilles*.
3. Do Step 1 of *Red Potatoes*.
4. Do Steps 1–4 of *Cuban Missiles*.
5. Do Step 2 of *Red Potatoes*.
6. Do Step 3 of *Grated Antilles*.
7. Do Steps 1–4 of *Havana Banana*.

WEDNESDAY

Cuban Missiles

1 Soak the raisins in a small bowl of warm water to plump. Peel and rinse the garlic. Rinse, trim, seed, and chop the bell pepper. Drain and slice the olives.

2 Heat the oil in a large skillet and sauté the garlic for 1 minute. Add the steaks and sauté until lightly browned, about 3 minutes per side.

3 Add the tomato sauce, the wine, the basil, the olives, and the bell pepper. Season to taste.

4 Drain the raisins and add them to the skillet. Mix to combine and simmer for 5 minutes more.

Red Potatoes

1 Scrub the potatoes. Place them in a large saucepan. Add the broth and enough water to cover the potatoes and bring to a boil. Cook until the potatoes are tender, 10 to 15 minutes.

2 Drain the potatoes and return them to the saucepan. Add the butter and the paprika, season to taste, and toss to combine.

Grated Antilles

1 Wash and dry the lettuce and tear it into bite-sized pieces. Peel and grate the onion. Peel, trim, halve, and grate the jicama. Peel, trim, and grate the carrots. Combine the ingredients in a large bowl.

2 In a small bowl, whisk together the oil, the vinegar, and the sugar. Season to taste.

3 Toss the salad with the dressing.

Havana Banana

1 Peel and quarter the bananas.

2 Place the powdered sugar in a shallow bowl.

3 In a medium skillet, melt the butter and sauté the bananas until they are lightly golden on both sides, about 5 minutes.

4 Remove from the skillet and roll in the powdered sugar.

THURSDAY

Bela Linguini

2 small shallots
1 pound fresh mushrooms
3 tablespoons fresh parsley (when chopped)
2 medium lemons
2 tablespoons butter
2 tablespoons olive oil
1/2 cup half-and-half
3 tablespoons dry white wine
Seasoning to taste
1 pound linguini
1/2 cup grated Parmesan cheese

Basil Rathbean

1 pound fresh green beans
2 tablespoons fresh basil leaves (when chopped)
2 tablespoons olive oil
1 teaspoon granulated sugar
Seasoning to taste

Gilbert Rolland

3 tablespoons butter
4 sourdough rolls
1 teaspoon dried thyme
Seasoning to taste

John Berrymore

1 pint fresh strawberries
1 pint fresh blueberries
2 tablespoons water
1 teaspoon cornstarch
1/4 cup currant jelly
1/2 cup whipped cream
4 prepared graham cracker tart shells
2 tablespoons powdered sugar

EQUIPMENT

Stockpot	Citrus grater
Small saucepan	Citrus juicer
Large covered skillet	Kitchen knives
Medium covered skillet	Measuring cups and spoons
Colander	Cooking utensils
Medium mixing bowl	

COUNTDOWN

1. Assemble the ingredients and the equipment.
2. Do Step 1 of *Gilbert Rolland*.
3. Do Step 1 of *Basil Rathbean*.
4. Do Steps 1–2 of *John Berrymore*.
5. Do Steps 1–6 of *Bela Linguini*.
6. Do Step 2 of *Gilbert Rolland*.
7. Do Step 2 of *Basil Rathbean*.
8. Do Step 7 of *Bela Linguini*.
9. Do Step 3 of *Gilbert Rolland*.
10. Do Step 3 of *John Berrymore*.

THURSDAY

Bela Linguini

1 Bring water to a boil in a stockpot.

2 Peel and mince the shallots. Rinse, pat dry, trim, and thinly slice the mushrooms. Rinse, stem, and chop the parsley. Grate the lemon peel and juice the lemons.

3 Melt the butter with the oil in a large skillet. Add the shallots and sauté for 1 minute. Add the mushrooms and the lemon peel and sauté until the mushrooms begin to soften, about 3 minutes. Add the lemon juice and cook for 1 minute.

4 Reduce the heat, add the half-and-half, and simmer for 1 minute.

5 Add the wine and simmer just until the mixture begins to thicken, about 3 minutes. Remove from the heat, stir in the parsley, and season to taste. Cover to keep warm.

6 Cook the linguini until it is almost tender 2 to 3 minutes if you are using fresh pasta, 6 to 7 minutes if you are using dry pasta.

7 Drain the linguini and return it to the stockpot. Add the mushroom mixture and toss to combine. Sprinkle with the cheese.

Basil Rathbean

1 Rinse and trim the green beans. Rinse, stem, and chop the basil.

2 In a medium skillet, heat the oil. Blend in the sugar. Add the beans, turning to coat. Sauté until crisp-tender, about 5 minutes. Remove from the heat. Stir in the basil, season to taste, cover, and steam for 1 minute.

Gilbert Rolland

1 Set the butter out to soften.

2 Cut the rolls in half lengthwise and toast lightly.

3 Combine the softened butter with the thyme and season to taste. Spread over the cut side of the rolls while still warm.

John Berrymore

1 Rinse, hull, and slice the strawberries. Rinse and pat dry the blueberries. Combine the berries in a medium bowl.

2 Combine the water, the cornstarch, and the jelly in a small saucepan and bring it to a boil, stirring, until the jelly melts and the mixture begins to thicken, about 1 minute. Remove from the heat and set aside.

3 Place 2 tablespoons of the whipped cream in the bottom of each tart shell. Spoon the fruit over the whipped cream and top with the jelly sauce. Dust with the powdered sugar.

FRIDAY

Chesapeake Cakes

¾ pound cooked crabmeat
1 small green bell pepper
1 small onion
3 eggs
1½ cups plain breadcrumbs
1 teaspoon white Worcestershire sauce
¼ teaspoon white pepper
Seasoning to taste
3 tablespoons vegetable oil

Potomac Peas

1½ pounds fresh green peas, unshelled
4 scallions (green onions)
2 tablespoons butter
1 teaspoon granulated sugar
Seasoning to taste

Baltomato Salad

1 medium head lettuce
4 medium tomatoes
1 medium cucumber
3 tablespoons fresh parsley (when chopped)
3 tablespoons olive oil
2 tablespoons red wine vinegar
½ teaspoon dried basil
Seasoning to taste

Black-Eyed Susans

1 package (3.4 ounces) instant vanilla pudding mix
2 cups milk
4 large ripe peaches
4 Hershey's kisses

EQUIPMENT

Electric mixer
2 large skillets
Large mixing bowl
Medium mixing bowl
2 small mixing bowls
Whisk

Vegetable peeler
Kitchen knives
Measuring cups and spoons
Cooking utensils

COUNTDOWN

1. Assemble the ingredients and the equipment.
2. Do Step 1 of *Black-Eyed Susans*.
3. Do Steps 1–4 of *Chesapeake Cakes*.
4. Do Steps 1–3 of *Baltomato Salad*.
5. Do Steps 1–2 of *Potomac Peas*.
6. Do Step 4 of *Baltomato Salad*.
7. Do Steps 2–3 of *Black-Eyed Susans*.

FRIDAY

Chesapeake Cakes

1 Flake the crabmeat, removing any pieces of shell and cartilage. Rinse, trim, seed, and mince the bell pepper. Peel and mince the onion.

2 Combine the crab, the bell pepper, and the onion in a large bowl.

3 In a small bowl, whip the eggs. Add the eggs to the crab mixture. Fold in the breadcrumbs, the Worcestershire sauce, and the white pepper. Season to taste.

4 Heat the oil in a large skillet. Place heaping tablespoons of the crab mixture in the oil and flatten the mixture into patties. Cook on both sides until golden, 4 to 6 minutes per side.

Potomac Peas

1 Shell the peas. Rinse, trim, and chop the scallions.

2 Melt the butter in a large skillet and sauté the peas and the scallions until they are crisp-tender, 2 to 3 minutes. Add the sugar and season to taste.

Baltomato Salad

1 Wash and dry the lettuce and distribute the leaves among individual salad plates.

2 Rinse, stem, and slice the tomatoes and arrange them over the lettuce. Peel, trim, and chop the cucumber and arrange the slices over the tomato. Rinse, stem, and chop the parsley.

3 In a small bowl, combine the oil, the vinegar, and the basil. Season to taste.

4 Drizzle the dressing over the salad and sprinkle with the parsley.

Black-Eyed Susans

1 In a medium bowl, beat the pudding mix with the milk until well blended, about 2 minutes. Spoon the mixture into individual dessert bowls and refrigerate until you are ready to serve.

2 Peel, halve, and pit the peaches and cut the halves into thin slices.

3 Arrange the slices around the edge of the puddings, face to face, to form petals. Place a Hershey's kiss in the middle, to form a flower.

WEEK TWO

Monday

Some Like It Hot
Call Me Bwoccoli
Film Rolls
Lemon Drop Kid

Tuesday

Sagebrush Soup
Casino Salad
Comstock Loaf
Black Rock Dessert

Wednesday

A Chick In Every Port
Overboard Orzo
Batten Down the Beans
Stowaways

Thursday

Pagoda Pork
Empress Rice
Most Important Pineapple
Mandarin Blossom Pudding

Friday

Pasta the Cheese
Two Cloves for Comfort
Halve No Pity
Done-In Dessert

STAPLES

- ☐ Butter
- ☐ Flour
- ☐ Cornstarch
- ☐ Granulated sugar
- ☐ Powdered sugar
- ☐ Olive oil
- ☐ Sesame oil
- ☐ Vegetable oil
- ☐ Apple cider vinegar
- ☐ Lemon juice
- ☐ Mayonnaise
- ☐ Soy sauce
- ☐ Tabasco sauce
- ☐ Worcestershire sauce
- ☐ Grated Parmesan cheese
- ☐ Chicken bouillon cube
- ☐ Bay leaf
- ☐ Dried marjoram
- ☐ Dried sage
- ☐ Dried tarragon
- ☐ Ground allspice
- ☐ Cayenne pepper
- ☐ Chili powder
- ☐ Whole cloves
- ☐ Ground cloves
- ☐ Ground ginger
- ☐ Ground nutmeg
- ☐ Paprika
- ☐ Black pepper
- ☐ Salt
- ☐ Peppermint extract

MEAT & POULTRY

1 1/2 pounds lean boneless pork loin (Th)

3 pounds chicken pieces (W)

FRESH PRODUCE

VEGETABLES

1 pound baking potatoes (T)

1 medium bunch broccoli (M)

1 small head cauliflower (Th)

1 pound green beans (W)

3/4 pound sugar-snap peas (F)

1/2 pound Chinese snow peas (Th)

2 small yellow zucchini (M)

2 medium carrots (T)

2 medium carrots (Th)

2 stalks celery (T)

2 stalks celery (Th)

1/2 pound mushrooms (Th)

1 small head red cabbage (T)

1 small head red leaf lettuce (T)

1 small ripe avocado (F)

1 large green bell pepper (T)

1 large onion (T)

1 medium onion (W)

4 scallions (green onions) (F)

1 clove garlic (M)

2 cloves garlic (W)

1 clove garlic (F)

HERBS

2 tablespoons basil leaves (when chopped) (F)

3 tablespoons chives (when chopped) (M)

2 tablespoons chives (when chopped) (Th)

3 tablespoons parsley (when chopped) (M)

2 tablespoons parsley (when chopped) (W)

FRUIT

1 large ripe honeydew melon (T)

4 large ripe apricots (F)

1 small ripe pineapple (Th)

1 pound seedless black grapes (T)

1 pint strawberries (F)

CANS, JARS & BOTTLES

SOUPS

1 can (14 ounces) beef broth (T)

1 can (14 ounces) chicken broth (W)

VEGETABLES

1 can (15 ounces) white beans (T)

1 can (15 ounces) sliced beets (T)

1 can (11 ounces) whole-kernel corn (W)

1 jar (7 ounces) roasted red peppers (F)

INTERNATIONAL FOODS

1 can (8 ounces) sliced water chestnuts (Th)

FRUIT

4 maraschino cherries (Th)

JUICES

3 cups tomato juice (T)

PACKAGED GOODS

PASTA, RICE & GRAINS

8 ounces orzo (W)

1 pound angel hair pasta (F)

1 cup long-grain white rice (Th)

BAKED GOODS

8 butterflake rolls (M)

1 loaf French bread (T)

1 loaf French bread (F)

DRIED FRUIT & NUTS

1/4 cup walnut pieces for garnish (F)

DESSERT & BAKING NEEDS

1 package (3 ounces) lemon gelatin (M)

1 package (3.4 ounces) instant vanilla pudding mix (Th)

1 package (7 ounces) lemon drop candies (M)

10 ounces toffee chips (F)

1/4 cup marshmallow crème for garnish (T)

1/4 cup flaked coconut for garnish (W)

WINE & SPIRITS

2 tablespoons dry sherry (T)

1 cup port or red wine (W)

REFRIGERATED PRODUCTS

DAIRY

2 tablespoons milk (M)

2 cups milk (Th)

2 tablespoons milk (F)

1/3 cup half-and-half (F)

1 container (6 ounces) mandarin orange yogurt (Th)

Whipped cream for garnish (M)

Whipped cream for garnish (W)

9 eggs (M)

4 eggs (F)

CHEESE

8 ounces Brie cheese (M)

3/4 cup shredded mozzarella cheese (F)

JUICES

2 tablespoons orange juice (M)

1/2 cup orange juice (W)

DELI

8 slices bacon (T)

FROZEN GOODS

DESSERTS

1 pint rocky road ice cream (T)

1 pint lime sherbet (W)

MONDAY

Some Like It Hot

3 tablespoons fresh parsley (when chopped)
3 tablespoons fresh chives (when chopped)
8 ounces Brie cheese
9 eggs
2 tablespoons milk
4 tablespoons butter
1 teaspoon Tabasco sauce
$\frac{1}{2}$ teaspoon dried tarragon
Seasoning to taste
$\frac{1}{2}$ teaspoon cayenne pepper

Call Me Bwoccoli

1 medium bunch broccoli
2 small yellow zucchini
1 tablespoon butter
2 tablespoons orange juice
Seasoning to taste

Film Rolls

1 clove garlic
4 tablespoons olive oil
$\frac{3}{4}$ teaspoon dried marjoram
8 butterflake rolls

Lemon Drop Kid

1 package (7 ounces) lemon drop candies
1$\frac{1}{4}$ cups water
1 package (3 ounces) lemon gelatin
Ice cubes
Whipped cream for garnish

EQUIPMENT

Blender	Whisk
Medium covered saucepan	Mallet
Large covered skillet	Plastic bag
Small skillet	Kitchen knives
Steamer insert	Measuring cups and spoons
Large mixing bowl	Cooking utensils
Small mixing bowl	

COUNTDOWN

1. Assemble the ingredients and the equipment.
2. Do Steps 1–5 of *Lemon Drop Kid*.
3. Do Steps 1–2 of *Some Like It Hot*.
4. Do Steps 1–3 of *Call Me Bwoccoli*.
5. Do Steps 3–5 of *Some Like It Hot*.
6. Do Steps 1–3 of *Film Rolls*.
7. Do Step 6 of *Lemon Drop Kid*.

MONDAY

Some Like It Hot

1 Rinse, stem, and chop the parsley. Rinse and chop the chives. Remove the rind from the Brie and chop the cheese into small pieces.

2 In a large bowl, whisk the eggs and milk together until light and frothy.

3 Melt the butter with the Tabasco sauce in a large skillet, turning the skillet to coat the bottom and sides evenly.

4 Pour the eggs into the skillet. Reduce the heat and simmer until the eggs have partially set, tilting the pan to cook evenly, about 3 minutes.

5 Add the Brie. Sprinkle with the parsley, the chives, and the tarragon and season to taste. Sprinkle with the cayenne, cover, and continue cooking until the cheese has melted and the eggs are fully set, 1 to 2 minutes.

Call Me Bwoccoli

1 Bring water to a boil in a medium saucepan. Rinse and trim the broccoli, discarding the tough ends, and cut into bite-sized florets. Rinse, trim, and julienne the zucchini.

2 Arrange the broccoli in a steamer insert. Place the insert in the saucepan, cover, and steam for 3 minutes. Add the zucchini and continue steaming until the vegetables are crisp-tender, about 3 minutes longer.

3 Drain the vegetables and return them to the saucepan. Add the butter and the orange juice and heat through. Season to taste and toss to combine. Cover to keep warm.

Film Rolls

1 Peel and mince the garlic.

2 Heat the oil in a small skillet and sauté the garlic for 1 minute. Blend in the marjoram.

3 Spread the mixture lightly between the sections of the rolls.

Lemon Drop Kid

1 Place the candies in a plastic bag and crush with a mallet.

2 Bring ¾ cup of the water to a boil.

3 Combine the boiling water and the gelatin in a blender. Cover and process until the gelatin is completely dissolved, about 30 seconds.

4 In a small bowl, combine the remaining ½ cup water with enough ice cubes to make 1¼ cups. Add the ice to the gelatin mixture and stir until it is partially melted. Blend at high speed for 30 seconds.

5 Sprinkle a tablespoon of the crushed candy into the bottom of individual dessert glasses. Pour the gelatin mixture over the candy and refrigerate until you are ready to serve.

6 Top each serving with a dollop of whipped cream and sprinkle with the remaining lemon candies.

TUESDAY

Sagebrush Soup

1 large onion
1 pound baking potatoes
2 stalks celery
2 medium carrots
1 large green bell pepper
8 slices bacon
1 can (15 ounces) white beans
3 cups tomato juice
1 can (14 ounces) beef broth
2 tablespoons dry sherry
1 teaspoon granulated sugar
1 teaspoon Worcestershire sauce
1 bay leaf
1 teaspoon dried sage
Seasoning to taste

Casino Salad

1 small head red leaf lettuce
1 small head red cabbage
1 can (15 ounces) sliced beets
3 tablespoons olive oil
2 tablespoons apple cider vinegar
1/2 teaspoon ground allspice
Seasoning to taste

Comstock Loaf

3 tablespoons butter
1/2 teaspoon paprika
1/4 teaspoon ground cloves
Seasoning to taste
1 loaf French bread

Black Rock Dessert

1 large ripe honeydew melon
1 pound seedless black grapes
1 pint rocky road ice cream
1/4 cup marshmallow crème for garnish

EQUIPMENT

Dutch oven	Pastry brush
Small saucepan	Ice cream scoop
Large mixing bowl	Kitchen knives
Small mixing bowl	Measuring cups and spoons
Whisk	
Vegetable grater	Cooking utensils
Vegetable peeler	

COUNTDOWN

1. Assemble the ingredients and the equipment.
2. Do Steps 1–4 of *Sagebrush Soup*.
3. Do Steps 1–2 of *Comstock Loaf*.
4. Do Steps 1–4 of *Casino Salad*.
5. Do Step 5 of *Sagebrush Soup*.
6. Do Steps 1–2 of *Black Rock Dessert*.

TUESDAY

Sagebrush Soup

1 Peel and chop the onion. Peel and cube the potatoes. Rinse, trim, and slice the celery. Peel, trim, and slice the carrots. Rinse, trim, seed, and chop the bell pepper. Chop the bacon. Rinse and drain the beans.

2 Sauté the bacon in a Dutch oven until almost crisp, about 8 minutes. Remove and drain on paper towels.

3 Remove all but 2 tablespoons of the bacon drippings. Sauté the onion in the remaining drippings until soft, about 5 minutes. Add the potatoes, the celery, the carrots, and the bell pepper and sauté for 3 minutes.

4 Add the beans, the tomato juice, the broth, the sherry, the sugar, the Worcestershire sauce, the bay leaf, and the sage. Return the bacon, season to taste, and bring the mixture to a boil. Cover, reduce the heat, and simmer until the vegetables are tender, about 25 minutes.

5 Remove the bay leaf before serving.

Casino Salad

1 Wash and dry the lettuce and distribute the leaves among individual salad plates.

2 Rinse, trim, quarter, and grate the cabbage into a large bowl. Drain the beets well.

3 In a small bowl, combine the oil, the vinegar, and the allspice. Season to taste.

4 Toss the cabbage with the dressing. Mound the cabbage over the lettuce leaves and spoon the beets over the top.

Comstock Loaf

1 Melt the butter in a small saucepan. Blend in the paprika and the cloves and season to taste.

2 Slice the bread and brush the butter mixture over the slices.

Black Rock Dessert

1 Quarter the melon, remove the seeds, and place the quarters on individual dessert plates. Rinse and stem the grapes.

2 Place a scoop of ice cream in the center of each melon quarter. Stud the ice cream with the grapes and top with a dollop of marshmallow crème.

WEDNESDAY

A Chick In Every Port

1 medium onion
2 cloves garlic
3 pounds chicken pieces
1/2 cup flour
2 teaspoons dried tarragon
1 teaspoon paprika
2 tablespoons vegetable oil
1 cup port or red wine
Seasoning to taste

Overboard Orzo

1 can (14 ounces) chicken broth
2 cups water
2 tablespoons fresh parsley (when chopped)
1 can (11 ounces) whole-kernel corn
8 ounces orzo
Seasoning to taste

Batten Down the Beans

1 pound fresh green beans
2 tablespoons butter
1 tablespoon lemon juice
1/2 teaspoon granulated sugar
1/2 cup water
Seasoning to taste

Stowaways

1/4 cup granulated sugar
2 tablespoons cornstarch
1/2 cup orange juice
1 pint lime sherbet
Whipped cream for garnish
1/4 cup flaked coconut for garnish

EQUIPMENT

Dutch oven	Shallow bowl
Large saucepan	Ice cream scoop
Small saucepan	Kitchen knives
Medium covered skillet	Measuring cups and spoons
Strainer	Cooking utensils

COUNTDOWN

1. Assemble the ingredients and the equipment.
2. Do Step 1 of *Stowaways*.
3. Do Steps 1–4 of *A Chick In Every Port*.
4. Do Steps 1–4 of *Overboard Orzo*.
5. Do Steps 1–3 of *Batten Down the Beans*.
6. Do Step 2 of *Stowaways*.

WEDNESDAY

A Chick In Every Port

1 Peel and slice the onion. Peel and mince the garlic. Rinse and pat dry the chicken pieces.

2 In a shallow bowl, combine the flour, the tarragon, and the paprika. Dredge the chicken in the flour mixture.

3 Heat the oil in a Dutch oven and sauté the onion and the garlic for 3 minutes. Add the chicken and sauté until the pieces are nicely browned on all sides, about 15 minutes.

4 Add the wine and season to taste. Cover, reduce the heat, and simmer until the chicken is tender and cooked through, about 30 minutes.

Overboard Orzo

1 Bring the broth and the water to a boil in a large saucepan.

2 Rinse, stem, and chop the parsley. Drain the corn.

3 Cook the orzo and the corn until the orzo is just tender, 6 to 7 minutes.

4 Drain the orzo and the corn, season to taste, and sprinkle with the parsley.

Batten Down the Beans

1 Rinse and trim the green beans.

2 Melt the butter with the lemon juice in a medium skillet. Blend in the sugar. Add the beans, tossing to coat, and cook for 2 minutes.

3 Add the water and season to taste. Reduce the heat, cover, and simmer until the beans are crisp-tender, about 7 minutes.

Stowaways

1 In a small saucepan, dissolve the sugar and the cornstarch in the orange juice. Bring the mixture to a boil and cook until slightly thickened, about 2 minutes. Remove from the heat and let the sauce cool to room temperature.

2 Place scoops of sherbet in individual dessert glasses and drizzle the sauce over the sherbet. Top with a dollop of whipped cream and a sprinkle of coconut.

THURSDAY

Pagoda Pork

1 1/2 pounds lean boneless pork loin
2 medium carrots
2 stalks celery
1 small head cauliflower
1/2 pound Chinese snow peas
1/2 pound fresh mushrooms
2 tablespoons cornstarch
1 chicken bouillon cube
1/4 cup hot water
1 tablespoon soy sauce
1/2 teaspoon ground ginger
2 tablespoons vegetable oil

Empress Rice

2 tablespoons fresh chives (when chopped)
1 can (8 ounces) sliced water chestnuts
1 cup long-grain white rice
2 cups water
1 teaspoon sesame oil

Most Important Pineapple

1 small fresh ripe pineapple
2 tablespoons lemon juice
2 tablespoons water
1 tablespoon cornstarch
1/2 teaspoon ground nutmeg

Mandarin Blossom Pudding

1 package (3.4 ounces) instant vanilla
   pudding mix
2 cups milk
1 container (6 ounces) mandarin orange
   yogurt
4 maraschino cherries

COUNTDOWN

1. Assemble the ingredients and the equipment.
2. Do Step 1 of *Mandarin Blossom Pudding*.
3. Do Steps 1–3 of *Empress Rice*.
4. Do Step 2 of *Mandarin Blossom Pudding*.
5. Do Steps 1–2 of *Most Important Pineapple*.
6. Do Steps 1–4 of the *Pagoda Pork*.
7. Do Step 3 of *Most Important Pineapple*.
8. Do Step 4 of *Empress Rice*.
9. Do Step 3 of *Mandarin Blossom Pudding*.

EQUIPMENT

Electric mixer
Wok
Double boiler
Small saucepan
Medium mixing bowl
Small mixing bowl
Whisk
Vegetable peeler
Waxed paper
Kitchen knives
Measuring cups and spoons
Cooking utensils

THURSDAY

Pagoda Pork

1 Slice the pork into thin strips. Peel, trim, and thinly slice the carrots. Rinse, trim, and slice the celery. Rinse and trim the cauliflower and cut into bite-sized florets. Rinse and string the snow peas. Rinse, pat dry, trim, and slice the mushrooms.

2 Place the pork on a sheet of waxed paper and coat with the cornstarch.

3 In a small bowl, dissolve the bouillon cube in the hot water. Blend in the soy sauce and the ginger.

4 Heat the oil in a wok. Stir-fry the pork slices for 2 minutes. Add the carrots, the celery, and the cauliflower and stir-fry for 2 minutes. Add the snow peas and the mushrooms and stir-fry for 2 minutes. Add the bouillon mixture, stirring to blend, and cook until the sauce begins to thicken, 1 to 2 minutes.

Empress Rice

1 Bring water to a boil in the bottom of a double boiler.

2 Rinse, trim, and chop the chives. Drain and chop the water chestnuts.

3 Combine the rice, the chives, the water chestnuts, the 2 cups water, and the oil in the top of the double boiler. Cover, reduce the heat, and simmer until all the liquid is absorbed and the rice is tender, 30 to 40 minutes.

4 Fluff the rice with a fork.

Most Important Pineapple

1 Cut a thick slice off the top and bottom of the pineapple. Remove the rind and the eyes. Cut the fruit lengthwise into spears, discarding the core. Arrange the spears on individual salad plates.

2 In a small saucepan, combine the lemon juice, the water, the cornstarch, and the nutmeg. Bring to a boil and whisk until blended, about 1 minute. Remove from the heat and let cool.

3 Drizzle the sauce over the pineapple.

Mandarin Blossom Pudding

1 In a medium bowl, beat the pudding mix and the milk until well blended, about 2 minutes. Pour into individual dessert dishes and let stand for 5 minutes.

2 Place spoonfuls of the yogurt on top of each pudding and swirl it into the pudding using a spiral motion. Refrigerate for at least 20 minutes.

3 Cut the cherries halfway through into quarters to resemble a flower. Place 1 cherry flower on top of each pudding.

FRIDAY

Pasta the Cheese

1 jar (7 ounces) roasted red peppers
4 scallions (green onions)
2 tablespoons fresh basil leaves
 (when chopped)
4 eggs
1/3 cup half-and-half
1/2 teaspoon chili powder
3/4 cup shredded mozzarella cheese
1/4 cup grated Parmesan cheese
1 pound angel hair pasta
1 tablespoon vegetable oil
Seasoning to taste

Two Cloves for Comfort

3/4 pound sugar-snap peas
2 tablespoons butter
2 whole cloves
Seasoning to taste

Halve No Pity

1 clove garlic
1 loaf French bread
1/4 cup mayonnaise
1 small ripe avocado
2 tablespoons lemon juice

Done-In Dessert

1 pint fresh strawberries
4 large ripe apricots
3 tablespoons powdered sugar
10 ounces toffee chips
1/2 teaspoon peppermint extract
2 tablespoons milk
1/4 cup walnut pieces for garnish

EQUIPMENT

Large saucepan	Medium mixing bowl
Small saucepan	Small mixing bowl
Large skillet	Whisk
Medium skillet	Kitchen knives
Baking sheet	Measuring cups and
Strainer	spoons
Large mixing bowl	Cooking utensils

COUNTDOWN

1. Assemble the ingredients and the equipment.
2. Do Step 1 of *Done-In Dessert*.
3. Do Step 1 of *Two Cloves for Comfort*.
4. Do Steps 1–3 of *Halve No Pity*.
5. Do Steps 1–6 of *Pasta the Cheese*.
6. Do Step 2 of *Two Cloves for Comfort*.
7. Do Steps 4–5 of *Halve No Pity*.
8. Do Steps 2–3 of *Done-In Dessert*.

FRIDAY

Pasta the Cheese

1 Bring water to a boil in a large saucepan.

2 Drain the peppers and cut them into thin strips. Rinse, trim, and chop the scallions. Rinse, stem, and chop the basil.

3 In a large bowl, combine the eggs, the half-and-half, the chili powder, the mozzarella cheese, and the Parmesan cheese. Whisk to blend.

4 Break the pasta into small pieces. Cook until it is almost tender, 1 to 2 minutes if you are using fresh pasta, 3 to 4 minutes if you are using dry pasta.

5 Drain the pasta.

6 Heat the oil in a large skillet. Add the pasta and the peppers. Pour the egg mixture over the pasta and season to taste. Fold in the scallions and the basil. Reduce the heat and simmer until the eggs are set, 3 to 4 minutes.

Too Cloves for Comfort

1 Rinse and string the snap peas.

2 Melt the butter in a medium skillet and sauté the cloves for 2 minutes. Add the snap peas and sauté until they are crisp-tender, 3 to 4 minutes. Season to taste. Remove the cloves before serving.

Halve No Pity

1 Peel and mince the garlic.

2 Split the bread in half lengthwise and spread with the mayonnaise.

3 Halve, pit, and peel the avocado. Place it in a small bowl and mash with the lemon juice and the garlic.

4 Preheat the broiler.

5 Spread the avocado mixture over the mayonnaise. Place the bread on a baking sheet and broil until hot and bubbly, 2 to 3 minutes.

Done-In Dessert

1 Rinse, hull, and pat dry the strawberries, cutting the large ones in half. Rinse, halve, pit, and chop the apricots. Combine the fruit in a medium bowl, sprinkle with the powdered sugar, and refrigerate until you are ready to serve.

2 Melt the toffee chips with the peppermint extract and the milk in a small saucepan.

3 Spoon the fruit into individual dessert dishes. Top with the toffee mixture and garnish with the nuts.

WEEK THREE

WEEK AT A GLANCE

Monday
Tipsy Tortellini
Carousing Salad
Upstanding Biscuits
Cautious Cake

Tuesday
San Andreas Fowl
Point Rice
Caulifornia
Calaveras County Pudding

Wednesday
Ragout of the Sea
Spinnaker Salad
Dinghy Bread
Scuttle the Sherbet

Thursday
Parton My Pasta
Minnie Pearls
Country Bread
Reba McIntoshes

Friday
Happy Hamburgers
The Dillighted Potato
Nuts to Nectarines

STAPLES

- ❏ Butter
- ❏ Bisquick
- ❏ Cornstarch
- ❏ Granulated sugar
- ❏ Dark brown sugar
- ❏ Powdered sugar
- ❏ Chocolate syrup
- ❏ Olive oil
- ❏ Vegetable oil
- ❏ Apple cider vinegar
- ❏ Raspberry vinegar
- ❏ White wine vinegar
- ❏ Lemon juice
- ❏ Dijon mustard
- ❏ Worcestershire sauce
- ❏ Grated Parmesan cheese
- ❏ Grated Romano cheese
- ❏ Plain breadcrumbs
- ❏ Bay leaf
- ❏ Dried oregano
- ❏ Dried tarragon
- ❏ Dried thyme
- ❏ Whole allspice
- ❏ Ground cinnamon
- ❏ Ground nutmeg
- ❏ Black pepper
- ❏ Salt
- ❏ Vanilla extract

MEAT & POULTRY

1 1/2 pounds lean ground beef (F)

1/2 pound Italian bulk sausage (Th)

4 boneless, skinless chicken breast halves (about 1 1/2 pounds) (T)

FISH

1 pound medium shrimp, shelled and deveined (W)

1/2 pound sea scallops (W)

1 pound mussels (W)

FRESH PRODUCE

VEGETABLES

1 1/2 pounds new red potatoes (F)

1 small bunch broccoli (W)

1 small head cauliflower (T)

1/2 pound green peas, unshelled (T)

4 large carrots (M)

2 large carrots (W)

2 stalks celery (F)

2 stalks celery (W)

1/2 pound mushrooms (W)

1 large head lettuce (W, F)

1 small head lettuce (M)

2 medium tomatoes (F)

2 medium tomatoes (W)

4 medium tomatoes (Th)

1 small orange bell pepper (T)

1 small yellow bell pepper (Th)

1 medium onion (F)

1 small onion (M)

1 small red onion (F)

4 small shallots (W)

3 scallions (green onions) (Th)

2 cloves garlic (M)

2 cloves garlic (W)

HERBS

1/4 cups basil leaves (when chopped) (Th)

1/4 cup chives (when chopped) (M)

3 tablespoons chives (when chopped) (W)

2/3 cup dill (when chopped) (F)

3 tablespoons dill (when chopped) (Th)

1/2 cup parsley (when chopped) (M)

3 tablespoons parsley (when chopped) (W)

FRUIT

1 small lemon (W)

1 large lime (T)

1 small lime (W)

4 large McIntosh apples (Th)

4 medium ripe nectarines (F)

CANS, JARS & BOTTLES

SOUPS

1 can (14 ounces) chicken broth (T)

VEGETABLES

2 cans (14 1/2 ounces each) Italian-style stewed tomatoes (M)

JUICES

1 can (6 ounces) tomato juice (F)

3 cups clam juice (W)

FRUIT

1 can (16 ounces) pitted dark cherries (M)

4 maraschino cherries for garnish (W)

DESSERT & BAKING NEEDS

1 cup plus 2 teaspoons evaporated milk (F)

1 jar (12 ounces) caramel topping (Th)

PACKAGED GOODS

PASTA, RICE & GRAINS

1 pound fettuccine (Th)

1 cup brown rice (T)

1 cup granola cereal (Th)

BAKED GOODS

1 loaf French bread (W)

1 loaf peasant bread (Th)

4 hamburger buns (F)

3 cups vanilla wafers (when crumbled) (F)

DRIED FRUIT & NUTS

4 raisins (T)

1/2 cup pecan bits (F)

DESSERT & BAKING NEEDS

1 package (3.4 ounces) instant pistachio pudding mix (T)

12 ounces white chocolate chips (F)

1 1/2 cups mini-marshmallows (F)

8 malted milk balls (T)

1 licorice whip (T)

1/4 cup flaked coconut for garnish (W)

WINE & SPIRITS

1/4 cup dry white wine (M)

1 cup dry white wine (W)

REFRIGERATED PRODUCTS

DAIRY

2/3 cup milk (M)

2 cups milk (T)

3 tablespoons milk (Th)

3 tablespoons half-and-half (Th)

Whipped cream for garnish (Th)

3 eggs (F)

CHEESE

1/4 cup shredded mozzarella cheese (M)

4 slices (1 ounce each) Cheddar cheese (F)

1 container (5 ounces) herbed cream cheese (Th)

DELI

12 ounces spinach tortellini with cheese (M)

FROZEN GOODS

VEGETABLES

1 package (10 ounces) pearl onions (Th)

BAKED GOODS

1 pound cake (M)

DESSERTS

1 pint vanilla ice cream (F)

1 pint pineapple sherbet (W)

MONDAY

Tipsy Tortellini

1 small onion
2 cloves garlic
1 tablespoon olive oil
2 cans (14½ ounces each) Italian-style
   stewed tomatoes
1 tablespoon dark brown sugar
¼ cup dry white wine
Seasoning to taste
12 ounces fresh spinach tortellini with
   cheese
¼ cup shredded mozzarella cheese

Carousing Salad

1 small head lettuce
4 large carrots
½ cup fresh parsley (when chopped)
3 tablespoons vegetable oil
2 tablespoons raspberry vinegar
1 teaspoon Dijon mustard
¼ teaspoon ground cinnamon
1 teaspoon granulated sugar
Seasoning to taste

Upstanding Biscuits

¼ cup fresh chives (when chopped)
2¼ cups Bisquick
⅔ cup milk

Cautious Cake

1 frozen pound cake
1 can (16 ounces) pitted dark cherries
2 tablespoons granulated sugar
1 tablespoon cornstarch
½ teaspoon ground nutmeg

EQUIPMENT

Stockpot	Whisk
Medium saucepan	Vegetable peeler
Small saucepan	Vegetable grater
Baking sheet	Kitchen knives
Colander	Measuring cups and
2 medium mixing	spoons
bowls	Cooking utensils
Small mixing bowl	

COUNTDOWN

1. Assemble the ingredients and the equipment.
2. Do Step 1 of *Cautious Cake*.
3. Do Steps 1–3 of *Tipsy Tortellini*.
4. Do Steps 1–2 of *Carousing Salad*.
5. Do Steps 2–3 of *Cautious Cake*.
6. Do Steps 1–3 of *Upstanding Biscuits*.
7. Do Steps 4–5 of *Tipsy Tortellini*.
8. Do Step 3 of *Carousing Salad*.
9. Do Step 4 of *Cautious Cake*.

MONDAY

Tipsy Tortellini

1 Peel and chop the onion. Peel and mince the garlic.

2 Heat the oil in a medium saucepan and sauté the onion and the garlic for 5 minutes. Add the tomatoes and the brown sugar. Bring the mixture to a boil and reduce the heat. Add the wine and simmer until the sauce begins to thicken, about 20 minutes. Season to taste.

3 Bring water to a boil in a stockpot.

4 Cook the tortellini until it is almost tender, about 5 minutes if you are using fresh pasta, about 10 minutes if you are using dry pasta.

5 Drain the tortellini. Pour the sauce over the pasta and sprinkle with the cheese.

Carousing Salad

1 Wash and dry the lettuce and distribute the leaves among individual salad plates. Peel, trim, and grate the carrots. Rinse, stem, and chop the parsley. Combine the carrots and the parsley in a medium bowl.

2 In a small bowl, combine the oil, the vinegar, the mustard, the cinnamon, and the sugar. Season to taste and toss with the carrots.

3 Spoon the mixture over the lettuce leaves.

Upstanding Biscuits

1 Preheat the oven to 450°F.

2 Rinse, trim, and chop the chives. In a medium bowl, combine the chives, the Bisquick, and the milk. Stir the mixture until just blended.

3 Drop the dough by tablespoons onto a baking sheet. Bake until golden, about 8 minutes.

Cautious Cake

1 Set the pound cake out to thaw.

2 Drain the cherries, reserving the liquid.

3 In a small saucepan, combine the reserved liquid, the sugar, the cornstarch, and the nutmeg. Bring the mixture to a boil and reduce the heat. Simmer until the sauce is thickened and glossy, about 2 minutes. Set aside.

4 Slice the cake and arrange the slices on individual dessert plates. Spoon the cherries over the slices and top with the sauce.

TUESDAY

San Andreas Fowl

4 boneless, skinless chicken breast halves
   (about 1 1/2 pounds)
1 large lime
1 teaspoon dried tarragon
1 tablespoon Dijon mustard
1 teaspoon Worcestershire sauce
2 tablespoons olive oil

Point Rice

1 small orange bell pepper
2 tablespoons butter
1 cup brown rice
1 can (14 ounces) chicken broth
1/2 cup water

Caulifornia

1 small head cauliflower
1/2 pound fresh green peas, unshelled
2 tablespoons butter
1/2 teaspoon dried thyme
1/4 cup water
1 teaspoon granulated sugar
Seasoning to taste

Calaveras County Pudding

1 package (3.4 ounces) instant pistachio
   pudding mix
2 cups milk
1 teaspoon vanilla extract
8 malted milk balls
4 raisins
1 licorice whip

EQUIPMENT

Electric mixer
Medium covered
   saucepan
Medium covered
   skillet
Medium mixing bowl
Shallow bowl
Whisk

Citrus grater
Citrus juicer
Pastry brush
Kitchen knives
Measuring cups and
   spoons
Cooking utensils

COUNTDOWN

1. Assemble the ingredients and the equipment.
2. Do Step 1 of *San Andreas Fowl.*
3. Do Step 1 of *Calaveras County Pudding.*
4. Do Steps 1–2 of *Point Rice.*
5. Do Step 1 of *Caulifornia.*
6. Do Steps 2–6 of *San Andreas Fowl.*
7. Do Step 2 of *Caulifornia.*
8. Do Step 3 of *Point Rice.*
9. Do Step 2 of *Calaveras County Pudding.*

TUESDAY

San Andreas Fowl

1 Prepare the grill or preheat the broiler.

2 Rinse and pat dry the chicken breasts.

3 Grate 2 tablespoons of lime peel and juice the lime.

4 In a shallow bowl, whisk together the lime peel, the lime juice, the tarragon, the mustard, the Worcestershire sauce, and the oil.

5 Dip the chicken breasts in the mixture, turning to coat well.

6 Grill or broil, brushing with the marinade, until the chicken is tender and opaque and the juices run clear, 5 to 10 minutes per side, depending on cooking method. Serve with the remaining marinade.

Point Rice

1 Rinse, trim, seed, and chop the bell pepper.

2 Melt the butter in a medium saucepan. Add the bell pepper and sauté until soft, about 4 minutes. Add the rice and mix to combine. Add the broth and the water. Bring to a boil, cover, reduce the heat, and simmer until the liquid is absorbed and the rice is tender, 40 to 45 minutes.

3 Fluff with a fork.

Caulifornia

1 Rinse and trim the cauliflower and cut into bite-sized florets. Shell the peas.

2 Melt the butter in a medium skillet. Add the cauliflower and sauté for 3 minutes. Add the peas, the thyme, the water, and the sugar. Season to taste, cover, and cook for 3 minutes.

Calaveras County Pudding

1 In a medium bowl, beat the pudding mix, the milk, and the vanilla until well blended, about 2 minutes. Pour the pudding into individual dessert dishes and refrigerate until you are ready to serve.

2 To make frog faces, place 2 malted milk balls on each pudding for the eyes. Place a raisin for each nose. Cut the licorice whip into quarters and use each piece to form a smiling mouth.

WEDNESDAY

Ragout of the Sea

2 cloves garlic
4 small shallots
2 large carrots
2 stalks celery
3 tablespoons fresh parsley (when chopped)
2 medium tomatoes
1 cup dry white wine
3 cups clam juice
1 bay leaf
3 whole allspice
1 pound medium shrimp, shelled and deveined
1/2 pound sea scallops
1 pound mussels
Seasoning to taste

Spinnaker Salad

1 large head lettuce
1 small bunch broccoli
1/2 pound fresh mushrooms
3 tablespoons olive oil
2 tablespoons white wine vinegar
1/2 teaspoon dried oregano
Seasoning to taste

Dinghy Bread

1 small lemon
3 tablespoons fresh chives (when chopped)
2 tablespoons olive oil
1 loaf French bread
1/4 cup grated Parmesan cheese

Scuttle the Sherbet

1 small lime
1 pint pineapple sherbet
1/4 cup flaked coconut for garnish
4 maraschino cherries for garnish

EQUIPMENT

Dutch oven	Vegetable peeler
2 medium covered saucepans	Citrus grater
	Citrus juicer
Steamer insert	Ice cream scoop
Baking sheet	Toothpicks
Strainer	Kitchen knives
2 small mixing bowls	Measuring cups and spoons
Whisk	
Vegetable brush	Cooking utensils

COUNTDOWN

1. Assemble the ingredients and the equipment.
2. Do Steps 1–4 of *Spinnaker Salad*.
3. Do Steps 1–3 of *Dinghy Bread*.
4. Do Steps 5–6 of *Spinnaker Salad*.
5. Do Step 1 of *Scuttle the Sherbet*.
6. Do Steps 1–4 of *Ragout of the Sea*.
7. Do Steps 4–5 of *Dinghy Bread*.
8. Do Steps 5–6 of *Ragout of the Sea*.
9. Do Step 7 of *Spinnaker Salad*.
10. Do Step 2 of *Scuttle the Sherbet*.

WEDNESDAY

Ragout of the Sea

1 Peel and mince the garlic. Peel and chop the shallots. Peel, trim, and thinly slice the carrots. Rinse, trim, and chop the celery. Rinse, stem, and chop the parsley. Rinse, stem, and chop the tomatoes.

2 In a Dutch oven, combine the garlic, the shallots, the carrots, the celery, ½ cup of the wine, the clam juice, the bay leaf, and the allspice. Bring to a boil, reduce the heat, and simmer for 10 minutes.

3 Rinse the shrimp. Rinse the scallops. Scrub the mussels and remove their beards, discarding any that do not close when tapped.

4 Place the mussels and the remaining ½ cup wine in a medium saucepan. Bring to a boil, cover, and cook just until the mussels open, about 5 minutes.

5 Add the shrimp and the scallops to the Dutch oven. Add the tomatoes and season to taste. Simmer until the shrimp turn bright pink, about 3 minutes. Remove the bay leaf and the allspice.

6 Drain the mussels, discarding any that do not open, and add them to the shrimp mixture. Garnish with the parsley.

Spinnaker Salad

1 Bring water to a boil in a medium saucepan.

2 Wash and dry the lettuce, reserving 4 leaves for use on Friday, and distribute the rest among individual salad plates.

3 Rinse and trim the broccoli, discarding the tough ends, and cut into bite-sized florets.

Rinse, pat dry, trim, and slice the mushrooms.

4 Arrange the broccoli in a steamer insert. Place the insert in the saucepan, cover, and cook until the florets are crisp-tender, 6 to 8 minutes.

5 Drain and rinse the broccoli under cold water and place in a large bowl. Add the mushrooms.

6 In a small bowl, combine the oil, the vinegar, and the oregano. Season to taste and toss with the vegetables.

7 Spoon the vegetables over the lettuce.

Dinghy Bread

1 Grate 1 tablespoon of lemon peel and juice the lemon. Rinse and chop the chives.

2 In a small bowl, combine the lemon juice, the lemon peel, the chives, and the oil.

3 Cut the bread in half lengthwise and place the halves on a baking sheet. Spread the cut sides with the lemon mixture and sprinkle with the cheese.

4 Preheat the broiler.

5 Broil until bubbly, about 2 minutes.

Scuttle the Sherbet

1 Cut the lime in half. Grate the peel from one half. Slice the second half.

2 Place scoops of the sherbet in individual dessert dishes. Top with the lime peel and the coconut. Place a slice of lime and a maraschino cherry on a toothpick and insert in the side of the sherbet.

THURSDAY

Parton My Pasta

3 scallions (green onions)
1/4 cup fresh basil leaves (when chopped)
1 container (5 ounces) herbed cream
   cheese
3 tablespoons half-and-half
1 pound fettuccine
1/2 pound Italian bulk sausage
Seasoning to taste
1/4 cup grated Romano cheese

Minnie Pearls

1 package (10 ounces) frozen pearl onions
4 medium tomatoes
1 small yellow bell pepper
2 tablespoons vegetable oil
1 tablespoon butter
1/4 cup water
Seasoning to taste

Country Bread

3 tablespoons butter
3 tablespoons fresh dill (when chopped)
1 teaspoon Worcestershire sauce
Seasoning to taste
1 loaf peasant bread

Reba McIntoshes

4 large McIntosh apples
1 jar (12 ounces) caramel topping
3 tablespoons milk
1 cup granola cereal
Whipped cream for garnish

COUNTDOWN

1. Assemble the ingredients and the equipment.
2. Do Step 1 of *Country Bread*.
3. Do Step 1 of *Minnie Pearls*.
4. Do Steps 1–2 of *Reba McIntoshes*.
5. Do Steps 1–2 of *Parton My Pasta*.
6. Do Step 2 of *Minnie Pearls*.
7. Do Steps 2–4 of *Country Bread*.
8. Do Step 3 of *Minnie Pearls*.
9. Do Steps 3–5 of *Parton My Pasta*.
10. Do Step 4 of *Minnie Pearls*.
11. Do Step 5 of *Country Bread*.
12. Do Step 3 of *Reba McIntoshes*.

EQUIPMENT

Blender	Colander
Stockpot	2 small mixing bowls
Large covered skillet	Kitchen knives
Medium covered skillet	Measuring cups and spoons
Small skillet	Cooking utensils
Baking sheet	

THURSDAY

Parton My Pasta

1 Bring water to a boil in a stockpot.

2 Rinse, trim, and chop the scallions. Rinse, stem, and chop the basil. Place the scallions, the basil, the cream cheese, and the half-and-half in a blender and process until well blended, 1 to 2 minutes.

3 Cook the fettuccine until it is almost tender, 2 to 3 minutes if you are using fresh pasta, 6 to 7 minutes if you are using dry pasta.

4 Brown the sausage in a small skillet, about 5 minutes. Drain on paper towels.

5 Drain the pasta and return it to the stockpot. Add the sausage and toss with the herbed sauce. Season to taste and sprinkle with the Romano cheese. Cover to keep warm.

Minnie Pearls

1 Set the onions in a small bowl of warm water to thaw.

2 Rinse, stem, and chunk the tomatoes. Rinse, trim, seed, and chop the bell pepper.

3 Heat the oil with the butter in a medium skillet. Add the onions, the tomatoes, and the bell pepper, tossing to coat. Add the water. Season to taste. Cover, reduce the heat, and simmer for 5 minutes.

4 Remove from the heat and keep warm.

Country Bread

1 Set the butter out to soften.

2 Rinse, stem, and chop the dill.

3 In a small bowl, combine the softened butter, the dill, and the Worcestershire sauce. Season to taste.

4 Preheat the broiler.

5 Cut the bread in half lengthwise and spread the cut sides with the butter mixture. Place on a baking sheet and broil until bubbly, 1 to 2 minutes.

Reba McIntoshes

1 Peel, core, and halve the apples.

2 In a large skillet, bring the caramel topping and the milk to a boil. Add the apples and turn them in the sauce to coat. Reduce the heat and simmer until the apples begin to soften, about 5 minutes. Cover and set aside.

3 Place the apples in individual dessert dishes. Fill the centers with the cereal. Spoon some of the sauce over the apples and top with a dollop of whipped cream.

FRIDAY

Happy Hamburgers

1 medium onion
1½ pounds lean ground beef
¾ cup plain breadcrumbs
1 egg
1 can (6 ounces) tomato juice
1 teaspoon Worcestershire sauce
Seasoning to taste
4 hamburger buns
2 medium tomatoes
4 slices (1 ounce each) Cheddar cheese
4 lettuce leaves (reserved from
    Wednesday)

The Dillighted Potato

2 eggs
1½ pounds new potatoes
1 small red onion
2 stalks celery
⅔ cup fresh dill (when chopped)
¼ cup olive oil
1 tablespoon Dijon mustard
1 tablespoon apple cider vinegar
Seasoning to taste

Nuts to Nectarines

4 medium ripe nectarines
2 tablespoons lemon juice
12 ounces white chocolate chips
1 cup plus 2 teaspoons evaporated milk
3 cups vanilla wafers (when crumbled)
1½ cups mini-marshmallows
½ cup pecan bits
1 cup powdered sugar
1 pint vanilla ice cream
¼ cup chocolate syrup for garnish

EQUIPMENT

Large covered saucepan	Vegetable brush
Medium saucepan	Vegetable peeler
Small saucepan	Ice cream scoop
9 x 9-inch baking pan	Plastic bag
2 large mixing bowls	Kitchen knives
Medium mixing bowl	Measuring cups and spoons
Small mixing bowl	Cooking utensils
Whisk	

COUNTDOWN

1. Assemble the ingredients and the equipment.
2. Do Steps 1–5 of *Nuts to Nectarines*.
3. Do Step 1 of *Happy Hamburgers*.
4. Do Steps 1–4 of *The Dillighted Potato*.
5. Do Step 2 of *Happy Hamburgers*.
6. Do Steps 5–7 of *The Dillighted Potato*.
7. Do Steps 3–5 of *Happy Hamburgers*.
8. Do Step 6 of *Nuts to Nectarines*.

FRIDAY

Happy Hamburgers

1 Prepare the grill or preheat the broiler.

2 Peel and mince the onion. Place in a large bowl. Add the ground beef, the bread-crumbs, the egg, the tomato juice, and the Worcestershire sauce. Season to taste, blend well, and form into round patties.

3 Grill or broil the patties to the desired doneness.

4 Split and toast the buns. Rinse, stem, and slice the tomatoes.

5 Place the patties on the buns. Top with the cheese, the reserved lettuce leaves, and the tomatoes.

The Dillighted Potato

1 Cover the eggs with water in a small saucepan. Bring the water to a boil and hard-cook the eggs, 10 to 12 minutes.

2 Scrub the potatoes and cut them into 1-inch cubes. Peel and chop the onion. Rinse, trim, and chop the celery. Rinse, stem, and mince the dill.

3 Drain the eggs and place them in the freezer for 10 minutes.

4 In a large saucepan, cover the potatoes with water. Bring the water to a boil, cover the saucepan, and cook the potatoes until they are tender, about 10 minutes.

5 Drain the potatoes and rinse them in cold water. Drain again and place in a large bowl.

6 In a small bowl, combine the oil, the mustard, and the vinegar. Season to taste.

7 Peel and chop the eggs. Add the eggs, the onion, the celery, and the dill to the potatoes and toss with the dressing.

Nuts to Nectarines

1 Grease a 9 x 9-inch baking pan.

2 Peel, halve, pit, and slice the nectarines and place them in a medium bowl. Sprinkle with the lemon juice to keep them from browning.

3 Melt the chocolate chips in a medium saucepan over very low heat. Slowly add 1 cup of the evaporated milk and blend well.

4 Place the vanilla wafers in a plastic bag and crumble them. In a large bowl, combine the vanilla crumbs, the marshmallows, the nuts, and the powdered sugar. Mix well.

5 Combine half of the melted chocolate with the crumb mixture and blend to coat. Turn the mixture into the baking pan and press evenly over the bottom. Add the remaining 2 teaspoons evaporated milk to the remaining melted chocolate and spread over the crumb mixture. Refrigerate until you are ready to serve.

6 Cut the brownies into large squares. Top with a scoop of ice cream, a drizzle of chocolate syrup, and the sliced nectarines.

WEEK FOUR

WEEK AT A GLANCE

Monday
Lewis and Cluck
Columbia River Rice
Cornvallis
Mount Hoods

Tuesday
Dillicious Fish
Parsnippity Potatoes
Swiss Miss
Pears on the Rum

Wednesday
Chili Chili Bang Bang
Fruiteous Potts
Eccentric Pie

Thursday
I Thigh For You
Tom Cruisecous
Bean Affleck
Antonio Bananaderas

Friday
Rock On By
Never Missed a Beet
Slaw Dancing
Rhubarb Rhythm

STAPLES

- ❑ Butter
- ❑ Granulated sugar
- ❑ Dark brown sugar
- ❑ Powdered sugar
- ❑ Chocolate sprinkles
- ❑ Silver shots
- ❑ Olive oil
- ❑ Vegetable oil
- ❑ Apple cider vinegar
- ❑ Rice vinegar
- ❑ Lemon juice
- ❑ Lime juice
- ❑ Honey
- ❑ Dried basil
- ❑ Dried dill
- ❑ Dried oregano
- ❑ Dried tarragon
- ❑ Cayenne pepper
- ❑ Ground cinnamon
- ❑ Ground cumin
- ❑ Paprika
- ❑ Black pepper
- ❑ White pepper
- ❑ Salt
- ❑ Brandy extract
- ❑ Rum extract
- ❑ Vanilla extract

MEAT & POULTRY

4 boneless, skinless chicken breast halves (about 1 1/2 pounds) (M)

1 1/2 pounds boneless, skinless chicken thighs (Th)

FISH

4 salmon fillets (about 1 1/2 pounds) (T)

4 rockfish or other white fish fillets (about 1 1/2 pounds) (F)

FRESH PRODUCE

VEGETABLES

1 1/2 pounds baking potatoes (T)

4 large ears sweet corn (M)

1 pound green beans (Th)

2 stalks celery (F)

1 medium parsnip (T)

1 bunch Swiss chard (T)

1 medium head cabbage (F)

1 medium head lettuce (W)

2 large tomatoes (Th)

1 medium cucumber (F)

1 large green bell pepper (W)

1 medium yellow bell pepper (F)

1 small onion (M)

1 medium sweet onion (Th)

1 clove garlic (W)

1 clove garlic (Th)

HERBS

3 tablespoons chives (when chopped) (T)

1/4 cup chives (when chopped) (F)

2 tablespoons parsley (when chopped) (M)

2 tablespoons parsley (when chopped) (T)

3 tablespoons parsley (when chopped) (Th)

3 tablespoons rosemary (when chopped) (M)

FRUIT

1 medium lemon (M)

1 medium lemon (T)

1 small lime (W)

2 medium oranges (W)

1 small ripe cantaloupe melon (Th)

2 large bananas (Th)

4 large ripe peaches (M)

4 large very ripe pears (T)

2 large stalks rhubarb (F)

1 pint blueberries (M)

1 pint raspberries (Th)

1 pint strawberries (F)

CANS, JARS & BOTTLES

SOUPS

1 can (14 ounces) chicken broth (M)

1 can (14 ounces) chicken broth (Th)

1 can (14 ounces) vegetable broth (T)

VEGETABLES

3 cans (15 ounces each) black beans (W)

1 can (15 ounces) julienne beets (F)

INTERNATIONAL FOODS

1 can (8 ounces) sliced water chestnuts (Th)

1 can (4 ounces) diced green chilies (W)

FRUIT

1 can (15 ounces) pineapple chunks (W)

SAUCES

1 can (8 ounces) tomato sauce

CONDIMENTS

1 jar (4 ounces) sliced pimientos (Th)

DESSERT & BAKING NEEDS

1/4 cup marshmallow crème for garnish (T)

PACKAGED GOODS

PASTA, RICE & GRAINS

1 cup long-grain white rice (M)

1 cup couscous (Th)

BAKED GOODS

1 prepared pie shell (W)

DRIED FRUIT & NUTS

2 tablespoons sliced almonds (T)

DESSERT & BAKING NEEDS

1 package (3.4 ounces) instant vanilla pudding mix (W)

1 package (3.4 ounces) instant chocolate pudding mix (W)

1/4 cup flaked coconut (Th)

WINE & SPIRITS

1/4 cup dry white wine (Th)

REFRIGERATED PRODUCTS

DAIRY

4 cups milk (W)

1/4 cup sour cream (W)

3/4 cup sour cream (F)

1 cup whipping cream (M)

Whipped cream for garnish (W)

FROZEN GOODS

BAKED GOODS

1 pound cake (M)

DESSERTS

1 pint strawberry ice cream (F)

MONDAY

Lewis and Cluck

4 boneless, skinless chicken breast halves
  (about 1 1/2 pounds)
3 tablespoons fresh rosemary (when
  chopped)
1/2 cup honey
Seasoning to taste

Columbia River Rice

1 small onion
1 medium lemon
2 tablespoons fresh parsley (when
  chopped)
2 tablespoons butter
1 cup long-grain white rice
1 can (14 ounces) chicken broth

Cornvallis

2 tablespoons butter
4 large ears fresh sweet corn
1/2 teaspoon paprika
Seasoning to taste

Mount Hoods

1 frozen pound cake
4 large ripe peaches
2 tablespoons lemon juice
1 pint fresh blueberries
1 cup whipping cream
2 tablespoons powdered sugar
1 teaspoon vanilla extract
1 tablespoon silver shots for garnish

EQUIPMENT

Electric mixer	Citrus juicer
Double boiler	Pastry brush
Small skillet	Kitchen knives
Medium mixing bowl	Measuring cups and
Small mixing bowl	spoons
Citrus grater	Cooking utensils

COUNTDOWN

1. Assemble the ingredients and the equipment.
2. Do Step 1 of *Mount Hoods.*
3. Do Step 1 of *Lewis and Cluck.*
4. Do Step 1 of *Cornvallis.*
5. Do Steps 1–4 of *Columbia River Rice.*
6. Do Steps 2–4 of *Mount Hoods.*
7. Do Steps 2–3 of *Lewis and Cluck.*
8. Do Steps 2–3 of *Cornvallis.*
9. Do Step 4 of *Lewis and Cluck.*
10. Do Step 4 of *Cornvallis.*
11. Do Step 5 of *Columbia River Rice.*
12. Do Step 5 of *Mount Hoods.*

MONDAY

Lewis and Cluck

1 Prepare the grill or preheat the broiler.

2 Rinse and pat dry the chicken breasts. Rinse, stem, and chop the rosemary.

3 Brush the chicken with some of the honey, sprinkle with some of the rosemary, and season to taste.

4 Grill or broil the chicken on one side until golden, 5 to 8 minutes. Turn, brush with the remaining honey, and sprinkle with the remaining rosemary. Grill or broil until tender and cooked through, 5 to 8 minutes longer.

Columbia River Rice

1 Peel and chop the onion. Grate 1 tablespoon of lemon peel and juice the lemon. Rinse, stem, and chop the parsley.

2 Melt the butter in a small skillet and sauté the onion for 5 minutes.

3 Bring water to a boil in the bottom of a double boiler.

4 Combine the onion, the rice, the broth, and the lemon juice in the top of the double boiler. Cover, reduce the heat, and simmer until all the liquid is absorbed and the rice is tender, 30 to 40 minutes.

5 Fold in the parsley and the lemon peel and fluff with a fork.

Cornvallis

1 Set the butter out to soften.

2 Carefully preserving the outer husks of the corn, remove the inner leaves and the corn silk.

3 In a small bowl, blend the butter with the paprika and season to taste. Spread the mixture on the corn. Close the outer husks back around the ears.

4 Cook the corn directly over the grill for 10 minutes, turning occasionally.

Mount Hoods

1 Chill a medium bowl and the beaters of an electric mixer for 10 minutes.

2 Set the pound cake out to thaw.

3 Peel, halve, pit, and slice the peaches and sprinkle them with the lemon juice to prevent browning. Rinse and pat dry the blueberries.

4 Whip the cream until stiff peaks form, about 3 minutes. Fold in the powdered sugar and the vanilla.

5 Cut the pound cake into 4 thick slices. Place the slices on individual dessert plates. Mound a quarter of the peach slices and a quarter of the blueberries onto each cake slice and cover the fruit with the whipped cream to represent a snowy peak. Garnish with the silver shots.

TUESDAY

Dillicious Fish

4 salmon fillets (about 1 1/2 pounds)
1 medium lemon
3 tablespoons fresh chives (when chopped)
2 teaspoons dried dill
1/2 teaspoon paprika
1/4 teaspoon white pepper
2 tablespoons vegetable oil
Seasoning to taste

Parsnippity Potatoes

1 1/2 pounds baking potatoes
1 medium parsnip
2 tablespoons fresh parsley (when chopped)
1 can (14 ounces) vegetable broth
3 tablespoons butter
Seasoning to taste

Swiss Miss

1 bunch Swiss chard
2 tablespoons butter
1 tablespoon lemon juice

Pears on the Rum

4 large very ripe pears
3 tablespoons butter
3 tablespoons dark brown sugar
1 teaspoon rum extract
1/4 cup marshmallow crème for garnish
2 tablespoons sliced almonds for garnish

EQUIPMENT

Electric mixer	Pastry brush
Large covered saucepan	Citrus grater
Medium covered saucepan	Citrus juicer
	Vegetable peeler
2 large skillets	Kitchen knives
Steamer insert	Measuring cups and spoons
Small mixing bowl	Cooking utensils

COUNTDOWN

1. Assemble the ingredients and the equipment.
2. Do Steps 1–2 of *Pears on the Rum*.
3. Do Steps 1–3 of *Parsnippity Potatoes*.
4. Do Steps 1–2 of *Dillicious Fish*.
5. Do Steps 1–2 of *Swiss Miss*.
6. Do Steps 4–5 of *Parsnippity Potatoes*.
7. Do Steps 3–5 of *Swiss Miss*.
8. Do Steps 3–4 of *Dillicious Fish*.
9. Do Step 3 of *Pears on the Rum*.

TUESDAY

Dillicious Fish

1 Rinse and pat dry the fish fillets. Grate 1 tablespoon of lemon peel and juice the lemon. Rinse, trim, and chop the chives.

2 In a small bowl, combine the lemon juice, the dill, the paprika, and the pepper. Brush the mixture over both sides of the fillets.

3 Heat the oil in a large skillet. Add the fish and cook until it flakes easily with a fork, 4 to 5 minutes per side.

4 Season to taste and garnish with the chives and the lemon peel.

Parsnippity Potatoes

1 Peel and quarter the potatoes. Peel, trim, and chunk the parsnip. Rinse, stem, and chop the parsley.

2 Reserve ¾ cup of the broth. Bring the remainder of the broth and water to a boil in a large saucepan.

3 Cook the potatoes and the parsnip until they are tender, 10 to 15 minutes.

4 Drain the potatoes and the parsnip and return them to the saucepan. Beat in the butter and the reserved broth until well blended. Season to taste and continue beating until the mixture is light and fluffy.

5 Sprinkle with the parsley and cover to keep warm.

Swiss Miss

1 Bring water to a boil in a medium saucepan.

2 Rinse and stem the Swiss chard and thinly slice it.

3 Arrange the Swiss chard in a steamer insert. Place the insert in the saucepan, cover, and steam for 2 minutes.

4 In a small saucepan, melt the butter with the lemon juice.

5 Drain the Swiss chard, turn it into the saucepan, and toss it with the butter mixture. Cover to keep warm.

Pears on the Rum

1 Peel, core, and slice the pears.

2 Melt the butter with the brown sugar in a large skillet. Blend in the rum extract. Add the pear slices and toss to coat and heat through, 2 to 3 minutes.

3 Arrange the pears on individual dessert plates. Top each serving with a dollop of marshmallow crème and a sprinkle of nuts.

WEDNESDAY

Chili Chili Bang Bang

1 clove garlic
1 large green bell pepper
1 small lime
3 cans (15 ounces each) black beans
1 can (4 ounces) diced green chilies
2 tablespoons olive oil
1 can (8 ounces) tomato sauce
2 teaspoons ground cumin
2 teaspoons dried basil
½ teaspoon dried oregano
¼ teaspoon cayenne pepper
Seasoning to taste
¼ cup sour cream for garnish

Fruiteous Potts

1 medium head lettuce
2 medium oranges
1 can (15 ounces) pineapple chunks
2 tablespoons vegetable oil
1 tablespoon rice vinegar
Seasoning to taste

Eccentric Pie

1 package (3.4 ounces) instant vanilla
   pudding mix
4 cups milk
1 package (3.4 ounces) instant chocolate
   pudding mix
1 prepared pie shell
Whipped cream for garnish
Chocolate sprinkles for garnish

EQUIPMENT

Electric mixer	Citrus grater
Dutch oven	Citrus juicer
2 medium mixing bowls	Kitchen knives
Small mixing bowl	Measuring cups and spoons
Whisk	Cooking utensils

COUNTDOWN

1. Assemble the ingredients and the equipment.
2. Do Steps 1–3 of *Eccentric Pie*.
3. Do Steps 1–2 of *Chili Chili Bang Bang*.
4. Do Steps 1–2 of *Fruiteous Potts*.
5. Do Step 3 of *Chili Chili Bang Bang*.
6. Do Step 3 of *Fruiteous Potts*.
7. Do Step 4 of *Eccentric Pie*.

WEDNESDAY

Chili Chili Bang Bang

1 Peel and mince the garlic. Rinse, trim, seed, and chop the bell pepper. Grate 1 tablespoon of lime peel and juice the lime. Rinse and drain the beans. Drain the chilies.

2 In a Dutch oven, heat the oil and sauté the garlic and the bell pepper until soft, about 4 minutes. Add the beans, the chilies, the tomato sauce, the lime juice, the cumin, the basil, the oregano, and the cayenne pepper. Season to taste and bring the mixture to a boil, stirring to combine. Cover, reduce the heat, and simmer for 10 minutes.

3 Top each serving with a dollop of sour cream and a sprinkle of lime peel.

Fruiteous Potts

1 Wash and dry the lettuce and distribute the leaves among individual salad plates to form cups. Peel and slice the oranges and place the slices in the lettuce cups. Drain the pineapple, reserving 3 tablespoons of the liquid. Add the pineapple to the oranges.

2 In a small bowl, combine the reserved pineapple liquid, the oil, and the vinegar. Season to taste.

3 Drizzle the dressing over the salad.

Eccentric Pie

1 In a medium bowl, beat the vanilla pudding mix with 2 cups of the milk until well blended, about 2 minutes. Place in the refrigerator for 10 minutes.

2 In a second medium bowl, beat the chocolate pudding mix with the remaining 2 cups milk until well blended, about 2 minutes. Place in the refrigerator for 10 minutes.

3 Spoon the vanilla pudding into one half of the pie shell. Spoon the chocolate mixture into the other half of the pie shell. Refrigerate the pie until you are ready to serve.

4 Garnish with dollops of whipped cream and sprinkles.

THURSDAY

I Thigh For You

1 1/2 pounds boneless, skinless chicken thighs
1 medium sweet onion
1 clove garlic
2 large tomatoes
3 tablespoons fresh parsley (when chopped)
1 jar (4 ounces) sliced pimientos
3 tablespoons vegetable oil
1/4 cup dry white wine
Seasoning to taste

Tom Cruisecous

2 tablespoons butter
1/4 teaspoon ground cinnamon
1 cup couscous
1 can (14 ounces) chicken broth
1/4 cup water

Bean Affleck

1 pound fresh green beans
1 can (8 ounces) sliced water chestnuts
1 tablespoon butter
1/2 teaspoon dried tarragon
Seasoning to taste

Antonio Bananaderas

2 large bananas
1 small ripe cantaloupe melon
1 pint fresh raspberries
2 tablespoons powdered sugar
2 tablespoons lime juice
1 teaspoon brandy extract
1/4 cup flaked coconut

EQUIPMENT

Blender

Medium covered
saucepan

2 large covered
skillets

Kitchen knives

Measuring cups and
spoons

Cooking utensils

COUNTDOWN

1. Assemble the ingredients and the equipment.
2. Do Steps 1–3 of *I Thigh For You.*
3. Do Step 1 of *Tom Cruisecous.*
4. Do Steps 1–3 of *Bean Affleck.*
5. Do Step 2 of *Tom Cruisecous.*
6. Do Steps 1–4 of *Antonio Bananaderas.*

THURSDAY

I Thigh For You

1 Rinse and pat dry the chicken thighs. Peel and chop the onion. Peel and mince the garlic. Rinse, stem, and chop the tomatoes. Rinse, stem, and chop the parsley. Drain the pimientos.

2 In a large skillet, heat the oil and sauté the onion and the garlic until the onion is soft, about 5 minutes. Add the chicken and sauté until it is golden, about 5 minutes per side. Add the tomatoes and the wine and cook until the tomatoes begin to soften, about 3 minutes.

3 Add the pimientos and the parsley. Season to taste. Bring the mixture to a boil, cover, and reduce the heat. Simmer until the chicken is tender, about 15 minutes.

Tom Cruisecous

1 In a medium saucepan, melt the butter with the cinnamon. Add the couscous and sauté until well coated, about 1 minute. Add the broth and the water and bring to a boil. Cover the saucepan, remove it from the heat, and let it stand until all the liquid is absorbed, at least 5 minutes.

2 Fluff with a fork before serving.

Bean Affleck

1 Bring a small amount of water to a boil in a large skillet.

2 Rinse and trim the green beans. Drain the water chestnuts. Arrange the beans in the skillet, cover, and cook until crisp-tender, about 6 minutes.

3 Drain the beans and return them to the skillet. Toss with the butter, the water chestnuts, and the tarragon. Season to taste and heat through.

Antonio Bananaderas

1 Peel and chunk the bananas. Quarter, seed, peel, and chunk the melon. Distribute the fruit among individual dessert bowls.

2 Rinse the raspberries.

3 In a blender, combine the raspberries, the powdered sugar, the lime juice, and the brandy extract. Puree until smooth.

4 Spoon the sauce over the fruit and sprinkle with the coconut.

FRIDAY

Rock On By

4 rockfish or other white fish fillets
   (about 1 1/2 pounds)
1/4 cup fresh chives (when chopped)
1 medium cucumber
1 tablespoon lemon juice
1 teaspoon granulated sugar
3/4 cup sour cream
Seasoning to taste
2 tablespoons vegetable oil
1/4 teaspoon paprika

Never Missed a Beet

1 can (15 ounces) julienne beets
1 tablespoon butter
1 teaspoon dark brown sugar
Seasoning to taste

Slaw Dancing

1 medium head cabbage
1 medium yellow bell pepper
2 stalks celery
3 tablespoons vegetable oil
2 tablespoons apple cider vinegar
1 teaspoon granulated sugar
1/2 teaspoon dried dill
Seasoning to taste

Rhubarb Rhythm

1 pint fresh strawberries
2 large stalks fresh rhubarb
1/2 cup granulated sugar
1 cup water
1 teaspoon vanilla extract
1 teaspoon ground cinnamon
1 pint strawberry ice cream

EQUIPMENT

Blender
2 medium covered
   saucepans
Large skillet
Large mixing bowl
Small mixing bowl
Whisk

Vegetable grater
Ice cream scoop
Kitchen knives
Measuring cups and
   spoons
Cooking utensils

COUNTDOWN

1. Assemble the ingredients and the equipment.
2. Do Steps 1–2 of *Slaw Dancing*.
3. Do Steps 1–3 of *Rhubarb Rhythm*.
4. Do Steps 1–2 of *Rock On By*.
5. Do Steps 1–2 of *Never Missed a Beet*.
6. Do Steps 3–4 of *Rock On By*.
7. Do Step 4 of *Rhubarb Rhythm*.

FRIDAY

Rock On By

1 Rinse and pat dry the fish fillets. Rinse, trim, and chop the chives. Peel, trim, and chunk the cucumber.

2 In a blender, combine the chives, the cucumber, the lemon juice, the sugar, and the sour cream and puree until smooth. Season to taste.

3 Heat the oil in a large skillet and sauté the fillets until they flake easily with a fork, 4 to 5 minutes per side.

4 Place a fillet on each plate and spoon the cucumber sauce over it. Garnish with a dash of paprika.

Never Missed a Beet

1 Drain the beets.

2 Melt the butter in a medium saucepan. Add the beets and the brown sugar, season to taste, and heat through, about 2 minutes. Cover to keep warm.

Slaw Dancing

1 Rinse, trim, quarter, and grate the cabbage. Rinse, trim, seed, and chop the bell pepper. Rinse, trim, and chop the celery. Combine the vegetables in a large bowl.

2 In a small bowl, whisk together the oil, the vinegar, the sugar, and the dill. Season to taste and toss with the salad.

Rhubarb Rhythm

1 Rinse, hull, and slice the strawberries. Rinse, trim, and dice the rhubarb.

2 In a medium saucepan, combine the rhubarb, the sugar, and the water and cook until the rhubarb is soft, 7 to 8 minutes.

3 Remove from the heat and stir in the strawberries, the vanilla, and the cinnamon. Cover to keep warm.

4 Place scoops of ice cream in individual dessert bowls and top with the warm sauce.

WEEK FIVE

WEEK AT A GLANCE

Monday
Flying Solo
Potato Puffs
Field of Greens
Bumpy Landing

Tuesday
Princeton Pasta
Garden of Eatin'
Boardwalk Bread
Jersey Bounce

Wednesday
Ginger Chicken
Top Hat Rice
Fred Astairagus
Fascinating Lady

Thursday
Blasé Bisque
In-Your-Face Sandwich
Understated Dessert

Friday
Small Fry
Afternoodle
Pint-Sized Salad
Real Crumby

STAPLES

- ☐ Butter
- ☐ Flour
- ☐ Cornstarch
- ☐ Granulated sugar
- ☐ Dark brown sugar
- ☐ Olive oil
- ☐ Vegetable oil
- ☐ Red wine vinegar
- ☐ Lemon juice
- ☐ Lime juice
- ☐ Dijon mustard
- ☐ Mayonnaise
- ☐ Grated Parmesan cheese
- ☐ Chicken bouillon cube
- ☐ Poppy seeds
- ☐ Dried dill
- ☐ Dried rosemary
- ☐ Dried savory
- ☐ Dried tarragon
- ☐ Ground cloves
- ☐ Ground ginger
- ☐ Black pepper
- ☐ Salt
- ☐ Orange extract
- ☐ Vanilla extract

MEAT & POULTRY

4 boneless, skinless chicken breast halves (about 1 1/2 pounds) (W)

FISH

4 sole fillets (about 1 1/2 pounds) (M)

1 1/2 pounds medium shrimp, shelled and deveined (F)

FRESH PRODUCE

VEGETABLES

1 1/2 pounds small new white potatoes (M)

1 large bunch broccoli (T)

1 pound green beans (M)

1 pound asparagus (W)

2 small Japanese eggplants (T)

1 small carrot (W)

2 stalks celery (M)

2 stalks celery (T)

1 stalk celery (Th)

1/2 pound mushrooms (F)

1 medium head green leaf lettuce (T)

1 medium head lettuce (F)

1 small head lettuce (Th)

2 large tomatoes (Th)

1 medium tomato (M)

2 medium tomatoes (T)

1 large ripe avocado (F)

1 medium cucumber (F)

1 medium red bell pepper (F)

1 medium red onion (T)

1 small shallot (M)

2 scallions (green onions) (T)

2 scallions (green onions) (Th)

2 scallions (green onions) (F)

2 cloves garlic (T)

1 clove garlic (F)

HERBS

3 tablespoons basil leaves (when chopped) (T)

1/4 cup chives (when chopped) (W)

2 tablespoons chives (when chopped) (F)

4 mint sprigs for garnish (Th)

2 tablespoons parsley (when chopped) (M)

2 tablespoons parsley (when chopped) (W)

3 tablespoons parsley (when chopped) (Th)

FRUIT

2 medium oranges (Th)

1 medium banana (M)

2 large ripe nectarines (W)

1 pint blackberries (M)

1 pint blueberries (T)

1 pint strawberries (Th)

CANS, JARS & BOTTLES

SOUPS

1 can (14 ounces) chicken broth (W)

1 can (14 ounces) chicken broth (Th)

1 can (10 1/2 ounces) onion soup (F)

VEGETABLES

1 can (28 ounces) stewed tomatoes (T)

1 jar (7 ounces) roasted red peppers (M)

1 jar (4 ounces) sliced pimientos (Th)

CONDIMENTS

1 jar (6 1/2 ounces) marinated artichoke hearts (F)

DESSERT & BAKING NEEDS

1/4 cup marshmallow crème for garnish (M)

1 jar (12 ounces) butterscotch topping (W)

PACKAGED GOODS

PASTA, RICE & GRAINS

1 pound linguini (T)

8 ounces broad egg noodles (F)

1 cup brown rice (W)

BAKED GOODS

1 loaf peasant bread (T)

12 slices sourdough bread (Th)

1 package (3 ounces) ladyfingers (W)

1 package (10 ounces) Oreo cookies (F)

DESSERT & BAKING NEEDS

1 package (3 ounces) raspberry gelatin (M)

1 package (3.4 ounces) instant cheesecake pudding mix (T)

6 ounces chocolate chips (F)

WINE & SPIRITS

1/4 cup dry white wine (Th)

1/4 cup dry white wine (F)

REFRIGERATED PRODUCTS

DAIRY

2 cups milk (T)

1 1/4 cups milk (Th)

1/4 cup milk (F)

Whipped cream for garnish (T)

Whipped cream for garnish (W)

2 eggs (T)

4 eggs (Th)

CHEESE

1/2 cup shredded Colby/Monterey Jack cheese (T)

4 slices Swiss cheese (Th)

JUICES

5 tablespoons orange juice (Th)

DELI

1/2 pound thinly sliced ham (Th)

1/2 pound thinly sliced turkey (Th)

FROZEN GOODS

VEGETABLES

1 package (10 ounces) green peas (T)

DESSERTS

1 pint vanilla ice cream (W)

1 pint chocolate chip ice cream (F)

MONDAY

Flying Solo

1 medium tomato
1 small shallot
4 sole fillets (about 1 1/2 pounds)
1 jar (7 ounces) roasted red peppers
2 tablespoons vegetable oil
2 teaspoons dried dill
Seasoning to taste

Potato Puffs

2 tablespoons fresh parsley (when chopped)
1 1/2 pounds small new white potatoes
1 teaspoon dark brown sugar
2 tablespoons butter

Field of Greens

1 pound fresh green beans
2 stalks celery
1 tablespoon butter
1/4 teaspoon ground cloves
1/4 teaspoon granulated sugar

Bumpy Landing

1 1/4 cups water
1 pint fresh blackberries
1 medium banana
1 package (3 ounces) raspberry gelatin
Ice cubes
1/4 cup marshmallow crème for garnish

EQUIPMENT

Blender	Steamer insert
Large covered saucepan	Vegetable brush
	Kitchen knives
Medium covered saucepan	Measuring cups and spoons
Large skillet	Cooking utensils

COUNTDOWN

1. Assemble the ingredients and the equipment.
2. Do Steps 1–3 of *Bumpy Landing*.
3. Do Steps 1–2 of *Potato Puffs*.
4. Do Step 1 of *Flying Solo*.
5. Do Steps 1–3 of *Field of Greens*.
6. Do Step 2 of *Flying Solo*.
7. Do Step 3 of *Potato Puffs*.
8. Do Step 4 of *Field of Greens*.
9. Do Step 4 of *Bumpy Landing*.

MONDAY

Flying Solo

1 Rinse, stem, and chop the tomato. Peel and chop the shallot. Rinse and pat dry the fish fillets. Drain and chop the roasted peppers.

2 Heat the oil in a large skillet and sauté the shallot for 1 minute. Add the tomato and sauté for 2 minutes. Add the fish, the roasted peppers, and the dill. Cook the fish until it flakes easily with a fork, 3 to 4 minutes per side. Season to taste.

Potato Puffs

1 Rinse, stem, and chop the parsley. Scrub and quarter the potatoes.

2 Place the potatoes and the brown sugar in a large saucepan and cover with water. Bring to a boil, cover, and cook until tender, about 10 minutes.

3 Drain the potatoes and return them to the saucepan. Toss with the butter and the parsley and cover to keep warm.

Field of Greens

1 Bring water to a boil in a medium saucepan.

2 Rinse and trim the green beans. Rinse and trim the celery and cut into thin strips the same length as the beans.

3 Arrange the beans and the celery in a steamer insert. Place the insert in the saucepan, cover, and cook until the vegetables are crisp-tender, about 8 minutes.

4 Drain the beans and celery. Return the vegetables to the saucepan and toss with the butter, the cloves, and the sugar. Cover to keep warm.

Bumpy Landing

1 Bring ¾ cup of the water to a boil.

2 Rinse the blackberries and peel and slice the banana. Place the fruit in individual dessert glasses.

3 Pour the boiling water into a blender. Add the gelatin. Cover and blend until the gelatin is dissolved, about 30 seconds. Combine the remaining ½ cup water with enough ice cubes to make 1¼ cups. Add to the blender, stir until the ice is partially melted, then blend at high speed for 30 seconds. Pour the mixture over the fruit. Refrigerate until you are ready to serve.

4 Garnish with the marshmallow crème.

TUESDAY

Princeton Pasta

2 cloves garlic
3 tablespoons fresh basil leaves \(when chopped)
2 medium tomatoes
2 small Japanese eggplants
2 tablespoons olive oil
1 can (28 ounces) stewed tomatoes
Seasoning to taste
1 pound linguini
1/2 cup shredded Colby/Monterey Jack cheese

Garden of Eatin'

1 package (10 ounces) frozen green peas
2 eggs
1 large bunch broccoli
1 medium red onion
2 stalks celery
1 medium head green leaf lettuce
1/2 cup mayonnaise
2 teaspoons Dijon mustard
2 tablespoons lemon juice
1/2 teaspoon dried savory
Seasoning to taste

Boardwalk Bread

3 tablespoons butter
2 scallions (green onions)
1 loaf peasant bread
1/4 cup grated Parmesan cheese

Jersey Bounce

1 package (3.4 ounces) instant cheesecake pudding mix
2 cups milk
1 pint fresh blueberries
Whipped cream for garnish

EQUIPMENT

Electric mixer
Stockpot
Medium saucepan
Small saucepan
Large covered skillet
Baking sheet
Colander
Large mixing bowl

Medium mixing bowl
2 small mixing bowls
Whisk
Pastry brush
Kitchen knives
Measuring cups and spoons
Cooking utensils

COUNTDOWN

1. Assemble the ingredients and the equipment.
2. Do Steps 1–2 of *Garden of Eatin'*.
3. Do Steps 1–3 of *Jersey Bounce*.
4. Do Step 1 of *Boardwalk Bread*.
5. Do Steps 3–10 of *Garden of Eatin'*.
6. Do Steps 1–3 of *Princeton Pasta*.
7. Do Steps 2–4 of *Boardwalk Bread*.
8. Do Steps 4–5 of *Princeton Pasta*.
9. Do Step 4 of *Jersey Bounce*.

TUESDAY

Princeton Pasta

1 Bring water to a boil in a stockpot.

2 Peel and mince the garlic. Rinse, stem, and chop the basil. Rinse, stem, and chop the fresh tomatoes. Rinse, trim, and thinly slice the eggplants.

3 Heat the oil in a large skillet. Add the garlic and sauté for 1 minute. Add the fresh tomatoes and the eggplants and sauté for 3 minutes. Add the canned tomatoes and the basil. Season to taste, cover, and reduce the heat. Simmer until heated through, about 5 minutes.

4 Cook the linguini until it is almost tender, 2 to 3 minutes if you are using fresh pasta, 6 to 7 minutes if you are using dry pasta.

5 Drain the linguini and toss with the sauce. Sprinkle with the cheese.

Garden of Eatin'

1 Set the peas in a small bowl of warm water to thaw.

2 In a small saucepan, cover the eggs with water. Bring the water to a boil and hard-cook the eggs, 10 to 12 minutes.

3 Drain the eggs and place them in the freezer to chill for 10 minutes.

4 Rinse and trim the broccoli discarding the tough ends, and cut into bite-sized florets. Peel and thinly slice the onion. Rinse, trim, and chop the celery. Wash and dry the lettuce and tear it into bite-sized pieces.

5 Bring water to a boil in a medium saucepan.

6 Cook the broccoli until it is crisp-tender, about 5 minutes.

7 Drain the broccoli and rinse it in cold water.

8 Combine the broccoli, the onion, the celery, the lettuce, and the peas in a large bowl.

9 In a small bowl, whisk together the mayonnaise, the mustard, the lemon juice, and the savory. Season to taste and toss with the salad.

10 Peel and slice the eggs and arrange them on top of the salad.

Boardwalk Bread

1 Melt the butter. Rinse, trim, and chop the scallions.

2 Preheat the broiler.

3 Cut the bread into thick slices and place the slices on a baking sheet. Brush the slices with the melted butter, sprinkle with the scallions, and top with the cheese.

4 Broil until bubbly, about 2 minutes.

Jersey Bounce

1 In a medium bowl, beat the pudding mix and the milk until well blended.

2 Rinse and dry the blueberries.

3 Layer the blueberries and the pudding in individual dessert glasses, reserving several blueberries for garnish. Refrigerate until you are ready to serve.

4 Top each parfait with a dollop of whipped cream and the reserved blueberries.

WEDNESDAY

Ginger Chicken

4 boneless, skinless chicken breast halves
 (about 1 1/2 pounds)
1/4 cup fresh chives (when chopped)
2 large ripe nectarines
1 1/2 teaspoons ground ginger
2 tablespoons vegetable oil
1 cup plus 2 tablespoons water
1 chicken bouillon cube
2 teaspoons cornstarch
1 teaspoon dark brown sugar
Seasoning to taste

Top Hat Rice

2 tablespoons fresh parsley (when
 chopped)
1 small carrot
2 tablespoons butter
1 cup brown rice
1 can (14 ounces) chicken broth
1/4 cup water

Fred Astairagus

1 teaspoon dried rosemary
1 pound fresh asparagus
1 tablespoon butter

Fascinating Lady

1 pint vanilla ice cream
1 package (3 ounces) ladyfingers
1 jar (12 ounces) butterscotch topping
Whipped cream for garnish

EQUIPMENT

Medium covered
 saucepan
Large covered skillet
Large skillet
9 x 9-inch glass
 baking dish
Whisk

Vegetable peeler
Vegetable grater
Plastic wrap
Kitchen knives
Measuring cups and
 spoons
Cooking utensils

COUNTDOWN

1. Assemble the ingredients and the
 equipment.
2. Do Step 1 of *Fascinating Lady*.
3. Do Steps 1–2 of *Top Hat Rice*.
4. Do Step 2 of *Fascinating Lady*.
5. Do Steps 1–3 of *Ginger Chicken*.
6. Do Steps 1–2 of *Fred Astairagus*.
7. Do Step 4 of *Ginger Chicken*.
8. Do Step 3 of *Fred Astairagus*.
9. Do Step 3 of *Top Hat Rice*.
10. Do Step 3 of *Fascinating Lady*.

WEDNESDAY

Ginger Chicken

1 Rinse and pat dry the chicken breasts. Rinse, trim, and chop the chives. Rinse, halve, pit, and slice the nectarines.

2 Sprinkle the ginger around a large skillet and heat for 1 minute. Add the oil and stir to combine. Add the chicken, turning to coat, and sauté until the pieces are opaque, about 4 minutes per side. Remove the chicken and cover to keep warm.

3 Add 1 cup of the water and the bouillon cube to the skillet and bring the mixture to a boil. Combine the cornstarch with the remaining 2 tablespoons water and add to the skillet. Blend in the brown sugar. Return the chicken and simmer until cooked through, about 15 minutes.

4 Add the nectarines to the skillet, turning to coat, and simmer until the liquid is reduced and slightly thickened, about 2 minutes. Season to taste and top with the chives.

Top Hat Rice

1 Rinse, stem, and chop the parsley. Peel, trim, and grate the carrot.

2 Melt the butter in a medium saucepan. Add the carrot and sauté for 2 minutes. Add the rice, stirring to combine. Add the broth and the water and bring to a boil. Cover, reduce the heat, and simmer until the liquid is absorbed and the rice is tender, about 40 minutes.

3 Fold in the parsley. Fluff with a fork.

Fred Astairagus

1 Bring a small amount of water and the rosemary to a boil in a large skillet.

2 Rinse the asparagus and remove the tough ends. Place the spears in the boiling water, cover, and steam until crisp-tender, 5 to 8 minutes, depending on thickness.

3 Drain the asparagus, return it to the skillet, and toss with the butter.

Fascinating Lady

1 Set the ice cream out to soften.

2 Separate the ladyfingers. Line a 9 x 9-inch baking dish with ladyfinger halves. Spread half of the softened ice cream over the ladyfingers. Add another layer of ladyfingers and top with the remaining ice cream. Cover with plastic wrap and place in the freezer until you are ready to serve.

3 Spoon the butterscotch topping over the ice cream and garnish with dollops of whipped cream.

THURSDAY

Blasé Bisque

3 tablespoons fresh parsley (when chopped)
1 jar (4 ounces) sliced pimientos
1 can (14 ounces) chicken broth
3 tablespoons butter
3 tablespoons flour
1 1/4 cups milk
1/4 cup dry white wine
Seasoning to taste

Understated Dessert

1 pint fresh strawberries
2 medium oranges
2 tablespoons granulated sugar
5 tablespoons orange juice
3 tablespoons lime juice
1 teaspoon orange extract
4 fresh mint sprigs for garnish

In-Your-Face Sandwich

4 eggs
1 small head lettuce
1 stalk celery
2 scallions (green onions)
2 large tomatoes
6 tablespoons mayonnaise
1/4 teaspoon lemon juice
1/4 teaspoon dried tarragon
Seasoning to taste
2 teaspoons Dijon mustard
12 slices sourdough bread
1/2 pound thinly sliced deli ham
4 slices Swiss cheese
1/2 pound thinly sliced deli turkey

EQUIPMENT

Blender
Large saucepan
Small saucepan
Large mixing bowl
Medium mixing bowl
Small mixing bowl
Whisk

Citrus grater
Toothpicks
Plastic wrap
Kitchen knives
Measuring cups and spoons
Cooking utensils

COUNTDOWN

1. Assemble the ingredients and the equipment.
2. Do Steps 1–3 of *Understated Dessert*.
3. Do Steps 1–2 of *Blasé Bisque*.
4. Do Steps 1–6 of *In-Your-Face Sandwich*.
5. Do Step 3 of *Blasé Bisque*.
6. Do Step 7 of *In-Your-Face Sandwich*.
7. Do Step 4 of *Understated Dessert*.

THURSDAY

Blasé Bisque

1 Rinse, stem, and chop the parsley. Drain the pimientos.

2 Place the pimientos and 1 cup of the broth in a blender and puree until smooth.

3 Melt the butter in a large saucepan. Blend in the flour. Add the pimiento mixture and blend well. Stir in the remaining broth. Gradually blend in the milk and the wine. Season to taste and simmer until heated through, about 5 minutes. Do not let boil. Garnish with the parsley.

In-Your-Face Sandwich

1 In a small saucepan, cover the eggs with water. Bring the water to a boil and hard-cook the eggs, 10 to 12 minutes.

2 Wash and dry the lettuce and separate it into leaves. Rinse, trim, and chop the celery. Rinse, trim, and chop the scallions. Rinse, stem, and cut the tomatoes into 8 slices.

3 Drain the eggs and place them in the freezer for 10 minutes.

4 Peel and chop the eggs and place them in a medium bowl. Add the celery and the scallions, 2 tablespoons of the mayonnaise, the lemon juice, and the tarragon. Season to taste and blend well.

5 In a small bowl, combine the remaining 4 tablespoons mayonnaise with the mustard.

6 Toast the bread.

7 Spread 4 slices of the toast with the mayonnaise mixture. Layer with a lettuce leaf, slices of ham, slices of cheese, slices of turkey, and a slice of tomato. Add a second slice of toast and spread with more of the mayonnaise mixture. Layer with another lettuce leaf, the egg salad, and the remaining tomato slices. Spread the remaining toast with the remaining mayonnaise mixture and place over the sandwiches. Cut the sandwiches in half diagonally and secure with toothpicks.

Understated Dessert

1 Rinse, hull, and slice the strawberries, reserving 4 whole berries for garnish.

2 Grate 1 tablespoon of the orange peel. Peel and section the oranges.

3 In a large bowl, combine the strawberries, the orange sections, the orange peel, the sugar, the orange juice, the lime juice, and the orange extract. Toss to blend. Cover with plastic wrap and refrigerate until you are ready to serve.

4 Spoon the fruit into individual dessert dishes and top with a whole strawberry and a sprig of mint for garnish.

FRIDAY

Small Fry

1 clove garlic
1/2 pound fresh mushrooms
1 medium red bell pepper
2 tablespoons fresh chives (when chopped)
1 1/2 pounds medium shrimp, shelled and deveined
1 jar (6 1/2 ounces) marinated artichoke hearts
1/4 cup dry white wine
3 tablespoons lemon juice
2 teaspoons butter
Seasoning to taste

Afternoodle

2 quarts water
1 can (10 1/2 ounces) onion soup
8 ounces broad egg noodles
2 tablespoons butter

Pint-Sized Salad

1 medium head lettuce
1 medium cucumber
1 large ripe avocado
2 scallions (green onions)
3 tablespoons olive oil
2 tablespoons red wine vinegar
1/2 teaspoon poppy seeds
Seasoning to taste

Real Crumby

1 package (10 ounces) Oreo cookies
6 ounces chocolate chips
1/4 cup milk
1 teaspoon vanilla extract
1 pint chocolate chip ice cream

EQUIPMENT

Wok	Mallet
Large saucepan	Plastic bag
Small saucepan	Ice cream scoop
Colander	Kitchen knives
Small mixing bowl	Measuring cups and spoons
Whisk	Cooking utensils
Vegetable peeler	

COUNTDOWN

1. Assemble the ingredients and the equipment.
2. Do Steps 1–2 of *Real Crumby*.
3. Do Step 1 of *Small Fry*.
4. Do Step 1 of *Afternoodle*.
5. Do Steps 1–2 of *Pint-Sized Salad*.
6. Do Step 2 of *Afternoodle*.
7. Do Step 2 of *Small Fry*.
8. Do Step 3 of *Afternoodle*.
9. Do Step 3 of *Pint-Sized Salad*.
10. Do Step 3 of *Real Crumby*.

FRIDAY

Small Fry

1 Peel and mince the garlic. Rinse, pat dry, trim, and thinly slice the mushrooms. Rinse, trim, seed, and slice the bell pepper. Rinse, trim, and chop the chives. Rinse and pat dry the shrimp. Drain the artichoke hearts, reserving the marinade.

2 Heat the reserved marinade in a wok. Add the garlic and stir-fry until golden, about 4 minutes. Add the mushrooms, tossing to coat, and stir-fry for 1 minute. Add the bell pepper and the artichoke hearts and stir-fry for 2 minutes. Add the shrimp and stir-fry until they turn bright pink, about 3 minutes. Add the wine and the lemon juice and simmer for 1 minute. Add the butter and the chives and season to taste.

Afternoodle

1 Bring the water and the soup to a boil in a large saucepan.

2 Cook the noodles in the soup mixture until they are almost tender, 6 to 7 minutes.

3 Drain, toss with the butter, and cover to keep warm.

Pint-Sized Salad

1 Wash and dry the lettuce and arrange the leaves on individual salad plates. Peel, trim, and slice the cucumber and arrange the slices over the lettuce. Halve, pit, peel, and slice the avocado and arrange the slices over the cucumber. Rinse, trim, and chop the scallions and sprinkle them over the salad.

2 In a small bowl, whisk together the oil, the vinegar, and the poppy seeds. Season to taste.

3 Drizzle the dressing over the salad.

Real Crumby

1 Place the cookies in a plastic bag and tap with a mallet until lightly crushed. Distribute half the crushed cookies among individual dessert glasses.

2 In a small saucepan, melt the chocolate chips with the milk and the vanilla, blending until smooth, about 5 minutes. Set aside.

3 Place scoops of ice cream over the crushed cookies, spoon the sauce over the ice cream, and top with the remaining cookie crumbs.

WEEK SIX

WEEK AT A GLANCE

Monday
Popeye Pasta
Olive Oyl Salad
Wimpy Bread
Bluto Brownies

Tuesday
Beef It Up
Rollovers
Mocha Tapioca

Wednesday
Errol Fin
The Prince and the Pilaf
Squashbuckler Salad
Douglas Pearbanks

Thursday
Loup Soup
The Salad Platte
Cornhuskers
Sand Hills

Friday
Macaroni Mumble
Humble Salad
Bumble Bread
Blackberry Grumble

STAPLES

- ☐ Butter
- ☐ Flour
- ☐ Bisquick
- ☐ Yellow cornmeal
- ☐ Baking powder
- ☐ Cornstarch
- ☐ Cream of tartar
- ☐ Granulated sugar
- ☐ Dark brown sugar
- ☐ Cocoa powder
- ☐ Olive oil
- ☐ Sesame oil
- ☐ Vegetable oil
- ☐ Red wine vinegar
- ☐ Rice vinegar
- ☐ Tarragon vinegar
- ☐ White wine vinegar
- ☐ Lemon juice
- ☐ Dijon mustard
- ☐ Honey
- ☐ Ketchup
- ☐ Steak sauce
- ☐ White Worcestershire sauce
- ☐ Grated Parmesan cheese
- ☐ Instant coffee
- ☐ Sesame seeds
- ☐ Dried basil
- ☐ Bay leaf
- ☐ Dried savory
- ☐ Ground allspice
- ☐ Ground cloves
- ☐ Cayenne pepper
- ☐ Dry mustard
- ☐ Ground nutmeg
- ☐ Paprika
- ☐ Black pepper
- ☐ Red pepper flakes
- ☐ Salt
- ☐ Lemon extract
- ☐ Vanilla extract

MEAT & POULTRY

1 1/2 pounds lean ground beef (T)

1 1/2 pounds boneless, skinless chicken breast (Th)

FISH

4 flounder or other firm white fish fillets (about 1 1/2 pounds) (W)

FRESH PRODUCE

VEGETABLES

1 1/2 pounds new red potatoes (T)

1 small bunch broccoli (F)

1 medium parsnip (T)

1 medium yellow zucchini (F)

2 medium zucchini (F)

1 small zucchini (W)

3 medium carrots (T)

1 medium carrot (F)

3 stalks celery (T)

5 large mushrooms (Th)

1 package (12 ounces) spinach (M)

1 medium head lettuce (M)

1 medium head lettuce (W)

1 small head lettuce (Th)

1 small head radicchio (Th)

4 large tomatoes (F)

3 medium tomatoes (M)

2 medium ripe avocados (Th)

2 small ripe avocados (M)

1 medium cucumber (Th)

1 large yellow bell pepper (T)

1 medium green bell pepper (W)

1 small bunch radishes (W)

1 small onion (W)

1 medium red onion (M)

1 medium red onion (F)

2 cloves garlic (M)

1 clove garlic (T)

1 clove garlic (F)

HERBS

1/2 cup chives (when chopped) (F)

1 small bunch cilantro (M)

2 tablespoons parsley (when chopped) (W)

2 tablespoons parsley (when chopped) (F)

FRUIT

1 large orange (Th)

1 small lemon (Th)

2 medium ripe pears (W)

3 pints blackberries (F)

CANS, JARS & BOTTLES

SOUPS

1 can (14 ounces) chicken broth (W)

2 cans (14 ounces each) chicken broth (Th)

1 can (10 1/2 ounces) beef broth (T)

1 can (10 1/2 ounces) beef consommé (Th)

VEGETABLES

1 can (11 ounces) whole-kernel corn (Th)

FRUIT

1 can (11 ounces) mandarin oranges (Th)

1 can (8 ounces) pineapple chunks (Th)

JUICES

1 can (12 ounces) pear nectar (W)

CONDIMENTS

2 tablespoons sweet pickle relish (W)

DESSERT & BAKING NEEDS

1/4 cup marshmallow crème for garnish (Th)

PACKAGED GOODS

PASTA, RICE & GRAINS

1 pound spaghetti (M)

4 ounces vermicelli (W)

12 ounces elbow macaroni (F)

1 cup long-grain white rice (W)

BAKED GOODS

2 hamburger buns (M)

1 loaf foccacia (F)

2 cups graham cracker crumbs (Th)

DRIED FRUIT & NUTS

1/2 cup walnut bits (M)

1/4 cup sliced almonds (Th)

DESSERT & BAKING NEEDS

1 package (3.4 ounces) instant lemon pudding mix (W)

1/3 cup instant tapioca (T)

2 squares (1 ounce each) semisweet chocolate (M)

6 ounces chocolate chips (M)

1/3 cup flaked coconut (W)

WINE & SPIRITS

1/3 cup dry white wine (M)

2 tablespoons dry sherry (W)

REFRIGERATED PRODUCTS

DAIRY

2/3 cup milk (T)

2/3 cup milk (Th)

1 cup milk (F)

1/3 cup half-and-half (M)

1 cup half-and-half (T)

Whipped cream for garnish (T)

Whipped cream for garnish (F)

2 eggs (M)

3 eggs (T)

1 egg (Th)

CHEESE

1 container (15 ounces) ricotta cheese (M)

1 container (5 ounces) herbed cream cheese (M)

6 ounces feta cheese (F)

DELI

1/2 pound bacon (M)

FROZEN GOODS

DESSERTS

1 pint butter pecan ice cream (Th)

MONDAY

Popeye Pasta

1/2 pound bacon
1 medium red onion
1 package (12 ounces) fresh spinach
1 small bunch fresh cilantro
1 container (15 ounces) ricotta cheese
1 container (5 ounces) herbed cream
   cheese
1/3 cup half-and-half
1/3 cup dry white wine
Seasoning to taste
1 pound spaghetti
1/2 cup grated Parmesan cheese

Olive Oyl Salad

1 medium head lettuce
3 medium tomatoes
2 small ripe avocados
1 tablespoon lemon juice
3 tablespoons olive oil
2 tablespoons tarragon vinegar
Seasoning to taste

Wimpy Bread

2 cloves garlic
2 tablespoons butter
1/2 teaspoon dry mustard
2 hamburger buns

Bluto Brownies

4 tablespoons butter
2 squares (1 ounce each) semisweet
   chocolate
3/4 cup granulated sugar
2 eggs
1/2 cup flour
1 teaspoon vanilla extract
6 ounces chocolate chips
1/2 cup walnut bits

EQUIPMENT

Stockpot	Small mixing bowl
Large saucepan	Whisk
2 large skillets	Kitchen knives
8 x 8-inch baking pan	Measuring cups and
Colander	spoons
Medium mixing bowl	Cooking utensils

COUNTDOWN

1. Assemble the ingredients and the equipment.
2. Do Steps 1–4 of *Bluto Brownies*.
3. Do Steps 1–3 of *Olive Oyl Salad*.
4. Do Steps 1–3 of *Popeye Pasta*.
5. Do Step 5 of *Bluto Brownies*.
6. Do Steps 4–6 of *Popeye Pasta*.
7. Do Steps 1–3 of *Wimpy Bread*.
8. Do Step 7 of *Popeye Pasta*.
9. Do Step 4 of *Olive Oyl Salad*.

MONDAY

Popeye Pasta

1 Bring water to a boil in a stockpot.

2 Dice the bacon. Peel and chop the onion. Rinse, stem, and chop the spinach. Rinse, stem, and chop the cilantro.

3 Sauté the bacon in a large skillet until almost crisp, about 10 minutes. Drain on paper towels. Reserve 2 tablespoons of the bacon drippings.

4 In a medium bowl, whisk together the ricotta cheese, the cream cheese, and the half-and-half.

5 Add the onion to the bacon drippings and sauté until it begins to soften, about 4 minutes. Add the spinach and sauté for 2 minutes. Add the wine and combine. Stir in the ricotta cheese mixture and heat through, about 3 minutes. Add the cilantro and season to taste. Return the bacon and heat through.

6 Cook the spaghetti until it is almost tender, 6 to 7 minutes.

7 Drain the pasta, toss it with the spinach mixture, and top with the Parmesan cheese.

Olive Oyl Salad

1 Wash and dry the lettuce and tear it into bite-sized pieces. Rinse, stem, and chop the tomatoes. Halve, pit, peel, and slice the avocados and sprinkle them with the lemon juice.

2 Distribute the lettuce among individual salad plates. Mound the tomatoes in the center. Place the avocado slices around the tomatoes.

3 In a small bowl, whisk together the oil and the vinegar. Season to taste.

4 Drizzle the dressing over the salad.

Wimpy Bread

1 Peel and mince the garlic.

2 Melt the butter in a large skillet and sauté the garlic with the mustard for 3 minutes.

3 Split the hamburger buns and toast them in the butter mixture, cut sides down, until golden, about 3 minutes.

Bluto Brownies

1 Preheat the oven to 350°F. Grease an 8 x 8-inch baking pan.

2 Melt the butter with the chocolate in a large saucepan, stirring to blend. Remove from the heat.

3 Gradually add the sugar. Beat in the eggs, one at a time, until well blended. Fold in the flour. Add the vanilla and beat well to combine. Stir in the chocolate chips and the walnut bits.

4 Pour the mixture into the baking pan and bake for 25 minutes. The top should be soft when touched.

5 Remove the brownies from the oven and let them cool before cutting.

TUESDAY

Beef It Up

1 clove garlic
1½ pounds new red potatoes
3 medium carrots
3 stalks celery
1 medium parsnip
1 large yellow bell pepper
2 tablespoons vegetable oil
1½ pounds lean ground beef
1 tablespoon Dijon mustard
2 tablespoons steak sauce
1 can (10½ ounces) beef broth
1 bay leaf
2 teaspoons ground allspice
¼ teaspoon cayenne pepper
Seasoning to taste

Rollovers

⅔ cup milk
¼ cup honey
2 tablespoons vegetable oil
1 egg
2 cups Bisquick
¼ teaspoon ground nutmeg

Mocha Tapioca

1 cup water
2 tablespoons cocoa powder
2½ tablespoons instant coffee
2 eggs
1 cup half-and-half
⅓ cup plus 2 tablespoons granulated sugar
⅓ cup instant tapioca
½ teaspoon cream of tartar
Whipped cream for garnish

EQUIPMENT

Electric mixer
Dutch oven
2 medium saucepans
Small saucepan
Muffin tin
2 medium mixing
  bowls

Vegetable brush
Vegetable peeler
Kitchen knives
Measuring cups and
  spoons
Cooking utensils

COUNTDOWN

1. Assemble the ingredients and the equipment.
2. Do Steps 1–6 of *Mocha Tapioca*.
3. Do Steps 1–2 of *Beef It Up*.
4. Do Steps 1–3 of *Rollovers*.
5. Do Step 3 of *Beef It Up*.
6. Do Step 7 of *Mocha Tapioca*.

TUESDAY

Beef It Up

1 Peel and mince the garlic. Scrub and cube the potatoes. Peel, trim, and slice the carrots. Rinse, trim, and chop the celery. Peel, trim, and cube the parsnip. Rinse, trim, seed, and chop the bell pepper.

2 Heat the oil in a Dutch oven. Add the garlic and sauté for 1 minute. Add the beef and sauté until it begins to brown, about 5 minutes. Stir in the mustard, the steak sauce, and the broth. Add the potatoes, the bay leaf, and the allspice. Cover, reduce the heat, and simmer for 15 minutes.

3 Add the cayenne pepper, the carrots, the celery, the parsnip, and the bell pepper. Season to taste and cook until the vegetables are crisp-tender, about 10 minutes. Remove the bay leaf before serving.

Rollovers

1 Preheat the oven to 400°F. Grease a muffin tin.

2 Combine the milk, the honey, the oil, and the egg in a medium bowl. Blend in the Bisquick and the nutmeg. Spoon the batter into the muffin cups.

3 Bake until golden, about 15 minutes.

Mocha Tapioca

1 Bring the water to a boil in a small saucepan. Add the cocoa powder and 2 tablespoons of the instant coffee and let stand to dissolve.

2 Separate the eggs, placing the egg whites in a medium bowl.

3 In a medium saucepan, combine the egg yolks, the half-and-half, ⅓ cup of the sugar, and the tapioca. Let stand for 5 minutes.

4 Beat the egg whites with the cream of tartar until frothy, about 2 minutes. Fold in the remaining 2 tablespoons sugar and beat until the egg whites are stiff and glossy, about 2 minutes more.

5 Add the coffee mixture to the tapioca and blend to combine. Bring to a boil, stirring, and cook for 1 minute. Remove from the heat.

6 Slowly pour the tapioca mixture into the egg whites and fold to combine. Spoon into individual dessert dishes and set aside.

7 Top each serving with a dollop of whipped cream and sprinkle with the reserved ½ tablespoon instant coffee.

WEDNESDAY

Errol Fin

4 flounder or other firm white fish fillets (about 1 1/2 pounds)
2 tablespoons fresh parsley (when chopped)
2 tablespoons dark brown sugar
1 tablespoon cornstarch
2/3 cup water
3 tablespoons ketchup
1 tablespoon rice vinegar
2 tablespoons sweet pickle relish
2 tablespoons vegetable oil
Seasoning to taste

The Prince and the Pilaf

1 small onion
3 tablespoons butter
4 ounces vermicelli
1 cup long-grain white rice
1 can (14 ounces) chicken broth
1/4 cup water
2 tablespoons dry sherry
Seasoning to taste
1/4 teaspoon ground cloves

Squashbuckler Salad

2 tablespoons sesame seeds
1 medium head lettuce
1 medium green bell pepper
1 small zucchini
1 small bunch radishes
3 tablespoons vegetable oil
2 tablespoons white wine vinegar
1/8 teaspoon red pepper flakes
Seasoning to taste

Douglas Pearbanks

2 medium ripe pears
1 tablespoon lemon juice
2 tablespoons butter
1/4 cup dark brown sugar
1/3 cup flaked coconut
1 package (3.4 ounces) instant lemon pudding mix
1 can (12 ounces) pear nectar

EQUIPMENT

Electric mixer
Medium covered saucepan
2 small saucepans
Large skillet
Small skillet
Large mixing bowl
Medium mixing bowl
2 small mixing bowls
Whisk
Vegetable brush
Kitchen knives
Measuring cups and spoons
Cooking utensils

COUNTDOWN

1. Assemble the ingredients and the equipment.
2. Do Steps 1–4 of *Douglas Pearbanks*.
3. Do Steps 1–3 of *Squashbuckler Salad*.
4. Do Steps 1–3 of *The Prince and the Pilaf*.
5. Do Steps 1–3 of *Errol Fin*.
6. Do Step 4 of *Squashbuckler Salad*.
7. Do Step 4 of *The Prince and the Pilaf*.
8. Do Step 4 of *Errol Fin*.
9. Do Step 5 of *The Prince and the Pilaf*.

WEDNESDAY

Errol Fin

1 Rinse and pat dry the fish fillets. Rinse, stem, and chop the parsley.

2 In a small saucepan, combine the brown sugar, the cornstarch, and the water and mix well. Blend in the ketchup and the vinegar. Cook the mixture until it begins to thicken slightly and is clear, about 2 minutes. Remove from the heat and stir in the pickle relish. Set aside.

3 Heat the oil in a large skillet. Sauté the fish, turning once, until it flakes easily with a fork, about 5 minutes per side.

4 Season to taste, top with the sauce, and sprinkle with the parsley.

The Prince and the Pilaf

1 Peel and chop the onion.

2 Melt the butter in a medium saucepan and sauté the onion for 3 minutes. Break the vermicelli into small pieces and sauté it for 1 minute. Add the rice and sauté until lightly golden, about 2 minutes.

3 Add the broth, the water, and the sherry and season to taste. Bring to a boil, cover, reduce the heat, and simmer until all the liquid is absorbed and the rice is tender, about 20 minutes.

4 Remove from the heat. Fold in the cloves and let stand, covered, for 5 minutes more.

5 Fluff with a fork.

Squashbuckler Salad

1 Place the sesame seeds in a small skillet and brown lightly, about 2 minutes, shaking the pan to cook evenly. Remove and set aside.

2 Wash and dry the lettuce and tear it into bite-sized pieces. Rinse, trim, seed, and slice the bell pepper into thin strips. Scrub, trim, and slice the zucchini. Rinse, trim, and slice the radishes. Combine the ingredients in a large bowl.

3 In a small bowl, combine the oil, the vinegar, and the pepper flakes. Season to taste.

4 Toss the salad with the dressing and sprinkle with the sesame seeds.

Douglas Pearbanks

1 Peel, core, and chop the pears. Place in a small bowl and sprinkle with the lemon juice.

2 Melt the butter in a small saucepan. Add the brown sugar and the coconut. Bring the mixture to a boil, stirring to blend. Remove from the heat.

3 In a medium bowl, beat the pudding mix and the nectar until well blended, about 2 minutes.

4 Spoon half of the pears into individual dessert glasses. Add a layer of the pudding, then a sprinkle of the coconut mixture. Add the remaining pudding and the remaining coconut mixture and top with the remaining pears. Refrigerate until you are ready to serve.

THURSDAY

Loup Soup

5 large fresh mushrooms
1 small lemon
2 cans (14 ounces each) chicken broth
1 can (10$\frac{1}{2}$ ounces) beef consommé
$\frac{1}{4}$ teaspoon sesame oil
1 teaspoon granulated sugar
Seasoning to taste

The Salad Platte

1$\frac{1}{2}$ pounds boneless, skinless chicken breast
1 small head lettuce
1 small head radicchio
1 medium cucumber
2 medium ripe avocados
1 large orange
1 can (11 ounces) mandarin oranges
1 can (8 ounces) pineapple chunks
1 teaspoon granulated sugar
3 tablespoons red wine vinegar
Seasoning to taste
$\frac{1}{4}$ cup sliced almonds

Cornhuskers

1 can (11 ounces) whole-kernel corn
$\frac{2}{3}$ cup milk
2 tablespoons vegetable oil
1 egg
1$\frac{1}{2}$ cups Bisquick
$\frac{3}{4}$ cup yellow cornmeal
$\frac{1}{4}$ teaspoon dried savory

Sand Hills

1 pint butter pecan ice cream
2 cups graham cracker crumbs
$\frac{1}{4}$ cup marshmallow crème for garnish

EQUIPMENT

Large saucepan
Medium saucepan
Muffin tin
Large mixing bowl
Medium mixing bowl
Small mixing bowl
Whisk
Vegetable peeler

Citrus grater
Citrus juicer
Ice cream scoop
Kitchen knives
Measuring cups and spoons
Cooking utensils

COUNTDOWN

1. Assemble the ingredients and the equipment.
2. Do Steps 1–2 of *The Salad Platte*.
3. Do Steps 1–5 of *Cornhuskers*.
4. Do Steps 3–6 of *The Salad Platte*.
5. Do Steps 1–3 of *Loup Soup*.
6. Do Step 7 of *The Salad Platte*.
7. Do Steps 1–3 of *Sand Hills*.

THURSDAY

Loup Soup

1 Rinse, pat dry, trim, and thinly slice the mushrooms. Juice half of the lemon. Thinly slice the other half.

2 In a large saucepan, combine the broth and the consommé. Bring just to a boil. Add the lemon juice, the mushrooms, the sesame oil, and the sugar. Season to taste and blend well. Reduce the heat and simmer until heated through, about 5 minutes.

3 Top each serving with a lemon slice.

The Salad Platte

1 Bring water to a boil in a medium saucepan.

2 Rinse and pat dry the chicken breast and cut into thin strips. Cook the chicken until it is opaque and tender, about 6 minutes.

3 Drain the chicken, rinse under cold water, and place in the refrigerator for 10 minutes.

4 Wash and dry the lettuce and tear it into bite-sized pieces. Wash, dry, and chop the radicchio. Peel, trim, and thinly slice the cucumber. Halve, pit, peel, and slice the avocados. Grate 1 tablespoon of the orange peel and juice the orange. Drain the mandarin oranges. Drain the pineapple.

5 In a large bowl, combine the lettuce, the radicchio, the cucumber, the avocados, the mandarin oranges, and the pineapple.

6 In a small bowl, whisk together the orange juice, the orange peel, the sugar, and the vinegar. Season to taste.

7 Distribute the salad among individual salad plates. Add the chicken and the almonds and spoon the dressing over the top.

Cornhuskers

1 Grease a muffin tin. Drain the corn.

2 In a medium bowl, combine the milk, the oil, and the egg. Fold in the Bisquick, the cornmeal, and the savory. Fold in the corn.

3 Spoon the batter into the muffin cups.

4 Preheat the oven to 400°F.

5 Bake the muffins until golden, 15 to 20 minutes.

Sand Hills

1 Place scoops of ice cream in individual dessert bowls.

2 Cover the ice cream with the graham cracker crumbs, patting lightly to adhere.

3 Top each "hill" with a dollop of marshmallow crème.

FRIDAY

Macaroni Mumble

1 medium red onion
1 clove garlic
2 medium zucchini
1 medium yellow zucchini
1 small bunch broccoli
1 medium carrot
6 ounces feta cheese
12 ounces elbow macaroni
3 tablespoons butter
3 tablespoons olive oil
1/2 teaspoon ground nutmeg
Seasoning to taste

Humble Salad

4 large tomatoes
1/2 cup fresh chives (when chopped)
2 tablespoons fresh parsley (when
   chopped)
3 tablespoons vegetable oil
2 tablespoons white wine vinegar
1/2 teaspoon white Worcestershire sauce
1/2 teaspoon Dijon mustard
Seasoning to taste

Bumble Bread

1 loaf foccacia
2 tablespoons olive oil
1 teaspoon dried basil
1/2 teaspoon paprika

Blackberry Grumble

3 pints fresh blackberries
1 1/4 cups granulated sugar
1/2 cup water
1 tablespoon cornstarch
1 teaspoon lemon juice
1 teaspoon lemon extract
2 cups flour
1 tablespoon baking powder
2 tablespoons butter
1 cup milk
Whipped cream for garnish

EQUIPMENT

Stockpot	Vegetable peeler
Large covered saucepan	Pastry brush
	Pastry blender
Large skillet	Aluminum foil
Colander	Kitchen knives
Medium mixing bowl	Measuring cups and spoons
Small mixing bowl	
Whisk	Cooking utensils

COUNTDOWN

1. Assemble the ingredients and the equipment.
2. Do Steps 1–5 of *Blackberry Grumble*.
3. Do Steps 1–3 of *Humble Salad*.
4. Do Steps 1–2 of *Macaroni Mumble*.
5. Do Step 6 of *Blackberry Grumble*.
6. Do Steps 1–3 of *Bumble Bread*.
7. Do Steps 3–6 of *Macaroni Mumble*.
8. Do Step 4 of *Humble Salad*.
9. Do Step 7 of *Blackberry Grumble*.

FRIDAY

Macaroni Mumble

1 Bring water to a boil in a stockpot.

2 Peel and chop the onion. Peel and mince the garlic. Rinse, trim, and chop the zucchini. Rinse and trim the broccoli, discarding the tough ends, and cut into bite-sized florets. Peel, trim, and slice the carrot. Crumble the cheese.

3 Cook the macaroni until it is almost tender, 8 to 10 minutes.

4 Melt the butter with the oil in a large skillet. Sauté the onion and the garlic for 1 minute. Add the zucchini, the broccoli, and the carrot and sauté until the vegetables are crisp-tender, about 5 minutes.

5 Drain the macaroni and return it to the stockpot.

6 Add the vegetables to the macaroni. Add the cheese and the nutmeg. Season to taste and toss to combine.

Humble Salad

1 Rinse, stem, and slice the tomatoes and arrange the slices on individual salad plates.

2 Rinse, trim, and chop the chives. Rinse, stem, and chop the parsley. Sprinkle both over the tomatoes.

3 In a small bowl, whisk together the oil, the vinegar, the Worcestershire sauce, and the mustard. Season to taste.

4 Drizzle over the tomatoes.

Bumble Bread

1 Preheat the oven to 350°F.

2 Split the foccacia in half lengthwise. Brush both halves with the oil and sprinkle with the basil and the paprika.

3 Wrap the loaf in aluminum foil and heat through, about 10 minutes.

Blackberry Grumble

1 Rinse the berries, removing the stems and any berries that are discolored.

2 In a large saucepan, combine 1 cup of the sugar, the water, the cornstarch, and the lemon juice and stir until dissolved. Add the berries and bring the liquid to a boil. Reduce the heat and simmer for 10 minutes.

3 Blend in the lemon extract.

4 In a medium bowl, combine the flour, the remaining ¼ cup sugar, and the baking powder. Add the butter and cut it in with a pastry blender until it resembles coarse meal. Slowly add the milk. Mix with a fork to form a stiff dough.

5 Drop the dough by spoonfuls onto the simmering berry mixture. Cover and simmer for 15 minutes. Do not peek!

6 Remove the saucepan from the heat and set aside.

7 Spoon the mixture into individual dessert dishes and garnish with dollops of whipped cream.

WEEK SEVEN

WEEK AT A GLANCE

Monday
Galloping Scallops
Posting Potatoes
Cantering Carrots
Toffee Trot

Tuesday
Exactly Right
Specifically Salad
Totally Dessert

Wednesday
Boise Burgers
Corn d'Alene
Pocatatoes
Appaloosas

Thursday
Grill Sergeant
Snappy Salute
No Loafing
At Ease Pudding

Friday
Super Soup
Terrific Tortellini
Scrumptious Scones
First–Class Fruit

STAPLES

- ❑ Butter
- ❑ Flour
- ❑ Baking powder
- ❑ Granulated sugar
- ❑ Dark brown sugar
- ❑ Powdered sugar
- ❑ Chocolate sprinkles
- ❑ Olive oil
- ❑ Vegetable oil
- ❑ Apple cider vinegar
- ❑ Red wine vinegar
- ❑ Rice vinegar
- ❑ Tarragon vinegar
- ❑ Lemon juice
- ❑ Dijon mustard
- ❑ Prepared horseradish
- ❑ Mayonnaise
- ❑ Worcestershire sauce
- ❑ Grated Parmesan cheese
- ❑ Bay leaf
- ❑ Dried dill
- ❑ Dried marjoram
- ❑ Dried tarragon
- ❑ Dried thyme
- ❑ Ground cardamom
- ❑ Ground cinnamon
- ❑ Italian seasoning
- ❑ Lemon-pepper seasoning
- ❑ Ground nutmeg
- ❑ Paprika
- ❑ Black pepper
- ❑ Salt
- ❑ Almond extract
- ❑ Rum extract

MEAT & POULTRY

1 1/2 pounds lean ground beef (W)

FISH

1 1/2 pounds sea scallops (M)
4 salmon steaks (about 1 1/2 pounds) (Th)

FRESH PRODUCE

VEGETABLES

1 1/2 pounds small new red potatoes (M)
1 1/2 pounds baking potatoes (W)
1/2 pound green beans (F)
1 small head cauliflower (F)
1/2 pound sugar-snap peas (Th)
4 whole ears corn (W)
1 pound baby carrots (M)
1 medium carrot (Th)
3 stalks celery (W)
2 stalks celery (F)
1 medium head red cabbage (Th)
1 medium head lettuce (T)
1 medium head lettuce (F)
1 medium cucumber (T)
1 small orange bell pepper (T)
1 small red bell pepper (F)
1 small green chili pepper (M)
1 medium onion (F)
1 small red onion (W)
4 scallions (green onions) (W)
4 scallions (green onions) (F)
2 cloves garlic (T)
2 cloves garlic (Th)
1 clove garlic (F)

HERBS

1/2 cup basil leaves (when chopped) (M)
1/4 cup chives (when chopped) (T)
2 tablespoons parsley (when chopped) (T)

2 tablespoons parsley (when chopped) (Th)

FRUIT

1 small ripe honeydew melon (F)
1/4 small seedless ripe watermelon (F)
2 medium bananas (M)
4 large baking apples (W)
4 ripe apricots (T)
2 medium ripe peaches (T)
4 ripe purple plums (T)
1 pint blueberries (F)

CANS, JARS & BOTTLES

SOUPS

1 can (10 1/2 ounces) chicken broth (M)
1 can (10 1/2 ounces) beef consommé (F)

VEGETABLES

1 can (14 1/2 ounces) diced tomatoes (F)
1 can (4 ounces) sliced mushrooms (F)

SAUCES

1 can (15 ounces) tomato sauce (T)

JUICES

1 can (6 ounces) tomato juice (F)
1 cup white grape juice (F)

SPREADS

1 jar (10 ounces) red currant jelly (T)

CONDIMENTS

1 jar (7 ounces) pitted green olives (T)

DESSERT & BAKING NEEDS

1 jar (12 ounces) toffee topping (M)

PACKAGED GOODS

PASTA, RICE & GRAINS

1 pound tricolor tortellini (F)

BAKED GOODS

1 loaf Italian bread (T)
4 hamburger buns (W)
4 small sourdough baguettes (Th)
1 angel food loaf cake (M)

DRIED FRUIT & NUTS

1 cup golden raisins (Th)
1/4 cup pecan bits (Th)

DESSERT & BAKING NEEDS

1 package (3 ounces) lime gelatin (Th)
2 cups mini-marshmallows (Th)

WINE & SPIRITS

1/2 cup dry white wine (Th)

REFRIGERATED PRODUCTS

DAIRY

1/2 cup buttermilk (F)
1/4 cup half-and-half (M)
1/2 cup sour cream (W)
1/2 cup whipping cream (T)
Whipped cream for garnish (M)
Whipped cream for garnish (Th)
9 eggs (T)
2 eggs (W)
2 eggs (F)

CHEESE

1 cup shredded Cheddar cheese (T)

JUICES

1/2 cup orange juice (F)

DELI

2 sweet pickes (W)

FROZEN GOODS

DESSERTS

1 pint rum raisin yogurt (W)
1 pint lime sherbet (F)

MONDAY

Galloping Scallops

1½ pounds sea scallops
½ cup fresh basil leaves (when chopped)
1 small green chili pepper
4 tablespoons vegetable oil
Seasoning to taste

Posting Potatoes

1½ pounds small new red potatoes
2 tablespoons butter
1 tablespoon flour
¼ cup half-and-half
1 teaspoon dried dill
Seasoning to taste

Cantering Carrots

1 pound baby carrots
1 can (10½ ounces) chicken broth
1 tablespoon butter
2 tablespoons granulated sugar
2 tablespoons apple cider vinegar
Seasoning to taste

Toffee Trot

2 medium bananas
1 angel food loaf cake
1 jar (12 ounces) toffee topping
Whipped cream for garnish
Chocolate sprinkles for garnish

EQUIPMENT

Large covered saucepan	Large mixing bowl
Medium covered saucepan	Vegetable brush
Small saucepan	Kitchen knives
Large skillet	Measuring cups and spoons
	Cooking utensils

COUNTDOWN

1. Assemble the ingredients and the equipment.
2. Do Step 1 of *Posting Potatoes*.
3. Do Steps 1–2 of *Cantering Carrots*.
4. Do Steps 1–2 of *Galloping Scallops*.
5. Do Steps 2–3 of *Posting Potatoes*.
6. Do Step 3 of *Cantering Carrots*.
7. Do Step 3 of *Galloping Scallops*.
8. Do Steps 1–2 of *Toffee Trot*.

MONDAY

Galloping Scallops

1 Rinse and pat dry the scallops. Rinse, stem, and chop the basil. Stem, halve, seed, and remove the vein of the chili pepper and mince.

2 In a large bowl, combine the scallops, the basil, the chili pepper, and 3 tablespoons of the oil.

3 Heat the remaining 1 tablespoon oil in a large skillet. Add the scallops and sauté until cooked through and opaque, 3 to 4 minutes. Add the marinade mixture, season to taste, and toss to heat through, about 2 minutes more.

Posting Potatoes

1 Scrub the potatoes. Place them in a large saucepan and cover with water. Bring the water to a boil and cook until the potatoes are tender, about 20 minutes.

2 Melt the butter in a small saucepan. Stir in the flour and blend. Slowly add the half-and-half, stirring constantly, about 2 minutes. Remove from the heat. Stir in the dill.

3 Drain the potatoes and return them to the saucepan. Toss the potatoes with the sauce, season to taste, and cover to keep warm.

Cantering Carrots

1 Rinse and trim the carrots.

2 In a medium saucepan, bring the broth to a boil. Add the butter, the sugar, and the carrots. Reduce the heat, cover, and simmer until the carrots are crisp-tender, about 10 minutes.

3 Drain the carrots and return them to the saucepan. Toss with the vinegar, season to taste, and cover until you are ready to serve.

Toffee Trot

1 Peel and slice the bananas. Slice the cake into individual servings.

2 Top the cake slices with the bananas and drizzle with the toffee topping. Garnish each serving with a dollop of whipped cream and top with the sprinkles.

TUESDAY

Exactly Right

2 cloves garlic
1/4 cup fresh chives (when chopped)
1 tablespoon vegetable oil
1 can (15 ounces) tomato sauce
9 eggs
1 cup shredded Cheddar cheese
1/2 teaspoon Italian seasoning
1 loaf Italian bread
Seasoning to taste

Specifically Salad

1 medium head lettuce
1 medium cucumber
2 tablespoons fresh parsley (when chopped)
1 small orange bell pepper
1 jar (7 ounces) pitted green olives
3 tablespoons olive oil
2 tablespoons red wine vinegar
1 teaspoon lemon juice
1 teaspoon Dijon mustard
Seasoning to taste

Totally Dessert

4 ripe purple plums
2 medium ripe peaches
4 ripe apricots
1/2 cup whipping cream
2 tablespoons powdered sugar
1 teaspoon almond extract
1 jar (10 ounces) red currant jelly

EQUIPMENT

Electric mixer
Small covered saucepan
Large covered skillet
Large mixing bowl
2 medium mixing bowls
Small mixing bowl

Whisk
Vegetable peeler
Plastic wrap
Kitchen knives
Measuring cups and spoons
Cooking utensils

COUNTDOWN

1. Assemble the ingredients and the equipment.
2. Do Step 1 of *Totally Dessert*.
3. Do Steps 1–2 of *Specifically Salad*.
4. Do Steps 2–4 of *Totally Dessert*.
5. Do Steps 1–6 of *Exactly Right*.
6. Do Step 3 of *Specifically Salad*.
7. Do Step 5 of *Totally Dessert*.

TUESDAY

Exactly Right

1 Peel and mince the garlic. Rinse, trim, and chop the chives.

2 Heat the oil in a large skillet and sauté the garlic for 1 minute. Add the tomato sauce and heat through.

3 Break each egg into the sauce and sprinkle with the cheese and the Italian seasoning. Cover, reduce the heat, and poach until the eggs are set and the cheese has melted, about 5 minutes.

4 Cut the bread into 1-inch-thick slices and lightly toast.

5 Distribute the toast among individual plates.

6 Carefully lift out the eggs and place them on the toast slices. Spoon the sauce over the eggs, season to taste, and sprinkle with the chives.

Specifically Salad

1 Wash and dry the lettuce and tear it into bite-sized pieces. Peel, trim, and chunk the cucumber. Rinse, stem, and chop the parsley. Rinse, trim, seed, and slice the bell pepper. Drain the olives and cut them in half. Combine the ingredients in a large bowl.

2 In a small bowl, whisk together the oil, the vinegar, the lemon juice, and the mustard. Season to taste.

3 Toss the salad with the dressing.

Totally Dessert

1 Chill a medium bowl and the beaters of an electric mixer for 10 minutes.

2 Rinse, halve, pit, and chop the plums. Peel, halve, pit, and chop the peaches. Rinse, halve, pit, and chop the apricots. Combine the fruit in a medium bowl, cover with plastic wrap, and refrigerate until you are ready to use.

3 Whip the cream until soft peaks form, about 2 minutes. Add the powdered sugar and beat until stiff, about 2 minutes longer. Fold in the almond extract. Refrigerate until you are ready to use.

4 Melt the jelly in a small saucepan. Cover and set aside.

5 Spoon half of the whipped cream into the bottom of individual dessert glasses. Top with the fruit. Add the remaining whipped cream. Top each serving with a spoonful of the warm jelly.

WEDNESDAY

Boise Burgers

1 1/2 pounds lean ground beef
Seasoning to taste
1 small red onion
2 tablespoons prepared horseradish
1/2 cup sour cream
1/2 teaspoon lemon-pepper seasoning
4 hamburger buns

Corn d'Alene

2 teaspoons granulated sugar
4 whole fresh ears of corn
2 tablespoons butter
1/4 teaspoon pepper
1/2 teaspoon dried tarragon
Seasoning to taste

Pocatatoes

2 eggs
1 1/2 pounds baking potatoes
4 scallions (green onions)
3 stalks celery
2 sweet pickles
Seasoning to taste
1/2 cup mayonnaise
1 teaspoon Dijon mustard
1 teaspoon granulated sugar
1 teaspoon rice vinegar
1 teaspoon paprika

Appaloosas

4 large baking apples
3 tablespoons butter
3/4 cup dark brown sugar
1/2 teaspoon ground nutmeg
1 teaspoon ground cinnamon
1 teaspoon rum extract
1 pint rum raisin frozen yogurt

EQUIPMENT

2 large saucepans
Small saucepan
Large covered skillet
Large mixing bowl
3 small mixing bowls
Whisk

Vegetable peeler
Ice cream scoop
Kitchen knives
Measuring cups and
  spoons
Cooking utensils

COUNTDOWN

1. Assemble the ingredients and the equipment.
2. Do Step 1 of *Boise Burgers.*
3. Do Steps 1–5 of *Pocatatoes.*
4. Do Steps 1–2 of *Appaloosas.*
5. Do Steps 2–4 of *Boise Burgers.*
6. Do Step 1 of *Corn d'Alene.*
7. Do Steps 6–8 of *Pocatatoes.*
8. Do Steps 5–7 of *Boise Burgers.*
9. Do Steps 2–3 of *Corn d'Alene.*
10. Do Step 3 of *Appaloosas.*

WEDNESDAY

Boise Burgers

1 Prepare the grill or preheat the broiler.

2 Form the ground beef into 4 patties. Season to taste.

3 Peel and slice the onion.

4 In a small bowl, combine the horseradish, the sour cream, and the lemon-pepper seasoning.

5 Grill or broil the hamburgers to taste.

6 Lay the hamburger buns on the coolest part of the grill for 2 minutes to toast while the hamburgers finish cooking.

7 Spread the horseradish mixture over the hamburger buns and place the hamburgers on the buns. Top with the onion slices.

Corn d'Alene

1 Bring water and the sugar to a boil in a large saucepan. Shuck the corn.

2 Cook the corn until crisp-tender, 2 to 3 minutes.

3 In a small bowl, combine the butter with the pepper and the tarragon. Season to taste and spread over the corn.

Pocatatoes

1 Cover the eggs with water in a small saucepan. Bring the water to a boil and hard-cook the eggs, 10 to 12 minutes.

2 Bring water to a boil in a large saucepan.

3 Peel and quarter the potatoes. Rinse, trim, and chop the scallions. Rinse, trim, and chop the celery. Chop the pickles.

4 Cook the potatoes until tender, about 20 minutes.

5 Drain the eggs, rinse them in cold water, and place them in the freezer for 10 minutes.

6 Drain the potatoes, rinse them in cold water, and cube them. Combine the potatoes, the scallions, the celery, and the pickles in a large bowl.

7 Peel and chop one of the eggs and add it to the bowl. Season to taste and refrigerate until you are ready to serve.

8 In a small bowl, combine the mayonnaise, the mustard, the sugar, and the vinegar and toss with the salad. Peel and slice the remaining egg, arrange it on top, and sprinkle with the paprika.

Appaloosas

1 Peel, core, and slice the apples.

2 Melt the butter in a large skillet and sauté the apples until they begin to soften, about 5 minutes. Add the brown sugar, the nutmeg, and the cinnamon and cook until the sugar has melted and the apples are tender, about 5 minutes more. Blend in the rum extract. Cover the skillet, remove it from the heat, and let stand.

3 Place scoops of frozen yogurt in individual dessert dishes and spoon the apple slices over the yogurt.

THURSDAY

Grill Sergeant

4 salmon steaks (about 1 1/2 pounds)
2 tablespoons fresh parsley (when
    chopped)
1/2 cup dry white wine
1/4 cup vegetable oil
2 tablespoons lemon juice
1/2 teaspoon dried thyme
1/2 teaspoon dried marjoram
Seasoning to taste

Snappy Salute

1 medium carrot
1 medium head red cabbage
1/2 pound sugar-snap peas
3 tablespoons butter
1/2 teaspoon ground cardamom
Seasoning to taste

No Loafing

2 cloves garlic
3 tablespoons olive oil
Seasoning to taste
4 small sourdough baguettes

At Ease Pudding

1 1/4 cups water
1 package (3 ounces) lime gelatin
Ice cubes
2 cups mini-marshmallows
1 cup golden raisins
Whipped cream for garnish
1/2 cup pecan bits for garnish

EQUIPMENT

Blender
Large covered skillet
9 x 13-inch glass
    baking dish
Small mixing bowl
Vegetable peeler
Vegetable grater

Pastry brush
Aluminum foil
Kitchen knives
Measuring cups and
    spoons
Cooking utensils

COUNTDOWN

1. Assemble the ingredients and the
   equipment.
2. Do Steps 1–3 of Grill Sergeant.
3. Do Steps 1–4 of At Ease Pudding.
4. Do Step 1 of Snappy Salute.
5. Do Steps 1–3 of No Loafing.
6. Do Step 4 of Grill Sergeant.
7. Do Step 4 of No Loafing.
8. Do Steps 2–3 of Snappy Salute.
9. Do Step 5 of At Ease Pudding.

THURSDAY

Grill Sergeant

1 Prepare the grill or preheat the broiler.

2 Rinse and pat dry the salmon steaks. Rinse, stem, and chop the parsley.

3 In a 9 x 13-inch baking dish, combine the wine, the oil, the lemon juice, the thyme, and the marjoram. Season to taste. Place the salmon steaks in the dish and marinate for 20 minutes, turning occasionally.

4 Place the steaks on the grill or under the broiler and cook, basting with the marinade, until the fish flakes easily with a fork, about 5 minutes per side. Sprinkle with the parsley.

Snappy Salute

1 Peel, trim, and slice the carrot. Rinse, trim, quarter, and coarsely grate the cabbage. Rinse and string the snap peas.

2 Melt the butter with the cardamom in a large skillet and sauté the carrot for 2 minutes. Add the cabbage and sauté for 3 minutes. Add the snap peas and sauté until they are crisp-tender and heated through, about 3 minutes. Season to taste.

3 Remove from the heat and cover to keep warm.

No Loafing

1 Peel and mince the garlic.

2 In a small bowl, combine the garlic and the oil. Season to taste.

3 Split the baguettes and place them on a sheet of aluminum foil.

4 Brush the cut sides with the garlic mixture. Seal the foil and place the baguettes on the grill to heat through, about 10 minutes.

At Ease Pudding

1 Bring ¾ cup of the water to a boil.

2 Pour the boiling water into a blender. Add the gelatin and blend until it is completely dissolved, about 30 seconds.

3 Combine the remaining ½ cup cold water with enough ice cubes to make 1¼ cups. Add the ice and the water to the gelatin and stir until the ice is partially melted, then blend for 30 seconds.

4 Distribute the marshmallows and the raisins among individual dessert glasses. Pour the gelatin mixture over the marshmallows and refrigerate until you are ready to serve.

5 Top each serving with a dollop of whipped cream and a sprinkle of nuts.

FRIDAY

Super Soup

1 clove garlic
1 medium onion
2 tablespoons butter
1 can (14½ ounces) diced tomatoes
1 can (6 ounces) tomato juice
1 can (10½ ounces) beef consommé
½ cup orange juice
1 bay leaf
Seasoning to taste

Terrific Tortellini

1 medium head lettuce
½ pound fresh green beans
1 small head cauliflower
2 stalks celery
1 small red bell pepper
4 scallions (green onions)
1 can (4 ounces) sliced mushrooms
1 pound tricolor tortellini
4 tablespoons olive oil
2 tablespoons tarragon vinegar
1 tablespoon lemon juice
1 teaspoon Dijon mustard
1 teaspoon Worcestershire sauce
Seasoning to taste
¼ cup grated Parmesan cheese

Scrumptious Scones

2 cups flour
1 tablespoon baking powder
1 tablespoon granulated sugar
4 tablespoons butter
2 eggs
½ cup buttermilk

First-Class Fruit

1 small ripe honeydew melon
¼ small ripe seedless watermelon
1 pint fresh blueberries
1 pint lime sherbet
1 cup white grape juice

EQUIPMENT

Electric mixer	2 small mixing bowls
Blender	Whisk
Stockpot	Melon baller
2 medium covered saucepans	Pastry blender
Steamer insert	Ice cream scoop
Baking sheet	Kitchen knives
Breadboard	Measuring cups and spoons
Colander	Cooking utensils
3 large mixing bowls	

COUNTDOWN

1. Assemble the ingredients and the equipment.
2. Do Step 1 of *First-Class Fruit*.
3. Do Steps 1–7 of *Terrific Tortellini*.
4. Do Steps 1–6 of *Scrumptious Scones*.
5. Do Steps 1–3 of *Super Soup*.
6. Do Step 8 of *Terrific Tortellini*.
7. Do Step 7 of *Scrumptious Scones*.
8. Do Steps 9–10 of *Terrific Tortellini*.
9. Do Step 4 of *Super Soup*.
10. Do Step 2 of *First-Class Fruit*.

FRIDAY

RECIPES

Super Soup

1 Peel and mince the garlic. Peel and mince the onion.

2 Melt the butter in a medium saucepan and sauté the garlic and the onion until soft, about 5 minutes. Scrape the mixture into a blender. Add the tomatoes and the tomato juice and puree until smooth.

3 Turn the tomato mixture into the saucepan. Blend in the consommé and the orange juice. Add the bay leaf and season to taste. Bring to a boil, cover, reduce the heat, and simmer until you are ready to serve.

4 Remove the bay leaf before serving.

Terrific Tortellini

1 Bring water to a boil in a stockpot. Bring water to a boil in a medium saucepan.

2 Wash and dry the lettuce, tear it into bite-sized pieces, and arrange it on a platter.

3 Rinse and trim the green beans and cut them into 2-inch-long pieces. Rinse, trim, and cut the cauliflower into bite-sized florets. Rinse, trim, and chop the celery. Rinse, trim, seed, and chop the bell pepper. Rinse, trim, and chop the scallions. Drain the mushrooms.

4 Arrange the beans and the cauliflower in a steamer insert and place the insert in the saucepan. Cover and steam until the vegetables are crisp-tender, about 7 minutes.

5 Remove the beans and the cauliflower and rinse them under cold water.

6 Combine the beans, the cauliflower, the celery, the bell pepper, the scallions, and the mushrooms in a large bowl. Place in the refrigerator to chill.

7 Cook the tortellini in the stockpot until it is almost tender, about 5 minutes if you are using fresh pasta, about 10 minutes if you are using dry pasta.

8 Drain and rinse under cold water. Add the pasta to the vegetables and refrigerate.

9 In a small bowl, combine the oil, the vinegar, the lemon juice, the mustard, and the Worcestershire sauce. Season to taste.

10 Toss the tortellini salad with the dressing and spoon over the lettuce. Top with the cheese.

Scrumptious Scones

1 Grease a baking sheet. Lightly flour a breadboard.

2 In a large bowl, combine the flour, the baking powder, and the sugar. Cut the butter in with a pastry blender until the mixture resembles coarse meal.

3 In a small bowl, beat the eggs with the buttermilk until well blended.

4 Stir the egg mixture gently into the flour mixture until blended and smooth.

5 Turn the dough onto the floured surface and knead for 1 minute. Pat the dough to a ¾-inch thickness. Cut into wedges and place on the baking sheet.

6 Preheat the oven to 425°F.

7 Bake the scones until lightly golden, about 15 minutes.

First-Class Fruit

1 Cut the honeydew melon in half and remove the seeds. Using a melon baller, scoop out the flesh of the honeydew and the watermelon. Rinse and dry the berries. Combine the fruit in a large bowl and refrigerate until you are ready to use.

2 Place scoops of sherbet in individual dessert bowls. Surround with the fruit. Pour the grape juice over the top.

WEEK EIGHT

Monday
Anchorage Away
Over-Bering Beets
Nome-Name Rolls
Glacial Grapes

Tuesday
Clark Gobble
Tabbouleh Bankhead
Vivian Leaf
Donald Krisp

Wednesday
Duke of Pork
Royal Rice
Prince of Kales
Queen Rum

Thursday
Chopin Stir
Ode to Choy
Haydn Seek Pudding

Friday
Hurry Curry
Lighthearted Rice
Public Appearances
The Poof Is In the Pudding

- ☐ Butter
- ☐ Flour
- ☐ Cornstarch
- ☐ Granulated sugar
- ☐ Dark brown sugar
- ☐ Chocolate syrup
- ☐ Silver shots
- ☐ Olive oil
- ☐ Sesame oil
- ☐ Vegetable oil
- ☐ Rice vinegar
- ☐ Lemon juice
- ☐ Honey
- ☐ Mayonnaise
- ☐ Soy sauce
- ☐ White Worcestershire sauce
- ☐ Celery seeds
- ☐ Poppy seeds
- ☐ Sesame seeds
- ☐ Dried dill
- ☐ Dried marjoram
- ☐ Dried sage
- ☐ Dried tarragon
- ☐ Curry powder
- ☐ Dry mustard
- ☐ Paprika
- ☐ Black pepper
- ☐ Poultry seasoning
- ☐ Salt
- ☐ Turmeric
- ☐ Almond extract
- ☐ Rum extract
- ☐ Vanilla extract

MEAT & POULTRY

1 1/2 pounds lean boneless pork loin (W)

1 1/2 pounds boneless, skinless turkey breast (T)

1 pound boneless, skinless chicken breast (Th)

FISH

3/4 pound cooked crabmeat (M)

3/4 pound cooked baby shrimp (M)

FRESH PRODUCE

VEGETABLES

2 small sweet potatoes (Th)

1 medium bunch broccoli (Th)

1 medium zucchini (W)

2 medium carrots (W)

4 stalks celery (T)

2 stalks celery (W)

1 stalk celery (F)

1 small bunch beets (M)

2 medium turnips (M)

1/2 pound mushrooms (W)

1 1/2 pounds baby bok choy (Th)

1 medium bunch kale (W)

1 medium head red leaf lettuce (M)

1 small head lettuce (T)

1 small head lettuce (F)

1 medium tomato (T)

1 medium cucumber (M)

2 medium red bell peppers (W)

1 small red bell pepper (M)

1 medium onion (W)

1 small onion (F)

1 small red onion (T)

2 scallions (green onions) (W)

1 clove garlic (M)

1 clove garlic (T)

1 clove garlic (W)

HERBS

3 tablespoons chives (when chopped) (M)

2 tablespoons chives (when chopped) (F)

2 tablespoons parsley (when chopped) (T)

2 tablespoons parsley (when chopped) (W)

FRUIT

1 large orange (Th)

1 large lemon (T)

1 large lime (W)

2 medium limes (F)

2 large tart apples (W)

4 ripe apricots (F)

2 medium ripe pears (F)

1/2 pound seedless green grapes (M)

1/2 pound seedless red grapes (M)

1 pint blueberries (W)

CANS, JARS & BOTTLES

SOUPS

1 can (14 ounces) chicken broth (W)

INTERNATIONAL FOODS

1 can (8 ounces) sliced water chestnuts (Th)

1 can (5 1/2 ounces) whole baby corn (Th)

FRUIT

1 can (11 ounces) mandarin oranges (T)

SPREADS

4 tablespoons orange marmalade (Th)

DESSERT & BAKING NEEDS

1 can (14 ounces) sweetened condensed milk (F)

PACKAGED GOODS

PASTA, RICE & GRAINS

1 cup long-grain white rice (W)

1 cup brown rice (F)

2 cups bulgar (T)

2 cups Rice Krispies cereal (T)

BAKED GOODS

4 crusty rolls (M)

4 shortbread tart shells (M)

1/2 cup graham cracker crumbs (F)

INTERNATIONAL FOODS

8 ounces soft Japanese soba noodles (Th)

4 almond cookies for garnish (Th)

DRIED FRUIT & NUTS

1/4 cup cashews (M)

DESSERT & BAKING NEEDS

1 package (3.4 ounces) instant coconut cream pudding mix (Th)

2/3 cup chocolate chips (T)

WINE & SPIRITS

3 tablespoons dry white wine (Th)

1/4 cup dry sherry (M)

1/4 cup dry sherry (W)

REFRIGERATED PRODUCTS

DAIRY

2 cups milk (Th)

1/4 cup milk (F)

4 cups buttermilk (M)

1 container (6 ounces) apple-cinnamon yogurt (W)

Whipped cream for garnish (M)

9 eggs (F)

CHEESE

1 package (8 ounces) cream cheese (F)

JUICES

1/4 cup orange juice (T)

2 tablespoons orange juice (F)

DELI

2 slices bacon (T)

FROZEN GOODS

VEGETABLES

1 package (10 ounces) green peas (T)

DESSERTS

1 pint vanilla frozen yogurt (M)

1 pint strawberry ice cream (T)

1 container (8 ounces) whipped topping (F)

MONDAY

Anchorage Away

3 tablespoons fresh chives (when chopped)
1 small red bell pepper
1 medium cucumber
3/4 pound cooked crabmeat
3/4 pound cooked baby shrimp
4 cups buttermilk
1/4 cup dry sherry
1 teaspoon white Worcestershire sauce
1/2 teaspoon dry mustard
1/4 teaspoon dried tarragon
1 teaspoon granulated sugar
Seasoning to taste

Over-Bering Beets

1 medium head red leaf lettuce
1 small bunch fresh beets
2 medium turnips
1/4 cup cashews
3 tablespoons vegetable oil
1 tablespoon lemon juice
2 tablespoons honey
Seasoning to taste

Nome-Name Rolls

1 clove garlic
4 crusty rolls
3 tablespoons butter
2 teaspoons poppy seeds

Glacial Grapes

1/2 pound seedless green grapes
1/2 pound seedless red grapes
1/2 teaspoon almond extract
1 pint vanilla frozen yogurt
4 shortbread tart shells
Whipped cream for garnish
Silver shots for garnish

EQUIPMENT

Small saucepan
Baking sheet
Large mixing bowl
Medium mixing bowl
4 small mixing bowls
Whisk
Vegetable peeler
Vegetable grater

Pastry brush
Ice cream scoop
Plastic wrap
Kitchen knives
Measuring cups and spoons
Cooking utensils

COUNTDOWN

1. Assemble the ingredients and the equipment.
2. Do Steps 1–4 of *Anchorage Away*.
3. Do Step 1 of *Glacial Grapes*.
4. Do Steps 1–4 of *Over-Bering Beets*.
5. Do Steps 1–4 of *Nome-Name Rolls*.
6. Do Step 5 of *Over-Bering Beets*.
7. Do Step 2 of *Glacial Grapes*.

MONDAY

Anchorage Away

1 Rinse, trim, and chop the chives. Rinse, trim, seed, and chop the bell pepper. Peel, trim, and finely chop the cucumber. Flake the crabmeat, and discard any bits of shell or cartilage.

2 In a large bowl, combine the chives, the bell pepper, the cucumber, the crabmeat, and the shrimp. Add the buttermilk and mix to combine.

3 In a small bowl, combine the sherry, the Worcestershire sauce, the mustard, the tarragon, and the sugar. Season to taste.

4 Add the sherry mixture to the buttermilk mixture and blend well. Cover with plastic wrap and chill for at least 20 minutes.

Over-Bering Beets

1 Wash and dry the lettuce and distribute the leaves among individual salad plates.

2 Trim and peel the beets and grate them into a small bowl. Trim and peel the turnips and grate them into a second small bowl. Finely chop the nuts.

3 Mound the beets and the turnips on the lettuce.

4 In a small bowl, whisk together the oil, the lemon juice, and the honey. Season to taste.

5 Drizzle the dressing over the salad and sprinkle with the nuts.

Nome-Name Rolls

1 Preheat the broiler.

2 Peel and mince the garlic. Split the rolls in half and place the split sides down on a baking sheet. Broil for 2 minutes.

3 Melt the butter in a small saucepan and sauté the garlic for 1 minute. Remove from the heat.

4 Turn the rolls over and brush the cut sides with the butter mixture and sprinkle with the poppy seeds. Return the rolls to the broiler and continue broiling until they are lightly golden, 1 to 2 minutes.

Glacial Grapes

1 Wash, dry, and stem the grapes and place them in a medium bowl. Toss them with the almond extract.

2 Place scoops of frozen yogurt in each tart shell. Spoon on the grapes. Top with a dollop of whipped cream and sprinkle with the silver shots.

TUESDAY

Clark Gobble

1½ pounds boneless, skinless turkey breast
1 clove garlic
1 can (11 ounces) mandarin oranges
1 cup flour
1 teaspoon poultry seasoning
1 teaspoon paprika
Seasoning to taste
1 tablespoon butter
2 tablespoons vegetable oil
3 tablespoons lemon juice
¼ cup orange juice
2 tablespoons honey
1 teaspoon white Worcestershire sauce

Tabbouleh Bankhead

2 tablespoons fresh parsley (when chopped)
1 medium tomato
1 large lemon
2 cups water
2 cups bulgar
2 tablespoons olive oil
Seasoning to taste

Vivian Leaf

1 package (10 ounces) frozen green peas
2 slices bacon
4 stalks celery
1 small red onion
1 small head lettuce
Seasoning to taste

Donald Krisp

2 tablespoons butter
⅔ cup chocolate chips
1 teaspoon vanilla extract
2 cups Rice Krispies cereal
1 pint strawberry ice cream
Chocolate syrup for garnish

EQUIPMENT

Dutch oven
Medium covered saucepan
Medium saucepan
Medium covered skillet
Pie plate
2 small mixing bowls

Citrus grater
Citrus juicer
Plastic bag
Kitchen knives
Measuring cups and spoons
Cooking utensils

COUNTDOWN

1. Assemble the ingredients and the equipment.
2. Do Steps 1–4 of *Donald Krisp*.
3. Do Steps 1–3 of *Tabbouleh Bankhead*.
4. Do Steps 1–4 of *Clark Gobble*.
5. Do Step 5 of *Donald Krisp*.
6. Do Steps 1–3 of *Vivian Leaf*.
7. Do Step 5 of *Clark Gobble*.
8. Do Step 4 of *Vivian Leaf*.
9. Do Step 4 of *Tabbouleh Bankhead*.
10. Do Step 6 of *Donald Krisp*.

TUESDAY

Clark Gobble

1 Rinse, pat dry, and cube the turkey. Peel and mince the garlic. Drain the mandarin oranges, reserving the liquid in a small bowl.

2 In a plastic bag, combine the flour, the poultry seasoning, and the paprika. Season to taste. Place the turkey in the bag and coat the cubes with the flour mixture.

3 Melt the butter with the oil in a Dutch oven. Add the garlic and sauté for 1 minute. Add the turkey and sauté until lightly browned, about 7 minutes.

4 To the reserved mandarin orange liquid, add the lemon juice, the orange juice, the honey, and the Worcestershire sauce. Pour the mixture over the turkey. Cover and simmer until the turkey is tender and cooked through, about 15 minutes.

5 Add the mandarin oranges, stirring to combine, and simmer for 5 minutes more.

Tabbouleh Bankhead

1 Rinse, stem, and chop the parsley. Rinse, stem, and chop the tomato. Grate 1 teaspoon of lemon peel and juice the lemon.

2 Bring the water to a boil in a medium saucepan.

3 Add the bulgar and the lemon juice to the boiling water. Cover and let stand for 20 minutes.

4 Add the tomato and the oil, season to taste, and blend well. Fluff with a fork and sprinkle with the parsley and the lemon peel.

Vivian Leaf

1 Set the peas in a small bowl of warm water to thaw.

2 Dice the bacon. Rinse, trim, and chop the celery. Peel and chop the onion. Wash and dry the lettuce, and distribute the leaves among individual salad plates.

3 Sauté the bacon in a medium skillet until crisp, about 5 minutes. Drain on paper towels.

4 In the bacon drippings, sauté the celery and the onion until soft, about 5 minutes. Add the peas and toss to combine. Season to taste.

5 Spoon the pea mixture over the lettuce leaves and top with the bacon.

Donald Krisp

1 Grease a pie plate.

2 In a medium saucepan, melt the butter with the chocolate chips over low heat, stirring to blend. Remove from the heat and fold in the vanilla and the cereal. Mix well.

3 Spread the mixture evenly in the pie plate, place it in the freezer, and chill at least 20 minutes.

4 Set the ice cream out to soften slightly.

5 Add the softened ice cream to the pie, smoothing over the chocolate mixture. Return it to the freezer.

6 To serve, cut the pie into wedges and drizzle with the chocolate syrup.

WEDNESDAY

Duke of Pork

1 clove garlic
1 medium onion
1 medium zucchini
2 medium red bell peppers
1/2 pound fresh mushrooms
1 1/2 pounds lean boneless pork loin
1 large lime
1/4 cup dry sherry
1 tablespoon dark brown sugar
1 teaspoon dried sage
Seasoning to taste

Royal Rice

2 tablespoons fresh parsley (when chopped)
2 scallions (green onions)
1 cup long-grain white rice
1 can (14 ounces) chicken broth
1 teaspoon turmeric
1/4 cup water

Prince of Kales

2 medium carrots
2 stalks celery
1 medium bunch kale
3 tablespoons olive oil
1 teaspoon granulated sugar
1/2 teaspoon celery seeds
1 teaspoon dried dill
Seasoning to taste

Queen Rum

2 large tart apples
1 tablespoon lemon juice
1 pint fresh blueberries
1 container (6 ounces) apple-cinnamon yogurt
2 tablespoons granulated sugar
2 teaspoons rum extract

EQUIPMENT

Double boiler
Medium skillet
Large mixing bowl
Medium mixing bowl
Small mixing bowl
8 bamboo skewers
Vegetable peeler

Plastic wrap
Pastry brush
Kitchen knives
Measuring cups and spoons
Cooking utensils

COUNTDOWN

1. Assemble the ingredients and the equipment.
2. Do Step 1 of *Queen Rum*.
3. Do Steps 1–3 of *Royal Rice*.
4. Do Steps 1–4 of *Duke of Pork*.
5. Do Step 1 of *Prince of Kales*.
6. Do Steps 5–6 of *Duke of Pork*.
7. Do Step 2 of *Prince of Kales*.
8. Do Step 4 of *Royal Rice*.
9. Do Steps 2–3 of *Queen Rum*.

WEDNESDAY

Duke of Pork

1 Prepare the grill or preheat the broiler.

2 Peel and mince the garlic. Peel and chop the onion. Rinse, trim, and chunk the zucchini. Rinse, trim, seed, and chunk the bell peppers. Rinse, pat dry, and stem the mushrooms. Cut the pork into 1½-inch cubes. Juice the lime.

3 In a medium bowl, combine the pork, the garlic, the onion, the lime juice, the sherry, and the brown sugar. Add the sage and season to taste. Toss to combine. Cover with plastic wrap and refrigerate for 10 minutes.

4 Soak 8 bamboo skewers in warm water for 10 minutes.

5 Remove the pork, reserving the marinade. Skewer the pork cubes alternately with the vegetables.

6 Grill or broil the kabobs, turning and brushing with the reserved marinade, until each side is cooked and the meat is no longer pink in the middle, 12 to 15 minutes.

Royal Rice

1 Bring water to a boil in the bottom of a double boiler.

2 Rinse, stem, and chop the parsley. Rinse, trim, and chop the scallions.

3 In the top of the double boiler, combine the scallions, the rice, the broth, the turmeric, and the ¼ cup water. Cover, reduce the heat, and simmer until all the liquid is absorbed and the rice is tender, 30 to 40 minutes.

4 Fluff the rice with a fork and sprinkle with the parsley.

Prince of Kales

1 Peel, trim, and slice the carrots. Rinse, trim, and slice the celery. Rinse, trim, and chop the kale.

2 Heat the oil in a medium skillet and sauté the carrots and the celery for 5 minutes. Add the kale and sauté for 2 minutes. Blend in the sugar, the celery seeds, and the dill. Season to taste and toss to combine.

Queen Rum

1 Peel, core, and thinly slice the apples. Place them in a large bowl and sprinkle with the lemon juice. Rinse and dry the blueberries. Add them to the apples and toss to blend. Cover with plastic wrap and chill in the refrigerator until you are ready to serve.

2 In a small bowl, combine the yogurt with the sugar and the rum extract.

3 Spoon the fruit into individual dessert dishes and top with dollops of the yogurt mixture.

THURSDAY

Chopin Stir

1 pound boneless, skinless chicken breast
1 medium bunch broccoli
2 small sweet potatoes
1 can (8 ounces) sliced water chestnuts
1 can (5½ ounces) whole baby corn
1 tablespoon cornstarch
2 tablespoons water
3 tablespoons dry white wine
2 tablespoons soy sauce
Seasoning to taste
2 tablespoons vegetable oil
1 tablespoon sesame oil
8 ounces soft Japanese soba noodles

Ode to Choy

1½ pounds baby bok choy
2 teaspoons sesame oil
2 teaspoons rice vinegar
1 tablespoon sesame seeds
Seasoning to taste

Haydn Seek Pudding

1 large orange
1 package (3.4 ounces) instant coconut
  cream pudding mix
2 cups milk
4 tablespoons orange marmalade
4 almond cookies for garnish

EQUIPMENT

Electric mixer	Vegetable peeler
Wok	Citrus grater
Medium covered skillet	Kitchen knives
Medium mixing bowl	Measuring cups and spoons
Small mixing bowl	Cooking utensils
Whisk	

COUNTDOWN

1. Assemble the ingredients and the equipment.
2. Do Steps 1–3 of *Haydn Seek Pudding*.
3. Do Step 1 of *Ode to Choy*.
4. Do Steps 1–3 of *Chopin Stir*.
5. Do Step 2 of *Ode to Choy*.
6. Do Steps 4–5 of *Chopin Stir*.
7. Do Step 4 of *Haydn Seek Pudding*.

THURSDAY

Chopin Stir

1 Rinse, pat dry, and cube the chicken breast. Rinse and trim the broccoli, discarding the tough ends, and cut into bite-sized florets. Peel and thinly slice the sweet potatoes. Drain the water chestnuts and the corn.

2 In a small bowl, combine the cornstarch, the water, the wine, and the soy sauce. Season to taste.

3 Heat the oils in a wok. Stir-fry the chicken until it is opaque, about 3 minutes.

4 Add the broccoli and the sweet potatoes and stir-fry for 3 minutes. Add the water chestnuts and the corn.

5 Add the soy sauce mixture to the wok and blend well. Add the noodles and stir-fry for 2 minutes.

Ode to Choy

1 Rinse and trim the bok choy.

2 Heat the oil in a medium skillet. Add the bok choy and the vinegar, toss to coat, and sauté for 1 minute. Add the sesame seeds and sauté for 2 minutes more. Season to taste. Cover to keep warm.

Haydn Seek Pudding

1 Grate 2 tablespoons of orange peel. Peel and section the orange and cut the sections in half. Place the orange in the bottom of individual dessert glasses.

2 In a medium bowl, combine the pudding mix and the milk and beat until well blended. Fold in the orange peel.

3 Pour the pudding over the oranges and top with a tablespoon of the marmalade. Refrigerate until you are ready to serve.

4 Garnish each pudding with an almond cookie.

FRIDAY

Hurry Curry

1 small onion
9 eggs
1/4 cup milk
1 teaspoon curry powder
Seasoning to taste
1 package (8 ounces) cream cheese
2 tablespoons butter

Lighthearted Rice

2 tablespoons fresh chives (when chopped)
1 stalk celery
1 cup brown rice
1 tablespoon lemon juice
2 cups water
1/2 teaspoon granulated sugar
1/4 teaspoon dried tarragon
1/4 teaspoon dried marjoram

Public Appearances

1 small head lettuce
2 medium ripe pears
4 ripe apricots
2 tablespoons orange juice
1/4 cup mayonnaise
1 teaspoon rice vinegar
Seasoning to taste

The Poof Is In the Pudding

2 medium limes
3 tablespoons butter
1/2 cup graham cracker crumbs
3 tablespoons granulated sugar
1 can (14 ounces) sweetened condensed milk
1 container (8 ounces) frozen whipped topping

EQUIPMENT

Double boiler
Large skillet
Small skillet
2 large mixing bowls
Medium mixing bowl
Small mixing bowl
Whisk

Citrus grater
Citrus juicer
Kitchen knives
Measuring cups and spoons
Cooking utensils

COUNTDOWN

1. Assemble the ingredients and the equipment.
2. Do Steps 1–3 of *The Poof Is In the Pudding*.
3. Do Steps 1–3 of *Lighthearted Rice*.
4. Do Steps 1–3 of *Public Appearances*.
5. Do Steps 1–5 of *Hurry Curry*.
6. Do Step 4 of *Public Appearances*.
7. Do Step 4 of *Lighthearted Rice*.
8. Do Step 4 of *The Poof Is In the Pudding*.

FRIDAY

Hurry Curry

1 Peel and mince the onion.

2 In a large bowl, combine the eggs, the milk, and the curry powder and whisk until frothy. Season to taste.

3 Cut the cream cheese into small pieces.

4 Melt the butter in a large skillet and sauté the onion for 3 minutes. Add the eggs and cook until almost set, about 3 minutes, lifting the edges to let the uncooked portion run under.

5 Sprinkle the cheese over half the eggs. Fold the other half over the cheese and continue cooking until the cheese is melted and the eggs are set, 2 to 3 minutes.

Lighthearted Rice

1 Bring water to a boil in the bottom of a double boiler.

2 Rinse, trim, and chop the chives. Rinse, trim, and finely chop the celery.

3 In the top of the double boiler, combine the rice, the lemon juice, the 2 cups water, the sugar, the tarragon, the marjoram, and the celery. Cover, reduce the heat, and simmer until all the liquid is absorbed and the rice is tender, 40 to 45 minutes.

4 Fold the chives into the rice and fluff with a fork.

Public Appearances

1 Wash and dry the lettuce and distribute the leaves among individual salad plates.

2 Rinse, core, and slice the pears and place them in a large bowl. Rinse, halve, pit, and chop the apricots. Toss the orange juice with the pear slices. Add the apricots to the pears.

3 In a small bowl, combine the mayonnaise and the vinegar. Season to taste.

4 Toss the fruit mixture with the dressing and spoon over the lettuce.

The Poof Is In the Pudding

1 Grate 2 tablespoons of lime peel. Juice the limes.

2 In a small skillet, melt the butter. Add the graham cracker crumbs and the sugar and stir to combine. Cook until the crumbs are a deep gold, about 2 minutes. Remove from the heat and set aside to cool.

3 In a medium bowl, combine the condensed milk, the lime juice, and the lime peel. Blend well. Fold in the whipped topping. Spoon into individual dessert glasses and refrigerate until you are ready to serve.

4 Top with the crumbs.

WEEK NINE

Monday

Ready, Set, Spaghetti
On–Your–Mark Salad
Bready or Not
Okay Sorbet

Tuesday

Pacific Pearadise
Outrigger Rice
Kilauea Karrots
Hana Banana

Wednesday

Margaret Hamilton
Lee J. Cob
Breada Garbo
Jack Lemon

Thursday

Caribbean Chicken
Jamaica Rice
Bermuda Triangle
Black Bart's Compote

Friday

Chiang Kai-Shrimp
Slaw Boat to China
Man Chu Pears

STAPLES

- ❑ Butter
- ❑ Cornstarch
- ❑ Granulated sugar
- ❑ Dark brown sugar
- ❑ Chocolate sprinkles
- ❑ Multicolored sprinkles
- ❑ Olive oil
- ❑ Sesame oil
- ❑ Vegetable oil
- ❑ Balsamic vinegar
- ❑ Red wine vinegar
- ❑ Rice vinegar
- ❑ White wine vinegar
- ❑ Lemon juice
- ❑ Dijon mustard
- ❑ Honey
- ❑ Ketchup
- ❑ Soy sauce
- ❑ Dried dill
- ❑ Cayenne pepper
- ❑ Ground cloves
- ❑ Ground cumin
- ❑ Ground ginger
- ❑ Lemon-pepper seasoning
- ❑ Dry mustard
- ❑ Ground nutmeg
- ❑ Paprika
- ❑ Black pepper
- ❑ Red pepper flakes
- ❑ Salt

MEAT & POULTRY

1 1/2 pounds lean ground beef (M)

1/2 pound lean cooked ham steak (W)

4 boneless, skinless chicken breast halves (about 1 1/2 pounds) (Th)

FISH

4 white fish fillets (about 1 1/2 pounds) (T)

1 1/2 pounds medium shrimp, shelled and deveined (F)

FRESH PRODUCE

VEGETABLES

1 small bunch broccoli (F)

4 whole ears corn (W)

1/4 pound Chinese snow peas (F)

1 pound medium carrots (T)

2 stalks celery (M)

1 stalk celery (T)

2 stalks celery (F)

1/2 pound mushrooms (W)

1/2 pound bean sprouts (F)

1 head Napa cabbage (F)

1 medium head lettuce (M)

1 medium head lettuce (W)

1 medium head lettuce (Th)

1 small tomato (F)

1 large ripe avocado (W)

1 medium cucumber (W)

1 large yellow bell pepper (W)

1 small green bell pepper (Th)

1 small red bell pepper (F)

1 small bunch radishes (W)

1 small diakon radish (F)

1 small onion (T)

1 medium Bermuda (sweet) onion (Th)

1 small shallot (M)

1 small shallot (F)

3 scallions (green onions) (W)

3 scallions (green onions) (Th)

1 clove garlic (M)

1 clove garlic (F)

HERBS

1 tablespoon chives (when chopped) (W)

1/4 cup cilantro (when chopped) (T)

2 tablespoons parsley (when chopped) (M)

2 tablespoons parsley (when chopped) (T)

3 tablespoons parsley (when chopped) (Th)

FRUIT

1 medium lime (Th)

2 large bananas (T)

2 small green apples (M)

2 ripe papayas (or small ripe cantaloupe melons) (Th)

1 medium ripe pear (T)

4 medium Asian pears (or crisp pears) (F)

1 pint raspberries (M)

1 pint blackberries (Th)

CANS, JARS & BOTTLES

SOUPS

1 can (14 ounces) vegetable broth (T)

1 can (14 ounces) vegetable broth (F)

1 can (14 ounces) chicken broth (Th)

VEGETABLES

1 can (15 ounces) black beans (Th)

FRUIT

1 can (8 ounces) pineapple tidbits (T)

SAUCES

1 can (8 ounces) tomato sauce (M)

SPREADS

2 tablespoons red currant jelly (Th)

DESSERT & BAKING NEEDS

1/4 cup marshmallow crème for garnish (M)

PACKAGED GOODS

PASTA, RICE & GRAINS

1 pound spaghetti (M)

1 cup wild rice (T)

1 cup long-grain white rice (Th)

BAKED GOODS

4 small pita bread rounds (M)

8 butterflake rolls (W)

4 individual meringue shells (M)

1 prepared shortbread pie shell (W)

INTERNATIONAL FOODS

12 ounces cellophane noodles (F)

DRIED FRUIT & NUTS

1/2 cup golden raisins (M)

DESSERT & BAKING NEEDS

1 package (3.4 ounces) instant lemon pudding mix (W)

1/4 cup flaked coconut (T)

WINE & SPIRITS

3 tablespoons dry white wine (F)

3 tablespoons dry sherry (T)

3 tablespoons dry sherry (Th)

REFRIGERATED PRODUCTS

DAIRY

1 1/4 cups milk (W)

1/4 cup sour cream (M)

1/4 cup sour cream (W)

1 cup plain yogurt (M)

Whipped cream for garnish (W)

8 eggs (W)

CHEESE

1 cup shredded Cheddar cheese (W)

JUICES

1 cup orange juice (T)

1 cup orange juice (Th)

DELI

1 pound bacon (W)

FROZEN GOODS

DESSERTS

1 pint raspberry sorbet (M)

MONDAY

Ready, Set, Spaghetti

2 tablespoons fresh parsley (when chopped)
1 clove garlic
2 tablespoons vegetable oil
1 1/2 pounds lean ground beef
1 can (8 ounces) tomato sauce
1 teaspoon paprika
1/4 teaspoon cayenne pepper
1/2 teaspoon ground cumin
1 pound spaghetti
1 cup plain yogurt
1/4 cup sour cream
Seasoning to taste

On-Your-Mark Salad

1 medium head lettuce
2 small green apples
2 stalks celery
1/2 cup raisins
3 tablespoons olive oil
2 tablespoons balsamic vinegar
1 teaspoon granulated sugar
Seasoning to taste

Bready or Not

1 small shallot
2 tablespoons olive oil
1 tablespoon lemon juice
Seasoning to taste
4 small pita bread rounds

Okay Sorbet

1 pint fresh raspberries
4 individual meringue shells
1 pint raspberry sorbet
1/4 cup marshmallow crème for garnish
Chocolate sprinkles for garnish

EQUIPMENT

Stockpot	Whisk
Small saucepan	Pastry brush
Large covered skillet	Ice cream scoop
Baking sheet	Kitchen knives
Colander	Measuring cups and
Large mixing bowl	spoons
2 small mixing bowls	Cooking utensils

COUNTDOWN

1. Assemble the ingredients and the equipment.
2. Do Step 1 of Okay Sorbet.
3. Do Steps 1–2 of On-Your-Mark Salad.
4. Do Steps 1–2 of Bready or Not.
5. Do Steps 1–5 of Ready, Set, Spaghetti.
6. Do Steps 3–4 of Bready or Not.
7. Do Step 6 of Ready, Set, Spaghetti.
8. Do Step 3 of On-Your-Mark Salad.
9. Do Steps 2–3 of Okay Sorbet.

MONDAY

Ready, Set, Spaghetti

1 Rinse, stem, and chop the parsley. Peel and mince the garlic.

2 Bring water to a boil in a stockpot.

3 Heat the oil in a large skillet and sauté the garlic for 1 minute. Add the ground beef and sauté until it is no longer pink, about 6 minutes. Stir in the tomato sauce, the paprika, the cayenne pepper, and the cumin. Cover, reduce the heat, and simmer for 10 minutes.

4 Cook the spaghetti in the stockpot until it is almost tender, 6 to 7 minutes.

5 Combine the yogurt and the sour cream in a small saucepan. Season to taste and heat through, but do not let boil.

6 Drain the pasta and arrange it on a platter. Pour the meat sauce over the pasta. Spoon the yogurt mixture over the meat sauce and sprinkle with the parsley.

On-Your-Mark Salad

1 Wash and dry the lettuce and tear it into bite-sized pieces. Rinse, core, and chop the apples. Rinse, trim, and chop the celery. Combine the ingredients in a large bowl. Mix in the raisins.

2 In a small bowl, whisk together the oil, the vinegar, and the sugar. Season to taste.

3 Toss the salad with the dressing.

Bready or Not

1 Peel and mince the shallot.

2 In a small bowl, combine the shallot, the oil, and the lemon juice. Season to taste.

3 Preheat the broiler.

4 Cut the pita bread rounds into pie-shaped wedges and brush them with the oil mixture. Place the wedges on a baking sheet and broil until lightly toasted, about 2 minutes.

Okay Sorbet

1 Rinse and pat dry the raspberries.

2 Place each meringue shell on a dessert plate.

3 Place scoops of sorbet in each shell, top with the berries, and garnish with the marshmallow crème and the sprinkles.

TUESDAY

Pacific Pearadise

4 white fish fillets (about 1 1/2 pounds)
1/2 teaspoon ground ginger
2 tablespoons soy sauce
1 teaspoon granulated sugar
3 tablespoons dry sherry
Seasoning to taste
1 small onion
1 medium ripe pear
1/4 cup fresh cilantro (when chopped)
2 tablespoons butter

Outrigger Rice

1 stalk celery
1 cup wild rice
1 tablespoon vegetable oil
1 can (14 ounces) vegetable broth
1 can (8 ounces) pineapple tidbits

Kilauea Karrots

1 pound medium carrots
2 tablespoons fresh parsley (when
   chopped)
2 tablespoons butter
1 tablespoon dark brown sugar
Seasoning to taste

Hana Banana

1/4 cup flaked coconut
2 large bananas
1 cup orange juice
1/4 cup water
2 tablespoons granulated sugar
1 teaspoon lemon juice
1/2 teaspoon ground nutmeg

EQUIPMENT

Blender	4 paper cups
2 medium covered saucepans	4 Popsicle sticks
Small saucepan	Kitchen knives
Large skillet	Measuring cups and spoons
Large shallow bowl	Cooking utensils
Vegetable peeler	

COUNTDOWN

1. Assemble the ingredients and the equipment.
2. Do Steps 1–3 of *Pacific Pearadise*.
3. Do Steps 1–3 of *Outrigger Rice*.
4. Do Steps 1–3 of *Hana Banana*.
5. Do Steps 1–3 of *Kilauea Karrots*.
6. Do Step 4 of *Hana Banana*.
7. Do Steps 4–5 of *Kilauea Karrots*.
8. Do Steps 4–6 of *Pacific Pearadise*.
9. Do Step 4 of *Outrigger Rice*.
10. Do Step 6 of *Kilauea Karrots*.

TUESDAY

Pacific Pearadise

1 Rinse and pat dry the fish fillets.

2 Combine the ginger, the soy sauce, the sugar, and the sherry in a large shallow bowl. Season to taste. Add the fish fillets and marinate for 10 minutes, turning occasionally.

3 Peel and chop the onion. Peel, core, and slice the pear. Rinse, stem, and chop the cilantro.

4 Melt half the butter in a large skillet and sauté the onion for 3 minutes. Add the pears and sauté for 2 minutes. Remove and reserve in a small saucepan.

5 Melt the remaining butter in the skillet. Drain the fillets, reserving the marinade, and cook in the skillet until they flake easily with a fork, 3 to 4 minutes per side.

6 Add the marinade to the saucepan and bring to a boil. Spoon the onion, the pear, and the sauce over the fish and garnish with the cilantro.

Outrigger Rice

1 Rinse, trim, and chop the celery. Rinse the wild rice.

2 Heat the oil in a medium saucepan. Add the celery, tossing to coat, and sauté for 1 minute. Stir in the rice and sauté for 1 minute.

3 Add the broth and the pineapple with its liquid and bring to a boil. Cover, reduce the heat, and simmer until all the liquid is absorbed and the rice is tender, about 45 minutes.

4 Fluff the rice before serving.

Kilauea Karrots

1 Peel, trim, and slice the carrots. Rinse, stem, and chop the parsley.

2 Bring water to a boil in a medium saucepan.

3 Cook the carrots until they are crisp-tender, about 5 minutes.

4 Drain the carrots and remove them from the saucepan.

5 Melt the butter with the brown sugar in the saucepan. Return the carrots, season to taste, and toss them in the butter mixture until they are well coated, about 2 minutes. Cover to keep warm.

6 Sprinkle with the parsley.

Hana Banana

1 Distribute the coconut among 4 paper cups.

2 Peel and chunk the bananas. In a blender, combine the bananas, the orange juice, the water, the sugar, the lemon juice, and the nutmeg. Blend well and pour into the paper cups.

3 Place in the freezer until partially frozen, about 10 minutes.

4 Remove from the freezer. Insert a Popsicle stick in the center of each cup and return to the freezer until you are ready to serve.

WEDNESDAY

Margaret Hamilton

8 eggs
1 pound bacon
$\frac{1}{2}$ pound lean cooked ham steak
1 medium head lettuce
1 medium cucumber
1 large ripe avocado
1 large yellow bell pepper
1 small bunch radishes
3 scallions (green onions)
$\frac{1}{2}$ pound fresh mushrooms
3 tablespoons olive oil
4 tablespoons white wine vinegar
1 teaspoon Dijon mustard
1 teaspoon granulated sugar
1 tablespoon ketchup
Seasoning to taste

Lee J. Cob

2 teaspoons granulated sugar
4 whole fresh ears of corn
1 tablespoon fresh chives (when chopped)
2 tablespoons butter
Seasoning to taste

Breada Garbo

2 tablespoons butter
8 butterflake rolls
1 cup shredded Cheddar cheese
1 teaspoon dried dill

Jack Lemon

1 package (3.4 ounces) instant lemon
   pudding mix
1 $\frac{1}{4}$ cups milk
$\frac{1}{4}$ cup sour cream
1 prepared shortbread pie shell
Whipped cream for garnish
Multicolored sprinkles for garnish

EQUIPMENT

Electric mixer
Large saucepan
Medium saucepan
Large skillet
Muffin tin
Large mixing bowl
Medium mixing bowl
Small mixing bowl

Whisk
Vegetable peeler
Pastry brush
Kitchen knives
Measuring cups and
   spoons
Cooking utensils

COUNTDOWN

1. Assemble the ingredients and the equipment.
2. Do Steps 1–2 of *Jack Lemon*.
3. Do Step 1 of *Breada Garbo*.
4. Do Steps 1–8 of *Margaret Hamilton*.
5. Do Steps 1–2 of *Lee J. Cob*.
6. Do Steps 2–3 of *Breada Garbo*.
7. Do Steps 3–4 of *Lee J. Cob*.
8. Do Step 4 of *Breada Garbo*.
9. Do Step 5 of *Lee J. Cob*.
10. Do Step 3 of *Jack Lemon*.

WEDNESDAY

Margaret Hamilton

1 Cover the eggs with water in a medium saucepan. Bring the water to a boil and hard-cook the eggs, 10 to 12 minutes.

2 Cut the bacon into 2-inch pieces. Cut the ham into thin strips. Sauté the bacon with the ham in a large skillet until the bacon is crisp and golden, about 7 minutes. Drain on paper towels.

3 Drain the eggs and put them in the freezer for 10 minutes.

4 Wash and dry the lettuce and distribute the leaves among individual salad plates.

5 Peel, trim, and chunk the cucumber. Halve, pit, peel, and slice the avocado. Rinse, trim, seed, and chop the bell pepper. Rinse, trim, and chop the radishes. Rinse, trim, and chop the scallions. Rinse, pat dry, trim, and slice the mushrooms. Combine the ingredients in a large bowl.

6 In a small bowl combine the oil, the vinegar, the mustard, the sugar, and the ketchup. Season to taste and toss with the salad.

7 Mound the salad over the lettuce. Add the bacon and the ham.

8 Peel and quarter the eggs and place them around the edges of the salad.

Lee J. Cob

1 Bring water and the sugar to a boil in a large saucepan.

2 Shuck the corn. Rinse, trim, and chop the chives.

3 Cook the corn until crisp-tender, 2 to 3 minutes.

4 Melt the butter.

5 Drain the corn, brush the ears with the melted butter, sprinkle with the chives, and season to taste.

Breada Garbo

1 Set the butter out to soften.

2 Without pulling them apart, gently separate the sections of the rolls. Spread the softened butter lightly between the sections. Sprinkle with the cheese and the dill.

3 Preheat the broiler.

4 Place the rolls in a muffin tin and broil until the cheese is hot and bubbly, about 2 minutes.

Jack Lemon

1 Combine the pudding mix, the milk, and the sour cream in a medium bowl and beat until well blended.

2 Pour the mixture into the prepared pie shell and refrigerate until you are ready to serve.

3 Top each serving with a dollop of whipped cream and garnish with the sprinkles.

THURSDAY

Caribbean Chicken

4 boneless, skinless chicken breast halves
   (about 1 1/2 pounds)
3 scallions (green onions)
1 medium lime
1 cup orange juice
1 teaspoon dry mustard
2 tablespoons honey
1/2 teaspoon cayenne pepper
1/2 teaspoon ground cumin
2 tablespoons vegetable oil
Seasoning to taste

Jamaica Rice

1 tablespoon butter
1 can (14 ounces) chicken broth
1/4 cup water
3 tablespoons dry sherry
1 cup long-grain white rice

Bermuda Triangle

1 medium head lettuce
1 medium Bermuda (sweet) onion
1 small green bell pepper
1 can (15 ounces) black beans
3 tablespoons olive oil
2 tablespoons red wine vinegar
1/4 teaspoon lemon-pepper seasoning
Seasoning to taste

Black Bart's Compote

2 ripe papayas (or small ripe cantaloupe
   melons)
1 pint fresh blackberries
1/4 cup granulated sugar
2 tablespoons red currant jelly
2 tablespoons water

EQUIPMENT

Double boiler	Whisk
Small covered saucepan	Citrus grater
	Citrus juicer
Large covered skillet	Kitchen knives
9 x 13-inch glass baking dish	Measuring cups and spoons
Medium mixing bowl	Cooking utensils
Small mixing bowl	

COUNTDOWN

1. Assemble the ingredients and the equipment.
2. Do Steps 1–2 of *Jamaica Rice*.
3. Do Steps 1–2 of *Caribbean Chicken*.
4. Do Steps 1–3 of *Bermuda Triangle*.
5. Do Step 3 of *Caribbean Chicken*.
6. Do Steps 1–2 of *Black Bart's Compote*.
7. Do Step 4 of *Bermuda Triangle*.
8. Do Step 3 of *Jamaica Rice*.
9. Do Step 4 of *Caribbean Chicken*.
10. Do Step 3 of *Black Bart's Compote*.

THURSDAY

Caribbean Chicken

1 Rinse and pat dry the chicken breasts. Rinse, trim, and chop the scallions. Grate 1 tablespoon of lime peel. Juice the lime.

2 Place the chicken breasts in a 9 x 13-inch baking dish. Add the lime peel, the lime juice, the orange juice, the mustard, the honey, the cayenne pepper, and the cumin. Marinate the chicken for 15 minutes, turning to coat.

3 Heat the oil in a large skillet. Reserving the marinade, add the chicken to the skillet and sauté until golden, about 5 minutes per side. Add the reserved marinade to the chicken. Season to taste, cover, reduce the heat, and simmer until the chicken is tender and cooked through, about 15 minutes.

4 Top with the scallions.

Jamaica Rice

1 Bring water to a boil in the bottom of a double boiler.

2 In the top of the double boiler, combine the butter, the broth, the ¼ cup water, the sherry, and the rice. Cover, reduce the heat, and simmer until all the liquid is absorbed and the rice is tender, 30 to 40 minutes.

3 Fluff with a fork before serving.

Bermuda Triangle

1 Wash and dry the lettuce and arrange the leaves on individual salad plates. Peel and thinly slice the onion. Rinse, trim, seed, and chop the bell pepper. Rinse and drain the beans.

2 Combine the onion, the bell pepper, and the beans in a medium bowl.

3 In a small bowl, whisk together the oil, the vinegar, and the lemon-pepper seasoning. Season to taste. Toss the bean mixture with the dressing.

4 Spoon the bean mixture over the lettuce.

Black Bart's Compote

1 Cut the papayas in half and scoop out the seeds. Place the halves on individual dessert plates.

2 Rinse the berries and put them in a small saucepan. Add the sugar, the jelly, and the water. Bring to a boil, reduce the heat, and simmer for 5 minutes. Remove from the heat and cover to keep warm.

3 Spoon the sauce over the papaya halves.

FRIDAY

Chiang Kai-Shrimp

1 small shallot
1 clove garlic
1 small bunch broccoli
2 stalks celery
1 small red bell pepper
1 1/2 pounds medium shrimp, shelled and deveined
2 tablespoons vegetable oil
1 teaspoon sesame oil
1 can (14 ounces) vegetable broth
1 tablespoon soy sauce
1 tablespoon granulated sugar
12 ounces cellophane noodles
2 tablespoons cornstarch
3 tablespoons water
Seasoning to taste

Slaw Boat to China

1 head Napa cabbage
1/4 pound Chinese snow peas
1 small daikon radish
1/2 pound fresh bean sprouts
1 small tomato
3 tablespoons vegetable oil
2 tablespoons rice vinegar
1 teaspoon granulated sugar
1/4 teaspoon red pepper flakes
Seasoning to taste

Man Chu Pears

4 medium Asian pears (or crisp pears)
1/4 cup dark brown sugar
1/4 cup water
3 tablespoons dry white wine
1/2 teaspoon ground cloves

EQUIPMENT

Wok	Whisk
Stockpot	Vegetable peeler
Medium covered skillet	Vegetable grater
Colander	Kitchen knives
Large mixing bowl	Measuring cups and spoons
Small mixing bowl	Cooking utensils

COUNTDOWN

1. Assemble the ingredients and the equipment.
2. Do Steps 1–2 of *Slaw Boat to China*.
3. Do Steps 1–2 of *Chiang Kai-Shrimp*.
4. Do Steps 1–3 of *Man Chu Pears*.
5. Do Steps 3–5 of *Chiang Kai-Shrimp*.
6. Do Step 4 of *Man Chu Pears*.

FRIDAY

Chiang Kai-Shrimp

1 Peel and mince the shallot. Peel and mince the garlic. Rinse and trim the broccoli, discarding the tough ends, and cut into bite-sized florets. Rinse, trim, and chop the celery. Rinse, trim, seed, and chop the bell pepper. Rinse and pat dry the shrimp.

2 Bring water to a boil in a stockpot.

3 Heat the oils in a wok. Add the garlic and stir-fry for 1 minute. Add the shallot, the broccoli, the celery, and the bell pepper and sauté for 2 minutes. Add the shrimp and stir-fry for 2 minutes. Add the broth, the soy sauce, and the sugar and sauté for 1 minute.

4 Cook the noodles in the stockpot for 1 minute. Drain and add to the wok.

5 Whisk together the cornstarch and the 3 tablespoons water. Add to the wok, stirring to blend, until the sauce begins to thicken, about 2 minutes. Season to taste.

Slaw Boat to China

1 Rinse, trim, and thinly slice the cabbage. Rinse, string, and very thinly slice the snow peas. Peel, trim, and grate the radish. Rinse and pat dry the bean sprouts. Rinse, stem, and chop the tomato. Combine the ingredients in a large bowl.

2 In a small bowl, whisk together the oil, the vinegar, the sugar, and the red pepper flakes. Season to taste and toss with the salad.

Man Chu Pears

1 Peel, core, and slice the pears.

2 In a medium skillet, combine the brown sugar and water. Bring to a boil and reduce the heat to a simmer. Add the pears, turning to coat. Add the wine and cook until the pears are crisp-tender, about 6 minutes.

3 Cover and set aside.

4 Sprinkle the pears with the cloves. Distribute them among individual dessert dishes and spoon the sauce over the top.

WEEK TEN

Monday
Yuma Omelet
Cactus Salad
Cocheese
Painted Dessert

Tuesday
Nothing to Cluck About
Zwonderful Zucchini
Tempting Tapioca

Wednesday
Savory Sole
Piquant Pilaf
Boozy Broccoli
Caramel Cake

Thursday
Prudent Pork
Hanky Pancakes
Crafty Carrots
Smart-Aleck Apples

Friday
They Died with Their Roots On
Don't Take This Pearsonally
It's Snowbody's Business

STAPLES

- ☐ Butter
- ☐ Baking powder
- ☐ Cream of tartar
- ☐ Granulated sugar
- ☐ Dark brown sugar
- ☐ Chocolate syrup
- ☐ Maple syrup
- ☐ Silver shots
- ☐ Olive oil
- ☐ Vegetable oil
- ☐ Rice vinegar
- ☐ Lemon juice
- ☐ Honey
- ☐ Prepared horseradish
- ☐ Plain breadcrumbs
- ☐ Instant coffee
- ☐ Chicken bouillon cube
- ☐ Dried basil
- ☐ Bay leaf
- ☐ Dried dill
- ☐ Dried marjoram
- ☐ Dried savory
- ☐ Dried tarragon
- ☐ Whole allspice
- ☐ Cayenne pepper
- ☐ Ground cinnamon
- ☐ Ground ginger
- ☐ Ground nutmeg
- ☐ Black pepper
- ☐ Poultry seasoning
- ☐ Salt
- ☐ Lemon extract
- ☐ Orange extract
- ☐ Vanilla extract

MEAT & POULTRY

4 loin pork chops (about 1 1/2 pounds) (Th)

4 boneless, skinless chicken breast halves (about 1 1/2 pounds) (T)

FISH

4 sole fillets (about 1 1/2 pounds) (W)

FRESH PRODUCE

VEGETABLES

1 1/2 pounds baking potatoes (Th)

1 large bunch broccoli (W)

1 small head cauliflower (F)

2 medium zucchini (T)

2 medium yellow zucchini (T)

1 pound baby carrots (Th)

2 stalks celery (F)

1 medium turnip (F)

1 medium parsnip (F)

1 package (10 ounces) spinach (M)

2 medium tomatoes (W)

1 medium green bell pepper (M)

1 medium red bell pepper (F)

1 medium yellow bell pepper (M)

1 medium yellow bell pepper (F)

2 large onions (F)

1 medium onion (Th)

1 large red onion (T)

1 large shallot (W)

1 medium shallot (M)

2 cloves garlic (M)

1 clove garlic (Th)

HERBS

3 tablespoons chives (when chopped) (Th)

3 tablespoons parsley (when chopped) (M)

2 tablespoons parsley (when chopped) (T)

FRUIT

1 medium lemon (W)

2 large bananas (F)

4 large baking apples (Th)

2 large ripe pears (M)

4 large ripe pears (F)

CANS, JARS & BOTTLES

SOUPS

1 can (14 ounces) vegetable broth (W)

VEGETABLES

1 can (11 ounces) whole-kernel corn (F)

SAUCES

1 can (8 ounces) tomato sauce (M)

1 can (8 ounces) whole cranberry sauce (F)

JUICES

1 cup clam juice (W)

PACKAGED GOODS

PASTA, RICE & GRAINS

8 ounces broad egg noodles (T)

1 cup quick-cooking barley (W)

1 cup granola cereal (Th)

BAKED GOODS

1 package (9 ounces) chocolate wafers (M)

DRIED FRUIT & NUTS

1 package (12 ounces) pitted prunes (Th)

2 tablespoons sliced almonds (W)

DESSERT & BAKING NEEDS

1 package (3.4 ounces) instant coconut cream pudding mix (F)

1/4 cup instant tapioca (T)

1 package (12 ounces) M&M's baking bits (M)

1/2 pound chocolate caramel candies (W)

WINE & SPIRITS

1 cup dry red wine (T)

1/4 cup dry white wine (W)

1/4 cup dry white wine (Th)

1 tablespoon crème de cacao (optional) (M)

REFRIGERATED PRODUCTS

DAIRY

2 tablespoons milk (W)

2 cups milk (F)

2 tablespoons sour cream (M)

3 tablespoons sour cream (W)

1 container (6 ounces) French vanilla yogurt (Th)

10 eggs (M)

1 egg (T)

1 egg (Th)

CHEESE

1 cup shredded Cheddar cheese (M)

2 cups shredded Colby/Monterey Jack cheese (F)

JUICES

1 1/2 cups orange juice (T)

DELI

1/2 pound Canadian bacon (T)

1 package (8 ounces) crescent rolls (F)

FROZEN GOODS

BAKED GOODS

1 pound cake (W)

PASTRY

1 sheet puff pastry (M)

DESSERTS

1 container (8 ounces) whipped topping (M)

1 container (8 ounces) whipped topping (F)

MONDAY

Yuma Omelet

1 medium shallot
2 cloves garlic
1 medium green bell pepper
1 medium yellow bell pepper
9 eggs
2 tablespoons sour cream
2 tablespoons olive oil
1 can (8 ounces) tomato sauce
1 teaspoon cayenne pepper
Seasoning to taste
3 tablespoons butter

Cactus Salad

1 package (10 ounces) fresh spinach
3 tablespoons fresh parsley (when chopped)
2 large ripe pears
3 tablespoons lemon juice
3 tablespoons vegetable oil
2 teaspoons honey
1/2 teaspoon dried basil
Seasoning to taste

Cocheese

1 sheet frozen puff pastry
1 egg
1 tablespoon water
1 cup shredded Cheddar cheese
Seasoning to taste

Painted Dessert

1 package (9 ounces) chocolate wafers
1 container (8 ounces) frozen whipped topping
3 tablespoons chocolate syrup
1 tablespoon instant coffee
1 tablespoon crème de cacao (optional)
1 package (12 ounces) M&M's baking bits

EQUIPMENT

2 large skillets	Whisk
Baking sheet	Rolling pin
Breadboard	Pastry brush
Large mixing bowl	Kitchen knives
2 medium mixing bowls	Measuring cups and spoons
2 small mixing bowls	Cooking utensils

COUNTDOWN

1. Assemble the ingredients and the equipment.
2. Do Steps 1–3 of *Painted Dessert*.
3. Do Steps 1–3 of *Cactus Salad*.
4. Do Steps 1–2 of *Yuma Omelet*.
5. Do Steps 1–6 of *Cocheese*.
6. Do Steps 3–5 of *Yuma Omelet*.
7. Do Step 4 of *Cactus Salad*.
8. Do Step 6 of *Yuma Omelet*.
9. Do Step 4 of *Painted Dessert*.

MONDAY

Yuma Omelet

1 Peel and chop the shallot. Peel and mince the garlic. Rinse, trim, seed, and chop the bell peppers.

2 In a medium bowl, whip the eggs with the sour cream.

3 Heat the oil in a large skillet. Add the shallot, the garlic, and the peppers and sauté until the shallot is soft, about 5 minutes. Add the tomato sauce and the cayenne pepper. Season to taste, reduce the heat, and simmer until heated through, about 3 minutes.

4 Melt the butter in another large skillet.

5 Pour the egg mixture into the skillet and cook until set, 3 to 4 minutes.

6 Top the eggs with the sauce.

Cactus Salad

1 Rinse, pat dry, and stem the spinach. Rinse, stem, and chop the parsley. Rinse, core, and chop the pears and sprinkle them with 1 tablespoon of the lemon juice.

2 Combine the spinach, the parsley, and the pears in a large bowl.

3 In a small bowl, combine the oil, the remaining 2 tablespoons lemon juice, the honey, and the basil. Season to taste.

4 Toss the salad with the dressing.

Cocheese

1 Set the pastry sheet out to soften.

2 Preheat the oven to 375°F. Grease a baking sheet. Flour a breadboard.

3 Beat the egg with the water in a small bowl until blended.

4 On the breadboard, with a rolling pin, smooth out the seams in the pastry sheet. Cut the sheet in half. Brush both halves with the egg mixture. Spread the cheese on one half and season to taste. Top with the other half.

5 Carefully cut the pastry into 1-inch-wide strips and seal all the edges. Twist the dough loosely three times. Place on the baking sheet.

6 Bake until the twists are puffed and golden, about 12 minutes.

Painted Dessert

1 Crumble the chocolate wafers.

2 In a medium bowl, combine ⅔ of the whipped topping, the chocolate syrup, the instant coffee, and the crème de cacao. Blend well.

3 Layer ⅓ of the mixture into dessert glasses, followed by 2 tablespoons of cookie crumbs. Repeat twice. Top with the remaining whipped topping. Refrigerate the parfaits until you are ready to serve.

4 Cover the tops of the parfaits with the M&M's baking bits.

TUESDAY

Nothing to Cluck About

4 boneless, skinless chicken breast halves
　　(about 1 1/2 pounds)
1/2 pound Canadian bacon
1 large red onion
2 tablespoons fresh parsley (when
　　chopped)
2 tablespoons butter
1 tablespoon vegetable oil
1 bay leaf
2 whole allspice
1/2 teaspoon poultry seasoning
1 cup dry red wine
1/2 cup water
1 chicken bouillon cube
Seasoning to taste
8 ounces broad egg noodles

Zwonderful Zucchini

2 medium zucchini
2 medium yellow zucchini
2 tablespoons butter
1/4 teaspoon dried marjoram
2 teaspoons dark brown sugar
Seasoning to taste

Tempting Tapioca

1 egg
1/4 teaspoon cream of tartar
3 tablespoons granulated sugar
1 1/2 cups orange juice
1/4 cup instant tapioca
1 teaspoon orange extract
1/2 teaspoon lemon extract

EQUIPMENT

Electric mixer	Medium mixing bowl
Dutch oven	Plastic wrap
Large saucepan	Kitchen knives
Medium saucepan	Measuring cups and
Large covered skillet	spoons
Colander	Cooking utensils

COUNTDOWN

1. Assemble the ingredients and the equipment.
2. Do Step 1 of Nothing to *Cluck About*.
3. Do Step 1 of *Zwonderful Zucchini*.
4. Do Steps 1–4 of *Tempting Tapioca*.
5. Do Steps 2–5 of *Nothing to Cluck About*.
6. Do Step 2 of *Zwonderful Zucchini*.
7. Do Steps 6–7 of *Nothing to Cluck About*.
8. Do Step 5 of *Tempting Tapioca*.

TUESDAY

Nothing to Cluck About

1 Rinse and pat dry the chicken breasts. Dice the Canadian bacon. Peel and thinly slice the onion. Rinse, stem, and chop the parsley.

2 Bring water to a boil in a large saucepan.

3 Melt the butter with the oil in a Dutch oven. Sauté the chicken until lightly browned, about 5 minutes per side. Remove the chicken and cover to keep warm. Add the bacon to the Dutch oven and sauté until lightly browned, about 7 minutes.

4 Add the onion, the bay leaf, the allspice, the poultry seasoning, the wine, the ½ cup water, and the bouillon cube to the Dutch oven. Lay the chicken breasts on top. Season to taste, cover, and simmer until the chicken is cooked through, 15 to 20 minutes.

5 Cook the noodles in the boiling water until almost tender, 5 to 6 minutes.

6 Remove the bay leaf and the allspice from the Dutch oven.

7 Drain the noodles and serve under the chicken. Sprinkle with the parsley.

Zwonderful Zucchini

1 Scrub, trim, and julienne the zucchini.

2 Melt the butter with the marjoram in a large skillet. Add the zucchini and sauté until crisp-tender, 3 to 4 minutes. Add the brown sugar, season to taste, and sauté until the zucchini is glazed, 2 to 3 minutes. Cover to keep warm.

Tempting Tapioca

1 Separate the egg, placing the yolk in a medium saucepan and the white in a medium bowl.

2 Beat the egg white with the cream of tartar until frothy, about 1 minute. Gradually add 2 tablespoons of the sugar and beat until the egg white is stiff and glossy, about 2 minutes. Cover with plastic wrap and refrigerate until you are ready to use.

3 Add the orange juice, the remaining 1 tablespoon sugar, and the tapioca to the egg yolk. Bring the mixture to a boil, reduce the heat, and simmer, stirring constantly, for 5 minutes.

4 Remove the saucepan from the heat, stir in the orange and lemon extracts and let stand. The mixture will thicken as it stands.

5 Swirl the tapioca mixture lightly into the egg white.

WEDNESDAY

Savory Sole

2 medium tomatoes
4 sole fillets (about 1 1/2 pounds)
1 cup clam juice
1 teaspoon dried savory
1 tablespoon prepared horseradish
3 tablespoons sour cream
Seasoning to taste

Piquant Pilaf

1 large shallot
1 medium lemon
1 tablespoon butter
1 can (14 ounces) vegetable broth
1 cup quick-cooking barley
Seasoning to taste

Boozy Broccoli

1 large bunch broccoli
2 tablespoons butter
1/4 cup dry white wine
1/2 teaspoon dried tarragon
Seasoning to taste

Caramel Cake

1 frozen pound cake
1/2 pound chocolate caramel candies
2 tablespoons milk
2 tablespoons sliced almonds for garnish

EQUIPMENT

Double boiler	Citrus grater
Medium covered saucepan	Citrus juicer
Large skillet	Kitchen knives
Medium covered skillet	Measuring cups and spoons
	Cooking utensils

COUNTDOWN

1. Assemble the ingredients and the equipment.
2. Do Steps 1–4 of *Caramel Cake*.
3. Do Step 1 of *Savory Sole*.
4. Do Step 1 of *Boozy Broccoli*.
5. Do Steps 1–3 of *Piquant Pilaf*.
6. Do Step 2 of *Boozy Broccoli*.
7. Do Step 2 of *Savory Sole*.
8. Do Steps 3–4 of *Boozy Broccoli*.
9. Do Steps 3–4 of *Savory Sole*.
10. Do Step 4 of *Piquant Pilaf*.

WEDNESDAY

Savory Sole

1 Rinse, stem, and chop the tomatoes. Rinse and pat dry the fish fillets.

2 Bring the clam juice to a boil in a large skillet. Reduce the heat to a simmer, add the fish, and poach until it flakes easily with a fork, about 6 minutes. Remove the fish and cover to keep warm.

3 Add the tomatoes, the savory, the horseradish, and the sour cream to the skillet. Season to taste, blend well, and heat through, about 1 minute.

4 Pour the sauce over the fish.

Piquant Pilaf

1 Peel and finely chop the shallot. Grate 1 tablespoon of lemon peel and juice the lemon.

2 Melt the butter in a medium saucepan. Add the shallot and sauté for 2 minutes.

3 Stir in the broth, the lemon juice, and the barley. Season to taste. Bring to a boil, cover, reduce the heat, and simmer until all the liquid is absorbed, about 25 minutes.

4 Stir in the lemon peel.

Boozy Broccoli

1 Rinse and trim the broccoli, discarding the tough ends, and cut into bite-sized florets.

2 Bring a small amount of water to a boil in a medium skillet. Add the broccoli, cover, and cook until crisp-tender, 6 to 8 minutes.

3 Drain the broccoli.

4 Melt the butter in the same skillet. Add the wine and the tarragon and cook, stirring, until the mixture comes to a boil, about 2 minutes. Return the broccoli and toss to coat and warm through. Season to taste.

Caramel Cake

1 Set the pound cake out to thaw.

2 Bring water to a boil in the bottom of a double boiler.

3 Melt the caramels with the milk in the top of the double boiler.

4 Spoon the caramel sauce over the top of the pound cake, letting it run down the sides. Sprinkle with the sliced almonds.

THURSDAY

Prudent Pork

1/4 cup dry white wine
1 package (12 ounces) pitted prunes
1 clove garlic
3 tablespoons fresh chives (when chopped)
1/2 cup flour
4 loin pork chops (about 1 1/2 pounds)
2 tablespoons vegetable oil
1 chicken bouillon cube
1/2 cup water
3 tablespoons rice vinegar
1 teaspoon ground cinnamon
Seasoning to taste

Hanky Pancakes

1 1/2 pounds baking potatoes
1 medium onion
1 egg
2 teaspoons baking powder
1/2 cup plain breadcrumbs
4 tablespoons vegetable oil
Seasoning to taste

Crafty Carrots

1 pound baby carrots
1 tablespoon butter
1 teaspoon dried dill
1/2 teaspoon ground ginger
1 teaspoon honey

Smart-Aleck Apples

4 large baking apples
1 cup granola cereal
1 teaspoon vanilla extract
1/2 cup maple syrup
1 container (6 ounces) French vanilla yogurt
1 teaspoon ground nutmeg

EQUIPMENT

Medium covered
    saucepan
2 large skillets
9 x 9-inch glass
    baking dish
Steamer insert
Large mixing bowl
Small mixing bowl

Vegetable peeler
Vegetable grater
Waxed paper
Kitchen knives
Measuring cups and
    spoons
Cooking utensils

COUNTDOWN

1. Assemble the ingredients and the equipment.
2. Do Step 1 of *Prudent Pork*.
3. Do Steps 1–4 of *Smart-Aleck Apples*.
4. Do Step 1 of *Hanky Pancakes*.
5. Do Steps 2–7 of *Prudent Pork*.
6. Do Steps 1–3 of *Crafty Carrots*.
7. Do Step 2 of *Hanky Pancakes*.
8. Do Step 4 of *Crafty Carrots*.
9. Do Step 8 of *Prudent Pork*.
10. Do Step 5 of *Smart-Aleck Apples*.

THURSDAY

Prudent Pork

1 Place the wine in a small bowl and soak the prunes for 10 minutes.

2 Peel and mince the garlic. Rinse, trim, and chop the chives.

3 Place the flour on a sheet of waxed paper and lightly dredge the pork chops.

4 Heat the oil in a large skillet and sauté the garlic for 1 minute.

5 Add the pork chops and brown them, 5 to 6 minutes per side. Remove the chops and cover to keep warm.

6 Add the prunes and the wine, the bouillon cube, the water, and the vinegar to the skillet. Bring the mixture to a boil, scraping any brown bits from the bottom of the skillet.

7 Return the pork chops to the skillet. Add the cinnamon, season to taste, and simmer until the pork is tender and white throughout, about 15 minutes.

8 Sprinkle with the chives.

Hanky Pancakes

1 Peel and grate the potatoes. Peel and grate the onion. Combine the ingredients in a large bowl. Add the egg, the baking powder, the breadcrumbs, and 2 tablespoons of the oil. Mix well and season to taste.

2 Heat the remaining 2 tablespoons oil in a large skillet. Spoon the potato mixture into the skillet to form pancakes and cook until golden on both sides, about 5 minutes.

Crafty Carrots

1 Bring water to a boil in a medium saucepan.

2 Rinse the carrots and trim if necessary.

3 Arrange the carrots in a steamer insert, place the insert in the saucepan, cover, and steam until the carrots are crisp-tender, about 10 minutes.

4 Drain the carrots and return them to the saucepan. Add the butter, the dill, the ginger, and the honey, tossing to coat, and cook for 1 minute.

Smart-Aleck Apples

1 Preheat oven to 375°F.

2 Rinse and core the apples. Prick several times with the tip of a sharp knife. Arrange the apples in a 9 x 9-inch baking dish.

3 Fill the cavities with the granola. Add a few drops of the vanilla to each apple and spoon the maple syrup over the tops.

4 Bake uncovered until the apples are tender, 20 to 25 minutes.

5 Top each apple with a dollop of the yogurt and sprinkle with the nutmeg.

FRIDAY

They Died with Their Roots On

2 large onions
1 small head cauliflower
1 medium red bell pepper
1 medium yellow bell pepper
1 medium turnip
1 medium parsnip
2 stalks celery
1 can (11 ounces) whole-kernel corn
1 package (8 ounces) crescent rolls
2 tablespoons butter
2 tablespoons vegetable oil
2 cups shredded Colby/Monterey Jack cheese
1/2 teaspoon dried savory
Seasoning to taste

Don't Take This Pearsonally

4 large ripe pears
2 large bananas
3 tablespoons butter
1 can (8 ounces) whole cranberry sauce
1/4 cup lemon juice

It's Snowbody's Business

1 container (8 ounces) frozen whipped topping
2 cups milk
1 package (3.4 ounces) instant coconut cream pudding mix
Silver shots for garnish

EQUIPMENT

Electric mixer	Vegetable peeler
Large covered skillet	Kitchen knives
Large skillet	Measuring cups and spoons
Pie plate	
Medium mixing bowl	Cooking utensils

COUNTDOWN

1. Assemble the ingredients and the equipment.
2. Do Steps 1–2 of *It's Snowbody's Business.*
3. Do Steps 1–3 of *They Died with Their Roots On.*
4. Do Step 3 of *It's Snowbody's Business.*
5. Do Steps 1–4 of *Don't Take This Pearsonally.*
6. Do Steps 4–6 of *They Died with Their Roots On.*
7. Do Step 4 of *It's Snowbody's Business.*

FRIDAY

RECIPES

They Died with Their Roots On

1 Preheat the oven to 375°F.

2 Peel and chop the onions. Rinse and trim the cauliflower and cut into bite-sized florets. Rinse, trim, seed, and chop the bell peppers. Peel, trim, and chop the turnip. Peel, trim, and chop the parsnip. Rinse, trim, and chop the celery. Drain the corn.

3 Unwrap the crescent rolls and separate into individual triangles. Press the triangles evenly into a pie plate in a single layer, overlapping to cover the bottom and sides. Bake for 7 minutes.

4 Melt 1 tablespoon of the butter with the oil in a large skillet and sauté the onions, the cauliflower, the bell peppers, the turnip, and the parsnip for 5 minutes. Add the celery and sauté for 5 minutes.

5 Remove the pie shell from the oven. Dot with the remaining 1 tablespoon butter and sprinkle with 1 cup of the cheese.

6 Add the corn and the savory to the skillet and season to taste. Fold in the remaining 1 cup cheese and blend to combine. Pour the mixture into the pie shell and return it to the oven. Bake until the crust around the edge is puffy and golden, the vegetables are hot, and the cheese is bubbly, about 5 minutes.

Don't Take This Pearsonally

1 Peel, core, and thinly slice the pears. Peel and slice the bananas.

2 Melt the butter in a large skillet. Add the cranberry sauce and cook until it is melted, about 1 minute.

3 Add the pears, the bananas, and the lemon juice. Reduce the heat and simmer until the pears are tender, about 5 minutes.

4 Cover to keep warm.

It's Snowbody's Business

1 Line individual dessert bowls with ⅔ of the whipped topping, smoothing over the sides and the bottoms. Place the bowls in the freezer for 15 minutes.

2 Combine the milk and the pudding mix in a medium bowl and beat for 2 minutes. Let stand for 10 minutes.

3 Remove the dessert bowls from the freezer and carefully spoon the pudding into the center of each bowl, mounding it in the center. Cover with the remaining whipped topping. Return the bowls to the freezer until you are ready to serve.

4 Sprinkle with the silver shots.

WEEK ELEVEN

Monday
Hooked on Halibut
Positively Pilaf
Groovy Green Beans
Cool Cake

Tuesday
Bamboo Beef
Nippon Noodles
Kabuki Koconut

Wednesday
Really Rigatoni
Certainly Salad
Unquestionably Bread
Definitely Dessert

Thursday
Keene On Chicken
Nashua Mashers
Ossipeas and Onions
Purple Lilacs

Friday
Scalloping Into the Sunset
Ricing to the Occasion
Beeting Around the Bush
Laying It On the Lime

STAPLES

- ☐ Butter
- ☐ Cornstarch
- ☐ Granulated sugar
- ☐ Dark brown sugar
- ☐ Powdered sugar
- ☐ Olive oil
- ☐ Sesame oil
- ☐ Vegetable oil
- ☐ Apple cider vinegar
- ☐ Raspberry vinegar
- ☐ Red wine vinegar
- ☐ Rice vinegar
- ☐ Lemon juice
- ☐ Lime juice
- ☐ Dijon mustard
- ☐ Honey
- ☐ Soy sauce
- ☐ Grated Parmesan cheese
- ☐ Plain breadcrumbs
- ☐ Sesame seeds
- ☐ Dried basil
- ☐ Dried dill
- ☐ Dried rosemary
- ☐ Ground allspice
- ☐ Ground cinnamon
- ☐ Ground cloves
- ☐ Ground ginger
- ☐ Ground nutmeg
- ☐ Black pepper
- ☐ Salt
- ☐ Almond extract
- ☐ Peppermint extract

MEAT & POULTRY

1 1/2 pounds lean beefsteak (T)
4 boneless, skinless chicken breast halves (about 1 1/2 pounds) (Th)

FISH

4 halibut or other white fish steaks (about 1 1/2 pounds) (M)
1 1/2 pounds sea scallops (F)

FRESH PRODUCE

VEGETABLES

1 1/2 pounds baking potatoes (Th)
1 large bunch broccoli (F)
1 pound green beans (M)
2 small Japanese eggplants (T)
2 medium carrots (T)
2 stalks celery (T)
1 stalk celery (F)
1/4 pound mushrooms (T)
1 medium head lettuce (W)
1 medium head lettuce (F)
1 large tomato (Th)
3 medium tomatoes (W)
1 medium cucumber (W)
1 large red bell pepper (T)
1 medium red onion (M)
1 small red onion (F)
3 scallions (green onions) (T)
2 scallions (green onions) (W)
3 cloves garlic (M)
1 clove garlic (W)
1 clove garlic (Th)
2 cloves garlic (F)

HERBS

3 tablespoons basil leaves (when chopped) (W)
1/4 cup chives (when chopped) (M)
1 tablespoon chives (when chopped) (W)
1/4 cup chives (when chopped) (F)
2 tablespoons dill (when chopped) (F)
2 tablespoons parsley (when chopped) (M)

3 tablespoons parsley (when chopped) (Th)

FRUIT

3 medium oranges (W)
1 small orange (Th)
1 small lemon (F)
3 medium bananas (W)
3 medium Asian pears (or crisp pears) (T)

CANS, JARS & BOTTLES

SOUPS

1 can (14 ounces) chicken broth (M)
1 can (14 ounces) chicken broth (Th)
1 can (14 ounces) vegetable broth (F)

VEGETABLES

1 can (15 ounces) julienne beets (F)

INTERNATIONAL FOODS

1 can (5 ounces) sliced bamboo shoots (T)

FISH

1 tin (2 ounces) anchovy fillets (W)

FRUIT

1 can (8 ounces) crushed pineapple (M)
1 can (11 ounces) mandarin oranges (T)
1 can (15 ounces) purple plums in syrup (Th)

CONDIMENTS

1 can (3 1/2 ounces) sliced black olives (W)
2 teaspoons capers (F)

PACKAGED GOODS

PASTA, RICE & GRAINS

1/2 cup capellini (when broken) (M)
1 pound rigatoni (W)
1 cup long-grain white rice (M)
1 cup wild rice (F)

BAKED GOODS

1 loaf Italian bread (W)
4 large sugar cookies (F)

INTERNATIONAL FOODS

8 ounces Japanese soba noodles (T)

DRIED FRUIT & NUTS

1/2 cup sliced almonds (M)
3 tablespoons walnut bits (W)
1/4 cup sliced almonds (Th)

DESSERT & BAKING NEEDS

1/2 cup flaked coconut (T)
6 ounces chocolate chips (F)

WINE & SPIRITS

1/4 cup dry white wine (Th)
1 cup dry white wine (F)
2 tablespoons dry sherry (T)
3 tablespoons brandy (W)

REFRIGERATED PRODUCTS

DAIRY

2 tablespoons milk (F)
1/2 cup half-and-half (F)
1 container (8 ounces) pineapple yogurt (M)
1/2 cup whipping cream (F)

CHEESE

1 package (8 ounces) cream cheese (M)
1/2 cup shredded mozzarella cheese (W)
1/4 pound sliced Swiss cheese (Th)

DELI

1/4 pound sliced ham (Th)

FROZEN GOODS

VEGETABLES

1 package (10 ounces) green peas and pearl onions (Th)

BAKED GOODS

1 pound cake (M)

DESSERTS

1 pint almond yogurt (Th)
1 pint lime sherbet (F)
1 container (8 ounces) whipped topping (T)

MONDAY

Hooked on Halibut

3 cloves garlic
2 tablespoons fresh parsley (when chopped)
4 halibut or other white fish steaks (about 1 1/2 pounds)
2 tablespoons lemon juice
1 teaspoon dried basil
2 tablespoons olive oil
Seasoning to taste

Positively Pilaf

1/4 cup fresh chives (when chopped)
3 tablespoons butter
1/2 cup sliced almonds
1/2 cup capellini (when broken)
1 cup long-grain white rice
1 can (14 ounces) chicken broth
1/4 cup water

Groovy Green Beans

1 pound fresh green beans
1 medium red onion
3 tablespoons butter
1/4 teaspoon pepper
1/4 cup raspberry vinegar
Seasoning to taste

Cool Cake

1 frozen pound cake
1 package (8 ounces) cream cheese
1 container (8 ounces) pineapple yogurt
1 can (8 ounces) crushed pineapple

EQUIPMENT

Electric mixer	Small mixing bowl
Medium covered saucepan	Whisk
Large covered skillet	Pastry brush
9 x 13-inch glass baking dish	Kitchen knives
Medium mixing bowl	Measuring cups and spoons
	Cooking utensils

COUNTDOWN

1. Assemble the ingredients and the equipment.
2. Do Steps 1–3 of *Cool Cake*.
3. Do Steps 1–3 of *Hooked on Halibut*.
4. Do Steps 1–4 of *Positively Pilaf*.
5. Do Steps 1–3 of *Groovy Green Beans*.
6. Do Step 4 of *Hooked on Halibut*.
7. Do Steps 4–5 of *Groovy Green Beans*.
8. Do Step 5 of *Positively Pilaf*.

MONDAY

Hooked on Halibut

1 Preheat the broiler.

2 Peel and mince the garlic. Rinse, stem, and chop the parsley. Rinse and pat dry the halibut steaks and arrange them in a 9 x 13-inch baking dish.

3 In a small bowl combine the garlic, the parsley, the lemon juice, the basil, and the oil. Season to taste. Pour over the halibut steaks and marinate for 20 minutes, turning once or twice to coat.

4 Drain the halibut steaks, reserving the marinade, and place them on a broiler pan. Brush them with some of the reserved marinade and broil for 5 minutes. Turn the steaks, brush with the remaining marinade, and continue broiling until the fish flakes easily with a fork, about 5 minutes more.

Positively Pilaf

1 Rinse, trim, and chop the chives.

2 Melt 1 tablespoon of the butter in a large skillet and sauté the almonds until lightly toasted, about 3 minutes. Remove them from the skillet and reserve.

3 Break the capellini into 1-inch pieces and sauté them in the skillet for 2 minutes. Remove the capellini and reserve.

4 Melt the remaining 2 tablespoons butter in the skillet. Add the rice and sauté until it is lightly browned, about 5 minutes. Return the almonds and the capellini to the skillet. Add the broth and the water and bring the mixture to a boil. Cover, reduce the heat, and simmer until all the liquid is absorbed and the rice is tender, about 20 minutes.

5 Sprinkle with the chives and fluff with a fork before serving.

Groovy Green Beans

1 Bring water to a boil in a medium saucepan.

2 Rinse and trim the green beans. Peel and thinly slice the onion and separate the slices into rings.

3 Cook the beans until they are crisp-tender, 5 to 6 minutes.

4 Drain the beans.

5 Melt the butter in the saucepan. Add the onion rings and cook until they begin to soften, about 4 minutes. Stir in the pepper and the vinegar. Return the green beans and cook until heated through, tossing to coat. Season to taste and cover to keep warm.

Cool Cake

1 Set the pound cake out to thaw. Set the cream cheese out to soften.

2 Combine the cream cheese, the yogurt, and the crushed pineapple with its liquid in a medium bowl and beat until well blended.

3 Split the cake in half lengthwise. Spread ⅓ of the pineapple mixture evenly on the bottom layer. Replace the top layer and spread the remainder of the mixture over the top and the sides of the cake. Refrigerate until you are ready to serve.

TUESDAY

Bamboo Beef

1 1/2 pounds lean beefsteak
2 stalks celery
3 scallions (green onions)
1/4 pound fresh mushrooms
2 small Japanese eggplants
2 medium carrots
1 large red bell pepper
1 can (5 ounces) sliced bamboo shoots
2 tablespoons cornstarch
2 tablespoons dry sherry
1 tablespoon soy sauce
1 tablespoon dark brown sugar
1/4 cup water
2 tablespoons vegetable oil
Seasoning to taste

Nippon Noodles

3 tablespoons rice vinegar
2 teaspoons sesame oil
1/2 teaspoon ground allspice
1 teaspoon ground ginger
Seasoning to taste
8 ounces Japanese soba noodles
2 tablespoons sesame seeds

Kabuki Koconut

1 container (8 ounces) frozen whipped
  topping
3 medium Asian pears (or crisp pears)
1 tablespoon lime juice
2 teaspoons almond extract
1 can (11 ounces) mandarin oranges
1/2 cup flaked coconut
2 tablespoons powdered sugar

EQUIPMENT

Wok
Large covered
  saucepan
2 medium mixing
  bowls
2 small mixing bowls
Colander

Whisk
Vegetable peeler
Plastic wrap
Kitchen knives
Measuring cups and
  spoons
Cooking utensils

COUNTDOWN

1. Assemble the ingredients and the equipment.
2. Do Steps 1–3 of *Kabuki Koconut.*
3. Do Steps 1–2 of *Bamboo Beef.*
4. Do Steps 1–4 of *Nippon Noodles.*
5. Do Steps 3–5 of *Bamboo Beef.*
6. Do Step 4 of *Kabuki Koconut.*

TUESDAY

Bamboo Beef

1 Trim any excess fat from the beef and cut across the grain into thin strips. Cut the strips into 2-inch pieces. Rinse, trim, and slice the celery. Rinse, trim, and slice the scallions. Rinse, pat dry, trim, and slice the mushrooms. Rinse, trim, and thinly slice the eggplants. Peel, trim, and thinly slice the carrots. Rinse, trim, seed, and chop the bell pepper. Drain the bamboo shoots.

2 In a small bowl, combine the cornstarch, the sherry, the soy sauce, the brown sugar, and the water.

3 Heat the oil in a wok.

4 Add the beef to the wok and stir-fry for 2 minutes. Add the eggplants and the carrots and stir-fry for 2 minutes. Add the celery, the mushrooms, the scallions, the bell pepper, and the bamboo shoots and stir-fry for 2 minutes. Mix well to combine.

5 Add the sauce and toss to blend. Season to taste.

Nippon Noodles

1 Bring water to a boil in a large saucepan.

2 In a small bowl, combine the vinegar, the oil, the allspice, and the ginger. Season to taste.

3 Cook the noodles until they begin to rise, about 1 minute.

4 Drain the noodles and return them to the saucepan. Add the vinegar mixture, tossing to coat, and heat through. Sprinkle with the sesame seeds and cover to keep warm.

Kabuki Koconut

1 Set the whipped topping out to soften.

2 Peel, core, and dice the pears. Place them in a medium bowl and sprinkle with the lime juice to keep them from browning. Cover with plastic wrap and refrigerate until you are ready to use.

3 In a medium bowl, blend the whipped topping with the almond extract. Drain and fold in the mandarin oranges. Refrigerate until you are ready to use.

4 Sprinkle the pears with the coconut and fold them into the whipped topping mixture. Blend in the powdered sugar and spoon into individual dessert dishes.

WEDNESDAY

Really Rigatoni

1 tin (2 ounces) anchovy fillets
1 clove garlic
3 tablespoons fresh basil leaves (when chopped)
3 medium tomatoes
1 pound rigatoni
2 tablespoons butter
1/2 cup shredded mozzarella cheese
Seasoning to taste

Certainly Salad

1 medium head lettuce
2 scallions (green onions)
1 medium cucumber
1 can (3 1/2 ounces) sliced black olives
3 tablespoons olive oil
2 tablespoons red wine vinegar
1 teaspoon Dijon mustard
Seasoning to taste

Unquestionably Bread

1 loaf Italian bread
1 tablespoon fresh chives (when chopped)
3 tablespoons butter
2 teaspoons dried dill
Seasoning to taste

Definitely Dessert

3 medium bananas
3 medium oranges
1/4 cup honey
3 tablespoons brandy
1 teaspoon ground nutmeg
3 tablespoons walnut bits

EQUIPMENT

Stockpot	Small mixing bowl
Small saucepan	Whisk
Large skillet	Vegetable peeler
9 x 9-inch glass baking dish	Pastry brush
Baking sheet	Kitchen knives
Colander	Measuring cups and spoons
Large mixing bowl	Cooking utensils

COUNTDOWN

1. Assemble the ingredients and the equipment.
2. Do Steps 1–3 of *Definitely Dessert*.
3. Do Steps 1–3 of *Unquestionably Bread*.
4. Do Steps 1–3 of *Really Rigatoni*.
5. Do Steps 1–2 of *Certainly Salad*.
6. Do Steps 4–6 of *Really Rigatoni*.
7. Do Steps 4–5 of *Unquestionably Bread*.
8. Do Step 3 of *Certainly Salad*.
9. Do Steps 4–5 of *Definitely Dessert*.

WEDNESDAY

Really Rigatoni

1 Bring water to a boil in a stockpot.

2 Drain, pat dry, and chop the anchovies. Peel and mince the garlic. Rinse, stem, and chop the basil. Rinse, stem, and chop the tomatoes.

3 Cook the rigatoni until it is almost tender, 8 to 10 minutes.

4 Drain the pasta.

5 Melt the butter in a large skillet and sauté the garlic for 1 minute. Add the tomatoes and sauté for 2 minutes. Add the pasta, tossing to coat, and sauté for 2 minutes more.

6 Fold in the anchovies and the basil. Add the cheese, season to taste, toss to combine, and heat through.

Certainly Salad

1 Wash and dry the lettuce and tear it into bite-sized pieces. Rinse, trim, and chop the scallions. Peel, trim, and slice the cucumber. Drain the olives. Combine the ingredients in a large bowl.

2 In a small bowl, whisk together the oil, the vinegar, and the mustard. Season to taste.

3 Toss the salad with the dressing.

Unquestionably Bread

1 Cut the bread in half lengthwise and place the halves on a baking sheet. Rinse, trim, and chop the chives.

2 In a small saucepan, melt the butter with the dill. Season to taste.

3 Brush the butter mixture on the cut sides of the bread. Sprinkle with the chives.

4 Preheat the broiler.

5 Broil until lightly toasted, 2 to 3 minutes.

Definitely Dessert

1 Butter a 9 x 9-inch baking dish.

2 Peel the bananas and slice them in half lengthwise. Peel and slice the oranges.

3 Place the orange slices and the banana halves in the baking dish. Drizzle with the honey and the brandy and sprinkle with the nutmeg and the nuts.

4 Preheat the broiler.

5 Broil until bubbly and heated through, about 5 minutes.

THURSDAY

Keene On Chicken

1 large tomato
3 tablespoons fresh parsley (when chopped)
4 boneless, skinless chicken breast halves (about 1½ pounds)
2 tablespoons butter
½ cup plain breadcrumbs
3 tablespoons grated Parmesan cheese
1 teaspoon dried basil
¼ pound sliced deli ham
¼ pound sliced Swiss cheese
¼ cup chicken broth
¼ cup dry white wine
Seasoning to taste

Nashua Mashers

1 clove garlic
1½ pounds baking potatoes
1½ cups chicken broth
2 tablespoons butter
½ teaspoon dried rosemary
Seasoning to taste

Ossipeas and Onions

1 package (10 ounces) frozen green peas and pearl onions
1 small orange
2 tablespoons butter
¼ cup water
1 teaspoon granulated sugar
Seasoning to taste

Purple Lilacs

1 can (15 ounces) purple plums in syrup
¼ cup dark brown sugar
1 teaspoon ground allspice
1 teaspoon ground nutmeg
½ teaspoon ground cinnamon
1 tablespoon butter
1 tablespoon almond extract
1 pint almond frozen yogurt
¼ cup sliced almonds

EQUIPMENT

Electric mixer	Vegetable peeler
Medium covered saucepan	Citrus grater
2 small saucepans	Citrus juicer
Medium covered skillet	Ice cream scoop
9 x 13-inch glass baking dish	Kitchen knives
2 small mixing bowls	Measuring cups and spoons
	Cooking utensils

COUNTDOWN

1. Assemble the ingredients and the equipment.
2. Do Step 1 of *Ossipeas and Onions*.
3. Do Steps 1–5 of *Keene On Chicken*.
4. Do Steps 1–2 of *Nashua Mashers*.
5. Do Steps 2–3 of *Ossipeas and Onions*.
6. Do Steps 1–2 of *Purple Lilacs*.
7. Do Step 3 of *Nashua Mashers*.
8. Do Step 3 of *Purple Lilacs*.

THURSDAY

RECIPES

Keene On Chicken

1 Preheat the oven to 350°F. Grease a 9 x 13-inch baking dish.

2 Rinse, stem, and cut the tomato into 4 even slices. Rinse, stem, and chop the parsley. Rinse and pat dry the chicken breasts and place them in the baking dish.

3 Melt the butter in a small saucepan. Blend in the breadcrumbs, the Parmesan cheese, the basil, and the parsley and set aside.

4 Top each chicken breast with a slice of ham. Lay a slice of Swiss cheese over the ham. Place a slice of tomato over the cheese. Sprinkle the breadcrumb mixture over the tomato slices.

5 Pour the broth and the wine around the chicken pieces. Season to taste and bake until the chicken is tender, about 30 minutes.

Nashua Mashers

1 Peel and mince the garlic. Peel and dice the potatoes.

2 Place the potatoes in a medium saucepan. Add 1 cup of the broth and enough water to cover the potatoes. Bring to a boil and cook until the potatoes are tender, 10 to 12 minutes.

3 Drain the potatoes and return them to the saucepan. Reduce the heat and shake the saucepan gently over low heat until the potatoes are dry. Beat in the remaining ½ cup broth. Add the butter, the rosemary, and the garlic and beat vigorously until the potatoes are light and fluffy. Season to taste and cover to keep warm.

Ossipeas and Onions

1 Set the peas and onions in a small bowl of warm water to thaw.

2 Grate 1 tablespoon of orange peel and juice the orange.

3 Melt the butter in a medium skillet. Add the peas and onions and sauté for 2 minutes. Add the orange juice and the ¼ cup water. Cover and simmer until heated through, about 2 minutes. Drain the peas. Add the sugar and the orange peel and season to taste.

Purple Lilacs

1 Drain the plums, reserving the syrup. Halve and pit the plums and place them in a small bowl.

2 In a small saucepan, combine the reserved syrup, the brown sugar, the allspice, the nutmeg, the cinnamon, and the butter and bring the mixture to a boil. Remove the saucepan from the heat, add the almond extract, and set aside.

3 Place scoops of frozen yogurt in individual dessert dishes. Top with the plums. Spoon the sauce over the top and sprinkle with the almonds.

FRIDAY

Scalloping Into the Sunset

1 1/2 pounds sea scallops
2 cloves garlic
1 large bunch broccoli
1 small lemon
2 tablespoons fresh dill (when chopped)
1/2 cup whipping cream
1/2 cup half-and-half
2 tablespoons Dijon mustard
Seasoning to taste
1 cup dry white wine

Ricing to the Occasion

1 stalk celery
1/4 cup fresh chives (when chopped)
1 cup wild rice
1 can (14 ounces) vegetable broth
1/2 cup water

Beeting Around the Bush

1 medium head lettuce
1 small red onion
1 can (15 ounces) julienne beets
3 tablespoons vegetable oil
3 tablespoons apple cider vinegar
1/2 teaspoon ground cinnamon
1 teaspoon ground cloves
1 teaspoon granulated sugar
Seasoning to taste
2 teaspoons capers

Laying It On the Lime

6 ounces chocolate chips
2 tablespoons milk
1/2 teaspoon peppermint extract
4 large sugar cookies
1 pint lime sherbet

EQUIPMENT

Double boiler	Small mixing bowl
Large saucepan	Whisk
Medium covered saucepan	Ice cream scoop
Small covered saucepan	Kitchen knives
Small saucepan	Measuring cups and spoons
Steamer insert	Cooking utensils

COUNTDOWN

1. Assemble the ingredients and the equipment.
2. Do Steps 1–3 of *Ricing to the Occasion*.
3. Do Steps 1–4 of *Beeting Around the Bush*.
4. Do Steps 1–2 of *Laying It On the Lime*.
5. Do Steps 1–7 of *Scalloping Into the Sunset*.
6. Do Step 4 of *Ricing to the Occasion*.
7. Do Step 5 of *Beeting Around the Bush*.
8. Do Step 3 of *Laying It On the Lime*.

FRIDAY

Scalloping Into the Sunset

1 Rinse and pat dry the scallops. Peel and mince the garlic. Rinse and trim the broccoli, discarding the tough ends, and cut into bite-sized florets. Slice the lemon. Rinse, stem, and chop the dill.

2 Bring a small amount of water to a boil in a medium saucepan. Arrange the broccoli and the garlic in a steamer insert. Place the insert in the saucepan, cover, and steam until the broccoli is crisp-tender, about 5 minutes.

3 Bring the whipping cream and the half-and-half to a boil in a small saucepan. Reduce the heat and simmer, stirring, until thickened, about 3 minutes. Stir in the dill and the mustard and season to taste. Blend well and cover to keep warm.

4 Drain the broccoli, return it to the saucepan, and cover to keep warm.

5 Combine the lemon slices and the wine in a large saucepan. Bring to a boil, add the scallops, and cook until they turn opaque, about 3 minutes.

6 Drain the scallops, discarding the lemon, and combine them with the broccoli.

7 Place spoonfuls of the mustard sauce on individual plates, swirling to cover the bottom of each plate, and top with the scallops and the broccoli.

Ricing to the Occasion

1 Bring water to a boil in the bottom of a double boiler.

2 Rinse, trim, and dice the celery. Rinse, trim, and chop the chives. Rinse the wild rice.

3 Combine the rice, the celery, the broth, and the ½ cup water in the top of the double boiler. Cover, reduce the heat, and simmer until all the liquid is absorbed and the rice is tender, about 45 minutes.

4 Fluff with a fork and sprinkle with the chives.

Beeting Around the Bush

1 Wash and dry the lettuce, tear it into bite-sized pieces, and distribute it among individual salad plates.

2 Peel and thinly slice the onion. Drain the beets.

3 In a small bowl, combine the oil, the vinegar, the cinnamon, and the cloves. Blend in the sugar and season to taste.

4 Arrange the beets on top of the lettuce and distribute the onions on top of the beets. Sprinkle with the capers.

5 Drizzle the dressing over each salad.

Laying It On the Lime

1 In a small saucepan, melt the chocolate chips with the milk, stirring until smooth, about 3 minutes.

2 Remove from the heat and blend in the peppermint extract. Let stand.

3 Place the cookies in individual dessert bowls. Top each cookie with a scoop of sherbet and drizzle with the sauce.

WEEK TWELVE

Monday
One-Night Strand
Head Over Peels
The Spooner the Batter
In Cake of Emergency

Tuesday
Boston Blackie
Sam'n Spade
Sherbet Holmes

Wednesday
Sweet Bird of Youth
Summer and Smoke
Suddenly Last Salad
The Rose Tapioca

Thursday
Dairy'n Delight
Puritan Peaches
Danbury Buns
Blue Law Cake

Friday
Clam Solo
Obi-Wan Kenobeans
Dark Vaders

- ☐ Butter
- ☐ Flour
- ☐ Baking powder
- ☐ Cornstarch
- ☐ Granulated sugar
- ☐ Dark brown sugar
- ☐ Powdered sugar
- ☐ Olive oil
- ☐ Vegetable oil
- ☐ Red wine vinegar
- ☐ Tarragon vinegar
- ☐ Lemon juice
- ☐ Lime juice
- ☐ Dijon mustard
- ☐ Mayonnaise
- ☐ Tabasco sauce
- ☐ Grated Parmesan cheese
- ☐ Dried basil
- ☐ Bay leaf
- ☐ Dried dill
- ☐ Dried marjoram
- ☐ Dried oregano
- ☐ Ground allspice
- ☐ Whole allspice
- ☐ Cayenne pepper
- ☐ Ground cinnamon
- ☐ Ground cumin
- ☐ Italian seasoning
- ☐ Lemon-pepper seasoning
- ☐ Ground nutmeg
- ☐ Black pepper
- ☐ Saffron threads
- ☐ Salt
- ☐ Peppermint extract
- ☐ Vanilla extract

MEAT & POULTRY

1 lean cooked ham steak (about 3/4 pound) (M)
1 pound Italian bulk sausage (Th)
4 boneless, skinless chicken breast halves (about 1 1/2 pounds) (W)

FISH

48 hard-shell clams (F)

FRESH PRODUCE

VEGETABLES

1/2 pound green beans (M)
1 medium zucchini (Th)
1 medium carrot (M)
2 stalks celery (W)
2 stalks celery (F)
1 medium portabello mushroom (W)
1 package (12 ounces) spinach (M)
1 medium head lettuce (W)
1 small head lettuce (F)
1 package (10 ounces) mixed salad greens (T)
2 medium tomatoes (T)
1 large ripe avocado (T)
1 medium cucumber (M)
4 medium cucumbers (W)
1 medium red bell pepper (W)
1 large onion (T)
1 small onion (F)
1 large sweet onion (W)
1 small red onion (F)
1 medium shallot (M)
4 scallions (green onions) (T)
4 cloves garlic (M)
2 cloves garlic (T)
1 clove garlic (Th)
1 clove garlic (F)

HERBS

2 tablespoons parsley (when chopped) (W)
1/4 cup parsley (when chopped) (F)
1/4 cup rosemary (when chopped) (Th)

FRUIT

2 medium oranges (T)
1 medium banana (T)

CANS, JARS & BOTTLES

SOUPS

2 cans (14 ounces each) chicken broth (T)

VEGETABLES

1 can (14 1/2 ounces) diced tomatoes (F)
2 cans (15 ounces each) black beans (T)
1 can (15 ounces) garbanzo beans (F)
1 can (11 ounces) whole-kernel white corn (T)
1 jar (7 ounces) roasted red peppers (M)
1 can (14 ounces) artichoke hearts (W)

FISH

2 cans (6 ounces each) salmon (T)

INTERNATIONAL FOODS

1 can (4 ounces) diced green chilies (T)
1 jar (12 ounces) salsa (T)

FRUIT

1 can (8 ounces) crushed pineapple (T)
1 can (29 ounces) sliced peaches (Th)

JUICES

8 ounces clam juice (F)

SPREADS

1/2 cup chunky peanut butter (M)
1/2 cup grape jelly (M)

DESSERT & BAKING NEEDS

2/3 cup marshmallow crème (F)

PACKAGED GOODS

PASTA, RICE & GRAINS

1 pound linguini (M)
1 pound spaghetti (F)
1 cup couscous (W)

BAKED GOODS

4 tostada crowns (T)
4 hamburger buns (Th)
1 pound cake (M)
1 angel food loaf cake (Th)

DRIED FRUIT & NUTS

1/4 cup pine nuts (M)
1/2 cup pecan pieces (F)

DESSERT & BAKING NEEDS

3 tablespoons instant tapioca (W)
1 square (1 ounce) semisweet chocolate (F)

WINE & SPIRITS

1/2 cup dry white wine (W)
1/2 cup dry red wine (F)
3 tablespoons dry sherry (T)

REFRIGERATED PRODUCTS

DAIRY

1/4 cup milk (M)
1/4 cup milk (Th)
1/4 cup milk (F)
1 1/4 cups sour cream (T)
2 tablespoons sour cream (W)
Whipped cream for garnish (W)
9 eggs (Th)

CHEESE

1 cup shredded mozzarella cheese (Th)
1/4 pound smoked Gouda cheese (W)
1/2 cup pepper Jack cheese (when grated) (F)

JUICES

1/4 cup orange juice (T)
1 cup orange juice (Th)

FROZEN GOODS

VEGETABLES

1 package (10 ounces) cut green beans (F)
1 package (10 ounces) chopped spinach (Th)

FRUIT

1 package (10 ounces) raspberries (W)
1 package (12 ounces) blueberries (Th)

DESSERTS

1 pint orange sherbet (T)
1 pint chocolate ice cream (F)

MONDAY

One-Night Strand

4 cloves garlic
1 medium shallot
1/2 pound fresh green beans
1 lean cooked ham steak (about 3/4 pound)
1 pound linguini
3 tablespoons olive oil
3 tablespoons lemon juice
1 teaspoon granulated sugar
1/8 teaspoon cayenne pepper
1/2 teaspoon Italian seasoning
Seasoning to taste

Head Over Peels

1/4 cup pine nuts
1 package (12 ounces) fresh spinach
1 medium cucumber
1 medium carrot
3 tablespoons vegetable oil
2 tablespoons red wine vinegar
1/4 teaspoon ground nutmeg
Seasoning to taste

The Spooner the Batter

4 tablespoons butter
1 jar (7 ounces) roasted red peppers
1 cup flour
1 teaspoon granulated sugar
1 tablespoon baking powder
1/4 cup milk

In Cake of Emergency

1 pound cake
1/2 cup chunky peanut butter
1/2 cup grape jelly

EQUIPMENT

Stockpot	Vegetable peeler
Medium skillet	Vegetable grater
Baking sheet	Pastry blender
Breadboard	Biscuit cutter
Colander	Kitchen knives
Large mixing bowl	Measuring cups and
Medium mixing bowl	spoons
Small mixing bowl	Cooking utensils
Whisk	

COUNTDOWN

1. Assemble the ingredients and the equipment.
2. Do Steps 1–4 of *Head Over Peels*.
3. Do Steps 1–2 of *One-Night Strand*.
4. Do Steps 1–7 of *The Spooner the Batter*.
5. Do Steps 3–5 of *One-Night Strand*.
6. Do Step 5 of *Head Over Peels*.
7. Do Steps 1–2 of *In Cake of Emergency*.

MONDAY

One-Night Strand

1 Bring water to a boil in a stockpot.

2 Peel and mince the garlic. Peel and chop the shallot. Rinse, trim, and julienne the green beans. Cut the ham into very thin strips.

3 Cook the linguini until it is almost tender, 2 to 3 minutes if you are using fresh pasta, 6 to 7 minutes if you are using dry pasta.

4 Heat the oil in a medium skillet and sauté the garlic and the shallot for 1 minute. Add the beans and sauté for 3 minutes. Add the ham strips and sauté for 2 minutes. Add the lemon juice, the sugar, the cayenne pepper, and the Italian seasoning. Season to taste and heat through.

5 Drain the pasta, return it to the stockpot, and toss it with the ham and bean mixture.

Head Over Peels

1 Preheat the oven to 350°F.

2 Place the pine nuts on a baking sheet and toast for 5 minutes.

3 Rinse, pat dry, stem, and chop the spinach. Peel, trim, and slice the cucumber. Peel, trim, and grate the carrot. Combine the spinach, the cucumber, and the carrot in a large bowl.

4 In a small bowl, combine the oil, the vinegar, and the nutmeg. Season to taste.

5 Toss the salad with the dressing and sprinkle with the pine nuts.

The Spooner the Batter

1 Increase the oven temperature to 425°F. Flour a breadboard.

2 Set the butter out to soften. Drain the red peppers, blot on paper towels, and chop.

3 Combine the flour, the sugar, and the baking powder in a medium bowl. Cut in the butter with a pastry blender until the mixture resembles coarse crumbs.

4 Blend in the milk. Fold in the peppers.

5 Place the dough on the breadboard and knead until the dough is smooth, 10 to 12 times.

6 Pat the dough out to a 1-inch thickness and cut with a biscuit cutter. Place the rounds on a baking sheet 1 inch apart.

7 Bake until the biscuits are golden and puffed, about 12 minutes.

In Cake of Emergency

1 Cut the cake into ¼-inch-thick slices.

2 Spread the peanut butter on half of the slices and the jelly on the other slices. Place the slices together to resemble peanut butter and jelly sandwiches and cut them in half diagonally.

TUESDAY

Boston Blackie

1 large onion
2 cloves garlic
2 cans (15 ounces each) black beans
1 can (11 ounces) whole-kernel white corn
2 bay leaves
2 whole allspice
2 cans (14 ounces each) chicken broth
1 teaspoon granulated sugar
3 tablespoons dry sherry
2 teaspoons ground cumin
Seasoning to taste
1/4 cup sour cream for garnish

Sam'n Spade

1 package (10 ounces) mixed salad greens
4 scallions (green onions)
2 medium tomatoes
1 large ripe avocado
2 cans (6 ounces each) salmon
1 can (4 ounces) diced green chilies
4 tostada crowns
1 cup sour cream
2 tablespoons mayonnaise
2 tablespoons lime juice
1 teaspoon dried dill
Seasoning to taste
1 jar (12 ounces) salsa

Sherbet Holmes

1 pint orange sherbet
2 medium oranges
1 medium banana
1 can (8 ounces) crushed pineapple
1/4 cup orange juice

EQUIPMENT

Blender
Large saucepan
Baking sheet
2 large mixing bowls
Vegetable grater

Kitchen knives
Measuring cups and
  spoons
Cooking utensils

COUNTDOWN

1. Assemble the ingredients and the equipment.
2. Do Steps 1–4 of *Sherbet Holmes*.
3. Do Steps 1–2 of *Boston Blackie*.
4. Do Steps 1–3 of *Sam'n Spade*.
5. Do Steps 3–4 of *Boston Blackie*.
6. Do Step 4 of *Sam'n Spade*.

TUESDAY

Boston Blackie

1 Peel and grate the onion. Peel and mince the garlic. Drain, rinse, and drain the beans. Drain the corn.

2 Combine the onion, the garlic, the bay leaves, the allspice, the beans, the corn, the broth, and the sugar in a large saucepan. Bring the mixture to a boil, reduce the heat, and simmer for 15 minutes.

3 Remove the allspice and the bay leaves from the saucepan. Puree half of the soup in a blender for 30 seconds and return it to the saucepan. Add the sherry and the cumin and season to taste. Bring the soup back to a boil and cook for 1 minute.

4 Garnish each serving with a dollop of sour cream.

Sam'n Spade

1 Preheat the oven to 350°F.

2 Rinse and dry the salad greens. Rinse, trim, and chop the scallions. Rinse, stem, and chop the tomatoes. Halve, pit, peel, and chop the avocado. Drain and flake the salmon. Drain the chilies. Combine the ingredients in a large bowl.

3 Place the tostada crowns on a baking sheet and crisp in the oven for 3 minutes.

4 In a small bowl, combine the sour cream, the mayonnaise, the lime juice, and the dill. Season to taste. Toss with salad.

5 Fill the tostada crowns with the salad and serve with the salsa.

Sherbet Holmes

1 Set the sherbet out to soften.

2 Peel and section the oranges and cut the sections in half. Peel and chunk the banana. Drain the pineapple.

3 Place the fruit in a blender with the orange juice and puree for 30 seconds. Pour the mixture into a large bowl. Fold in the sherbet and blend well.

4 Spoon the mixture into individual dessert glasses and place in the freezer until you are ready to serve.

WEDNESDAY

Sweet Bird of Youth

4 boneless, skinless chicken breast halves
   (about 1 1/2 pounds)
1/2 cup dry white wine
1 teaspoon lemon-pepper seasoning
1 large sweet onion
1 medium red bell pepper
1 medium fresh portabello mushroom
1 can (14 ounces) artichoke hearts
3 tablespoons butter
Seasoning to taste

Summer and Smoke

2 stalks celery
2 tablespoons fresh parsley (when
   chopped)
1/4 pound smoked Gouda cheese
2 tablespoons vegetable oil
2 tablespoons lemon juice
1 1/2 cups water
1 teaspoon saffron threads
1 cup couscous
Seasoning to taste

Suddenly Last Salad

1 medium head lettuce
4 medium cucumbers
1/2 cup mayonnaise
2 tablespoons sour cream
1/2 teaspoon granulated sugar
1 tablespoon tarragon vinegar
1/2 teaspoon Dijon mustard
Seasoning to taste

The Rose Tapioca

1 package (10 ounces) frozen raspberries
1/2 cup granulated sugar
1/2 cup water
3 tablespoons instant tapioca
1 teaspoon vanilla extract
Whipped cream for garnish

EQUIPMENT

Medium covered
   saucepan
Medium saucepan
Large skillet
9 x 9-inch glass
   baking dish
2 small mixing bowls

Whisk
Vegetable peeler
Cheese grater
Kitchen knives
Measuring cups and
   spoons
Cooking utensils

COUNTDOWN

1. Assemble the ingredients and the equipment.
2. Do Step 1 of *Sweet Bird of Youth*.
3. Do Steps 1–3 of *Suddenly Last Salad*.
4. Do Steps 1–3 of *The Rose Tapioca*.
5. Do Steps 2–4 of *Sweet Bird of Youth*.
6. Do Steps 1–5 of *Summer and Smoke*.
7. Do Step 4 of *Suddenly Last Salad*.
8. Do Step 4 of *The Rose Tapioca*.

WEDNESDAY

Sweet Bird of Youth

1 Rinse and pat dry the chicken breasts. Place the chicken in a 9 x 9-inch baking dish. Add the wine and the lemon-pepper seasoning. Marinate, turning once or twice, for 15 minutes.

2 Peel and thinly slice the onion. Rinse, trim, seed, and slice the bell pepper. Rinse, pat dry, and slice the mushroom. Drain and quarter the artichoke hearts.

3 Melt the butter in a large skillet. Drain the chicken, reserving the marinade, and brown lightly on both sides, about 5 minutes per side.

4 Remove the chicken and keep it warm. Add the onion and the bell pepper to the skillet and sauté for 3 minutes. Add the artichokes and the reserved marinade and blend well. Season to taste. Add the mushroom and cook for 3 minutes. Return the chicken to the skillet and cook through, about 15 minutes more.

Summer and Smoke

1 Rinse, trim, and chop the celery. Rinse, stem, and chop the parsley. Grate the cheese.

2 Heat the oil in a medium saucepan. Add the celery and sauté for 1 minute. Add the lemon juice and the water. Bring the mixture to a boil.

3 Add the saffron and the couscous and season to taste. Cover the saucepan and remove it from the heat. Let stand until all the liquid has been absorbed, about 5 minutes.

4 Sprinkle the cheese over the couscous and cover until the cheese has melted, about 5 minutes more

5 Fluff with a fork and sprinkle with the parsley.

Suddenly Last Salad

1 Wash and dry the lettuce and distribute the leaves among individual salad plates.

2 Peel, trim, and thinly slice the cucumbers. Arrange the slices over the lettuce leaves.

3 In a small bowl, combine the mayonnaise, the sour cream, the sugar, the vinegar, and the mustard. Season to taste.

4 Spoon the dressing over the salad.

The Rose Tapioca

1 Place the package of raspberries in a small bowl of warm water to thaw slightly.

2 In a medium saucepan, combine the berries, the sugar, the ½ cup water, and the tapioca and let stand for 5 minutes.

3 Bring the mixture to a boil, stirring constantly, and cook for 2 minutes. Remove from the heat. Blend in the vanilla. Spoon the mixture into individual dessert bowls and set aside.

4 Top with dollops of whipped cream.

THURSDAY

Dairy'n Delight

1 package (10 ounces) frozen chopped
  spinach
1 clove garlic
1 medium zucchini
1 tablespoon olive oil
1 pound Italian bulk sausage
9 eggs
3/4 cup grated Parmesan cheese
1/2 teaspoon dried basil
1/4 teaspoon dried marjoram
Seasoning to taste
1 cup shredded mozzarella cheese

Puritan Peaches

1 can (29 ounces) sliced peaches
1 cup orange juice
2 tablespoons dark brown sugar
2 tablespoons cornstarch
2 tablespoons cold water
1 teaspoon ground nutmeg

Danbury Buns

1/4 cup fresh rosemary (when chopped)
4 hamburger buns
3 tablespoons olive oil
Seasoning to taste

Blue Law Cake

1 package (12 ounces) frozen blueberries
4 tablespoons butter
1/2 cup powdered sugar
1/4 cup milk
1 teaspoon ground cinnamon
1/4 teaspoon ground allspice
1 angel food loaf cake

EQUIPMENT

Medium saucepan	2 small mixing bowls
Small saucepan	Whisk
Large skillet	Pastry brush
9 x 13-inch glass baking dish	Kitchen knives
Baking sheet	Measuring cups and spoons
Large mixing bowl	Cooking utensils

COUNTDOWN

1. Assemble the ingredients and the equipment.
2. Do Steps 1–3 of *Blue Law Cake*.
3. Do Steps 1–6 of *Dairy'n Delight*.
4. Do Steps 1–2 of *Danbury Buns*.
5. Do Steps 1–3 of *Puritan Peaches*.

THURSDAY

Dairy'n Delight

1 Preheat the oven to 350°F. Grease a 9 x 13-inch baking dish.

2 Set the spinach in a small bowl of very warm water to thaw. Peel and mince the garlic. Scrub, trim, and chop the zucchini.

3 Heat the oil in a large skillet and sauté the sausage until it is well browned, about 10 minutes. Remove the sausage and drain it on paper towels.

4 Add the garlic and the zucchini to the skillet and sauté until the zucchini begins to soften, about 3 minutes. Stir in the spinach and heat through, about 1 minute.

5 In a large bowl, whip the eggs with the Parmesan cheese, the basil, and the marjoram. Season to taste. Stir in the sausage and the zucchini mixture. Pour the mixture into the baking dish and top with the mozzarella cheese.

6 Bake until the eggs are set, about 25 minutes.

Puritan Peaches

1 Drain the peaches and place them in a medium saucepan. Add the orange juice and the brown sugar.

2 Combine the cornstarch and the water and add it to the saucepan. Bring the mixture to a boil and cook until the sauce begins to thicken, about 5 minutes.

3 Dust each serving with the nutmeg.

Danbury Buns

1 Rinse, stem, and chop the rosemary. Split the hamburger buns. Brush the cut sides with the oil. Sprinkle with the rosemary. Season to taste.

2 Place the buns on a baking sheet and bake at 350°F until lightly golden and heated through, about 10 minutes.

Blue Law Cake

1 Set the package of blueberries in a small bowl of warm water to thaw.

2 Melt the butter in a small saucepan. Blend in the powdered sugar, the milk, the cinnamon, and the allspice and cook until the mixture begins to thicken, about 1 minute.

3 Spoon the mixture over the cake, letting it run down the sides. Cover the top with the blueberries.

FRIDAY

Clam Solo

1 small onion
2 stalks celery
1 clove garlic
1/4 cup fresh parsley (when chopped)
2 tablespoons olive oil
48 fresh hard-shell clams
8 ounces clam juice
1/2 cup dry red wine
1 can (14 1/2 ounces) diced tomatoes
1/2 teaspoon dried oregano
1/2 teaspoon Tabasco sauce
Seasoning to taste
1 pound spaghetti

Obi-Wan Kenobeans

1 package (10 ounces) frozen cut green
  beans
1/2 cup pepper Jack cheese (when grated)
1 small head lettuce
1 small red onion
1 can (15 ounces) garbanzo beans
3 tablespoons olive oil
2 tablespoons red wine vinegar
1/2 teaspoon dried basil
Seasoning to taste

Dark Vaders

1 square (1 ounce) semisweet chocolate
2/3 cup marshmallow crème
1/4 cup milk
1 teaspoon peppermint extract
1 pint chocolate ice cream
1/2 cup pecan pieces

EQUIPMENT

Stockpot	Whisk
Large covered saucepan	Cheese grater
2 medium saucepans	Vegetable brush
Large skillet	Ice cream scoop
Colander	Kitchen knives
Large mixing bowl	Measuring cups and spoons
Small mixing bowl	Cooking utensils

COUNTDOWN

1. Assemble the ingredients and the equipment.
2. Do Step 1 of *Dark Vaders*.
3. Do Steps 1–5 of *Obi-Wan Kenobeans*.
4. Do Steps 1–8 of *Clam Solo*.
5. Do Steps 6–7 of *Obi-Wan Kenobeans*.
6. Do Step 2 of *Dark Vaders*.

FRIDAY

Clam Solo

1 Bring water to a boil in a stockpot.

2 Peel and chop the onion. Rinse, trim, and mince the celery. Peel and mince the garlic. Rinse, stem, and chop the parsley.

3 Heat the oil in a large skillet. Sauté the onion, the celery, and the garlic for 4 minutes.

4 Scrub the clams, discarding any with open shells that do not close when tapped.

5 Heat the clam juice and the wine in a large saucepan. Add the clams, cover, and cook until the clams open, about 5 minutes.

6 Discard any clams that do not open. Combine the clams and their cooking liquids with the onion, the celery, and the garlic. Add the tomatoes, the oregano, and the Tabasco sauce. Season to taste and heat through.

7 Cook the spaghetti until it is almost tender, 6 to 7 minutes.

8 Drain the pasta and top it with the clam sauce. Sprinkle with the parsley.

Obi-Wan Kenobeans

1 Place the green beans in a medium saucepan. Cover with water and bring to a boil. Cook for 1 minute, remove the saucepan from the heat, drain the beans, and set aside.

2 Grate the cheese.

3 Wash and dry the lettuce and distribute the leaves among individual salad plates.

4 Peel and thinly slice the onion. Drain the garbanzo beans. Combine the onion and the garbanzo beans in a large bowl.

5 Add the green beans to the bowl. Blend in the cheese.

6 In a small bowl, combine the oil, the vinegar, and the basil. Season to taste.

7 Toss the vegetables with the dressing and spoon over the lettuce.

Dark Vaders

1 In a medium saucepan, combine the chocolate, the marshmallow crème, and the milk. Cook, stirring, until the chocolate is melted and the mixture is well blended, about 3 minutes. Stir in the peppermint extract and set aside.

2 Place scoops of ice cream in individual dessert dishes and top with the sauce. Sprinkle with the nuts.

WEEK THIRTEEN

WEEK AT A GLANCE

Monday
According to Foil
Pinochle Pilaf
Double Dilling
Four of a Kind

Tuesday
Pygmalion
The Daikon's Disciple
G. B. Slaw
Candida Apples

Wednesday
Betta Fettuccine
Sue-Kissed Salad
Be My Loaf
One For My Honey

Thursday
Blue Hen Special
Dover Doodles
Small Wonders

Friday
Finocchio
Vegepetto Pilaf
Jiminy Croccoli
Cleo Cake

STAPLES

❑ Butter
❑ Flour
❑ Bisquick
❑ Cornstarch
❑ Cream of tartar
❑ Granulated sugar
❑ Dark brown sugar
❑ Powdered sugar
❑ Multicolored sprinkles
❑ Olive oil
❑ Vegetable oil
❑ Balsamic vinegar
❑ Rice vinegar
❑ Lemon juice
❑ Lime juice
❑ Dijon mustard
❑ Honey
❑ Prepared horseradish
❑ Tabasco sauce
❑ Worcestershire sauce
❑ Plain breadcrumbs
❑ Caraway seeds
❑ Celery seeds
❑ Dried basil
❑ Dried dill
❑ Dried rosemary
❑ Dried sage
❑ Dried tarragon
❑ Cayenne pepper
❑ Ground ginger
❑ Ground nutmeg
❑ Black pepper
❑ Red pepper flakes
❑ Salt
❑ Almond extract
❑ Orange extract
❑ Vanilla extract

MEAT & POULTRY

4 loin pork chops (about 1 1/2 pounds) (T)

4 boneless, skinless chicken breast halves (about 1 1/2 pounds) (Th)

FISH

4 white fish fillets (about 1 1/2 pounds) (M)

4 salmon fillets (about 1 1/2 pounds) (F)

FRESH PRODUCE

VEGETABLES

1 medium bunch broccoli (F)

1 small head cauliflower (T)

1 pound asparagus (T)

2 medium zucchini (Th)

2 stalks celery (T)

1 package (10 ounces) spinach (W)

1 medium head red cabbage (T)

1 head romaine lettuce (M)

1 small head Boston lettuce (W)

2 medium tomatoes (M)

1 medium ripe avocado (M)

1 medium cucumber (M)

1 medium daikon radish (T)

1 medium onion (W)

1 small onion (Th)

1 small shallot (F)

4 scallions (green onions) (M)

3 scallions (green onions) (T)

3 scallions (green onions) (Th)

2 cloves garlic (M)

2 cloves garlic (W)

1 clove garlic (F)

HERBS

1/4 cup chives (when chopped) (M)

3 tablespoons chives (when chopped) (T)

2 tablespoons dill (when chopped) (M)

3 tablespoons parsley (when chopped) (M)

3 tablespoons parsley (when chopped) (W)

2 tablespoons parsley (when chopped) (F)

FRUIT

2 medium oranges (W)

1 small lemon (W)

1 small ripe honeydew melon (W)

4 large soft apples (T)

1/2 pound seedless red grapes (W)

CANS, JARS & BOTTLES

SOUPS

1 can (14 ounces) chicken broth (M)

1 can (14 ounces) chicken broth (Th)

1 can (14 ounces) vegetable broth (F)

VEGETABLES

1 can (14 1/2 ounces) crushed tomatoes (T)

1 jar (7 ounces) roasted red peppers (W)

1 can (11 ounces) whole-kernel corn (Th)

FRUIT

1 can (16 ounces) goose-berries in syrup (M)

1 can (11 ounces) mandarin oranges (M)

1 can (8 ounces) pineapple chunks (M)

1 can (8 ounces) pineapple tidbits (F)

1 can (16 ounces) pitted dark cherries (M)

PACKAGED GOODS

PASTA, RICE & GRAINS

1 pound fettuccine (W)

8 ounces fine egg noodles (Th)

1/2 cup vermicelli (when broken) (F)

1/2 cup brown rice (F)

1 cup quick-cooking barley (M)

BAKED GOODS

1 loaf Italian bread (W)

1 package brown-and-serve rolls (Th)

4 large sugar cookies (W)

DRIED FRUIT & NUTS

1/3 cup chopped dates (F)

1/2 cup walnut bits (T)

1/4 cup sliced almonds (Th)

DESSERT & BAKING NEEDS

1 package (8 ounces) caramel candies (T)

1/2 cup flaked coconut (F)

WINE & SPIRITS

1/4 cup dry white wine (M)

3 tablespoons dry white wine (Th)

2 tablespoons dry sherry (Th)

REFRIGERATED PRODUCTS

DAIRY

1/2 cup milk (F)

1/2 cup whipping cream (T)

1/4 cup plain yogurt (Th)

2 eggs (M)

3 eggs (W)

1 egg (F)

CHEESE

4 ounces feta cheese (W)

4 ounces blue cheese (Th)

DELI

4 slices bacon (Th)

FROZEN GOODS

DESSERTS

1 pint vanilla yogurt (T)

1 container (8 ounces) whipped topping (M)

MONDAY

According to Foil

4 white fish fillets (about 1 1/2 pounds)
1/4 teaspoon cayenne pepper
Seasoning to taste
2 cloves garlic
4 scallions (green onions)
3 tablespoons fresh parsley (when chopped)
2 medium tomatoes
4 tablespoons olive oil
1/2 teaspoon dried tarragon
1/4 cup dry white wine

Pinochle Pilaf

1/4 cup fresh chives (when chopped)
2 tablespoons butter
1 cup quick-cooking barley
1/2 teaspoon celery seeds
1 can (14 ounces) chicken broth
1/4 cup water

Double Dilling

2 eggs
1 head romaine lettuce
1 medium cucumber
2 tablespoons fresh dill (when chopped)
1 medium ripe avocado
3 tablespoons lemon juice
3 tablespoons vegetable oil
1/2 teaspoon granulated sugar
1/2 teaspoon Dijon mustard
Seasoning to taste

Four of a Kind

1 can (16 ounces) gooseberries in syrup
1 can (11 ounces) mandarin oranges
1 can (8 ounces) pineapple chunks
1 can (16 ounces) pitted dark cherries
1 container (8 ounces) frozen whipped topping
2 tablespoons powdered sugar
1 tablespoon lime juice
1 teaspoon almond extract
Multicolored sprinkles for garnish

EQUIPMENT

Medium covered saucepan	Whisk
Small saucepan	Vegetable peeler
Medium skillet	Pastry brush
Baking sheet	Aluminum foil
2 large mixing bowls	Kitchen knives
Medium mixing bowl	Measuring cups and spoons
Small mixing bowl	Cooking utensils

COUNTDOWN

1. Assemble the ingredients and the equipment.
2. Do Step 1 of *Double Dilling*.
3. Do Steps 1–4 of *Four of a Kind*.
4. Do Steps 2–4 of *Double Dilling*.
5. Do Steps 1–6 of *According to Foil*.
6. Do Steps 1–3 of *Pinochle Pilaf*.
7. Do Step 7 of *According to Foil*.
8. Do Step 5 of *Double Dilling*.
9. Do Step 4 of *Pinochle Pilaf*.
10. Do Step 8 of *According to Foil*.
11. Do Step 5 of *Four of a Kind*.

MONDAY

According to Foil

1 Preheat the oven to 450°F. Cut four 12-inch sheets of aluminum foil.

2 Rinse and pat dry the fish fillets. Sprinkle the fillets with the cayenne pepper and season to taste.

3 Peel and mince the garlic. Rinse, trim, and slice the scallions into 3 pieces each. Rinse, stem, and chop the parsley. Rinse, stem, and chop the tomatoes.

4 Brush the foil squares with 2 tablespoons of the oil. Lay the fish fillets in the center of the prepared foil squares.

5 Heat the remaining 2 tablespoons oil in a medium skillet. Add the garlic, the scallions, the tomatoes, and the tarragon and sauté until the scallions begin to soften, about 3 minutes.

6 Spoon the mixture over the fish fillets. Drizzle the wine evenly over the fish. Fold the edges of the foil to seal tightly.

7 Place the packets on a baking sheet and bake until the packets begin to puff up, about 10 minutes.

8 Cut the packets open and sprinkle with the parsley.

Pinochle Pilaf

1 Rinse, trim, and chop the chives.

2 Melt the butter in a medium saucepan and sauté the barley and the celery seeds for 2 minutes.

3 Add the broth and the water. Bring the mixture to a boil, stirring to blend well. Cover, reduce the heat, and simmer until the barley is tender, 20 to 25 minutes.

4 Drain the barley and sprinkle with the chives.

Double Dilling

1 Cover the eggs with water in a small saucepan. Bring the water to a boil and hard-cook the eggs, 10 to 12 minutes.

2 Drain the eggs and set them in the freezer for 10 minutes.

3 Wash and dry the lettuce and tear it into bite-sized pieces. Peel, trim, and slice the cucumber. Rinse, stem, and chop the dill. Halve, pit, peel, and slice the avocado and sprinkle with a tablespoon of the lemon juice.

4 In a small bowl, whisk together the oil, the remaining 2 tablespoons lemon juice, the sugar, and the mustard. Season to taste.

5 Peel and quarter the eggs. Combine the lettuce, the cucumber, and the avocado in a large bowl and toss with the dressing. Add the egg quarters and sprinkle with the dill.

Four of a Kind

1 Drain the gooseberries, reserving ¼ cup of the syrup.

2 Drain the oranges, the pineapple, and the cherries. Combine the fruit in a large bowl.

3 Place the reserved syrup in a medium bowl. Add the whipped topping, the powdered sugar, the lime juice, and the almond extract and whisk to combine.

4 Spoon half of the fruit into individual dessert glasses. Add half of the whipped topping mixture, then the remaining fruit, and top with the remaining topping. Refrigerate until you are ready to serve.

5 Garnish with the sprinkles.

TUESDAY

Pygmalion

3 tablespoons fresh chives (when chopped)
2 tablespoons olive oil
4 loin pork chops (about 1 1/2 pounds)
1 can (14 1/2 ounces) crushed tomatoes
1 tablespoon balsamic vinegar
2 teaspoons Worcestershire sauce
1/2 teaspoon Tabasco sauce
1/2 teaspoon dried sage
2 tablespoons dark brown sugar
Seasoning to taste

The Daikon's Disciple

1 medium daikon radish
1 pound fresh asparagus
2 tablespoons butter
1/2 teaspoon dried rosemary
Seasoning to taste

G. B. Slaw

1 medium head red cabbage
1 small head cauliflower
2 stalks celery
3 scallions (green onions)
2 teaspoons caraway seeds
2 tablespoons vegetable oil
2 tablespoons rice vinegar
1 teaspoon granulated sugar
Seasoning to taste

Candida Apples

1 package (8 ounces) caramel candies
1/2 cup whipping cream
1 teaspoon vanilla extract
4 large soft apples
1 pint vanilla frozen yogurt
1/2 cup walnut bits

EQUIPMENT

Double boiler	Vegetable grater
2 large skillets	Ice cream scoop
Large mixing bowl	Kitchen knives
Small mixing bowl	Measuring cups and
Whisk	spoons
Vegetable peeler	Cooking utensils

COUNTDOWN

1. Assemble the ingredients and the equipment.
2. Do Steps 1–2 of *Candida Apples*.
3. Do Steps 1–2 of *Pygmalion*.
4. Do Steps 1–3 of *G. B. Slaw*.
5. Do Steps 3–4 of *Pygmalion*.
6. Do Steps 1–2 of *The Daikon's Disciple*.
7. Do Steps 5–6 of *Pygmalion*.
8. Do Step 3 of *Candida Apples*.

TUESDAY

Pygmalion

1 Rinse, trim, and chop the chives.

2 Heat the oil in a large skillet and cook the pork chops, turning once, until they are browned on the outside and white and tender on the inside, 20 to 25 minutes.

3 Remove the chops and cover to keep warm.

4 In the same skillet, combine the tomatoes, the vinegar, the Worcestershire sauce, the Tabasco sauce, the sage, and the brown sugar. Season to taste and cook until the sauce is reduced by half, about 10 minutes.

5 Return the pork chops to the skillet, coat with the sauce, and simmer until heated through, about 2 minutes.

6 Garnish with the chives.

The Daikon's Disciple

1 Trim, peel, and thinly slice the daikon. Rinse the asparagus, cut off the tough ends, and slice the spears diagonally into 1-inch pieces.

2 Melt the butter with the rosemary in a large skillet. Sauté the daikon and the asparagus until crisp-tender, about 5 minutes. Season to taste.

G. B. Slaw

1 Rinse, trim, quarter, and grate the cabbage. Rinse and trim the cauliflower and cut into bite-sized florets. Rinse, trim, and chop the celery. Rinse, trim, and chop the scallions. Combine the ingredients in a large bowl. Stir in the caraway seeds.

2 In a small bowl, combine the oil, the vinegar, and the sugar. Season to taste.

3 Toss the salad with the dressing.

Candida Apples

1 Bring water to a boil in the bottom of a double boiler.

2 Combine the caramel candies and the cream in the top of the double boiler and cook, stirring, until the candy is melted and the sauce is blended and smooth. Stir in the vanilla, remove from the heat, and cover to keep warm.

3 Rinse and core the apples and cut each apple into 6 wedges. Fan the wedges out on individual dessert plates. Top with a scoop of frozen yogurt and drizzle with the caramel sauce. Sprinkle with the nuts.

WEDNESDAY

Betta Fettuccine

3 tablespoons fresh parsley (when chopped)
1 medium onion
2 cloves garlic
1 package (10 ounces) fresh spinach
1 jar (7 ounces) roasted red peppers
4 ounces feta cheese
2 tablespoons olive oil
1/4 teaspoon red pepper flakes
1/2 teaspoon dried basil
1 pound fettuccine

Sue-Kissed Salad

1 small head Boston lettuce
1 small ripe honeydew melon
2 medium oranges
1/2 pound seedless red grapes
3 tablespoons vegetable oil
2 tablespoons lemon juice
1 teaspoon granulated sugar
Seasoning to taste

Be My Loaf

3 tablespoons butter
1 loaf Italian bread
2 tablespoons Dijon mustard
1 teaspoon celery seeds
1 teaspoon prepared horseradish

One For My Honey

1 small lemon
3 eggs
3 tablespoons honey
1/2 teaspoon cream of tartar
1/8 teaspoon salt
1/2 teaspoon orange extract
4 large sugar cookies

EQUIPMENT

Electric mixer	Citrus grater
Stockpot	Citrus juicer
Large skillet	Melon baller
Baking sheet	Kitchen knives
Colander	Measuring cups and
Medium mixing bowl	spoons
3 small mixing bowls	Cooking utensils
Whisk	

COUNTDOWN

1. Assemble the ingredients and the equipment.
2. Do Step 1 of *Be My Loaf*.
3. Do Steps 1–5 of *One For My Honey*.
4. Do Steps 1–3 of *Sue-Kissed Salad*.
5. Do Steps 1–2 of *Betta Fettuccine*.
6. Do Steps 2–4 of *Be My Loaf*.
7. Do Steps 3–5 of *Betta Fettuccine*.
8. Do Step 5 of *Be My Loaf*.
9. Do Step 4 of *Sue-Kissed Salad*.
10. Do Step 6 of *One For My Honey*.

WEDNESDAY

Betta Fettuccine

1 Bring water to a boil in a stockpot.

2 Rinse, stem, and chop the parsley. Peel and chop the onion. Peel and mince the garlic. Rinse, pat dry, stem, and chop the spinach. Drain and blot the roasted peppers and cut them into thin strips. Crumble the cheese.

3 Heat the oil in a large skillet and sauté the onion, the garlic, and the red pepper flakes for 3 minutes. Add the roasted peppers and sauté for 5 minutes. Add the spinach and the basil and sauté until heated through, 2 to 3 minutes.

4 Cook the fettuccine until it is almost tender, 2 to 3 minutes if you are using fresh pasta, 6 to 7 minutes if you are using dry pasta.

5 Drain the pasta and return it to the stockpot. Toss with the sauce and stir in the parsley and the cheese.

Sue-Kissed Salad

1 Wash and dry the lettuce and distribute the leaves among individual salad plates.

2 Cut the melon in half and remove the seeds. Using a melon baller, scoop out the melon. Peel and thinly slice the oranges. Rinse stem, and halve the grapes. Arrange the fruit over the lettuce.

3 In a small bowl, whisk together the oil, the lemon juice, and the sugar. Season to taste.

4 Drizzle the dressing over the salad.

Be My Loaf

1 Set the butter out to soften.

2 Slice the bread in half lengthwise, lay it on a baking sheet, and spread the cut sides with the softened butter.

3 In a small bowl, combine the mustard, the celery seeds, and the horseradish. Spread the mixture over the bread.

4 Preheat the broiler.

5 Broil the bread until the topping is bubbly, 2 to 3 minutes.

One For My Honey

1 Grate the lemon peel. Squeeze 1 tablespoon of the juice.

2 Separate the eggs, placing the whites in a medium bowl and the yolks in a small bowl.

3 Add the honey to the egg yolks and beat until frothy, about 2 minutes. Fold in the lemon peel and the lemon juice.

4 Beat the egg whites with the cream of tartar for 1 minute. Add the salt and beat the whites until stiff, about 2 minutes. Fold the egg yolk mixture into the egg whites. Fold in the orange extract.

5 Spoon the mixture into individual dessert glasses and refrigerate until you are ready to serve.

6 Serve with a sugar cookie on the side.

THURSDAY

Blue Hen Special

1 small onion
2 medium zucchini
4 slices bacon
4 boneless, skinless chicken breast halves
    (about 1 1/2 pounds)
4 ounces blue cheese
2 tablespoons butter
1/2 cup plain breadcrumbs
1 tablespoon lemon juice
3 tablespoons flour
1/2 cup chicken broth
3 tablespoons dry white wine
Seasoning to taste

Small Wonders

4 tablespoons butter
1/2 cup dark brown sugar
2 tablespoons water
1 teaspoon almond extract
1/4 cup sliced almonds
1 package brown-and-serve rolls

Dover Doodles

3 scallions (green onions)
1 can (11 ounces) whole-kernel corn
1 1/4 cups chicken broth
2 tablespoons butter
1/4 cup plain yogurt
2 tablespoons dry sherry
2 teaspoons granulated sugar
Seasoning to taste
8 ounces fine egg noodles

EQUIPMENT

Large saucepan	Aluminum foil
Small saucepan	Waxed paper
2 large skillets	Kitchen knives
9 x 13-inch baking dish	Measuring cups and spoons
Muffin tin	Cooking utensils
Strainer	

COUNTDOWN

1. Assemble the ingredients and the equipment.
2. Do Steps 1–4 of *Small Wonders*.
3. Do Steps 1–7 of *Blue Hen Special*.
4. Do Step 5 of *Small Wonders*.
5. Do Step 8 of *Blue Hen Special*.
6. Do Steps 1–5 of *Dover Doodles*.
7. Do Step 6 of *Small Wonders*.

THURSDAY

Blue Hen Special

1 Peel and mince the onion. Scrub, trim, and thinly slice the zucchini. Dice the bacon. Crumble the cheese. Rinse and pat dry the chicken breasts.

2 Lightly grease a 9 x 13-inch baking dish.

3 Melt the butter in a large skillet and sauté the onion until soft, about 3 minutes.

4 Add the zucchini to the skillet and sauté for 2 minutes. Add the breadcrumbs, the blue cheese, and the lemon juice and blend well. Spread the mixture in the bottom of the baking dish.

5 Add the bacon to the skillet and sauté until crisp, about 7 minutes. Drain on paper towels. Discard all but 3 tablespoons of fat from the skillet.

6 Place the flour on a sheet of waxed paper and dredge the chicken breasts in it, coating well. Sauté the chicken in the bacon drippings until golden, about 5 minutes per side. Arrange the chicken on top of the zucchini mixture.

7 Add the broth and the wine to the skillet, season to taste, bring to a boil, and pour over the chicken. Sprinkle the bacon on top.

8 Cover the baking dish with a sheet of aluminum foil and bake at 400°F for 20 minutes.

Dover Doodles

1 Rinse, trim, and chop the scallions. Drain the corn.

2 Bring water and the broth to a boil in a large saucepan.

3 Melt the butter in a large skillet and sauté the scallions for 2 minutes. Add the corn and sauté for 2 minutes more. Stir in the yogurt, the sherry, and the sugar. Season to taste and heat through, about 3 minutes.

4 Cook the noodles until they are almost tender, 3 to 4 minutes.

5 Drain the noodles and combine them with the corn mixture.

Small Wonders

1 Preheat the oven to 400°F. Grease a muffin tin.

2 Melt the butter in a small saucepan. Add the brown sugar, the water, and the almond extract. Stir to combine and bring the mixture to a boil.

3 Spoon the mixture into the muffin cups. Sprinkle some of the sliced almonds into each cup. Press a roll, top side down, over the almonds.

4 Bake for 15 minutes.

5 Remove from the oven and let stand to cool.

6 Invert onto a plate to serve.

FRIDAY

MENU

Finocchio

4 salmon fillets (about 1 1/2 pounds)
1 small shallot
1 can (8 ounces) pineapple tidbits
1/2 teaspoon ground ginger
1 1/2 teaspoons cornstarch
1 tablespoon granulated sugar
Seasoning to taste
2 tablespoons butter

Vegepetto Pilaf

1 clove garlic
2 tablespoons fresh parsley (when chopped)
3 tablespoons vegetable oil
1/2 cup vermicelli (when broken)
1/2 cup brown rice
1 can (14 ounces) vegetable broth
1 cup water
1 teaspoon ground nutmeg
Seasoning to taste

Jiminy Croccoli

1 medium bunch broccoli
2 tablespoons butter
2 tablespoons balsamic vinegar
1 teaspoon dried dill
Seasoning to taste

Cleo Cake

1 1/2 cups Bisquick
1 egg
1/2 cup milk
1/3 cup chopped dates
3 tablespoons honey
1/2 cup flaked coconut

EQUIPMENT

Electric mixer
2 medium covered saucepans
Small covered saucepan
Medium skillet
8 x 8-inch baking pan

Steamer insert
Medium mixing bowl
Kitchen knives
Measuring cups and spoons
Cooking utensils

COUNTDOWN

1. Assemble the ingredients and the equipment.
2. Do Steps 1–2 of Cleo Cake.
3. Do Steps 1–4 of Vegepetto Pilaf.
4. Do Steps 1–2 of Jiminy Croccoli.
5. Do Steps 1–2 of Finocchio.
6. Do Step 5 of Vegepetto Pilaf.
7. Do Step 3 of Jiminy Croccoli.
8. Do Steps 3–4 of Finocchio.
9. Do Step 6 of Vegepetto Pilaf.
10. Do Step 3 of Cleo Cake.

FRIDAY

Finocchio

1 Rinse and pat dry the fish fillets. Peel and chop the shallot.

2 Drain the pineapple, reserving the liquid. Combine the reserved liquid, the ginger, the cornstarch, and the sugar in a small saucepan. Add the pineapple chunks and season to taste. Bring to a boil and cook for 1 minute. Cover, remove from the heat, and let stand.

3 Melt the butter in a medium skillet and sauté the shallot until it is soft, about 4 minutes. Add the fish and cook until it flakes easily with a fork, 3 to 4 minutes per side.

4 Spoon the sauce over the fish.

Vegepetto Pilaf

1 Peel and mince the garlic. Rinse, stem, and chop the parsley.

2 Heat the oil in a medium saucepan and sauté the garlic for 1 minute.

3 Break the vermicelli into 1-inch pieces and sauté until golden brown, about 5 minutes.

4 Add the rice, the broth, the water, and the nutmeg and season to taste. Cover, reduce the heat, and simmer until all the liquid is absorbed and the rice is tender, about 20 minutes.

5 Remove from the heat and let stand for 10 minutes.

6 Fluff the rice with a fork and sprinkle with the parsley.

Jiminy Croccoli

1 Bring a small amount of water to a boil in a medium saucepan.

2 Rinse and trim the broccoli, discarding the tough ends, and cut into spears. Arrange the broccoli in a steamer insert. Place the insert in the saucepan, cover, and steam until the spears are crisp-tender, about 5 minutes.

3 Drain the broccoli. Melt the butter in the saucepan. Return the broccoli, add the vinegar, and toss to coat. Add the dill and season to taste. Cover to keep warm.

Cleo Cake

1 Preheat the oven to 350°F. Grease and flour an 8 x 8-inch baking pan.

2 In a medium bowl, combine the Bisquick, the egg, and the milk. Beat until smooth, about 2 minutes. Fold in the dates. Pour the mixture into the pan and bake until a toothpick inserted in the center comes out clean, about 30 minutes.

3 Spoon the honey over the top of the warm cake and garnish with the coconut.

AUTUMN

WEEK AT A GLANCE

Monday
Pie-Eyed
Peas Pass the Corn
Just Desserts

Tuesday
Soused Carolina
Pinopolis Pilaf
Charleston Chokes
Butteree Pie

Wednesday
Tie One On
Whatever Romaines
Bready, Set, Go
Phony Spumoni

Thursday
Hang Chow Chicken
Porcelain Rice
Lychee Laughter

Friday
In Cod We Trust
The Couscous Creation
Evegetables
Adam's Apple

STAPLES

- ❐ Butter
- ❐ Flour
- ❐ Baking powder
- ❐ Cornstarch
- ❐ Cream of tartar
- ❐ Granulated sugar
- ❐ Dark brown sugar
- ❐ Olive oil
- ❐ Sesame oil
- ❐ Vegetable oil
- ❐ White wine vinegar
- ❐ Lemon juice
- ❐ Soy sauce
- ❐ Mayonnaise
- ❐ Worcestershire sauce
- ❐ Caraway seeds
- ❐ Poppy seeds
- ❐ Dried basil
- ❐ Dried dill
- ❐ Dried tarragon
- ❐ Dried thyme
- ❐ Cayenne pepper
- ❐ Chinese 5-spice
- ❐ Ground cinnamon
- ❐ Curry powder
- ❐ Italian seasoning
- ❐ Lemon-pepper seasoning
- ❐ Ground nutmeg
- ❐ Paprika
- ❐ Black pepper
- ❐ Salt
- ❐ Turmeric
- ❐ Almond extract
- ❐ Rum extract
- ❐ Vanilla extract

MEAT & POULTRY

1 1/2 pounds lean ground beef (M)

1 1/2 pounds boneless, skinless chicken breast (Th)

FISH

4 halibut or other white fish steaks (about 1 1/2 pounds) (T)

4 cod fillets (about 1 1/2 pounds) (F)

FRESH PRODUCE

VEGETABLES

1 1/2 pounds baking potatoes (M)

1 pound Brussels sprouts (Th)

3/4 pound green peas, unshelled (M)

1/2 pounds green beans (Th)

1/4 pound Chinese snow peas (Th)

2 medium carrots (Th)

2 medium carrots (F)

2 stalks celery (M)

3 stalks celery (W)

2 stalks celery (Th)

2 medium parsnips (F)

1 small head red cabbage (W)

1 small head romaine lettuce (W)

1 medium tomato (M)

1 small cucumber (W)

1 medium red bell pepper (Th)

1 small green bell pepper (M)

1 medium onion (M)

1 medium red onion (T)

1 small shallot (F)

4 scallions (green onions) (W)

3 scallions (green onions) (Th)

1 clove garlic (T)

1 clove garlic (W)

3 cloves garlic (F)

HERBS

1/2 cup chives (when chopped) (W)

1/4 cup parsley (when chopped) (T)

2 tablespoons parsley (when chopped) (W)

3 tablespoons parsley (when chopped) (F)

FRUIT

1 large lemon (F)

2 large sweet apples (F)

CANS, JARS & BOTTLES

SOUPS

1 can (14 ounces) vegetable broth (F)

1 can (10 1/2 ounces) beef broth (T)

1 can (10 1/2 ounces) chicken broth (Th)

VEGETABLES

1 can (14 1/2 ounces) Italian-style stewed tomatoes (W)

1 can (11 ounces) whole-kernel corn (M)

FRUIT

1 can (8 ounces) pineapple chunks (Th)

1 jar (6 ounces) maraschino cherries (Th)

INTERNATIONAL FOODS

1 can (11 ounces) lychee nuts in syrup (Th)

SAUCES

1 can (8 ounces) tomato sauce (M)

CONDIMENTS

1 can (3 1/2 ounces) sliced black olives (W)

2 teaspoons capers (F)

PACKAGED GOODS

PASTA, RICE & GRAINS

1 pound bow-tie pasta (W)

1 cup long-grain white rice (Th)

1 cup brown rice (T)

1 cup couscous (F)

BAKED GOODS

1 loaf Italian bread (W)

1 package (6 ounces) seasoned croutons (M)

1 prepared shortbread pie shell (T)

INTERNATIONAL FOODS

1 package (4 ounces) rice noodles (Th)

DRIED FRUIT & NUTS

1 container (7 ounces) mixed candied fruit (W)

1/2 cup sliced almonds (W)

1/2 cup walnut bits (F)

DESSERT & BAKING NEEDS

1 package (3.4 ounces) instant vanilla pudding mix (W)

1/4 cup marshmallow crème for garnish (Th)

WINE & SPIRITS

1 cup dry sherry (T)

REFRIGERATED PRODUCTS

DAIRY

2 cups milk (T)

2 cups milk (W)

1/2 cup half-and-half (M)

1/4 cup plain yogurt (T)

Whipped cream for garnish (M)

Whipped cream for garnish (W)

Whipped cream for garnish (F)

2 eggs (M)

3 eggs (T)

2 eggs (F)

CHEESE

1 cup Colby/Monterey Jack cheese (M)

8 ounces feta cheese (W)

FROZEN GOODS

VEGETABLES

1 package (10 ounces) artichoke hearts (T)

FRUIT

1 package (10 ounces) raspberries (M)

DESSERTS

1 pint raspberry ripple ice cream (M)

1 pint boysenberry sorbet (F)

MONDAY

Pie-Eyed

1 medium onion
1 small green bell pepper
1 medium tomato
1 package (6 ounces) seasoned croutons
2 eggs
1 1/2 pounds lean ground beef
Seasoning to taste
1 can (8 ounces) tomato sauce
1/4 teaspoon Worcestershire sauce
1/8 teaspoon cayenne pepper
1 cup shredded Colby/Monterey Jack
   cheese
1 1/2 pounds baking potatoes
1/2 cup half-and-half
3 tablespoons butter
1/2 teaspoon paprika for garnish

Peas Pass the Corn

2 stalks celery
3/4 pound fresh green peas, unshelled
1 can (11 ounces) whole-kernel corn
1 tablespoon butter
1/2 teaspoon dried thyme
1/2 teaspoon granulated sugar

Just Desserts

1 package (10 ounces) frozen raspberries
1 1/2 teaspoons cornstarch
2 teaspoons granulated sugar
1 pint raspberry ripple ice cream
Whipped cream for garnish

EQUIPMENT

Electric mixer	Vegetable grater
Large saucepan	Mallet
Small saucepan	Ice cream scoop
Medium skillet	Plastic bag
Deep-dish pie plate	Kitchen knives
2 medium mixing bowls	Measuring cups and spoons
Small mixing bowl	Cooking utensils
Vegetable peeler	

COUNTDOWN

1. Assemble the ingredients and the equipment.
2. Do Step 1 of *Just Desserts*.
3. Do Steps 1–6 of *Pie-Eyed*.
4. Do Step 1 of *Peas Pass the Corn*.
5. Do Steps 7–8 of *Pie-Eyed*.
6. Do Steps 2–3 of *Just Desserts*.
7. Do Step 2 of *Peas Pass the Corn*.
8. Do Steps 9–13 of *Pie-Eyed*.
9. Do Step 4 of *Just Desserts*.

MONDAY

Pie-Eyed

1 Preheat the oven to 375°F. Grease a deep-dish pie plate.

2 Peel and grate the onion. Rinse, trim, seed, and chop the bell pepper. Rinse, stem, and slice the tomato. Place the croutons in a plastic bag and crumble them with a mallet.

3 Beat 1 egg lightly in a medium bowl. Add the onion, the ground beef, and 1 cup of the croutons. Season to taste. Mix in the tomato sauce, the Worcestershire sauce, and the cayenne pepper and blend well. Place the mixture in the pie plate and press it evenly into the bottom and the sides.

4 Beat the remaining egg in another medium bowl. Add the remaining croutons and the bell pepper. Fold in the cheese.

5 Spread the cheese mixture over the beef mixture. Arrange the tomato slices over the top.

6 Bake until the beef is cooked through and the top is lightly browned, about 40 minutes.

7 Bring water to a boil in a large saucepan.

8 Peel and dice the potatoes. Boil the potatoes until they are tender, 10 to 15 minutes.

9 Drain the potatoes and return them to the saucepan. Reduce the heat and shake the saucepan gently over the burner until the potatoes are dry. Slowly beat in the half-and-half until the potatoes are smooth and fluffy. Blend in the butter and season to taste.

10 Top the pie with the potatoes, using the back of a spoon to make swirls. Sprinkle with the paprika.

11 Preheat the broiler.

12 Place the pie under the broiler and broil until the potatoes are just golden, about 2 minutes.

13 To serve, cut into pie-shaped wedges.

Peas Pass the Corn

1 Rinse, trim, and chop the celery. Shell the peas. Drain the corn.

2 Melt the butter in a medium skillet and sauté the celery for 1 minute. Add the peas and the thyme and sauté for 3 minutes. Stir in the corn and the sugar. Toss to combine and heat through, about 1 minute.

Just Desserts

1 Set the frozen raspberries in a small bowl of warm water to thaw.

2 Drain the berries, reserving 2 tablespoons of the juice, and combine the reserved juice with the cornstarch and sugar in a small saucepan.

3 Add the berries to the cornstarch mixture, bring to a boil, and cook, stirring, until the juice is clear and has thickened, about 2 minutes. Remove from the heat and set aside until you are ready to use.

4 Place scoops of ice cream in individual dessert bowls. Spoon the sauce over the ice cream and garnish with a dollop of whipped cream.

TUESDAY

Soused Carolina

1 medium red onion
4 halibut or other white fish steaks (about 1½ pounds)
1 cup dry sherry
¼ cup flour
½ teaspoon paprika
Seasoning to taste
¼ cup mayonnaise
¼ cup plain yogurt
1 teaspoon dried dill

Pinopolis Pilaf

¼ cup fresh parsley (when chopped)
1 clove garlic
2 tablespoons vegetable oil
1 cup brown rice
1 can (10½ ounces) beef broth
¾ cup water
1 tablespoon caraway seeds
Seasoning to taste

Charleston Chokes

1 package (10 ounces) frozen artichoke hearts
2 tablespoons butter
1 teaspoon granulated sugar
1 teaspoon ground nutmeg
2 tablespoons lemon juice
Seasoning to taste

Butteree Pie

¾ cup dark brown sugar
3 tablespoons cornstarch
2 cups milk
3 eggs
3 tablespoons butter
1 teaspoon rum extract
¼ teaspoon cream of tartar
¼ cup granulated sugar
1 shortbread pie shell

EQUIPMENT

Electric mixer
Medium covered saucepan
Medium saucepan
Medium covered skillet
9 x 13-inch glass baking dish

Large shallow bowl
Large mixing bowl
2 small mixing bowls
Kitchen knives
Measuring cups and spoons
Cooking utensils

COUNTDOWN

1. Assemble the ingredients and the equipment.
2. Do Step 1 of *Charleston Chokes.*
3. Do Steps 1–3 of *Butteree Pie.*
4. Do Steps 1–3 of *Soused Carolina.*
5. Do Steps 1–3 of *Pinopolis Pilaf.*
6. Do Steps 4–7 of *Butteree Pie.*
7. Do Steps 4–8 of *Soused Carolina.*
8. Do Step 2 of *Charleston Chokes.*
9. Do Step 9 of *Soused Carolina.*
10. Do Step 4 of *Pinopolis Pilaf.*

TUESDAY

Soused Carolina

1 Grease a 9 x 13-inch baking dish.

2 Peel and thinly slice the onion. Rinse and pat dry the halibut steaks.

3 Place the onion in the bottom of the baking dish. Add the halibut and pour the sherry over the top. Marinate, turning occasionally, for 15 minutes.

4 In a large shallow bowl, combine the flour and the paprika and season to taste.

5 Drain any remaining sherry from the baking dish. Dredge the halibut steaks in the flour mixture and return them to the dish, arranging them over the onion slices.

6 In a small bowl, combine the mayonnaise, the yogurt, and the dill.

7 Preheat the broiler.

8 Broil the fish until golden, about 5 minutes.

9 Turn the fish over and spread the mayonnaise mixture over the top. Continue broiling until the sauce begins to bubble and the fish flakes easily with a fork, about 5 minutes longer.

Pinopolis Pilaf

1 Rinse, stem, and chop the parsley. Peel and mince the garlic.

2 Heat the oil in a medium saucepan and sauté the garlic and the rice for 2 minutes.

3 Add the broth, the water, and the caraway seeds and season to taste. Cover, reduce the heat, and simmer until all the liquid is absorbed and the rice is tender, 40 to 45 minutes.

4 Fluff the rice with a fork.

Charleston Chokes

1 Set the artichoke hearts in a small bowl of warm water to thaw.

2 Melt the butter in a medium skillet. Add the artichokes, the sugar, the nutmeg, and the lemon juice. Season to taste and sauté until heated through, 5 to 6 minutes. Cover to keep warm.

Butteree Pie

1 In a medium saucepan, combine the brown sugar and the cornstarch. Gradually add the milk, stirring to blend. Bring to a boil and cook for 2 minutes. Remove from the heat.

2 Separate the eggs, placing the whites in a large bowl. Add the yolks, one at a time, to the brown sugar mixture, beating well after each addition.

3 Return the saucepan to the heat and cook the mixture, stirring, for 2 minutes. Remove from the heat, stir in the butter and the rum extract, and refrigerate for 10 minutes.

4 Preheat the oven to 350°F.

5 Beat the egg whites with the cream of tartar until soft peaks form, about 1 minute. Gradually add the granulated sugar and beat until stiff peaks form, about 2 minutes.

6 Pour the brown sugar mixture into the pie shell. Top with the meringue, being sure the meringue seals the cream mixture completely.

7 Bake until lightly golden, 10 to 12 minutes.

WEDNESDAY

Tie One On

1 clove garlic
4 scallions (green onions)
2 tablespoons fresh parsley (when chopped)
1 can (3½ ounces) sliced black olives
8 ounces feta cheese
1 pound bow-tie pasta
2 tablespoons olive oil
1 can (14½ ounces) Italian-style stewed tomatoes
½ teaspoon lemon-pepper seasoning
Seasoning to taste

Whatever Romaines

1 small head romaine lettuce
1 small head red cabbage
½ cup fresh chives (when chopped)
3 stalks celery
1 small cucumber
3 tablespoons vegetable oil
2 tablespoons white wine vinegar
1 teaspoon dried basil
Seasoning to taste

Bready, Set, Go

3 tablespoons butter
1 loaf Italian bread
1 teaspoon Italian seasoning
1 tablespoon poppy seeds

Phony Spumoni

1 package (3.4 ounces) instant vanilla pudding mix
2 cups milk
1 container (7 ounces) mixed candied fruit
1 tablespoon almond extract
Whipped cream for garnish
½ cup sliced almonds for garnish

EQUIPMENT

Electric mixer	Whisk
Stockpot	Vegetable peeler
Medium skillet	Aluminum foil
Colander	Kitchen knives
Large mixing bowl	Measuring cups and
Medium mixing bowl	spoons
2 small mixing bowls	Cooking utensils

COUNTDOWN

1. Assemble the ingredients and the equipment.
2. Do Step 1 of *Phony Spumoni*.
3. Do Steps 1–2 of *Whatever Romaines*.
4. Do Steps 1–5 of *Bready, Set, Go*.
5. Do Steps 1–3 of *Tie One On*.
6. Do Step 6 of *Bready, Set, Go*.
7. Do Steps 4–5 of *Tie One On*.
8. Do Step 3 of *Whatever Romaines*.
9. Do Step 2 of *Phony Spumoni*.

WEDNESDAY

Tie One On

1 Bring water to a boil in a stockpot.

2 Peel and mince the garlic. Rinse, trim, and chop the scallions. Rinse, stem, and chop the parsley. Drain the olives. Crumble the cheese.

3 Cook the pasta until it is almost tender, 8 to 10 minutes.

4 Heat the oil in a medium skillet and sauté the garlic for 1 minute. Add the scallions and sauté for 2 minutes. Add the tomatoes and the olives and bring to a boil.

5 Drain the pasta and return it to the stockpot. Toss with the tomato mixture. Add the cheese, the lemon-pepper seasoning, and the parsley. Season to taste and toss to combine.

Whatever Romaines

1 Wash and dry the lettuce and tear it into bite-sized pieces. Rinse, trim, quarter, and chop the cabbage. Rinse, trim, and chop the chives. Rinse, trim, and chop the celery. Peel, trim, and slice the cucumber. Combine the ingredients in a large bowl.

2 In a small bowl, combine the oil, the vinegar, and the basil. Season to taste.

3 Toss the salad with the dressing.

Bready, Set, Go

1 Set the butter out to soften.

2 Slice the bread loaf in half lengthwise.

3 In a small bowl, blend the butter with the Italian seasoning and spread the mixture on both cut halves. Sprinkle with the poppy seeds.

4 Reassemble the loaf and wrap it in a sheet of aluminum foil.

5 Preheat the oven to 350°F.

6 Bake the loaf until heated through, about 10 minutes.

Phony Spumoni

1 Combine the pudding mix and the milk in a medium bowl and beat until well blended. Fold in the candied fruit and the almond extract. Spoon into individual serving dishes and refrigerate until you are ready to serve.

2 Top each pudding with a dollop of whipped cream and sprinkle with the sliced almonds.

THURSDAY

Hang Chow Chicken

1 1/2 pounds boneless, skinless chicken breast
1 pound Brussels sprouts
1/2 pound fresh green beans
1 medium red bell pepper
2 stalks celery
2 medium carrots
1/4 pound Chinese snow peas
3 scallions (green onions)
2 tablespoons vegetable oil
1 teaspoon sesame oil
1 tablespoon cornstarch
2 tablespoons water
2 tablespoons soy sauce
1 can (8 ounces) pineapple chunks
Seasoning to taste

Porcelain Rice

1 cup long-grain white rice
1 can (10 1/2 ounces) chicken broth
1 cup water
1/2 teaspoon Chinese 5-spice
2 teaspoons turmeric
1 package (4 ounces) rice noodles

Lychee Laughter

1 can (11 ounces) lychee nuts in syrup
1 jar (6 ounces) maraschino cherries
1 tablespoon cornstarch
1 pint boysenberry sorbet
1/4 cup marshmallow crème for garnish

EQUIPMENT

Wok	Vegetable peeler
Double boiler	Ice cream scoop
Medium saucepan	Kitchen knives
Small saucepan	Measuring cups and
Strainer	spoons
Small mixing bowl	Cooking utensils
Whisk	

COUNTDOWN

1. Assemble the ingredients and the equipment.
2. Do Steps 1–3 of *Lychee Laughter*.
3. Do Steps 1–2 of *Porcelain Rice*.
4. Do Steps 1–2 of *Hang Chow Chicken*.
5. Do Steps 3–5 of *Porcelain Rice*.
6. Do Steps 3–4 of *Hang Chow Chicken*.
7. Do Step 4 of *Lychee Laughter*.

THURSDAY

Hang Chow Chicken

1 Rinse and pat dry the chicken and cut it into thin strips.

2 Rinse and trim the Brussels sprouts and cut them in half. Rinse, trim, and slice the green beans into 2-inch pieces. Rinse, trim, seed, and chop the bell pepper. Rinse, trim, and slice the celery. Peel and slice the carrots. Rinse and string the snow peas. Rinse, trim, and slice the scallions.

3 Heat both oils in a wok. Add the chicken and stir-fry until the strips are white, 3 to 4 minutes. Add the Brussels sprouts, the beans, the bell pepper, the celery, and the carrots and stir-fry for 3 minutes. Add the snow peas and stir-fry for 1 minute.

4 In a small bowl, combine the cornstarch and the water. Add the soy sauce and blend well. Add the mixture to the wok. Add the undrained pineapple. Stir-fry until the sauce is thick and clear, about 2 minutes. Season to taste and sprinkle with the scallions.

Porcelain Rice

1 Bring water to a boil in the bottom of a double boiler.

2 Place the rice, the broth, the 1 cup water, the Chinese 5-spice, and half of the turmeric in the top of the double boiler. Cover, reduce the heat, and simmer until all the liquid is absorbed and the rice is tender, 30 to 40 minutes.

3 Bring water to a boil in a medium saucepan.

4 Break the rice noodles into small pieces. Add the noodles and the remaining turmeric to the saucepan. Combine and cook for 1 minute.

5 Drain the noodles and fold them into the rice. Cover to keep warm.

Lychee Laughter

1 Drain the lychees, reserving 3 tablespoons of the syrup.

2 Reserve 4 whole maraschino cherries and 1 tablespoon of the liquid. Drain and chop the remaining cherries. Combine the cherries and the lychees in a small bowl.

3 Combine the reserved lychee syrup with the reserved maraschino cherry liquid and the cornstarch in a small saucepan. Bring the mixture to a boil, stirring to combine, and cook until the mixture thickens and runs clear, about 1 minute. Remove from the heat and set aside.

4 Place half of the fruit in the bottom of individual dessert glasses. Top with a scoop of sorbet. Add the remaining fruit. Spoon the syrup over the top and garnish with dollops of marshmallow crème and the reserved maraschino cherries.

FRIDAY

In Cod We Trust

4 cod fillets (about 1 1/2 pounds)
1 small shallot
1 large lemon
2 tablespoons olive oil
2 teaspoons capers
1/2 teaspoon curry powder
1/2 teaspoon dried thyme
Seasoning to taste

The Couscous Creation

3 tablespoons fresh parsley (when chopped)
3 cloves garlic
3 tablespoons butter
1 can (14 ounces) vegetable broth
1/4 teaspoon dried tarragon
1 cup couscous

Evegetables

2 medium parsnips
2 medium carrots
2 tablespoons butter
1 teaspoon granulated sugar
Seasoning to taste

Adam's Apple

2 large sweet apples
2 teaspoons lemon juice
2 eggs
1 1/2 teaspoons vanilla extract
1/2 cup walnut bits
1 cup flour
3/4 cup dark brown sugar
2 teaspoons baking powder
1/2 teaspoon ground cinnamon
1/2 teaspoon ground nutmeg
Whipped cream for garnish

EQUIPMENT

2 medium covered saucepans
9 x 13-inch glass baking dish
Pie plate
Steamer insert
Large mixing bowl
Small mixing bowl

Whisk
Vegetable peeler
Citrus juicer
Aluminum foil
Kitchen knives
Measuring cups and spoons
Cooking utensils

COUNTDOWN

1. Assemble the ingredients and the equipment.
2. Do Steps 1–4 of *Adam's Apple*.
3. Do Steps 1–4 of *In Cod We Trust*.
4. Do Steps 1–3 of *Evegetables*.
5. Do Steps 1–3 of *The Couscous Creation*.
6. Do Step 5 of *In Cod We Trust*.
7. Do Step 4 of *The Couscous Creation*.
8. Do Step 4 of *Evegetables*.
9. Do Step 5 of *Adam's Apple*.

FRIDAY

In Cod We Trust

1 Grease a 9 x 13-inch baking dish.

2 Rinse and pat dry the fish fillets. Peel and mince the shallot. Juice the lemon.

3 In a small bowl, combine the shallot, the lemon juice, the oil, the capers, the curry powder, and the thyme. Season to taste.

4 Arrange the fillets in the baking dish. Pour the marinade mixture over the fish and let stand for 20 minutes, turning occasionally.

5 Cover the dish with aluminum foil and bake at 350°F until the fish flakes easily with a fork, 10 to 12 minutes.

The Couscous Creation

1 Rinse, stem, and chop the parsley. Peel and mince the garlic.

2 Melt the butter in a medium saucepan and sauté the garlic for 2 minutes. Add the broth and the tarragon and bring the mixture to a boil.

3 Add the couscous. Stir to combine. Cover and remove from the heat. Let stand until all the liquid has been absorbed, about 10 minutes.

4 Add the parsley. Fluff with a fork.

Evegetables

1 Bring water to a boil in a medium saucepan.

2 Peel, trim, and julienne the parsnips. Peel, trim, and julienne the carrots.

3 Arrange the vegetables in a steamer insert. Place the insert in the saucepan, cover, and steam until the vegetables are crisp-tender, about 10 minutes.

4 Drain the vegetables and return them to the saucepan. Add the butter and the sugar, and toss to coat. Season to taste and cover to keep warm.

Adam's Apple

1 Preheat the oven to 350°F. Grease a pie plate.

2 Rinse, core, and coarsely chop the apples. Sprinkle with the lemon juice.

3 In a large bowl, whip the eggs until frothy. Add the vanilla, the walnuts, and the chopped apples. Fold in the flour, the brown sugar, the baking powder, the cinnamon, and the nutmeg. Blend well to combine.

4 Pour the mixture into the pie plate. Bake until lightly browned and a toothpick inserted in the center comes out clean, 30 to 35 minutes.

5 Serve with dollops of whipped cream.

WEEK TWO

Monday

Broccoli Turtles
Deer Fruit
Monkey Muffins
Chocolate Moosetake

Tuesday

Chick du Soleil
Sideshow Squash
Three-Ring Spinach
Banana and Bailey

Wednesday

Ham a Nice Day
Peasing Personality
Salad Isn't So
Pudding On the Ritz

Thursday

Boothbay Bisque
Down East Slaw
Mainestream Muffins
Auburnt Cake

Friday

Drunken Pasta
Sober Salad
Italian Loafer
Idle Grapefruit

☐ Butter
☐ Flour
☐ Baking powder
☐ Baking soda
☐ Granulated sugar
☐ Dark brown sugar
☐ Powdered sugar
☐ Corn syrup
☐ Chocolate syrup
☐ Multicolored sprinkles
☐ Olive oil
☐ Vegetable oil
☐ Balsamic vinegar
☐ Rice vinegar
☐ Lemon juice
☐ Honey
☐ Mayonnaise
☐ Grated Parmesan cheese
☐ Seasoned breadcrumbs
☐ Instant coffee
☐ Sesame seeds
☐ Dried basil
☐ Dried oregano
☐ Ground cinnamon
☐ Curry powder
☐ Italian seasoning
☐ Ground nutmeg
☐ Black pepper
☐ White pepper
☐ Salt
☐ Orange extract
☐ Rum extract
☐ Vanilla extract

MEAT & POULTRY

1 1/2 pounds lean cooked ham steak (W)

4 boneless, skinless chicken breast halves (about 1 1/2 pounds) (T)

FISH

1/2 pound cooked lobster meat (or crab) (Th)

1/2 pound cooked baby shrimp (Th)

FRESH PRODUCE

VEGETABLES

1 1/2 pounds small new red potatoes (W)

1 medium butternut squash (T)

1/2 pound asparagus (F)

3 medium carrots (F)

2 stalks celery (M)

1 package (10 ounces) spinach (T)

1 medium head cabbage (Th)

1 medium head lettuce (W)

1 small head lettuce (F)

3 medium tomatoes (W)

2 medium tomatoes (F)

2 medium ripe avocados (W)

2 medium cucumbers (F)

1 small red bell pepper (F)

1 small green bell pepper (Th)

1 medium onion (Th)

2 large sweet onions (W)

1 medium red onion (F)

1 small red onion (F)

1 clove garlic (T)

2 cloves garlic (W)

2 cloves garlic (F)

HERBS

3 tablespoons chives (when chopped) (Th)

1/2 cup dill (when chopped) (F)

3 tablespoons parsley (when chopped) (T)

1/4 cup parsley (when chopped) (Th)

FRUIT

2 medium grapefruit (F)

4 medium bananas (T)

2 medium red apples (M)

2 ripe kiwifruit (M)

1/2 pound seedless red grapes (M)

CANS, JARS & BOTTLES

VEGETABLES

1 can (28 ounces) crushed tomatoes (M)

1 can (11 ounces) whole-kernel corn (Th)

1 can (15 ounces) cream-style corn (Th)

1 can (4 ounces) whole button mushrooms (F)

INTERNATIONAL FOODS

1 can (8 ounces) sliced water chestnuts (T)

SPREADS

1/4 cup strawberry jam (T)

CONDIMENTS

1 can (4 ounces) sliced black olives (W)

PACKAGED GOODS

PASTA, RICE & GRAINS

24 jumbo pasta shells (M)

1 pound fettuccine (F)

BAKED GOODS

1 loaf Italian bread (F)

1 angel food loaf cake (Th)

DESSERT & BAKING NEEDS

1 package (3.4 ounces) instant vanilla pudding mix (W)

1 cup chocolate chips (W)

WINE & SPIRITS

1 cup dry white wine (F)

2 tablespoons dry sherry (Th)

1 tablespoon Grand Marnier (M)

REFRIGERATED PRODUCTS

DAIRY

2 cups milk (W)

1 cup milk (Th)

1/2 cup half-and-half (F)

2 cups half-and-half (Th)

1 cup plain yogurt (M)

1 cup whipping cream (M)

Whipped cream for garnish (W)

1 egg (M)

1 egg (T)

1 egg (Th)

CHEESE

1 cup small-curd cottage cheese (M)

1/2 pound Swiss cheese (M)

1/2 cup shredded mozzarella cheese (F)

JUICES

1 cup orange juice (Th)

FROZEN GOODS

VEGETABLES

1 package (10 ounces) chopped broccoli (M)

1 package (10 ounces) green peas (W)

DESSERTS

1 pint strawberry ice cream (T)

MONDAY

Broccoli Turtles

1 package (10 ounces) frozen chopped broccoli
½ pound Swiss cheese
24 jumbo pasta shells
1 cup small-curd cottage cheese
1 teaspoon Italian seasoning
Seasoning to taste
1 can (28 ounces) crushed tomatoes

Deer Fruit

1 medium head lettuce
2 medium red apples
2 stalks celery
½ pound seedless red grapes
2 ripe kiwifruit
3 tablespoons mayonnaise
2 tablespoons lemon juice
1 tablespoon honey
Seasoning to taste

Monkey Muffins

2 cups flour
1 tablespoon baking powder
½ teaspoon baking soda
½ teaspoon salt
2 teaspoons dried basil
2 teaspoons dried oregano
1 cup plain yogurt
⅓ cup vegetable oil
1 egg

Chocolate Moosetake

1 cup whipping cream
1 teaspoon orange extract
2 tablespoons powdered sugar
¾ cup chocolate syrup
1 tablespoon Grand Marnier

EQUIPMENT

Electric mixer	3 small mixing bowls
Stockpot	Whisk
9 x 13-inch glass baking dish	Cheese grater
Muffin tin	Aluminum foil
Colander	Kitchen knives
3 large mixing bowls	Measuring cups and spoons
Medium mixing bowl	Cooking utensils

COUNTDOWN

1. Assemble the ingredients and the equipment.
2. Do Step 1 of Chocolate Moosetake.
3. Do Steps 1–6 of Broccoli Turtles.
4. Do Step 2 of Chocolate Moosetake.
5. Do Steps 1–4 of Monkey Muffins.
6. Do Steps 7–9 of Broccoli Turtles.
7. Do Step 5 of Monkey Muffins.
8. Do Steps 1–4 of Deer Fruit.

MONDAY

Broccoli Turtles

1 Place the broccoli in a small bowl of warm water to thaw.

2 Bring water to a boil in a stockpot.

3 Grate the Swiss cheese.

4 Cook the shells in the boiling water until just tender, about 10 minutes.

5 In a large bowl, combine the broccoli, the cottage cheese, the Swiss cheese, and the Italian seasoning. Season to taste.

6 Pour 2 cups of the crushed tomatoes in the bottom of a 9 x 13-inch baking dish.

7 Preheat the oven to 375°F.

8 Drain the shells and run them under cold water to cool.

9 Spoon the broccoli mixture into the shells and place open side up in the dish. Pour the remaining tomatoes over and around the shells. Cover the dish with aluminum foil and bake until the shells are heated through and the cheese has melted, about 20 minutes.

Deer Fruit

1 Wash and dry the lettuce and distribute the leaves among individual salad plates.

2 Rinse, core, and chop the apples. Rinse, trim, and chop the celery. Rinse, stem, and halve the grapes. Peel and slice the kiwifruit. Combine the fruit in a large bowl and place over the lettuce.

3 In a small bowl, whisk together the mayonnaise, the lemon juice, and the honey. Season to taste.

4 Drizzle the dressing over the salad.

Monkey Muffins

1 Grease a muffin tin.

2 In a large bowl, combine the flour, the baking powder, the baking soda, the salt, the basil, and the oregano.

3 In a small bowl, combine the yogurt, the oil, and the egg.

4 Fold the yogurt mixture into the flour mixture just until moistened. Fill the muffin cups ⅔ full.

5 Bake the muffins at 375°F until golden, 15 to 20 minutes.

Chocolate Moosetake

1 Chill a medium bowl and the beaters of an electric mixer for 10 minutes.

2 Whip the cream until soft peaks form. Fold in the orange extract and the powdered sugar. Add the chocolate syrup and beat until the cream is thick and glossy, about 2 minutes. Fold in the Grand Marnier and spoon into individual dessert dishes. Place in the freezer until you are ready to serve.

TUESDAY

Chick du Soleil

4 boneless, skinless chicken breast halves
    (about 1 1/2 pounds)
1 clove garlic
3 tablespoons fresh parsley (when
    chopped)
1/2 cup flour
Seasoning to taste
1 egg
2 tablespoons water
1 cup seasoned breadcrumbs
1/4 cup sesame seeds
3 tablespoons vegetable oil

Sideshow Squash

1 medium butternut squash
2 tablespoons butter
2 tablespoons dark brown sugar
1/2 teaspoon ground cinnamon

Three-Ring Spinach

1 package (10 ounces) fresh spinach
1 medium red onion
1 can (8 ounces) sliced water chestnuts
2 tablespoons butter
Seasoning to taste

Banana and Bailey

4 medium bananas
3 tablespoons butter
2 tablespoons granulated sugar
1 teaspoon ground nutmeg
1 pint strawberry ice cream
1/4 cup strawberry jam

EQUIPMENT

Large covered
    saucepan
Medium covered
    saucepan
Large skillet
Medium covered
    skillet
9 x 13-inch glass
    baking dish
Steamer insert

3 large shallow
    bowls
Whisk
Ice cream scoop
Aluminum foil
Kitchen knives
Measuring cups and
    spoons
Cooking utensils

COUNTDOWN

1. Assemble the ingredients and the
   equipment.
2. Do Steps 1–5 of Chick du Soleil.
3. Do Steps 1–3 of Sideshow Squash.
4. Do Steps 1–2 of Three-Ring Spinach.
5. Do Steps 1–2 of Banana and Bailey.
6. Do Step 6 of Chick du Soleil.
7. Do Step 3 of Three-Ring Spinach.
8. Do Step 4 of Sideshow Squash.
9. Do Step 3 of Banana and Bailey.

TUESDAY

Chick du Soleil

1 Preheat the oven to 350°F. Grease a 9 x 13-inch baking dish.

2 Rinse and pat dry the chicken breasts. Peel and mince the garlic. Rinse, stem, and chop the parsley.

3 Set out 3 large shallow bowls. Combine the flour and the parsley in the first bowl. Season to taste. Whisk together the egg and the water in the second bowl. Combine the breadcrumbs and the sesame seeds in the third bowl.

4 Heat the oil in a large skillet and sauté the garlic for 1 minute.

5 Dip the chicken breasts in the flour mixture, then the egg mixture, and then the breadcrumb mixture. Sauté until lightly browned, about 5 minutes per side. Place the chicken in the baking dish, cover with aluminum foil, and bake for 15 minutes.

6 Remove the foil and bake for 5 minutes longer.

Sideshow Squash

1 Bring water to a boil in a medium saucepan.

2 Cut the squash in half. Remove the seeds and fibers, peel, and cut into bite-sized pieces.

3 Arrange the squash in a steamer insert, place the insert in the saucepan, cover, and steam until it is tender, about 10 minutes.

4 Drain the squash and return it to the saucepan. Add the butter, the brown sugar, and the cinnamon. Blend well and cover to keep warm.

Three-Ring Spinach

1 Rinse, pat dry, and stem the spinach. Peel and thinly slice the onion. Drain the water chestnuts.

2 Melt the butter in a large saucepan. Add the onion and sauté until it softens, about 5 minutes. Stir in the water chestnuts and toss to combine. Add the spinach and cook, covered, until it is wilted, about 1 minute.

3 Uncover the saucepan and cook, stirring, until the liquid has evaporated, about 1 minute. Season to taste and cover to keep warm.

Banana and Bailey

1 Peel and chunk the bananas.

2 Melt the butter with the sugar in a medium skillet. Add the bananas, tossing to coat. Sprinkle with the nutmeg and simmer until the bananas are heated through, about 2 minutes. Remove from the heat and cover to keep warm.

3 Spoon some of the bananas into individual dessert glasses. Add scoops of ice cream and top with more bananas and a dollop of jam.

WEDNESDAY

Ham a Nice Day

1 ½ pounds small new red potatoes
1 ½ pounds lean cooked ham steak
2 large sweet onions
2 tablespoons butter
2 tablespoons vegetable oil
Seasoning to taste

Peasing Personality

1 package (10 ounces) frozen green peas
2 cloves garlic
2 tablespoons butter
½ teaspoon white pepper
Seasoning to taste
1 tablespoon balsamic vinegar

Salad Isn't So

1 medium head lettuce
2 medium ripe avocados
3 tablespoons lemon juice
3 medium tomatoes
1 can (4 ounces) sliced black olives
3 tablespoons olive oil
Seasoning to taste

Pudding On the Ritz

1 package (3.4 ounces) instant vanilla
   pudding mix
2 cups milk
1 cup chocolate chips
1 tablespoon instant coffee
Whipped cream for garnish

EQUIPMENT

Electric mixer	Whisk
Large saucepan	Vegetable brush
Large skillet	Kitchen knives
Medium covered skillet	Measuring cups and spoons
Medium mixing bowl	Cooking utensils
2 small mixing bowls	

COUNTDOWN

1. Assemble the ingredients and the equipment.
2. Do Step 1 of *Peasing Personality*.
3. Do Steps 1–2 of *Pudding On the Ritz*.
4. Do Step 2 of *Peasing Personality*.
5. Do Steps 1–4 of *Salad Isn't So*.
6. Do Steps 1–5 of *Ham a Nice Day*.
7. Do Steps 3–4 of *Peasing Personality*.
8. Do Step 5 of *Salad Isn't So*.
9. Do Step 3 of *Pudding On the Ritz*.

WEDNESDAY

Ham a Nice Day

1 Scrub and halve the potatoes. Cover them with water in a large saucepan. Bring to a boil and cook until the potatoes are almost tender, about 10 minutes.

2 Cube the ham. Peel and thinly slice the onions.

3 Melt the butter with the oil in a large skillet. Sauté the onions until they are golden, about 10 minutes.

4 Drain the potatoes, add them to the skillet, and season to taste. Sauté until the potatoes are golden, about 8 minutes.

5 Add the ham and combine. Cook until the ham is heated through, about 5 minutes.

Peasing Personality

1 Set the package of peas in a small bowl of warm water to thaw.

2 Peel and mince the garlic.

3 Melt the butter in a medium skillet and sauté the garlic for 2 minutes. Add the peas and the white pepper, season to taste, and toss until heated through.

4 Drizzle with the balsamic vinegar and cover to keep warm.

Salad Isn't So

1 Wash and dry the lettuce and distribute the leaves among individual salad plates.

2 Halve, pit, peel, and slice the avocados and sprinkle them with 1 tablespoon of the lemon juice. Rinse, stem, and slice the tomatoes. Drain the olives.

3 In a small bowl, combine the oil with the remaining 2 tablespoons lemon juice and season to taste.

4 Alternate the avocado slices and the tomato slices on each salad. Top with the olives.

5 Drizzle the salad with the dressing.

Pudding On the Ritz

1 In a medium bowl, combine the pudding mix and the milk and beat until well blended. Divide the pudding in half. Add half of the chocolate chips to one half of the pudding. Add the instant coffee to the second half of the pudding.

2 Spoon the remaining chocolate chips into individual dessert glasses. Top with alternating layers of each pudding, ending with the coffee mixture on top. Refrigerate until you are ready to serve.

3 Top each serving with a dollop of whipped cream.

THURSDAY

Boothbay Bisque

1 medium onion
3 tablespoons fresh chives (when chopped)
½ pound cooked lobster meat (or crab)
1 can (11 ounces) whole-kernel corn
3 tablespoons butter
3 tablespoons flour
1 can (15 ounces) cream-style corn
1 teaspoon curry powder
2 cups half-and-half
1 cup milk
2 tablespoons dry sherry
½ pound cooked baby shrimp
Seasoning to taste

Down East Slaw

1 medium head green cabbage
1 small green bell pepper
¼ cup fresh parsley (when chopped)
3 tablespoons vegetable oil
2 tablespoons lemon juice
1 teaspoon honey
Seasoning to taste

Mainestream Muffins

4 tablespoons butter
2 cups flour
2 tablespoons granulated sugar
1 tablespoon baking powder
½ teaspoon salt
1 egg
1 cup orange juice

Auburnt Cake

⅔ cup water
⅔ cup granulated sugar
1 teaspoon vanilla extract
2 tablespoons corn syrup
½ teaspoon ground cinnamon
1 angel food loaf cake

EQUIPMENT

Large saucepan
Medium skillet
Muffin tin
2 large mixing bowls
Medium mixing bowl
Small mixing bowl

Whisk
Vegetable grater
Kitchen knives
Measuring cups and
   spoons
Cooking utensils

COUNTDOWN

1. Assemble the ingredients and the equipment.
2. Do Steps 1–3 of *Auburnt Cake*.
3. Do Steps 1–2 of *Down East Slaw*.
4. Do Steps 1–7 of *Mainestream Muffins*.
5. Do Steps 1–4 of *Boothbay Bisque*.
6. Do Step 4 of *Auburnt Cake*.

THURSDAY

Boothbay Bisque

1 Peel and finely chop the onion. Rinse and chop the chives. Flake the lobster. Drain the whole-kernel corn.

2 Melt the butter in a large saucepan and sauté the onion until soft, about 5 minutes. Blend in the flour.

3 Reduce the heat to a simmer and add the whole-kernel corn, the cream-style corn, and the curry powder. Stir in the half-and-half, the milk, and the sherry. Add the lobster and the shrimp, season to taste, and mix to combine. Simmer until hot, but do not let boil.

4 Garnish with the chives.

Down East Slaw

1 Rinse, trim, quarter, and grate the cabbage. Rinse, trim, seed, and chop the bell pepper. Rinse, stem, and chop the parsley. Combine the ingredients in a large bowl.

2 In a small bowl, whisk together the oil, the lemon juice, and the honey. Season to taste and toss with the slaw.

Mainestream Muffins

1 Preheat the oven to 425°F. Grease a muffin tin.

2 Melt the butter.

3 In a large bowl, combine the flour, the sugar, the baking powder, and the salt.

4 Whip the egg in a medium bowl. Add the butter and the orange juice and mix well.

5 Make a well in the center of the flour mixture. Pour the egg mixture into the flour mixture and fold to combine.

6 Spoon the mixture into the muffin cups.

7 Bake until the muffins are golden, 20 to 25 minutes.

Auburnt Cake

1 Bring the water to a boil.

2 Heat the sugar in a medium skillet, stirring constantly, until golden brown and melted, about 3 minutes.

3 Slowly pour the boiling water into the sugar and whisk until the sugar is dissolved, about 2 minutes. Add the vanilla, the corn syrup, and the cinnamon and whisk until well blended, about 1 minute. Remove from the heat and set aside to cool.

4 Drizzle the burnt sugar over the angel food cake.

FRIDAY

Drunken Pasta

2 cloves garlic
2 medium tomatoes
1/2 cup fresh dill (when chopped)
1/2 pound fresh asparagus
1 small red bell pepper
4 tablespoons butter
2 tablespoons flour
1 cup dry white wine
1/2 cup half-and-half
1 can (4 ounces) whole button mushrooms
1 pound fettuccine
Seasoning to taste
Grated Parmesan cheese for garnish

Sober Salad

1 small head lettuce
3 medium carrots
2 medium cucumbers
3 tablespoons vegetable oil
2 tablespoons rice vinegar
1 teaspoon granulated sugar
1/4 teaspoon dried basil
Seasoning to taste

Italian Loafer

1 small red onion
1 loaf Italian bread
2 tablespoons olive oil
1/2 cup shredded mozzarella cheese

Idle Grapefruit

2 tablespoons butter
2 medium grapefruit
2 tablespoons dark brown sugar
2 teaspoons rum extract
Multicolored sprinkles for garnish

EQUIPMENT

Stockpot	Whisk
Medium covered saucepan	Vegetable peeler
Large skillet	Vegetable grater
Steamer insert	Grapefruit knife
2 baking sheets	Pastry brush
Colander	Kitchen knives
Medium mixing bowl	Measuring cups and spoons
Small mixing bowl	Cooking utensils

COUNTDOWN

1. Assemble the ingredients and the equipment.
2. Do Steps 1–2 of *Idle Grapefruit*.
3. Do Steps 1–3 of *Sober Salad*.
4. Do Steps 1–4 of *Drunken Pasta*.
5. Do Steps 1–5 of *Italian Loafer*.
6. Do Steps 5–8 of *Drunken Pasta*.
7. Do Step 4 of *Sober Salad*.
8. Do Steps 3–5 of *Idle Grapefruit*.

FRIDAY

Drunken Pasta

1 Bring water to a boil in a stockpot.

2 Peel and mince the garlic. Rinse, stem, and chop the tomatoes. Rinse, stem, and chop the dill. Rinse, cut off the tough ends, and slice the asparagus into 2-inch pieces. Rinse, trim, seed, and chunk the bell pepper.

3 Bring water to a boil in a medium saucepan.

4 Arrange the asparagus and the bell pepper in a steamer insert, place the insert in the saucepan, cover, and steam for 3 minutes.

5 Remove from the heat and set aside.

6 Melt the butter in a large skillet. Add the garlic and sauté until soft, about 3 minutes. Add the flour and blend until smooth. Slowly add the wine and blend well. Add the half-and-half and the tomatoes, mixing to combine. Add the dill, the asparagus, the bell pepper, and the mushrooms with their liquid. Reduce the heat and simmer until heated through, about 5 minutes. Do not let boil.

7 Cook the pasta in the stockpot until it is almost tender, 2 to 3 minutes if you are using fresh pasta, 6 to 7 minutes if you are using dry pasta.

8 Drain the pasta. Return it to the stockpot. Toss with the vegetables and season to taste. Add the cheese and toss again.

Sober Salad

1 Wash and dry the lettuce and distribute the leaves among individual salad plates.

2 Peel, trim, and grate the carrots. Peel, trim, and slice the cucumbers. Combine both in a medium bowl.

3 In a small bowl, whisk together the oil, the vinegar, the sugar, and the basil. Season to taste and toss with the carrots and cucumbers.

4 Spoon the carrots and cucumbers over the lettuce.

Italian Loafer

1 Preheat the oven to 350°F.

2 Peel and mince the onion.

3 Slice the bread in half lengthwise and place, cut side up, on a baking sheet.

4 Brush the cut sides with the oil. Sprinkle with the onion and the cheese.

5 Bake until the bread is heated through and the cheese is melted and bubbly, about 10 minutes.

Idle Grapefruit

1 Set the butter out to soften.

2 Cut the grapefruit in half. Remove the seeds and loosen the sections with a grapefruit knife. Place the halves on a baking sheet.

3 Preheat the broiler.

4 Spread each grapefruit half with the butter, sprinkle with the brown sugar, and drizzle with the rum extract. Broil until the grapefruit halves are heated through and bubbly, 2 to 3 minutes.

5 Garnish with the sprinkles.

WEEK THREE

Monday
Nothing to Cheese At
Shallot Be Zucchini?
All Puffed Up
Good Little Brownies

Tuesday
Hawkeyed Sausage
State Fair Salad
Ames to Be Pudding

Wednesday
Slippery Salmon
Rough Rice
Smooth Succotash
Marbled Fruit

Thursday
Soup Opera
The Guiding Linguini
One Loaf to Live
Dates of Our Lives

Friday
C'est la Gruyère
Marquis de Salad
Beaucoup Biscuits
Eiffel Towers

STAPLES

- ☐ Butter
- ☐ Flour
- ☐ Baking powder
- ☐ Yellow cornmeal
- ☐ Cornstarch
- ☐ Granulated sugar
- ☐ Dark brown sugar
- ☐ Powdered sugar
- ☐ Chocolate sprinkles
- ☐ Multicolored sprinkles
- ☐ Olive oil
- ☐ Vegetable oil
- ☐ Red wine vinegar
- ☐ Lemon juice
- ☐ Lime juice
- ☐ Dijon mustard
- ☐ Worcestershire sauce
- ☐ White Worcestershire sauce
- ☐ Grated Parmesan cheese
- ☐ Dried basil
- ☐ Dried oregano
- ☐ Cayenne pepper
- ☐ Italian seasoning
- ☐ Ground nutmeg
- ☐ Paprika
- ☐ Black pepper
- ☐ Saffron threads
- ☐ Salt
- ☐ Vanilla extract

MEAT & POULTRY

1½ pounds Italian sausage (T)

FISH

4 salmon fillets (about 1½ pounds) (W)

FRESH PRODUCE

VEGETABLES

1 pound small new red potatoes (T)
2 medium zucchini (M)
2 stalks celery (T)
2 stalks celery (W)
1 package (10 ounces) spinach (F)
1 small head red cabbage (F)
1 small head lettuce (F)
1½ pounds tomatoes (Th)
2 medium tomatoes (M)
2 medium orange bell peppers (T)
1 large onion (T)
3 small sweet onions (F)
1 small shallot (M)
3 scallions (green onions) (Th)
1 clove garlic (Th)
1 clove garlic (T)
2 cloves garlic (W)

HERBS

4 tablespoons basil leaves (when chopped) (Th)
3 tablespoons chives (when chopped) (W)
2 tablespoons chives (when chopped) (M)
2 tablespoons parsley (when chopped) (Th)
3 tablespoons parsley (when chopped) (M)

FRUIT

1 small lemon (Th)
2 large oranges (F)
2 medium bananas (W)
2 large cooking apples (T)
2 large ripe pears (Th)
2 small ripe pears (F)

1 ripe pineapple (W)
1 cup cranberries (F)
¼ pound seedless black grapes (F)

CANS, JARS & BOTTLES

SOUPS

1 can (14 ounces) vegetable broth (W)
1 can (10½ ounces) beef consommé (Th)
1 can (10½ ounces) chicken broth (Th)
1 can (10½ ounces) chicken broth (T)

VEGETABLES

1 can (15 ounces) cream-style corn (W)

FRUIT

1 can (16 ounces) pitted dark cherries (W)

DESSERT & BAKING NEEDS

1 can (14 ounces) sweetened condensed milk (F)

PACKAGED GOODS

PASTA, RICE & GRAINS

1 pound linguini (Th)
1 pound elbow macaroni (M)
1 cup brown rice (W)

BAKED GOODS

1 loaf Italian bread (Th)
1 package (16 ounces) seasoned stuffing mix (T)

DRIED FRUIT & NUTS

½ cup chopped dates (Th)
½ cup walnut bits (M)
½ cup pecan bits (W)

DESSERT & BAKING NEEDS

1 package (3.4 ounces) instant white chocolate pudding mix (T)
1 package (3.4 ounces) cook-and-serve chocolate pudding mix (M)

2 Snickers candy bars (2.7 ounces each) (F)

WINE & SPIRITS

¼ cup dry white wine (Th)
2 tablespoons dry sherry (Th)
4 teaspoons crème de menthe (T)

REFRIGERATED PRODUCTS

DAIRY

2 cups milk (T)
¾ cup milk (F)
¼ cup plus 2 tablespoons milk (M)
½ cup half-and-half (Th)
3 tablespoons sour cream (Th)
Whipped cream for garnish (T)
Whipped cream for garnish (F)
4 eggs (F)
3 eggs (M)

CHEESE

½ pound Gruyère cheese (F)
1 container (15 ounces) ricotta cheese (M)

JUICES

½ cup orange juice (F)
3 tablespoons orange juice (W)

DELI

1 package (8 ounces) refrigerated biscuits (M)

FROZEN GOODS

VEGETABLES

1 package (10 ounces) cut green beans (Th)
1 package (10 ounces) green peas and pearl onions (T)
1 package (10 ounces) lima beans (W)

PASTRY

1 sheet puff pastry (F)

DESSERTS

1 pint chocolate yogurt (F)

MONDAY

Nothing to Cheese At

3 tablespoons fresh parsley (when chopped)
1 pound elbow macaroni
3 tablespoons butter
1 container (15 ounces) ricotta cheese
1 teaspoon ground nutmeg
1 teaspoon Dijon mustard
Seasoning to taste
1/2 cup grated Parmesan cheese

Shallot Be Zucchini?

2 medium zucchini
1 small shallot
2 medium tomatoes
2 tablespoons olive oil
1 teaspoon dried basil
Seasoning to taste

All Puffed Up

2 tablespoons fresh chives (when chopped)
1 egg
2 tablespoons milk
1 teaspoon Italian seasoning
1/8 teaspoon paprika
1 package (8 ounces) refrigerated biscuits

Good Little Brownies

6 tablespoons butter
2/3 cup granulated sugar
2 eggs
1/4 cup milk
1 teaspoon vanilla extract
1/2 cup flour
1 package (3.4 ounces) cook-and-serve chocolate pudding mix
1 teaspoon baking powder
1/2 cup walnut bits
1/4 cup powdered sugar

EQUIPMENT

Electric mixer	Medium mixing bowl
Stockpot	Small mixing bowl
Large covered skillet	Whisk
Pie plate	Kitchen knives
Muffin tin	Measuring cups and spoons
Colander	Cooking utensils
Large mixing bowl	

COUNTDOWN

1. Assemble the ingredients and the equipment.
2. Do Steps 1–4 of Good Little Brownies.
3. Do Step 1 of Shallot Be Zucchini?
4. Do Steps 1–2 of Nothing to Cheese At.
5. Do Steps 1–4 of All Puffed Up.
6. Do Steps 3–4 of Nothing to Cheese At.
7. Do Step 2 of Shallot Be Zucchini?
8. Do Step 5 of Nothing to Cheese At.
9. Do Step 5 of Good Little Brownies.

MONDAY

Nothing to Cheese At

1 Bring water to a boil in a stockpot.

2 Rinse, stem, and chop the parsley.

3 Cook the macaroni until it is almost tender, 8 to 10 minutes.

4 Drain the pasta and return it to the stockpot. Blend in the butter, tossing to melt. Blend in the ricotta cheese, the nutmeg, and the mustard. Season to taste and simmer until the mixture is heated through, about 3 minutes.

5 Sprinkle with the parsley and the Parmesan cheese.

Shallot Be Zucchini?

1 Scrub, trim, and slice the zucchini. Peel and chop the shallot. Rinse, stem, and chop the tomatoes.

2 Heat the oil in a large skillet and sauté the shallot for 1 minute. Add the zucchini and sauté for 1 minute. Add the tomatoes and the basil, cover, and cook until the zucchini is crisp-tender and the tomatoes are heated through, about 2 minutes more. Season to taste.

All Puffed Up

1 Grease a pie plate.

2 Rinse, trim, and chop the chives.

3 In a small bowl, combine the chives, the egg, the milk, the Italian seasoning, and the paprika. Separate the biscuits and arrange them in the pie plate. Pour the egg mixture over the biscuits.

4 Increase the oven temperature to 450°F. Bake the biscuits until golden, 12 to 15 minutes.

Good Little Brownies

1 Preheat the oven to 350°F. Grease a muffin tin.

2 In a large bowl, cream the butter with the sugar until fluffy. Add the eggs, one at a time, and beat well. Add the milk and the vanilla.

3 In a medium bowl, combine the flour, the pudding mix, and the baking powder. Add the flour mixture to the egg mixture, stirring to combine. Spoon the batter into the muffin cups.

4 Sprinkle the nuts on top and bake until a toothpick inserted in the center comes out clean, 20 to 25 minutes.

5 Dust with the powdered sugar.

TUESDAY

Hawkeyed Sausage

1 ½ pounds Italian sausage
1 tablespoon olive oil
1 large onion
2 stalks celery
2 medium orange bell peppers
2 large cooking apples
2 tablespoons butter
1 tablespoon dark brown sugar
1 can (10 ½ ounces) chicken broth
Seasoning to taste
1 package (16 ounces) seasoned stuffing
  mix

State Fair Salad

1 pound small new red potatoes
1 clove garlic
1 package (10 ounces) frozen green peas
  and pearl onions
¼ cup vegetable oil
3 tablespoons red wine vinegar
1 teaspoon dried oregano
2 teaspoons Dijon mustard
1 teaspoon granulated sugar
Seasoning to taste
1 teaspoon paprika

Ames to Be Pudding

1 package (3.4 ounces) instant white
  chocolate pudding mix
2 cups milk
4 teaspoons crème de menthe
Whipped cream for garnish
Multicolored sprinkles for garnish

EQUIPMENT

Electric mixer
Large saucepan
Large skillet
2-quart casserole
Medium mixing bowl
Small mixing bowl

Whisk
Vegetable brush
Kitchen knives
Measuring cups and
  spoons
Cooking utensils

COUNTDOWN

1. Assemble the ingredients and the
   equipment.
2. Do Step 1 of *Hawkeyed Sausage.*
3. Do Steps 1–2 of *Ames to Be Pudding.*
4. Do Steps 2–6 of *Hawkeyed Sausage.*
5. Do Steps 1–2 of *State Fair Salad.*
6. Do Steps 7–9 of *Hawkeyed Sausage.*
7. Do Steps 3–6 of *State Fair Salad.*
8. Do Step 3 of *Ames to Be Pudding.*

TUESDAY

Hawkeyed Sausage

1 Place the sausage in the freezer for 10 minutes.

2 Preheat the oven to 350°F. Butter a 2-quart casserole.

3 Slice the sausage.

4 Heat the oil in a large skillet and sauté the sausage until browned, about 10 minutes.

5 Peel and chop the onion. Rinse, trim, and chop the celery. Rinse, trim, seed, and chop the bell peppers. Peel, core, and slice the apples.

6 Remove the sausage from the skillet, drain on paper towels, and discard the drippings.

7 Melt the butter in the same skillet and sauté the onion, the celery, the bell peppers, and the apples until the onion is soft, about 5 minutes. Add the brown sugar and toss to coat. Add the broth and season to taste.

8 Return the sausage and blend well. Stir in all but 1 cup of the stuffing mix and toss to combine. Pour into the casserole and top with the remaining stuffing.

9 Bake until the top is lightly browned and the casserole is heated through, about 20 minutes.

State Fair Salad

1 Scrub the potatoes and cut the larger ones in half. Peel and chop the garlic.

2 Cover the potatoes with water in a large saucepan. Bring to a boil and cook until almost tender, about 10 minutes.

3 Add the frozen peas and onions, stir to combine, and cook until hot, about 5 minutes.

4 In a small bowl, combine the garlic, the oil, the vinegar, the oregano, the mustard, and the sugar. Season to taste.

5 Drain the potatoes and the peas and onions and return them to the saucepan. Add the dressing and toss to coat.

6 Sprinkle with the paprika.

Ames to Be Pudding

1 In a medium bowl, beat the pudding mix with the milk until well blended.

2 Spoon the mixture into individual dessert dishes. Swirl a teaspoon of the crème de menthe into each pudding and refrigerate until you are ready to serve.

3 Top each pudding with a dollop of whipped cream and garnish with the sprinkles.

WEDNESDAY

Slippery Salmon

4 salmon fillets (about 1 1/2 pounds)
3 tablespoons fresh chives (when chopped)
2 tablespoons butter
3 tablespoons lemon juice
1 teaspoon Worcestershire sauce
1/2 teaspoon paprika
Seasoning to taste

Rough Rice

2 cloves garlic
2 tablespoons vegetable oil
1 cup brown rice
1 can (14 ounces) vegetable broth
3 tablespoons orange juice
1 teaspoon white Worcestershire sauce
1/2 cup pecan bits

Smooth Succotash

1 package (10 ounces) frozen lima beans
2 stalks celery
3 tablespoons butter
1 can (15 ounces) cream-style corn
Seasoning to taste

Marbled Fruit

1 ripe pineapple
2 medium bananas
1 can (16 ounces) pitted dark cherries
2 tablespoons lime juice
1 teaspoon cornstarch

EQUIPMENT

Medium covered
  saucepan
Medium saucepan
Small saucepan
9 x 13-inch glass
  baking dish
2 small mixing bowls

Whisk
Aluminum foil
Plastic wrap
Kitchen knives
Measuring cups and
  spoons
Cooking utensils

COUNTDOWN

1. Assemble the ingredients and the equipment.
2. Do Step 1 of Smooth Succotash.
3. Do Steps 1–3 of Rough Rice.
4. Do Steps 1–2 of Slippery Salmon.
5. Do Steps 1–2 of Marbled Fruit.
6. Do Steps 3–4 of Slippery Salmon.
7. Do Steps 2–3 of Smooth Succotash.
8. Do Step 5 of Slippery Salmon.
9. Do Step 4 of Rough Rice.
10. Do Steps 3–4 of Marbled Fruit.

WEDNESDAY

Slippery Salmon

1 Rinse and pat dry the fish fillets. Rinse, trim, and chop the chives.

2 Melt the butter in a 9 x 13-inch baking dish. Add the lemon juice, the Worcestershire sauce, and the paprika. Season to taste. Add the fillets and marinate for 15 minutes, turning to coat once or twice.

3 Preheat the oven to 400°F.

4 Cover the dish with aluminum foil and bake until the fish flakes easily with a fork, about 10 minutes.

5 Top with the chives.

Rough Rice

1 Peel and mince the garlic.

2 Heat the oil in a medium saucepan and sauté the garlic for 2 minutes. Add the rice and sauté for 1 minute. Add the broth, the orange juice, and the white Worcestershire sauce and stir to combine.

3 Cover, reduce the heat, and simmer until all the liquid is absorbed and the rice is tender, 40 to 45 minutes.

4 Fold in the nuts and fluff with a fork.

Smooth Succotash

1 Set the lima beans in a small bowl of warm water to thaw.

2 Rinse, trim, and chop the celery.

3 Melt the butter in a medium saucepan. Sauté the celery until it is crisp-tender, about 4 minutes. Add the lima beans and sauté for 2 minutes. Add the corn and season to taste. Simmer until the vegetables are heated through, about 5 minutes.

Marbled Fruit

1 Cut the pineapple in quarters. Remove the rind and slice off the core. Arrange the quarters on individual dessert plates.

2 Peel and slice the bananas. Drain the cherries, reserving the liquid, and combine them in a small bowl with the bananas. Sprinkle with 1 tablespoon of the lime juice, cover the bowl with plastic wrap, and set aside.

3 In a small saucepan, combine the reserved cherry liquid with the cornstarch and the remaining 1 tablespoon lime juice and heat until the cornstarch is dissolved and the mixture begins to thicken, about 1 minute.

4 Spoon the fruit mixture over the pineapple and top with the sauce.

THURSDAY

Soup Opera

1 1/2 pounds tomatoes
4 tablespoons fresh basil leaves (when chopped)
1 clove garlic
2 tablespoons olive oil
1 can (10 1/2 ounces) beef consommé
1/2 cup half-and-half
2 tablespoons dry sherry
Seasoning to taste

The Guiding Linguini

1 package (10 ounces) frozen cut green beans
3 scallions (green onions)
1 pound linguini
2 tablespoons butter
1/4 cup dry white wine
1 tablespoon saffron threads
1 can (10 1/2 ounces) chicken broth
Seasoning to taste

One Loaf to Live

2 tablespoons fresh parsley (when chopped)
2 tablespoons olive oil
1/8 teaspoon cayenne pepper
1 loaf Italian bread

Dates of Our Lives

2 large ripe pears
1 small lemon
1/2 cup chopped dates
3 tablespoons sour cream
2 tablespoons dark brown sugar

EQUIPMENT

Blender	Whisk
Stockpot	Citrus grater
Medium saucepan	Citrus juicer
Large skillet	Aluminum foil
8 x 8-inch glass baking dish	Kitchen knives
Colander	Measuring cups and spoons
3 small mixing bowls	Cooking utensils

COUNTDOWN

1. Assemble the ingredients and the equipment.
2. Do Step 1 of *The Guiding Linguini*.
3. Do Steps 1–2 of *Soup Opera*.
4. Do Steps 1–5 of *Dates of Our Lives*.
5. Do Steps 1–3 of *One Loaf to Live*.
6. Do Step 3 of *Soup Opera*.
7. Do Steps 2–4 of *The Guiding Linguini*.
8. Do Steps 4–5 of *Soup Opera*.
9. Do Step 4 of *One Loaf to Live*.
10. Do Steps 5–6 of *The Guiding Linguini*.
11. Do Step 6 of *Soup Opera*.

THURSDAY

Soup Opera

1 Rinse, stem, and quarter the tomatoes. Rinse, stem, and chop the basil. Peel and mince the garlic.

2 Heat the oil with the garlic in a medium saucepan. Add the tomatoes and 2 table-spoons of the basil and sauté until the tomatoes begin to soften, 10 to 12 minutes.

3 Remove the saucepan from the heat.

4 Place the tomato mixture in a blender, add the consommé, and puree until smooth.

5 Return the mixture to the saucepan. Blend in the half-and-half and the sherry and season to taste. Simmer until hot, but do not let boil, about 5 minutes.

6 Garnish with the remaining 2 tablespoons basil.

The Guiding Linguini

1 Set the green beans in a small bowl of warm water to thaw.

2 Bring water to a boil in a stockpot.

3 Rinse, trim, and chop the scallions.

4 Cook the linguini in the stockpot until it is almost tender, 2 to 3 minutes if you are using fresh pasta, 6 to 7 minutes if you are using dry pasta.

5 Melt the butter in a large skillet. Add the wine and the saffron, bring to a boil, and cook for 2 minutes. Add the broth, the beans, and the scallions, reduce the heat, and simmer for 1 minute.

6 Drain the pasta and return it to the stockpot. Add the green bean mixture and toss to combine. Season to taste.

One Loaf to Live

1 Rinse, stem, and chop the parsley.

2 In a small bowl, combine the oil, the cayenne pepper, and the parsley.

3 Cut the bread in half lengthwise. Spread the parsley mixture over the cut sides of the bread. Reassemble the loaf and wrap it in a sheet of aluminum foil.

4 Bake at 350°F until heated through, about 10 minutes.

Dates of Our Lives

1 Preheat the oven to 350°F.

2 Rinse, halve, and core the pears.

3 Grate 2 teaspoons of lemon peel and juice the lemon. Place the pears in an 8 x 8-inch baking dish. Fill the centers with the dates. Sprinkle with the lemon juice.

4 In a small bowl, combine the sour cream and the brown sugar. Spoon the mixture over the pears and sprinkle with the lemon peel.

5 Bake until the pears are hot and have begun to soften, 15 to 20 minutes.

FRIDAY

C'est la Gruyère

1 sheet frozen puff pastry
3 small sweet onions
1 package (10 ounces) fresh spinach
1 small head red cabbage
1/2 pound Gruyère cheese
4 eggs
1 tablespoon flour
1 tablespoon yellow cornmeal
1 teaspoon ground nutmeg
Seasoning to taste
4 tablespoons butter

Marquis de Salad

1 cup fresh cranberries
1/2 cup orange juice
1/2 cup granulated sugar
1 small head lettuce
2 small ripe pears
2 large oranges
1/4 pound seedless black grapes

Beaucoup Biscuits

2 cups flour
2 tablespoons granulated sugar
4 teaspoons baking powder
1/4 teaspoon salt
1/3 cup butter
3/4 cup milk

Eiffel Towers

2 Snickers candy bars (2.7 ounces each)
1 can (14 ounces) sweetened condensed milk
1 pint chocolate frozen yogurt
2 cups crushed ice
Whipped cream for garnish
Chocolate sprinkles for garnish

EQUIPMENT

Blender	Cheese grater
Small saucepan	Pastry blender
2-quart casserole	Biscuit cutter
Baking sheet	Kitchen knives
Breadboard	Measuring cups and
2 large mixing bowls	spoons
Medium mixing bowl	Cooking utensils

COUNTDOWN

1. Assemble the ingredients and the equipment.
2. Do Steps 1–4 of *Eiffel Towers.*
3. Do Steps 1–7 of *C'est la Gruyère.*
4. Do Steps 1–4 of *Beaucoup Biscuits.*
5. Do Steps 1–5 of *Marquis de Salad.*
6. Do Step 5 of *Eiffel Towers.*

FRIDAY

C'est la Gruyère

1 Preheat the oven to 375°F. Grease a 2-quart casserole.

2 Set the sheet of puff pastry out to thaw.

3 Peel and chop the onions. Rinse, pat dry, stem, and chop the spinach. Rinse, trim, quarter, and chop the cabbage. Combine the vegetables in a large bowl.

4 Grate the cheese.

5 Combine the eggs, the flour, the cornmeal, and the nutmeg in a medium bowl. Season to taste and blend well. Pour the mixture over the vegetables. Toss to combine. Fold in the grated cheese and place the mixture in the casserole. Dot with the butter.

6 Trim the pastry to fit loosely over the top of the casserole.

7 Bake until the pastry is golden and the vegetables are cooked through, about 30 minutes.

Marquis de Salad

1 Rinse the cranberries, discarding any that are soft or discolored, and place them in a small saucepan. Add the orange juice and the sugar, bring to a boil, and cook until the cranberries begin to pop, about 5 minutes.

2 Wash and dry the lettuce and distribute the leaves among individual salad plates.

3 Remove the cranberry mixture from the heat and set aside to cool.

4 Rinse, core, and slice the pears. Peel and slice the oranges and cut the slices in half. Rinse, stem, and halve the grapes. Arrange the fruit over the lettuce.

5 Top with the cranberry mixture.

Beaucoup Biscuits

1 Flour a breadboard. Grease a baking sheet.

2 In a large mixing bowl, combine the flour, the sugar, the baking powder, and the salt. Add the butter and blend with a pastry blender until the dough is crumbly and the size of coarse meal. Add the milk and mix with a fork to combine.

3 Turn the dough onto the breadboard and knead until smooth, 8 to 10 times. Pat to ½-inch thickness and cut the dough with a biscuit cutter or glass dipped in flour. Place the biscuits on the baking sheet.

4 Bake at 375°F until the biscuits are golden brown on top, about 15 minutes.

Eiffel Towers

1 Break the candy bars into small pieces.

2 Combine the candy bars, the condensed milk, and the frozen yogurt in a blender and process for 30 seconds.

3 Add half of the crushed ice and blend for 1 minute. Add the remaining ice and blend for 1 minute.

4 Pour the mixture into individual dessert glasses and refrigerate until you are ready to serve.

5 Garnish with dollops of whipped cream and top with the sprinkles.

WEEK FOUR

Monday

Finger Lake Fish
Syracusecous
Brooklyn Broccoli
The Bronx Bananas

Tuesday

Humpty Dumpty Omelet
Peter Rabbit Food
Little Miss Muffins
Simple Simon Pie

Wednesday

Fowl Weather Friend
Raindrop Rice
Boots 'n' Brussels
Slicker Sorbet

Thursday

Dog-Gone Good
Super Sauce
Better Bread
Yummy Yogurt

Friday

Spaghetti Already
Split-Second Salad
Nimble Nibbles
A Shot In the Dark

STAPLES

- ☐ Butter
- ☐ Flour
- ☐ Baking powder
- ☐ Baking soda
- ☐ Granulated sugar
- ☐ Dark brown sugar
- ☐ Corn syrup
- ☐ Chocolate syrup
- ☐ Silver shots
- ☐ Multicolored sprinkles
- ☐ Olive oil
- ☐ Vegetable oil
- ☐ Balsamic vinegar
- ☐ Red wine vinegar
- ☐ Tarragon vinegar
- ☐ White wine vinegar
- ☐ Lemon juice
- ☐ Mayonnaise
- ☐ Soy sauce
- ☐ Worcestershire sauce
- ☐ Grated Parmesan cheese
- ☐ Caraway seeds
- ☐ Poppy seeds
- ☐ Dried basil
- ☐ Dried dill
- ☐ Ground cinnamon
- ☐ Ground nutmeg
- ☐ Paprika
- ☐ Black pepper
- ☐ Red pepper flakes
- ☐ White pepper
- ☐ Salt
- ☐ Vanilla extract

MEAT & POULTRY

3 pounds chicken pieces (W)

FISH

4 white fish fillets (about 1 1/2 pounds) (M)

FRESH PRODUCE

VEGETABLES

1 pound baking potatoes (T)
1 medium bunch broccoli (M)
1 small head cauliflower (T)
1 pound Brussels sprouts (W)
2 Japanese eggplants (F)
4 medium carrots (T)
1 stalk celery (T)
2 stalks celery (F)
1 medium head lettuce (F)
4 medium tomatoes (F)
1 small cucumber (F)
1 small green bell pepper (T)
1 small orange bell pepper (M)
1 medium onion (T)
1 small onion (F)
1 small shallot (M)
2 scallions (green onions) (M)
1 clove garlic (M)
2 cloves garlic (T)
2 cloves garlic (W)
2 cloves garlic (F)

HERBS

1 tablespoon dill (when chopped) (Th)
2 tablespoons parsley (when chopped) (W)
3 tablespoons parsley (when chopped) (F)
1 tablespoon thyme (when chopped) (Th)

FRUIT

2 large oranges (M)
4 mandarin oranges (W)
1 small lemon (Th)
2 medium bananas (M)
4 large cooking apples (Th)

CANS, JARS & BOTTLES

SOUPS

1 can (14 ounces) vegetable broth (M)
1 can (14 ounces) chicken broth (W)

VEGETABLES

1 can (14 1/2 ounces) diced tomatoes (Th)
1 jar (22 ounces) sauerkraut (Th)
1 can (11 ounces) whole-kernel corn (Th)

FRUIT

1 can (15 ounces) apricot halves (T)
1 can (29 ounces) sliced peaches (W)

FISH

1 tin (2 ounces) anchovy fillets (F)

CONDIMENTS

1 jar (2 ounces) diced pimientos (F)

DESSERT & BAKING NEEDS

1/4 cup marshmallow crème for garnish (F)

PACKAGED GOODS

PASTA, RICE & GRAINS

1 pound spaghetti (F)
1 cup long-grain white rice (W)
1 cup couscous (M)
1 1/4 cups All-Bran cereal (T)

BAKED GOODS

1 loaf pumpernickel bread, unsliced (Th)
1 prepared shortbread pie shell (T)
1 package (9 ounces) sugar cookies (Th)
1 package (9 ounces) chocolate cookies (F)

DRIED FRUIT & NUTS

1/4 cup golden raisins (T)
1/4 cup pecan bits (M)
1/4 cup walnut bits (T)

DESSERT & BAKING NEEDS

1 package (3.4 ounces) instant chocolate pudding mix (F)
6 ounces white chocolate chips (W)
1 cup cinnamon chips (Th)
24 large marshmallows (T)

REFRIGERATED PRODUCTS

DAIRY

1/4 cup milk (M)
1 1/4 cups milk (F)
1 1/4 cups milk (T)
1 cup buttermilk (F)
3/4 cup sour cream (F)
2 containers (8 ounces each) coffee yogurt (Th)
1 cup whipped cream (T)
Whipped cream for garnish (M)
9 eggs (T)
1 egg (F)

CHEESE

2 cups shredded Colby/Monterey Jack cheese (T)

JUICES

3 tablespoons orange juice (W)
1/2 cup orange juice (T)

DELI

1 1/2 pounds all-beef frankfurters (Th)

FROZEN GOODS

BAKED GOODS

1 pound cake (M)

DESSERTS

1 pint raspberry sorbet (W)

MONDAY

Finger Lake Fish

2 large oranges
1 clove garlic
4 white fish fillets (about 1 1/2 pounds)
3 tablespoons butter
1/2 teaspoon dried basil
Seasoning to taste

Syracusecous

2 scallions (green onions)
2 tablespoons butter
1 cup couscous
1 can (14 ounces) vegetable broth
2 tablespoons balsamic vinegar
1 tablespoon dried dill
Seasoning to taste

Brooklyn Broccoli

1 medium bunch broccoli
1 small orange bell pepper
1 small shallot
2 tablespoons vegetable oil
Seasoning to taste

The Bronx Bananas

1 frozen pound cake
1/2 cup dark brown sugar
1 tablespoon corn syrup
1/4 cup milk
1/2 teaspoon vanilla extract
1/2 teaspoon ground nutmeg
2 medium bananas
1 tablespoon lemon juice
Whipped cream for garnish
1/4 cup pecan bits for garnish

EQUIPMENT

2 medium covered saucepans
Small saucepan
Large skillet
Medium skillet
Citrus grater

Citrus juicer
Kitchen knives
Measuring cups and spoons
Cooking utensils

COUNTDOWN

1. Assemble the ingredients and the equipment.
2. Do Steps 1–3 of *The Bronx Bananas*.
3. Do Step 1 of *Finger Lake Fish*.
4. Do Steps 1–2 of *Brooklyn Broccoli*.
5. Do Steps 1–2 of *Syracusecous*.
6. Do Steps 3–5 of *Brooklyn Broccoli*.
7. Do Step 2 of *Finger Lake Fish*.
8. Do Step 3 of *Syracusecous*.
9. Do Step 4 of *The Bronx Bananas*.

MONDAY

Finger Lake Fish

1 Grate 2 tablespoons of orange peel. Juice both oranges. Peel and mince the garlic. Rinse and pat dry the fish fillets.

2 Melt the butter in a large skillet and sauté the garlic for 1 minute. Add the fish and cook for 2 minutes on each side. Add the orange peel, the orange juice, and the basil and cook until the fish flakes easily with a fork, 3 to 4 minutes. Season to taste.

Syracusecous

1 Rinse, trim, and chop the scallions.

2 Melt the butter in a medium saucepan. Add the couscous and toss to coat. Add the broth and the vinegar and bring to a boil. Cover and remove from the heat. Let stand for about 10 minutes.

3 Add the dill and the scallions, season to taste, and fluff with a fork.

Brooklyn Broccoli

1 Bring water to a boil in a medium saucepan.

2 Rinse and trim the broccoli, discarding the tough ends, and cut into bite-sized florets. Rinse, trim, and seed the bell pepper and cut into thin strips. Peel and chop the shallot.

3 Cook the broccoli until it is crisp-tender, about 5 minutes.

4 Heat the oil in a medium skillet and sauté the shallot and the bell pepper until soft, about 4 minutes.

5 Drain the broccoli and return it to the saucepan. Add the bell pepper and the shallot, season to taste, and sauté until heated through, about 1 minute. Cover to keep warm.

The Bronx Bananas

1 Set the pound cake out to thaw.

2 In a small saucepan, combine the brown sugar, the corn syrup, the milk, the vanilla, and the nutmeg. Slowly bring the mixture to a boil. Remove from the heat and set aside.

3 Peel and slice the bananas and sprinkle with the lemon juice. Cover with plastic wrap and set aside.

4 Arrange the banana slices on the top of the cake and spoon the sauce over the bananas. Garnish with dollops of whipped cream and a sprinkle of pecans.

TUESDAY

Humpty Dumpty Omelet

2 cloves garlic
1 medium onion
1 pound baking potatoes
1 small green bell pepper
1 small head cauliflower
3 tablespoons olive oil
8 eggs
1/4 cup milk
1/2 cup grated Parmesan cheese
1 teaspoon dried basil
Seasoning to taste
2 cups shredded Colby/Monterey Jack cheese

Peter Rabbit Food

4 medium carrots
1 stalk celery
1 can (15 ounces) apricot halves
1/4 cup walnut bits
1/4 cup golden raisins
1/2 cup mayonnaise
1 teaspoon white wine vinegar
1/4 teaspoon ground cinnamon
Seasoning to taste

Little Miss Muffins

1 cup flour
1/4 cup dark brown sugar
1 tablespoon baking powder
1/2 teaspoon baking soda
1/4 teaspoon salt
1 1/4 cups All-Bran cereal
1 cup milk
1 egg
1/4 cup vegetable oil

Simple Simon Pie

24 large marshmallows
1/2 cup orange juice
1 cup whipped cream
1 prepared shortbread pie shell
Multicolored sprinkles for garnish

EQUIPMENT

Medium saucepan	Small mixing bowl
Large skillet	Whisk
9 x 13-inch glass baking dish	Vegetable peeler
Muffin tin	Vegetable grater
3 large mixing bowls	Kitchen knives
2 medium mixing bowls	Measuring cups and spoons
	Cooking utensils

COUNTDOWN

1. Assemble the ingredients and the equipment.
2. Do Steps 1–2 of *Simple Simon Pie*.
3. Do Steps 1–7 of *Humpty Dumpty Omelet*.
4. Do Steps 1–4 of *Little Miss Muffins*.
5. Do Step 3 of *Simple Simon Pie*.
6. Do Steps 1–3 of *Peter Rabbit Food*.
7. Do Step 4 of *Simple Simon Pie*.

TUESDAY

Humpty Dumpty Omelet

1 Peel and mince the garlic. Peel and chop the onion. Peel and slice the potatoes. Rinse, trim, seed, and chop the bell pepper. Rinse and trim the cauliflower and cut into bite-sized florets.

2 Heat the oil in a large skillet. Sauté the potatoes until they are golden, 8 to 10 minutes.

3 Preheat the oven to 350°F. Grease a 9 x 13-inch baking dish.

4 Whip the eggs in a large bowl with the milk and the Parmesan cheese. Add the basil and season to taste.

5 Add the garlic, the onion, the bell pepper, and the cauliflower to the potatoes. Cover and cook for 3 minutes, tossing to blend.

6 Place the potato mixture in the baking dish. Pour the egg mixture over the potatoes and sprinkle with the Colby/Monterey Jack cheese.

7 Bake until the eggs are set, 25 to 30 minutes.

Peter Rabbit Food

1 Peel, trim, and grate the carrots. Rinse, trim, and chop the celery. Drain and chop the apricots. Combine the ingredients in a medium bowl. Mix in the nuts and the raisins.

2 In a small bowl, whisk together the mayonnaise, the vinegar, and the cinnamon. Season to taste.

3 Toss the salad with the dressing.

Little Miss Muffins

1 Grease a muffin tin.

2 In a large bowl, combine the flour, the brown sugar, the baking powder, the baking soda, the salt, and the bran cereal.

3 In a medium bowl, combine the milk, the egg, and the oil. Mix well and pour into the dry ingredients. Spoon the batter into the muffin cups.

4 Bake at 350°F until the muffins are golden, 15 to 20 minutes.

Simple Simon Pie

1 Combine the marshmallows and the orange juice in a medium saucepan and simmer until the marshmallows are melted, about 5 minutes.

2 Scrape the mixture into a large bowl and refrigerate for 10 minutes.

3 Fold the whipped cream into the marshmallow mixture and spoon it evenly into the pie shell. Place in the freezer until you are ready to serve.

4 Garnish with the sprinkles.

WEDNESDAY

Fowl Weather Friend

3 pounds chicken pieces
2 cloves garlic
1 can (29 ounces) sliced peaches
2 tablespoons soy sauce
1/2 teaspoon ground cinnamon
Seasoning to taste

Raindrop Rice

2 tablespoons fresh parsley (when
  chopped)
1 cup long-grain white rice
1 can (14 ounces) chicken broth
1/4 cup water
1/8 teaspoon paprika
1/4 teaspoon white pepper

Boots 'n' Brussels

1 pound Brussels sprouts
2 tablespoons butter
2 tablespoons lemon juice
Seasoning to taste

Slicker Sorbet

4 fresh mandarin oranges
6 ounces white chocolate chips
3 tablespoons orange juice
1 pint raspberry sorbet

EQUIPMENT

Double boiler	Ice cream scoop
Large saucepan	Kitchen knives
Small saucepan	Measuring cups and
9 x 13-inch glass	spoons
baking dish	Cooking utensils
Small mixing bowl	

COUNTDOWN

1. Assemble the ingredients and the
   equipment.
2. Do Steps 1–3 of *Raindrop Rice.*
3. Do Steps 1–4 of *Fowl Weather Friend.*
4. Do Steps 1–2 of *Slicker Sorbet.*
5. Do Steps 1–4 of *Boots 'n' Brussels.*
6. Do Step 4 of *Raindrop Rice.*
7. Do Step 3 of *Slicker Sorbet.*

WEDNESDAY

Fowl Weather Friend

1 Preheat the oven to 375°F. Butter a 9 x 13-inch baking dish.

2 Rinse and pat dry the chicken pieces and arrange them in a single layer in the baking dish. Peel and mince the garlic.

3 Drain the liquid from the peaches into a small bowl. Add the garlic, the soy sauce, and the cinnamon. Pour the mixture over the chicken and bake until lightly browned, about 15 minutes.

4 Turn and baste the chicken. Reduce the oven temperature to 350°F. Add the peach slices, season to taste, and continue cooking until the chicken is tender, about 25 minutes.

Raindrop Rice

1 Bring water to a boil in the bottom of a double boiler.

2 Rinse, stem, and chop the parsley.

3 Combine the rice, the broth, the ¼ cup water, the paprika, and the white pepper in the top of the double boiler. Cover, reduce the heat, and simmer until all the liquid is absorbed and the rice is tender, 30 to 40 minutes.

4 Fold in the parsley and fluff with a fork.

Boots 'n' Brussels

1 Bring water to a boil in a large saucepan.

2 Rinse and trim the Brussels sprouts. If they are large, cut them in half.

3 Cook the sprouts until they are crisp-tender, 8 to 10 minutes.

4 Drain the sprouts. Add the butter and the lemon juice, season to taste, and toss to combine.

Slicker Sorbet

1 Peel and section the oranges and set them aside.

2 In a small saucepan, combine the chocolate chips and the orange juice and simmer until melted and smooth, about 3 minutes. Remove from the heat and cover to keep warm.

3 Place scoops of sorbet in individual dessert bowls, arrange the orange sections around the sorbet, and drizzle with the sauce.

THURSDAY

Dog-Gone Good

1½ pounds all-beef frankfurters
1 jar (22 ounces) sauerkraut
1 can (11 ounces) whole-kernel corn
1 can (14½ ounces) diced tomatoes
½ cup dark brown sugar

Super Sauce

4 large cooking apples
1 small lemon
1 cup water
2 tablespoons granulated sugar
½ teaspoon ground nutmeg

Better Bread

1 tablespoon fresh dill (when chopped)
1 tablespoon fresh thyme (when chopped)
1 loaf pumpernickel bread, unsliced
¼ cup olive oil
1 teaspoon caraway seeds

Yummy Yogurt

1 package (9 ounces) sugar cookies
2 containers (8 ounces each) coffee yogurt
1 cup cinnamon chips

EQUIPMENT

Medium saucepan
2-quart casserole
Citrus grater
Citrus juicer
Pastry brush
Aluminum foil

Plastic bag
Kitchen knives
Measuring cups and spoons
Cooking utensils

COUNTDOWN

1. Assemble the ingredients and the equipment.
2. Do Step 1 of *Yummy Yogurt*.
3. Do Steps 1–2 of *Super Sauce*.
4. Do Steps 1–4 of *Dog-Gone Good*.
5. Do Steps 1–3 of *Better Bread*.
6. Do Step 3 of *Super Sauce*.
7. Do Step 2 of *Yummy Yogurt*.

THURSDAY

Dog-Gone Good

1 Preheat the oven to 350°F.

2 Rinse and pat dry the frankfurters and cut them into ¼-inch-thick slices. Drain the sauerkraut. Drain the corn.

3 Arrange the frankfurters in the bottom of a 2-quart casserole. Top with the sauerkraut. Layer the corn over the sauerkraut. Spoon the tomatoes over the corn. Sprinkle with the brown sugar.

4 Bake until hot and bubbly, about 25 minutes.

Super Sauce

1 Peel, core, and chop the apples. Grate 1 teaspoon of lemon peel and juice the lemon.

2 In a medium saucepan, combine the apples with the water. Bring to a boil, reduce the heat, and simmer, stirring occasionally, until the apples are tender, about 20 minutes.

3 Remove the saucepan from the heat. Blend in the sugar, the lemon juice, and the nutmeg. Sprinkle with the lemon peel.

Better Bread

1 Rinse, stem, and chop the dill. Rinse, stem, and chop the thyme.

2 Split the pumpernickel loaf in half lengthwise. Brush the cut sides with the oil. Sprinkle with the thyme and the dill. Top with the caraway seeds. Reassemble the loaf and wrap it in aluminum foil.

3 Bake at 350°F until heated through, about 15 minutes.

Yummy Yogurt

1 Place the cookies in a plastic bag and crumble them.

2 Place half the cookie crumbs in the bottom of individual dessert glasses. Add a layer of yogurt. Sprinkle with half of the cinnamon chips. Repeat.

FRIDAY

Spaghetti Already

1 small onion
2 cloves garlic
3 tablespoons fresh parsley (when chopped)
4 medium tomatoes
2 Japanese eggplants
1 tin (2 ounces) anchovy fillets
2 tablespoons olive oil
1 tablespoon red wine vinegar
1 teaspoon granulated sugar
1/8 teaspoon red pepper flakes
Seasoning to taste
1 pound spaghetti

Split-Second Salad

1 medium head lettuce
2 stalks celery
1 small cucumber
1 jar (2 ounces) diced pimientos
3 tablespoons olive oil
2 tablespoons tarragon vinegar
1/2 teaspoon granulated sugar
1/2 teaspoon Worcestershire sauce
Seasoning to taste

Nimble Nibbles

4 tablespoons butter
1 3/4 cups flour
1 tablespoon granulated sugar
1 tablespoon baking powder
1/2 teaspoon baking soda
1/2 teaspoon salt
1 cup buttermilk
1 egg
2 tablespoons warm water
2 tablespoons poppy seeds

A Shot In the Dark

1 package (9 ounces) chocolate cookies
2 tablespoons butter
1 package (3.4 ounces) chocolate instant pudding mix
1 1/4 cups milk
3/4 cup sour cream
1/4 cup marshmallow crème
Silver shots for garnish
2 tablespoons chocolate syrup

EQUIPMENT

Electric mixer	Small mixing bowl
Stockpot	Whisk
Small saucepan	Vegetable peeler
Large covered skillet	Plastic bag
Muffin tin	Kitchen knives
Colander	Measuring cups and spoons
2 large mixing bowls	Cooking utensils
2 medium mixing bowls	

COUNTDOWN

1. Assemble the ingredients and the equipment.
2. Do Steps 1–3 of *A Shot In the Dark*.
3. Do Steps 1–2 of *Split-Second Salad*.
4. Do Steps 1–7 of *Nimble Nibbles*.
5. Do Steps 1–5 of *Spaghetti Already*.
6. Do Step 3 of *Split-Second Salad*.
7. Do Step 4 of *A Shot In the Dark*.

FRIDAY

Spaghetti Already

1 Bring water to a boil in a stockpot.

2 Peel and chop the onion. Peel and mince the garlic. Rinse, stem, and chop the parsley. Rinse, stem, and dice the tomatoes. Rinse, trim, and slice the eggplants. Drain, blot, and chop the anchovies.

3 Heat the oil in a large skillet and sauté the onion for 1 minute. Add the garlic, the tomatoes, and the eggplants and sauté until the eggplants and tomatoes begin to soften, about 5 minutes. Stir in the vinegar, the anchovies, the sugar, and the red pepper flakes. Season to taste, cover, reduce the heat, and simmer for 3 minutes longer.

4 Cook the spaghetti in the boiling water until it is almost tender, 6 to 7 minutes.

5 Drain the pasta and return it to the stockpot. Toss with the tomato mixture and sprinkle with the parsley.

Split-Second Salad

1 Wash and dry the lettuce and tear it into bite-sized pieces. Rinse, trim, and chop the celery. Peel, trim, and chop the cucumber. Drain the pimientos. Combine the ingredients in a large bowl.

2 In a small bowl, combine the oil, the vinegar, the sugar, and the Worcestershire sauce. Season to taste.

3 Toss the salad with the desssing.

Nimble Nibbles

1 Preheat the oven to 400°F. Grease a muffin tin.

2 Melt the butter.

3 In a large bowl, combine the flour, the sugar, the baking powder, the baking soda, and the salt.

4 In a medium bowl, combine the buttermilk, the egg, the water, and the melted butter. Blend well.

5 Stir the egg mixture into the flour mixture until just combined.

6 Spoon the batter into the muffin cups. Sprinkle with the poppy seeds.

7 Bake until a wooden toothpick inserted in the center of a muffin comes out clean, about 20 minutes.

A Shot In the Dark

1 Place the cookies in a plastic bag and crush them.

2 Melt the butter in a small saucepan. Add the cookie crumbs and mix well. Distribute the crumbs among individual dessert bowls, pressing them into the bottoms and up the sides.

3 In a medium bowl, beat the pudding mix, the milk, and the sour cream until well blended. Spoon the mixture into the dessert bowls and refrigerate until you are ready to serve.

4 Top each pudding with a dollop of marshmallow crème and a drizzle of chocolate syrup.

WEEK FIVE

WEEK AT A GLANCE

Monday
Cheese Whiz
Gadzucchs
Fiddle-Faddle Fruit

Tuesday
Engagin' Cajun
Calamity Corn
Gullible Grapes
Cherry Flip

Wednesday
Pennsylvania Avenue Pasta
House Salad
Capitol Muffins
The Supreme Torte

Thursday
Bewitchin' Chicken
Appealing Potatoes
Peach Sorcery

Friday
Tuna In Tomorrow
Same Time, Same Salad
Commercial Crumble

STAPLES

- ❑ Butter
- ❑ Flour
- ❑ Baking powder
- ❑ Granulated sugar
- ❑ Dark brown sugar
- ❑ Powdered sugar
- ❑ Chocolate syrup
- ❑ Olive oil
- ❑ Vegetable oil
- ❑ Red wine vinegar
- ❑ White wine vinegar
- ❑ Lemon juice
- ❑ Dijon mustard
- ❑ White Worcestershire sauce
- ❑ Grated Parmesan cheese
- ❑ Chicken bouillon cube
- ❑ Caraway seeds
- ❑ Celery seeds
- ❑ Dried dill
- ❑ Dried oregano
- ❑ Dried thyme
- ❑ Ground allspice
- ❑ Cayenne pepper
- ❑ Chili powder
- ❑ Ground cinnamon
- ❑ Ground nutmeg
- ❑ Paprika
- ❑ Black pepper
- ❑ Red pepper flakes
- ❑ White pepper
- ❑ Salt
- ❑ Rum extract
- ❑ Vanilla extract

MEAT & POULTRY

3 pounds chicken pieces (Th)

FISH

4 red snapper fillets (about 1 1/2 pounds) (T)

FRESH PRODUCE

VEGETABLES

12 small new red potatoes (Th)
1 medium head cauliflower (T)
1 medium spaghetti squash (W)
3 medium zucchini (M)
1/4 pound mushrooms (W)
1 package (10 ounces) spinach (F)
1 medium head lettuce (W)
3 medium tomatoes (F)
1 small ripe avocado (W)
1 medium cucumber (W)
1 large green bell pepper (F)
1 small red bell pepper (W)
1 medium onion (M)
1 large red onion (W)
4 scallions (green onions) (F)
1 clove garlic (T)
2 cloves garlic (W)
1 clove garlic (F)

HERBS

3 tablespoons basil leaves (when chopped) (W)
1/4 cup chives (when chopped) (T)
2 tablespoons parsley (when chopped) (M)
2 tablespoons parsley (when chopped) (T)
2 tablespoons parsley (when chopped) (Th)

FRUIT

1 large orange (M)
4 medium oranges (W)
1 large lime (Th, F)
1 small lime (T)
2 medium tart apples (F)

1/4 pound seedless green grapes (T)

CANS, JARS & BOTTLES

VEGETABLES

1 jar (4 ounces) sun-dried tomatoes in oil (W)

FRUIT

1 can (15 ounces) apricot halves (M)
1 can (15 ounces) purple plums (M)
1 can (16 ounces) pitted dark cherries (T)
1 can (15 ounces) peach halves (Th)
1 can (8 ounces) crushed pineapple (F)
1 can (15 ounces) whole cranberry sauce (F)
1 maraschino cherry (Th)

FISH

2 cans (6 ounces each) solid white tuna (F)
1 tin (2 ounces) anchovy fillets (F)

SPREADS

1/2 cup raspberry jam (W)
1/2 cup apricot preserves (W)

CONDIMENTS

1 jar (4 ounces) pimiento-stuffed green olives (F)

PACKAGED GOODS

PASTA, RICE & GRAINS

1 pound linguini (W)
1 cup rolled oats (F)

BAKED GOODS

4 small Boboli pizza crusts (F)
12 salted crackers (Th)
2 cups seasoned croutons (F)

DRIED FRUIT & NUTS

8 currants (Th)

DESSERT & BAKING NEEDS

1 package (3 ounces) cherry gelatin (T)

1 cup mini-marshmallows (M)
2 squares (1 ounce each) unsweetened chocolate (W)

WINE & SPIRITS

1/4 cup dry white wine (W)
2 tablespoons Grand Marnier (M)

REFRIGERATED PRODUCTS

DAIRY

1 cup milk (W)
1 cup milk (Th)
1 cup half-and-half (M)
1/2 cup buttermilk (Th)
Whipped cream for garnish (F)
4 eggs (M)
2 eggs (W)
1 egg (F)

CHEESE

8 ounces Swiss cheese (M)
1 package (3 ounces) cream cheese (Th)
1 1/2 cups shredded mozzarella cheese (F)

JUICES

1/2 cup orange juice (M)

DELI

6 ounces Canadian bacon, sliced (M)

FROZEN GOODS

VEGETABLES

1 package (10 ounces) whole-kernel corn (T)
1 package (10 ounces) green peas (Th)

BAKED GOODS

1 pound cake (W)

PASTRY

1 unbaked pie shell (M)

DESSERTS

1 container (8 ounces) whipped topping (T)

MONDAY

MENU

Cheese Whiz

1 frozen unbaked pie shell
1 medium onion
2 tablespoons fresh parsley (when
   chopped)
8 ounces Swiss cheese
6 ounces Canadian bacon, sliced
4 eggs
1 cup half-and-half
1/2 teaspoon ground nutmeg
Seasoning to taste

Gadzucchs

3 medium zucchini
2 tablespoons butter
1 teaspoon granulated sugar
2 teaspoons dried dill
Seasoning to taste

Fiddle-Faddle Fruit

1 large orange
1 can (15 ounces) apricot halves
1 can (15 ounces) purple plums
1/2 cup orange juice
1/4 cup dark brown sugar
2 tablespoons Grand Marnier
1 teaspoon ground allspice
1 cup mini-marshmallows

EQUIPMENT

Medium covered   Vegetable brush
   skillet   Cheese grater
Medium skillet   Citrus grater
Glass pie plate   Kitchen knives
Medium mixing bowl   Measuring cups and
Small mixing bowl   spoons
Whisk   Cooking utensils

COUNTDOWN

1. Assemble the ingredients and the
   equipment.
2. Do Steps 1–3 of Cheese Whiz.
3. Do Steps 1–4 of Fiddle-Faddle Fruit.
4. Do Steps 4–7 of Cheese Whiz.
5. Do Steps 1–2 of Gadzucchs.
6. Do Step 8 of Cheese Whiz.

MONDAY

Cheese Whiz

1 Set the pie shell out to thaw.

2 Prick the bottom with a fork.

3 Peel and mince the onion. Rinse, stem, and chop the parsley. Grate the cheese. Cut the bacon slices into quarters.

4 Cook the bacon in a medium skillet until lightly browned, about 5 minutes. Remove the bacon, drain on paper towels, and lay in the bottom of the pie shell.

5 Sauté the onion in the bacon drippings until lightly browned, about 5 minutes. Drain well and place on top of the bacon.

6 Reduce the oven temperature to 375°F.

7 In a medium bowl, beat the eggs lightly with the half-and-half. Add the cheese and the nutmeg, and season to taste. Pour evenly over the onion-bacon mixture and bake until a knife inserted in the center comes out clean, about 25 minutes.

8 Garnish with the parsley.

Gadzucchs

1 Scrub, trim, and chop the zucchini.

2 Melt the butter in a medium skillet. Add the zucchini, the sugar, and the dill. Cover, reduce the heat, and simmer for 2 minutes. Season to taste. Remove from the heat and keep warm.

Fiddle-Faddle Fruit

1 Preheat the oven to 400°F.

2 Grate 1 tablespoon of orange peel. Peel and slice the orange and place the slices in the bottom of a pie plate.

3 Drain the apricots and the plums and add them to the orange slices.

4 In a small bowl, combine the orange juice, the brown sugar, and the Grand Marnier. Stir in the allspice. Pour the mixture over the fruit. Sprinkle with the marshmallows and bake until the fruit is hot and the marshmallows are lightly browned, about 10 minutes.

TUESDAY

Engagin' Cajun

4 red snapper fillets (about 1 1/2 pounds)
2 tablespoons fresh parsley (when chopped)
3 tablespoons vegetable oil
1 tablespoon paprika
2 teaspoons dried thyme
1/4 teaspoon cayenne pepper
1 teaspoon chili powder
1/4 teaspoon red pepper flakes
Seasoning to taste

Calamity Corn

1 package (10 ounces) frozen whole-kernel corn
1/4 cup fresh chives (when chopped)
1 clove garlic
1 tablespoon butter
1 tablespoon granulated sugar
1/4 teaspoon celery seeds
3 tablespoons white wine vinegar
1/2 teaspoon white Worcestershire sauce
Seasoning to taste

Gullible Grapes

1 medium head cauliflower
1/4 pound seedless green grapes
1 small lime
2 tablespoons butter
Seasoning to taste

Cherry Flip

1 3/4 cups water
1 package (3 ounces) cherry gelatin
1 container (8 ounces) frozen whipped topping
1 can (16 ounces) pitted dark cherries
1/4 cup chocolate syrup for garnish

EQUIPMENT

Medium covered saucepan	Whisk
Small saucepan	Citrus grater
Large covered skillet	Citrus juicer
Medium covered skillet	Pastry brush
	Kitchen knives
Steamer insert	Measuring cups and spoons
2 small mixing bowls	Cooking utensils

COUNTDOWN

1. Assemble the ingredients and the equipment.
2. Do Step 1 of *Calamity Corn*.
3. Do Steps 1–2 of *Cherry Flip*.
4. Do Step 1 of *Gullible Grapes*.
5. Do Step 2 of *Calamity Corn*.
6. Do Step 3 of *Cherry Flip*.
7. Do Step 1 of *Engagin' Cajun*.
8. Do Step 2 of *Gullible Grapes*.
9. Do Steps 3–4 of *Calamity Corn*.
10. Do Step 3 of *Gullible Grapes*.
11. Do Steps 2–6 of *Engagin' Cajun*.
12. Do Step 4 of *Cherry Flip*.

TUESDAY

Engagin' Cajun

1 Rinse and pat dry the fish fillets. Rinse, stem, and chop the parsley.

2 Brush the fish on both sides with half of the oil. Place the remaining oil in a large skillet.

3 In a small bowl, combine the paprika, the thyme, the cayenne pepper, the chili powder, and the red pepper flakes and season to taste.

4 Coat the fish on both sides with the mixture.

5 Heat the oil and cook the fish until it flakes easily with a fork, 3 to 4 minutes per side.

6 Garnish with the parsley.

Calamity Corn

1 Set the corn in a small bowl of warm water to thaw.

2 Rinse, trim, and chop the chives. Peel and mince the garlic.

3 Melt the butter in a medium skillet and sauté the garlic for 1 minute. Add the corn, the sugar, and the celery seeds and simmer for 5 minutes.

4 Stir in the vinegar and the Worcestershire sauce and season to taste. Simmer until heated through, about 3 minutes more.

5 Stir in the chives and cover to keep warm.

Gullible Grapes

1 Rinse and trim the cauliflower and cut it into bite-sized florets. Rinse and stem the grapes. Grate 1 tablespoon of lime peel and juice the lime.

2 Bring water to a boil in a medium saucepan. Arrange the cauliflower in a steamer insert, place the insert in the saucepan, cover, and steam until the florets are crisp-tender, 4 to 5 minutes.

3 Drain the cauliflower. Melt the butter with the lime juice in the saucepan. Add the grapes and toss to coat. Return the cauliflower, season to taste, and toss to combine. Sprinkle with the lime peel and cover to keep warm.

Cherry Flip

1 Bring 1 cup of the water to a boil in a small saucepan.

2 Dissolve the gelatin in the boiling water. Add the remaining ¾ cup water and set the saucepan in the freezer until the gelatin has thickened, about 10 minutes.

3 Place half of the whipped topping in the bottom of individual dessert glasses. Add half of the thickened gelatin. Add the cherries. Top with the remaining gelatin and chill until you are ready to serve.

4 Top each serving with the remaining whipped topping and drizzle the chocolate syrup over the top.

WEDNESDAY

Pennsylvania Avenue Pasta

1 medium spaghetti squash
1 large red onion
2 cloves garlic
1/4 pound fresh mushrooms
1 small red bell pepper
3 tablespoons fresh basil leaves (when chopped)
1 jar (4 ounces) sun-dried tomatoes in oil
1/4 cup dry white wine
1 chicken bouillon cube
1/2 cup water
1 pound linguini
1/2 cup grated Parmesan cheese
Seasoning to taste

House Salad

1 medium head lettuce
4 medium oranges
1 small ripe avocado
1 medium cucumber
3 tablespoons vegetable oil
2 tablespoons white wine vinegar
1 teaspoon granulated sugar
1/4 teaspoon ground cinnamon
Seasoning to taste

Capitol Muffins

1 1/2 cups flour
1 tablespoon baking powder
2 teaspoons caraway seeds
1 teaspoon salt
1/4 cup dark brown sugar
1 cup milk
1/3 cup vegetable oil
2 eggs

The Supreme Torte

1 frozen pound cake
1 cup dark brown sugar
2 squares (1 ounce each) unsweetened chocolate
3 tablespoons butter
1/2 cup water
4 tablespoons powdered sugar
1 teaspoon rum extract
1/2 cup raspberry jam
1/2 cup apricot preserves

EQUIPMENT

Stockpot	Whisk
Small saucepan	Vegetable brush
Large skillet	Vegetable peeler
Muffin tin	Kitchen knives
Colander	Measuring cups and spoons
Large mixing bowl	Cooking utensils
2 small mixing bowls	

COUNTDOWN

1. Assemble the ingredients and the equipment.
2. Do Steps 1–4 of *The Supreme Torte*.
3. Do Steps 1–3 of *House Salad*.
4. Do Step 1 of *Pennsylvania Avenue Pasta*.
5. Do Steps 5–6 of *The Supreme Torte*.
6. Do Steps 1–4 of *Capitol Muffins*.
7. Do Steps 2–9 of *Pennsylvania Avenue Pasta*.
8. Do Step 4 of *House Salad*.

WEDNESDAY

Pennsylvania Avenue Pasta

1 Bring water to a boil in a stockpot.
2 Scrub, quarter, and seed the squash. Cook in the boiling water until almost tender, about 5 minutes.
3 Peel and chop the onion. Peel and mince the garlic. Rinse, pat dry, trim, and slice the mushrooms. Rinse, trim, seed, and chop the bell pepper. Rinse, stem, and chop the basil. Drain and chop the tomatoes, reserving 2 tablespoons of the oil.
4 Remove the squash from the stockpot and scrape the flesh and fibers out with a fork.
5 Bring additional water to a boil in the stockpot.
6 Heat the reserved oil in a large skillet and sauté the onion and the garlic for 4 minutes. Add the mushrooms and the bell pepper and sauté for 5 minutes. Add the tomatoes and sauté for 2 minutes. Add the wine, the bouillon cube, the water, and the squash and toss to combine and heat through.
7 Cook the linguini in the stockpot until almost tender, 2 to 3 minutes if you are using fresh pasta, 6 to 7 minutes if you are using dry pasta.
8 Drain the pasta and return it to the stockpot.
9 Add the basil to the skillet. Fold in the cheese and season to taste. Simmer until the cheese is melted, about 2 minutes. Toss the pasta with the squash mixture.

House Salad

1 Wash and dry the lettuce and distribute the leaves among individual salad plates. Peel and thinly slice the oranges. Halve, pit, peel, and slice the avocado. Peel, trim, and slice the cucumber.
2 Arrange the orange slices over the lettuce. Add the avocado and the cucumber.
3 In a small bowl, combine the oil, the vinegar, the sugar, and the cinnamon. Season to taste.
4 Drizzle the dressing over the salad.

Capitol Muffins

1 Preheat the oven to 375°F. Grease a muffin tin.
2 Combine the flour, the baking powder, the caraway seeds, and the salt in a large bowl.
3 In a small bowl, combine the brown sugar, the milk, and the oil. Add the eggs and beat to blend. Fold the milk mixture into the flour mixture. Spoon the batter evenly into the muffin cups.
4 Bake until the muffins are golden and firm to the touch, 15 to 20 minutes.

The Supreme Torte

1 Set the pound cake out to thaw.
2 Slice the cake lengthwise into 3 layers.
3 Combine the brown sugar, the chocolate, the butter, and the water in a small saucepan. Heat until the chocolate has melted, about 3 minutes.
4 Remove from the heat and let cool.
5 Add the powdered sugar, a tablespoon at a time, to thicken, beating well after each addition. Fold in the rum extract.
6 Spread the raspberry jam over the bottom layer of the cake. Spread the apricot preserves over the middle layer. Assemble the cake and spread the top and sides of the cake with the chocolate frosting.

THURSDAY

Bewitchin' Chicken

12 salted crackers
2 tablespoon fresh parsley (when chopped)
1/4 cup grated Parmesan cheese
1/2 teaspoon dried oregano
1/2 teaspoon dried thyme
3 pounds chicken pieces
1/2 cup buttermilk
2 tablespoons butter
1 tablespoon vegetable oil
Seasoning to taste

Appealing Potatoes

12 small new red potatoes
1 package (10 ounces) frozen green peas
1 teaspoon granulated sugar
2 tablespoons butter
1 1/2 tablespoons flour
1 cup milk
1/4 teaspoon white pepper
1/4 teaspoon ground nutmeg
Seasoning to taste

Peach Sorcery

1 large lime
1 can (15 ounces) peach halves
1 maraschino cherry
1 package (3 ounces) cream cheese
8 currants

EQUIPMENT

Large covered saucepan
Medium saucepan
9 x 13-inch baking pan
Large shallow bowl
Medium mixing bowl
Small mixing bowl
Vegetable brush
Citrus grater
Citrus juicer
Plastic bag
Kitchen knives
Measuring cups and spoons
Cooking utensils

COUNTDOWN

1. Assemble the ingredients and the equipment.
2. Do Steps 1–7 of *Bewitchin' Chicken*.
3. Do Steps 1–5 of *Peach Sorcery*.
4. Do Step 8 of *Bewitchin' Chicken*.
5. Do Steps 1–8 of *Appealing Potatoes*.

THURSDAY

Bewitchin' Chicken

1 Preheat the oven to 375°F.

2 Place the crackers in a plastic bag and crush them. Rinse, stem, and chop the parsley.

3 In a medium bowl, combine the crackers, the parsley, the Parmesan cheese, the oregano, and the thyme and blend well.

4 Rinse and pat dry the chicken pieces.

5 Place the buttermilk in a large shallow bowl. Dip the chicken pieces in the buttermilk and then in the cracker mixture.

6 Melt the butter with the oil in a 9 x 13-inch baking pan. Add the chicken pieces, turning to coat. Season to taste.

7 Bake the chicken for 15 minutes.

8 Turn the chicken and continue to bake until the pieces are browned and the juices run clear when pierced with a fork, about 25 minutes.

Appealing Potatoes

1 Bring water to a boil in a large saucepan.

2 Scrub the potatoes and peel a thin strip around the middle of each one.

3 Cook the potatoes until they are firm but tender, 8 to 10 minutes.

4 Place the peas in a medium saucepan. Sprinkle with the sugar. Add water just to cover and cook until the peas are thawed and heated through, about 3 minutes.

5 Drain the peas well.

6 Drain the potatoes, return them to the saucepan, add the peas, and cover to keep warm.

7 Melt the butter in the medium saucepan. Add the flour and blend well. Slowly add the milk, stirring constantly to keep the mixture smooth. Add the white pepper and the nutmeg and season to taste.

8 When the mixture is hot and bubbling, pour it over the peas and potatoes and toss well to coat.

Peach Sorcery

1 Grate 3 tablespoons of lime peel. Juice 2 tablespoons of lime juice and reserve it for use on Friday.

2 Drain the peaches, reserving 2 tablespoons of the liquid. Cut the maraschino cherry into quarters.

3 Place the cream cheese in a small bowl. Add the reserved liquid and blend well.

4 Place the peach halves, hollow side up, on individual dessert dishes. Spoon a tablespoon of the cream cheese mixture into each hollow and smooth to form a half round for a face. Add the lime peel to form hair around each face. Add the currants for eyes and a small bit of the maraschino cherry for a mouth.

5 Refrigerate until you are ready to serve.

FRIDAY

Tuna In Tomorrow

1 large green bell pepper
4 scallions (green onions)
3 medium tomatoes
1 jar (4 ounces) pimiento-stuffed
   green olives
2 cans (6 ounces each) solid white tuna
1 tin (2 ounces) anchovy fillets
4 small Boboli pizza crusts
¼ cup olive oil
3 tablespoons white wine vinegar
1½ teaspoons Dijon mustard
½ teaspoon dried oregano
Seasoning to taste
1½ cups shredded mozzarella cheese

Same Time, Same Salad

1 package (10 ounces) fresh spinach
1 clove garlic
1 egg
¼ cup vegetable oil
2 tablespoons lime juice (reserved from
   Thursday)
1 tablespoon red wine vinegar
Seasoning to taste
2 cups seasoned croutons

Commercial Crumble

2 medium tart apples
1 tablespoon lemon juice
1 cup rolled oats
½ cup dark brown sugar
½ cup flour
½ teaspoon ground cinnamon
⅓ cup butter
1 teaspoon vanilla extract
1 can (8 ounces) crushed pineapple
1 can (15 ounces) whole cranberry sauce
Whipped cream for garnish

E Q U I P M E N T

Small saucepan
9 x 9-inch glass
   baking dish
Baking sheet
Large mixing bowl
Medium mixing bowl
2 small mixing bowls

Whisk
Pastry blender
Kitchen knives
Measuring cups and
   spoons
Cooking utensils

C O U N T D O W N

1. Assemble the ingredients and the
   equipment.
2. Do Steps 1–5 of *Commercial Crumble.*
3. Do Steps 1–3 of *Same Time, Same
   Salad.*
4. Do Steps 1–5 of *Tuna In Tomorrow.*
5. Do Step 4 of *Same Time, Same Salad.*
6. Do Step 6 of *Commercial Crumble.*

FRIDAY

Tuna In Tomorrow

1 Increase the oven temperature to 450°F.

2 Rinse, trim, seed, and thinly slice the bell pepper. Rinse, trim, and chop the scallions. Rinse, stem, and chop the tomatoes. Drain and slice the olives. Drain and flake the tuna. Drain and chop the anchovies.

3 Set the Boboli pizza crusts on a baking sheet and cover them with the tuna and the anchovies. Add the bell pepper, the scallions, the tomatoes, and the olives.

4 In a small bowl, combine the oil, the vinegar, the mustard, and the oregano. Season to taste, spoon the dressing over the Boboli, and sprinkle with the cheese.

5 Bake until the cheese has melted and the pizzas are heated through, 10 to 12 minutes.

Same Time, Same Salad

1 Rinse, pat dry, and stem the spinach and place it in a large bowl. Peel and mince the garlic.

2 Bring water to a boil in a small saucepan. Add the egg and cook for 1 minute. Remove the egg, rinse in cold water, and set aside.

3 In a small bowl, combine the garlic, the oil, the lime juice, the vinegar, and the egg. Season to taste and blend well.

4 Toss the salad with the dressing. Add the croutons and toss again to combine.

Commercial Crumble

1 Preheat the oven to 350°F. Grease a 9 x 9-inch baking dish.

2 Peel, core, and chop the apples. Place them in the baking dish and sprinkle with the lemon juice.

3 In a medium bowl, combine the rolled oats, the brown sugar, the flour, and the cinnamon. Cut in the butter and mix until crumbly. Fold in the vanilla.

4 Drain the pineapple and spread it over the apples. Spoon the cranberry sauce over the pineapple and sprinkle with the oat mixture.

5 Bake until the apples are tender and the top is golden, about 30 minutes.

6 Top with dollops of whipped cream.

WEEK SIX

Monday
Altoona
Liberty Bells
Mellon Melon
Plain and Fancy

Tuesday
Tomato Beginnings
Not Exactly Eggs Benedict
Fruit Conclusions

Wednesday
Side Chick
Silly Sprouts
Just Peachy

Thursday
Pucker-Up Pasta
Triple-Threat Salad
Poppy Sticks
Toasty Surprise

Friday
Beanie Baby Soup
Plain Jane Salad
Munchy Muffins
Pumpkin Pillows

STAPLES
- ❑ Butter
- ❑ Flour
- ❑ Baking powder
- ❑ Baking soda
- ❑ Yellow cornmeal
- ❑ Cornstarch
- ❑ Granulated sugar
- ❑ Dark brown sugar
- ❑ Olive oil
- ❑ Vegetable oil
- ❑ Balsamic vinegar
- ❑ White wine vinegar
- ❑ Lemon juice
- ❑ Dijon mustard
- ❑ Honey
- ❑ Mayonnaise
- ❑ Worcestershire sauce
- ❑ Grated Parmesan cheese
- ❑ Poppy seeds
- ❑ Bay leaf
- ❑ Dried dill
- ❑ Dried savory
- ❑ Dried tarragon
- ❑ Ground allspice
- ❑ Ground cinnamon
- ❑ Ground cloves
- ❑ Whole cloves
- ❑ Ground ginger
- ❑ Dry mustard
- ❑ Ground nutmeg
- ❑ Black pepper
- ❑ Salt
- ❑ Almond extract
- ❑ Vanilla extract

MEAT & POULTRY

1 1/2 pounds lean cooked ham steak (T)

1 1/2 pounds boneless, skinless chicken breast (W)

FISH

4 tuna steaks or other firm-fleshed fish (about 1 1/2 pounds) (M)

FRESH PRODUCE

VEGETABLES

1 medium baking potato (F)

1 pound Brussels sprouts (W)

2 medium zucchini (Th)

1 medium yellow zucchini (F)

3 medium carrots (Th)

2 medium carrots (F)

2 stalks celery (W)

2 stalks celery (F)

1 medium head lettuce (Th)

1 small head lettuce (M)

1 package (10 ounces) mixed salad greens (F)

2 large tomatoes (T)

1 medium cucumber (F)

1 small red bell pepper (M)

1 small yellow bell pepper (M)

1 medium onion (M)

2 medium onions (F)

1 medium red onion (Th)

2 scallions (green onions) (F)

2 cloves garlic (Th)

2 cloves garlic (W)

2 cloves garlic (F)

HERBS

2 tablespoons chives (when chopped) (T)

1/4 cup chives (when chopped) (M)

2 tablespoons parsley (when chopped) (Th)

3 tablespoons parsley (when chopped) (W)

3 tablespoons parsley (when chopped) (F)

FRUIT

1 large lemon (Th)

1 small ripe honeydew melon (M)

1 medium ripe cantaloupe melon (M)

2 medium tart green apples (T)

2 medium ripe pears (T)

CANS, JARS & BOTTLES

SOUPS

1 can (14 ounces) vegetable broth (T)

1 can (14 ounces) vegetable broth (F)

1 can (14 ounces) beef broth (M)

VEGETABLES

1 can (14 1/2 ounces) diced tomatoes (T)

1 can (14 1/2 ounces) diced tomatoes (F)

1 can (15 ounces) whole beets (Th)

1 can (15 ounces) white beans (F)

1 can (15 ounces) red kidney beans (F)

FRUIT

1 can (15 ounces) sliced peaches (W)

FISH

2 cans (6 ounces each) whole baby clams (Th)

JUICES

1 can (6 ounces) tomato juice (T)

1 cup apple juice (T)

8 ounces clam juice (M)

SPREADS

1/4 cup orange marmalade (W)

1 jar (10 ounces) grape jelly (Th)

CONDIMENTS

1 jar (2 ounces) diced pimientos (W)

DESSERT & BAKING NEEDS

1 cup canned pumpkin (F)

PACKAGED GOODS

PASTA, RICE & GRAINS

1 pound linguini (Th)

1/2 pound orzo (M)

1 cup long-grain white rice (W)

1/2 cup rolled oats (F)

BAKED GOODS

4 English muffins (T)

DRIED FRUIT & NUTS

1/4 cup sliced almonds (Th)

1 cup pecan bits (M)

DESSERT & BAKING NEEDS

1 package (3.4 ounces) instant vanilla pudding mix (W)

1 package (3.4 ounces) instant coconut cream pudding mix (F)

1/4 cup flaked coconut (F)

WINE & SPIRITS

1/2 cup dry white wine (M)

2 tablespoons dry sherry (T)

1/4 cup dry sherry (F)

REFRIGERATED PRODUCTS

DAIRY

1 1/2 cups milk (W)

1 1/2 cups milk (F)

1 cup half-and-half (W)

1 cup buttermilk (F)

Whipped cream for garnish (W)

8 eggs (T)

1 egg (F)

JUICES

1/4 cup orange juice (M)

DELI

1 package refrigerated breadsticks (Th)

FROZEN GOODS

VEGETABLES

1 package (10 ounces) chopped spinach (T)

BAKED GOODS

1 pound cake (Th)

PASTRY

1 sheet puff pastry (M)

MONDAY

Altoona

4 tuna steaks or other firm-fleshed fish
   (about 1 1/2 pounds)
1 medium onion
2 tablespoons vegetable oil
8 ounces clam juice
1/2 cup dry white wine
2 tablespoons lemon juice
1 tablespoon Worcestershire sauce
1/2 teaspoon dry mustard
1/2 teaspoon dried dill
1/2 teaspoon ground nutmeg
Seasoning to taste
1 tablespoon cornstarch

Liberty Bells

1 quart water
1 can (14 ounces) beef broth
1 small red bell pepper
1 small yellow bell pepper
1/4 cup fresh chives (when chopped)
1/2 pound orzo
3 tablespoons butter
Seasoning to taste

Mellon Melon

1 small head lettuce
1 small ripe honeydrew melon
1 medium ripe cantaloupe melon
1/4 cup orange juice
1 tablespoon honey
1 teaspoon ground ginger

Plain and Fancy

1 sheet frozen puff pastry
2 tablespoons butter
2/3 cup dark brown sugar
2 tablespoons ground cinnamon
1 cup pecan bits

EQUIPMENT

Medium saucepan	Whisk
3 small saucepans	Rolling pin
Medium skillet	Pastry brush
9 x 13-inch glass baking dish	Waxed paper
Baking sheet	Kitchen knives
Breadboard	Measuring cups and spoons
Strainer	Cooking utensils
Large shallow bowl	

COUNTDOWN

1. Assemble the ingredients and the equipment.
2. Do Step 1 of *Plain and Fancy*.
3. Do Steps 1–2 of *Altoona*.
4. Do Steps 2–6 of *Plain and Fancy*.
5. Do Step 3 of *Altoona*.
6. Do Steps 1–2 of *Mellon Melon*.
7. Do Step 4 of *Altoona*.
8. Do Steps 1–3 of *Liberty Bells*.
9. Do Step 3 of *Mellon Melon*.
10. Do Steps 4–5 of *Liberty Bells*.
11. Do Step 5 of *Altoona*.
12. Do Step 4 of *Mellon Melon*.

MONDAY

Altoona

1 Rinse and pat dry the fish steaks. Peel and mince the onion.

2 In a 9 x 13-inch baking dish, combine the onion, the oil, the clam juice, the wine, the lemon juice, the Worcestershire sauce, the mustard, the dill, and the nutmeg. Season to taste. Add the fish steaks and marinate for 15 minutes, turning several times to coat.

3 Preheat the broiler.

4 Drain the fish, reserving the marinade in a small saucepan, and broil until the fish flakes easily with a fork, about 15 minutes.

5 Add the cornstarch to the reserved marinade and bring the mixture to a boil, whisking until the sauce turns clear and begins to thicken, about 5 minutes. Serve with the fish.

Liberty Bells

1 Bring the water and the broth to a boil in a medium saucepan.

2 Rinse, trim, seed, and chop the bell peppers. Rinse, trim, and chop the chives.

3 Cook the orzo until it is almost tender, about 10 minutes.

4 Melt 1 tablespoon of the butter in a medium skillet and sauté the peppers for 3 minutes.

5 Melt the remaining 2 tablespoons butter in the skillet. Drain the orzo and toss it with the butter and the peppers. Season to taste and fold in the chives.

Mellon Melon

1 Wash and dry the lettuce and arrange the leaves on individual salad plates.

2 Cut the melons in half and seed them. Slice them into thin wedges and remove the rinds. Arrange the wedges over the lettuce in alternating colors.

3 In a small saucepan, combine the orange juice with the honey and the ginger. Cook, stirring, until the honey is melted and the sauce is just warm.

4 Pour the sauce over the melons.

Plain and Fancy

1 Set the puff pastry out to thaw.

2 Preheat the oven to 400°F. Flour a breadboard.

3 Melt the butter in a small saucepan.

4 In a large shallow bowl, combine the brown sugar and the cinnamon. Spread the nuts on a sheet of waxed paper.

5 Roll out the puff pastry and cut it into 1 x 3-inch sticks. Brush both sides of the sticks very lightly with the melted butter, dip both sides into the sugar mixture, and then coat both sides with the nuts. Give each stick a twist in the middle and place it on a baking sheet.

6 Bake the cinnamon twists until they are golden, about 10 minutes.

TUESDAY

Tomato Beginnings

2 tablespoons chives (when chopped)
1 can (14½ ounces) diced tomatoes
1 can (14 ounces) vegetable broth
1 can (6 ounces) tomato juice
1 teaspoon granulated sugar
1 teaspoon Worcestershire sauce
2 tablespoons dry sherry
Seasoning to taste

Fruit Conclusions

2 medium tart green apples
2 medium ripe pears
2 tablespoons lemon juice
1 cup apple juice
½ teaspoon ground allspice
1 tablespoon honey

Not Exactly
Eggs Benedict

1 package (10 ounces) frozen chopped
   spinach
1½ pounds lean cooked ham steak
2 large tomatoes
4 English muffins
2 tablespoons butter
½ cup water
⅔ cup mayonnaise
1 teaspoon dried tarragon
2 tablespoons lemon juice
Seasoning to taste
8 eggs

EQUIPMENT

Blender	Strainer
Large covered skillet	Small mixing bowl
2 medium covered saucepans	Whisk
Medium saucepan	Kitchen knives
Small covered saucepan	Measuring cups and spoons
Baking sheet	Cooking utensils

COUNTDOWN

1. Assemble the ingredients and the equipment.
2. Do Step 1 of *Not Exactly Eggs Benedict.*
3. Do Steps 1–3 of *Tomato Beginnings.*
4. Do Step 1 of *Fruit Conclusions.*
5. Do Steps 2–9 of *Not Exactly Eggs Benedict.*
6. Do Step 4 of *Tomato Beginnings.*
7. Do Step 2 of *Fruit Conclusions.*

TUESDAY

Tomato Beginnings

1 Rinse, trim, and chop the chives.

2 Place the tomatoes, the broth, the tomato juice, the sugar, and the Worcestershire sauce in a blender and puree for 1 minute.

3 Transfer the mixture to a medium saucepan. Blend in the sherry, season to taste, cover, reduce the heat, and simmer until hot, about 5 minutes.

4 Top with the chives.

Not Exactly Eggs Benedict

1 Set the spinach in a small bowl of very warm water to thaw.

2 Preheat the broiler.

3 Cut the ham steak into 8 portions. Rinse and stem the tomatoes and cut them into 8 even slices.

4 Split the muffins and spread them very lightly with 1 tablespoon of the butter. Arrange the halves on a baking sheet and place them under the broiler until lightly browned, about 1 minute.

5 Top each muffin with a piece of ham and broil for 3 minutes. Top the ham with a slice of tomato and broil for 2 minutes. Turn off the broiler, leaving the muffins inside to keep warm.

6 In a medium saucepan, combine the spinach and the ½ cup water. Bring to a boil, cook for 2 minutes, and drain thoroughly. Return the spinach to the saucepan and cover to keep warm.

7 In a small saucepan, combine the mayonnaise, the tarragon, and the lemon juice. Season to taste and heat through, but do not boil. Cover the sauce to keep warm.

8 Bring a small amount of water to a boil. Melt the remaining 1 tablespoon butter in a large skillet. Break the eggs into the skillet and cook them for 1 minute. Drizzle the boiling water over the eggs, cover, and cook until the whites are set, 3 to 4 minutes.

9 Place a portion of spinach and an egg on each muffin. Top with a dollop of sauce.

Fruit Conclusions

1 Rinse, core, and thinly slice the apples. Rinse, core, and thinly slice the pears. Arrange the slices on individual dessert plates and sprinkle with 1 tablespoon of the lemon juice to keep them from browning.

2 In a medium saucepan, combine the apple juice, the allspice, the honey, and the remaining 1 tablespoon lemon juice. Bring the mixture just to a boil, whisking to blend, and spoon over the fruit.

WEDNESDAY

Side Chick

1 cup long-grain white rice
2½ cups water
1½ pounds boneless, skinless chicken breast
2 cloves garlic
2 stalks celery
3 tablespoons fresh parsley (when chopped)
1 jar (2 ounces) diced pimientos
2 tablespoons butter
1 cup half-and-half
3 tablespoons Dijon mustard
Seasoning to taste

Silly Sprouts

1 pound Brussels sprouts
2 tablespoons butter
1 tablespoon dark brown sugar
1 teaspoon dried savory
Seasoning to taste

Just Peachy

1 package (3.4 ounces) instant vanilla pudding mix
1½ cups milk
1 teaspoon almond extract
1 can (15 ounces) sliced peaches
¼ cup orange marmalade
Whipped cream for garnish

COUNTDOWN

1. Assemble the ingredients and the equipment.
2. Do Step 1 of *Just Peachy.*
3. Do Steps 1–5 of *Side Chick.*
4. Do Steps 2–3 of *Just Peachy.*
5. Do Steps 1–4 of *Silly Sprouts.*
6. Do Steps 6–7 of *Side Chick.*
7. Do Step 4 of *Just Peachy.*

EQUIPMENT

Electric mixer
Double boiler
Medium covered saucepan
Small saucepan
Large covered skillet
Medium mixing bowl
Kitchen knives
Measuring cups and spoons
Cooking utensils

WEDNESDAY

Side Chick

1 Bring water to a boil in the bottom of a double boiler.

2 In the top of the double boiler, combine the rice and the 2¼ cups water. Cover, reduce the heat, and simmer until all the liquid is absorbed, and the rice is tender, 30 to 40 minutes.

3 Rinse, pat dry, and cube the chicken. Peel and mince the garlic. Rinse, trim, and chop the celery. Rinse, stem, and chop the parsley. Drain the pimientos.

4 Melt the butter in a large skillet and sauté the garlic and the celery for 1 minute. Add the chicken and sauté until tender and opaque, about 5 minutes. Remove the chicken from the skillet.

5 Blend the half-and-half and the mustard into the skillet. Season to taste. Bring to a boil. Cover, reduce the heat, and simmer until the mixture reduces and begins to thicken, about 3 minutes.

6 Return the chicken to the skillet, stir in the pimientos, cover, and simmer until heated through, about 5 minutes.

7 Spoon the chicken and the sauce over the rice. Garnish with the parsley.

Silly Sprouts

1 Bring water to a boil in a medium saucepan.

2 Rinse, trim, and halve the Brussels sprouts.

3 Cook the sprouts until they are crisp-tender, about 5 minutes.

4 Drain the sprouts. Add the butter, the brown sugar, and the savory. Season to taste, toss to coat, and cover to keep warm.

Just Peachy

1 In a medium bowl, combine the pudding mix, the milk, and the almond extract. Beat until well blended, about 2 minutes. Pour the mixture into individual dessert bowls and refrigerate for 10 minutes.

2 Drain the peaches, reserving 3 tablespoons of the liquid, and arrange the slices on top of the pudding.

3 In a small saucepan, heat the marmalade with the reserved peach liquid until melted. Spoon the mixture over the peach slices and refrigerate until you are ready to serve.

4 Garnish with dollops of whipped cream.

THURSDAY

Pucker-Up Pasta

1 medium red onion
2 cloves garlic
2 tablespoons parsley (when chopped)
2 cans (6 ounces each) whole baby clams
1 large lemon
2 tablespoons butter
2 tablespoons olive oil
1 pound linguini
1 tablespoon flour
1/4 teaspoon ground cloves
Seasoning to taste
1/2 cup grated Parmesan cheese

Triple-Threat Salad

1 medium head lettuce
3 medium carrots
2 medium zucchini
1 can (15 ounces) whole beets
1/4 cup olive oil
3 tablespoons white wine vinegar
1 teaspoon Worcestershire sauce
1 teaspoon Dijon mustard
Seasoning to taste

Poppy Sticks

2 tablespoons poppy seeds
1 package refrigerated breadsticks
2 tablespoons vegetable oil

Toasty Surprise

1 frozen pound cake
1/4 cup sliced almonds
1 jar (10 ounces) grape jelly

EQUIPMENT

Stockpot	Vegetable peeler
Medium skillet	Vegetable grater
2 baking sheets	Pastry brush
Colander	Waxed paper
5 small mixing bowls	Kitchen knives
Whisk	Measuring cups and
Citrus grater	spoons
Citrus juicer	Cooking utensils
Vegetable brush	

COUNTDOWN

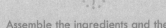

1. Assemble the ingredients and the equipment.
2. Do Steps 1–4 of *Toasty Surprise*.
3. Do Steps 1–3 of *Poppy Sticks*.
4. Do Step 1 of *Pucker-Up Pasta*.
5. Do Steps 1–4 of *Triple-Threat Salad*.
6. Do Step 4 of *Poppy Sticks*.
7. Do Steps 2–6 of *Pucker-Up Pasta*.
8. Do Step 5 of *Triple-Threat Salad*.
9. Do Steps 5–7 of *Toasty Surprise*.

THURSDAY

Pucker-Up Pasta

1 Bring water to a boil in a stockpot.

2 Peel and chop the onion. Peel and mince the garlic. Rinse, stem, and chop the parsley. Drain the clams, reserving the liquid. Grate 1 tablespoon of lemon peel and juice the lemon.

3 In a medium skillet, melt the butter with the oil. Add the onion and the garlic and sauté until the onion is tender, about 5 minutes.

4 Cook the linguini in the stockpot until just tender, 2 to 3 minutes if you are using fresh pasta, 6 to 7 minutes if you are using dry pasta.

5 In a small bowl, combine the flour with the reserved clam juice and whisk well to blend. Add the mixture to the onion and garlic. Add the lemon peel, the lemon juice, and the cloves and season to taste. Add the clams and cook until hot, 2 to 3 minutes.

6 Drain the pasta. Pour the sauce over the pasta. Sprinkle with the parsley and the cheese.

Triple-Threat Salad

1 Wash and dry the lettuce and arrange the leaves on individual salad plates.

2 Peel, trim, and grate the carrots. Scrub, trim, and grate the zucchini. Drain and grate the beets. Place each vegetable in a separate small bowl.

3 In a small bowl, whisk together the oil, the vinegar, the Worcestershire sauce, and the mustard. Season to taste.

4 Blend ⅓ of the dressing into each of the vegetables and refrigerate until you are ready to serve.

5 Mound a portion of each vegetable over the lettuce on each plate.

Poppy Sticks

1 Preheat the oven to 375°F.

2 Sprinkle the poppy seeds on a sheet of waxed paper.

3 Cut the breadstick dough into sticks and brush them lightly with the oil. Roll them in the poppy seeds until they are well coated.

4 Arrange the sticks on a baking sheet and bake until they are golden brown, 10 to 12 minutes.

Toasty Surprise

1 Set the pound cake out to thaw partially.

2 Preheat the broiler.

3 Lay the almonds on a baking sheet and broil until lightly toasted, 1 to 2 minutes.

4 Remove the almonds and reserve.

5 Reheat the broiler.

6 Cut the pound cake into ½-inch-thick slices, place the slices on the baking sheet, and toast until just golden, about 3 minutes.

7 Arrange the toasted cake slices on individual dessert plates, spread with the jelly, and top with the toasted almonds.

FRIDAY

Beanie Baby Soup

1 clove garlic
2 medium onions
8 whole cloves
1 medium baking potato
2 medium stalks celery
1 medium yellow zucchini
2 medium carrots
3 tablespoons parsley (when chopped)
1 can (15 ounces) white beans
1 can (15 ounces) red kidney beans
2 tablespoons olive oil
1 bay leaf
1 can (14 1/2 ounces) diced tomatoes
1 can (14 ounces) vegetable broth
1/4 cup dry sherry
Seasoning to taste

Plain Jane Salad

1 package (10 ounces) mixed salad greens
2 scallions (green onions)
1 medium cucumber
1 clove garlic
3 tablespoons olive oil
2 tablespoons balsamic vinegar
Seasoning to taste

Munchy Muffins

1 cup flour
1 tablespoon baking powder
1/2 teaspoon baking soda
1/2 cup yellow cornmeal
1/2 cup rolled oats
1 cup buttermilk
1 egg
1/3 cup dark brown sugar
4 tablespoons butter

Pumpkin Pillows

1 package (3.4 ounces) instant coconut
   cream pudding mix
1 1/2 cups milk
1 cup canned pumpkin
1 teaspoon ground cinnamon
1 teaspoon ground allspice
1 teaspoon vanilla extract
1/4 cup flaked coconut

EQUIPMENT

Electric mixer	Vegetable brush
Dutch oven	Vegetable peeler
3 large mixing bowls	Kitchen knives
2 small mixing bowls	Measuring cups and
Muffin tin	spoons
Whisk	Cooking utensils

COUNTDOWN

1. Assemble the ingredients and the equipment.
2. Do Steps 1–2 of *Pumpkin Pillows*.
3. Do Steps 1–2 of *Beanie Baby Soup*.
4. Do Steps 1–5 of *Munchy Muffins*.
5. Do Steps 1–2 of *Plain Jane Salad*.
6. Do Step 3 of *Beanie Baby Soup*.
7. Do Step 3 of *Pumpkin Pillows*.

FRIDAY

Beanie Baby Soup

1 Peel and mince the garlic. Peel the onions. Chop 1 onion. Cut the remaining onion in half and stud the halves with the cloves. Peel and dice the potato. Rinse, trim, and slice the celery. Scrub, trim, and dice the zucchini. Peel, trim, and chunk the carrots. Rinse, stem, and chop the parsley. Drain the beans.

2 Heat the oil in a Dutch oven. Add the garlic and the chopped onion and sauté until the onion is soft, about 5 minutes. Add the studded onion halves, the potato, the celery, the zucchini, the carrots, the beans, the bay leaf, the tomatoes, the broth, and the sherry. Bring to a boil, cover, reduce the heat, and simmer until the vegetables are crisp-tender, about 20 minutes.

3 Remove the studded onion halves and the bay leaf. Season to taste. Sprinkle with the chopped parsley.

Plain Jane Salad

1 Rinse and dry the salad greens. Rinse, trim, and chop the scallions. Peel, trim, and slice the cucumber. Combine the ingredients in a large bowl.

2 Peel and mince the garlic. In a small bowl, whisk the garlic with the oil and the vinegar. Season to taste and toss with the salad.

Munchy Muffins

1 Preheat the oven to 400°F. Grease a muffin tin.

2 In a small bowl, combine the flour, the baking powder, and the baking soda.

3 In a large bowl, combine the cornmeal, the oats, the buttermilk, the egg, and the brown sugar.

4 Melt the butter and add it to the cornmeal mixture. Fold in the flour mixture until just blended.

5 Fill the muffin cups. Bake until the muffins are golden, about 15 minutes.

Pumpkin Pillows

1 In a large bowl, beat the pudding mix and the milk until well blended. Fold in the pumpkin, the cinnamon, the allspice, and the vanilla.

2 Pour the pudding into individual dessert bowls and refrigerate until you are ready to serve.

3 Top each pudding with a sprinkle of coconut.

WEEK SEVEN

Monday

Love My Linguini
Tomato Top-Off
Pita-Pita-Pita
Chocolate Bears

Tuesday

Shanghai the Salmon
Capture the Rice
Seize the Peas
Filch the Fruit

Wednesday

Meat Me In St. Louis
St. Jo Potato
Show Me the Beans
Bluebirds

Thursday

Ali Baba's Chicken
Scheherazade's Soba
Fairytale Fruit
Once Upon a Tempura

Friday

Grab the Crab
Snatch the Salad
Finger the Fruit

- Butter
- Flour
- Cornstarch
- Granulated sugar
- Dark brown sugar
- Powdered sugar
- Olive oil
- Sesame oil
- Vegetable oil
- Red wine vinegar
- Rice vinegar
- Lemon juice
- Dijon mustard
- Honey
- Soy sauce
- Grated Parmesan cheese
- Plain breadcrumbs
- Seasoned breadcrumbs
- Sesame seeds
- Dried basil
- Dried dill
- Dried rosemary
- Dried savory
- Dried thyme
- Ground cardamom
- Ground cinnamon
- Ground ginger
- Italian seasoning
- Ground nutmeg
- Black pepper
- Salt
- Rum extract

MEAT & POULTRY

2 pounds lean ground beef (W)

1 1/2 pounds boneless, skinless chicken thighs (Th)

FISH

4 salmon steaks (about 1 1/2 pounds) (T)

FRESH PRODUCE

VEGETABLES

1 1/2 pounds baking potatoes (W)

1 pound green beans (W)

1 pound Chinese snow peas (T)

2 stalks celery (Th)

3 stalks celery (F)

1/2 pound mushrooms (M)

1/2 pound mushrooms (T)

1 package (10 ounces) spinach (F)

1 small head lettuce (M)

3 large tomatoes (M)

2 medium tomatoes (F)

1 small green bell pepper (F)

1 small onion (F)

1 small red onion (M)

1 small leek (T)

2 scallions (green onions) (T)

4 scallions (green onions) (W)

3 scallions (green onions) (Th)

3 cloves garlic (M)

2 cloves garlic (T)

1 clove garlic (W)

2 cloves garlic (Th)

HERBS

2 tablespoons chives (when chopped) (F)

2 tablespoons parsley (when chopped) (M)

2 tablespoons parsley (when chopped) (T)

2 tablespoons parsley (when chopped) (F)

FRUIT

2 medium oranges (T)

2 mandarin oranges (Th)

2 medium bananas (T)

1 small ripe honeydew melon (F)

1 small ripe cantaloupe melon (F)

1 medium apple (T)

1 medium ripe pear (T)

2 large Asian pears (or crisp pears) (Th)

2 ripe kiwifruit (F)

CANS, JARS & BOTTLES

SOUPS

1 can (14 ounces) beef broth (T)

1 can (14 ounces) vegetable broth (Th)

1 can (10 1/2 ounces) beef broth (W)

1 can (11 ounces) tomato bisque (W)

1 can (10 3/4 ounces) cream of celery soup (F)

VEGETABLES

1 can (14 ounces) quartered artichoke hearts (M)

FISH

2 cans (6 ounces each) crabmeat (F)

SAUCES

1 can (8 ounces) tomato sauce (M)

CONDIMENTS

1 jar (2 ounces) diced pimientos (F)

1 can (3 1/2 ounces) sliced black olives (F)

DESSERT & BAKING NEEDS

1/4 cup marshmallow crème for garnish (F)

PACKAGED GOODS

PASTA, RICE & GRAINS

1 pound linguini (M)

1 cup long-grain white rice (T)

2 cups couscous (F)

BAKED GOODS

2 small pita bread rounds (M)

1 angel food loaf cake (W)

8 Oreo cookies (M)

INTERNATIONAL FOODS

8 ounces Japanese soba noodles (Th)

DRIED FRUIT & NUTS

8 raisins (M)

1 cup chopped dates (T)

1/2 cup sliced almonds (F)

DESSERT & BAKING NEEDS

4 cinnamon candies (M)

1/4 cup flaked coconut (M)

WINE & SPIRITS

1/2 cup dry white wine (T)

3 tablespoons dry sherry (Th)

1/4 cup dry sherry (F)

2 tablespoons vermouth (T)

REFRIGERATED PRODUCTS

DAIRY

1/2 cup half-and-half (T)

1/4 cup sour cream (M)

1/4 cup sour cream (W)

1 egg (W)

2 eggs (Th)

JUICES

1/2 cup orange juice (T)

DELI

8 slices bacon (M)

FROZEN GOODS

FRUIT

1 package (12 ounces) blueberries (W)

DESSERTS

1 pint chocolate ice cream (M)

1 pint vanilla ice cream (Th)

MONDAY

Love My Linguini

8 slices bacon
2 cloves garlic
1 small red onion
1/2 pound fresh mushrooms
2 tablespoons fresh parsley (when chopped)
1 can (14 ounces) quartered artichoke hearts
1 can (8 ounces) tomato sauce
1/4 cup sour cream
1 pound linguini
2 teaspoons Italian seasoning
Seasoning to taste
1/3 cup grated Parmesan cheese

Tomato Top-Off

1 small head lettuce
3 large tomatoes
1 clove garlic
3 tablespoons olive oil
1 tablespoon red wine vinegar
1 tablespoon lemon juice
1/2 teaspoon dried dill
Seasoning to taste

Pita-Pita-Pita

2 tablespoons butter
2 small pita bread rounds
1/2 teaspoon dried thyme
1/4 teaspoon dried savory
Seasoning to taste

Chocolate Bears

1 pint chocolate ice cream
1/2 cup flaked coconut
2 teaspoons ground cinnamon
4 cinnamon candies
8 raisins
8 Oreo cookies

EQUIPMENT

Blender	Whisk
Stockpot	Kitchen knives
Large skillet	Measuring cups and spoons
2 baking sheets	
Colander	Cooking utensils
2 small mixing bowls	

COUNTDOWN

1. Assemble the ingredients and the equipment.
2. Do Steps 1–3 of *Chocolate Bears*.
3. Do Steps 1–3 of *Pita-Pita-Pita*.
4. Do Steps 1–3 of *Tomato Top-Off*.
5. Do Steps 4–5 of *Chocolate Bears*.
6. Do Steps 1–5 of *Love My Linguini*.
7. Do Steps 4–5 of *Pita-Pita-Pita*.
8. Do Step 6 of *Love My Linguini*.
9. Do Step 4 of *Tomato Top-Off*.
10. Do Step 6 of *Chocolate Bears*.

MONDAY

Love My Linguini

1 Bring water to a boil in a stockpot.

2 Dice the bacon. Peel and mince the garlic. Peel and chop the onion. Rinse, pat dry, trim, and slice the mushrooms. Rinse, stem, and chop the parsley. Drain and chop the artichoke hearts.

3 Sauté the bacon in a large skillet until crisp, about 10 minutes. Drain on paper towels.

4 Cook the linguini until it is almost tender, 2 to 3 minutes if you are using fresh pasta, 6 to 7 minutes if you are using dry pasta.

5 Sauté the garlic in the bacon drippings for 1 minute. Add the onion, the mushrooms, and the artichoke hearts and sauté for 3 minutes. Add the tomato sauce, the sour cream, and the bacon. Heat through, but do not let boil.

6 Drain the pasta and return it to the stockpot. Add the artichoke mixture, the Italian seasoning, and the parsley. Season to taste and toss to combine. Sprinkle with the cheese.

Tomato Top-Off

1 Wash and dry the lettuce and arrange the leaves on individual salad plates.

2 Rinse, stem, and slice the tomatoes and arrange the slices over the lettuce. Peel and mince the garlic.

3 In a small bowl, combine the garlic, the oil, the vinegar, the lemon juice, and the dill. Season to taste.

4 Spoon the dressing over the tomatoes.

Pita-Pita-Pita

1 Set the butter out to soften.

2 Place the pita rounds on a baking sheet.

3 In a small bowl, combine the butter, the thyme, and the savory. Season to taste and spread the mixture evenly over the bread.

4 Preheat the broiler.

5 Broil until lightly browned, about 2 minutes. Cut in wedges to serve.

Chocolate Bears

1 Preheat the oven to 350°F.

2 Set the ice cream out to soften slightly.

3 Spread the coconut in a single layer on a baking sheet and toast lightly, about 5 minutes.

4 Place the ice cream in a blender. Add the cinnamon and process for 1 minute.

5 Distribute the ice cream among individual dessert bowls and refreeze until you are ready to use.

6 Sprinkle the coconut over the ice cream. Place a cinnamon candy in the center of each serving for a nose. Add 2 raisins for eyes. Place 2 cookies on end for ears.

TUESDAY

Shanghai the Salmon

4 salmon steaks (about 1 1/2 pounds)
2 cloves garlic
4 tablespoons butter
1 cup plain breadcrumbs
1/2 cup dry white wine
2 tablespoons vermouth
1/2 cup half-and-half
Seasoning to taste

Capture the Rice

2 tablespoons fresh parsley (when
   chopped)
1 small leek
2 tablespoons butter
1 cup long-grain white rice
1 can (14 ounces) beef broth
1/4 cup water
1 tablespoon lemon juice
Seasoning to taste

Seize the Peas

1 pound Chinese snow peas
1/2 pound fresh mushrooms
2 scallions (green onions)
2 tablespoons vegetable oil
1/2 teaspoon dried thyme
Seasoning to taste

Filch the Fruit

2 medium bananas
2 medium oranges
1 medium apple
1 medium ripe pear
1 cup chopped dates
1/2 cup orange juice
2 tablespoons honey
1 teaspoon ground nutmeg

EQUIPMENT

Medium covered saucepan	Whisk
Small saucepan	Plastic wrap
Medium skillet	Kitchen knives
Large mixing bowl	Measuring cups and spoons
Medium mixing bowl	Cooking utensils
Small mixing bowl	

COUNTDOWN

1. Assemble the ingredients and the equipment.
2. Do Step 1 of *Filch the Fruit*.
3. Do Steps 1–3 of *Capture the Rice*.
4. Do Steps 1–4 of *Shanghai the Salmon*.
5. Do Steps 1–2 of *Seize the Peas*.
6. Do Step 5 of *Shanghai the Salmon*.
7. Do Step 3 of *Seize the Peas*.
8. Do Step 6 of *Shanghai the Salmon*.
9. Do Step 4 of *Capture the Rice*.
10. Do Step 2 of *Filch the Fruit*.

TUESDAY

Shanghai the Salmon

1 Preheat the broiler.

2 Rinse and pat dry the salmon steaks. Peel and mince the garlic.

3 Melt half the butter in a small saucepan. Blend in the garlic and the breadcrumbs.

4 Broil the salmon steaks on one side for 5 minutes.

5 Turn the salmon over and spread the breadcrumb mixture evenly over the steaks. Broil until the fish flakes easily with a fork and the breadcrumbs are golden brown, about 5 minutes more.

6 Combine the wine and the vermouth in the saucepan. Bring to a boil, reduce the heat, add the half-and-half, and simmer until slightly thickened. Add the remaining 2 tablespoons butter and season to taste. Pour over the salmon fillets.

Capture the Rice

1 Rinse, stem, and chop the parsley. Thoroughly rinse the leek, discarding the root end and the tough outer leaves. Cut into thin slices.

2 Melt the butter in a medium saucepan. Sauté the leek and the parsley for 3 minutes. Add the rice and sauté 2 minutes more.

3 Add the broth, the water, and the lemon juice. Season to taste, cover the saucepan, and reduce the heat. Simmer until all the liquid is absorbed and the rice is tender, about 20 minutes.

4 Fluff the rice with a fork.

Seize the Peas

1 Place ice water in a medium bowl.

2 Rinse and string the snow peas and add them to the ice water. Rinse, pat dry, trim, and slice the mushrooms. Rinse, trim, and chop the scallions.

3 Heat the oil in a medium skillet and stir-fry the mushrooms for 2 minutes. Drain the snow peas and add them to the skillet. Stir-fry for 1 minute. Add the scallions and the thyme, season to taste, and toss to combine.

Filch the Fruit

1 Peel and diagonally slice the bananas. Peel and section the oranges. Rinse, core, and slice the apple. Rinse, core, and slice the pear. Combine the fruit in a large bowl. Add the dates and sprinkle with 1 tablespoon of the orange juice. Cover with plastic wrap and refrigerate until you are ready to serve.

2 In a small bowl, combine the remaining orange juice, the honey, and the nutmeg. Pour the mixture over the fruit and toss to combine.

WEDNESDAY

Meat Me In St. Louis

1 clove garlic
4 scallions (green onions)
2 pounds lean ground beef
1/2 cup seasoned breadcrumbs
1 egg
1/4 cup sour cream
1/4 cup water
2 teaspoons dried dill
Seasoning to taste
1 can (11 ounces) tomato bisque

St. Jo Potato

1 1/2 pounds baking potatoes
1 can (10 1/2 ounces) beef broth
2 tablespoons butter
Seasoning to taste

Show Me the Beans

1 pound fresh green beans
2 tablespoons vegetable oil
1 teaspoon dried basil
1/2 teaspoon granulated sugar
Seasoning to taste

Bluebirds

1 package (12 ounces) frozen blueberries
1/2 cup granulated sugar
1 tablespoon cornstarch
2 tablespoons water
1 tablespoon lemon juice
2 teaspoons rum extract
1 angel food loaf cake

EQUIPMENT

Electric mixer
Large covered saucepan
Medium saucepan
Medium covered skillet
Loaf pan

Large mixing bowl
Small mixing bowl
Vegetable peeler
Kitchen knives
Measuring cups and spoons
Cooking utensils

COUNTDOWN

1. Assemble the ingredients and the equipment.
2. Do Steps 1–4 of *Meat Me In St. Louis*.
3. Do Steps 1–3 of *Bluebirds*.
4. Do Steps 1–2 of *St. Jo Potato*.
5. Do Step 1 of *Show Me the Beans*.
6. Do Step 3 of *St. Jo Potato*.
7. Do Step 2 of *Show Me the Beans*.
8. Do Step 4 of *Bluebirds*.

WEDNESDAY

Meat Me In St. Louis

1 Preheat the oven to 400°F.

2 Peel and mince the garlic. Rinse, trim, and mince the scallions.

3 In a large bowl, combine the garlic, the scallions, the ground beef, the breadcrumbs, the egg, the sour cream, the water, and the dill. Season to taste and mix well.

4 Place the beef mixture in a loaf pan, spread the soup over the top and bake until it is no longer pink inside, about 50 minutes.

St. Jo Potato

1 Peel and cube the potatoes.

2 Bring the broth and enough water to cover the potatoes to a boil in a large saucepan and cook until the potatoes are tender, 10 to 15 minutes.

3 Drain the potatoes, reserving the cooking liquid. Return the potatoes to the saucepan, reduce the heat, and shake gently over the burner until they are dry. Add the butter and beat until the potatoes are soft. Gradually add just enough of the reserved cooking liquid to beat until fluffy. Season to taste and cover to keep warm.

Show Me the Beans

1 Rinse and trim the green beans.

2 Heat the oil in a medium skillet. Add the green beans, the basil, and the sugar, tossing to coat, and sauté the beans until they are crisp-tender, 6 to 8 minutes. Remove from the heat, season to taste, and cover to keep warm.

Bluebirds

1 Set the blueberries in a small bowl of warm water to thaw.

2 Combine the sugar, the cornstarch, and the 2 tablespoons water in a medium saucepan, blending well. Bring the mixture to a boil and add the lemon juice and the rum extract. Cook, stirring, until the mixture thickens and becomes clear, about 2 minutes.

3 Stir in the blueberries. Mix to combine and heat through, about 1 minute. Remove from the heat and set aside.

4 Slice the cake and place the slices on individual dessert plates. Spoon the sauce over the cake.

THURSDAY

Ali Baba's Chicken

2 cloves garlic
1 1/2 pounds boneless, skinless chicken thighs
1 teaspoon ground ginger
1/4 cup soy sauce
2 tablespoons honey
2 tablespoons rice vinegar
1 egg
1/4 cup flour
1/4 cup sesame seeds
2 tablespoons butter
2 tablespoons vegetable oil

Scheherazade's Soba

3 scallions (green onions)
2 stalks celery
2 teaspoons sesame oil
1 can (14 ounces) vegetable broth
8 ounces Japanese soba noodles
3 tablespoons dry sherry
Seasoning to taste

Fairytale Fruit

2 large Asian pears (or crisp pears)
2 fresh mandarin oranges
1/2 cup water
1 tablespoon dark brown sugar
1 teaspoon ground nutmeg

Once Upon a Tempura

1 pint vanilla ice cream
1 egg
1 cup water
1 1/4 cups flour
1 cup vegetable oil
2 tablespoons powdered sugar

EQUIPMENT

Wok
Medium covered
  saucepan
Medium saucepan
Medium skillet
9 x 13-inch glass
  baking dish
2 large shallow bowls
Medium mixing bowl

Small mixing bowl
Whisk
Waxed paper
Ice cream scoop
Kitchen knives
Measuring cups and
  spoons
Cooking utensils

COUNTDOWN

1. Assemble the ingredients and the equipment.
2. Do Steps 1–2 of *Once Upon a Tempura.*
3. Do Steps 1–7 of *Ali Baba's Chicken.*
4. Do Steps 1–2 of *Fairytale Fruit.*
5. Do Step 8 of *Ali Baba's Chicken.*
6. Do Step 3 of *Fairytale Fruit.*
7. Do Steps 1–4 of *Scheherazade's Soba.*
8. Do Step 3 of *Once Upon a Tempura.*

THURSDAY

Ali Baba's Chicken

1 Peel and mince the garlic. Rinse and pat dry the chicken thighs and place them in a 9 x 13-inch baking dish.

2 In a small bowl, combine the garlic, the ginger, the soy sauce, the honey, and the vinegar. Pour the mixture over the chicken and marinate for 20 minutes, turning occasionally.

3 Preheat the oven to 400°F.

4 Beat the egg in a large shallow bowl. Combine the flour and the sesame seeds in a second shallow bowl.

5 Drain the chicken and discard the marinade. Melt the butter with the oil in the baking dish.

6 Dip the chicken in the egg, then coat it in the flour mixture.

7 Return the chicken to the baking dish in a single layer, turning to coat in the butter mixture. Bake until the chicken is lightly browned, about 15 minutes.

8 Turn the thighs and bake until tender and cooked through, about 10 minutes more.

Scheherazade's Soba

1 Rinse, trim, and thinly slice the scallions. Rinse, trim, and chop the celery.

2 Heat the oil in a medium skillet and sauté the celery for 2 minutes. Add the scallions and cook for 1 minute. Remove the skillet from the heat and set aside.

3 Bring the broth to a boil in a medium saucepan. Add the soba noodles and cook until they are almost tender, 2 to 3 minutes.

4 Drain the noodles and return them to the saucepan. Add the sherry. Fold in the celery and the scallions and season to taste. Heat through.

Fairytale Fruit

1 Peel, core, and slice the pears. Peel and section the oranges.

2 Combine the pears and the oranges in a medium saucepan. Add the water and the brown sugar, bring to a boil, and cook until the pears begin to soften and the oranges are heated through, about 5 minutes.

3 Sprinkle with the nutmeg and cover to keep warm.

Once Upon a Tempura

1 Place 4 large scoops of ice cream on a sheet of waxed paper and freeze until they are very hard, at least 15 minutes.

2 Combine the egg and the water in a medium bowl. Add the flour and beat until smooth. Refrigerate until you are ready to use.

3 Heat the oil in a wok. Remove the ice cream balls from the freezer, dip them into the egg batter, and fry until golden, about 2 minutes. Sprinkle with the powdered sugar.

FRIDAY

MENU

Grab the Crab

1¾ cups water
2 cups couscous
3 stalks celery
1 small onion
1 small green bell pepper
2 tablespoons fresh parsley (when chopped)
1 jar (2 ounces) diced pimientos
2 cans (6 ounces each) crabmeat
1 can (3½ ounces) sliced black olives
2 tablespoons vegetable oil
¼ cup dry sherry
½ teaspoon dried rosemary
½ teaspoon dried basil
1 can (10¾ ounces) cream of celery soup
Seasoning to taste
½ cup sliced almonds

Snatch the Salad

1 package (10 ounces) fresh spinach
2 tablespoons fresh chives (when chopped)
2 medium tomatoes
3 tablespoons olive oil
2 tablespoons red wine vinegar
½ teaspoon granulated sugar
1 teaspoon Dijon mustard
Seasoning to taste

Finger the Fruit

1 small ripe honeydew melon
1 small ripe cantaloupe melon
2 ripe kiwifruit
2 tablespoons lemon juice
3 tablespoons powdered sugar
½ teaspoon ground cardamom
¼ cup marshmallow crème for garnish

EQUIPMENT

Dutch oven
Medium covered saucepan
Large shallow bowl
Large mixing bowl
Small mixing bowl
Whisk

8 skewers
Plastic wrap
Kitchen knives
Measuring cups and spoons
Cooking utensils

COUNTDOWN

1. Assemble the ingredients and the equipment.
2. Do Steps 1–2 of *Finger the Fruit*.
3. Do Steps 1–2 of *Snatch the Salad*.
4. Do Steps 1–3 of *Grab the Crab*.
5. Do Step 3 of *Snatch the Salad*.
6. Do Step 4 of *Grab the Crab*.
7. Do Step 3 of *Finger the Fruit*.

FRIDAY

Grab the Crab

1 Bring the water to a boil in a medium saucepan. Add the couscous and stir to combine. Cover, remove from the heat, and let stand for 5 minutes.

2 Rinse, trim, and dice the celery. Peel and chop the onion. Rinse, trim, seed, and chop the bell pepper. Rinse, stem, and chop the parsley. Drain the pimientos. Drain and flake the crabmeat, discarding any bits of shell or cartilage. Drain the olives.

3 Heat the oil in a Dutch oven and sauté the celery, the onion, and the bell pepper until the onion is soft, about 5 minutes. Add the crabmeat, the pimientos, the olives, and the sherry. Add the couscous, the rosemary, and the basil and blend well. Add the soup and season to taste. Simmer until the mixture is hot and bubbly, about 10 minutes.

4 Top with the parsley and the almonds.

Snatch the Salad

1 Rinse, pat dry, and stem the spinach. Rinse, trim, and chop the chives. Rinse, stem, and quarter the tomatoes. Combine the ingredients in a large bowl.

2 In a small bowl, whisk together the oil, the vinegar, the sugar, and the mustard. Season to taste.

3 Toss the salad with the dressing.

Finger the Fruit

1 Quarter and seed the melons, remove the rinds, and cut into chunks. Peel and slice the kiwifruit.

2 Alternate melon chunks and kiwifruit slices on 8 skewers. Sprinkle with the lemon juice. Place on a plate, cover with plastic wrap, and refrigerate until you are ready to use.

3 Combine the powdered sugar and the cardamom in a large shallow bowl. Roll the fruit sticks in the sugar mixture and spoon the marshmallow crème over the top.

WEEK EIGHT

Monday
Utahragon Soup
Provocative Avocados
Loganberry Frost

Tuesday
Fowl Play
Orzo They Say
The Premeditated Pimiento
Captive Cranberries

Wednesday
Coddle Up a Little Closer
Bundling Babies
Smoochy Zucchini
Not Tonight, Honey

Thursday
Button Your Lip
Rice 'n' Easy
Jelly Beans
Precious Pumpkin

Friday
Strata Various
Grape Flute Salad
Clarinut

STAPLES

- ☐ Butter
- ☐ Flour
- ☐ Granulated sugar
- ☐ Dark brown sugar
- ☐ Powdered sugar
- ☐ Maple syrup
- ☐ Silver shots
- ☐ Olive oil
- ☐ Vegetable oil
- ☐ Red wine vinegar
- ☐ White wine vinegar
- ☐ Lemon juice
- ☐ Dijon mustard
- ☐ Honey
- ☐ Mayonnaise
- ☐ Worcestershire sauce
- ☐ Grated Romano cheese
- ☐ Seasoned breadcrumbs
- ☐ Dried basil
- ☐ Bay leaf
- ☐ Dried dill
- ☐ Dried oregano
- ☐ Dried thyme
- ☐ Cayenne pepper
- ☐ Ground cinnamon
- ☐ Lemon-pepper seasoning
- ☐ Dry mustard
- ☐ Ground nutmeg
- ☐ Paprika
- ☐ Black pepper
- ☐ Salt
- ☐ Vanilla extract

MEAT & POULTRY

2 lean cooked ham steaks (about $1/2$ pound each) (M)

4 loin pork chops (about $1 1/2$ pounds) (Th)

3 pounds chicken pieces (T)

FISH

4 cod fillets (about $1 1/2$ pounds) (W)

FRESH PRODUCE

VEGETABLES

$1 1/2$ pounds small new potatoes (W)

1 large bunch broccoli (F)

3 small zucchini (W)

2 stalks celery (T)

1 medium head romaine lettuce (T)

1 small head red leaf lettuce (F)

4 large tomatoes (M)

8 medium tomatoes (F)

2 medium ripe avocados (M)

1 large red bell pepper (M)

1 small green bell pepper (T)

1 large onion (M)

1 large onion (Th)

1 medium onion (F)

1 small onion (W)

1 large red onion (M)

1 small red onion (T)

2 scallions (green onions) (T)

2 cloves garlic (T)

2 cloves garlic (M)

1 clove garlic (W)

HERBS

2 tablespoons chives (when chopped) (W)

3 tablespoons chives (when chopped) (Th)

$1/2$ cup parsley (when chopped) (T)

2 tablespoons parsley (when chopped) (W)

$1/4$ cup tarragon (when chopped) (M)

FRUIT

1 large pink grapefruit (F)

2 mandarin oranges (T)

2 medium very ripe pears (W)

1 package (12 ounces) cranberries (F)

CANS, JARS & BOTTLES

SOUPS

1 can (14 ounces) chicken broth with roasted garlic (T)

1 can (14 ounces) chicken broth (M)

1 can (14 ounces) chicken broth (Th)

1 can ($10 1/2$ ounces) beef consommé (M)

VEGETABLES

1 can ($14 1/2$ ounces) diced tomatoes (W)

1 can (4 ounces) whole button mushrooms (Th)

FRUIT

1 can (8 ounces) whole cranberry sauce (T)

1 can (15 ounces) loganberries (M)

1 can (15 ounces) apricot halves (F)

JUICES

2 cups tomato juice (M)

SPREADS

$1/4$ cup orange marmalade (Th)

CONDIMENTS

1 jar (2 ounces) diced pimientos (T)

DESSERT & BAKING NEEDS

1 cup canned pumpkin (Th)

PACKAGED GOODS

PASTA, RICE & GRAINS

1 cup orzo (T)

$1/2$ cup vermicelli (when broken) (Th)

1 cup long-grain white rice (Th)

BAKED GOODS

4 super size English muffins (M)

12 slices white bread (F)

4 prepared graham cracker tart shells (F)

DRIED FRUIT & NUTS

$1/4$ cup pecan bits (F)

DESSERT & BAKING NEEDS

1 package (3.4 ounces) instant vanilla pudding mix (T)

WINE & SPIRITS

1 cup dry white wine (Th)

$1/4$ cup dry sherry (M)

1 tablespoon Grand Marnier (W)

REFRIGERATED PRODUCTS

DAIRY

$1 1/4$ cups milk (T)

2 cups milk (Th)

$1 1/2$ cups milk (F)

$3/4$ cup sour cream (T)

$1/2$ cup sour cream (Th)

Whipped cream for garnish (Th)

3 eggs (Th)

6 eggs (F)

CHEESE

8 slices (1 ounce each) Swiss cheese (M)

1 cup shredded Cheddar cheese (F)

1 cup shredded Colby/Monterey Jack cheese (F)

JUICES

$1/4$ cup orange juice (W)

2 tablespoons orange juice (F)

DELI

$1/2$ pound bacon (M)

FROZEN GOODS

VEGETABLES

1 package (10 ounces) baby lima beans (Th)

BAKED GOODS

1 pound cake (W)

DESSERTS

1 pint vanilla yogurt (M)

1 pint butter pecan ice cream (F)

MONDAY

Utahragon Soup

1 large onion
4 large tomatoes
1/4 cup fresh tarragon (when chopped)
1 tablespoon olive oil
1 can (14 ounces) chicken broth
1 can (10 1/2 ounces) beef consommé
2 cups tomato juice
1 teaspoon dried thyme
1 bay leaf
1/4 cup dry sherry
Cayenne pepper
Seasoning to taste

Loganberry Frost

1 can (15 ounces) loganberries
2 tablespoons powdered sugar
1 pint vanilla frozen yogurt
Silver shots for garnish

Provocative Avocados

1/2 pound bacon
1 large red bell pepper
2 cloves garlic
1 large red onion
2 medium ripe avocados
2 tablespoons lemon juice
2 lean cooked ham steaks (about 1/2 pound
  each)
4 super size English muffins
3 tablespoons mayonnaise
1 tablespoon Dijon mustard
8 slices (1 ounce each) Swiss cheese

EQUIPMENT

Blender	Whisk
Large covered saucepan	Ice cream scoop
Medium skillet	Kitchen knives
Baking sheet	Measuring cups and spoons
2 small mixing bowls	Cooking utensils

COUNTDOWN

1. Assemble the ingredients and the equipment.
2. Do Steps 1–3 of *Utahragon Soup*.
3. Do Steps 1–6 of *Provocative Avocados*.
4. Do Steps 4–5 of *Utahragon Soup*.
5. Do Step 7 of *Provocative Avocados*.
6. Do Steps 1–2 of *Loganberry Frost*.

MONDAY

Utahragon Soup

1 Peel and slice the onion. Rinse, stem, and quarter the tomatoes. Rinse, stem, and chop the tarragon.

2 Heat the oil in a large saucepan and sauté the onion until it is soft, about 5 minutes. Add the tomatoes, the tarragon, the broth, the consommé, the tomato juice, the thyme, the bay leaf, the sherry, and the cayenne pepper. Season to taste.

3 Bring to a boil, cover, reduce the heat, and simmer, stirring occasionally, for 20 minutes.

4 Remove the bay leaf.

5 Place half of the soup mixture in a blender and puree for 1 minute. Return to the saucepan, blend well, and heat through.

Provocative Avocados

1 Preheat the oven to 400°F.

2 Cook the bacon in a medium skillet until crisp, about 8 minutes. Drain on paper towels, reserving 3 tablespoons of the drippings.

3 Rinse, trim, seed, and slice the bell pepper. Peel and mince the garlic. Peel and thinly slice the onion. Halve, pit, peel, and slice the avocados and sprinkle them with the lemon juice. Cut each ham steak into quarters. Split the muffins in half.

4 In a small bowl, combine the mayonnaise, the garlic, and the mustard. Spread the mixture on the muffin halves.

5 Sauté the bell pepper and the onion in the reserved bacon drippings until they are soft, about 5 minutes.

6 Place the muffins on a baking sheet. Layer each half with the bacon, the bell pepper, the onion, the ham, the avocados, and the cheese.

7 Bake in the oven until the muffins are hot and the cheese begins to melt, about 5 minutes.

Loganberry Frost

1 Drain the loganberries, reserving 3 tablespoons of the liquid. Combine the reserved liquid and the powdered sugar in a small bowl.

2 Distribute the loganberries among individual dessert bowls, top with scoops of frozen yogurt, drizzle the sauce over the top, and garnish with the silver shots.

TUESDAY

Fowl Play

1/2 cup fresh parsley (when chopped)
1 clove garlic
3 pounds chicken pieces
2 cups seasoned breadcrumbs
1 cup grated Romano cheese
3 tablespoons butter
2 teaspoons Dijon mustard
1 teaspoon Worcestershire sauce
Seasoning to taste

Orzo They Say

1 small red onion
1 tablespoon vegetable oil
1 can (14 ounces) chicken broth with
    roasted garlic
1 quart water
1 cup orzo
Seasoning to taste

The Premeditated Pimiento

1 medium head romaine lettuce
2 stalks celery
1 small green bell pepper
2 scallions (green onions)
1 clove garlic
1 jar (2 ounces) diced pimientos
3 tablespoons olive oil
2 tablespoons white wine vinegar
1/2 teaspoon granulated sugar
1/2 teaspoon lemon-pepper seasoning
Seasoning to taste

Captive Cranberries

2 fresh mandarin oranges
1 1/4 cups milk
1 package (3.4 ounces) instant vanilla
    pudding mix
3/4 cup sour cream
1 can (8 ounces) whole cranberry sauce

EQUIPMENT

Electric mixer	Medium mixing bowl
Medium saucepan	Small mixing bowl
Small saucepan	Whisk
9 x 13-inch glass baking dish	Kitchen knives
Large shallow bowl	Measuring cups and spoons
Large mixing bowl	Cooking utensils

COUNTDOWN

1. Assemble the ingredients and the equipment.
2. Do Steps 1–6 of *Fowl Play.*
3. Do Steps 1–3 of *Captive Cranberries.*
4. Do Steps 1–2 of *Orzo They Say.*
5. Do Steps 1–2 of *The Premeditated Pimiento.*
6. Do Step 3 of *Orzo They Say.*
7. Do Step 3 of *The Premeditated Pimiento.*

TUESDAY

Fowl Play

1 Preheat the oven to 375°F. Grease a 9 x 13-inch baking dish.

2 Rinse, stem, and chop the parsley. Peel and mince the garlic. Rinse and pat dry the chicken pieces.

3 In a large shallow bowl, combine the parsley, the breadcrumbs, and the cheese.

4 Melt the butter in a small saucepan. Add the garlic, the mustard, and the Worcestershire sauce. Season to taste and heat through, about 2 minutes.

5 Dip the chicken pieces in the butter mixture, then roll them in the breadcrumb mixture.

6 Arrange the chicken in the baking dish. Pour the remaining butter mixture over the top. Bake, occasionally basting with the juices, until the chicken is tender, about 40 minutes.

Orzo They Say

1 Peel and finely chop the onion.

2 Heat the oil in a medium saucepan and sauté the onion for 3 minutes. Add the broth and the water and bring the mixture to a boil. Add the orzo and cook until almost tender, about 8 minutes.

3 Drain the orzo and season to taste.

The Premeditated Pimiento

1 Wash and dry the lettuce and tear it into bite-sized pieces. Rinse, trim, and slice the celery. Rinse, trim, seed, and thinly slice the bell pepper. Rinse, trim, and chop the scallions. Peel and chop the garlic. Drain the pimientos. Combine the ingredients in a large bowl.

2 In a small bowl, whisk together the oil, the vinegar, the sugar, and the lemon-pepper seasoning. Season to taste.

3 Toss the salad with the dressing.

Captive Cranberries

1 Peel and section the mandarin oranges.

2 In a medium bowl, combine the milk and the pudding mix and beat until the mixture is well blended, about 2 minutes. Fold in the sour cream.

3 Drain any liquid from the cranberry sauce and discard it. Mash the cranberries with a fork. Spoon into the bottom of individual dessert glasses. Top with the pudding. Garnish with the mandarin orange sections. Refrigerate until you are ready to serve.

WEDNESDAY

Coddle Up a Little Closer

1 clove garlic
4 cod fillets (about 1 1/2 pounds)
1 teaspoon lemon-pepper seasoning
2 tablespoons mayonnaise
2 tablespoons Dijon mustard
1 tablespoon dried dill
2 tablespoons butter
Seasoning to taste

Bundling Babies

1 1/2 pounds small new potatoes
2 tablespoons fresh chives (when chopped)
1 tablespoon lemon juice
1 tablespoon vegetable oil
1/2 teaspoon dried basil
Seasoning to taste

Smoochy Zucchini

1 small onion
3 small zucchini
2 tablespoons parsley (when chopped)
1 can (14 1/2 ounces) diced tomatoes
2 tablespoons olive oil
1 teaspoon dried oregano
Seasoning to taste

Not Tonight, Honey

1 frozen pound cake
1/3 cup honey
1/4 cup orange juice
1 tablespoon Grand Marnier
2 tablespoons butter
2 medium very ripe pears

EQUIPMENT

Medium saucepan	Vegetable brush
Small covered saucepan	Vegetable peeler
2 large covered skillets	Kitchen knives
Small mixing bowl	Measuring cups and spoons
Whisk	Cooking utensils

COUNTDOWN

1. Assemble the ingredients and the equipment.
2. Do Step 1 of *Not Tonight, Honey.*
3. Do Step 1 of *Smoochy Zucchini.*
4. Do Steps 1–2 of *Coddle Up a Little Closer.*
5. Do Step 2 of *Not Tonight, Honey.*
6. Do Steps 1–3 of *Bundling Babies.*
7. Do Step 3 of *Coddle Up a Little Closer.*
8. Do Step 2 of *Smoochy Zucchini.*
9. Do Step 4 of *Bundling Babies.*
10. Do Step 3 of *Smoochy Zucchini.*
11. Do Step 3 of *Not Tonight, Honey.*

WEDNESDAY

Coddle Up a Little Closer

1 Peel and chop the garlic. Rinse and pat dry the fish fillets and sprinkle with the lemon-pepper seasoning.

2 In a small bowl, combine the mayonnaise, the mustard, and the dill.

3 Melt the butter in a large skillet and sauté the garlic for 1 minute. Add the fish, cover the skillet, and cook for 3 minutes. Turn the fish and spread the mayonnaise mixture evenly over the fillets. Season to taste and cook until the fish flakes easily with a fork, about 3 minutes more.

Bundling Babies

1 Bring water to a boil in a medium saucepan.

2 Scrub the potatoes and prick them with a fork. Rinse, trim, and chop the chives.

3 Cook the potatoes until tender, 12 to 15 minutes.

4 Drain the potatoes and return them to the saucepan. Add the lemon juice and the oil and toss to coat. Add the basil and the chives, season to taste, and combine.

Smoochy Zucchini

1 Peel and thinly slice the onion. Scrub, trim, and thinly slice the zucchini. Rinse, trim, and chop the parsley. Drain the tomatoes.

2 Heat the oil in a large skillet and sauté the onion for 4 minutes. Add the zucchini and sauté for 2 minutes. Add the tomatoes and the oregano, season to taste, reduce the heat, cover, and simmer until hot, about 3 minutes.

3 Sprinkle with the parsley.

Not Tonight, Honey

1 Set the pound cake out to thaw.

2 In a small saucepan, combine the honey, the orange juice, the Grand Marnier, and the butter. Bring the mixture to a boil. Cover, remove from the heat, and set aside.

3 Slice the pound cake into individual servings. Peel, core, and thinly slice the pears and arrange them on top of the cake. Drizzle the sauce over the cake.

THURSDAY

Button Your Lip

4 loin pork chops (about 1 1/2 pounds)
Seasoning to taste
3 tablespoons flour
3 tablespoons fresh chives (when chopped)
1 can (4 ounces) whole button mushrooms
2 tablespoons vegetable oil ·
1 cup dry white wine
1/2 cup sour cream

Rice 'n' Easy

1 large onion
1/2 cup vermicelli (when broken)
4 tablespoons butter
1 cup long-grain white rice
1 can (14 ounces) chicken broth
1/2 cup water
Seasoning to taste

Jelly Beans

1 package (10 ounces) frozen baby lima
    beans
1/2 cup water
2 tablespoons butter
1/4 cup orange marmalade
Seasoning to taste

Precious Pumpkin

2 cups milk
1 teaspoon butter
3 eggs
1/2 cup dark brown sugar
1/4 teaspoon salt
1 cup canned pumpkin
1/2 teaspoon ground nutmeg
1/2 teaspoon ground cinnamon
1 teaspoon vanilla extract
Whipped cream for garnish

EQUIPMENT

Large saucepan
2 large covered
    skillets
Medium skillet
1-quart casserole
9 x 9-inch baking pan

Whisk
Kitchen knives
Measuring cups and
    spoons
Cooking utensils

COUNTDOWN

1. Assemble the ingredients and the equipment.
2. Do Steps 1–3 of *Precious Pumpkin*.
3. Do Steps 1–3 of *Button Your Lip*.
4. Do Steps 1–4 of *Rice 'n' Easy*.
5. Do Step 4 of *Button Your Lip*.
6. Do Step 1 of *Jelly Beans*.
7. Do Step 5 of *Button Your Lip*.
8. Do Step 2 of *Jelly Beans*.
9. Do Step 5 of *Rice 'n' Easy*.
10. Do Step 6 of *Button Your Lip*.
11. Do Step 4 of *Precious Pumpkin*.

THURSDAY

Button Your Lip

1 Trim any excess fat from the pork chops and season them to taste. Dust the chops with the flour. Rinse, trim, and chop the chives. Drain the mushrooms.

2 Heat the oil in a large skillet and cook the chops until they are browned on both sides, about 10 minutes.

3 Add the wine to the skillet and bring it to a boil. Reduce the heat, cover, and simmer until the pork is tender, about 20 minutes.

4 Add the mushrooms to the skillet. Simmer for 5 minutes.

5 Remove the pork and the mushrooms. Add the sour cream and the chives to the skillet, scraping up any brown bits from the bottom of the pan. Stir to combine and heat through, about 2 minutes.

6 Spoon the sauce over the pork chops.

Rice 'n' Easy

1 Peel and mince the onion. Break up the vermicelli into 2-inch pieces.

2 Melt half of the butter in a large skillet and sauté the onion until soft, about 5 minutes. Remove the onion and set aside.

3 Melt the remaining 2 tablespoons butter in the skillet. Add the rice and the vermicelli and sauté until the rice becomes opaque and the vermicelli turns golden, 3 to 4 minutes.

4 Add the broth and the water to the skillet. Return the onion. Season to taste. Cover, reduce the heat, and simmer until all the liquid is absorbed and the rice is tender, about 20 minutes.

5 Fluff with a fork.

Jelly Beans

1 Place the frozen lima beans in a medium skillet with the water and cook until heated through and tender, about 5 minutes.

2 Drain the beans. Add the butter and the marmalade, season to taste, and toss to combine.

Precious Pumpkin

1 Preheat the oven to 350°F.

2 Place the milk in a large saucepan and scald (small bubbles will form around the edge of the pan). Remove from the heat. Add the butter. Add the eggs, one at a time, whisking to blend. Add the brown sugar, the salt, the pumpkin, the nutmeg, the cinnamon, and the vanilla. Blend well.

3 Pour the mixture into a 1-quart casserole. Set the dish in a 9 x 9-inch baking pan and fill the pan halfway with hot water. Bake the custard until a knife inserted in the center comes out clean, 20 to 25 minutes.

4 Top each serving with a dollop of whipped cream.

FRIDAY

Strata Various

1 medium onion
1 large bunch broccoli
8 medium tomatoes
12 slices white bread
1 cup shredded Cheddar cheese
6 eggs
1 1/2 cups milk
1/4 teaspoon paprika
1/4 teaspoon dry mustard
Seasoning to taste
1 cup shredded Colby/Monterey Jack
   cheese

Grape Flute Salad

1 small head red leaf lettuce
1 large pink grapefruit
1 package (12 ounces) fresh cranberries
2 tablespoons orange juice
2 teaspoons honey
1 tablespoon red wine vinegar

Clarinut

1 can (15 ounces) apricot halves
2 tablespoons butter
1/4 cup pecan bits
1/3 cup maple syrup
1 pint butter pecan ice cream
4 prepared graham cracker tart shells

EQUIPMENT

Small saucepan	Strainer
9 x 13-inch glass baking dish	Ice cream scoop
Medium mixing bowl	Kitchen knives
Small mixing bowl	Measuring cups and spoons
Whisk	Cooking utensils

COUNTDOWN

1. Assemble the ingredients and the equipment.
2. Do Steps 1–5 of *Strata Various*.
3. Do Steps 1–2 of *Clarinut*.
4. Do Step 6 of *Strata Various*.
5. Do Steps 1–4 of *Grape Flute Salad*.
6. Do Step 7 of *Strata Various*.
7. Do Step 5 of *Grape Flute Salad*.
8. Do Step 3 of *Clarinut*.

FRIDAY

Strata Various

1 Grease a 9 x 13-inch baking dish.

2 Peel and chop the onion. Rinse and trim the broccoli, discarding the tough ends, and cut into bite-sized florets. Rinse, stem, and slice the tomatoes.

3 Place half of the bread in the bottom of the baking dish. Sprinkle with the Cheddar cheese. Arrange the broccoli over the cheese and add the onion. Top with the remaining bread.

4 In a medium bowl, combine the eggs, the milk, the paprika, and the mustard and season to taste. Pour the mixture over the bread. Cover and let stand for 10 minutes.

5 Preheat the oven to 375°F.

6 Bake the casserole for 30 minutes.

7 Arrange the tomatoes over the bread. Sprinkle with the Colby/Monterey Jack cheese and continue baking until hot and bubbly, about 5 minutes more.

Grape Flute Salad

1 Wash and dry the lettuce and distribute the leaves among individual salad plates.

2 Peel and section the grapefruit and arrange the sections over the lettuce.

3 Wash the cranberries, discarding any that are soft or discolored. Slice the cranberries in half and mound them over the grapefruit sections.

4 In a small bowl, whisk together the orange juice, the honey, and the vinegar.

5 Spoon the dressing over each salad.

Clarinut

1 Drain the apricots.

2 Melt the butter with the pecans in a small saucepan and cook for 2 minutes. Add the maple syrup, blend well, and cook for 1 minute more. Remove and set aside.

3 Place scoops of ice cream in individual tart shells, add the apricots, and spoon the sauce over the top.

WEEK NINE

Monday
It Used to Be Fusilli
Soon to Be Salad
Born to Be Biscuits
The Crust of the Matter

Tuesday
The Fish Marquette
Slaw Sainte Marie
Huron a Roll

Wednesday
Currier and Chives
Whistler's Muffin
Norman Rockwells

Thursday
A Berry Nice Chicken
The Right Stuff
Snips and Sprouts
Almost Splits

Friday
Shrimp and Save
Salad In a Mint
Chocolate Dollar

- ☐ Butter
- ☐ Flour
- ☐ Bisquick
- ☐ Baking powder
- ☐ Granulated sugar
- ☐ Powdered sugar
- ☐ Cocoa powder
- ☐ Olive oil
- ☐ Vegetable oil
- ☐ Apple cider vinegar
- ☐ Balsamic vinegar
- ☐ Red wine vinegar
- ☐ Lemon juice
- ☐ Dijon mustard
- ☐ Ketchup
- ☐ Mayonnaise
- ☐ Grated Parmesan cheese
- ☐ Celery seeds
- ☐ Sesame seeds
- ☐ Dried marjoram
- ☐ Dried oregano
- ☐ Curry powder
- ☐ Ground nutmeg
- ☐ Paprika
- ☐ Black pepper
- ☐ Poultry seasoning
- ☐ Red pepper flakes
- ☐ Salt
- ☐ Almond extract
- ☐ Vanilla extract

MEAT & POULTRY

1 1/2 pounds mild Italian sausage (M)

4 cube steaks (about 1 1/2 pounds) (W)

4 boneless, skinless chicken breast halves (about 1 1/2 pounds) (Th)

FISH

4 white fish fillets (about 1 1/2 pounds) (T)

1 1/2 pounds large shrimp, shelled and deveined (F)

FRESH PRODUCE

VEGETABLES

4 large baking potatoes (T)

1 pound Brussels sprouts (Th)

1 pound baby carrots (W)

2 stalks celery (M)

1 stalk celery (Th)

2 medium parsnips (Th)

1/2 pound mushrooms (M)

4 medium mushrooms (Th)

1 small head green cabbage (T)

1 small head red cabbage (T)

1 medium head lettuce (M)

1 medium head lettuce (F)

3 medium tomatoes (M)

2 medium tomatoes (F)

1 medium cucumber (M)

1 medium cucumber (F)

3 medium red bell peppers (M)

1 small red bell pepper (T)

1 large onion (M)

1 medium onion (Th)

2 medium onions (F)

1 small red onion (M)

1 small shallot (Th)

3 scallions (green onions) (T)

3 scallions (green onions) (F)

2 cloves garlic (M)

2 cloves garlic (T)

2 cloves garlic (W)

3 cloves garlic (F)

HERBS

3 tablespoons chives (when chopped) (W)

2 sprigs mint (F)

3 tablespoons parsley (when chopped) (T)

FRUIT

2 small ripe cantaloupe melons (W)

2 medium bananas (Th)

2 medium tart apples (W)

1/4 pound seedless red grapes (W)

CANS, JARS & BOTTLES

SOUPS

1 can (14 ounces) chicken broth (F)

1 can (10 3/4 ounces) golden mushroom soup (W)

FRUIT

1 can (8 ounces) pineapple tidbits (W)

1 can (16 ounces) whole cranberry sauce (Th)

4 maraschino cherries for garnish (Th)

SAUCES

1 can (6 ounces) tomato paste (M)

DESSERT & BAKING NEEDS

1 can (20 ounces) cherry pie filling (M)

1/4 cup caramel topping for garnish (Th)

1 jar (7 ounces) marshmallow crème (F)

2 squares (1 ounce each) unsweetened chocolate (F)

PACKAGED GOODS

PASTA, RICE & GRAINS

1 pound fusilli (M)

1 cup couscous (F)

BAKED GOODS

1 package (8 ounces) seasoned stuffing mix (Th)

1 prepared shortbread pie shell (M)

DRIED FRUIT & NUTS

1/2 cup sliced almonds (T)

1 cup sliced almonds (F)

DESSERT & BAKING NEEDS

1 cup rock or other hard candy (W)

WINE & SPIRITS

1/2 cup dry white wine (Th)

1/2 cup dry red wine (M)

REFRIGERATED PRODUCTS

DAIRY

2/3 cup milk (W)

1 cup milk (F)

2/3 cup half-and-half (M)

1 container (6 ounces) vanilla yogurt (W)

1/2 cup whipped cream (T)

Whipped cream for garnish (M)

1 egg (T)

1 egg (W)

1 egg (F)

FROZEN GOODS

VEGETABLES

1 package (10 ounces) green peas (W)

PASTRY

4 puff pastry shells (T)

DESSERTS

1 pint vanilla yogurt (Th)

MONDAY

It Used to Be Fusilli

1½ pounds mild Italian sausage
1 large onion
2 cloves garlic
3 medium red bell peppers
3 medium tomatoes
2 tablespoons vegetable oil
1 can (6 ounces) tomato paste
½ cup dry red wine
½ teaspoon red pepper flakes
Seasoning to taste
1 pound fusilli
½ cup grated Parmesan cheese

Soon to Be Salad

1 medium head lettuce
1 medium cucumber
2 stalks celery
½ pound fresh mushrooms
¼ cup olive oil
3 tablespoons balsamic vinegar
½ teaspoon dried oregano
Seasoning to taste

Born to Be Biscuits

1 small red onion
2 tablespoons butter
2 cups Bisquick
⅔ cup half-and-half
1 tablespoon sesame seeds

The Crust of the Matter

1 can (20 ounces) cherry pie filling
1 tablespoon lemon juice
1 prepared shortbread pie shell
Whipped cream for garnish
Ground nutmeg for garnish

EQUIPMENT

Stockpot	Vegetable peeler
Large covered skillet	Vegetable grater
Medium skillet	Biscuit cutter
Small skillet	Kitchen knives
Baking sheet	Measuring cups and spoons
Breadboard	Cooking utensils
Colander	
2 medium mixing bowls	

COUNTDOWN

1. Assemble the ingredients and the equipment.
2. Do Steps 1–2 of *The Crust of the Matter.*
3. Do Step 1 of *It Used to Be Fusilli.*
4. Do Steps 1–2 of *Soon to Be Salad.*
5. Do Steps 2–5 of *It Used to Be Fusilli.*
6. Do Steps 1–6 of *Born to Be Biscuits.*
7. Do Step 6 of *It Used to Be Fusilli.*
8. Do Step 3 of *Soon to Be Salad.*
9. Do Step 7 of *It Used to Be Fusilli.*

MONDAY

It Used to Be Fusilli

1 Place the sausage in the freezer for 10 minutes to chill.

2 Peel and chop the onion. Peel and mince the garlic. Rinse, trim, seed, and chop the bell peppers. Rinse, stem, and chop the tomatoes. Slice the sausage into ¼-inch-thick rounds.

3 Bring water to a boil in a stockpot.

4 Heat 1 tablespoon of the oil in a large skillet and sauté the sausage until it is browned, about 10 minutes. Remove the sausage and blot it on paper towels.

5 Heat the remaining 1 tablespoon oil and sauté the onion and the garlic for 3 minutes. Add the bell peppers and the tomatoes and sauté until the peppers are soft, about 5 minutes. Add the tomato paste and the wine, stirring to combine. Add the red pepper flakes and season to taste. Return the sausage, cover the skillet, and simmer for 10 minutes.

6 Cook the fusilli in the stockpot until it is almost tender, 8 to 10 minutes.

7 Drain the pasta, top it with the sausage mixture, and sprinkle with the cheese.

Soon to Be Salad

1 Wash and dry the lettuce and distribute the leaves among individual salad plates. Peel, trim, and slice the cucumber and arrange the slices over the lettuce.

2 Rinse, trim, and chop the celery. Rinse, pat dry, trim, and thinly slice the mushrooms.

3 In a medium skillet, heat the oil with the vinegar and the oregano. Season to taste. Add the celery and the mushrooms and sauté for 1 minute. Spoon the mushroom mixture over the lettuce and cucumber.

Born to Be Biscuits

1 Preheat the oven to 425°F. Flour a breadboard.

2 Peel and grate the onion.

3 Melt the butter in a small skillet and sauté the onion until tender, about 3 minutes. Remove from the heat and set aside.

4 Combine the Bisquick and the half-and-half in a medium bowl. Turn the mixture out onto the breadboard and knead gently until smooth, 8 to 10 times. Pat the dough out to a ¼-inch thickness. Cut with a biscuit cutter and place the biscuits on a baking sheet.

5 Make an indentation in the top of each biscuit. Spoon a teaspoon of the onion mixture into the center of each biscuit and sprinkle with the sesame seeds.

6 Bake until golden, 10 to 12 minutes.

The Crust of the Matter

1 In a medium bowl, combine the cherry pie filling and the lemon juice. Pour the mixture into the pie shell.

2 Top with dollops of whipped cream and sprinkle with the nutmeg. Refrigerate until you are ready to serve.

TUESDAY

The Fish Marquette

4 white fish fillets (about 1 1/2 pounds)
4 large baking potatoes
2 cloves garlic
3 tablespoons fresh parsley (when chopped)
4 tablespoons vegetable oil
Seasoning to taste

Slaw Sainte Marie

1 small red bell pepper
1 small head green cabbage
1 small head red cabbage
3 scallions (green onions)
1/2 cup mayonnaise
2 teaspoons granulated sugar
3 tablespoons apple cider vinegar
1 teaspoon celery seeds
Seasoning to taste

Huron a Roll

4 frozen puff pastry shells
1 egg
1 tablespoon water
1/4 cup granulated sugar
1 teaspoon almond extract
1/2 cup whipped cream
1/2 cup sliced almonds
Powdered sugar for garnish

EQUIPMENT

Electric mixer
2 baking sheets
Large mixing bowl
2 medium mixing bowls
2 small mixing bowls
Whisk
Vegetable peeler
Vegetable grater
Pastry brush
Plastic wrap
Kitchen knives
Measuring cups and spoons
Cooking utensils

COUNTDOWN

1. Assemble the ingredients and the equipment.
2. Do Steps 1–8 of *Huron a Roll.*
3. Do Steps 1–4 of *The Fish Marquette.*
4. Do Steps 1–2 of *Slaw Sainte Marie.*
5. Do Steps 5–6 of *The Fish Marquette.*
6. Do Step 9 of *Huron a Roll.*

TUESDAY

The Fish Marquette

1 Increase the oven temperature to 450°F.

2 Rinse and pat dry the fish fillets. Peel and julienne the potatoes. Peel and mince the garlic. Rinse, stem, and chop the parsley.

3 Place the oil in a medium bowl. Add the garlic and the potatoes and toss lightly to coat. Lay the potato slices in a single layer on a baking sheet. Season to taste.

4 Bake until the potatoes are golden, about 12 to 15 minutes.

5 Turn the potatoes over and bake for 5 minutes more.

6 Brush the fish with any remaining oil and garlic mixture. Lay the fish fillets over the potatoes and bake until the fish flakes easily with a fork, about 8 minutes. Season to taste and garnish with the parsley.

Slaw Sainte Marie

1 Rinse, trim, seed, and thinly slice the bell pepper. Rinse, trim, quarter, and grate the cabbage. Rinse, stem, and chop the scallions. Combine the ingredients in a large bowl.

2 In a small bowl, combine the mayonnaise, the sugar, the vinegar, and the celery seeds. Season to taste and toss with the slaw.

Huron a Roll

1 Preheat the oven to 400°F.

2 Set the pastry shells on a baking sheet.

3 Separate the egg, putting the white in a medium bowl and the yolk in a small bowl.

4 Whip the egg yolk with the water and brush the mixture over the pastry shells.

5 Bake until puffed, about 15 minutes.

6 Beat the egg white until light and fluffy, about 2 minutes. Gradually add the granulated sugar and beat until the mixture is thick and glossy, about 2 minutes more. Fold in the almond extract. Fold in the whipped cream. Cover with plastic wrap and refrigerate until you are ready to use.

7 Remove the pastry shells from the oven and lift off the tops, setting them beside the puffs. Place the almonds in the shells, return the baking sheet to the oven, and bake for 5 minutes more.

8 Remove the pastries from the oven and let cool.

9 Fill the pastries with the whipped cream mixture. Replace the tops and dust with the powdered sugar.

WEDNESDAY

Currier and Chives

1 package (10 ounces) frozen green peas
2 cloves garlic
1 pound baby carrots
3 tablespoons fresh chives (when chopped)
2 tablespoons vegetable oil
4 cube steaks (about 1 1/2 pounds)
1/2 cup water
1 can (10 3/4 ounces) golden mushroom soup
1 1/2 teaspoons curry powder
Seasoning to taste

Whistler's Muffin

2 medium tart apples
2 cups Bisquick
3 tablespoons granulated sugar
3 tablespoons vegetable oil
1 egg
2/3 cup milk

Norman Rockwells

1 cup rock or other hard candy
2 small ripe cantaloupe melons
1/4 pound seedless red grapes
1 can (8 ounces) pineapple tidbits
1 container (6 ounces) vanilla yogurt

EQUIPMENT

Medium covered saucepan
Large covered skillet
Muffin tin
2 large mixing bowls
2 small mixing bowls
Whisk
Vegetable grater

Melon baller
Mallet
Plastic bag
Kitchen knives
Measuring cups and spoons
Cooking utensils

COUNTDOWN

1. Assemble the ingredients and the equipment.
2. Do Steps 1–4 of *Norman Rockwells*.
3. Do Steps 1–3 of *Whistler's Muffin*.
4. Do Steps 1–8 of *Currier and Chives*.
5. Do Steps 4–5 of *Whistler's Muffin*.
6. Do Steps 9–10 of *Currier and Chives*.
7. Do Step 5 of *Norman Rockwells*.

WEDNESDAY

Currier and Chives

1 Set the peas in a small bowl of warm water to thaw.

2 Bring water to a boil in a medium saucepan.

3 Peel and mince the garlic. Rinse and trim the carrots. Rinse, trim, and chop the chives.

4 Cook the carrots until they are crisp-tender, about 10 minutes.

5 Heat the oil in a large skillet and sauté the garlic for 1 minute. Brown the cube steaks, about 3 minutes per side.

6 Drain the carrots, return them to the saucepan, and cover to keep warm.

7 Remove the steaks and cover to keep warm.

8 Add the ½ cup water, the soup, and the curry powder to the skillet. Heat through and stir to blend. Return the steaks to the skillet. Cover and cook until the beef is tender, about 5 minutes, turning occasionally.

9 Add the peas and the carrots to the skillet, season to taste, and simmer for 2 minutes.

10 Garnish with the chives.

Whistler's Muffin

1 Grease a muffin tin.

2 Rinse, quarter, core, and grate the apples.

3 Combine the apples, the Bisquick, the sugar, the oil, the egg, and the milk in a large bowl. Blend well.

4 Increase the oven temperature to 400°F.

5 Spoon the batter into the muffin cups. Bake until the muffins are golden, about 15 minutes.

Norman Rockwells

1 Place the rock candy in a plastic bag and crush with a mallet.

2 Cut the melons in half and remove the seeds. Using a melon baller, hollow out the halves and place the balls in a large bowl. Place the melon shells in individual dessert bowls.

3 Rinse and stem the grapes and add them to the melon balls. Drain the pineapple, reserving 2 tablespoons of the liquid, and add the tidbits to the melon balls and grapes.

4 In a small bowl, combine the yogurt with the reserved pineapple liquid. Toss with the fruit and fill the melon shells.

5 Top with the crushed rock candy.

THURSDAY

A Berry Nice Chicken

1 medium onion
4 boneless, skinless chicken breast halves
    (about 1 1/2 pounds)
1 tablespoon butter
1/3 cup ketchup
1 can (16 ounces) whole cranberry sauce
1 tablespoon apple cider vinegar
1 tablespoon Dijon mustard

The Right Stuff

1 small shallot
1 stalk celery
4 medium fresh mushrooms
2 tablespoons butter
1 package (8 ounces) seasoned stuffing mix
1 teaspoon poultry seasoning
1/2 cup dry white wine
Seasoning to taste

Snips and Sprouts

2 medium parsnips
1 pound Brussels sprouts
1 tablespoon butter
1/2 teaspoon dried marjoram
1/4 teaspoon paprika

Almost Splits

2 medium bananas
1 pint vanilla frozen yogurt
1/4 cup caramel topping for garnish
4 maraschino cherries for garnish

EQUIPMENT

Large skillet	Vegetable peeler
Large covered skillet	Ice cream scoop
Small skillet	Kitchen knives
9 x 13-inch glass baking dish	Measuring cups and spoons
9 x 9-inch baking dish	Cooking utensils
Large mixing bowl	

COUNTDOWN

1. Assemble the ingredients and the equipment.
2. Do Step 1 of *A Berry Nice Chicken*.
3. Do Step 1 of *The Right Stuff*.
4. Do Step 2 of *A Berry Nice Chicken*.
5. Do Steps 2–3 of *The Right Stuff*.
6. Do Steps 3–4 of *A Berry Nice Chicken*.
7. Do Steps 1–3 of *Snips and Sprouts*.
8. Do Steps 4–5 of *The Right Stuff*.
9. Do Step 5 of *A Berry Nice Chicken*.
10. Do Step 4 of *Snips and Sprouts*.
11. Do Steps 1–2 of *Almost Splits*.

THURSDAY

A Berry Nice Chicken

1 Preheat the oven to 350°F. Grease a 9 x 13-inch baking dish.

2 Peel and chop the onion. Rinse and pat dry the chicken breasts.

3 Melt the butter in a large skillet and sauté the onion until it is soft, about 5 minutes. Add the ketchup, the cranberry sauce, the vinegar, and the mustard and whisk gently to blend. Reduce the heat and simmer for 3 minutes.

4 Arrange the chicken breasts in the baking dish in a single layer. Spread with half the sauce and bake for 15 minutes.

5 Spoon the remaining sauce over the chicken and bake until the chicken is cooked through, 10 to 15 minutes.

The Right Stuff

1 Grease a 9 x 9-inch baking dish.

2 Peel and chop the shallot. Rinse, trim, and chop the celery. Rinse, pat dry, trim, and chop the mushrooms.

3 Melt the butter in a small skillet. Add the shallot and the celery and sauté until soft, about 5 minutes. Add the mushrooms and sauté for another 2 minutes.

4 In a large bowl, combine the stuffing mix with the celery mixture, the poultry seasoning, and the wine. Blend well and season to taste.

5 Pour the mixture into the baking dish and bake at 350°F until golden brown, 15 to 20 minutes.

Snips and Sprouts

1 Peel and trim the parsnips and cut them into 1/4-inch-thick slices. Wash and trim the Brussels sprouts.

2 Bring water to a boil in a large skillet.

3 Add the parsnips and the sprouts, cover, and cook until the vegetables are crisp-tender, 8 to 10 minutes.

4 Drain the vegetables. Toss them with the butter and the marjoram and sprinkle with the paprika. Cover to keep warm.

Almost Splits

1 Peel and slice the bananas and distribute them among individual dessert bowls.

2 Place scoops of yogurt over the bananas, drizzle with the caramel topping, and top with a maraschino cherry.

FRIDAY

Shrimp and Save

2 medium onions
3 cloves garlic
1½ pounds large shrimp, shelled and
  deveined
1 cup sliced almonds
1 tablespoon butter
1 can (14 ounces) chicken broth
2 tablespoons lemon juice
1 cup couscous
3 tablespoons olive oil
Seasoning to taste

Salad In a Mint

1 medium head lettuce
2 medium tomatoes
3 scallions (green onions)
1 medium cucumber
2 sprigs fresh mint
3 tablespoons vegetable oil
2 tablespoons red wine vinegar
1 teaspoon dried oregano
Seasoning to taste

Chocolate Dollar

1 cup flour
2 teaspoons baking powder
¼ teaspoon salt
1 cup granulated sugar
1 egg
1 cup milk
2 squares (1 ounce each) unsweetened
  chocolate
2 tablespoons butter
1 teaspoon vanilla extract
1 jar (7 ounces) marshmallow crème
1 tablespoon cocoa powder for garnish

EQUIPMENT

Medium covered saucepan	2 small mixing bowls
Small saucepan	Vegetable peeler
Large skillet	Whisk
Small skillet	Kitchen knives
Round cake pan	Measuring cups and spoons
2 large mixing bowls	Cooking utensils

COUNTDOWN

1. Assemble the ingredients and the equipment.
2. Do Steps 1–6 of *Chocolate Dollar*.
3. Do Steps 1–2 of *Salad In a Mint*.
4. Do Steps 1–6 of *Shrimp and Save*.
5. Do Step 3 of *Salad In a Mint*.
6. Do Step 7 of *Chocolate Dollar*.

FRIDAY

Shrimp and Save

1 Peel and chop the onions. Peel and mince the garlic. Rinse and pat dry the shrimp.

2 Spread the almonds in a small skillet and toast until golden, stirring often, about 2 minutes. Set aside.

3 Melt the butter in a medium saucepan. Add the broth and the lemon juice and bring to a boil.

4 Stir in the couscous, cover, and remove from the heat. Let stand for 10 minutes.

5 Heat the oil in a large skillet and sauté the onions for 5 minutes. Add the garlic and sauté until the onions are golden brown, about 5 minutes.

6 Add the shrimp to the skillet and sauté until they turn bright pink, about 3 minutes. Mix in the almonds and season to taste. Fluff the couscous and add it to the skillet.

Salad In a Mint

1 Wash and dry the lettuce and tear it into bite-sized pieces. Rinse, stem, and chop the tomatoes. Rinse, trim, and chop the scallions. Peel, trim, and slice the cucumber. Combine the ingredients in a large bowl. Rinse, stem, and chop the mint.

2 In a small bowl, combine the oil, the vinegar, the oregano, and the mint. Season to taste.

3 Toss the salad with the dressing.

Chocolate Dollar

1 Preheat the oven to 350°F. Grease a round cake pan.

2 In a large bowl, combine the flour, the baking powder, the salt, and the sugar.

3 In a small bowl, mix together the egg and the milk.

4 Slowly melt the chocolate with the butter in a small saucepan.

5 Beat the egg mixture into the flour mixture and blend well. Blend in the chocolate mixture and the vanilla.

6 Pour the batter into the cake pan and bake until a toothpick inserted in the center comes out clean, about 35 minutes.

7 Frost the cake with the marshmallow crème and sprinkle with the cocoa powder.

WEEK TEN

Monday
Omelet Go
Zoot Fruit
Dough Re Me
Anonymousse

Tuesday
Egg Wynn
W. C. Fields
Molly Pecans
Zasu Pits

Wednesday
Honey Bee Chicken
Mount Ricemore
Pasque the Peas
Berry My Heart at Wounded Knee

Thursday
Sole What?
Yam Good
It's Bean Swell
Bears Repeating

Friday
Meatless In Seattle
Microchips
Monorolls
Ferryboat Fruit

- ☐ Butter
- ☐ Flour
- ☐ Baking powder
- ☐ Baking soda
- ☐ Cornstarch
- ☐ Cream of tartar
- ☐ Granulated sugar
- ☐ Chocolate syrup
- ☐ Maple syrup
- ☐ Multicolored sprinkles
- ☐ Olive oil
- ☐ Vegetable oil
- ☐ Apple cider vinegar
- ☐ Tarragon vinegar
- ☐ White wine vinegar
- ☐ Dijon mustard
- ☐ Honey
- ☐ Worcestershire sauce
- ☐ Grated Parmesan cheese
- ☐ Poppy seeds
- ☐ Dried basil
- ☐ Dried dill
- ☐ Dried oregano
- ☐ Dried tarragon
- ☐ Dried thyme
- ☐ Ground allspice
- ☐ Ground cinnamon
- ☐ Ground cloves
- ☐ Ground nutmeg
- ☐ Paprika
- ☐ Black pepper
- ☐ Salt
- ☐ Brandy extract

MEAT & POULTRY

4 boneless, skinless chicken breast halves (about 1½ pounds) (W)

FISH

4 sole fillets (about 1½ pounds) (Th)

FRESH PRODUCE

VEGETABLES

4 small yams (Th)
1 large bunch broccoli (F)
1 pound green beans (Th)
1 pound sugar-snap peas (W)
2 medium eggplants (T)
2 medium zucchini (F)
2 medium carrots (F)
2 stalks celery (F)
1 medium head lettuce (T)
1 medium head lettuce (F)
2 small ripe avocados (T)
2 medium cucumbers (F)
1 small yellow bell pepper (Th)
1 small bunch radishes (F)
1 small onion (M)
1 small onion (W)
1 medium sweet onion (T)
1 medium red onion (F)
1 medium shallot (Th)
4 scallions (green onions) (M)
2 scallions (green onions) (W)
2 cloves garlic (T)
1 clove garlic (W)
2 cloves garlic (F)

HERBS

2 tablespoons parsley (when chopped) (T)
3 tablespoons parsley (when chopped) (F)

FRUIT

2 large oranges (T)
1 large lemon (W)
2 large bananas (T)

2 medium ripe pears (F)
½ pound seedless red grapes (T)
½ pound seedless green grapes (Th)

CANS, JARS & BOTTLES

SOUPS

1 can (14 ounces) vegetable broth (W)

VEGETABLES

1 jar (7 ounces) roasted red peppers (T)
1 can (11 ounces) whole-kernel white corn (W)

FRUIT

1 can (15 ounces) pink grapefruit sections (M)
1 can (11 ounces) mandarin oranges (M)
1 can (15 ounces) sliced peaches (M)
1 can (15 ounces) almond-flavored apricots (F)

SAUCES

1 can (8 ounces) tomato sauce (W)

JUICES

½ cup apple juice (T)
½ cup white grape juice (T)

CONDIMENTS

1 jar (3 ounces) pimiento-stuffed green olives (T)

DESSERT & BAKING NEEDS

1 can (14 ounces) sweetened condensed milk (Th)
6 ounces chocolate chips (Th)

PACKAGED GOODS

PASTA, RICE & GRAINS

1 pound fettuccine (T)
1 pound rotini (F)
1 cup brown rice (W)

BAKED GOODS

1 small loaf rye bread (M)
1 cup corn chips (when crumbled) (F)
2 cups graham cracker crumbs (Th)

DRIED FRUIT & NUTS

½ pound prunes (T)
1 cup pecan bits (T)
½ cup shelled unsalted pumpkin seeds (W)

WINE & SPIRITS

½ cup dry red wine (T)
2 tablespoons dry sherry (Th)
1 tablespoon Kahlúa (M)

REFRIGERATED PRODUCTS

DAIRY

1 cup milk (W)
1 cup half-and-half (M)
½ cup half-and-half (Th)
1 cup whipping cream (M)
9 eggs (M)
1 egg (T)
2 eggs (W)

CHEESE

12 ounces pepper Jack cheese (M)
½ cup shredded mozzarella cheese (T)
1 container (15 ounces) ricotta cheese (F)

DELI

8 slices bacon (M)
1 package (8 ounces) refrigerated crescent rolls (F)

FROZEN GOODS

FRUIT

1 package (10 ounces) raspberries (W)

DESSERTS

1 pint caramel frozen yogurt (F)

MONDAY

Omelet Go

8 slices bacon
4 scallions (green onions)
12 ounces pepper Jack cheese
9 eggs
1 cup half-and-half
Seasoning to taste

Zoot Fruit

1 can (15 ounces) pink grapefruit sections
1 can (11 ounces) mandarin oranges
1 can (15 ounces) sliced peaches
2 tablespoons apple cider vinegar
1 teaspoon ground cloves
2 teaspoons ground cinnamon

Dough Re Me

4 tablespoons butter
1 small loaf rye bread
1/2 teaspoon paprika
1 small onion

Anonymousse

1 cup whipping cream
1 tablespoon Kahlùa
2/3 cup chocolate syrup
Multicolored sprinkles for garnish

EQUIPMENT

Electric mixer	Small mixing bowl
Medium covered saucepan	Whisk
Medium skillet	Cheese grater
9 x 13-inch glass baking dish	Aluminum foil
Large mixing bowl	Kitchen knives
Medium mixing bowl	Measuring cups and spoons
	Cooking utensils

COUNTDOWN

1. Assemble the ingredients and the equipment.
2. Do Step 1 of *Dough Re Me*.
3. Do Step 1 of *Anonymousse*.
4. Do Steps 1–2 of *Omelet Go*.
5. Do Step 2 of *Anonymousse*.
6. Do Steps 3–6 of *Omelet Go*.
7. Do Steps 2–5 of *Dough Re Me*.
8. Do Steps 1–3 of *Zoot Fruit*.
9. Do Step 7 of *Omelet Go*.
10. Do Step 3 of *Anonymousse*.

MONDAY

Omelet Go

1 Preheat the oven to 350°F. Grease 9 x 13-inch baking dish.

2 Dice the bacon. Rinse, trim, and chop the scallions. Grate the cheese.

3 Sauté the bacon in a medium skillet until crisp, about 10 minutes.

4 Drain the bacon on paper towels. Sauté the scallions in the bacon drippings until soft, about 2 minutes.

5 Combine the eggs and the half-and-half in a large bowl and whip until smooth and light. Season to taste. Add the bacon and the scallions. Stir in half of the cheese. Pour the mixture into the baking dish.

6 Bake until the mixture is lightly browned, about 25 minutes.

7 Sprinkle with the remaining cheese and continue to bake until the cheese is melted, about 5 minutes more.

Zoot Fruit

1 Drain the grapefruit. Drain the mandarin oranges.

2 Place the grapefruit and the oranges in a medium saucepan. Add the undrained peaches. Stir in the vinegar, the cloves, and the cinnamon.

3 Bring the mixture to a boil and cook for 2 minutes. Remove from the heat and cover to keep warm.

Dough Re Me

1 Set the butter out to soften.

2 Cut the bread into ¾-inch-thick slices, but not quite all the way through.

3 In a small bowl, combine the softened butter with the paprika.

4 Peel and thinly slice the onion. Spread the butter lightly onto the cut surfaces of the bread and slip a slice of onion into each cut.

5 Wrap the bread in aluminum foil and bake at 350°F for 20 minutes.

Anonymousse

1 Chill a medium bowl and the beaters of an electric mixer for 10 minutes.

2 Whip the cream until soft peaks form, about 2 minutes. Add the Kahlùa and continue to beat until stiff, about 3 minutes more. Fold in the chocolate syrup. Spoon the mixture into individual dessert glasses and freeze until you are ready to serve.

3 Top each mousse with a splash of sprinkles.

TUESDAY

Egg Wynn

2 medium eggplants
2 cloves garlic
2 tablespoons fresh parsley (when chopped)
1 jar (7 ounces) roasted red peppers
1 jar (3 ounces) pimiento-stuffed green olives
1/2 teaspoon dried oregano
1 pound fettuccine
1/2 cup dry red wine
Seasoning to taste
1/2 cup shredded mozzarella cheese

W. C. Fields

1 medium head lettuce
2 large oranges
2 small ripe avocados
1 medium sweet onion
3 tablespoons vegetable oil
2 tablespoons white wine vinegar
1 tablespoon honey
Seasoning to taste

Molly Pecans

2 cups flour
1 tablespoon baking powder
1/2 teaspoon baking soda
1/2 teaspoon salt
1/2 cup apple juice
1/2 cup maple syrup
1 egg
1/3 cup vegetable oil
1 cup pecan bits

Zasu Pits

2 cups water
1/2 pound dried prunes
2 large bananas
1/2 pound seedless red grapes
2 tablespoons butter
1 teaspoon granulated sugar
1/2 teaspoon ground allspice
1/2 cup white grape juice
1/2 teaspoon ground cinnamon

EQUIPMENT

Stockpot
Large covered skillet
Medium covered skillet
Muffin tin
Colander
Large mixing bowl
2 medium mixing bowls

2 small mixing bowls
Whisk
Kitchen knives
Measuring cups and spoons
Cooking utensils

COUNTDOWN

1. Assemble the ingredients and the equipment.
2. Do Step 1 of *Zasu Pits.*
3. Do Steps 1–4 of *Molly Pecans.*
4. Do Step 2 of *Zasu Pits.*
5. Do Steps 1–3 of *W. C. Fields.*
6. Do Steps 1–3 of *Egg Wynn.*
7. Do Step 5 of *Molly Pecans.*
8. Do Steps 3–6 of *Zasu Pits.*
9. Do Steps 4–7 of *Egg Wynn.*
10. Do Step 4 of *W. C. Fields.*
11. Do Step 7 of *Zasu Pits.*

TUESDAY

Egg Wynn

1 Rinse and trim the eggplants and cut them into ½-inch cubes. Peel and mince the garlic. Rinse, stem, and chop the parsley. Drain the roasted peppers, reserving 3 tablespoons of the oil. Pat dry and quarter the peppers. Drain the olives and slice them in half.

2 Heat the reserved oil in a large skillet and sauté the garlic with the eggplants and the oregano for 10 minutes.

3 Bring water to a boil in a stockpot.

4 Cook the fettuccine until it is almost tender, 2 to 3 minutes if you are using fresh pasta, 6 to 7 minutes if you are using dry pasta.

5 Add the wine to the skillet, cover, reduce the heat, and simmer for 5 minutes.

6 Add the roasted peppers and the olives to the skillet. Heat through. Season to taste.

7 Drain the pasta. Spoon the eggplant mixture over the pasta and top with the parsley and the cheese.

W. C. Fields

1 Wash and dry the lettuce and arrange the leaves on individual salad plates.

2 Peel and section the oranges and cut the sections in half. Halve, pit, peel, and chunk the avocados. Peel and thinly slice the onion. Combine the ingredients in a medium bowl.

3 In a small bowl, whisk together the oil, the vinegar, and the honey. Season to taste.

4 Toss the orange mixture with the dressing and spoon over the lettuce.

Molly Pecans

1 Preheat the oven to 400°F. Grease a muffin tin.

2 In a large bowl, combine the flour, the baking powder, the baking soda, and the salt.

3 In a small bowl, whisk together the apple juice, the maple syrup, the egg, and the oil. Add the egg mixture to the flour mixture and blend well. Fold in the nuts.

4 Spoon the batter into the muffin cups.

5 Bake until the muffins are golden, 15 to 18 minutes.

Zasu Pits

1 Bring the water to a boil.

2 Place the prunes in a medium bowl and pour the boiling water over them. Set aside.

3 Peel and chunk the bananas. Rinse and stem the grapes and cut them in half.

4 Drain the prunes. Melt the butter with the sugar and the allspice in a medium skillet and sauté the prunes, the bananas, and the grapes until they are lightly glazed, about 5 minutes.

5 Add the grape juice and bring the mixture to a boil. Reduce the heat and simmer until the liquid begins to thicken, about 5 minutes.

6 Remove the skillet from the heat and cover to keep warm.

7 Spoon the fruit into individual dessert dishes and sprinkle with the cinnamon.

WEDNESDAY

Honey Bee Chicken

4 boneless, skinless chicken breast halves
   (about 1 1/2 pounds)
1 small onion
1 clove garlic
1 can (8 ounces) tomato sauce
1/4 cup honey
1/4 cup white wine vinegar
1 tablespoon Worcestershire sauce
1 teaspoon paprika
Seasoning to taste

Mount Ricemore

2 scallions (green onions)
2 tablespoons butter
1 cup brown rice
1 can (14 ounces) vegetable broth
1/2 cup water
1/2 cup shelled unsalted pumpkin seeds

Pasque the Peas

1 pound sugar-snap peas
1 can (11 ounces) whole-kernel white corn
1 teaspoon Dijon mustard
1 tablespoon apple cider vinegar
1/2 teaspoon dried tarragon
1/2 teaspoon dried basil
1/2 teaspoon granulated sugar
Seasoning to taste

Berry My Heart at Wounded Knee

1 package (10 ounces) frozen raspberries
1 large lemon
2 eggs
1 cup granulated sugar
2 tablespoons flour
1/4 teaspoon salt
1 cup milk
1/4 teaspoon cream of tartar
2 tablespoons butter

EQUIPMENT

Electric mixer
Medium covered
   saucepan
Medium saucepan
9 x 13-inch glass
   baking dish
1-quart casserole
9 x 9-inch baking pan
Large mixing bowl

Medium mixing bowl
2 small mixing bowls
Whisk
Citrus grater
Citrus juicer
Kitchen knives
Measuring cups and
   spoons
Cooking utensils

COUNTDOWN

1. Assemble the ingredients and the equipment.
2. Do Steps 1–7 of *Berry My Heart at Wounded Knee*.
3. Do Steps 1–4 of *Honey Bee Chicken*.
4. Do Steps 1–2 of *Mount Ricemore*.
5. Do Steps 1–4 of *Pasque the Peas*.
6. Do Step 3 of *Mount Ricemore*.

WEDNESDAY

Honey Bee Chicken

1 Grease a 9 x 13-inch baking dish.

2 Rinse and pat dry the chicken breasts. Peel and thinly slice the onion. Peel and mince the garlic. Arrange the chicken in the baking dish. Sprinkle the onion and the garlic on top.

3 In a small bowl, combine the tomato sauce, the honey, the vinegar, the Worcestershire sauce, and the paprika. Season to taste.

4 Pour the mixture over the chicken and bake at 375°F for 25 minutes.

Mount Ricemore

1 Rinse, trim, and chop the scallions.

2 Melt the butter in a medium saucepan and sauté the scallions for 1 minute. Add the rice and sauté for 3 minutes more. Stir in the broth and the water. Bring to a boil, reduce the heat, and cover. Simmer until all the liquid is absorbed and rice is tender, about 40 minutes.

3 Fluff the rice and fold in the pumpkin seeds.

Pasque the Peas

1 Rinse and string the snap peas. Drain the corn.

2 Bring water to a boil in a medium saucepan.

3 Cook the snap peas for 2 minutes.

4 Drain the snap peas and return them to the saucepan. Add the corn, the mustard, the vinegar, the tarragon, the basil, and the sugar. Stir to combine and heat through. Season to taste.

Berry My Heart at Wounded Knee

1 Set the raspberries in a small bowl of warm water to thaw.

2 Preheat the oven to 375°F.

3 Grate 2 tablespoons of lemon peel. Juice the lemon. Separate the eggs, placing the yolks in a large bowl and the whites in a medium bowl.

4 Beat the yolks. Add the sugar, the flour, the salt, the lemon peel, the lemon juice, and the milk. Beat to combine for 1 minute.

5 Beat the egg whites with the cream of tartar until stiff, about 2 minutes.

6 Melt the butter and add it to the egg yolk mixture. Fold in the egg whites. Fold in the berries. Spoon the mixture into a 1-quart casserole.

7 Set the casserole in a 9 x 9-inch baking pan half-filled with hot water and bake until the pudding is set and golden on top, about 40 minutes.

THURSDAY

Sole What?

4 sole fillets (about 1 1/2 pounds)
1/2 pound seedless green grapes
1/3 cup flour
1 teaspoon ground nutmeg
3 tablespoons butter
1/2 cup half-and-half
2 tablespoons dry sherry
Seasoning to taste

Yam Good

4 small yams
2 tablespoons butter
1 teaspoon ground cinnamon

It's Bean Swell

1 pound fresh green beans
1 medium shallot
1 small yellow bell pepper
2 tablespoons vegetable oil
1/2 teaspoon dried basil
Seasoning to taste
1/4 cup water

Bears Repeating

2 cups graham cracker crumbs
1 can (14 ounces) sweetened condensed milk
1/4 cup chocolate syrup
6 ounces chocolate chips
1 teaspoon brandy extract
1/4 teaspoon salt

EQUIPMENT

Large skillet
Medium covered skillet
9 x 9-inch glass baking dish
Medium mixing bowl
Vegetable brush

Waxed paper
Aluminum foil
Kitchen knives
Measuring cups and spoons
Cooking utensils

COUNTDOWN

1. Assemble the ingredients and the equipment.
2. Do Steps 1–3 of Yam Good.
3. Do Steps 1–2 of Sole What?
4. Do Step 4 of Yam Good.
5. Do Steps 1–3 of Bears Repeating.
6. Do Step 1 of It's Bean Swell.
7. Do Step 3 of Sole What?
8. Do Steps 2–3 of It's Bean Swell.
9. Do Steps 4–5 of Sole What?
10. Do Step 5 of Yam Good.
11. Do Step 6 of Sole What?

THURSDAY

Sole What?

1 Rinse and pat dry the fish fillets. Rinse and stem the grapes.

2 Place the flour on a sheet of waxed paper. Dredge both sides of the fish fillets in the flour, shaking off and reserving the excess. Sprinkle the fillets with the nutmeg.

3 Melt the butter in a large skillet and cook the fish until it is golden on both sides and flakes easily with a fork, 3 to 4 minutes per side.

4 Carefully remove the fish and cover to keep warm.

5 Blend the reserved flour with the half-and-half and add it to the skillet. Blend in the sherry and simmer for 5 minutes.

6 Fold in the grapes. Season to taste and pour the sauce over the fish.

Yam Good

1 Preheat the oven to 425°F.

2 Scrub the yams and prick them along the top with a fork.

3 Place the yams on a sheet of aluminum foil and bake for 15 minutes.

4 Reduce the oven temperature to 350°F and continue baking until the potatoes are soft, about 30 minutes.

5 Split the yams down the middle. Add a dollop of butter and dust with the cinnamon.

It's Bean Swell

1 Rinse, trim, and slice the green beans into 2-inch lengths. Peel and chop the shallot. Rinse, trim, seed, and chunk the bell pepper.

2 Heat the oil in a medium skillet and sauté the shallot for 1 minute. Add the beans, the bell pepper, and the basil. Season to taste and toss to coat.

3 Add the water, cover, and reduce the heat. Simmer until the vegetables are crisp-tender, about 7 minutes.

Bears Repeating

1 Grease a 9 x 9-inch baking dish.

2 In a medium bowl, combine the cracker crumbs, the condensed milk, the chocolate syrup, the chocolate chips, the brandy extract, and the salt. Spread the mixture evenly in the pan.

3 Bake at 350°F until the top of the brownies starts to brown and crust, 30 to 35 minutes.

FRIDAY

Meatless In Seattle

1 large bunch broccoli
2 medium carrots
2 stalks celery
1 medium red onion
2 medium zucchini
2 cloves garlic
3 tablespoons fresh parsley (when chopped)
1 pound rotini
2 tablespoons vegetable oil
1 container (15 ounces) ricotta cheese
1/2 teaspoon dried oregano
Seasoning to taste
1/4 cup grated Parmesan cheese

Microchips

1 medium head lettuce
2 medium cucumbers
1 small bunch radishes
3 tablespoons olive oil
2 tablespoons tarragon vinegar
1/2 teaspoon dried thyme
Seasoning to taste
1 cup corn chips (when crumbled)

Monorolls

2 tablespoons butter
1 teaspoon dried dill
1 package (8 ounces) refrigerated crescent rolls
1/2 teaspoon poppy seeds

Ferryboat Fruit

2 medium ripe pears
1 can (15 ounces) almond-flavored apricots
1/2 teaspoon ground cinnamon
1/2 teaspoon ground nutmeg
1 tablespoon cornstarch
1 pint caramel frozen yogurt

EQUIPMENT

Stockpot	Vegetable brush
2 small saucepans	Vegetable peeler
Large covered skillet	Pastry brush
Baking sheet	Ice cream scoop
Colander	Kitchen knives
Large mixing bowl	Measuring cups and
Small mixing bowl	spoons
Whisk	Cooking utensils

COUNTDOWN

1. Assemble the ingredients and the equipment.
2. Do Steps 1–2 of *Ferryboat Fruit*.
3. Do Steps 1–2 of *Microchips*.
4. Do Steps 1–4 of *Monorolls*.
5. Do Steps 1–6 of *Meatless In Seattle*.
6. Do Step 3 of *Microchips*.
7. Do Step 3 of *Ferryboat Fruit*.

FRIDAY

Meatless in Seattle

1 Bring water to a boil in a large stockpot.

2 Rinse and trim the broccoli and cut into bite-sized florets, discarding the tough ends. Peel, trim, and slice the carrots. Rinse, trim, and chop the celery. Peel and chop the onion. Scrub, trim, and slice the zucchini. Peel and mince the garlic. Rinse, stem, and chop the parsley.

3 Cook the rotini until it is almost tender, 8 to 10 minutes.

4 Heat the oil in a large skillet and sauté the garlic for 1 minute. Add the onion, the broccoli, the carrots, the celery, and the zucchini and toss to coat. Cover, reduce the heat, and simmer until the vegetables are crisp-tender, about 5 minutes.

5 Drain the pasta and return it to the stockpot. Add the ricotta cheese, mix, and heat through. Add the vegetables and the oregano and season to taste.

6 Sprinkle with the parsley and the Parmesan cheese.

Microchips

1 Wash and dry the lettuce and tear it into bite-sized pieces. Peel and slice the cucumber. Trim and slice the radishes. Combine in a large bowl.

2 In a small bowl, combine the oil, the vinegar, and the thyme. Season to taste.

3 Toss the salad with the dressing. Crumble the corn chips and sprinkle on top.

Monorolls

1 Preheat the oven to 375°F.

2 Melt the butter in a small saucepan. Blend in the dill.

3 Unroll the dough and separate it into 8 triangles. Brush the butter mixture on the insides of the triangles. Sprinkle with the poppy seeds. Starting at the shortest side of the triangle, roll to the opposite point. Arrange seam side down on a baking sheet.

4 Bake until golden, 11 to 13 minutes.

Ferryboat Fruit

1 Peel, halve, and core the pears and place them on individual dessert plates. Drain the apricots, reserving the liquid.

2 In a small saucepan, whisk together the reserved apricot liquid, the cinnamon, the nutmeg, and the cornstarch and heat until smooth and thick, about 3 minutes. Set aside.

3 Place a scoop of frozen yogurt into each pear cavity. Top with the apricots and drizzle with the sauce.

WEEK ELEVEN

Monday

Hail Halibut
Colossal Couscous
I Came, I Slaw, I Conquered
Forum Flip

Tuesday

Wichita Thigh Man
Kornsas
South Wind Salad
Topeka Pie

Wednesday

Red Hairing
Misdirected Salad
French Fraud
Pear Pretense

Thursday

Ham's Off
Calculating Carrots
Cagey Crisp

Friday

Barley Noticeable
Scarcely Salad
Undetectably Cake

STAPLES

- ☐ Butter
- ☐ Flour
- ☐ Granulated sugar
- ☐ Dark brown sugar
- ☐ Chocolate syrup
- ☐ Olive oil
- ☐ Vegetable oil
- ☐ Balsamic vinegar
- ☐ Raspberry vinegar
- ☐ Rice vinegar
- ☐ White wine vinegar
- ☐ Lemon juice
- ☐ Dijon mustard
- ☐ Honey
- ☐ Mayonnaise
- ☐ Worcestershire sauce
- ☐ Poppy seeds
- ☐ Dried basil
- ☐ Bay leaf
- ☐ Dried dill
- ☐ Dried oregano
- ☐ Dried tarragon
- ☐ Dried thyme
- ☐ Ground allspice
- ☐ Cayenne pepper
- ☐ Ground cinnamon
- ☐ Lemon-pepper seasoning
- ☐ Paprika
- ☐ Black pepper
- ☐ Salt
- ☐ Rum extract
- ☐ Vanilla extract

MEAT & POULTRY

1 1/2 pounds boneless, skinless chicken thighs (T)

FISH

4 halibut or other white fish steaks (about 1 1/2 pounds) (M)

FRESH PRODUCE

VEGETABLES

1 pound baking potatoes (F)
2 large carrots (F)
1 pound baby carrots (Th)
1 stalk celery (M)
2 stalks celery (Th)
2 stalks celery (F)
1 medium parsnip (M)
1 small turnip (F)
1/2 pound mushrooms (W)
1 small head red cabbage (M)
1 small head lettuce (T)
1 small head romaine lettuce (W)
1 small head Boston lettuce (F)
1 large tomato (T)
3 medium tomatoes (W)
1 large ripe avocado (F)
2 medium cucumbers (T)
2 medium red bell peppers (W)
1 bunch radishes (T)
1 large onion (F)
1 medium onion (Th)
1 small red onion (M)
1 small red onion (T)
1 medium shallot (T)
2 scallions (green onions) (M)
2 scallions (green onions) (T)
1 clove garlic (M)
2 cloves garlic (T)
2 cloves garlic (W)

HERBS

1 tablespoon chives (when chopped) (W)
2 tablespoons parsley (when chopped) (W)

FRUIT

1 small lemon (M)
1 small lemon (Th)
2 medium oranges (F)
1 large grapefruit (F)
2 mandarin oranges (M)
2 medium bananas (M)
4 large ripe pears (W)

CANS, JARS & BOTTLES

SOUPS

1 can (10 1/2 ounces) chicken broth (T)
1 can (10 1/2 ounces) beef consommé (Th)

VEGETABLES

1 can (28 ounces) diced tomatoes (F)
2 cans (11 ounces each) whole-kernel corn (T)
1 can (14 ounces) quartered artichoke hearts (W)

FRUIT

4 maraschino cherries (F)

JUICES

1 1/4 cups cranberry juice (M)

CONDIMENTS

2 tablespoons capers (W)

DESSERT & BAKING NEEDS

1 can (20 ounces) apple pie filling (Th)
1 jar (12 ounces) toffee topping (W)
1 cup marshmallow crème (F)

PACKAGED GOODS

PASTA, RICE & GRAINS

1 pound angel hair pasta (W)
1 package (6 ounces) curry-flavored couscous (M)
1 1/2 cups red lentils (F)
1 cup quick-cooking barley (F)

BAKED GOODS

1 loaf French bread (W)
1 loaf country bread (F)

1 1/2 cups cornbread stuffing mix (Th)
1 prepared shortbread pie shell (T)
4 individual sponge cake shells (F)
1 package (9 ounces) vanilla wafers (Th)

DRIED FRUIT & NUTS

1/2 cup raisins (Th)
2 tablespoons sliced almonds for garnish (M)
1/2 cup pecan bits (W)
1/2 cup walnut bits (Th)

DESSERT & BAKING NEEDS

1 package (3 ounces) strawberry gelatin (M)
1 package (3.4 ounces) instant cheese cake pudding mix (T)

REFRIGERATED PRODUCTS

DAIRY

1 3/4 cups milk (T)
1/2 cup sour cream (Th)
1/2 cup plain yogurt (M)
Whipped cream for garnish (M)

CHEESE

1/2 cup shredded Colby/Monterey Jack cheese (M)
8 slices Swiss cheese (Th)

DELI

8 slices deli ham (about 1 pound) (Th)

FROZEN GOODS

VEGETABLES

1 package (10 ounces) green peas and pearl onions (W)

DESSERTS

1 pint chocolate cherry frozen yogurt (F)

MONDAY

Hail Halibut

2 scallions (green onions)
1 small lemon
4 halibut or other white fish steaks (about 1 1/2 pounds)
1/2 cup plain yogurt
1/2 cup shredded Colby/Monterey Jack cheese
1 teaspoon lemon-pepper seasoning
Seasoning to taste

Colossal Couscous

1 clove garlic
1 1/4 cups water
1 package (6 ounces) curry-flavored couscous
Seasoning to taste

I Came, I Slaw, I Conquered

1 small head red cabbage
1 medium parsnip
1 small red onion
1 stalk celery
1/4 cup vegetable oil
3 tablespoons rice vinegar
1 teaspoon honey
Seasoning to taste

Forum Flip

1 1/4 cups cranberry juice
2 medium bananas
2 fresh mandarin oranges
1 package (3 ounces) strawberry gelatin
Ice cubes
Whipped cream for garnish
2 tablespoons sliced almonds for garnish

EQUIPMENT

Blender
Medium covered saucepan
Small saucepan
9 x 13-inch glass baking dish
Large mixing bowl
2 small mixing bowls

Vegetable peeler
Vegetable grater
Whisk
Kitchen knives
Measuring cups and spoons
Cooking utensils

COUNTDOWN

1. Assemble the ingredients and the equipment.
2. Do Steps 1–5 of *Forum Flip*.
3. Do Steps 1–5 of *Hail Halibut*.
4. Do Steps 1–3 of *Colossal Couscous*.
5. Do Steps 1–2 of *I Came, I Slaw, I Conquered*.
6. Do Step 4 of *Colossal Couscous*.
7. Do Step 6 of *Hail Halibut*.
8. Do Step 6 of *Forum Flip*.

MONDAY

Hail Halibut

1 Preheat the oven to 350°F. Grease a 9 x 13-inch baking dish.

2 Rinse, trim, and chop the scallions. Slice the lemon.

3 Rinse and pat dry the halibut steaks and place them in the baking dish.

4 In a small bowl, combine the yogurt, the cheese, the lemon-pepper seasoning, and the scallions. Season to taste and pour the mixture over the fish.

5 Bake until the fish flakes easily with a fork, about 15 minutes.

6 Garnish with the lemon slices.

Colossal Couscous

1 Peel and mince the garlic.

2 Bring the water to a boil in a medium saucepan.

3 Add the couscous and the garlic, season to taste, and stir to combine. Cover, remove from the heat, and let stand for 10 minutes.

4 Fluff with a fork.

I Came, I Slaw, I Conquered

1 Rinse, trim, quarter, and grate the cabbage. Peel, trim, and grate the parsnip. Peel and grate the onion. Rinse, trim, and dice the celery. Combine the ingredients in a large bowl.

2 In a small bowl, combine the oil, the vinegar, and the honey. Season to taste and toss with the vegetables.

Forum Flip

1 Bring ¾ cup of the cranberry juice to a boil in a small saucepan.

2 Peel and slice the bananas. Peel and section the mandarin oranges.

3 Pour the hot cranberry juice into a blender. Add the gelatin. Cover and blend until the gelatin is dissolved, about 30 seconds.

4 Combine the remaining ½ cup cranberry juice with enough ice cubes to make 1¼ cups. Add the mixture to the blender, stir until the ice is partially melted, and blend for 30 seconds.

5 Pour the mixture into individual dessert glasses, add the bananas and oranges, and refrigerate until you are ready to serve.

6 Top with dollops of whipped cream and sprinkle with the sliced almonds.

TUESDAY

Wichita Thigh Man

1 1/2 pounds boneless, skinless chicken thighs
2 cloves garlic
1 medium shallot
3 tablespoons vegetable oil
1 can (10 1/2 ounces) chicken broth
1 tablespoon dried tarragon
2 tablespoons lemon juice
Seasoning to taste

Kornsas

1 small red onion
1 large tomato
2 cans (11 ounces each) whole-kernel corn
2 tablespoons butter
1 teaspoon granulated sugar
1/2 teaspoon dried oregano
Seasoning to taste

South Wind Salad

1 small head lettuce
2 scallions (green onions)
2 medium cucumbers
1 bunch radishes
3 tablespoons olive oil
2 tablespoons raspberry vinegar
1 teaspoon Worcestershire sauce
1 teaspoon Dijon mustard
Seasoning to taste

Topeka Pie

1 package (3.4 ounces) instant cheesecake
  pudding mix
1 3/4 cups milk
1 prepared shortbread pie shell
Chocolate syrup for garnish

EQUIPMENT

Electric mixer	Whisk
Large covered skillet	Vegetable peeler
Medium skillet	Kitchen knives
2 medium mixing bowls	Measuring cups and spoons
Small mixing bowl	Cooking utensils

COUNTDOWN

1. Assemble the ingredients and the equipment.
2. Do Step 1 of *Topeka Pie*.
3. Do Steps 1–4 of *Wichita Thigh Man*.
4. Do Steps 1–3 of *South Wind Salad*.
5. Do Steps 1–3 of *Kornsas*.
6. Do Step 4 of *South Wind Salad*.
7. Do Step 2 of *Topeka Pie*.

TUESDAY

Wichita Thigh Man

1 Rinse and pat dry the chicken thighs. Peel and mince the garlic. Peel and chop the shallot.

2 Heat the oil in a large skillet and sauté the garlic and the shallot for 2 minutes.

3 Add the chicken and cook until golden, 5 to 6 minutes per side.

4 Add the broth, the tarragon, and the lemon juice. Season to taste, cover, and simmer until the chicken is tender and the flavors have blended, about 15 minutes.

Kornsas

1 Peel and chop the onion. Rinse, stem, and chop the tomato. Drain the corn.

2 Melt the butter in a medium skillet and sauté the onion until soft, about 5 minutes.

3 Add the corn and toss to combine. Add the sugar and the oregano and season to taste. Fold in the tomato and heat through, about 2 minutes.

South Wind Salad

1 Wash and dry the lettuce and arrange the leaves on individual salad plates.

2 Rinse, trim, and chop the scallions. Peel, trim, and thinly slice the cucumbers. Rinse, trim, and slice the radishes. Combine the cucumbers, the radishes, and the scallions in a medium bowl.

3 In a small bowl, combine the oil, the vinegar, the Worcestershire sauce, and the mustard. Season to taste.

4 Toss the vegetables with the dressing and spoon over the lettuce.

Topeka Pie

1 In a medium bowl, beat the pudding mix and the milk until well blended, about 2 minutes. Pour the mixture into the pie shell and refrigerate until you are ready to serve.

2 Slice the pie and drizzle the slices with chocolate syrup.

WEDNESDAY

Red Hairing

1 package (10 ounces) frozen green peas
   and pearl onions
2 medium red bell peppers
4 tablespoons olive oil
3 medium tomatoes
2 cloves garlic
1 pound angel hair pasta
1/4 teaspoon cayenne pepper
1/2 teaspoon dried basil
Seasoning to taste

Misdirected Salad

1 small head romaine lettuce
1/2 pound fresh mushrooms
1 can (14 ounces) quartered artichoke
   hearts
1/3 cup mayonnaise
2 tablespoons white wine vinegar
2 teaspoons Dijon mustard
1 teaspoon Worcestershire sauce
2 tablespoons capers
Seasoning to taste

French Fraud

1 loaf French bread
2 tablespoons fresh parsley (when
   chopped)
1 tablespoon fresh chives (when chopped)
1/2 teaspoon dried tarragon
1/4 cup butter
1 tablespoon lemon juice

Pear Pretense

4 large ripe pears
2 tablespoons lemon juice
1 jar (12 ounces) toffee topping
1 teaspoon rum extract
1/2 cup pecan bits

EQUIPMENT

Blender
Stockpot
Small saucepan
Large skillet
2 baking sheets
Colander
Large mixing bowl
2 small mixing bowls

Whisk
Pastry brush
Plastic bag
Kitchen knives
Measuring cups and
   spoons
Cooking utensils

COUNTDOWN

1. Assemble the ingredients and the equipment.
2. Do Steps 1–2 of *Misdirected Salad*.
3. Do Steps 1–3 of *Red Hairing*.
4. Do Step 1 of *Pear Pretense*.
5. Do Steps 1–2 of *French Fraud*.
6. Do Steps 4–8 of *Red Hairing*.
7. Do Step 3 of *French Fraud*.
8. Do Steps 9–10 of *Red Hairing*.
9. Do Step 3 of *Misdirected Salad*.
10. Do Steps 2–3 of *Pear Pretense*.

WEDNESDAY

Red Hairing

1 Preheat the broiler.

2 Set the peas and onions in a small bowl of warm water to thaw.

3 Rinse and trim the bell peppers and cut them in half lengthwise. Remove the seeds. Arrange the peppers on a baking sheet, cut side down, brush them with 1 tablespoon of the oil, and broil until they begin to turn black, 3 to 4 minutes.

4 Turn the peppers over, brush with another tablespoon of the oil, and broil 2 minutes longer.

5 Seal the peppers in a plastic bag to cool.

6 Rinse, stem, seed, and quarter the tomatoes. Place the tomatoes in a blender and puree until smooth, about 1 minute. Set aside.

7 Peel and mince the garlic. Peel the bell peppers, discarding the burnt skin. Chop into bite-sized pieces.

8 Cook the pasta in the stockpot until it is almost tender, about 2 minutes if you are using fresh pasta, 3 to 4 minutes if you are using dry pasta.

9 Heat the remaining 2 tablespoons oil in a large skillet. Add the garlic, the cayenne pepper, and the basil and sauté for 1 minute. Add the peas and onions and the bell peppers and sauté for 1 minute. Add the tomato puree, season to taste, and bring to a boil.

10 Drain the pasta and toss with the sauce.

Misdirected Salad

1 Wash and dry the lettuce and tear it into bite-sized pieces. Rinse, pat dry, trim, and thinly slice the mushrooms. Drain the artichokes. Combine the ingredients in a large bowl.

2 In a small bowl, whisk together the mayonnaise, the vinegar, the mustard, and the Worcestershire sauce. Mix in the capers and season to taste.

3 Toss the salad with the dressing.

French Fraud

1 Slice the bread in half lengthwise.

2 Rinse, stem, and chop the parsley. Rinse, trim, and chop the chives. In a blender, combine the parsley, the chives, the tarragon, the butter, and the lemon juice. Blend until fluffy and smooth, about 1 minute.

3 Spread the mixture on both cut halves of the bread, place the bread on a baking sheet, and broil until it begins to turn golden, about 2 minutes.

Pear Pretense

1 Rinse, core, and slice the pears. Arrange them on individual dessert plates and sprinkle with the lemon juice.

2 Heat the toffee topping with the rum extract in a small saucepan and drizzle it over the pears.

3 Top with the nuts.

THURSDAY

Ham's Off

1 package (10 ounces) frozen chopped
   spinach
1 medium onion
2 stalks celery
3/4 cup water
4 tablespoons vegetable oil
1 1/2 cups cornbread stuffing mix
1/2 cup sour cream
Seasoning to taste
8 slices Swiss cheese
8 slices deli ham (about 1 pound)
1/2 teaspoon paprika
3 tablespoons flour
1 can (10 1/2 ounces) beef consommé

Calculating Carrots

1 small lemon
1 pound baby carrots
2 tablespoons butter
1 teaspoon dried dill
Seasoning to taste

Cagey Crisp

1 package (9 ounces) vanilla wafers
1 can (20 ounces) apple pie filling
1/2 teaspoon vanilla extract
1 teaspoon ground cinnamon
2 tablespoons dark brown sugar
1/2 cup raisins
1/2 cup walnut bits
2 tablespoons butter

EQUIPMENT

Medium covered
  saucepan
Medium covered
  skillet
9 x 13-inch glass
  baking dish
9 x 9-inch glass
  baking dish
Large mixing bowl

Medium mixing bowl
Small mixing bowl
Citrus grater
Citrus juicer
Plastic bag
Kitchen knives
Measuring cups and
  spoons
Cooking utensils

COUNTDOWN

1. Assemble the ingredients and the
   equipment.
2. Do Steps 1–6 of *Cagey Crisp*.
3. Do Steps 1–9 of *Ham's Off*.
4. Do Steps 1–3 of *Calculating Carrots*.

THURSDAY

Ham's Off

1 Set the package of spinach in a small bowl of very warm water to thaw.

2 Grease a 9 x 13-inch baking dish.

3 Peel and mince the onion. Rinse, trim, and dice the celery.

4 Bring the water and 1 tablespoon of the oil to a boil in a medium saucepan. Blend in the cornbread stuffing mix. Remove from the heat, cover, and let stand for 5 minutes.

5 Add the onion and the celery and set aside.

6 Squeeze the spinach dry. Combine the spinach and the sour cream in a large bowl. Add the stuffing mixture and season to taste.

7 Place a slice of cheese on each slice of ham. Place ¼ cup of the spinach mixture in the center of each cheese slice, roll up the cheese and ham, and place seam side down in the baking dish. Sprinkle with the paprika.

8 Heat the remaining 3 tablespoons oil in the saucepan. Add the flour and stir to combine. Slowly add the consommé and simmer until thickened, about 5 minutes.

9 Remove the mixture from the heat and pour over the ham slices. Bake at 350°F until the cheese is melted and the ham rolls are heated through, 15 to 20 minutes.

Calculating Carrots

1 Grate 2 teaspoons of lemon peel. Juice the lemon. Rinse and trim the carrots.

2 Bring a small amount of water and the carrots to a boil in a medium skillet. Cover the skillet, reduce the heat, and simmer until the carrots are crisp-tender, about 10 minutes, checking to make sure the water does not boil away.

3 Pour off any remaining water. Add the butter, the lemon juice, and the dill. Season to taste and toss to coat and heat through, about 1 minute. Garnish with the lemon peel.

Cagey Crisp

1 Preheat the oven to 350°F. Grease a 9 x 9-inch baking dish.

2 Place the cookies in a plastic bag and crumble them.

3 In a medium bowl, combine the apple pie filling, the vanilla, the cinnamon, and the brown sugar.

4 Fold in the raisins and the nuts and pour the mixture into the baking dish.

5 Sprinkle the cookie crumbs over the top and dot with the butter.

6 Bake until hot and bubbly, about 20 minutes.

FRIDAY

MENU

Barley Noticeable

1½ cups red lentils
1 large onion
2 large carrots
1 pound baking potatoes
2 stalks celery
1 small turnip
2 tablespoons vegetable oil
4 cups water
1 cup quick-cooking barley
1 teaspoon dried thyme
1 can (28 ounces) diced tomatoes
1 bay leaf
Seasoning to taste
1 loaf country bread

Scarcely Salad

1 small head Boston lettuce
2 medium oranges
1 large grapefruit
1 large ripe avocado
3 tablespoons vegetable oil
2 tablespoons balsamic vinegar
¼ teaspoon ground allspice
1 teaspoon poppy seeds
Seasoning to taste

Undetectably Cake

1 pint chocolate cherry frozen yogurt
4 individual sponge cake shells
1 cup marshmallow crème
4 maraschino cherries

EQUIPMENT

Dutch oven
Large covered
  saucepan
Small mixing bowl
Whisk
Vegetable peeler

Ice cream scoop
Kitchen knives
Measuring cups and
  spoons
Cooking utensils

COUNTDOWN

1. Assemble the ingredients and the equipment.
2. Do Step 1 of *Barley Noticeable*.
3. Do Step 1 of *Scarcely Salad*.
4. Do Steps 2–4 of *Barley Noticeable*.
5. Do Step 2 of *Scarcely Salad*.
6. Do Step 5 of *Barley Noticeable*.
7. Do Steps 3–4 of *Scarcely Salad*.
8. Do Step 6 of *Barley Noticeable*.
9. Do Steps 1–2 of *Undetectably Cake*.

FRIDAY

RECIPES

Barley Noticeable

1 Bring water to a boil in a large saucepan.

2 Place the lentils in the saucepan, cover, reduce the heat, and simmer until slightly crunchy, about 20 minutes.

3 Peel and chop the onion. Peel, trim, and slice the carrots. Peel and dice the potatoes. Rinse, trim, and chop the celery. Peel, trim, and chop the turnip.

4 Heat the oil in a Dutch oven and sauté the onion for 3 minutes. Add the 4 cups water, the carrots, the potatoes, the celery, the turnip, the barley, the thyme, the tomatoes, and the bay leaf. Bring the mixture to a boil, reduce the heat, and simmer for 10 minutes.

5 Stir in the lentils, season to taste, and cook until the vegetables are tender, about 10 minutes.

6 Remove the bay leaf. Serve with chunks of country bread.

Scarcely Salad

1 Wash and dry the lettuce and arrange the leaves on individual salad plates.

2 Peel and slice the oranges and cut the slices in half. Peel and section the grapefruit. Halve, pit, peel, and slice the avocado. Arrange the oranges, the grapefruit, and the avocado over the lettuce.

3 In a small bowl, whisk together the oil, the vinegar, the allspice, and the poppy seeds. Season to taste.

4 Drizzle the dressing over the salad.

Undetectably Cake

1 Place scoops of the frozen yogurt in the sponge cake shells.

2 Top each serving with a dollop of marshmallow crème and garnish with a maraschino cherry.

WEEK TWELVE

WEEK AT A GLANCE

Monday
Commonwealth Chicken
Orzo Rico
Plantation Parsnips
San Juan Sundae

Tuesday
Consommé-hem
Crab Pockets
Bean Sleeves
Unzipped Bananas

Wednesday
Till We Meat Again
Loaf of My Life
The Object of My Confection

Thursday
Penne Name
Also Known as Salad
Nom de Plum

Friday
Gillbert and Sullivan
The Potatoes of Penzance
Now I Am the Captain of the
    Zucchini
Nankee Pooding

STAPLES

- ❒ Butter
- ❒ Flour
- ❒ Granulated sugar
- ❒ Dark brown sugar
- ❒ Powdered sugar
- ❒ Cocoa powder
- ❒ Olive oil
- ❒ Vegetable oil
- ❒ Red wine vinegar
- ❒ White wine vinegar
- ❒ Lemon juice
- ❒ Lime juice
- ❒ Dijon mustard
- ❒ Honey
- ❒ Ketchup
- ❒ Mayonnaise
- ❒ Grated Parmesan cheese
- ❒ Plain breadcrumbs
- ❒ Dried basil
- ❒ Bay leaf
- ❒ Dried dill
- ❒ Dried oregano
- ❒ Dried rosemary
- ❒ Dried tarragon
- ❒ Whole allspice
- ❒ Ground nutmeg
- ❒ Paprika
- ❒ Black pepper
- ❒ White pepper
- ❒ Salt
- ❒ Almond extract
- ❒ Vanilla extract

MEAT & POULTRY

- 1 lean sirloin steak (about 1 1/2 pounds) (W)
- 1 1/2 pounds spicy Italian sausage (Th)
- 4 boneless, skinless chicken breast halves (about 1 1/2 pounds) (M)

FISH

- 1 1/2 pounds cooked crabmeat (T)
- 4 white fish fillets (about 1 1/2 pounds) (F)

FRESH PRODUCE

VEGETABLES

- 4 medium sweet potatoes (F)
- 1 pound green beans (T)
- 4 small zucchini (F)
- 2 stalks celery (M)
- 2 stalks celery (T)
- 2 stalks celery (Th)
- 1 pound parsnips (M)
- 1/4 pound mushrooms (Th)
- 1 medium head lettuce (Th)
- 1 small bunch endive (Th)
- 4 medium tomatoes (W)
- 1 medium ripe avocado (F)
- 1 medium cucumber (Th)
- 1 medium green bell pepper (Th)
- 1 medium red bell pepper (Th)
- 2 large onions (W)
- 1 medium onion (Th)
- 1 small onion (T)
- 1 small red onion (M)
- 2 scallions (green onions) (T)
- 2 scallions (green onions) (W)
- 3 scallions (green onions) (Th)
- 2 cloves garlic (M)
- 1 clove garlic (T)
- 1 clove garlic (Th)
- 3 cloves garlic (F)

HERBS

- 3 tablespoons chives (when chopped) (T)
- 2 tablespoons parsley (when chopped) (W)
- 1/4 cup parsley (when chopped) (F)

FRUIT

- 1 large orange (M)
- 1 small lemon (M)
- 3 medium bananas (T)
- 1 large tart green apple (M)
- 1 pound purple plums (Th)

CANS, JARS & BOTTLES

SOUPS

- 1 can (14 ounces) chicken broth (M)
- 1 can (10 1/2 ounces) beef consommé (T)

VEGETABLES

- 1 can (14 1/2 ounces) diced tomatoes (Th)
- 1 jar (7 ounces) roasted red peppers (T)

FRUIT

- 1 can (15 ounces) sliced peaches (W)
- 1 can (15 ounces) apricot halves (W)
- 1 can (8 ounces) pineapple chunks (W)

JUICES

- 2 cans (6 ounces each) clamato juice (T)
- 1 can (6 ounces) tomato juice (T)
- 1 cup apple cider (F)

SPREADS

- 1/4 cup orange marmalade (M)

CONDIMENTS

- 1 jar (6 1/2 ounces) marinated artichoke hearts (W)

PACKAGED GOODS

PASTA, RICE & GRAINS

- 1 pound penne pasta (Th)
- 1/2 pound orzo (M)

BAKED GOODS

- 1 loaf Italian bread (W)
- 4 large croissants (T)
- 1 prepared shortbread pie shell (W)

DRIED FRUIT & NUTS

- 1/4 cup walnut bits (T)

DESSERT & BAKING NEEDS

- 1 package (3.4 ounces) instant white chocolate pudding mix (F)
- 1/4 cup flaked coconut (W)

WINE & SPIRITS

- 2 tablespoons dry sherry (T)
- 2 tablespoons dry sherry (F)
- 1/2 cup Marsala wine (M)
- 2 tablespoons rum (M)
- 2 tablespoons Kahlùa (F)

REFRIGERATED PRODUCTS

DAIRY

- 2 cups milk (F)
- 1/2 cup sour cream (F)
- Whipped cream for garnish (F)

CHEESE

- 12 ounces Jarlsberg cheese (T)
- 1 container (8 ounces) pineapple cream cheese (W)

JUICES

- 1/2 cup orange juice (W)

FROZEN GOODS

DESSERTS

- 1 pint vanilla ice cream (M)
- 1 container (8 ounces) whipped topping (Th)

MONDAY

Commonwealth Chicken

4 boneless, skinless chicken breast halves
(about 1 1/2 pounds)
1 small lemon
2 cloves garlic
1/4 cup flour
Seasoning to taste
2 tablespoons butter
2 tablespoons olive oil
2/3 cup chicken broth
1/2 cup Marsala wine
3 tablespoons grated Parmesan cheese

Orzo Rico

2 stalks celery
1 small red onion
2 tablespoons butter
1 teaspoon dried dill
1 cup chicken broth
1/2 pound orzo
Seasoning to taste

Plantation Parsnips

1 pound parsnips
1 large tart green apple
2 tablespoons lemon juice
3 tablespoons butter
2 tablespoons dark brown sugar
1/4 teaspoon ground nutmeg
Seasoning to taste

San Juan Sundae

1 large orange
1/4 cup orange marmalade
2 tablespoons rum
1 tablespoon butter
1 pint vanilla ice cream

EQUIPMENT

Medium covered
saucepan
Small saucepan
Large covered skillet
Large skillet
Medium skillet
Strainer
Large shallow bowl

Vegetable peeler
Citrus grater
Citrus juicer
Ice cream scoop
Kitchen knives
Measuring cups and
spoons
Cooking utensils

COUNTDOWN

1. Assemble the ingredients and the equipment.
2. Do Steps 1–2 of *San Juan Sundae.*
3. Do Step 1 of *Orzo Rico.*
4. Do Step 1 of *Plantation Parsnips.*
5. Do Steps 1–4 of *Commonwealth Chicken.*
6. Do Step 2 of *Plantation Parsnips.*
7. Do Steps 2–4 of *Orzo Rico.*
8. Do Step 3 of *Plantation Parsnips.*
9. Do Step 5 of *Commonwealth Chicken.*
10. Do Step 5 of *Orzo Rico.*
11. Do Steps 6–7 of *Commonwealth Chicken.*
12. Do Step 4 of *Plantation Parsnips.*
13. Do Step 3 of *San Juan Sundae.*

MONDAY

Commonwealth Chicken

1 Rinse and pat dry the chicken breasts. Grate 2 teaspoons of lemon peel and juice the lemon. Peel and mince the garlic.

2 Place the flour in a shallow bowl and season to taste. Dredge the chicken in the seasoned flour. Shake off any excess.

3 Melt the butter with the oil in a large skillet. Add the garlic and sauté for 1 minute. Add the chicken and cook until it is golden, about 5 minutes per side.

4 Add the broth and the wine. Bring to a boil, cover, reduce the heat, and simmer for 10 minutes.

5 Add the cheese and simmer uncovered until the cheese has melted, about 3 minutes.

6 Remove the chicken and cover to keep warm. Continue cooking the pan juices until they are reduced by half, about 5 minutes.

7 Add the lemon juice and lemon peel and bring to a boil, scraping up any brown bits from the bottom of the skillet. Return the chicken to the skillet and coat with the sauce.

Orzo Rico

1 Rinse, trim, and dice the celery. Peel and chop the onion.

2 Bring water to a boil in a medium saucepan.

3 Melt the butter in a medium skillet and sauté the celery and the onion with the dill until the onion is soft, about 5 minutes. Remove from the heat and cover to keep warm.

4 Add the broth to the boiling water, return to a boil, and cook the orzo until it is tender, 8 to 10 minutes.

5 Drain the orzo and return it to the saucepan. Add the celery mixture, season to taste, toss to combine, and cover to keep warm.

Plantation Parsnips

1 Trim, peel, and julienne the parsnips. Rinse, core, and slice the apple and sprinkle the slices with the lemon juice.

2 Bring water to a boil in a large skillet.

3 Cook the parsnips in the boiling water until crisp-tender, 8 to 10 minutes.

4 Drain the skillet. Add the butter, the apple, the brown sugar, and the nutmeg to the parsnips. Season to taste and sauté until the apples and the parsnips are heated through and begin to soften, about 5 minutes.

San Juan Sundae

1 Grate 2 teaspoons of orange peel and juice the orange.

2 In a small saucepan, combine the orange juice, the orange marmalade, the rum, and the butter. Stir to combine. Bring the mixture to a boil, cook for 1 minute, remove from the heat, and set aside.

3 Spoon scoops of ice cream into individual dessert dishes. Top with the sauce and sprinkle with the orange peel.

TUESDAY

Consommé-hem

2 scallions (green onions)
1 can (10½ ounces) beef consommé
2 cans (6 ounces each) clamato juice
1 can (6 ounces) tomato juice
½ teaspoon dried rosemary
¼ teaspoon white pepper
1 teaspoon granulated sugar
¼ cup lemon juice
2 tablespoons dry sherry
Seasoning to taste

Crab Pockets

4 large fresh baked croissants
1 clove garlic
2 stalks celery
3 tablespoons fresh chives (when chopped)
12 ounces Jarlsberg cheese
1½ pounds cooked crabmeat
1 jar (7 ounces) roasted red peppers
1 tablespoon lemon juice
½ cup mayonnaise
2 teaspoons dried dill
Seasoning to taste

Bean Sleeves

1 pound fresh green beans
1 small onion
¼ cup granulated sugar
3 tablespoons ketchup
2 tablespoons red wine vinegar

Unzipped Bananas

¼ cup walnut bits
3 medium bananas
3 tablespoons lime juice
2 tablespoons honey
2 tablespoons butter

EQUIPMENT

Medium covered saucepan	Large mixing bowl
Medium covered skillet	Cheese grater
Small skillet	Kitchen knives
Baking sheet	Measuring cups and spoons
	Cooking utensils

COUNTDOWN

1. Assemble the ingredients and the equipment.
2. Do Steps 1–3 of *Unzipped Bananas*.
3. Do Step 1 of *Consommé-hem*.
4. Do Steps 1–2 of *Bean Sleeves*.
5. Do Steps 1–5 of *Crab Pockets*.
6. Do Step 2 of *Consommé-hem*.
7. Do Steps 3–6 of *Bean Sleeves*.
8. Do Step 3 of *Consommé-hem*.

TUESDAY

Consommé-hem

1 Rinse, trim, and chop the scallions.

2 Combine the consommé, the clamato juice, the tomato juice, the rosemary, and the white pepper in a medium saucepan. Bring the mixture to a boil and add the sugar, the lemon juice, and the sherry. Season to taste, cover, reduce the heat, and simmer for 10 minutes.

3 Garnish with the chopped scallions.

Crab Pockets

1 Preheat the oven to 350°F.

2 Cut the croissants in half lengthwise and set the halves on a baking sheet.

3 Peel and mince the garlic. Rinse, trim, and dice the celery. Rinse, trim, and chop the chives. Grate the cheese. Flake the crabmeat and discard any shell or cartilage. Drain, blot, and chop the roasted peppers.

4 In a large bowl, combine the lemon juice, the mayonnaise, the dill, the garlic, the celery, the chives, the crab, the roasted peppers, and half of the cheese. Season to taste and blend well.

5 Spoon the mixture onto the croissant halves. Sprinkle with the remaining cheese and bake until the crab mixture is hot and bubbling, about 10 minutes.

Bean Sleeves

1 Rinse and trim the green beans. Peel and slice the onion.

2 Bring water to a boil in a medium skillet.

3 Add the beans and the onion to the skillet, cover, and cook until the beans are bright green and crisp-tender, 6 to 8 minutes.

4 Drain the beans and the onion.

5 Combine the sugar, the ketchup, and the vinegar in the skillet. Cook until the sugar has dissolved and the mixture is blended, about 1 minute.

6 Return the beans and the onions and toss to coat well and heat through.

Unzipped Bananas

1 Finely chop the walnuts. Peel the bananas and cut them into chunks.

2 Combine the lime juice, the honey, and the butter in a small skillet. Add the bananas, tossing to coat, and heat through.

3 Place the banana chunks on individual dessert plates. Spoon the sauce over the bananas and sprinkle with the nuts. Set aside until you are ready to serve.

WEDNESDAY

Till We Meat Again

1 lean sirloin steak (about 1 1/2 pounds)
2 large onions
2 tablespoons vegetable oil
1 teaspoon dried oregano
Seasoning to taste
1 tablespoon black pepper

Loaf of My Life

1 loaf Italian bread
2 tablespoons fresh parsley (when chopped)
2 scallions (green onions)
4 medium tomatoes
1 jar (6 1/2 ounces) marinated artichoke hearts
2 tablespoons red wine vinegar
1 teaspoon Dijon mustard
1/2 teaspoon dried basil
1 teaspoon granulated sugar
Seasoning to taste

The Object of My Confection

1 container (8 ounces) pineapple cream cheese
1 can (15 ounces) sliced peaches
1 can (15 ounces) apricot halves
1 can (8 ounces) pineapple chunks
1/2 cup orange juice
2 tablespoons powdered sugar
1 teaspoon almond extract
1 prepared shortbread pie shell
1/4 cup flaked coconut for garnish

EQUIPMENT

9 x 13-inch baking pan
9 x 13-inch glass baking dish
Large mixing bowl
3 small mixing bowls
Whisk

Pastry brush
Aluminum foil
Kitchen knives
Measuring cups and spoons
Cooking utensils

COUNTDOWN

1. Assemble the ingredients and the equipment.
2. Do Steps 1–2 of *The Object of My Confection*.
3. Do Steps 1–2 of *Till We Meat Again*.
4. Do Steps 1–6 of *Loaf of My Life*.
5. Do Steps 3–5 of *Till We Meat Again*.
6. Do Steps 3–4 of *The Object of My Confection*.
7. Do Steps 7–8 of *Loaf of My Life*.
8. Do Step 6 of *Till We Meat Again*.

WEDNESDAY

Till We Meat Again

1 Trim any excess fat from the steak. Peel and thinly slice the onions.

2 Combine the oil and the oregano in a small bowl and season to taste.

3 Place the steak in a 9 x 13-inch baking pan. Brush with some of the oil mixture. Broil for 5 minutes.

4 Turn the steak. Sprinkle with the pepper. Top with the onions and drizzle the remaining oil over the top. Continue broiling until done to taste, about 10 minutes for medium rare.

5 Thinly slice the steak across the grain and serve with the onions.

Loaf of My Life

1 Preheat the broiler.

2 Cut the bread into 8 thick slices. Rinse, stem, and chop the parsley. Rinse, trim, and chop the scallions. Rinse, stem, and slice the tomatoes and place them in a 9 x 13-inch baking dish.

3 Drain and mince the artichoke hearts, reserving the marinade in a small bowl. Arrange the artichokes over the tomatoes.

4 Add the vinegar, the mustard, the basil, and the sugar to the reserved marinade. Season to taste and blend well. Pour the mixture over the tomatoes.

5 Broil the tomatoes until hot and bubbly, about 4 minutes.

6 Remove the tomatoes from the broiler and cover with aluminum foil to keep warm.

7 Toast the bread.

8 Top the toast with the tomato slices and the artichokes. Sprinkle with the parsley and the scallions.

The Object of My Confection

1 Set the cream cheese out to soften.

2 Drain the peaches, the apricot halves, and the pineapple chunks. Place the fruit in a large bowl.

3 In a small bowl, combine the cream cheese and the orange juice and blend until smooth. Fold in the powdered sugar and the almond extract.

4 Spoon the fruit into the pie shell. Top with the cream cheese mixture and sprinkle with the coconut. Refrigerate until you are ready to serve.

THURSDAY

Penne Name

1 1/2 pounds spicy Italian sausage
1 clove garlic
1 medium onion
1 medium green bell pepper
1 medium red bell pepper
1/4 pound fresh mushrooms
1 pound penne
3 tablespoons olive oil
1 can (14 1/2 ounces) diced tomatoes
1 teaspoon dried basil
Seasoning to taste

Nom de Plum

1 pound fresh purple plums
1/4 cup dark brown sugar
2 tablespoons lemon juice
1/4 cup water
1 teaspoon vanilla extract
1 container (8 ounces) whipped topping
1 teaspoon ground nutmeg

Also Known as Salad

1 medium head lettuce
1 small bunch endive
2 stalks celery
3 scallions (green onions)
1 medium cucumber
3 tablespoons vegetable oil
2 tablespoons white wine vinegar
1 teaspoon granulated sugar
1/2 teaspoon dried tarragon
Seasoning to taste
1/2 teaspoon paprika for garnish

EQUIPMENT

Stockpot	Whisk
Medium covered saucepan	Vegetable peeler
Large skillet	Kitchen knives
Colander	Measuring cups and spoons
Large mixing bowl	Cooking utensils
Small mixing bowl	

COUNTDOWN

1. Assemble the ingredients and the equipment.
2. Do Step 1 of *Penne Name*.
3. Do Steps 1–2 of *Nom de Plum*.
4. Do Steps 1–2 of *Also Known as Salad*.
5. Do Step 3 of *Nom de Plum*.
6. Do Steps 2–7 of *Penne Name*.
7. Do Step 3 of *Also Known as Salad*.
8. Do Step 4 of *Nom de Plum*.

THURSDAY

Penne Name

1 Set the sausage in the freezer for 10 minutes.

2 Peel and mince the garlic. Peel and chop the onion. Rinse, trim, seed, and thinly slice the bell peppers. Rinse, pat dry, and thinly slice the mushrooms.

3 Bring water to a boil in a stockpot.

4 Cut the sausage into ½-inch-thick slices and sauté in a large skillet until lightly browned on all sides, about 10 minutes. Drain the sausage on paper towels.

5 Cook the penne in the boiling water until it is almost tender, 8 to 10 minutes.

6 Heat the oil in the skillet and sauté the garlic for 1 minute. Add the onion and the bell peppers and sauté for 5 minutes. Add the mushrooms, the tomatoes, and the basil and season to taste. Return the sausage, toss to combine, and simmer until the mixture is heated through, about 5 minutes.

7 Drain the pasta and toss with the sauce.

Also Known as Salad

1 Wash and dry the lettuce and tear it into bite-sized pieces. Rinse, pat dry, and chop the endive. Rinse, trim, and chop the celery. Rinse, trim, and chop the scallions. Peel, trim, and chop the cucumber. Combine the ingredients in a large bowl.

2 In a small bowl, combine the oil, the vinegar, the sugar, and the tarragon. Season to taste.

3 Toss the salad with the dressing and sprinkle with the paprika.

Nom de Plum

1 Rinse, halve, and pit the plums.

2 Place the plums, the brown sugar, the lemon juice, and the water in a medium saucepan. Bring to a boil, cover, reduce the heat, and simmer until the plums are soft, about 10 minutes.

3 Remove the saucepan from the heat and set aside.

4 Combine the vanilla with the whipped topping. Fold in the plums and spoon the mixture into individual dessert glasses. Sprinkle with the nutmeg.

FRIDAY

Gillbert and Sullivan

4 white fish fillets (about 1 1/2 pounds)
1 clove garlic
1 medium ripe avocado
2 tablespoons lemon juice
1/4 cup fresh parsley (when chopped)
2 tablespoons dry sherry
1/2 cup sour cream
3 tablespoons flour
1/4 cup plain breadcrumbs
Seasoning to taste
3 tablespoons vegetable oil

The Potatoes of Penzance

4 medium sweet potatoes
2 tablespoons butter
1 cup apple cider
Seasoning to taste

Now I Am the Captain of the Zucchini

1 cup water
4 small zucchini
2 cloves garlic
1 bay leaf
3 whole allspice
3 tablespoons olive oil
2 tablespoons lemon juice
Seasoning to taste

Nankee Pooding

1 package (3.4 ounces) instant white chocolate pudding mix
2 cups milk
2 tablespoons Kahlùa
Whipped cream for garnish
1 tablespoon cocoa powder

EQUIPMENT

Electric mixer	Medium mixing bowl
Large covered saucepan	Vegetable brush
	Kitchen knives
Medium covered saucepan	Measuring cups and spoons
Large skillet	Cooking utensils
2 large shallow bowls	

COUNTDOWN

1. Assemble the ingredients and the equipment.
2. Do Step 1 of *Nankee Pooding*.
3. Do Steps 1–2 of *The Potatoes of Penzance*.
4. Do Steps 1–2 of *Gillbert and Sullivan*.
5. Do Steps 1–3 of *Now I Am the Captain of the Zucchini*.
6. Do Steps 3–5 of *The Potatoes of Penzance*.
7. Do Steps 4–5 of *Now I Am the Captain of the Zucchini*.
8. Do Steps 3–5 of *Gillbert and Sullivan*.
9. Do Step 2 of *Nankee Pooding*.

FRIDAY

Gillbert and Sullivan

1 Rinse and pat dry the fish fillets. Peel and mince the garlic. Halve, pit, peel, and thinly slice the avocado and sprinkle with the lemon juice to prevent browning. Rinse, stem, and chop the parsley.

2 Combine the sherry and the sour cream in a shallow bowl. Combine the flour and the breadcrumbs in a second shallow bowl. Season to taste.

3 Heat the oil with the garlic in a large skillet.

4 Dip the fish in the sour cream mixture, then coat with the breadcrumb mixture. Sauté the fish, turning once, until it is lightly browned and crisp, about 3 minutes per side.

5 Top the fillets with the avocado slices and sprinkle with the parsley.

The Potatoes of Penzance

1 Bring water to a boil in a large saucepan. Scrub and quarter the potatoes.

2 Cook the potatoes until they are almost tender, about 10 minutes.

3 Drain the potatoes and rinse them in cold water to cool. Peel the potatoes and cut them into thin slices.

4 Melt the butter in the saucepan. Add the potatoes and toss to coat. Add the apple cider and season to taste. Bring to a boil and heat through, about 2 minutes.

5 Remove from the heat. Drain and cover to keep warm.

Now I Am the Captain of the Zucchini

1 Bring the water to a boil in a medium saucepan.

2 Scrub and trim the zucchini and cut them in half lengthwise. Peel the garlic.

3 Add the garlic, the bay leaf, and the allspice to the water. Add the zucchini, return to a boil, reduce the heat, and simmer until the zucchini is tender, 5 to 7 minutes.

4 Drain the zucchini and discard the garlic, the bay leaf, and the allspice.

5 Return the zucchini to the saucepan. Add the oil and the lemon juice, season to taste, and toss to combine and heat through. Cover to keep warm.

Nankee Pooding

1 In a medium bowl, combine the pudding mix and the milk and beat until well blended, about 2 minutes. Fold in the Kahlùa, pour into individual dessert bowls, and refrigerate until you are ready to serve.

2 Place a dollop of whipped cream on each pudding and dust lightly with the cocoa powder.

WEEK THIRTEEN

WEEK AT A GLANCE

Monday
Last Gasp Pasta
So Long Salad
Bye For Now Bread
See Ya Tomallow

Tuesday
Dickens' Chickens
A Christmas Carrot
The Pickwick Peppers
Oliver Twists
Grape Expectations

Wednesday
Ohi-On the Hog
Chillisquashie
Buckeye Salad
Dayton Delight

Thursday
Whimsical White Fish
Pixie Potatoes
Playful Peas and Onions
Queen of Tarts

Friday
Exit Gracefully
Fruit Finale
Chocolate Curtain Call

STAPLES

- ❏ Butter
- ❏ Flour
- ❏ Cornstarch
- ❏ Granulated sugar
- ❏ Dark brown sugar
- ❏ Cocoa powder
- ❏ Olive oil
- ❏ Vegetable oil
- ❏ Rice vinegar
- ❏ White wine vinegar
- ❏ Lemon juice
- ❏ Dijon mustard
- ❏ Honey
- ❏ Mayonnaise
- ❏ Poppy seeds
- ❏ Sesame seeds
- ❏ Dried basil
- ❏ Dried dill
- ❏ Dried marjoram
- ❏ Dried sage
- ❏ Ground allspice
- ❏ Cayenne pepper
- ❏ Ground cinnamon
- ❏ Ground ginger
- ❏ Italian seasoning
- ❏ Ground nutmeg
- ❏ Paprika
- ❏ Black pepper
- ❏ Salt
- ❏ Almond extract
- ❏ Brandy extract
- ❏ Vanilla extract

MEAT & POULTRY

4 loin pork chops (about 1 1/2 pounds) (W)

3 pounds chicken pieces (T)

FISH

4 white fish fillets (about 1 1/2 pounds) (Th)

FRESH PRODUCE

VEGETABLES

1 1/2 pounds small new red potatoes (Th)

3/4 pound sugar-snap peas (Th)

2 large acorn squash (W)

1 medium yellow zucchini (M)

4 medium carrots (T)

2 stalks celery (M)

2 stalks celery (W)

1 stalk celery (F)

1 medium turnip (M)

1 medium head red leaf lettuce (M)

1 medium head lettuce (W)

2 medium tomatoes (Th)

1 medium cucumber (M)

2 large green bell peppers (T)

2 large red bell peppers (T)

1 small daikon radish (M)

1 small bunch radishes (W)

1 medium onion (M)

1 small onion (F)

1/2 pound baby boiling onions (Th)

2 medium leeks (T)

1 clove garlic (M)

2 cloves garlic (T)

1 clove garlic (Th)

1 clove garlic (F)

HERBS

2 tablespoons chives (when chopped) (Th)

3 tablespoons parsley (when chopped) (W)

3 tablespoons parsley (when chopped) (Th)

FRUIT

1 medium ripe cantaloupe melon (F)

1 medium ripe honeydew melon (F)

2 large ripe red pears (W)

3/4 pound seedless red grapes (T)

CANS, JARS & BOTTLES

SOUPS

1 can (14 ounces) chicken broth (W)

1 can (14 ounces) vegetable broth (Th)

VEGETABLES

1 can (28 ounces) diced tomatoes (F)

1 can (14 1/2 ounces) stewed tomatoes (M)

1 can (11 ounces) whole-kernel corn (M)

INTERNATIONAL FOODS

1 can (8 ounces) sliced water chestnuts (W)

FRUIT

6 maraschino cherries (W)

JUICES

1 1/2 cups white grape juice (T)

CONDIMENTS

1 jar (6 1/2 ounces) marinated artichoke hearts (W)

1 jar (7 ounces) pitted green olives (Th)

1 jar (2 ounces) diced pimientos (Th)

2 tablespoons capers (Th)

DESSERT & BAKING NEEDS

1 container (7 ounces) Hershey's Magic Shell (F)

PACKAGED GOODS

PASTA, RICE & GRAINS

1 pound spaghetti (M)

1 cup instant rice (W)

1 1/2 cups corn flakes (T)

BAKED GOODS

1 loaf sourdough bread (M)

1 loaf French bread (F)

4 individual graham cracker tart shells (Th)

4 large chocolate chip cookies (F)

DRIED FRUIT & NUTS

1 cup chopped dates (W)

1/4 cup raisins (W)

1 cup walnut bits (M)

1/2 cup peanuts (F)

2 tablespoons sliced almonds (Th)

DESSERT & BAKING NEEDS

1 package (18 ounces) chocolate cake mix (M)

1 package (3.4 ounces) instant coconut cream pudding mix (Th)

1 envelope unflavored gelatin (T)

2 cups mini-marshmallows (M)

1/2 cup chocolate chips (T)

1/2 cup flaked coconut (F)

WINE & SPIRITS

1/4 cup dry white wine (Th)

1 tablespoon dry sherry (W)

REFRIGERATED PRODUCTS

DAIRY

1 1/3 cups milk (M)

1 1/4 cups milk (Th)

3/4 cup sour cream (Th)

Whipped cream for garnish (T)

Whipped cream for garnish (Th)

3 eggs (M)

8 eggs (F)

CHEESE

8 ounces shredded Colby/Montery Jack cheese (M)

JUICES

1 cup orange juice (F)

DELI

6 slices bacon (M)

1 package (8 ounces) refrigerated crescent rolls (T)

FROZEN GOODS

FRUIT

1 package (10 ounces) raspberries (F)

BAKED GOODS

1 pound cake (W)

DESSERTS

1 pint chocolate chip ice cream (F)

1 carton (8 ounces) whipped topping (W)

MONDAY

Last Gasp Pasta

6 slices bacon
1 clove garlic
1 medium onion
1 medium yellow zucchini
1 can (11 ounces) whole-kernel corn
1 can (14½ ounces) stewed tomatoes
½ teaspoon Italian seasoning
Seasoning to taste
1 pound spaghetti
8 ounces shredded Colby/Monterey Jack
   cheese

So Long Salad

1 medium head red leaf lettuce
1 medium cucumber
1 medium turnip
1 small daikon radish
2 stalks celery
3 tablespoons olive oil
2 tablespoons white wine vinegar
1 teaspoon granulated sugar
Seasoning to taste
1 teaspoon paprika for garnish

Bye For Now Bread

1 loaf sourdough bread
3 tablespoons butter
1 teaspoon dried sage
Seasoning to taste
2 teaspoons poppy seeds

See Ya Tomallow

2 cups water
1 package (18 ounces) chocolate cake mix
3 eggs
½ cup vegetable oil
1⅓ cups milk
1 teaspoon vanilla extract
1 cup walnut bits
2 cups mini-marshmallows
1 cup dark brown sugar
1 cup cocoa powder

EQUIPMENT

Electric mixer	Whisk
Stockpot	Vegetable brush
Small saucepan	Vegetable peeler
Large covered skillet	Pastry brush
9 x 13-inch baking pan	Aluminum foil
Colander	Kitchen knives
2 large mixing bowls	Measuring cups and spoons
Small mixing bowl	Cooking utensils

COUNTDOWN

1. Assemble the ingredients and the equipment.
2. Do Steps 1–4 of *See Ya Tomallow*.
3. Do Steps 1–2 of *Bye For Now Bread*.
4. Do Steps 1–2 of *So Long Salad*.
5. Do Steps 1–4 of *Last Gasp Pasta*.
6. Do Step 5 of *See Ya Tomallow*.
7. Do Step 3 of *Bye For Now Bread*.
8. Do Step 5 of *Last Gasp Pasta*.
9. Do Step 3 of *So Long Salad*.
10. Do Step 6 of *Last Gasp Pasta*.
11. Do Step 6 of *See Ya Tomallow*.

MONDAY

Last Gasp Pasta

1 Chop the bacon. Peel and mince the garlic. Peel and chop the onion. Scrub, trim, and slice the zucchini. Drain the corn.

2 Sauté the bacon in a large skillet until crisp, about 10 minutes. Drain on paper towels.

3 Bring water to a boil in a stockpot.

4 Remove all but 2 tablespoons of the bacon drippings from the skillet. Add the garlic and the onion and sauté for 3 minutes. Add the zucchini and sauté for 3 minutes. Add the corn, the tomatoes, and the Italian seasoning. Season to taste. Cover, reduce the heat, and simmer until heated through, about 10 minutes.

5 Cook the pasta in the stockpot until it is almost tender, 6 to 7 minutes.

6 Drain the pasta and place it on a large serving platter. Top with the sauce and sprinkle with the bacon and the cheese.

So Long Salad

1 Wash and dry the lettuce and tear it into bite-sized pieces. Peel, trim, and thinly slice the cucumber. Peel, trim, and halve the turnip and cut it into thin slices. Rinse, trim, and thinly slice the radish. Rinse, trim, and slice the celery. Combine the ingredients in a large bowl.

2 In a small bowl, combine the oil, the vinegar, and the sugar. Season to taste.

3 Toss the salad with the dressing. Sprinkle with the paprika.

Bye For Now Bread

1 Split the bread loaf in half lengthwise.

2 Melt the butter in a small saucepan. Blend in the sage and season to taste. Brush the butter mixture on the cut sides of the bread and sprinkle with the poppy seeds. Reassemble the loaf and wrap it in aluminum foil.

3 Bake at 350°F until heated through, about 10 minutes.

See Ya Tomallow

1 Preheat the oven to 350°F. Grease a 9 x 13-inch baking pan. Bring the water to a boil.

2 Combine the cake mix, the eggs, the oil, the milk, and the vanilla in a large bowl. Beat on low speed for 1 minute. Beat on high speed for 3 minutes. Fold in the nuts and set aside.

3 Sprinkle the marshmallows on the bottom of the baking pan. Sprinkle with the brown sugar and the cocoa powder. Pour the boiling water over the mixture. Slowly add the cake batter.

4 Bake until the cake begins to pull away from the sides of the pan and is firm on top, about 40 minutes.

5 Remove and set aside to cool.

6 Invert the cake onto a large plate so that the marshmallow becomes the topping.

TUESDAY

Dickens' Chickens

3 pounds chicken pieces
1 1/2 cups corn flakes
2 cloves garlic
1 cup mayonnaise
Seasoning to taste

A Christmas Carrot

4 medium carrots
2 medium leeks
2 cups water
3 tablespoons butter
1/2 teaspoon ground nutmeg
Seasoning to taste

The Pickwick Peppers

2 large green bell peppers
2 large red bell peppers
2 tablespoons vegetable oil
1/2 teaspoon dried marjoram
Seasoning to taste
1/2 teaspoon sesame seeds

Oliver Twists

2 tablespoons butter
1/2 teaspoon Dijon mustard
1/2 teaspoon honey
1 package (8 ounces) refrigerated crescent
   rolls

Grape Expectations

1 envelope unflavored gelatin
1 1/2 cups white grape juice
3 ice cubes
3/4 pound seedless red grapes
1/2 cup chocolate chips
Whipped cream for garnish

EQUIPMENT

2 small saucepans	Vegetable peeler
Medium covered skillet	Plastic bag
Medium skillet	Pastry brush
9 x 13-inch glass baking dish	Kitchen knives
Baking sheet	Measuring cups and spoons
2 large shallow bowls	Cooking utensils

COUNTDOWN

1. Assemble the ingredients and the equipment.
2. Do Steps 1–6 of *Dickens' Chickens*.
3. Do Steps 1–2 of *A Christmas Carrot*.
4. Do Steps 1–3 of *Oliver Twists*.
5. Do Step 7 of *Dickens' Chickens*.
6. Do Step 3 of *A Christmas Carrot*.
7. Do Steps 1–4 of *Grape Expectations*.
8. Do Step 4 of *Oliver Twists*.
9. Do Steps 1–3 of *The Pickwick Peppers*.

TUESDAY

Dickens' Chickens

1 Preheat the oven to 400°F.

2 Rinse and pat dry the chicken pieces.

3 Crush the corn flakes in a plastic bag and turn them into a large shallow bowl.

4 Peel and mince the garlic. In another shallow bowl, combine the garlic with the mayonnaise and blend well.

5 Dip the chicken pieces in the mayonnaise and roll to coat in the corn flake crumbs. Arrange the chicken pieces in a single layer in a 9 x 13-inch baking dish. Season to taste.

6 Bake for 15 minutes.

7 Turn the chicken pieces. Reduce the oven temperature to 350°F and continue baking until the chicken is tender and golden, about 30 minutes.

A Christmas Carrot

1 Peel and trim the carrots and cut them into thick slices. Wash the leeks thoroughly, rinsing several times. Trim, remove the root ends and the tough outer leaves, and cut into thick slices.

2 Bring the water to a boil in a medium skillet. Add the carrots and cook for 5 minutes. Add the leeks. Cover the skillet, reduce the heat, and simmer until the leeks and the carrots are crisp-tender, 5 to 7 minutes.

3 Drain and remove the vegetables. Melt the butter with the nutmeg in the skillet and season to taste. Return the carrots and the leeks and toss to combine and heat through. Cover to keep warm.

The Pickwick Peppers

1 Rinse, trim, seed, and cut the bell peppers into strips.

2 Heat the oil with the marjoram in a medium skillet and sauté the peppers until they are crisp-tender, about 3 minutes.

3 Season to taste and toss with the sesame seeds.

Oliver Twists

1 Melt the butter in a small saucepan. Blend in the mustard and the honey.

2 Unroll and separate the dough. Brush the triangles on one side with the butter mixture. Starting at the narrow end, roll the triangles up and gently twist them twice.

3 Arrange the twists on a baking sheet.

4 Add the pan to the oven and bake the twists at 350°F until lightly golden, 10 to 12 minutes.

Grape Expectations

1 In a small saucepan, soften the gelatin with ¾ cup of the grape juice. Add the remaining ½ cup juice and bring to a boil, stirring. Cook until the gelatin is completely dissolved, 3 to 4 minutes.

2 Remove the saucepan from the heat, add the ice cubes, and stir until the mixture is smooth and slightly thickened, about 2 minutes. Set aside.

3 Rinse, stem, and halve the grapes.

4 Layer half the gelatin into individual dessert glasses. Top with half of the grapes and half of the chocolate chips. Repeat. Garnish with whipped cream and refrigerate until you are ready to serve.

WEDNESDAY

Ohi-On the Hog

2 large ripe red pears
1 tablespoon lemon juice
1/4 cup flour
1 teaspoon dried basil
Seasoning to taste
4 loin pork chops (about 1 1/2 pounds)
2 tablespoons vegetable oil
1 can (14 ounces) chicken broth
1 teaspoon ground cinnamon
1 tablespoon dry sherry

Chillisquashie

1 cup water
1 cup instant rice
2 large acorn squash
2 stalks celery
3 tablespoons fresh parsley (when chopped)
1 can (8 ounces) sliced water chestnuts
Seasoning to taste
1/4 cup dark brown sugar
4 tablespoons butter

Buckeye Salad

1 medium head lettuce
1 small bunch radishes
1 jar (6 1/2 ounces) marinated artichoke hearts
2 tablespoons rice vinegar
1/2 teaspoon granulated sugar
1/4 teaspoon dried sage
Seasoning to taste

Dayton Delight

1 frozen pound cake
1 carton (8 ounces) frozen whipped topping
6 maraschino cherries
1 teaspoon brandy extract
1/4 cup raisins
1 cup chopped dates

EQUIPMENT

Medium covered saucepan
Large covered skillet
9 x 13-inch glass baking dish
Large shallow bowl
Medium mixing bowl

Small mixing bowl
Whisk
Kitchen knives
Measuring cups and spoons
Cooking utensils

COUNTDOWN

1. Assemble the ingredients and the equipment.
2. Do Step 1 of *Dayton Delight*.
3. Do Steps 1–5 of *Chillisquashie*.
4. Do Steps 1–4 of *Ohi-On the Hog*.
5. Do Steps 1–3 of *Buckeye Salad*.
6. Do Steps 2–5 of *Dayton Delight*.
7. Do Steps 5–8 of *Ohi-On the Hog*.

WEDNESDAY

Ohi-On the Hog

1 Peel, quarter, core, and cut the pears into ¼-inch-thick slices. Sprinkle with the lemon juice.

2 In a large shallow bowl, combine the flour and the basil. Season to taste and blend well. Coat both sides of the pork chops with the mixture, shaking off any excess.

3 Heat the oil in a large skillet and cook the chops until they are browned on both sides, 5 to 6 minutes per side.

4 Add ½ cup of the broth to the skillet. Cover, reduce the heat, and simmer until the chops are tender and no longer pink inside, 15 to 20 minutes.

5 Remove the chops and cover to keep warm.

6 Add the remaining broth to the skillet and bring it to a boil. Add the pears, cover, reduce the heat, and simmer for 5 minutes.

7 Remove the pears and arrange them over the pork.

8 Blend the cinnamon and the sherry into the broth and cook for 1 minute, scraping up any brown bits from the bottom. Spoon the sauce over the pork and pears.

Chillisquashie

1 Bring the water to a boil in a medium saucepan. Add the rice, cover, remove from the heat, and let stand for 5 minutes.

2 Preheat the oven to 375°F.

3 Cut the squash in half lengthwise. Scoop out the seeds and stringy fibers. Rinse, trim, and mince the celery. Rinse, stem, and chop the parsley. Drain and chop the water chestnuts.

4 Combine the rice, the celery, the parsley, and

the water chestnuts in a medium bowl. Season to taste.

5 Sprinkle the brown sugar in the squash cavities. Spoon in the rice mixture. Dot with the butter. Set the squash in a 9 x 13-inch baking dish. Carefully add water around the squash and bake until the squash is tender, about 40 minutes.

Buckeye Salad

1 Wash and dry the lettuce and arrange the leaves on individual salad plates.

2 Rinse, trim, and slice the radishes. Drain the artichokes, reserving the marinade. Arrange the radishes and the artichokes over the lettuce.

3 In a small bowl, whisk together the reserved marinade, the vinegar, the sugar, and the sage. Season to taste and drizzle over the salad.

Dayton Delight

1 Set the pound cake out to thaw. Set the frozen topping out to soften.

2 Chop the cherries.

3 Fold the brandy extract into the whipped topping.

4 Cut the pound cake in half horizontally. Spread ¼ of the frosting on the cut surface of the bottom layer. Place the top layer back on the cake and frost the top and sides.

5 Decorate the cake with the cherries, the raisins, and the dates.

THURSDAY

MENU

Whimsical White Fish

3 tablespoons fresh parsley (when chopped)
1 clove garlic
2 medium tomatoes
1 jar (2 ounces) diced pimientos
1 jar (7 ounces) pitted green olives
4 white fish fillets (about 1 1/2 pounds)
2 tablespoons olive oil
2 tablespoons capers
1/4 teaspoon ground ginger
1/2 cup vegetable broth
1/4 cup dry white wine
1/8 teaspoon cayenne pepper
Seasoning to taste

Pixie Potatoes

2 cups water
1 1/4 cups vegetable broth
1 teaspoon dried dill
1 1/2 pounds small new red potatoes
2 tablespoons fresh chives (when chopped)
2 tablespoons olive oil
1 tablespoon lemon juice
Seasoning to taste

Playful Peas and Onions

3/4 pound sugar-snap peas
1/2 pound baby boiling onions
2 tablespoons butter
1 teaspoon granulated sugar
1/2 teaspoon ground allspice
Seasoning to taste

Queen of Tarts

1 package (3.4 ounces) instant coconut cream pudding mix
1 1/4 cups milk
3/4 cup sour cream
1 teaspoon almond extract
4 individual graham cracker tart shells
Whipped cream for garnish
2 tablespoons sliced almonds for garnish

EQUIPMENT

Electric mixer	Medium mixing bowl
Large saucepan	Vegetable brush
Large skillet	Kitchen knives
Medium skillet	Measuring cups and
9 x 13-inch glass	spoons
baking dish	Cooking utensils

COUNTDOWN

1. Assemble the ingredients and the equipment.
2. Do Steps 1–2 of *Queen of Tarts*.
3. Do Steps 1–5 of *Whimsical White Fish*.
4. Do Steps 1–3 of *Pixie Potatoes*.
5. Do Steps 1–2 of *Playful Peas and Onions*.
6. Do Step 4 of *Pixie Potatoes*.
7. Do Step 6 of *Whimsical White Fish*.

THURSDAY

Whimsical White Fish

1 Preheat the oven to 350°F. Butter a 9 x 13-inch baking dish.

2 Rinse, stem, and chop the parsley. Peel and mince the garlic. Rinse, stem, and chop the tomatoes. Drain the pimientos. Drain the olives.

3 Rinse and pat dry the fish fillets and place them in a single layer in the baking dish.

4 Heat the oil in a medium skillet. Sauté the garlic for 2 minutes. Add the tomatoes, the pimientos, the olives, the capers, the ginger, the broth, the wine, and the cayenne pepper. Season to taste. Bring to a boil, stirring to blend. Remove from the heat and pour over the fish fillets.

5 Bake until the fish flakes easily with a fork, about 15 minutes.

6 Sprinkle with the parsley.

Pixie Potatoes

1 Bring the water, the broth, and the dill to a boil in a large saucepan.

2 Scrub the potatoes. Rinse, trim, and chop the chives.

3 Cook the potatoes until they are tender, 10 to 15 minutes.

4 Drain the potatoes and return them to the saucepan. Add the oil, the lemon juice, and the chives. Season to taste and toss to coat.

Playful Peas and Onions

1 Rinse and string the snap peas. Peel the onions.

2 Melt the butter in a large skillet and sauté the onions for 4 minutes. Add the snap peas, the sugar, and the allspice. Season to taste and sauté until the snap peas are crisp-tender, 3 to 4 minutes.

Queen of Tarts

1 In a medium bowl, beat the pudding mix with the milk and the sour cream until well blended. Fold in the almond extract and distribute the mixture among the tart shells.

2 Top the tarts with a dollop of whipped cream and sprinkle with the almonds. Refrigerate until you are ready to serve.

FRIDAY

Exit Gracefully

1 clove garlic
1 small onion
1 stalk celery
1 tablespoon vegetable oil
1 can (28 ounces) diced tomatoes
2 teaspoons dried basil
$1/2$ teaspoon ground cinnamon
1 teaspoon granulated sugar
Seasoning to taste
1 loaf French bread
4 tablespoons butter
8 eggs

Fruit Finale

1 package (10 ounces) frozen raspberries
1 cup orange juice
2 teaspoons cornstarch
1 medium ripe honeydew melon
1 medium ripe cantaloupe melon

Chocolate Curtain Call

4 large chocolate chip cookies
1 pint chocolate chip ice cream
1 container (7 ounces) Hershey's Magic Shell
$1/2$ cup peanuts
$1/2$ cup flaked coconut

EQUIPMENT

Medium covered saucepan
Medium saucepan
Large covered skillet
Ice cream scoop

Kitchen knives
Measuring cups and spoons
Cooking utensils

COUNTDOWN

1. Assemble the ingredients and the equipment.
2. Do Steps 1–2 of *Fruit Finale*.
3. Do Steps 1–3 of *Exit Gracefully*.
4. Do Steps 3–4 of *Fruit Finale*.
5. Do Steps 4–7 of *Exit Gracefully*.
6. Do Steps 1–2 of *Chocolate Curtain Call*.

FRIDAY

Exit Gracefully

1 Peel and mince the garlic. Peel and chop the onion. Rinse, trim, and dice the celery.

2 Heat the oil in a medium saucepan and sauté the garlic, the onion, and the celery for 5 minutes.

3 Add the tomatoes, the basil, the cinnamon, and the sugar. Season to taste, cover, reduce the heat, and simmer for 20 minutes.

4 Cut the bread into 8 thick slices. With a spoon, hollow out a small cavity in the center of each slice.

5 Melt the butter in a large skillet. Lay the bread slices, cavity side down, and cook until golden, about 3 minutes.

6 Turn the bread slices over. Break an egg into each cavity, cover, and cook until the whites are set and the eggs are cooked through, about 4 minutes.

7 With a spatula, transfer the egg toasts to individual dinner plates and top with the tomato sauce.

Fruit Finale

1 Place the raspberries in a medium saucepan. Add the orange juice and the cornstarch. Bring to a boil and cook, stirring occasionally, for 5 minutes.

2 Place the berries in the refrigerator to cool.

3 Slice the melons and remove the seeds and rinds.

4 Arrange alternating slices of melon on individual salad plates and top with the raspberries.

Chocolate Curtain Call

1 Place the cookies on individual dessert plates.

2 Place the peanuts in a plastic bag and crush with a mallet.

3 Place scoops of ice cream over the cookies. Drizzle with the Magic Shell. Top with the coconut and the peanuts.

INDEX

BREADS

BISCUITS

BREADSTICKS

BUNS

FLAT BREADS

LOAVES

MAIN DISH PIES

MEAT

QUICHE

SALADS

MAIN COURSE SALADS

SIDE SALADS

SANDWICHES

SEAFOOD

SKILLET DISHES

SOUPS

VEGETARIAN DISHES

METRIC EQUIVALENCIES

Liquid and Dry Measure Equivalencies

CUSTOMARY	METRIC
¼ teaspoon	1.25 milliliters
½ teaspoon	2.5 milliliters
1 teaspoon	5 milliliters
1 tablespoon	15 milliliters
1 fluid ounce	30 milliliters
¼ cup	60 milliliters
⅓ cup	80 milliliters
½ cup	120 milliliters
1 cup	240 milliliters
1 pint *(2 cups)*	480 milliliters
1 quart *(4 cups, 32 ounces)*	960 milliliters *(.96 liter)*
1 gallon *(4 quarts)*	3.84 liters
1 ounce *(by weight)*	28 grams
¼ pound *(4 ounces)*	114 grams
1 pound *(16 ounces)*	454 grams
2.2 pounds	1 kilogram *(1,000 grams)*